T0354536

My SUPERMAN

Living for tomorrow.

DAVID O. IDAHOSA

Order this book online at www.trafford.com
or email orders@trafford.com

Most Trafford titles are also available at major online book retailers.

Dickens, in his book "THE GREAT EXPECTATIONS", said, Heaven we need never be ashamed
of our tears, for they are rain upon the blinding dust of earth, overlying our hard hearts.

Printed in the United States of America.

ISBN: 978-1-4669-4820-4 (sc)
ISBN: 978-1-4669-4809-9 (e)

Trafford rev. 08/13/2012

 www.trafford.com

North America & international
toll-free: 1 888 232 4444 (USA & Canada)
phone: 250 383 6864 ♦ fax: 812 355 4082

CHAPTER 1

ALL DAVID'S LIFE, HE HAS always wanted to be a writer—a prolific and successful writer. Maybe he thought he was not competent enough. And at the same time, he was having a strong passion for music. Music was his everything. His life was music and music was his life. About becoming a musician, he had tried everything he could since it was a thing he could not do without, but becoming a musician was far more than becoming a writer.

David was a good reader. He has read many great books, and upon the many books he read, he came to understand that creativity was his way of life. Although his principal reason for wanting to be an artist was for him to become sententious and being able to communicate with other writers and spreading the words to other people who hunger and thirst for it—whether by writing or singing or painting—to him, it is all the same. He once read in a book that "A man is fed not that he may be fed, but that he might work," which he came to interpret on his own that he is not reading because he like to, but for him to procure knowledge, and this knowledge which later became inspiration for him to be creative.

Actually, we can see, if God became the first Person to create and set a precedent for other artists, why would God not be in favor of those who intend to be like him? God himself is an artist and at the same time, a scientist. The bible and other religions books tells us that God made man—which is to say he sculpted man—and that is art. He later breathe life into him—which is science. God made man in His own image, which is to say, man is like God, as God will always love man and want him to be like him.

So, after all and all, David then took the will to become a writer since he rediscovered pleasure when reading. Reading amuses and diverts him, so he think of other people who read. He once said, "I cannot in the life of me imagine why some folks would not like to read. Those who do not read, might not conceive what in life the already lost."

David here is two: 1st David and 2nd David. When he is with other people, he is one, but sometimes when he is with himself, he will automatically become two. He has always secluded himself, living a solitary life, while most people thought of him to be self-exiled. He thought people who are happy should just move on to be happy and let those who prefer to be alone to remain alone all by themselves. He said, "The more friends he was having, the farther he was walking away from his dream." His conception about folks who live an enjoyable and comfortable life with no problems and responsibilities was too absurd. He thought these folks might not be able to explain what life really is. It might seem not logical or sensible, but it is a good thing to see one find a definition of life for himself, since life itself is a mystery which no scientist can explore. He said he could not grasp how and what made him to walk into the history of mankind that later captured the essence of his self-education. He said, "How in the life of mankind to see that it is a terrible thing to see one man laid down his life for others."

CHAPTER 2

F RIDAY MORNING WAS THE LAST day of the month as it was also the last day of the year. David, an African immigrant living in Spain, woke up from his bed at about 05:00 a.m, brushed his teeth, showered with a very warm water since the weather outside was very cold, and approximately, three degrees centigrade. To shower in the morning before going to work was not a thing he was habituated. But he did so that day so as to keep his body warm. He slipped on his blue jeans trouser, a t-shirt, then a sweater, and on top of that, a warm anorak jacket. To match, he wore his sneakers, preparing to go to work.

As he was accustomed to smoking a cigarette before parting for work, so he thought he was still having some in one of the packet he found on the floor of his room, but there was nothing inside when he checked it. 'This is an obnoxious day,' he murmured to himself.

As he left the door of the house ajar, stepping across the threshold, he found that it was rainy outside. Since there was nothing he could do about it, so he covered his head with the hood of his jacket, and with an umbrella, he moved on, meanwhile, he was to walk nine hundred meters to get to the train station where he could get a train. Waiting for the train to come, he met one of his friends who also was going to work and was waiting for the rain as well. They shook hands just the way they always do while in Africa. 'Hey whats up brother,' greeted David, first. 'I dey fine,' replied the boy. 'Cold dey today o my brother,' said David, again to the boy. 'I bow o, wetin man go do now? man not fit say cold dey, make him not go work.' replied the boy.

As they waited and continued to converse, speaking pidgin English—English mostly spoken by many west African countries colonized by the British. When the train finally arrived, they went inside and were sitting opposite to each other. 'We are about to commence a new year,' said the boy to David, looking at him to see if he was responding to his questions. 'What do you think about it?' he asked for the second time. David full of too many things running around his brain, was not listening. But the boy struck him on his lap and shouted louder, 'hey brother! wetin be the matter with you? we dey both sit down here, *and I said something, yet you not dey hear me.'* 'Oh! were you talking to me? asked David, waiting a bit and proceeding with what he intended to say, as he watched the boy looked at him in disgust. 'I thought you were talking to the other man sitting there,' said David, again, wiping his eyes with the back of his right hand. 'No,' said the boy. 'I was talking to you. I was saying, we are about to commence with another year.' 'Yes,' said David. 'I mean, what do you think about this country?' asked the boy again. 'Do you think we will be able to survive this economic crisis here in Spain? Actually, David being whom he is, was really not prepared to edify anyone about an arduous journey the country would have to go, which was inevitable, as long as the government was not able to provide a new strategy to confront the crisis.

It is true people say, "You do not run away from your problems, you have to confront it." Agreed. But he said he disagreed to agree that the socialist party which was in power in Spain, was capable of setting the country free from the crisis. The Zapatero's administration was not doing anything, but was just debating on the next step to take after landing the country into a deep hole. The intrinsic truth was that the prime minister, Zapatero, was indeed a good man, but he was not brainy enough to have been able to prevent the crisis. Although, there were economic and financial crisis everywhere around the globe at that particular time, but the one in Spain was just more than economic and financial crisis. David said, he saw how Zapatero was constantly lying to the citizens to get his political stand, and his political strategies to get the economy back in track, were not functioning. He said earlier that Zapatero was a good man, who would have preferred to always help the citizens by giving them more chances and opportunities. As a socialist, immediately he was voted in as the prime minister, he was on the brink of a revolution; he legalized same-sex marriage, brought the Spanish troops back from Iraq because he said he understood the war was unjustifiable. It baffled David to see how much his administration was spending little of what they have to help others who were in need; he also helped lots of illegal immigrants to become legal, even if they were to pay more than they were earning to get the documents—which was a way for the government to make money from the immigrants. What he was doing was worth praising, as it was a thing already forbidden in most European countries.

All David could say to the other boy who was willing to know what he was thinking about the New Year and the crisis in Spain, was that, God will be in control. But he knew in his mind that, "God helps those who help themselves."

When David finally stepped down from the train, he trekked a hundred and fifty meters to the place he was working, which cannot be referred to as work but begging. Yes, begging, if he might use the right word—it was begging.

He had decided to take this job, because there was nothing he could do to earn a living. There was no job and no government assistance from any source. What they normally do was to show a parking space to the drivers, and after parking, they might be given 1.00 euro or more, but usually 1.00 euro or less. Some might give then twenty cents, while some might also give them nothing. Some who thought these immigrants were exploiting the government of the state by doing this, would want to draw a scene by calling the police, because they understood it to be illegal. It was illegal, but it was their only means of survival. Since most of the immigrants doing it were illegal in the country, so whenever the police were called for, what they do is to ask them to present their documents out, if found illegal, they will be taken to the police station where the police would have to thumbprint them and give them some papers that will set a deadline for their expulsion to leave the country. Although, they were all also provided with a government legal assistant who then will later files an appeal to the court—to see if they will be given any chance to live in the country—and this was going on every time like this. But, immediately the police understand that any of them was legal, all they do is to advise him not to insult anybody, and also to be very careful, since some of their citizens were not happy to be seeing what they were seeing. Some of these people were also claiming they were forced to be paying, which actually was true and false. True, because some were being obliged by some of them to be paying. False, because many of them were pouring insults on them and were asking them to go back to their countries. Although, David also tried the best he could to lecture his colleagues on the issue of how illegal immigrants will never be given the opportunities like that to beg and earn money on the street. From David's point of view, he could see that some of these people who were giving them money, were doing it voluntarily because they understood that they were suffering and needed aids. Some of them were also coming to give them clothes and food, knowing they were in need. He, being a person who had been to many other countries in Europe, knew it was a great privilege for them to be doing what they were doing in Spain, as it will never be permitted in Germany or Holland or France or Norway or Sweden. But he also understood that, while you are a refugee in these countries mentioned, the government will be responsible for your welfare. The governments of these countries were always responsible for the payments of the house rents and feeding for these immigrants, and as well, encouraging them to get some type of educational training to get a great paying job—helping them build their future. In Spain it was different. The very day these immigrants seek asylum, the same day they are to start thinking of where to go and live—whether they are to go meet their fellow country people so as to be told what to do or they will be kept in a refugee camp, where they are being deprived of their privileges as refugees. In reality, many of these immigrants were complaining of how human rights were being violated by the Spanish government, and for that reason, they were all fleeing Spain to other countries. It was also being noticed that most of the aids given to immigrants in Spain were from the churches and other voluntary organizations. Spaniards are said to be very sympathetic, but the truth was that the economy was not good enough for the citizens. David said he could see them as people who were willing to help, but the fact that they were not having enough, not to think of rendering out to others—this was making most immigrants sees them as selfish people, and to David, that was not true. He fathomed what was going on in Spain, he comprehend that the citizens are not that contented with their lives, but they are always filled with a conceit of their own importance, and were always looking at the immigrants with contempt, and the conception that they were better than these other people living with them was always there.

David who had actually traveled to other countries and had met many Spaniards living there as immigrants looking for a better way of life, leaving their countries, their families and friends. Many of them whom David had met with in Holland, Belgium, Swiss, Norway, Sweden and many more who were said to be living in Germany, U.k. and many other European countries. Most of them who said to have left the country during the regime of Franco, the dictator who said to had ruled and ruined the country for thirty-nine years.

David said he believe begging is out of necessity. And it will be foolish if anyone decide to take it as a job, because of the humiliation they get from it. He saw that he lacked confidence in himself by begging people to give him something which he he believed he could have if he was working. Every time he was going to do this parking of cars while he wait for people to give him money or insults probably because of the economic crisis, he was always sad. Many were concerned about the fact that they were blacks and were not supposed to be living in Spain. One of the lad told him he was lucky Franco was not alive, because he would have been seeing himself digging his own grave for coming to live in Spain. Another man also did ask them if they could please let them live their lives in peace by voluntarily getting their belongings and leave the country. David was overcome with remorse when he was told this, but there was nothing he could do about it, except to ignore him, because he believed people like that were ignorance that needed to travel out of Spain to other places to see how their fellow country people were living in other countries—so that they could learn how to respect others no matter the situation they find them.

So, when David arrived at his so-called place of work, he thought he will be able to go home that day with at least 15.00 euros or more. But he waited and waited with the other boys until at about 02:00 p.m when he still was unable to get 2.00 euros. Stunned by the feelings of hopelessness, he decided to return back home so that he could create time to do some hard thinking about his life.

When David finally arrived home and was all alone by himself, then appeared 2nd David. 'Do you think you deserve to be living this kind of life that you are living?' he asked. 'No, I really do not think so,' replied 1st David. 'Yes, you do not, you deserve better than becoming a beggar. You are young, smart, intelligent and full of charisma, then, why not do something better with your life? Or maybe you like getting humiliated every time by everybody.' And after he said that, he disappeared, leaving him there alone to think about what he just told him. It was at this very time he knew what he should be doing, so he picked up a pen and a notebook and started to write, putting celebration outside his life, even when it was the last day of the year when everybody were celebrating.

He came to learn that he was the only solution to his own problems, and that there was no one he could wait for to tell him what his desires were and how he could be seeing himself as a human being. Then, he said to himself, "If you want something, you have to put yourself in the way of getting it."

A week after this, as he walked himself into one of the betting-house in Torrejon de Ardoz, Madrid. He did not actually entered the place to bet, but to shake hands and converse with some his country people since he was too lonely and was living a boring life at home. There appeared, eight policemen unlooked for, dressing on khaki suits and jeans, and were showing their I D cards. *'Nadie se mueva, policia!'* As the betting-house was filled with immigrants—who were mainly blacks, the policemen took a premature decision that crime was going on there, and this decision was based on ignorance and prejudice—which was also inhuman and degrading. Everyone there were requested to present their documents since that was the only charge the could rely on. With voices very high as the black people were challenging them, the few Romanians and South Americans there were also claiming their rights as parts of European citizens. "We really do pretend that we hate each other, whereas we do. But by pretending, we have been able to tolerate and live with each other peacefully. It was so obvious the way the Spanish police in Madrid were harassing the immigrants and deporting those without documents back to their countries. Before the economic crisis, the hatred was there but hidden in everyone of them, until they all finally were given the authorization to harass and deport them. David said he found it so formidable to explain to himself why "People decidedly puts their blames on other people, whereas they are the cause of their own problems."

After the police finished searching almost all of them to know whether some were with drugs or fake currency or whatsoever that they were suspecting them of, some were granted leave. Because of how David was calm, the police noticed something suspicious in his behavior; they believed he was dangerous. One of them swiftly called him closer and asked him to present his document. David told him he just gave it his colleague who had first demanded for it. But the young man still was unsatisfied, so he demanded for his wallet, *'dame tu cartera,'* he said to him. David gave him his wallet, and after much checking and checking, he came closer to him and said, *'manos arriba!'* David raised his two hands up, and the policeman searched him very well from head to toe and yet nothing was found with him. David swiftly brought out a piece of paper that was hidden in his wallet and presented it to the policeman, letting him know it was given to him by the police as well. After the young man read it, he asked him, *'estas alguna vez detenido?'* 'Si,' answered David, walking closer to the policeman and trying to explain the meaning of the paper he presented to them—which actually was a document issued to him at the police station, to make him understand that he is having a permanent residence permit in Spain and no matter the crime he will commit, he will never be deported, instead he will be jailed or treated like a Spaniard. The policeman told him not to fret himself about anything, but he urged him to be patience and not to utter any word. After David had waited until almost everybody held with him were all gone, so he went to meet the policeman again and asked him, *'no se porque stoy detenido aqui, yo tambien quiero salir fuera como el resto.'* The other policemen walked closer to where he was to attend to him, seeing that he was rude and was speaking better Spanish that the rest Nigerians there. One of the policemen later asked him if he speaks English, not knowing that he was making a great mistake. David replied him, saying 'yes, I do speak English.' Then, the policeman said to him, 'look! in your country, foreigners and citizens are being extorted everyday. Every policeman there are corrupt just like the governments are.' 'Do not mention that,' yelled David. 'You do not have to tell me there is corruption and bribery in my country. I knew that already. But I believe there is corruption here in Spain as well. Even in the U.s. there is corruption there too. So, please you do not have to be telling me there is problems in my country when actually there are more problems here already that you people are unwilling to identify not to talk of how to get a solution to them. Or do you not know there are very many Spaniards living in other countries?' As he continued to edify these policemen about the problems in the country, and when he was asked to shut his mouth by one of them, he refused. They decided to delay him, and he became very incommoded, as he was waiting and waiting for them to give him his document and grant him leave like the rest. He was speaking in Spanish, and at the same time, speaking in English and was asking them to do whatever they wish because he said he had seen more than enough to keep on keeping quiet. So, he thought it was the right time for him to lecture them things about life since he believed they were never willing to learn. After more than one hour that he was detained inside the betting-house, he was later given his document and was granted leave. So he left, shaking the policeman whom they had both disputed—who was so astonished by the shaking, comparing it to the manner he had talked to them before.

Walking home alone, he began to converse with himself—a thing he found pleasure in doing. And anytime he was doing this, he thought it was a way for him to be interacting with his soul. He later went far to write a poem when he arrived home that day.

MY SOUL'S MY BEST FRIEND.

I might thought it to be a mistake,
While I'm waiting for the best.
Do you care to know
What I'm passing through?
Heaven's door's closed over me,
The Earth's about to swallow me.
Sometimes I wish I've got wings
So I can easily fly.
When to structure, my aims,
A sabotage, always their aims.

In trouble when I am.
To talk to, when there is none.
To my soul, I have to talk,
Because my soul is my best friend.

Now that we cannot make it here,
I'm thinking of a new strategy.
You wanna take me with you,
So we should be going back home.
If only we've got one.
Where's my home now?
Where do I call my home?

CHAPTER 3

D AVID WAS BORN INTO A polygamous family of seventeen. His father, Idahosa, his step mother, his mother, three brothers, four sisters, four half-brothers and three half-sisters—of which he was the thirteenth child of his father and the sixth of his mother.

The Idahosa family were living in Benin-city, the capital city of Edo state which was twenty miles far from Lagos, the financial and industrial capital of the country, Nigeria—the country with the largest population in Africa.

At the time David mother gave birth to him, his father was already at his sixties. His mother, Veronica named him Osamudiame in their native language, which means, GOD STANDS FOR ME. Her husband, Idahosa was always sick, and because of that, he had to travel to almost every cities and villages in the country, looking for means and sources and to all hospitals and native herbalists around the country, and yet, he could not find a cure for a stomach ulcer that was destroying him. He was neither a Christian, nor was he a Muslim or an idol worshiper, since these were the three main religions in the country at that time. But he believed in everything as long as he understand that God is in everywhere. Maybe he came to adopt this suspension of disbelief, because of the stomach ulcer's problems he was incurring which was rough and tumble for him. He was not a saint nor was he a sinner, but he never ceased to believe in one thing, the golden rule of "Do onto others as you would want to be done to you," which he took to be his philosophy of life, and this he tried all possibly means to extend to all his children. In other words, he could be described as a man who believe in many or all gods, he was a pantheist. He once said to David—Look! my son, life is not how we look at it, it is something more than the way we look at it to be. Choose your own God, it does not matter where you find it. He could neither writer, nor could he read his own name, but he was full of education; he was an example of a defined illiteracy.

David's father was born into a monogamous family of seven including his father and mother. He was name Idahosa, meaning—I hope in God. He once mentioned to David, that according to their superstitious beliefs, "A child's destiny walks according to his/her name." This, in David's later life in the future, has led him to think of changing his name, Osamudiame to become David, because he read in the bible how great the name was, and moreover, he saw that his own native name was too long to be pronounced by many people living in civilized countries.

David's family was born into a poor family who lived inside the farm near a village. Since Idahosa was a great storyteller, he was able to narrate the story of his life to him and his other children. How he was born and how his parents migrated from the city to go live inside a farm, because they needed to farm to outlast the periodic widespread-severe famine that almost send them to their graves. In the city, asIdahosa had said, the whole family and the entire people in the place where his father was born, were said-to-be bronze casters. They were using clay molds for casting bronze statues—they were all artists. But his father and mother decided to go and live in a different part of the world, leaving behind their artistic life to become farmers. At this period, everyone were having the right to take a land and start farming without another person interfering, so said, David's father.

When his father arrived at that village, since they were not having a house of their own and there was nobody they knew that was going to harbor them, so they went to meet the head of the village who was ordained chief by inheritance by the villagers. The chief, then instructed men and women to render Idahosa's father a help to construct his mud and bamboo sticks house which he said did not take them a week. So when Idahosa's father gave birth to him, he was named in their native language, Idahosa, to say, they trust and hope in God, the giver of everything.

David's father who was the eldest son of the five children they were having, became a strong and hard-working man, a persevering man, and was also a diligent person who was able to ensure a better life for his own parents and two brothers and two sisters. He became a home builder and was specialized in handmade brick working and scaffolding; he also became a building contractor. In those days, there were buildings with mud houses, so Idahosa was able to bring his family who were living inside the farm all alone by themselves to the village where he built a house for them to live with the other villagers. Not quite long, he decided to go live in the city, as he was making more money in his professional building jobs. But after a few time, the parents died, and David's father said he mourned them so much that he almost lost his sight.

He later married at his twenties, and then after he had three children with his first wife, he decided to marry his second wife—since having many wives at that time—to them, was a count of wealth. He married the second wife who later left him, because she confessed of being a witch, according to what David's father said.

After his second marriage failed, he did on his own volition, with pleasure and without fear of contradiction, moved away from his house in the village, allowing his other brothers and sisters live there and went to live in the city with his wife and children. During this time, Nigeria was still a country under the British colony and the people were all hoping to have their independence soon, making them think of coming near the city to live. He then laid a foundation for his third house and started building it, meanwhile he was already living in his second house in the city. He decided to have another house which was more closer to the city center, as the more money he was having and the progress he was making, the more he loved to walk closer to civilization. His wife then gave birth to another four, making it to be seven children and they were all living happily until at a time he met another woman and made her his second wife, which was the beginning of his stressful life events.

David was told by his father that at this very time, he decided to marry his second that was supposed to be his third wife who appeared to be the most wonderful person on Earth and is also the mother of David. And immediately he married her, that was when his stomach ulcer started developing into a strange sickness he could not find a cure to, all throughout is lifetime.

David's mother, Veronica had her first son with another man before, but she lost him. So when she got married to his father and had a daughter, she named her Mary, because Mary was said to be the mother of Jesus Christ, and she had decided to christened her with a Christian name, since they were at the beginning of the Christian era in Africa. Veronica could read and write but not very good. The little she could understand about education, was what made his father fell in love with her.

His mother was born into a polygamous family. Her father was holding a chieftaincy title, meaning she was a well-to-do man. She, her younger sister, and her younger brother who later died at the age of forty after having had four kids, were all born of the same mother and were still very young when their father died, which made their mother moved away, leaving her children, not minding how they might survive in the village to go marry a wealthy man in the city. According to what David was told, Veronica's mother, after having three other children for the man he went to marry, she was chased with a cutlass out of the house by the man. But after a short period of time, her second husband died and she became a widow for the second time.

David's mother later had eight children, including David and her first daughter, Mary, while his father kept scrambling and tussling, looking for a cure to his stomach ulcer, which he never found.

A week before David was born, from what he was told, his family lost a great man that was said to be his eldest half-brother. He died of kidney failure, and was survived by three children, one of them who was born the same day with David, but later died at his early age. David's father, who never was opportune, in the nick of time to have education, sworn with his life to reverse this and to possess the power to ensure a good education for all his children. But how was he going to do this when he was always sick and was spending the little money he was earning to save his life? So, that was the reason he was unable to fulfill that promise despite how much he tried. His first daughter became his first child, and she got married to a wealthy man whom actually nobody knew the type of job he was doing or how he met with his fortune, but was well-feathered and was a member of the moneyed class, with a luxurious lifestyle. It was later, when David grew up that he came to fathom how his eldest half-sister and her children and husband were always talking about money and wealth and it was the most essential part of their lives and was also the only good thing they believed. David saw that they were lured by the smell of filthy lucre and were happy with their lives.

His father was getting too old with the stomach ulcer sickness he could not find a cure to and soon became apparent that he was going to die. There was no hospital he did not attend, and there was no traditional herbalist with lots of experience that he did not visit. He once said to David and some of his other brothers when he was telling them about his life, since he was a good storyteller—both the story of his life and that of the impostors whom he knew. He said he ate every leaves from the forest, some which were poisonous and some which were not—and he was convinced by some herbalists who were having the experience in this profession and some others who were just impostors and were doing everything to make money. He said he did everything just for his stomach ulcer to get cured; he became older and was less vigorous and was much afraid of death, but more concerned about how David and his other brothers and sisters were to survive without him being alive. He love them so much, because he said they were giving him hope every time he was seeing them.

It came to a time when he stood as a guarantor for his nephew to borrow some money from a moneylender who warned them of how he was going to increase the interest if they ever fail to pay back in a given time. His nephew indeed failed to pay back, because he had an accident with the same car he bought with the money. Since there was no insurance company at that time, his nephew ran away, leaving the debts for David's father to pay. Things then turned from bad to worse for him. So he started paying and was trying out different means on how to raise money to pay off the debt. It was not just paying the debt that bothered him most, but the interest. He knew he had to sell most of his properties, and that was exactly what he did. He could not meet up to raise the money, neither could he cater for his family, nor send them to school, the way he has promised. He loved education and has always said to his children, "Education is the key to success and the doorway to a better future." Since he was illiterate, he thought it will be the best thing for him to render to his children according to how serious they want it, so as for them not to undergo the same degradation he too undergone during his youth. But all the good plans he contrived became a nightmare. Anything anybody does to amuse him, was only to cross with him. Actually, his rational explanation for standing as a guarantor for his nephew was to help him succeed in life. It is true they say, "Good people suffers from severe afflictions, while evildoers relish life more, each day and every day." David said he could not imagine how in life someone could hurt a man with a good heart like his father. The peculiar thing about everything was that, his brother, the father of the man that landed him into this life of hardship and toil, never fret himself about it. "We do know who our enemies are when we strike a bad patch."—which goes with the saying, "A friend in need is a friend indeed." The only friends that he could have during this hard time, were his four youngest male children he had with his second wife and the last born of his first wife. And thanks to his best friend, a lady who did the best she could, borrowing him money with less interest so he could pay off the debt, in return, he sold most of his landed properties to her. They both became two good friends. With joint effort, they both invested in agriculture. David's father, knowing that the building of houses were no longer profitable the way it usually was, as there arise new methods of building houses with bricks, and moreover, younger people with innovation then took control as better professional builders. David's father undeniably, with open arms, welcomed and admitted the new image and platonic idea that was drawing close to civilization. He made his debut as a good farmer and investor by investing on poultry and livestock farming—which was prolific. With his work being of a consistently high standard and his children being of a great consolation to him during all these time of a huge obstacle and frustration, he was able to regain his sensation of pleasure which is very important to every normal person for improving their physical and mental well being. This felicity is what energized him to be able to move on—though with his impeccable manners.

With the little profits he made from his livestock and poultry home industry, he was able to go to his village to re-invest in agriculture, this time not the way his father did, but in a larger scale. He was having lots of landed properties in his village, so that made it more easier for him. All he did was to cultivate the land and planted maize, yam, cassava, pepper, and so many other vegetables, but he flatly declined to accept that the village was a better place for him to live—for that, taking care of the farm became a difficult task, since he would have to go everyday with a bicycle to the farm which was four miles from the city where he was living. Yet he did not yield up, even when the stomach ulcer he was suffering from still was incurable. Physically and mentally, he was stronger than ever. His two wives, David's mother and his step-mother were hundred percent in support and were always at his back. David said sometimes when he glanced at this, he was able to draw a comparison of his father's life with Bob Marley's saying, "Tis, he who fight and run away, live to fight another day," as he was a great fan of this artist and love the inspiration he gets from his music.

After much sacrifices of time and energy to improve his financial situation, David's father was able to realize the goodness of being capable to restore yourself as a man and as a leader in resisting every tremendous spot of trouble. Although he did this with the family's supports he received. He has always blamed himself for being foolish to stand as a guarantor for another man to borrow money. But to David, it was not foolishness, it was just that he was only trying to be good, because he said he believe anyone can fall a victim, as every human being born by a woman is fallible.

The West African countries experiences uniformly high temperatures all year round, but there are two major seasons—the dry season and the rainy season. The dry season is when everywhere become drier and sunnier with less rain and less cloud cover and the temperature climbs as high as thirty-three to thirty-six degree centigrade. While the rainy season is when there is more rainfall and the temperature is in-between twenty-two to twenty-five degree centigrade.

It was on Monday morning in the middle of October, the beginning of the next dry season—at the time the sun was very hot and everywhere were dusty, that he was almost suffocating to death. David was dressed in khaki shorts and shirt and sanders to match. He was with his mother and they were both walking to his new school which was almost opposite his house. When they arrived there, they were asked to be on queue with the other pupils and their parents for registration of the new pupils to be admitted that year. Many women were there, holding their children close to them, with strident voices from different angles, making many unable to hear the instructions they were given. But all of them accustomed to it easily, as it was their culture. Women and their children with them were moving around from one place to the other in the random zigzag motion. Other pupils were going out of the school while others were coming in. Noise, noise and noise. For admission of new pupils, it was to be in the headmasters office, and some of the teachers attending to them were practically biased. It was said that some of them were demanding bribes and some parents were offering them so as for their kids to be admitted. Another way out was when you are related to any of them working there.

In those days, most children in Africa were born at home, which is to say, there was no way they could have a birth certificate which was only issued to children that were born in the hospitals. This was making admission for children born of poor parents more complicated. The only way to show that the child was old enough to be admitted, was to ask them to put their hands across their heads and allowing their hands to touch their ears at the other side of their heads. David who was six-and-a-half-year old, was able to touch his ear with his hand at the other side across his head, which gave him the chance to be admitted, as he was born at home and was without a birth certificate. Meanwhile, there were other pupils who were also admitted even as they could not touch their ears with their hands, but due to their parents position of influence or by bribery, things went all well for them. In Nigeria, it is always said that corruption pays more than honesty, and that was David's first time to be experiencing it.

After David was admitted, he was so excited that when he arrived home, he went bragging with some of his friends who were yet not able to start. The next day, at about 12.30 p.m, he was already in school with his mother. They were given lists of books to buy and a prospectus of the school and were also given instructions on the type and color of school uniforms they were to be putting on.

It came to the time when he finally started the school, and when he did, he saw that most of the pupils that were admitted with him, were mainly the ones that had previously attended a day care or a nursery school, but he also came to understand that he was better than many of them.

His first day in school was horrible, as it was something new to him. He thought it was a new way for him to be staying away from his family and be closer to kids like himself. From Mondays to Fridays, he was always with a table and a chair on his head, dressed on his school uniform of dark green khaki shorts and shirt with white collar, walking to school alone. Things were becoming strange to him since he was no longer having enough time to play with the other kids in their yard. He discovered that illumination can only come from learning and it was very interesting to him, which made him started to derive meanings from what his father was preaching to them about education being the doorway to a better future. He thought he saw that the school headmaster and the other teachers were living far better than his parents were. In spite that his father was poor, but he loved him and comprehend the situation he was. He wanted to be seeing his father dressed like the headmaster, but he knew that was going to be impossible. And to make it possible, he thought it will be better if he start to dream like Joseph the dreamer in the bible and get his father out of the impoverished life he was living and make him live the life he wished for him to live. He saw that education was the only means and the only remedy he could be that Joseph.

One afternoon, when he was dressed on his school uniform, with a chair and a table on his head and was about to cross the road to his school, a car almost hit him, but the driver of the car was very careful to have been able to hold the break. When the man came out of the car, he started insulting him and was also insulting his parents who were not there with him for having left him to be crossing the road by himself. Other people who saw it ran quickly to the scene and advised him to return back to his house, but he refused and left them to where he was going to, because he did not want to miss a day without learning. He cherished the friendship of his classmates and always wanted to be seeing them. His first year in that school was like a volcano. Many a time, he witnessed his vital force hanging around his classroom while his body will be at home. He thought of not returning home several times when the school was closed, most particularly on Fridays after his school hours, knowing that he would not be seeing his friends till the next week on Monday, and moreover, because he would be asked by his father on Saturdays to assist him on the farm jobs, which he would have to walk twenty kilometers, waking up as early as 05.00 a.m.

Farming was his father only source of income, and anybody who was not willing to assist him, was actually proclaiming independence and would have to provide for himself every of his/her needs.

Farming in Africa was essentially based on manual labor and it was indeed the most strenuous work to do. At a time, David and his other brothers became inured to this arduous labor of farming and were happy about it, seeing it as a profession. It also came to a time when he was asking his father for permission to go work in the farm alone, making his father became very proud of him as he was also very brilliant in school.

His first term result was not too good and he came out 23rd out of 60 pupils in his class, and yet he was unhappy. But his form teacher cheered him up and praised him. After then, he knew he had to study harder to get close to the other pupils who were better than him. When the second term result came out, he was 19. The third term came and he took 4th, and that term was for them to be promoted to a higher grade.

The second year came, and he was glad he was with the same classmates that were in his previous class; he was doing what he knew will make him attain a better position than he had before. Despite that he was spending most of the weekends in assisting his father to be doing the farm work, but he was also improving his thinking and writing ability. The first term of his second year, he came out 3rd, and second term, he came out 2nd and third term, he came out 3rd again. The third year, he came out 1st from the first term to the third term. When he got to his fourth grade, he came out 1st for the four terms. This made some of his classmates worried, as the secret behind his success was undisclosed to them—which later drove them into a tempest in a teacup, at the end, leading them to jealousy and hatred. This became intractable for David. He was confused about this problem that he thought the best way to deal with it was to be friendly with them, but the more he tried to be, the more they were hating him.

He was one of the smallest child in his class if not the smallest, and he was also the most brilliant among all of them. In some British schools, an older or more intelligent pupil were elected to have some authority over younger pupils and some other responsibilities and advantage. Since Nigeria was colonized by the British, so they adopted most of their culture respectively at schools. When he was elected as the class prefect, most of the grown-up pupils became very rude to him and there was no way he could authorized them to do anything or else he will be beaten up after school, so he decided to quit the job, seeing that it was more than him, and also to be able to focus more on his studies, knowing there is an impact of education in improving the quality of life. Most of the girls in his classroom and generally around the school, were anxious to know him, as there were widespread rumors about him being the most brilliant pupil in the school even when he was at his fourth grade, still waiting for another two grades.

During this time, as a child he was beginning to apprehend the meaningful consequences one can accumulate from publicization or rather ostentation. He was not at the initial time aware of the peril he was imposing on himself till then. Although he could understand how unfortunate it was for him to be impecunious and to have come from a poor home. He was beginning to see how he was detesting himself for being alive, due to the fact that he could not withstand the jealousy and hatred that were coming from his classmates, friends at home, and also his brothers and sisters. His controversial life which he was unwilling to abandon was becoming very boring, yet so many girls were dying to know him. These were all contributing to his adversity, bringing tears of anguish to his eyes. There came a time when he started thinking everybody around him were talking about him anywhere he was. But even if all these were happening, there was still one thing that was still amusing him and made him believe he was from the profundity of his misery, it was reading. Reading was the only way he could see himself as human. While other kids were having fun, he will be studying, thinking fun makes people vulnerable.

One night, he dreamed he was alone, reading a novel which was very interesting. Some of his classmates came to ask him to follow them to play, but he refused, and as he did, they started shouting and laughing and making those strange noises and playing games, but he tried to stop them, and as he tried, he found their laughter and noisy games more coarse and vulgar. Immediately he screamed and woke up from sleep. His mother also woke up from sleep, asking him what the problem was. It was then, he understood he was dreaming. From that day on, he knew he would have to be very careful about how he play with his friends.

They say, "No money, no honey." "Living in poverty seemed to be like living with cancer you cannot cure." His devotion to study was not for him to be unique, but because he thought it was the only way for him to eradicate the poverty which engulfed him and his family. In the farm, every day, he and his other brothers and his father were working tediously for many hours so that his father could be able to raise money to pay all his debts and also to pay their school fees.

When he got to the fifth grade, he drastically changed some many things about himself by spending much time with his friends, playing football and participating in other sports and games—making him develop skills in different sports and acrobatics. Fun is good, so he thought—as he started having it. Yet, every time he thinks about the difficult tasks ahead of him, he will start to shed tears. Although that year was a remarkable year, as everything returned back to normal and his family were able to afford a better quality of life by enlarging their farmland, harvesting large amount of grains and other foodstuffs and making more money, but all with the supports of every members of the family.

It was a day before the last day of the school term, when all the pupils were to leave for their holidays which was to be for one month. David was alone on top of his father's unfinished building with a flat concrete roof that was also near their house. He was always going there to relax and also to read—a thing he was customary for. It was really a nice place to relax and read because of the bright sun and most especially, the cool breeze. He was unable to read the novel he was holding in his hands, due to the too much thinking he was doing about the next day and how his school examination result was going to be, knowing he had spent too much time having fun than studying throughout the term. He was also thinking about his parents who were already in the village and were waiting for them to come over to join them immediately they get their exam results. He saw his heart filled with sadness and he could not do anything to alter the situation.

The next day, when he arrived at school, the name of the girl sitting close to him in the class came out 1st and another boy whose parents were tenants in his father's second house, came out 2nd, while he was in the 3rd position. He started crying, and people around there came to cheer him up. He said he was crying not just because of the result, but because he was asked to go and live in the village with his parents to join them to work in the farm all through that month of holiday, which was like sending a soldier to go fight a war. He said he hated travelling to go live in the village for so many reasons. First, because there was no electric power for light, no water except the people has to go to the stream, and also, the roads were bad. Secondly, according to what he was told, most of the people there were said-to-be witches and wizards who were having the power to turn human beings into goat meats and eat them at nights. Seeing a cat at night was an omen of bad luck, especially when it happened to be black. There was also a belief that most of these witches and wizards were possessing the power of transforming themselves into cats at nights, which was very dreary to the many youths living in the cities that has come to live there. All these miserable feelings David was developing inside him, motivated him to start augmenting a hymn of hate towards his parents. Although loathing them was a thing he could not do, because he understood how they wanted him and his other brothers and sisters to succeed in life, so he thought despising them would be a better way.

He and his immediate elder sister, Tina, and two other of his brothers and sisters, one older and two younger, all arrived at their village at about 06:00 p.m, after trekking for five hours from the city. Seeing that their mother had already prepared their best meal for them, which was rice and stew—a meal that could only be eaten by rich people anytime and every time, but can only be eaten by the poor at the time of celebration, probably on Christmas and New-years days or on Easter day or sometimes on Sundays or when celebrating the country's Independence day, which is every October 1st. Preparing rice and stew at that time was much more expensive than preparing any other meal and was meant for mainly the rich people, because of the high cost of living, and as the country's economy was in an inflationary spiral of wage and price increase and the lack of job opportunities. It was at this same time, David said when he grew up and was living in Europe, he came to ascertain the reason why most people living in poor countries had decided to believe more in the existence of a supernatural Being than the people in rich and developed countries. He said he could understand that these poor people are left with no choice than to believe, since they could see it to be the only means to survive their everyday hardship. To many people living in rich countries, belief is probabilistic, since many have come to believe more in evolution, which to these poor people in the third-world countries is a taboo.

The next day after they arrived in the village, they started going to the farm, and it was every morning by 05:00 a.m that their father normally come to wake all of them up to get prepared to go to the farm. They were always the first people to leave to the farm and also the last to return back home. It was seen that they were working more than the people in the village. Sometimes, their father would have to hire more workers to assist them to do the farm work, since his farm was extremely large and they were unable to do everything all alone by themselves. Everything were going on smoothly despite the fact that they were working too much and not having time to rest. David was in fact a young boy with sensation of pleasure, thrilled and full of exaltation; he was just like every normal kids again, until one evening, at about

07:00 p.m when he, his father, and his other three brothers were still in the farm, waiting for the rain to cease so they could go home. It was almost dark and the only source of light was the sun and no electricity in the village. They all waited and waited till 09:00 p.m and the rain was still falling heavily. Since they could not wait longer, the father ordered them to get up and walk through the rain to their house, as they were shivering in the cold. As they arrived home, their mother was so happy, because she was starting to be afraid that something horrible had happened to them. But something struck his heart when he was asked to come pound the yam since it was his turn to do so, meanwhile his other brothers and sister had showered and went to their neighbor's house to play with the other children there, because there was a glass gaslight in that house, making many children go there to play. In that village of a population of approximately two thousand people, there were three of that type of glass gaslight, and they were owned by the head of the village. Then, the man supposing to be the richest in the village, since his children were doctors, lawyers and business men living in the city. The third person was the man who owned the house close to his father's house—a man who was working in the city and was a very good man with a wife and six children who were also good to David's father and his family.

Immediately David picked up the pestle and dropped it inside the mortar to start pounding, his lost memory came back to him, knowing at some deep level that what he was doing was wrong, by thinking his parents were exploiting them, probably his father whom with his brothers and sister's aids, had been able to secure a large amount of money for the payment of his debt. Although he continued to pound the yam, but his mother was staring at him, knowing already he was worried and something was wrong. So she asked him, 'my son, I hope you are fine,' and David answered him, 'yes mama.' 'I really cannot believe you are fine, since I know all these works are too much for you and your brothers and sister. You see! your father and I do love you all and want everyone of you to have education so that you might not suffer the way we are suffering now. We are proud of all of you and we appreciate the hard work you are doing, but we cannot say it out.' As the words went deeply into David's ears, sinking down to his heart, he was stunned, dumb struck, seeing his mother to be a good psychologist. Instantly, he came to expound his view on the proverb his father had said sometime ago that, "A good timber tree does not grow with comfort. The stronger the wind blows it everyday and night, the stronger the tree becomes." He came to understand that his father was not exploiting them, instead, he was trying to make them to be strong so as to be able to cater for themselves in the future time. After he finished the pounding at about 12:20 midnight, his mother went to call his other brothers and sister to come eat. They all ate the food, spent some hours of storytelling and listening, since it was a native habit to them every night before going to bed. They slept late that night, knowing the next day was a day strictly forbidden for people to go to the farm, since it was said to be so according to a fable told to them by their ancestors of how it was a day the dead had chosen to visit the Earth and later return back to their different homes. It was also said that many people who declined to comply to this fable by going to work in the farm, never return back home alive. At later time when David grew older, he decided to put himself to a test by going to work in the farm on this strictly forbidden day, but nothing happened to him. Even his father did the same so many times and nothing happened. But most villagers had later came to denounced this and also said their tradition were fading away because of the new religion and culture brought to them by their colonial masters.

The one month holiday David spent with his family in the village was incredible, at a time he was unwilling to return back to the city, because there in the village, it was all fun every time. He was getting to love and show some interest in the many jokes, tales, fables, and parables his father was telling them. He was also enjoying the plenty of fresh food and meat and vegetables that were surplus for them to eat. And there was something that amuses him most that he love to do and that he never had the chance to do in the city—that was, going to the stream to swim with many girls and boys of his age and also older people. It was all fun, even at his later life in the future, when he came to take his memory back to this particular time and considered it the most happiest time of his life, because he said it made him to understand the importance of living close to nature.

CHAPTER 4

ONE MONTH HOLIDAY PASSED AND David was back at school again. At first it seemed boring to him basically because he thought it was better for him to live in the village with less stress, and there were events that he loved that amuses him, so also were hard work and good companionship. But, as time went on, after he regained his senses in school, he discerned the beauty of the white men world known as civilization, he embraced it again.

It came to the last year of his primary school days and he was in his sixth grade; he knew he would have to be more serious about his studies so that he could shine once again.

In his new class, there were two form teachers, because the class was grouped A and B together. The male teacher was a younger man than any other teacher he has ever had, while the female teacher was the youngest he has also ever had. After another one month, they became three. The new teacher was a bit older and more experienced, as he had spent more time than the rest others in the teaching profession. At that time, the teachers that were mainly employed to teach in the country's primary schools were teachers with teacher's training course. But it was said that these three teachers were the best in the school and were still studying in the universities, but have come to teach so that they could raise money to return back to school to further their studies. The younger male teacher, though with intellectualism, was also taking his position as a teacher in having affairs with the mature female pupils in the class who were all less than fifteen years. David's elder sister was among these girls, as she repeated that class, making her and David to become classmates. After sometimes, the older teacher included himself into this wrong doing and filthy attitudes of abusing and molesting these girls, since they were both in privileged position to make them pass their exams. But, as for the female teacher, she was pretty, smart, prudish, and was with psychic organism. She was the kind of woman that will conform to certain standard adopted by any man with ambition for will and pleasure. She was the kind of woman, when with a man, would make him despise evil and live a prudent life.

David's father had always said things about women that David took to his heart and learn from it. He said, "Behind any successful man, there is a woman. But it has to be a good woman, as many women might want to exploit you, while some might help you to succeed." So anytime David looked at this female teacher, he sees in her, the woman that can help him succeed in life. But he understood there was no way he could have her, due to the fact that he was too young to be thinking of having a relationship with a woman twice his age. What he could not help to resist, was the temptation to always shot her a sideways glance. At a time she reckoned that he was interested in her. So she called him one day, asking him to see her in camera. When he went to see her, she asked him the reason he was always staring at her, but he denied he was. She then cautioned him to stop doing what he was doing and also told him she was old enough to be his eldest sister. When he was about to leave, she called him back and said to her, 'look! I like you because you are a clever boy and I would be more happier to see you focus on your education. If you know why you are here, you will understand what I am talking about.' There was no way he could deny it this time, instead he made her understood how he felt anytime he was seeing her.

Actually David was good at arithmetic more than any other subject, but since she became his form teacher, so many things about him changed—meaning he was transformed and driven into a world of literature and he has seemed to be moving into the realms of fantasy. She made him loved her and he was loving her with all his heart. She became everything he was thinking about and everything he was dreaming about everywhere, every minute every hour. He also dreamed that he married her and took her with him to swim in their village stream. Although he was so young and never understood what love was. He has never even seen a woman naked before, but he was falling in love with a woman twice his age. To him, it was not for sexual reason, but it was because he thought she was attracted to him morally and spiritually. She was possessing every qualities of a veritable artist. She was also a good singer with her voice like that of an angel. She was having a passion for painting and drawing as she was for literature. When she was not teaching, she will be reading a novel, and he has seen her with different novels which made him think she has come to take him to the world he wished to go live. So many times she looked at him and feel sorry for him, knowing he was lost with her love. She called him several times and asked him about his family and his life. They later became friends, but secretly. She was also a devoted Christian and a member of a choir in her church. She wrote many Christian songs and taught them several times how to sing. Even when the other male teacher tried flirting with her to seduce her, thinking she was like other strumpets, she never fell for him. And anytime David was seeing her discussing with the male teacher, he would come to conclusion that he was telling her things about love, and it was making him jealous. But, as for her, she was that pretty young lady who remained what she was and never wore make-ups to make her face look more attractive. She was always plaiting her hair in different African hairstyles, but mostly cornrows. She was natural and was having the beauty of a true African queen.

Later in David's future life at the time he was held behind bars in Italy, he was able to relax his brain and think all about his life—from his childhood to the time he was there. Then he wrote this poem for her, despite he also wrote this same poem and sent it to one American girl, Donna whom he was dating online, lying that he wrote it for her just for him to win her love. In accordance with fact, he wrote it for the woman he had loved with all his heart and never set his eyes on her again.

WHEN AM I GOING TO SEE YOU AGAIN.

Love, people say is blind.
But true love is also hard to find.
When I found you, I found love.
And it made me to stay alive,
Driving me to go and live
In the places I've never been.
The things making me see,
All that I'd never seen.

Your love my strength,
Your love my dream.
To see not, your love I lived.
To have not, your love I lived.
Heaven and Earth, your love was to me.

You came to give me life,
So I can see the light
That shines behind my eyes.
Down I was and started to grieve,
When me, you came to make believe.
So high I can fly to touch the sky,
For your love, if not I'm lost.
For your love, if not I'm nobody.
Will I ever see you again my love?

This poem is prodigiously evocative of his childhood life. He wrote it so it can remind him of the woman he had first known and loved. The woman who taught and encouraged him that, by reading, he could be able to dream bigger to achieve an optimum life. She also taught him and the other pupils to learn moral way of life and also to be wise. During one of her lecture, she told them a story about a wise man and a foolish man, a story David said he never forgot. It was a story about a wise man who built his house upon the rock, and when the rain came trembling down and the floods were going up, but yet the house stood still. Meanwhile, the foolish man also built his house upon the sand, and when the rain came trembling down and the floods were going up, the house fell flat. At the end of the story, she advised them to be like the wise man who built his house upon the rock, even when the rain and storm and winds come upon it, it will remain strong. She also told them another story of how Noah in the bible was drunk and naked, and when some of his children saw him, they mocked him. But when the others saw him, they swiftly got some robes to cover him up. Later when Noah became conscious and heard of this, he cursed those who saw him drunk and naked and were mocking him, while he blessed the others who covered him up with a robe. She later referred Africa and other poor countries to be the generations of those that were cursed, as she also referred the westerners to the generations of those that were blessed. This woman, who actually was a strong believer of the Christian faith, was able to teach them every parables that were said by Jesus Christ in the new testaments. She made them understand that the parables and the whole bible indeed was a metaphor that captures the complexity of real life humans are living. She also advised them to always comply to the commandments of God in the bible. Apart from teaching them to fear and respect God, she also taught them about Shakespeare and the many plays he wrote.

One day, she wrote on the the blackboard with a chalk, THE COMING OF THE WHITE PEOPLE INTO AFRICA PROVE MORE BLESSING THAN A CURSE. After she wrote it, she then asked them to write an argumentative essay on this topic, meaning it was either anyone was to uphold it or oppose it. This in David's later life, had become a debate he is still grappling to find the answer to. He said he could neither uphold it, nor could he oppose it, because he saw in it the advantages and the disadvantages of the white people coming to Africa. Though this lady made him understand that there were more advantages than disadvantages. She also told them many other stories and kept repeating the story of Noah in the bible and how he got drunk and was mocked by some of his children. Throughout David's life, he never ceased to find out whether it is just a fallacy or a fact. But most time when he seek a clarification about this theme, he just could not apprehend it. This also contributed to the reason he led himself into a life expedition. Not to mention who this woman was, but she played a great role and had major influence on his life. David has come to believe in most of the things she taught him, to the length he had wanted to practice some of the thing she preached to him. First he started reading the bible, particularly, the new testament. He was always reading about the parables of Jesus Christ and tried to find some interpretations to them all by himself. To him, he came to see the bible as a gateway to understanding life and everything in it. The prophecies of the book, is to him a thing we should not ignore no matter how much we have devoted our lives to science and technology. He said he is saying this, because the bible has created in him an imaginary fear, and mostly, these could be found in the book of Revelation. At his later future, as life became more complex for him and he became more adventurous with more developed ideas, living in advanced industrialized cities, so he decided to let this imagination run away with him. In spite that he never saw her again or was never going to see her, and no matter where he was or where he is, the picture of her face was always there, and no matter how he tried to erase it, it was always there.

That year which was his last year in the primary school—also said to be some of his most memorable year, as it was of prime importance to his life. That year, he has read many books including books written by the westerners. Since it was his first time of reading books like that, he found it more interesting and yearned for more. He read many short plays written by William Shakespeare, like the TEMPEST, MACBETH, MUCH ADO ABOUT NOTHING, THE MERCHANT OF VENICE and many others. Although at first, he started reading books written by African writers, and among these great books were, the LION AND THE JEWEL, written by Wole Soyinka, the first African to have won a noble prize for literature. He also read, THINGS FALL APART, written by Chinua Achebe, another great writer he love to read his books. He has read many other books written by Africans, like THE GODS ARE NOT TO BLAME, written by Ola Rotimi. One other book that he read repeatedly more than six times was, DIZZY ANGEL and many others that he said he cannot remember their names not to mention the names of the people who wrote them. Out of all these books that he read, he fell in love with Dickens and Shakespeare writings more than he did to other writers. He said he saw Shakespeare as a progenitor of modern playwright with a level of proficiency. He saw that many of the plays and poems Shakespeare wrote, were filled with resonant imagery. And, as he derives pleasure from his writings, he kept reading and was going deeper and deeper.

His first term exam result at school was great. He came out first with a total mark scored which was 380 out of 400. After then, they went on holiday which was short and was just two weeks. This time, his father, his mother, his sister, Tina and his two younger brothers, all traveled to the village, leaving him and his elder brother behind in the city. His father paid for an extra lecture outside the school for the both of them. The lecture which was to be taken throughout the holiday period, was for them to be able to study harder since they were both having a very important exam to take.

His elder brother was to take the Junior Secondary School (J.S.S) exam, while he himself was to to take the Common Entrance exam to transit from his primary school level to a secondary school level. They both needed to study harder, since it was not just an ordinary exams like the rest. Meanwhile, this idea of taking an extra lecture from some university post-graduate students was brought by his elder brother, Ken who was four years older than him and was his mother first male child.

He was named Kennedy after the late president Kennedy of the United States of America who was assassinated. Kennedy was also the owner of all the novels he was reading, as he, David was always experiencing a lack of confidence when demanding money from his father to purchase books. He was always pitying his father, thinking of how he could be able to payoff his debt, and for that reason, he has always wanted to assist him in doing the farm works even when he never asked him to. But, as for Ken—the short name David love to call him, he was the man who cares about himself more than he care for others. He was always fighting for his self-interest. Despite how his father was suffering, Ken never ceased to demand for money from him. Since their father has promised to give them education no matter the situation, so he never declined his assistance to them, since he came to take it to be an obligation. He began to take advantage of his father's ignorance and was demanding for more money from the poor old man every time. What baffled David most was that, the money he was being given was not all for books, but also it was a way for him to purchase new outfits for himself. This to David point of view, was inhuman. He thought it will be better if he put an end to it. But just as he was trying, he was lured into participating in the same acts simply by purchasing some new electronic sets which were bought by Ken and placed inside the room they were both living. David, who saw that it was good to have these material things inside their room, swiftly welcomed the idea and was automatically becoming part his brother's team.

From David's childhood, he has loved music. He was told, at the age of three, he had started murmuring songs and dancing every time the music was playing. So he got thrilled and adhered to this new way of life which his brother, Ken has just introduced. Their father on the other side was able to payoff most of his debts and started erecting a new building, which was his fourth house. David said, when he saw how is father was suffering and was still struggling to erect this new house, he thought he was insane. So one day, he decided to have a discussion with his mother about this issue, but dumbfounded, he heard his mother say his father was doing it because of them. She said his father was afraid he was going to die, and for that reason he has planned to build these houses for them to have a place to live in, since he was having two wives and many children. Hearing this, David shed tears. He saw that his brother was a moron not to have seen all what the old man was planning to do for them. He regarded him to be ungrateful, greedy calf who thinks himself to be smart but not. Although, in his later future, he came to fathom that his father did not actually did what he was doing for him, but he did it for himself, as he became old and was feeding with the rents. But he also did it for Ken and others, who were lazy to fight to achieve a better life rather than look onto their father's properties, as they were the first male children of the both wives to inherit these properties according to their native custom and belief.

During the two weeks holiday, David and Ken were always traveling to meet their family in the village every Friday evening to return back to the city every Sunday evening. It was a good time for him, because he was beginning to attain new information, understandings, and skills in education. His too much devotion to studying made him started to think, with a little imagination he could transform the lives his family were living to a better one. One of the post-graduate student who was teaching them, was always praising him because he saw in him, a healthy intellectual curiosity to explore, discover, and cultivate new talents and interests. He advised him to keep it up and never to deviate from it and also to not associate himself too much with many other kids who were always smoking cigarettes and marijuana and roaming about the school building were the lecturing was held. With these post-graduate students, he was able to learn harder mathematics which was for secondary school students. He was also able to learn better English language, and then, his country and the world history and current affairs. He was also taught biography of the many great men who fought for his country and many other African countries to gain independence—this which later motivated him, as time went on to want to dig deep into history.

Ken, on the other hand was about to become an adult. He was just a little more than sixteen, and was beginning to feel like a man and was at the third grade of his time in the secondary school. Although he repeated one class at his sixth grade in the primary school. This same Ken, whom David, with comprehensibility, was skeptical about his chances of succeeding in life, was his elder brother and at the same time, to his best knowledge, his best friend. They were always doing their home assignments together and discussing about the novels they have read. And, since they were living in the same room, they became friends even to an extent, they were gossiping about the same women.

David loved his brother and tried to assist him in many ways he could. But, as time went on, the moment he started to read about Cain and Abel in the bible, he came to take it personally and was able to interpret the clear differences between him and his elder brother. He saw that he was always in a conviction to the contrary of his elder brother's doctrine which was only a way leading to devastation of everything he was trying to build.

The three weeks they both spent in the city alone while their parents and their other brothers and sister were in the village, was splendid and sensational. He was able to read all the many books he had wanted to read and was able to study hard as he had wanted to. His skills in sport and acrobatics were also improved. He became one of the best footballer and acrobat in the street where they were living. Though, he learned everything from Ken, but at a time he became better than him, and were competing with many other youths who were coming from the nearby streets. He became famous and everybody in his street including his brother, were proud of him. They both enlisted in a football team organized by some other grown up boys in their street and held matches with other teams from the nearby streets. He was having enough fun, forgetful of the vulnerability. But he came to discover something unique about himself, which he sees as a gift from God. He saw that he was able to do anything he set his mind to doing, and even do it better than other people who have been doing it. It also astonished many of his friends including his brother of how he was developing skills in everything he was doing. In response to this, many girls were seeing him as a genius and were falling in love with him.

It was said to be a beginning of a new era, as David's older half-brother who was the fifth born of his father's children successfully traveled abroad. At this time of the eighties when very few people were having their relations in Europe, mainly Germany or west Germany the way it was called then. Despite that he was able to read all the great books and studied and participated in sport activities and was also seeing himself to be one of the most happiest person on Earth to be seeing that his elder brother was in Germany, many things still made him feel guilty and full of remorse—and it was simply because he was not living with his family in the village. He said he was missing the fun he usually have when going to the stream to swim with many other boys and girls, the tales and fables he was told by his father and other old men and women that was compelling him to approve of their superstitious beliefs. And most of all, how he usually go to the toilet inside the bush and then, using some dropped leaves from rubber plants to clean his anus. Initially it seemed primitive to him, but it was fun. He also later found it difficult to go to poop in the pit latrines in the village, as there were always flies flying around him anytime he tried to do so. So, it was more comfortable, warm, and safe going to poop inside the bush. To him, it never seemed unwise as in his later life, it made him to be able to distinguish between primitiveness and civilization and also to recognize the sensibility and insensibility of the both sides.

After the holiday, everybody were returned back to school, just the way David's family also returned back to the city. It was then, his father was informed that Sunny, his son has traveled abroad. Looking at him, David could see how he was so excited and delighted about the news. His father, without having to waste much time, went to meet his first daughter who was married to a rich man, since they were said to be responsible for the necessary funds for the successive change of place and life of the young man called, Sunny. Although this story was later changed as time passed when it was revealed that David's father was among the sponsors. David's oldest half-sister who was married to a rich man was said to have also contributed a great deal to this. Most of the money and other aids were also said to have come from Sunny's friends who were living abroad. Sunny was having too many friends when he was at home—some of them who were living in the U.s. and U.k. and they were always coming to visit him whenever they return from abroad. Some of them who were recognized as their family relations who had once stayed in his father's house before traveling abroad. Sunny who was the most educated amid the other brothers and sisters David has, attended a technical college after he completed his secondary school and later became a technician, using one of the stores in his father's house to be a workshop which he was not paying for. Every time David sees Sunny, he just kept asking himself why he did not proceed further with education to become a physician or a lawyer. He thought he could see him to be a person with the power, capable of changing the wretched situation of his family to become something different. But instead, Sunny was very busy dating different women, dissipating the little money he was earning from his job on them. He was not doing anything to favor his father, but he was always stealing from him and was causing him more distress and soreness. He became very perfect in sneaking into his father's bedroom by cutting the ceiling in his bedroom and passing through the roof only to go steal the little money and other valuable materials hidden by his father. He was the clever thief, the way David always referred him to be, but later when he traveled abroad, he became the figure head of the family whom everyone of them were looking onto, believing he was going to wipe away their every tears.

Although, David's father had pretended his son had with inexplicability, fortuitously made that trip to abroad without his consent and assistance—which actually was not true, but was a way to make them think of struggling to help themselves and not to wait for him. Even, when his father and Sunny were always seen as cat and rat before he left to abroad, but he was seen lamenting when he left—he was lamenting for not having contributed much for the trip. David said he was able to glimpsed how much love and affection his father had secretly concealed from Sunny when he was at home with them, but, when he left them, he saw how his father, including every member of his family felt his absence.

The eldest son of all was an habitual criminal who at many a time been convicted of theft and jailed. He was called Moses—who was supposed to have led them out of Egypt if actually he understood the significance of his name in the bible. Although, he was popularly known as Boma, and he was nothing but a nuisance. Many times, Boma had met his father's friends who offered him a driving job, based on the trust and assurance of his father. But after some period of working with them, he would decide to sell the vehicles and run away, letting his father being held responsible. These were among the many debts his father suffered to work for to pay. For these reasons, his father hated Sunny and Boma, because they were not assisting him in doing his farm work, but were always causing him trouble. David said he was always seeing himself in the middle of heaven and hell when he watch his father with anger, cursing his older brothers, repeating some words of incantations, and also saying their children will always treat them the way they have treated him. David saw that his father hated Boma more than he hated any other person on Earth, as he was his first male child after the the one who was supposed to be first, died of kidney failure. Sunny was useful in many ways, because he was educated and was always rendering him helps when it come to reading letters for him and fixing the doors and windows or getting some electronic sets or electrical works repaired, which sometimes he charges him more than he was supposed to pay for buying the tools needed for doing the job. Sunny was so brainy which made his father looked miserable and felt sick when he left. Despite that they were both cat and rat that they were, but he has always planned of how to finance his trip to abroad, as everybody at that time were seeing it to be a lucrative business.

They say, "Hope is a thing of the heart. A thing we cannot see, but can only feel." Traveling to abroad was Sunny only hope and dream, but he kept it to himself, not willingly wanting to give it up maybe for another option in spite the fact that he knew it had distracted his attention away from furthering his education. Even at the time of his distress and confusion, one thing he hoped for, was traveling abroad. But he thought he was keeping it to himself, not knowing everyone of them in his family already knew what his plan in life was. David said he saw how Sunny and his friends were discussing about this subject matter that he came to believe it was the only dream anyone of them could dream, and it was to them, like—dream a dream and you must achieve it or else . . . .

CHAPTER 5

RETURNING BACK TO SCHOOL FROM the holiday, virtually all pupils in his school were still not in their readiness to receive lectures. The teachers were trying on their possibly best to re-organize them by making them change their seats. As for David, he was full of delight instantly as he saw the lady he has been dreaming to see—that was his female form teacher. The two weeks holiday that passed, to him was depth of misery, because he could not see her face. Everyday, he wished he could look into her eyes, but all of a sudden, he saw himself sitting face to face, gazing into her eyes. Although this was not the first time it had happened that he was having a teacher and a pupil secret affair. At the age of ten, at his fourth grade, his female teacher who was a wanton hussy, called him to ask him about his life and how he became so brilliant, but she was looking into his eyes. He immediately felt something emotional for her—something relating to sex, and she knew it and kept doing what she was doing to make him continuously feel it. This way he had first learn how to feel something for a woman, but he never loved her until he met this lady whom he came to love spiritually and could not have her or even utter it out to her that he was in love with her.

When he saw her coming towards where he was sitting, he quickly stood up and greeted her, 'good morning, mam,' and she responded, 'good morning my dear, how are you?' 'Fine, thank you,' he replied. 'How was your holiday?' she asked him again. 'Fine mam,' he replied her again. 'I am so glad you are,' she said. 'She will never know how much I have been missing her and wanting to see this her pretty face,' he murmured to himself. Looking at her as she walk to go sit in her seat, he could see how pretty she really was, making him believe, seeing her everyday will give him joy and steal his grief. She was as he was always thinking in his heart—the one born to make him happy.

The second term commenced with him poised eagerly with enthusiasm, knowing he was preparing for his last exam—the Common Entrance exam. He was with self-appointed task, cheerfully, wanting to say good-bye to his primary school life and as he envisioned himself a new student in one of best secondary school in the city where he was living—living the life of the BIG BOYS, a name people in the secondary schools were popularly known for. With much determination and plans, he was better than ever because he had studied harder during the holiday period. He was already taught most of what he was to be taught in the class. When the female teacher he was in love with noticed this, she called him to ask him how he did it. He went on to explain everything to her, and he saw that she was impressed. 'You do not need to tell me you are prepared for the Common Entrance examination, I already knew you are, so keep it up,' she said to him and asked him to go and have his seat.

The second term exam came and he came out first, scoring 400 out of the total marks of 400. The secret lore of this, was that he has been taught everything by the post-graduate students. With this he came to take the plunge and walk closer to a particular interest to elaborate on the subject matter of how money can buy almost everything. He saw himself able to buy knowledge with money, as the post-graduate students had given him enough knowledge just for the little money he paid. From what he learnt from this, in his later future life he was enraged, when he was watching in a television, a man getting interviewed about a book he wrote, entitled, AFRICANS ARE LESS INTELLIGENT THAN WESTERNERS. The man went further to elaborate on this issue, claiming blacks are less intelligent than the whites. Although, David said he never think of how to read the book to understand the reason why he claimed a title like that for his book, but from what he believed and from what he has experienced, he could see that the man is totally wrong and he could be referred to as a racist. He said he said this because he cannot see a hungry child being capable of learning what a child fed thrice a day could learn. Or he could put it in a different but yet more similar way. "Whom among us will not want to feed our stomach first before feeding our brain?" To David, he said he sees everybody to be intelligent, as he also sees that everything comes from a source. "To be intelligent also depends on the environmental and financial influence of an individual, as no man is born to be foolish." It is said that talent comes naturally, but with the influence of something—something relating to the financial, physical, and mental well-being of a person. Because, a person who is sick or starving can never be wise, as he/she is totally incapable of acting upon his/her dream. From talent, wisdom is acknowledge. Most people describe wisdom as the ability to make sensible decisions and give advises because of the experience and knowledge possessed by an individual. While they describes talent as the natural ability to do something well. Some claim talent is from the devil, while others claim it to be from God. It is one man who has been able to define it properly. He said, "Talent is neither from God, nor from the devil. Talent comes from the natural surrounding we live. Our entrenched interest in driving to our visions and imaginations improved to become a skill. In other words, we say, too much concentration on a particular thing makes us understand it better. This is mostly referred to as, practice makes perfect. Talent is in everyone of us. All we need to do is to build and shape it to become what we want it to be." David said he could get to the bottom of this theory to understand that, we cannot expect a man born and raised up in the amazon forest to be as smart as a man who was born in Tokyo, Japan with close access to computers and robots. This is not to withstand theoretically, why David with a passion for adventure has always disapproved of the notions of so many youths of nowadays who prefer an easy life that is full of pleasure, but that can cause them harms in the end—the primrose path, the way it is mostly referred to. His passion for adventure was unveiled to him during his childhood. This, he had later launched into a task throughout his childhood, adolescence, and adulthood, so as to think of a way to eradicate poverty from his life and the life of his unborn children and children's children. He saw that to be poor is like to be sick, and for this reasons most people including him refer to poverty to be financial sickness. Not only that it is said but it also a fact that three-quarters of the population of Africans live in poverty. As many teenagers are forced to cater for themselves without any support from their parents or the government or from any organization. Instead of concentrating on their studies, they will be concentrating on how to feed. "In accordance to fact, we the people of the world are so egocentric, lost in treasure, and sunk in iniquity that we have chosen to ignore the adversity engulfing the poor and the less privileged and even mock them with it when we are not ignoring it." Do we not think it to be inhuman for a man to take another man's adversity to be the butt of his joke? For the nemesis for this might be extended to these peoples children's children, from one generation to another. This, undeniably is egomania—an exaggeration of egoism.

Just when David was still speculating about the reasons why things like this happens, then walked in involuntarily, 2nd David, the ideologist, with a great intellectual exercise, and he said to 1st David, 'stop complaining about how people mock you because of your poverty. The crucial thing is for you to find a way out of that poverty. "People mock you so that you can realize your problems and get a solution to it." Or did not father used to tell us that, "Anyone who mocks us of our poverty life is telling us that we are weak and need to work harder." Why are you now fretting yourself about this when you should be finding a solution to your problems?' 'Yes, father did said that, but do you not also think we can also assist each other at the time of anyone's need? replied 1st David. After he finished saying that, he raised his head up to see that his soul, 2nd David, the ideologist was nowhere to be found.

After David's second term, he thought it will be better for him to study with the post graduate student throughout the holiday once again, but unfortunately for him, they all returned back to their various schools. His father was able to seize this opportunity to take them to the village to work in the farm. David, who was not happy about this idea, only found himself unable disapprove of it, since he was to obey and comply to his father's every will and decisions.

When he finally arrived at the village with his family, it took him just some few days to be oblivious of the life he was living in the city and face reality that he was in the village again to do the farm work. He became happy again, not thinking much about his life and influence on education. He and his elder brother, Ken were getting closer, just when their friendship was also becoming stronger. They both honor the glory of this friendship which was a strategy for them to extract money from their father and go live in the city.

David's plan was never to leave his father in the village and go live in the city when actually there were enough work for them in the farm, and probably because of the enough fun he was having there already. But Ken who was too determined to leave, promised him a new way of life that will yield better life with much fun. And after much confrontation with their father, they were finally given the privilege and money to go live in the city. As they left, David already foreseen how they were going to indulge themselves in a serious misfortune. But he also wanted to see the light again and read a good novel and experience the pleasure of a good music from the radio once again.

Back in the city, he came to comprehend the sweet reason why Ken had been so anxious to come over to live there—and the reason was that he was in love with a girl living opposite their house. At this time, he and Ken had moved into the room which their older half-brother, Sunny left. With Ken being able to extract enough money from their father, he was able to put the room in the best form that he wanted. It was then he started teaching David how to lie to extract money from their father. With the enough money they were having, they were able to purchase a good radio tape player. Ken, who believed everything and everywhere in the room should be cleaned every time, was spending all his time shining and polishing it six times each day which was making David feel uncomfortable. He knew initially it was going to be a difficult life for him to live with Ken in the same room, but he wanted to experience that life and see how difficult it was going to be. He understood the way Ken was cleaning everywhere was a plan of campaign to make him leave the room for him alone, yet he never relinquished the idea of leaving even when he believed himself to be so unfortunate to be having a brother like him that could never be trustworthy. He instantly knew his brother was using him for his own purpose, and he was seeing everything about him so absurd. He thought he reckon that he was a person who would want to live a life of dynamism, but to his astonishment, he saw him as being retrogressive, and it was making him develop more hatred for him. He also saw him to be weak, cowardly, treacherous, and unprincipled. He knew he had hated him since he understood he was the kind who would want to suck every blood out of you until you are dead. From him he also learned to lie and steal.

So, David was coming to regret what motivated him to leave the village to come to the city to meet with the tragic and uncomfortable life he was living with his brother who promised him everything and at the end of it, he was being humiliated. He felt abashed and thought it will be better for him to return back to his family in the village. And, when everything continued without change, he came to recall that this was the beginning of the misfortune he foreseen when he first arrived.

But he was glad that he was experiencing this kind of life, since it was an opportunity for him to apprehend to not ever put his trust in any human being.

After some weeks passed, their parents returned back to the city, since the schools were resumed and all the pupils were also back. It was their last and most difficult exam which they were to face as primary school pupils. Everybody were getting prepared, so was David. The exam was scheduled for the next few days which was just one single day, and it was on Saturday. There were much revisions to do, so the school teachers were doing the best they could to get them prepared by revising with them everything they were taught before.

It was on Saturday morning, all the final year pupils with their mathematics sets on their hands, were assembled, awaiting consciously for the headmaster to come and instruct them of the rules and regulations, which anybody who fails to comply with, will be expelled from the exam hall and from the school. Although he later came to understand this was a strategy to scare them not to cheat.

David from a distance, could see Miss B, the name he preferred to call his form teacher whom he was secretly in love with and could not utter it out to her or to any other person. He saw her discussing with some other teachers and wanted to call her so that she could wish him good luck, but he could not. He tried to dispose himself in a position where she could see him, but she was eventually laughing and chatting with some of her colleagues. This made him felt ill-conditioned, believing he was going to lose her forever. Not quite long, the headmaster dropped in to give the instructions and they were later asked to go to their different classes and they all marched to their classrooms, sitting by numbers given to them alphabetically according to their surnames. David and his elder sister were to be in the same class and also in the same role, but the teacher in charge who was brought from another school, decided to change them, meanwhile they were left in the same classroom. To David, the exam was so simple, as he was being taught almost everything, so instead of him fretting himself, he was meditating on how he was going to be in the secondary school without knowing the whereabouts of Miss B. As he was meditating, the other pupils sitting close to him were scuffling with their brain to get the answers to the objective questions. When he came back to life from his meditation, knowing he was too young for Miss B and that it will be better if he move on with his life, so he started answering the questions which did not take him thirty minutes out of the two hours they were given.

Immediately he completely answered the questions to his satisfaction, he gave room to the other pupils sitting close to him so as for them to copy, but he was so cautious not to let them copy everything. They did the same throughout with the other three subjects. Maths, English, Social studies, and Bible knowledge were the only four subjects they were instructed to take in that exam. After they left and were discussing about the exam while walking home, successfully claiming victory even when the answer sheets were still not yet been transferred to where the examiners were to mark them. Most of the girls who sat close to him were coming to thank him for his generosity. Inside him, he was the most happiest person living on Earth, as he looked at himself to be a hero; he wished he could see Miss B to narrate everything to her, but she was not there to hear him; he looked at the sky to see if he could see her face, and her face was not there. He knew he was to wait till the next Monday to see her.

On Monday morning after the exam, he was in his class with the other pupils, having a discussion with some of his friends about the exam, meanwhile the class turned out to be substantially noisy since all the teachers were absent. He could not meditate because of the too much of noise, so he took an excuse from the class prefect to go and urinate. The class prefect who was his friend refused to allow him go out because he was upset about what happened on the day of the exam. He was definitely upset because some information were passed to him of how David made everybody in his class copied from him. He was jealous and discontented the way he was being lauded for his generosity by everybody in the class. When David heaved a sigh and stood up for the second time, calling on the prefect's name loudly, 'Victor, are you going to allow me go out to urinate?' The boy who was with a heart of stone, answered him saying, 'you are not going anywhere. You can urinate where you are if you want. But going out of this classroom, you are prohibited.' To David's astonishment, he saw other boys and girls going out and coming in. Instantly he fathomed the reason why this was happening. But he thought it was not worth the aggravation for him to be detested and punished for his generosity for others by his own friend—a boy he has long ascertained to be a foe and was only pretending to be a friend. The boy was said to be Victor and he was from Delta state—the state known to be the treasure Base of the Nation, simply because that is where most of the oil in Nigeria is refined. Victor who was living with his aunt and her husband who were both tenants in David's father's house, was a clever boy with ambition and was three years older than David. He was constantly denouncing how the people in the city where David was born and where he too had come to live and was referring to them as lazy fools. Although David was observing him and came to understand he was envying his talent of being capable of doing everything he laid his hands on. He and David were good friends indeed, but Victor has tried all his possibly best to keep that friendship and love him, but he could not even when he forced himself to—he could not because of the enviousness. The same boy who edified David on how to start a relationship with a woman, since he has been doing it with so many girls and David was still not prepared to lose his virginity.

Victor's aunt and husband owned a television and they were always working, leaving him at home to be taking care of their newly born little baby. David who was not having any access to his father's television, was constantly present at his friend's house. Several times they would watch the television together, study together, shower together, and even walk to school together. But why the hatred? why? why? This became a question David was persistently and repeatedly asking himself even at his later life when he was already grown up. But he could not possibly provide a confutation to it even with much subsequent experiments. This made him to write a poem at the time he was in prison in Italy, since he could not confide in any of his friends.

FRIENDS.

So many friends I have always had.
With my enemies, I'm more than petrified.
My actual friend, how can I know?
In my guilty acts, why forgive me not?
Perfect as God no one, is it not said?
So to me, your love manifest please

To fortify me to reach the mountain peak.
Tomorrow, something I'm waiting.
What it brings, I do know not.
Me as a child of the living God,
I was born to do it.
Or should I say, it is my destiny.

So many places I've been.
He teniendo muchos amigos.
Truthful to me some were.
Destruction, to some were their aims.
This to you, I'm saying.
Love me or hate me, you either do.
The things I do, I'm confident,
Cos, my Lord already set for me a mission.

Six days after David'd Common Entrance exam, the result was out. It was rumored at first that he passed the exam with a distinction. To him, there was no need for any excitement, because he knew how much he really deserved it. The next two days came, which was on Monday. As David arrived at school, all eyes were on him. He thought if heaven could open his mouth and swallow him, and when he tried to raise his head up, all he could see was everybody staring at him, thinking him to be the hero the school had long dreamed of. To an extent, other pupils from the morning section were all in search of the most intelligent pupil in the entire school. It was said that he scored almost the total marks of the exam. His result was different from that of the three other pupils in the morning section who also passed with a distinction. All the teachers were also staring at him and thinking he was the genius to inspire other pupils in the school. Deep inside of him, he was trying to delineate a situation when he is so excited at the prospect of attending a secondary school. He was seeing that his dream was turning into a reality. He became delirious with joy, but was oblivious of the dream that he thought could be more better for him—the dream when he was seeing himself swimming in the stream in his village with Miss B, and after then, they both went home—and at home, it was there in his heart the exaltation of emotion above logical reasoning, as he scent the delectable smell of the freshly food she was cooking for the both of them. He knew in his heart, he was born to love her as she had always wanted him to succeed in life; but he also understood that she has always wanted him not to ever think about it since he was too young to be thinking of having a relationship, most especially with a woman many years older than him.

Almost all the pupils that were in the same classroom with him on the day of their exam had a remarkable scores, and they were showing gratitude for what he did for allowing them copy from him. Even his elder sister was. His best friend, Harrison whom he has always confide in even when he could not confide in his brother, was also there and was always at his back. Harrison who was to him, a elder brother and a friend, has defended him so many times when other boys and girls tried to beat him up because he was stubborn and wayward. Harrison has also took him home to feed him several times like he was his younger brother. They were two great friends whom many other people believed to be brothers. They had many times studied and worked together but never discussed anything relating to sex unlike Victor. He saw that the empathy between the two of them was so obvious that he thought they were brothers that their both parents had decided to separate them from each other. Throughout his life even when he became an adult, he said he was never able to find a friend as trustworthy as Harrison was, even when he later disappointed him.

The day of the school send-off party came and everybody were flip-flopping and fluttering here and there and transposing food, drinks and other things from one place to another. Many pupils who were to participate in the different programs schematized by the school authority, were all filled with passions and spasms of anxiety, dressing on their most expensive attires, meanwhile David was all by himself solo, dressing on his school uniform, as he was profoundly confused about everything and was meditating on how he will be attending the secondary school. He was too preoccupied with the thoughts of who was to finance his education, knowing that his father was old and sick and might die at anytime. In is later future, this made him to come oppose the idea of many Africans who practice primogeniture. He said he has come to loathe many Africans that have decided to have many children they cannot cater for, because it has with no lie, caused a great damage to the lives of many innocent African children.

As he sat down on the chair watching the plays, cultural dance, and other activities performed by different sets of pupils, he thought he heard some people called his name and it was so clamorous that he could not listen attentively. He tried to fathom what exactly was going on around him, and suddenly, he saw their headmaster staring deep at him and calling his name again. It was then his psyche which had traveled one hundred and ninety kilometers ahead of him, came back to him—and he swiftly stood up and went to stand in front of the audience including the parents and families of the pupils. Although his parents and families were not there because he did not inform them, believing it was not necessary. But many people who were in the same street with him were there since the school was opposite their house—which is to say, the school was built in the same street where his father's house was also built, and it was named Saint Savior after one of the missionaries who first traveled to their country—a name he was later known for when he grew up and was working as an apprentice.

Standing in front of a crowded audience of about seven hundred people was like jumping into the mouth of an hippopotamus, knowing you might not be coming out. Though, as unsocial person, he was shy, sedate and quiet. Then came the headmaster who announced his name as the most intelligent student of the school and was presented with some books and novels and pen for his secondary school career. There were big hands of applause and praises. Parents, teachers, pupils, and all invited guests cheered him up. But all he could do was to look down, and immediately he raised his head up, with a shrewd idea, gazed directly at the lady he loved, the lady who made him believe, "You can earn everything you work hard for." This is for you, he said in faintness to himself.

As he left the audience and went out of the building where the party was held that was also a church, many of the young boys and girls were staring at him. He said he could see into their hearts as the girls were wishing if he could be theirs, while the boys were wishing if they could be as intelligent as he was, but none of them was wise enough to get to the bottom of his heart to see what he was passing through. Though his heart was filled to the brim with rapture and sensation of pleasure, but he could see that he was walking close to a life more difficult than the one he has lived before which was also not far from the road to LET ME SEE IF I WILL MAKE IT. He said he came to understand life a bit and think with his own experience, it will be better to also advise many youths of what is better for them. He said, "Anybody, whom with good fortune happens to have their parents financial assistance to study, should please take it seriously and study hard so they could succeed, as not everyone could have this same opportunity."

Later when he grew up and was already living in Europe, and when he came to recollect back the memory of his childhood as a young boy who thought education was to be a priority in life, but he was later seeing himself committing crimes, he was always on the verge of tears of pains and joy, as it was a proof for a commencement of the external verities of his life. So, he decided to write this poem while he was in the penitentiary in Italy.

LIKE A HEAVEN.

Like a heaven, was my process.
A night-mare my dreams became, reaching there.
Scuffle and struggle to survive, I have.
Almost lifeless, until I was.
Like a strange man marching as he strums.
Stumble, fell, rise and fell, stumble and rise again.
Try to be myself, help myself, but I could not.
With all hopes lost, my fate I intended to conceive.
That are dreadful, trifling and mucking,
I adhered doing with the villains.
In me then stood the greed, living mischievously.
Made me so the system, so get me wrong not.

Exhaustion, frustration, then confusion.
The way I paved in the penitentiary.
A better future, seeking wisdom to obtain.
Had a lot in my brain, just did fathom not.

To rebuild myself I have, back to the real world,
Physically, mentally, technically, logically, and financially.
Explain better, I cannot. Life is full of misery.
Everything they say, please believe not.

Like a heaven, you've not arrived at.
Darker than the dark paradise,
Better than the beautiful hell.
Apprehend it, to be there you have to.
Comprehend it, to study it you have to.

CHAPTER 6

I T WAS A COLD DARK night, in the jungle of Nador, near Tetuan, the border town of Morocco with Spain. At about 11:15 p.m on Thursday. More than fifty Sub-Saharan Africans including David, were waiting quietly for instructions from some Moroccan guides who were specialized in smuggling immigrants and drugs into the Spanish territory of Ceuta. These smugglers were paid 600.00 to 800.00 dollars by each of the passengers, while the middle men who were Nigerians and Ghanaian were paid 500.00 to 1,000.00 dollars for bringing the connections between the passengers and the guides.

In this jungle, where David and the other passengers were hiding quietly, as they were cautioned by the guides not to talk and only to demonstrate with their hands. Not more than sixty meters far from them, were another group of passengers who were also waiting, and not far from that group, were also another group and another group and another group. There were also other groups with fewer passengers and did not pay to be smuggled since they believed they could beat the border to Spain all by themselves to get to the camp.

The border was demarcated with concrete fences of about three feet high from the ground level, tied round with barbed wires to the height of about fifteen feet. Under the fence, there were few drainage channels. Closed to the demarcation, there every time, were the Spanish *guardia civiles* (civil guardians) at the Spanish side, and at the Moroccan side, were the Moroccan *gendarmerie*. David said he found it formidably challenging to fathom how people were still possibly penetrating through this border without being caught. Yes, this to him was impossibility becoming possibility, when he came to interpret his father's parable of "Everything is made from something." His father has also said, "It is when there is a hole in a tree, that is when ants sees it and pass through the hole to go dwell inside." He also said, "It is the rat that lives in a house, that knows there are foods in that house before going to inform and invites other rats outside to come join in the looting." In the sense, David's father was saying, "Your enemies are lying close to you." David who has always listened to his father speak in parables and on his own, tried to interpret the meanings, came to understand many things about life more than many children have.

From the jungle, on top of the mountain where they were hiding, they could look straight to Ceuta. They were seeing the lights shining just like they were seeing the lights of heaven shining and hoping in not quite long, they will be there in heaven to talk to their God and show their gratitude. Seeing the lights shining and seeing the barbed wires fence were making them think they were seeing the demarcation between heaven and hell.

Ceuta, a town formerly owned by the Moroccans many years ago, but is presently governed by the Spanish. With the Spanish territory, it is separated by the Mediterranean sea with the Moroccans. It is also separated by the concrete fence and barbed wires with a direct entry gate which is guarded by the Spanish *guardia civiles* and the Moroccan *gendarmeries*. Although there has constantly be disputes between the both sides on who governs it and who does not. But for the people living there, if asked to vote, probably eighty percents of them would preferred to be Spanish as they already are.

At that very time, it seemed the Spanish government needed immigrants, as they just became a stronger member of the European Union countries and were expanding on new infrastructural development—maybe taking it as a plan to ingratiate themselves with the rest countries of the Union or to create jobs and also to build their economy. This in the later time, came to drive the country into an inglorious moment as it resulted into an instantaneous collapse of the countries economy. Farming was previously their major source of income. But, as they moved to construction, it was understood that there will be less people to work in the farm, so they thought of carrying out a plan to allow immigrants come into the country to work. For this reason, a refugee camp was setup at the extreme end of the city of Ceuta and Melilla. Anybody who was able to penetrate in was to be treated and issued a working and a residence permits to work and live in the country. But these refugees were allowed to stay one month and some weeks in these camps before they could be transferred to the peninsular by boats with 1,000.00 pesetas (6.00 euros) given to them by the Spanish government of the Ministry of works and Immigration.

David and the other passengers were still waiting patiently to be instructed by the guides on what to do. They were tired and starving and were left with some few Moroccan breads and little water to drink. After having waited for six days and nothing happened due to the fact that there were too many guards patrolling the barbed wires, which means there was no way they could easily be smuggled in. These smugglers who were all working as a team, were said to be living in Ceuta and Tetuan, and they were all Moroccans working with the assistance of some of the Moroccan *gendarmeries*. It was also said that few Spanish *guardia civiles* were involved as well. The Moroccan *gendarmeries* patrolling the fenced barbed wires were said to be the ones to be passing information to the smugglers only by sending them text messages on phone to let them know when there was a chance for them to carry out their operations. It was also said that everyone participating in this operation were entitled to some amount of money according to the numbers of passengers smuggled in.

This was the fourth time David was making an attempt to beat the border to go to the refugee camp. The first time he did was when he paid one Ghanaian who was working as the middle man and was the negotiator, the sum of 1,000.00 dollars. He was taken with another twenty people who were mostly girls to the jungle and handled to some Moroccan guides. After spending two weeks there with no hope of being able to smuggle them in, one of the guides took a drastic decision and asked them to follow him directly to the gate. It was like running to meet your enemies in a battle field to fight them without holding any weapon. It was insane and it was suicidal. But, as the guide with command *yala yala* asked them to follow him, they all followed him, facing the gate where the Spanish *guardia civiles* were all standing in front, with guns in their hands, and one of the smugglers who was already at the the other side of the gate said-to-be the Spanish territory, began to shout *yala, yala* and running and was being chased by the *guardia civiles* . This indeed was a strategy to for him to distract their attentions so that the passengers could climb the gate which was almost twenty feet high to come down at the other side and run. As everybody—boys and girls were running, stampeding towards the gate, initially the policemen and the guards were stunned by fear since it was unusual. But, when they saw the people climbing the gate and were jumping down into their own territory while they were at guard, they knew they have to do something. So, they all left the guides who they were chasing after to concentrate on getting hold of the passengers.

As David got closer to the gate, he was startled with what he was seeing and could not move further, instead he was watching, thinking it to be a movie. He saw that some of the boys were brutally beaten and the guides were running around the police who were chasing them. He looked at everything and thought it was a war, but one thing that stood in his mind was—is it worth dying for? Before he could think of running back, he saw the Moroccan *gendarmeries* running after him and getting hold of him and started to beat him up almost to the point of death. This, in his later life in Europe, became a melancholy within his memory that he was unable to get rid off. He came to actually acknowledged the bitterness and tears achieved after much sacrifices of lives to live in a better society which most youths could dream of.

It is true that Africa is one of the largest continent in the world, and as historians have said civilization started from Egypt which is in Africa. David said he read that ancient Egypt civilization was formed around 3150 B.C (according to conventional Egyptian chronology) with the political unification of upper and lower Egypt under the first pharaoh. This great Empire was said to have later fell to the Roman Empire and became a Roman province. The success of this ancient Egypt civilization came partly from its ability to adapt to the conditions of the Nile Valley. The predictable flooding and controlled irrigation of the fertile valley produced surplus crops, which fueled social development and culture. With resources to spare, the administration sponsored mineral exploitation of the valley and surrounding desert regions, the early development of an independent writing system, the organization of collective construction and agricultural projects, trade with surrounding regions, and a military intended to defeat foreign enemies affirm Egyptian dominance. Motivating and organizing these activities was a bureaucracy of elite scribes, religious leaders and administrators under the control of a pharaoh who ensured the co-operation and unity of the Egyptian people in context of an elaborate system of religious beliefs. The many achievements of this great ancient Empire include quarrying, surveying and construction techniques that facilitated the building of monumental pyramids, temples and obelisks; a system of mathematics, a practical and effective system of medicine, irrigation and agricultural production techniques. The first know ships were also said to have been built by these same Egyptians.

David thought he could see that civilization which started in Egypt became an inspiration to other great Empires like that of the Greeks and Romans who then acted upon it and developed it into a higher and better standard. In the sense, the civilization which started in Egypt has contributed a great idea to our modern day world. All these David tried to explain to himself and saw that if Egypt is in Africa and started civilization, meaning civilization started from Africa. But, it could be of a big disgrace to see that this Africa still remains the poorest and less civilized continent among the six continents in our planet, Earth. Why is it so? Is it that the world want it so or is it because the leaders have decided to choose the path of corruption as a way of life and let greed dwell in their hearts? But most of all, David has constantly looked to the theory of why we should continuously blame others for our problems, instead of trying to identify our problems and how to find a solution to it. So, he came to write a poem to explain how he sees these Africans and come to believe most of the problems engulfing them are simply caused by the same Africans with their leaders leading the ways.

O' AFRICA, MY AFRICA.

They say you're the first continent
And remain you now, the darkest continent.
That I'm a part of you, I'm proud.
But, I'm ashamed to say it loud
That in you, that ceased to exist is civilization.
When to bestow upon, all you intend the next generation,
Is nothing than a lake of frustration.

The greed seem not to show the light,
You have to take it from the sight
That there are much more to accomplish.
Not seeing that you're really foolish.

O' Africa, my Africa.
Might be this the time,
In you the beauty, you should bring out

For the world to see.
Too long, do wait not
Cos, they are moving too fast.

The comic truth, no one ever uphold your betterment.
Of your existence, every action like a volcano.
Witnessed they have, all your sufferment.
Standing now that you are on your own,
To the wonderland, you need to send your ghost.
At the old tradition and religions stop to peep,
If a devastation is where it lead.

Blessed thy land is with natural things,
Make use then, you should, of the good things.
Stop the conflicts and listen to the radio,
Where they go, you can roll with them.

David said he came to think of writing this poem because, he
saw the calamity and dejection imposed on them as Africans by their
leaders. No one is truly delight to live illegally in another man's country
"How humiliating and degrading it is to see that you live in a foreign
land where people detests and disregards you deliberately because of
your identity, religion, or your color of race."

CHAPTER 7

B ACK TO THE TIME DAVID was beaten and arrested by the Moroccan *gendarmeries*, all of them (boys and girls) who were caught trying to jump the gate into the Spanish territory, were detained and sent to prison for one week. The prison where they were sent to was not to be referred to as a prison, it will be better if it is described as hell—it was a very large two storey building with about fifty cells up and down. In every each cell, was twelve to fifteen prisoners held together. They were all fed once in everyday with one loaf of Moroccan bread for each of them. There was not a single chair, no bed, and no foam, but there was a loo, which means nobody was ever allowed to step out. Anyone who would have to poop, would have to do it in the presence of all the other eleven to fourteen prisoners watching. As there was no bed, no foam, no chair, there was still no space for the prisoners to stretch their legs. So, none of them even thought of making the attempt to sleep. All they could do was to sit down with their legs half-stretched and doze. The worst thing about that prison was the millions of bedbugs that were having their houses built in every of the bed sheet that they were given to sit down. They were all tortured only to frighten them not to repeat what they did, and they all knew it was only going to make them stronger and plan on how to reach their various destinations. Everyday to every prisoner there was like hell and was like a thousand days back at the time they were at home. Being that the prison was densely populated, some of the prisoners were then allowed to be freed and deported not to their countries of origin but to the border between Morocco and Algeria and left there in the wild Savannah land that was mainly dominated by scorpions and snakes. As they were left there in the border by the Moroccan police and were cautioned never to make any attempt of coming back to Morocco, most of them decided to return back to Morocco while others went to Magnaya, Algeria, a border town with Morocco where they could be able to refresh and look for how to invigorate themselves and restock some food for another journey to go and beat the border between Morocco and Spain once again. This was David's first time of making that attempt and he was caught and beaten up and treated badly and sent back, but he refuses to relinquish. He tried and tried again until this fourth time.

David who was so confident of succeeding this time, inside him, he began to pray to his God. He prayed, 'O' God, if it is your will for me to step my feet into that land, let Thy will be done and I know I will definitely prevail. But if it is not Thy will, I know anyhow I try, I will not prevail.' He said this prayer silently with confidence but he also recalled the last time in his life that he has said a prayer, and more over, all the sins he has committed without asking God for forgiveness. But now that he was in a a very formidable situation, that was when he knew he has to call on God. Before he started praying to his God to help him, he first said, 'O' merciful God. Forgive me for the sins I have committed. You are the only One that can make a way when there is no way.' At the end of the prayer, he said, 'O' Lord, because I believe in your name, I know You will see me through this, and if I am able to succeed, I will glorify Thy name and worship you with all my life. I know I am not worthy to have Your blessings.' He then went on to quote from the book of Psalm 50:15, saying, 'And call upon me in the day of trouble; I will deliver thee, and thou shall glorify me,' and again, he said, 'These are Your words, O' Lord and I am calling upon Your name. Please deliver me so I can glorify Thy name.' As he opened his eyes, he saw that one of the guides was also praying, bowing down his head and prostrating as Muslims according to the Muslim way of praying. David said he was stunned seeing what he thought was a dream, and he then asked himself, "Is it so with people who believe in God, to commit sins and pray for God to assist them?"

At about 04:00 a.m, immediately the guide stopped praying, he instructed all of them to follow him, with the word *yala yala*. They were all creeping along with the him, thinking he was going towards where the drainage was so as to pass through it to the other side. But, to their astonishment, they saw two other guides already cut a round hole of about fifty inches wide in the barbed wires, and was waiting for them to come pass it. With haste, they were all passing through the drainage and running as fast as they could to the place where more than nine taxis were already parked and waiting for them. Those who arrived there first, got into the taxi and were driven to where the camp was located and they were dropped there. Getting there, they met some

African refugees mostly Nigerians, who later took them along to the gate of the camp. And, at the gate where everybody enterring were to present a card issued to all the refugees inside to show they were already there before, and if not, they might be arrested and deported back to Morocco. Although, before then, they were already given some cards owned by some Nigerians to present to the police there at the gate, but at the end, as they were able to enter the camp successfully, they were asked to pay for the cards, which they did. It was the rules there, and it was what they were supposed to do. It was said to be, "Use what you have to get what you want,"—at this time, it was already 07:00 a.m and very early in the morning.

After more than two hours that they arrived, the office was already opened for registration. David was standing in a queue with some other refugees from different countries like Morocco, Algeria, Ghana, Mali, Senegal, and Cameroon. In spite that Moroccans were not allowed to seek asylum there because of the agreement the country was having with Spain, but there were still very many of them, claiming to be Tunisians or Algerians. As David was standing and waiting to be registered and be issued a refugee card, he was praying secretly and silently, murmuring the prayers under his breath. He kept praying and praying, until he got to where the man who was to register them was sitting.

First, he was asked his name and surnames, followed by his date of birth, father and mother's name and surnames. After that, his fingerprint were taken by the police, and at the end, he was issued a refugee card that will enable him to stay in the camp legally—maybe for one and a half month, before he will be transferred to the peninsular.

When they finished with the registration, they were given an address in the city center, and were told to go there for vaccination, and also for urine and blood sample test—which was to be the next day. Flushed with a shiver of excitement that he was going to be accepted and issued a document to go live and work in Europe, which was very fascinating, he screamed with joy, and tears were coming out of his eyes.

Instantly, when he left the registration office, he went straight to the phone booth where he met more than twenty people waiting to also call their families in Europe and in Africa. Although, he was penniless, so he pleaded for people there to help him out. Surprisingly for him, he saw four of his friends who were already there in the camp for long. They were so glad when they saw him. One of them whom David did lend some money at the time they were in Morocco, when after much adverse circumstances, and by the fear of starvation and was helpless, he was discouraged, and as he could not overcome it, he decided to return back to his country. But David, who was so determined, decided to lend him some money and encouraged him to reject that idea and move on, using a phrase, "Brother, no retreat, no surrender. Europe, here we come."

'Oh! my big brother, I so much appreciate what you did for me. I really do not know how to thank you,' said the boy. David, embracing him again, said 'You do not need to thank me, just thank God. Do you remember the assurance I gave you that we are going to have this victory? Now, how do you feel?' 'Real good, brother, real good. It is good to have faith,' said the boy. David walked closer to him, and with a low voice, he said 'Yes it is. Let me tell you something about life if you can listen, "The one thing you must do to ensure success after much scuffling, is for you to believe in yourself, who you are and what you are capable of." The boy, wanting David to also know that he too was having the dream of coming to Europe and was determined to do everything to get there, if not that he was not having anyone who was financially supporting him, he said, 'As you may know, coming to Europe has always been a dream to me. "I see no reason why I can see the light in heaven shinning, and then I cannot step my feet in that land where the light is shinning from." Immediately he said this, David fathomed he was believing Europe to be heaven, and he laughed along with the other boys who were also there laughing at how their friend was describing Europe as heaven on Earth. They all kept laughing and cheering David up, calling him names, saying he is to be compared to Joseph the dreamer. Then, one of them swiftly brought out is cell phone and gave it to him to call.

Having the phone in his hand, he called his elder sister, Tina who was living in Spain and was married to a Spaniard in the northern part of Spain—the base country, and was also the person who sponsored his trip to where he was. He called, waiting for almost three minutes for her sister to pick the call, and when she picked and heard his voice, she screamed with joy. 'Where are you calling from,' she asked. 'I am calling from Ceuta, I am already here.' 'O.k, now, how can I reach you so that I can send some money to you?' 'Of course, you can reach me with this phone number. It belongs to a friend of mine, and anytime you call,

just tell him you want to speak with me, and I will be given the phone.'
'Fine, I will call you now.' She cut the phone and called, asking him how
she could send him some money. He told her to send the money to him
through Western Union, with his name as the receiver. 'O.k' she said. 'I
am going to call mama to tell her you have finally succeeded in getting
to Ceuta, and I will send the money on Monday, because there is no
way you can receive it now over there.

After talking to his sister, he gave the cell phone back to the owner.
And with joy and happiness, they all went to sit at the beach which was
not far from the camp. Sitting there, they were singing and clapping
and smoking hashish and drinking beer. It was just a dream come true,
so it was worth celebrating. They were all celebrating, not knowing this
was just the beginning of another new journey that might be requiring
more effort than the one they just accomplished.

The refugee camp was situated in the midst of rocks and trees in a
wide valley, with about two hundred refugee and relief tents and other
smaller tents, and it was fenced round with barbed wires about five
meters high. There was also a gate where three or four policemen
usually stand with guns in their hands. Inside this camp, were mostly
Nigerians and Senegalese and many other immigrants from other
African countries. Many immigrants who were living in Germany,
Holland, France, and other European countries for many years without
documents, were also using this opportunity to come there to get the
documents just only for them to be legal in Europe. Later in David's
future life when he was living in Europe, he could see how much the
Spanish government has really helped them by issuing these documents
to them, as it made many of them to possess a valid document to work in
Spain and also to allow them to travel to every countries in Europe said
to be in the Schengen. It is a fact to say that the vast majority of African
immigrants living in Europe—legal or illegal, passed through Spain, as
it became the newly discovered route to Europe, to the extent that most
other countries like Holland, Germany, Switzerland, and Luxembourg
became very annoyed and were blaming the Spanish government.
Although, this later drew concerns among European Union member
states to fund and invest to secure and tighten the border between
Morocco and Spain.

Actually Spain has helped most immigrants, mostly Africans to realize their dreams of coming to Europe, since coming to Europe by flight was very expensive and difficult in regard to the strict European laws of declining to issue out visas easily to them. But, as time went by, with the assistance of the Union, Spain was able to secure and tighten their border with Morocco, making people coming both by sea and by land to be finding it difficult to penetrate.

Getting to Spain, most of these immigrants, particularly Nigerians, as they arrive, they still intend to move ahead to the countries of their choice, knowing that the Spanish economy was not really too good, and there were few chances and opportunities for employments. Despite that they intend to leave to other countries, but they all knew right there in their hearts how much Spain has rendered to them, and they understand they owe the country a debt of gratitude. This actually did motivate David when he was in prison in Italy to come to write a poem to show how he feel to see how Spain made him and many others realized their dream of coming to Europe. VIVA ESPANA.

VIVA ESPANA.

You're Spain,
The doorway to many immigrants destiny.
Seeing my future, I first saw your light,
This light, I traced to cast my visions.
In your many ways I love.
In your many ways I also loathe.
A friend than a foe, to me, you remain.
In the peninsular where you are,
Your sacred values and language
Spreading to the four corners of the Earth.
You and me, no matter what becomes,
Siempre, lo tengo en mi corazon.

CHAPTER 8

D AVID'S ARRIVAL IN CEUTA AND meeting his friends was a joyous moment he had never experienced before. Immediately after they left the beach, his friends took him to one of the local restaurant inside the camp which was owned by a Nigerian, so that he could eat a good African meal instead of him to be standing in a queue and be waiting to be served some Spanish food and bread. After he finished eating, he asked his friends why they were not interested in going to stand in a queue with the other immigrants. But they all told him it was too stressful and noisy because of the too many people wanting to be served food, and the worst of all, they said they disliked the French speaking Africans attitudes of always trying to confront them anytime they are trying to cheat them. Although this food they were being served by the Spanish Refugee Council, were good food and were always brought to them by some companies with some skilled cooking techniques located in the city center. The food which was meant to feed everybody in the camp, were always later shared among other immigrants except the Nigerians who believed by going there to stand in a queue is a waste of time. Undisputedly, they were confident of being able to take their own responsibilities, not wanting to be a liability to the Refugee Council, who never asked them to be doing what they were doing. Actually, some of them were not accustomed to these European food, while most of them preferred they could spend their money to have what they want. But, where was the money coming from? Yes, this was a question most of the police and guards were asking each other. Why would they want to travel abroad if everything is well with them in their country? The attitudes of WE CAN CARE FOR OURSELVES became so apparent, and it was with the spirit of conspicuous consumption, and was attracting the police, guards and the Refugee Council's attention. It was provocative and was making other immigrants and the Spaniards dislike them. And, because of this, the Refugee Council decided to turn to the favor of other immigrants and to support them, ruling the Nigerians out. They were given more days than the other immigrants to stay in the camp before being transferred to the peninsular. Giving them documents became more strict, and more restraints were imposed as they were all dissatisfied with the situation, basically, since the Nigerians were unable to be hiding their pride, not forgetting they were illegal immigrants, and by pretending to be having a different life, so as for them to get what they came there for and leave to have a better life ahead of them, with documents in their hands.

Money were still pouring in from their families and relations living abroad, particularly in Europe. They were shopping in many of the supermarkets extravagantly and were spending lavishly on clothes and shoes and phones and other things. Although, most of them were also living in Europe before, and had come there for the documents, knowing that to be the only means they could achieve the good life they dreamed of in Europe. It was said that they spent thousands of dollars on the trips, as they were smuggled into boats and ships coming from Algeciras, the last city in Spain, to Ceuta by some Spanish sailors and boat drivers, with hope and belief they will be issued a residence and a working permit to live, work, and travel around Europe. Getting to Ceuta, they were all spending the money they have long saved while working in Europe, since they were beginning to see hope of becoming legal in Europe at the time all their hopes were lost.

Every Fridays were said to be the days for transfer, and at least ten to fifteen Nigerians and other immigrants were transferred from the camp. Nigerians were organizing themselves and spending money in purchasing cans of beer, dry gins, and whiskeys to held parties and celebrate. Despite that they were seen to be wayward and too proud by the policemen and guards there in the camp, but they were also supported and lauded by the same people when it come to the time of celebration. Some of the policemen knew most of the girls were prostitutes, so they were using that privilege in having sex with them and paying them for it, since that was their major aim of leaving their countries to Europe. As for the girls, they were able to be seducing the policemen and extracting money from them and letting them have what they were paying for. In that camp, it was everyday sex and fun, fun and sex, sex, sex, sex, fun, fun and sex and fun.

The next day came, and it was David's second day in the camp—and it was on Saturday. He decided to move from the government built tent to the smaller, two-person backpacking tent that was owned by one of his friend, Festus, and was almost at the extreme end of the camp just ten meters away from the fenced barbed wires.

Early in the morning, he and his friend both went to where milk and other food items were shared as long as they were able to join others in standing in a queue. In the long queue, there were always policemen with batons trying to calm them and to prevent disputes and contentions between the refugees as they drag the food since it was inadequate to meet everybody needs. Everything went very fast unexpectedly for David. Immediately he was given the milk and food he went there for, he left with his friend to the camp to drop everything and left again to meet his other friends who took him to a place inside the bush near the camp, where they all went to smoke hashish and drink beer. Meanwhile, as he was drinking and smoking, he was also thinking about the new tent he was sharing with his friend, because of how his friend's elder half-brother was coming there to inconvenient and make them uncomfortable by coming with his girlfriend to have sex with her. He saw that his friend was not always present in the camp, and for this reason, he ignored the idea of confronting his elder half-brother, instead he was advising him to join in his plan—this plan which when David first heard of it, was like sending a man an errand to go ravage another man who was trying to find a way to get to the camp where they were already and knew how tough and rough it was for them to get there. He was beginning to think his friend to be evil and too money-conscious, for having a thing like that in his mind and doing it to get little money that was not enough for him to feed for months.

It was on Sunday, the third day since he arrived there. It was a day for worshiping God as Christians. He dressed himself up and left to the church—a hall built for the refugees to be receiving the Spanish language lessons from Mondays to Sundays, while on Sundays, it will be converted into a church.

As he walked into the church, he saw that it was already crammed full of people who were there to praise and thank God, for helping them to see the light they have been dreaming to see—seeing it, and also standing with their two feet in the land from where the light was shining. In this very church, majority of the people attending it were Nigerians and some few Ghanaian. Despite how people were coming to the camp and also departing, the church remained constant and was always full of people every on Sundays—and was said to be developing rapidly since one year of its inception. The leaders were all Nigerians, most of them said be very treacherous and have committed acts of impiety during the time they were in Morocco, knowing that nobody was willing to rescue them as the situation got worse and they were fraught with difficulties. Many of them later confessed that it was a thing they never intend to do, but due to some extenuating circumstances whereby they have eventually driven themselves into the depth of despair and were overwhelmed with deep sense of it, so they were left with just one choice—to do whatever they had to do to survive and accomplish their dreams of getting to Europe. Many a time he took a look back at this theme and examine his fellow Nigerians, he sees them as men driven by ferocious determination to succeed—whether by crime or by honesty.

After some minutes, he saw the church service commenced, and people were praying, and after that the leader of the church or pastor who was a very learned person and was with good English grammar, started preaching and quoting from the bible, advising them to repent of their sins. After that, more prayers were said while some were seeing visions or claiming they were, then at the end, they all started singing and dancing and praising God—a thing that amuses him most. He was beginning to see himself as a man filled with the Holy spirit the way others claim they were. He started singing along with the song and was dancing and praising God. At the end of the church service, he vowed to God that he was prepared to be serving Him with all his life and becoming His instrument to win more souls to His Kingdom by preaching His word to the world.

It was 05:00 a.m, Monday morning, David was already preparing himself to go to the city center for the urine and blood sample test, and also for vaccination. Firstly, he went to shower, which took him almost one hour, because of how he had to wait for some others who were there before him and were very many. In the bathhouse, there were always disputes between the refugees, because of how the Muslims were complaining of people getting naked. Although the bathhouse was divided by a wall—one for the women and the other for the men. But most of these girls declined to abide to the rules, as they defied the police and guards by exposing their body indecently to every men around or close to the bathhouse, and also coming to shower several times with some of their boyfriends. This actually became a very big issue this Muslims were unable to deal with, but only for them to complain and complain, saying it indicate a sign of evil spirit. As for the Nigerians, they were more happier, seeing these girls coming around to expose their body to them as they try to do whatever they could to have and nail them, if possible inside the bathhouse. And, as for the Ghanaian, they were ready to give their lives for it. But, it was later, David came to find out how many of these Moroccans and Senegalese who in public places were claiming it as a taboo for seeing the nude of women said not to be their wives, but at nights, were paying these Nigerian girls to be having sex with them.

At the bathhouse, as David went to shower and was waiting for his turn, he stood motionless by the door and was watching and studying everything that were taking place inside. It was to him like a movie, seeing how these girls were trying to seduce the boys, and as the Muslims among them complain and complain about the incident to the police and guards. To him, the show was hilarious and he knew he could not afford the money to pay for it if he was charged to pay. He was about to laugh out, when suddenly he realized he was about to provoke a resentment. He quickly shut his mouth and waited until it got to his turn to shower. When he immersed himself in the warm water, he could feel inside of him, a new beginning of his adventure, but he could not help comprehend how he managed to get to where he was, so he started singing and praising God while showering, forgetting there were other people there.

Before 09:00 a.m, he was already at the gate of the laboratory where he was asked to present his urine and blood sample for analysis. With many other refugees standing and waiting in a queue, he wanted to leave, but he knew if he did, there will be a price he would have to pay, so he waited just like the rest. Not too long, he finally had the chance to get inside and present everything, and after he presented his urine sample and some blood were taken from him, he was asked to leave to another room for the vaccination. After then he was given a yellow card, even if he was not told whether he was healthy or not, but inside him, he believed he was, simply because of the yellow card. He was also told he was to wait for the result of the analysis which might take two weeks before he could see it pasted in the notice board. After he left and was so delighted, so he called his sister with the money he was given by his friend just to tell her about the good news. His sister who was so excited to hear his voice again, quickly gave him a number which he could use to collect the money she already sent to him at the Western Union office that was located there in the city center. Immediately, he wrote the numbers on a piece of paper and was poised to leave to the office where he was to go collect the money; he saw a boy walked up to him, telling him he was a having a phone to sell just because he heard him telling his sister on phone that he was going to spend the money in purchasing a phone. As David refused to chit-chat with him, he was aggrieved and started nagging, having that delusional thinking. He came up pouring different kind of insults on him. But, David was able to exercise considerable restraint by ignoring the insults, saying to himself, "Silence is the best way to answer a fool."

After he received the money, he made an abrupt change of mind to go purchase a cell phone, instead of returning back to the camp as he once planned to do. He walked into a shop and purchased a very cheap and easy use cell phone. And, as he walked out of the shop, took by surprise, he saw an electronic shop, then he quickly went inside to glance at the many electronics inside and found a walk-man which he has always wanted to have, since music was the only thing he thought could help him live that glorious moment to the full at that very particular time of his life.

Having bought the cellphone and a walk-man, he decided to buy a jacket since autumn was just beginning and he was experiencing what cold looks like for the first time. He bought a jacket with a hood, a body warmer jacket, two pairs of jeans trouser, and an adidas-made baseball cap. When he looked at the things he bought, he was starting to believe this was an auspicious beginning of his new life in Europe.

When he returned back to the camp, he met his friends who cheered him up, and snatching away from him the thing he bought just to inspect them—to see how much they worth. Meanwhile, he has announced to them that he was having some hashish he bought already with him—making all of them believed the world was theirs, knowing they were about to go get high. They all started singing and were celebrating just as if they had won a lottery. But before he could try and get his things back from them, he caught a glimpse of one of his friends using his cellphone to be making gratuitous calls to Africa. He quickly went to meet him and asked him to handover the phone back to him. The boy did as he was told, but he did with dissatisfaction. After he was given his phone back, he stood and watched the boy, and then something evil walked freely into his mind, and was saying, kill this dude man, kill this dude. As he watched, one of his friend walked closer to him and said, 'brother, let us leave this man here, and let us go smoke the hell off.' When David heard this, he quickly recollect where he was, and that he was about to kill somebody if actually he was having a gun with him. Later in his future life, he said he came to understand why many Americans find themselves in a situation whereby killing become an addict to them. He said he came to understand the reason why legal possession of arms can cause more violence than when they are not, because he said he understand that, "Some people really deserve to die, as they cease to think of how to prevent it, believing themselves to be more wiser by causing other people pains to please themselves."

After he listened to his friend, he came to where the boy was again, and was still standing motionless and watching him even when his other friends were calling him to come with them to go and smoke, with his implicit feelings making him assume that his friend was guilty and he deserved to be killed. When his ghost finally return back to him, he saw other people looking at him as if he was in a trauma, and was causing a great scene with it. He tried as much to control his temper, getting his things back into a bag and left with his other friends to their favorite smoking spot to smoke the hashish that he was having with him. But, as he tried to check the credit remaining in his phone, he saw that it was empty, and immediately, the memory of killing the boy came back to him.

CHAPTER 9

E XHAUSTED AFTER A WHOLE DAY of shopping, drinking, singing, disputing, and drug-smoking, e trod cautiously and quietly back to the tent which he was sharing with his friend, Festus, who actually had left since 05:00 a.m, and was just returning back home. 'Where have you been?' He asked his friend. 'I have been all day hustling,' replied Festus. 'You mean you were executing your plans?' Asked David, again. 'Oh, man, it has been a rough day. I have not been able to get anything, even a penny.' David looking at him, felt pity for him, and then said to him, 'common now, let us go and eat in a restaurant.' They both went to their favorite local restaurant where they were served rice and stew and meat, which David did pay for. When they finished eating and were going back to the tent, he brought out the things he bought that he took with him in a bag and showed them to him and also explained everything that happened on his absence—how his friend took his phone and was using it to call his families in Africa, when he who owns it could not call his families in Africa with it. Deeply saddened, Festus told him to follow him so that they could go and meet the boy to confront him again. He said, 'this is so awful. How can someone do a thing like this to a person he calls his friend, and yet you could not injure him? Now, I am going to ask him the reason he did what he did.' 'No need, let us not wake a dead matter up. It has passed,' replied David, walking towards where their tent was and pleading with his friend to let them forget about the past and face the future. As they entered the tent, they sat there conversing until the both of them were tired and said goodnight to each other and fell asleep.

The next morning, at about 08:00 a.m, when David woke up, he saw that Festus was no longer there. He has left to do his hustling and bustling work as he usually refer it to be. After brushing his teeth and using water to wash his face, David walked straight into the nearby bush, passing through the hole already been cut in the barbed wires long ago by an anonymous person. Getting to the bush, he looked around to see if there were anybody staring at him, and when he saw that there was nobody, he pulled off his trouser and underwear and started emptying the solid waste matter from his stomach. Although, it was just a thing that he always love to do when ever he is in a place where there are many people using the toilet and messing it up, and he has always disliked going to the lavatory where people might be hearing him make all the funny noises, which is very disgusting, making him unable to poop the way he would have want to. After he finished pooping, he cleansed his anus with the water he brought along with him in a bottle. He later walked to their favorite smoking spot, with his walk-man and wearing the earphone in his two ears, he sat down and was listening to Tupac's Shakur's music and smoking the already wrapped hashish he also brought along.

To him, at that time, Tupac's music was great source of inspiration, and he was seeing how he was entrusting himself to it. He was seeing himself walking along the same pathway with the rap artist. Throwing himself into this pathway was easy, but where it leads to, that was unknown to him. At first, he was seeing Tupac as his mentor and believing in every word he said; he was seeing him as a living legend—the black Jesus, someone who smoked as he too smoke, drink as he was drinking; he was seeing him as a messenger from God who died after having fulfilled his dream; he was seeing him as the one to inspire and lead him and many poor kids out of the poverty lives they were living. He saw him as a hero who had come to make him believe more in his dream and also strengthen him with his lyrics to keep moving, no matter the obstacles. He saw that Tupac, who was so ambitious in life had later succeeded in becoming a famous rap musician, with money always in his hands and pockets, living luxurious life. This actually had motivated him to started thinking of how to become a musician, instead of becoming a wealthy African with a profession of designing and structuring metal gates—which he already started back in his country, but only wanting to come to Europe to improve his skills and raise money to purchase some of the very expensive materials and tools to take back to home and invest in a large company. But, as he has always love adventure and was continuously listening to Tupac's lyrics, he came to fathom how the rap artist was always talking about the hardship and the dangerous life—that was not meant for him—but he found himself living it, and he was using it as lyrics in telling stories. David came to realize he can also be like him and be making money by telling his stories through music, as he believed music to be a very easy way to breakthrough to achieve success.

Later in David's future life, when he came to take time to sit and to watch many documentaries about the life and death of this rap artist, on his own, he came to believe he could explain clearly, the interesting facts about Tupac's music to many youngsters, most especially blacks. He said he could understand what his message was truly about—it was truly about how to keep dreaming and not stopping, no matter the hardship and temptations, until you achieve that dream. This can be better explained in many of his songs.

To David, even from the beginning of rap music, no rap artist will be as good as Tupac. He was unique, just as everything about him was also unique, and for this reason most people, including David were seeing him as a visionary. In the history of rap music, Tupac remains the greatest rap musician and his legends will never die. But as David grew up and was able to get to the bottom of this subject matter, he was seeing him as an artist who was luring people with the stories of his life to be like him, and at the same time, he was making money. This could be understood when he said he was turning words into money. Tupac was smart, and because he read a lot, and was very well inspired and was able to put this inspiration into music, he became what he was. Although, many a time David said he sit and look back to his life and how it was almost ruined by the lyrics of this rap artist, he loathe him and never want to talk about him. But the problem is, no matter how old he become and how he will choose to live his life, there is no way he could forget about him even when he is always seeing him as evil. He came to see that he was never the black Jesus he claimed to be, since there was never a time he was preaching about love and peace, except for him to preach about how he intend to kill his friend and have sex with his wife just because they quarreled. Moreover, David came to understand that this rap artist never left to visit people starving in Africa or in India or in Afghanistan or in Vietnam, yet he was claiming to be black and was planning on how to terminate the life of his fellow blacks. Notwithstanding his evil deeds, but he had also played a great role in the life of many young people around the world, including David. For this reason, David said he could see him as the good, the bad, the ugly.

Anytime he said he sees rap artists like Jay-z, Snoop Dogg, Dr Dre, P. Diddy, Eminem, 50 cents and many others, and how they all became millionaires and are living the fabulous life they have yearned for, he would remember Tupac and think of the good life he should be living, if he had not let death be is friend. Although, he could be seen by many to be a real thug who lived by gun and had declared death on himself by gun, forgetting there were too many good things in life to be enjoyed, since he was still very young and healthy. From some of his lyrics, he was able to tell people that it is only God that can judge anyone of us—showing that he also believed in God. But if he did, why then did he declared death on his friend, who later became his worst enemy. He forgot it is only this same God he talk about in almost all his music, that is the maker of life and no one has the right to take another's own or else he is against God.

The other side of him also revealed how smart and intelligent he was, because of how he came to believe that women must be respected—and this, we can hear in one of his music when he said, YOU KNOW IT MAKES ME UNHAPPY WHEN BROTHERS MAKE BABIES, AND LEAVE A YOUNG MOTHER TO BE PAPPY. AND SINCE WE ALL CAME FROM A WOMAN, GET OUR NAMES FROM A WOMAN, AND OUR GAME FROM A WOMAN. I WONDER WHY WE TAKE FROM OUR WOMEN, WHY WE RAPE OUR WOMEN, DO WE HATE OUR WOMEN? I THINK IT'S TIME TO KILL FOR OUR WOMEN, TIME TO HEAL OUR WOMEN, BE REAL TO OUR WOMEN. AND IF WE DON'T, WE'LL HAVE A RACE OF BABIES THAT WILL HATE THE LADIES THAT MAKE THE BABIES.

But after having praised women for their role as child bearer, he was also describing them as bitches. David who took time to listen to almost all of his songs and watched his music videos and also his documentaries, then came to comprehend the complexity of being a thug—which is to say, being a thug is evil, and it makes you not think like normal human beings do. To David, it is a painful thing to see that Tupac was killed. He meant a lot to many artists like him. His creative power was so unique that we can never in life see a man like that again. But why the violence and the insulting and crude words that sent him to his grave? Then we will all have to live that for God to judge, just as he said, ONLY GOD CAN JUDGE.

After David has read Tupac's biography and compared it with his own life of no bed of roses, he was able to expound his views on the sufferings and travails bestowed upon many young kids born into poverty. This he saw, and came to object the idea of holding to blame Tupac's attitudes of being arrogant. Knowing all these, he came to comprehend that, "We should not judge people, most distinctively when we do not know anything about them." From his own momentous and critical experience in life, he came to believe that crime can also be a product of the law and as a the lack of social benefits, misbehavior as side-effects of social repression.

Extracting meanings from critical theory and taking a deep look at David's future life in Europe, you could be touched, as he was seen as a man, who, no matter what people were doing or saying to distract his attention from what he believed was appropriate for him to be doing, he kept moving in dreams, even when he got to the top and still did not know it. He had the will drawn to himself. Lions were roaring and about to get him, as he walked along the pavement, quivering, quavering, shivering, stuttering, shuddering, trembling, shaking, and quaking. He fell and rose to his feet and fell and rose again and again. Not a soul thought he could survive the tragedy, till angels came down from heaven to rescue him. But one advice he took from his father was, "He who knows how to trade will always be prosperous," and this has so much helped him to overcome the many tragedies that befell him.

David, still sitting and smoking hashish and listening to Tupac's music and was fantasizing on the future life he was going to live in Europe. Suddenly, one of his friend touched him at the back and said, 'man, what are you thinking about? I have been here for almost five minutes watching you smoke and listen to your music without you knowing it.' 'Man, I was in a deep meditation and not aware of somebody watching me' replied David. 'You do not need to think too much. We are already in Europe, and there is a need for us to appreciate what God has done for us. Europe is not like Africa where there is no hope. The most important thing of all, is that we all will be transferred with documents to live and work and even travel around the continent. I am quite sure it will be better than the life we were living in Morocco.' 'I know that,' replied David, stretching his hand to offer his friend the hashish he was smoking. 'I am so happy I finally made it to get to this place even when I thought there was no way I could. The God that made a way for me to come here will also make a way for me over there, I know that. I am so glad that I am here, brother.' 'Oh, guess what? My name is in the list of the people to be transferred on Friday,' said the boy. 'You are really not sure of what you are saying. You cannot tell me you are living me here,' said David. 'Man, I am leaving you here because I came here before you and I have to leave before you. But you do not need to fret much, you will be transferred one day, and we will meet there in Spain.' 'Where in Spain will you be going to live?' asked David. 'Madrid,' said the boy. 'Madrid. What about Valencia? Someone told me there are less jobs in Madrid, and in Valencia, there are very many farm works to do to raise money. And, since we are new people in Europe, I think that will be good for us to start life.' 'Forget it,' said the boy, annoyingly, as he finished smoking the hashish David offered him and was wrapping another one that he brought along with him. 'I am not going to Spain to work. I am going there to transact good business and make good money.' 'What type of business is that?' asked David, smiling reluctantly. 'Look, boy, I am going to be into drug business, o.k?' said the boy, putting his wrapped hashish in his mouth and light it up with fire. 'But, people who do that type of business usually get caught easily and be sent to prison,' said David, this time he was trying to be a good adviser. 'Boy, wake up, I actually do not relish the prospect of getting up everyday as early as 06:00 a.m to get dressed and go to work in the farm inside the cold weather.' Being that it was David first time of hearing that, did not believe what the boy was saying, and he asked him again, 'how do you know that?' 'My friend that was transferred there told me that. As for me, I want to be on a fast lane and make quick money and return back to Africa to invest there.' 'Great, you are right.' He relinquished the hope of trying to convince him to try and get himself a job when he arrive in Spain.

After some minutes without the both of them talking to each other, the boy said to him, 'by the way, why are you listening to Tupac's music when you cannot act like him? He impertinently snatched the walk-man and earphone from David, and putting the earphone in his two ears, as the music was playing, he started singing along with it. He kept singing and was not in the mood to return the walk-man back to David, who actually was watching in amazement and did not know how to tell him to. Meanwhile, David who was already intoxicated with the hashish he was smoking, could see his ghost departing from him. Then, another thing he could see was a huge white grey haired man at his eighties, dressing in white robes, and was sitting on a throne made of gold. But when he looked to the other side, he saw another black monster with red robes all around him, but his age was not able to guess. As he could not move from where he was standing, he watched the monster walked closer to him, 'what have you come to do here you little creature?' with an imperious voice, he demanded. 'I have come to seek my fate, and to know what is best for me to do with it,' replied David, boldly. The monster laughed out loudly, ah! ah! ah! ah!. 'You mean, you want to know what you should do in life to achieve the good life that you want? Yes, replied David, stepping backward and with gait. 'You really should not ask anybody to tell you what to do now that you have been able to succeed in getting to Europe. Anything that will give you money, do it and return back to your country as quick as possible and live like a king there.' 'Thank you, I will stick to this advice and use it,' said David. He turned to leave, and as he turned, he saw the white grey haired man again, and the man said to him with a soft and quiet voice, 'Oh, my son, life they say is tough but not too tough. If you make it easy, it will be easy. But, if you make it hard, it will be hard. Life is how you make it. Do what is good and abstain from evil my son. Try and go read Psalm 1:1-6, in your bible so that you can understand what I am asking you to do with your life.'

Seized with fear, David could see his own lips move up and down and words uttering out from it, 'are you my God and my Creator? Who are you?' He knelt down in supplication. 'I am your God and Creator. Go now and do the right thing.'

Still sitting down with his wrapped hashish in his hand, David saw that he was already surrounded by four other boys, including the one that they were both discussing before, without any of them knowing or wanting to know about the haunted experience he just had. They were all celebrating with hashish in their hands and singing send-off songs to their friend who was to be transferred soon to the peninsular.

Leaving his friends behind and walking alone to go back to his tent to relax and to figure out what his aim of traveling abroad really was. With his mind already full, and with abstract and imageless thoughts, he was unable to distinguish between what was real and what was not. When he finally managed to reached their tent and saw that Festus, his friend had still not arrived, he sat down on the thick blanket they were given by the Refugee authority which they had also turned some into mattress by putting six to seven of them together and lying it on the floor.

'Is that God I just saw not quite long?' he was asking himself. 'Oh. by the way, is it true that people say God is white and the devil is black? he was referring to many pictures and painting of the Roman catholic church he had seen before hanged mostly in some of the catholic churches in his country. 'This is not just an imagination, I just saw God who just advised me to abstain from evil, and the devil who who was advising me to do anything to make quick money and return back home and enjoy my life.' As he was conversing with himself, suddenly something struck him in his mind, and a voice said to him, 'go and read Psalm 1:1-6.' So, he quickly picked up the bible where it was hidden under the pillow and opened to the Psalm 1:1-6, and started reading.

After when he finished reading where he was told to read by his own God that he thought he just saw, he quickly recall so many times he has been to churches and experience similar things he just experienced. Although he has read the bible several time but also came to understand that, reading the bible is one thing, but understanding it and and interpreting it in the right way is another. As he tried to interpret what he just read to himself, he found himself astonished by the complexity of the quotes in the bible and the metaphorical meanings we drive from them. The more he tried interpreting these quotes, the more he was hearing Tupac's music inside his head, so he picked up his walk-man again and started playing it and singing along with the music just as his friend just did.

Yes, he finally concluded that Tupac was the one to lead him. 'I will do what I will have to do to make it quickly and return back to my country with precious metal and live that splendiferous life,' thinking that was how the rap artist made it, but it also faded from his mind that the same Tupac whom everyone of them were trying to imitate, was also a person who later decided to choose to quit drug-dealings and fast lane money-making so as to focus on his musical career, turning his tears of anguish and grief into inspiration to write songs.

Despite that he loved and loathe this rap artist, later in his future life, when he really came to apply his studies and assimilate his biography and his lyrics, and with intellectual curiosity, comparing it with how many youths wants to hear his lyrics and act like him, it came to appear to him that everything were just about money and fame. He was a genius who created a different world for himself instead of living all his life in jail because of crime. He will always remain a legend.

After two days that he thought he saw his God Whom no other person could see except him alone, he was still thinking of how he could be interpreting these quotes he was reading in the bible, since he was beginning to take it to be a hobby. Although, as this confused issue kept running around in hi brain, he thought he could use this opportunity to to learn not to entrust all his life to any religion book, so he decided not to be referring everything he was doing in life with what are written in the bible, instead, to be referring it to humanities and social science. He also came to comprehend that, "Believing too much in what we read in religions books can lead us to extremism, making us refrain from concentrating on reality, and at the end, making us to substitute failure for success."

The day his friend was to be transferred came, and everybody were celebrating. During this celebration, many of the girls were using this opportunity in getting themselves close to the men of their choices. It was true that in that camp, there were more women than men. Every time, two or three girls were seen fighting over one boy. They were all prepared to have sex, and have it full to their throats. It was sex everywhere and they were happy having it every time like it was a curse to them. Actually, most of them were thinking it was the right time for them to look for their future husband there in the camp, while others were seeing it as just a fun and pleasure thing. Jocularly, David and some of his friends had always come into conclusion that most of the girls were practicing prostitution there, since that was exactly what they were going to Europe to do to pay their pimps and also to assist their impoverished families. Sex to many of them, was like eating bred and butter, forgetting they could be infected with any venereal disease or they might get pregnant, and if that happens, their pimps will definitely send them to their graves. Many of them were also giving their hearts to the boys who were ready to squeeze and dump them. They forgot the heart is a precious thing that one has to be careful with. For David, it was a difficult thing to deal with, seeing how much most of these girls really hated him, since he was not friendly and was not easily seduced. Meanwhile, at this time, majority of them were not aware of the existence of gays and lesbians, if not they might had referred him to be one.

That night, as the send-off party was still going on, one of David's friend, the same boy whom they were both smoking hashish at the very time his ghost left him to the place where he saw his God and his devil. The boy called him to tell him about the deal he was having with some other boys that night. Telling him this—was actually because he wanted to know if he was having some friends in Madrid who could help him to sell the hashish he was to take there the next morning. 'I am not having anybody there,' said David to the boy. 'O.k, I would have to look for another person who is having his family or friend over there,' replied the boy, walking away. David tried to make him stop, inquiring from him, 'are you going to swallow and take the hashish there?' 'Look, now that you said you are not having anybody there in Madrid, so please, forget about all these questions,' replied the boy, but, as he was about to walk away, he stopped again and came back to meet him where he was still standing in awe, and with an intense anger, he asked him, 'By the way, have you come to Europe to play or have you come to make money?' David, stupefied and silent, did not know how to respond to the question he was being asked. 'Brother! wake up,' said the boy again. 'Our fathers and forefathers were all living for years in a perpetual state of fear, and that is the reason we their children are suffering now. If you want to continue to live in fear, that is for you. But, as for me, I am leaving fear aside to go get the things that belongs to me, and that is my reason for leaving Africa to come to Europe.' He left, without waiting to hear what David was about to utter. David, still stupefied and silent, was alone on his own, and since he was already intoxicated with the little alcohol he was offered in addition to the hashish he smoked, and also with the thoughts of the perplexity of life and how it could be solved, he stood where he was unable to move an inch until he went down slowly and sat down on the filthy floor where he was standing. He was wondering why he was experiencing what he never wished for himself. He could really imagine how he came to initiate himself into this life that he was starting to live that he was always unwilling to live that he understood, with no doubt, was going to lead him into an inglorious ending.

CHAPTER 10

T HE NEXT DAY CAME, AND it was on Saturday early morning at about 09:30 a.m. It was raining so bad that almost everybody in the camp were unable to go outside except for the people who were to be transferred that morning to the peninsular, that were already moved with a bus provided by the Refugee authority to the seaport with very few people assisting them to bid them goodbye. David and his friend, Festus were together inside their small tent and were discussing about the things that were happening inside the camp. David, who actually thought it to be a rumor when he first heard that balls of hashish wrapped with a transparent plastic material called cellophane, were given to people to swallow so that they might take it to the peninsular without being caught by the police. So, he quickly came up with that topic to be discussed so as to be enlightened about it. 'Is it true that people usually succeed in getting the hashish there without being caught?' he asked. 'Yes, it is true,' responded Festus. 'Why is it not detected by the police?' he inquired. 'Oh, it is because of the cellophane used in wrapping them. There is no way the police or the computer can detect any drug wrapped with that cellophane.' 'Are you implying, even if it were to be cocaine?' he asked curiously. 'I said, nothing hidden under that cellophane can be detected by their so-called computer or whatever they call it,' replied Festus. 'O.k, I think I am about to start buying this idea of drug trafficking,' said David. 'What about you Festus? Are you going to swallow these things on the day you will be transferred?' 'Do you think I am a coward? Look, man. I need money, and that is why I have took the risk to come to this place. You see, you hardly get caught if you try it, because most of these Spanish policemen there knows it, but they are pretending not to. They only want to allow us to do it, because they already know some of us might not be having anybody there in the peninsular to harbor us when we arrive there, so they believe, with the little money we will be paid, we can then start life with it on our own.'

David, sitting and listening to this unverified supposition formulated by his friend, was already convinced that he was going to be a part of the dream team, whom their intention were to make real good money. He then said to Festus, 'tomorrow, I want to go with you to do the hustling and bustling thing.' 'Yeah, you have finally come to your senses. Do not fret yourself, I will be taking you with me to my working place tomorrow, just count on me.'

The next morning, at about 05:00 a.m, David was woken up by his friend. He wanted to return back to bed, but Festus who was so desperate to make money that day, said something that gave him strength to follow him. He said, "A coward dies a thousand deaths. A soldier dies but once." To prove not to be a coward, he decided to get up from sleep, got himself prepared, and they both set on their hustling and bustling Promethean job they already assigned for themselves.

With haste, they both walked themselves into the bush, searching everywhere around to see if there were immigrants trying to find their ways to the camp. They were walking and searching for more than two hours without finding anybody. David was already exhausted and wanted to return back to the camp, but Festus who was accustomed to this, urged him to wait for more minutes. He insisted they should take another road where he said he believed he could find them. Then, there arise a little disagreement between the two of them—whether to keep searching or to return back to the camp. As they finally agreed to keep searching, they heard some noises not too far from where they were. So, they kept quiet and hid themselves under some leaves of trees and were waiting for the people making the noises to get near them. For more than ten minutes, they were still where they were and were waiting, until finally, they heard the chatting noise more louder than it was before, so they came out from where they were hiding, and immediately the group of starving and filthy illegal immigrants saw them, they all broke into a trot and disappeared and were hiding themselves around the corners of the bush. But David and Festus were calling them with the little French they could speak, to come out from where they were hiding, promising to help take them to the camp. After much promises and promises, the scattered immigrants came out and walk closer to them with joy, hoping they had met Africans like them who were to give them aids and show them how to get to the camp. Festus, who for long has took this to be his profession, called all of them together and advised them to follow his instructions, and after that, with his voice as soft as that of a woman, he asked them to empty their pockets. The money and passports, he told them were proof they were coming from Morocco, and if caught with them by the Spanish guards, they will be deported back to Morocco. When they heard they were going to be deported, they all brought everything out and handled it over to them. Meanwhile they had both promised to return these things back to them the next day after they might been registered.

Festus and David led them through the bush until they arrived close to the barbed wires that were used in fencing the camp and was having a big round hole cut in it for long by unknown person just to ease the passing of people inside the camp and also for new immigrants who are trying to penetrate into the camp. Then, they told them to move forward on their own to the camp and promised to return everything back to them, while the two of them went to pass through the gate and went to relax themselves inside their tent with their minds filled with joy and happiness, as they were counting the money which actually served them for two weeks—enough for them to twice in the local restaurant everyday.

Later that day, when evening came, David's was relaxing inside the tent alone, still thinking of how he was going to swallow the balls of hashish the day he will be transferred. Suddenly, his phone rang, and, as he picked it, he heard the voice of his friend, the same boy who was transferred the previous day to the peninsular. The boy had actually called to inform him of his success, and also to encourage him to take the same risk to become successful like him. He was bragging with the money he was having with him, and when David heard this, he knew nothing was going to stop him from not taking that risk to succeed. The boy also told him he was already living in Madrid with the money he got from selling the hashish he stole from the owner, by refusing to go deliver it to the person whom he was sent to.

This information he received, and with the money he made by going into the bush with Festus for the hustling and bustling business, totally made him to think of how to recast his view of himself in relation to how he see life and in the pursuit of wealth. For this reason, he later came to write a poem while he was in prison in Italy.

THE PATHWAY

Wild and perilous, the pathway I'm to take.
To reach my goal, even with my life held at stake.
Not to blow the fire off in a hurry, but I'm obliged
To be setting things right, pushing my decisions to collide.
To the future, while I walk to bite even with no teeth,
As I might not forget, life could be bitter and sweet.

David and Festus did actually succeeded in extracting money from these other immigrants by promising to return it back to them after they might have been registered, which was far from the truth that they were going to keep the money, and believing they were never going to be seen again by these same immigrants. But it all became a nightmare as David was walking to the bathhouse one morning to shower, carrying with him a bucket full of water, when someone tapped him at the shoulder, *'mon ami, commet allez-vous?'* the boy greeted, smiling. *'Je ne vous connaisse?'* asked David, anxiously wanting to leave, but the boy tapped him again at the back, shouting, *'voileur! voleur!'* In not less than two minutes, more than twenty Malians and senegalese arrived at the scene, speaking to each other in their dialect. Some of the Nigerians who were close to them came in order to settle the dispute, but immediately they were told what happened, they all turned against David and were in support of those boys, because most of them had had the same problems before. David who was struggling from the grip of the boy, managed to escape and started to run like an antelope that was caught by a lion and was ready to be served as a meal. He ran as fast as he could, jumping across the barbed wires and continued to run until he was disappeared from view, finally succeeding in propelling himself into the nearby bush. He did not know what else to do than to sit himself down on the sandy floor, folding his hands around his body since the weather was a bit cold at about fifteen degree centigrade. His legs were shaken as he had left his foot-wears behind when he tried to escape from the lion whom he had once treated like a cow.

Still sitting down where he was, not being able to move any of his leg further, first, because he was afraid some one might still be running after him and might be hiding to see him move. Secondly, because he was almost frozen to death. Something strange happened and he thought he could see the boy or rather his ghost moving around him. When he opened his mouth to shout, he could not close it, or he thought he was shouting and nobody came to rescue him. 'Do not be afraid,' said the boy, placing his right hand on his shoulder. 'Who are you?' asked David, exhausted. "Ah! Ah! Ah,' giggled the boy, nervously as he walked closer to him. 'Do you really want to know who exactly I am? Look, you seemed tired and I think you do need a rest. But let me inform you. I am your angel, your second life and your soul. In anyway you might look at it, I have come to always be around you and anytime you want to talk to anybody about your problems, I will always be here for you. But I do not think I need you,' replied David. You might think you do not, but you do. You are going to Europe where you are not going to be told what to and what not to do by your father or mother or your brothers or sisters. You are going to be on your own, so, I am always going to be there with you.' David was stunned by silence because he could not actually figure out what was happening to him. 'Let me advise you of one thing. Do not turn away from God. Do not let yourself get confused with the quotes from the bible. The bible is not written for people to read and learn how to do evil, instead, for correcting man's mistakes. In 2 Timothy 3:15-16, it says, "All scriptures in the bible is inspired of God and beneficial for teaching, for reproving, for setting things straight, for disciplining in righteousness." 'Are you saying I should become an instrument of God by reading the bible and preaching it to others?' asked David. 'I am not telling you what to become. I am only saying you should deviate from evil,' said the boy, turning his back on David, and was about to walk away. He turned again to face him and said, 'Do not forget in the book of Matthew 7:19, it says "Every tree that bringeth not forth good fruit is hewn down, and cast into the fire." David could watch the boy as he quoted that last scripture to him and turned and walked away. This was when he realize there were two David, even when he has met and discussed with him before and thought it was an imagination, but was already coming to see that the other David has always been with him right from his birth, but he just did not grasp his presence in something close to reality.

That afternoon when he returned back to the camp, it was rumored that the boys who were looking for him have gone to file a report at the office. Festus, his friend returned back late in the evening, fatigued

and exhausted and wanted to go to bed. 'Hey Festy! what's the matter?'
'nothing, it is just that I am very tired and I want to sleep,' replied Festus.
'Did you hear what happened this morning?' asked David, sitting down
with a blanket round his body and peeping through the little hole in
the tent to see if any body was coming to get him. '*Wetin be the problem?*'
asked Festus, in pidgin english. '*O boy, I tire o. This people want to put
sand sand for my garry o.*' said David '*Who be this people sef?*' asked festus,
again. '*No be this Francophone people wey we take their money that day,*'
replied David. '*You mean say this people see you, and them come hold you?*'
Festus fretful, sitting himself well so he could see that it was not just
a dream that David is telling him they were been haunted by the evil
things they did. '*Man, forget this people. Them not fit do anything. You sef
too dey fear,*' said Festus, trying to get his confidence back and to make
David not to be scared. '*I want sleep o, if you like make you dey fear those
useless Francophone people.*' '*O boy, this na serious matter if you not know,
becos, if them report us, we not go get documents here, and them fit come put
us for prison o,*' said David. '*Forget that thing, this people not fit do anything,*'
responded Festus as he fell to bed and slept off, forgetting many people
had had this same problem before, mostly Moroccans and Nigerians,
and after been reported of theft and extortion, they might later be
denied of documents to be transferred to the peninsular, and even if
they were transferred, but with no document—which will deprive them
of the rights and privileges to live and work there.

David, still sitting down alone watching his friend sleep, was already
in a confused state of mind, not knowing what to do. He could see
himself as a fool who, because of greed, was about to lose everything in
life that he dreamed of. He sat there and was unable to sleep and unable
to move his body, replenished with strength, but with his heart filled to
the brim with fear and hopelessness and was overwhelmed by feelings
of guilt. It came straight to his mind, a quote by the great William
Shakespeare in the play, Julius Caesar, "The evil that men do lives after
them; the good is oft interred with their bones." For this, later in his
future life, he came to write this poem.

LIFE WITH VICTORY

What is it, that seeketh thy soul?
That bringeth not to thee, a life of everlasting.
Instead, hindereth thy way to a happy ending.
In thee, it dwell, if thou thinketh so,
The true meaning of life with victory
That causeth not pains and sufferings.

Many days had passed and David's heart was still bumping, thinking, one day he was going to be called by the camp authority and summoned. He met with almost all the boys they extorted money from and apologized to them, trying to convince them how regretful he was. Most of them did accept his apologies while most of them threatened to file a report about it to the camp authority. But David vowed never to do it again and had kept to his vow. His friend, Festus, left the camp and was being transferred to the peninsular, leaving him behind. He was then associating himself with new friends and was waiting for the day his name will be included on the list of the people to be transferred. He became interested in going to the football field to watch people play. Most of them who were very determined to become footballers in Europe and were competing with skills and tenacity, hopefully they might be seen by some good coaches who might help them bring to reality their dreams to change their destiny. But at the end, nothing went as expected for any of them. Many of these people who were current about European football, understood Spain to be a country that love football since they also were good in investing in this sport, having some of the best football clubs in Europe and in the world like Real Madrid and Barcelona football clubs. They also thought that most of the French national team that won the world cup were immigrants—some who were born there and some who were selected by some good coaches who watched them play at the time they were in the refugee camp, so they were told. They were all in a mood of cautious optimism, but forgetting Spain was not France in terms of giving an immigrant a chance and an opportunity like that.

It was on friday morning, late November, as he walkd to the notice board where list of names of the people to be transferred were placed.

Getting there, he saw that most of the people whom they both arrived the camp, were celebrating. 'What is the matter?' he asked. 'Oh, have you not checked the list?' asked one of the boys, jumping up and down, screaming—my name is on the list. 'O.k. But, why not go outside so that other people can as well take a look at it?' asked David, as he managed to squeeze himself through the crowded myriad of people waiting to check their names on the list. From a distance, he could see on the list, a name almost like his. He tried to get closer to assure himself that it was his name, but the more he tried getting closer, the more he was getting farther as he was being pushed backward. He finally gave up the idea of vigorously trying to penetrate through the crowded myriad of people, instead he waited for everybody to finish and then walk carefully closer, but unluckily for him he saw that the list was been torn. It's hard to tell why most people's fortune is always tragic. Throughout David's life, this has been part of him. Misfortune, and he has tried in every way he could to avoid it, but it kept coming and coming. Although he later discovered the solution to this misfortune by trying to be a good person. "The more good things he was doing, the more this misfortune was running away from him and being replaced by good fortune." The sayings that "Good things come to those who do good things, and to those who do bad things, bad things will come to haunt them."—is a thing we the people of the world has always not think of before we proceed in doing the things that we know could hurt other people.

In David's later life in the future, he had also come to be able to penetrate and get to the bottom, driven by his own will to learn and coming to comprehend the fact that, "It is better to be close to the saints than to be close to the sinners, as getting close to the saints gives you an opportunity of becoming a better person, while getting close to the sinners makes you sin more, and sins can leads to death."

Still checking the list on the board, he thought he saw his surname, but when he got closer to check it properly, he saw that it was the surname of another person. He kept checking, blaming himself for being too patient at the time he first arrived there. He saw that the floor were filled with torn pieces of papers that the list was written, and when he picked up one of these pieces of paper to glance through with no hope left to see what was written on it, the very first one that his hand reached for, was the one which is name was written. 'Oh my God! my name is here,' he screamed with joy, leaping himself up high and landing back to the floor with one of his finger fractured. He did not actually realize how fractured his finger was as he moved swiftly passed some other immigrants who were also moaning and groaning with happiness. He could not explain the reason he was running and where he was running to, but he kept running until he got close to the beach and finally decided to stop to inform some of his friends who were running after him to verify if truly he had seen his name on the the list, knowing already why he was running. 'I have finally seen my name,' he kept screaming and panting. His friends were happy for him. He could not actually believe it was happening after he had lost his faith, blaming God inside him, the reason He created him as a human being.

The whole camp that night was full of newly arrived immigrants and celebrations and jubilation of the ones to be transferred to the peninsular. Music, drinks, and sex were the proof of the celebrations most especially among the Nigerians. But the reasons for the celebration were that some of them were to be thrown into a paradise that they have long dreamed of. Frankly speaking, they all thought it wrong, if not all, but majority did. There is no wonder they say,"The life of distress begins with a lot of excitement."

Later that evening, after David had returned from the office of the Spanish government delegate that was responsible for issuing them the residence and working permits—which was situated in the city center. He went alone into the bush, sitting on one of the stone laid on the ground and started thinking of what to do. Inside his mind, a voice spoke to him, 'pray and thank the Lord God for this wonderful work He has done for you.' Holding the documents he was given in his two hands and raising them high to the sky, he knelt down and prayed, 'O Lord, I thank you for what you have done for me. I will always believe in you. You are my God and my creator. Lead me O'Lord so I might not get lost. Marvelous God, you are the one I put my trust on, and I know you will never fail me.' He then said the Lord's prayer in addition, 'Our father, who art in heaven, hallowed be thy name. Thy kingdom come. Thy will be done, on Earth as it is in heaven. Give us this day our daily bread. And forgive us our trespasses, as we forgive those who trespass against us. And lead us not into temptation, but deliver us from evil. For thine is the kingdom, the power and the glory, forever and ever. Amen.' Immediately he finished saying these prayers, he stood up and turned to leave. But, suddenly, 2nd David was already in front of him. 'What are you doing here?' asked 1st David. 'I have come to congratulate you. Congratulation.' He held out his hand for a shake. 'I really do not think I need you in everything I am doing,' said 1st David. 'You do need me,' replied 2nd David. 'I have come now to warn you not to do the thing you intend to do this night.' 'What is that?' 'Don't pretend you do not know what I am talking about.' 'I actually do not know what you are talking about,' replied 1st David, stepping one leg forward, wanting to leave. 'Look 1st David, if you try to go swallow that thing to take to where you are going to, you will have a big problem and you will be thrown into prison. Remember what I told you the other time. Read Matthew 7:19 again.' and after he said that, he vanished into the sky. David again was left alone to choose which way to go—to go to Spain peacefully with no money in his hand, or to go with drugs inside his stomach, if he succeed, he will be paid a reasonable amount of money that will help him start a new life there. But another thing was that he was told the wrapped hashish can get loosed—which might destroy his intestines and get him killed. 'Which way do I take now?' he asked himself, calling for 2nd David to help him suggest what to do, when automatically, a boy appeared from a nearby bush and walked close to him—asking him who he was talking to. 'I was not talking to anybody, I was just singing,' said David, walking passed the boy whom he had known at the the time they were in Morocco, who later said, *Take life easy, O boy, make you not go dey talk to yourself, like say you don dey craze.* But David ignored him and left.

It was 10:00 p.m, two hours before then, David hosted five of his friends who were very close to him and were good in smoking. He bought some hashish from one Moroccan boy, and then, twelve cans of beer. They all smoke and drank, gathering themselves together, jubilating and singing songs they normally sing while smoking drugs. After then, they all moved to go and meet other people who were celebrating too—so as to join them, but David left them all to go and meet the man who was to take him to the place where he was to go and swallow the wrapped hashish.

There he was, in a dark or rather dim room with a bowl full of hundreds of wrapped hashish—say, ten grams in one, and a bottle of coke in his hand, waiting to swallow them with it. His memory leaped away from him instantly, flying back to a day before that day. He could see everything again. How his elder sister who just got married and has been responsible for his trip to abroad—has promised to send him some money so that he can use it for transporting himself to her house from the camp. He did not actually ask for that money, but his sister ex-boyfriend who came to meet him in the camp, did. When David first met the boy, they were both happy to meet again since it was long they never saw each other. Back at the time they were in their country, the boy has quit coming to ask David and his elder brother, Ken, the whereabout of their sister, as they had both refused to tell him—making him give up. But the boy believed she has traveled abroad, because, the girl (David's sister) informed him before. The reason why David and his elder brother refused to tell him was because they were afraid that their sister might forget about helping them first before helping her boyfriend, just for her to keep her relationship with the boy—and this was happening to many families whom their daughter had traveled abroad. So, when the boy met David in the camp, there was no way he could keep it as a secret, believing his sister to be married and will not be much concerned about the boy. But, at later on, the boy has been so smart, calling the girl every time, demanding money from her. David who had given him his sisters phone number, was now regretting the reason he did so, even when he had seen this same boy several times with different girls in the camp where they were together. The most astonished thing was that, his sister was later promising to send him money through the same boy. To David, that was so absurd and disgraceful. He decided to take the risk to traffic drugs, instead of him to accept that money. He has always loved adventure and wanting to try something new, and this was the right time for him to prove himself again as a man. "A man lives because he wish to live. A man does not live because he was instructed to live." "We cannot wait for people to constantly give us what to eat. We must look for what to eat by ourselves." "No one would want to see the fire burning and get close to it, knowing he will be burnt. But what if the thing that can make you survive and live for a hundred years is close to you to take—and at the same time close to the fire. What will you do then?"

David who was left feeling disgruntled at the way he was treated by his sister, decided to commit himself into the devil's hand, not fretting about what the consequences might be. He saw that he was left with no choice. His friend once told him before when he newly arrived in that camp, that "A coward dies many times before his final death. A soldier die but once." I am not a coward, and I will not be one, he said to himself. As his memory flew back, wanting to return back to where it leaped from, someone he could not see properly since the room was dark, touched him at his back. 'Do it quickly man.' It was at this time he could recollect the reason why they were all gathered there in the dark room.

They say, "The longer you stay in the dark, the more brighter it appears to you, and the more clearly you see." When he tried to look around him, he saw that there were more people than he thought. There were about eight boys and four girls whom their faces he could recognize, and immediately he saw those girls, fear was instantly replaced by confidence and hope to break through the door of freedom and success that was locked behind him. 'I want to be free to be able to live the kind of life that I know will be suitable for me. I am not going to depend on my sister for anything,' he murmured these words to himself. He watched all of them swallowing the wrapped hashish in form of a cylinder with both edges spherical—let say, three millimeters long and one and a half millimeters round. He picked up one of the hundred that was in his bowl, but when he put it in his mouth, he vomited it out again, because it was too rigid to pass through his throat; he continued to try even as he continued to vomit it out, as he was already beginning to have a soar in his throat. He quickly asked where the toilet was, and the Moroccan who owns the house pointed it to him. He ran as fast as he could hurriedly to the door to leave the house, but he was instructed not to open the door until every one of them finished swallowing what they came there for. He was ordered to sit down and watch. He then walked to the toilet, and when he put on the light there and tried to look at the mirror, then appeared 2nd David. 'Aha ha,' he let out a loud guffaw which no one was hearing except him alone. 'Did I not warned you not to come over here?' he asked, annoyingly. Then he went on and said, 'I am so sorry 2nd David, I should have listen to your advice before, I never thought it to be as so a formidable task.' 'It is not a task,' replied 2nd David. 'You brought this to yourself, nobody forced you to. You wanted to try something new. You said you do not want to be depending on your sister and that you are ashamed to accept the money she sent to you through her boyfriend. "Look if you think you are ashamed to do anything because you do not want people to mock you, what they will do is to weep and mourn for you when you are dead." 'Please, do not talk about death. I can see even girls swallow it, I see no reason why I cannot.' 'If everybody can, that does not mean everybody should,' said 2nd David. "You are trying to be other people, and by doing so, you can never be who you really are, and you will always live by the will of other people whom you are trying to be like." '1st David, there is one more thing that I have to say to you, "Just be yourself no matter the situation. Do not try to change who you really are by doing that—that are awry, I tell you, you will have everything in life that you have dreamed of." 'But are you saying I should not go and try again to see if I can swallow these balls so by tomorrow I will be thinking of getting paid when I reach to deliver it to the owner?' 'For the last time, I have to say this,' said 2nd David, raising his voice louder, 'will you ever learn?' "The thing that you have long wish to do that gives you pleasure, is now becoming a sense of impending doom, with your future prospect seeming to look dim." 'It is up to you,' he turned away and vanished, passing through the mirror where he entered from. 'What are you still doing inside the toilet? if you know you cannot swallow these things, why did you have to bother yourself to come here? every other person here have finished, even the girls, and you are there hiding in the bathroom. You are a coward,' screamed the Nigerian boy who brought them there. David who was quiet and did not know what else to do since he was ashamed to come out of the toilet, but the word, COWARD sounded like someone just hit him on the head with a hammer. He could not resist that word, COWARD, so he opened the door and came out of the toilet, demanding for another soft drink—which he thought might help him swallow the balls easily and better. And immediately he was given some orange juice, he started by drinking it first and putting the balls along with it in his mouth. He swallowed the first one, second, third, until fifty without stopping. The Moroccan boy who owns the apartment and the Nigerian boy who brought them there, both watched him in amazement. 'I am done, I do not think I can take more than this.' 'You tried,' said the Nigerian boy, paying him a compliment, because he never thought he will be able to swallow one of it not to say as that much as fifty. This compliment, at David's later life, he came to understand that the more he was able to swallow and delivered, the more money the boy might be paid. That is the deal. His job was to control the business by getting people to traffic the drugs and by communicating with the people they were to deliver it to, period, without even touching it or trying to swallow it to know how clumsy and burdensome it is to the people who are doing it. David, in his future life, he also came to see the drug traffickers to be the most unintelligent, senseless, ludicrous, insane and greediest people living on the planet, Earth. What they do that they think is the right thing for them to do as to make money to be in an exalted position in life, is nothing but foolishness by working for another man to eat, sacrificing their lives for another human being, giving themselves as slaves to another man to be used like a tool. It is stupid, and it is because people has made greed rule over them.

David was able to swallow fifty out of the one hundred balls he was given. He then went home with the rest of the other people who were there with him at the place they went to swallow the hashish. Immediately he arrived home, he fell on his blankets-made-bed, wanting to sleep since he was very weak and weary, but he could not sleep because the hashish he had swallowed had become a problem, causing his stomach to ache. It was turning his intestine and he could not resist it, so he sat down. Sitting down really did ease the pains, so he sat till it was 05:00 a.m when everybody that were to be transferred that day were all getting ready to leave the camp to the seaport. He quickly went to shower and got himself ready, with a bag containing two trousers and one t-shirt and a sweater.

At the camp's gate, they were all called by their names and surnames and anybody whose name was called, could get into the bus that was already waiting for them to leave the camp. Getting to the seaport, the same list was called and everyone on board were given a seat to sit down and watch a movie. It was great for almost all of them since it was their first time of traveling with a ship, but those with drugs inside their stomach found it miserable as they were eager to get to their destinations to quickly discharged everything.

It took the ship just forty five minutes to get them to Algeciras, the first town in Spain that you reach after the Mediterranean sea. As they all arrived there—that was presumably the last place the Spanish government completed their responsibilities, so anyone who was having a family or friends should call them so they can render them help on where to go or how to survive in the country, but those without families or friends were to look for a way out themselves. And for this reason of no one to care for you if you cannot care for yourself, many of them had forcibly took the decision of trafficking the drugs so that when they get paid, they might be able to start life with the little money.

Waiting for someone to come over to get them to their destination where they can go and discharge the hashish, David and the other boys and girls were still waiting, while the policemen came to ask them what the problem was, but they refused to let them know who they were waiting for. After awhile as they were still waiting and waiting, news came to them that a boy had been arrested because he could not resist the hashish he had swallowed, so he started vomiting and was later rushed to the hospital for a surgical operation. Everyone who were at the seaport, became afraid because they thought the police might be suspecting them too of the same crime. But the police just passed by without even looking at them, then David recalled what his friend, Festus, had told him before, that the police knew about it, and that they just overlook it not to be a serious crime, knowing they need the little money to start up life in Europe.

CHAPTER 11

I T WAS HIS FIRST YEAR in the secondary school. It was a year he thought he was to join the big boys as they normally calls it while he was still in the primary school. His coming to this school was actually to prove himself a good scholar so as to attain success in his future life. But, along the way, he was totally transformed into a different thing close to a weird and wonderful creature living beneath the Earth.

After he passed his primary school common entrance examination and scored the best marks, he was to wait till the school resume again—which took about three weeks. While waiting, he was spending more time, assisting his father with the farm work, knowing he would have to need some money to start this new school. His father, on the other hand was prepared to take the responsibilities in any form, but to make sure he was able to give him education which on his own, he never had the chance to get. He was prepared to do anything, thinking he had seen his son very hungry and wanting to eat from the fruit of knowledge and wisdom. That same year had been a good year. His father made an enormous harvest and sold a lot of it, raising a reasonable amount of money to send his children to school. Meanwhile, David and his sister were to start their secondary schools which is a higher step for them to be, but more expensive. Although, Kennedy, his elder brother was to be promoted to a senior secondary school, which also is more expensive than the junior secondary school—the very one he will be leaving.

Sometimes, when David was alone, he will sit down and start to think of this whole thing. Whether his father was capable of taking these responsibilities for the three of them and their three younger ones who were still in the primary school. The more he was thinking about this theme and whether posterity will think of his father as a great man, the more his love and affection for education was fading away, and the more his anger and hatred for his father for having too many children was growing inside of him.

The school resumed with all the students excited to be promoted to a higher class. An interview was conducted among every students that passed the the final year primary school examination popularly known as the common entrance exam. During the interview, David was asked the three favorite secondary schools he would like to attend, and he had chosen (I.C.C) Immaculate Conception College, as his first choice, Edo College, as the second choice and Western Boys High School, as the third choice. These three schools he had chosen, were all single schools for boys only. I.C.C, was founded by Bishop Patrick J. Kelly, one of the missionaries that visited Nigeria in the year 1944. It was said to be a school for the kids whom their father were rich, particularly at that time when the government schools were the only schools you can find in the country. Edo College, which was established in 1937 with a quality of its products that gave the school strength. Some of its products that excelled academically throughout the country, and it was a school attended by the Oba (the king), which brought an advance and written notification and a flourish of trumpet image to the school. Western Boys High School, the last of his choice, was a school he had sometimes admired, because most of the students were with an attitude of mind for fighting. Confident, sometimes aggressive behavior were included making many other students from other schools respect and fear them. Many use to refer to them as students with attitudes.

When the school resumed, every students that knew he passed the exam were to go to any of the school he chose during the interview. David with hope and expectation, buoyantly went straight to I.C.C to check the list pasted on the notice board to see if he was admitted. He has heard of great people who have attended this school, and wanted to be just like them since his father had also approved of it. He arrived there with some of his friends who were there for the same reason to check the list, vigorously passing through the midst of the multitudes who were there not for a different reason but also to check the list. He was at the front of everybody, although he was among the smallest but also was among the smartest. He checked and checked and checked and checked repeatedly to see if he was not seeing very well, but it all happened that his name was not on the list. He squeezed himself out of the multitudes again with his two eyes full of tears. He thought of going to the ministry of education to ask them the reason why his name was not on the list; he also thought of what to tell his father at home, knowing how happy his father would be if he went home with good news that he saw his name on the list of the students that were admitted into that school that year. He was still crying when his friends came to meet him to cheer and encourage him not to fret himself too much, and to move ahead and go to Edo college, his second choice—which was not very far from where they were. He was told by some people that the school, I.C.C, was a school most rich people would want their kids to attend, so they were prepared to do anything to get them there, either by bribing or by using their influence.

In not more than twenty minutes, he and his friends were already at the front gate of Edo college, after walking eight hundred meters. It was David first time of stepping his feet pass the gate. Though, so many times he passed by the gate and has always admired the buildings in it, probably because it was the best buildings that any of the schools in the state had ever had. It was rumored that the school was not built for secondary school students, instead it was meant to be a university campus, but because the king ordered it so, since that was the school he attended. The one thing that has always appalled David about the school, was that there were very wicked and dangerous senior student in the school—and mostly how criminals were coming to hide in the moat that was at the back of the building of the school. About the moat, it had been a myth David had tried to learn more about when he was growing up. The moat was also at the back of their house and it has served them and a lot of people near their house as a dust-bin that can never be full. When he and some of his other brothers asked their father long time ago how it had come into existence, they were told a fable that some thousand years ago, the supposed king, a giant who was a brother to the king, had hit his foot on the ground with vexation because he was denied the king's throne, because the people saw him to be a fool and believed he could not rule them and as he kept hitting his foot on the ground, the moat became wider and wider and longer and longer. David could not substantially believe this fable, but he could not disbelieve it also since there were no written documents to prove how the moats came into existence. It was later when he grew older and was already in Europe, that he came across a book written about the history of the city and the existence of the moats, that he came to discern that, a one time Oba (king) had ordered the moats to be dug round the city, during the second half of the 15th century. The earthworks served as preventive measure against the people who were coming to trouble the new city and also afforded control of access to the capital which had nine gates that were shut at nights. It was finalized around 1460, and at that time being the world's largest earthwork.

David and his friends passed through the gate of the school, walking towards an open field where the list of the newly admitted students were placed—which was not far from the principals office. As they reached, they saw that the place was already full of very few boys with no uniforms on them, but with a very high numbers of boys with uniforms on, meaning they were already students there in the school. He and his friends were so keen on seeing the list to see if they could find their names, but when they move closer, they were restrained by some of the students who were standing there like pickets who were paid for to make sure violent does not breakout. 'Where are you going to?' asked one of the boys. 'Please, I just want to see if my name is on the list,' replied David. 'Wow, you are very rude, I think you should have to be careful here, because we are the big boys in this school and I am here to see the list if my younger brother's name is here,' said the boy, wanting to focus on looking at the board where the list were pasted. But when he finished looking with an absolute self-sufficient, without seeing his younger brother's name, he walked out of the congested crowd and was walking towards the building where his class was situated. David who was so blissfully happy and was rejoicing that he had seen his name on the list, even leaving his friends behind, did not know the time he walked pass the boy. 'Hey you! come here,' with a voice of compulsion. David waited promptly and efficiently, knowing where he was and having heard about the school and how the new students are being treated by the senior student. 'Why are you so excited,' he asked, waving his hand to inform some of his other friends who were passing-by to come join him, and when they saw him with a new student, they all ran, coming to meet him. 'Why are you rejoicing,' he repeated. 'Oh, I am so glad that my name is on the list,' replied David, shaking, not knowing what to do—whether to run or to stay. He was afraid to run because it was his first time of going there and getting inside the school compound and he does not know which way to take out, not to mention the fastest way to escape so that he might not be caught if chased by these boys. He was afraid to stay because he knew something was going to happen to him—what, that is what he could not predict. When the other boys drew nearer, the boy who had called him, ordered him to kneel down. 'Your name is on the list and my younger brother's name was not there and I have been going there since two days now to see if it will appear one day, and you are here, rejoicing and you had the guts to answer for all the other boys whom I do not know if they are your friends and I do not even care to know.' Please, I am sorry. I thought you asked us where we were going to, that is why I answered.' 'You answered,' roared the boy like a lion, only to install fear on him. 'You are still talking,' said another. 'We are talking and you are talking, now tell me who is the senior?' asked one of them. 'No, he is trying to prove a good leadership by answering for his friends,' said another. Immediately he heard this last word, it was then he knew the offence he had committed. Trying to be a leader by answering for all of them. I am so sorry, I did not know it to be like that,' said David, putting his hands together to beg them, and as he was begging and praying to God to rescue him, one of the boy hit him on the head with some of the books he was holding on his hand. 'Stubborn boy,' he said, spitting out saliva on the floor. 'You will die. We will be the one to kill you. You can go and report this, o.k, but if you do, just make sure you are not coming to this school.' 'No, I would not,' said David. 'Shut up your filthy mouth, you idiot.' 'I told you, you should keep your mouth shut when your senior is talking to you.' It was then he understand that, when a senior student is talking to you, you should have to keep your mouth shut, because, talking or arguing with him might lead to a great offence which you might be punished for. 'How much is with you?' asked one of them, waving his hand to tell him to stand up, and with the same hand, trying to search him exactly the same way a police does to a man who just committed a felony. After the search, they could not find a dime with him, so they asked him to run as fast as he could without looking back, which he did. As he ran, not looking back, he went straight to where his friends were—who were still trying to see if they could find their names on the list. He walked closer to the congested and noisy crowd, and as he walk, he tried to acquire a meaning from the incident, but he understood that he had just learn a lesson, which was, "To become a leader, you are bound to face so many difficulties which might endanger your life." He had also come to face the reality—that leadership is a thing you can impose on yourself by working hard towards to achieve it, but it can also be a thing that imposes itself on you—meaning, leadership can be born and it can be made.

Harrison, David's best friend who was among his friends that came with him to see if his name was on the the list just like David, came running towards him, joyfully singing like he just won a gold medal. 'My name is here, I am a student of this school.' 'We made it,' said David, running to go meet his best friend too. They embraced each other with tears falling from their eyes. 'I told you this is the place for us to come, not I.C.C.' 'Yeah, you said it.' They were both so happy that David even forgot to tell him what he just encountered.

After much rejoice, David and Harrison, both decided to go and look for their other friends who came with them, but they could not find them, because the place was crowded with too many people—majority of them being students and parents who came to help their younger ones or their friends or their children to check the list.

David was on the list—this, he was very sure of, because he had seen it and it was very clear that it was his name, but something appeared to him—how will he be able to be coming to this school, knowing it was far from his house which was three miles. The transportation was going to be a very problematic issue that he would have to consider. As he tried to explain to Harrison, his friend about this, he received a very encouraging words. 'Look, we can always make it by walking. It is not far from us. I know a lot of people who are living close to us and still study here.' 'O.k,' said David, since he understood his friend who was not used to trekking was becoming the person to be saying this to a man like him who is used to trekking eight miles before to farm.

That day, when he arrived home late to deliver the good news to his parents who as well has arrived home late from their farm work. Everybody in the house were busy trying to get things organized. His mother was in the kitchen, preparing some food for his father who was already inside the bathroom that was built at the backyard of the house and was been used by almost forty people that were living in his father two houses since the both houses were close and the water system and shower in the new house were all ram-shackled and were never been reconditioned. There were very few lamps available in the house as there was no light due to power failure, which is just a normal thing in the most populous country in Africa, Nigeria, since he was born into this wicked and greedy world as he always thought it to be.

He could not deliver the good news to anyone which he was anxious to do. He was to wait until his father will finish eating and come out of the house to the front yard which was a commonplace for them to sit at nights. Meanwhile, as he was waiting, his mother who had served him his food came to realize that he was there with her. 'Hey! Osamudiame,' I have forgotten to ask you about your admission. Did you find your name in I.C.C?' she asked him in their native language. 'No, I did not, but I found it in Edo college and I think I am glad I did.' His mother who was so delighted to have heard this, congratulated him by adding more food to his food so as for him to eat and be satisfied. In less than thirty minutes, the news reached his father and every other people that were living in the whole house, including the tenants. His father later called him that night to congratulate him, and later asked him about everything relating to his admission and how he was preparing to start the new school. He saw that his admission into this new school was generally reckoned a success by his both parents and other members of his family, making him gain a recognition for his years of hard work of study during his primary school days. After he left everybody and went inside the room his father gave to him and Kennedy, his elder brother who was already very envious of his younger brother's success, because he was attending a mixed secondary school that was not much recognized and was less regarded by people and most of all, was newly founded and was near to their house. It was understood that—that school actually was not competitive with the other schools. That night was presumed to have been a joyful night for David, but it was Ken who messed it up for him maybe out of enviousness or out of challenge. It has been a thing between the two of them for so many years. Meanwhile David had tried to make his elder brother quit thinking he was in a challenge with him, but he had failed, trying to convince him. That night, they both quarreled over a subject matter of how the room should always be cleaned and tidied—which David and the other people who had come to settle them, including their parents, all knew was an excuse. This situation intrinsically did drove David to quickly take a new decision to leave his boring brother to go on a journey of self-discovering.

The next day came and David and his friends were already walking to their new hope-to-be school to get some more details about what to be done next to be admitted into the school. As they walk, chanting and exchanging opinions, reminiscing about their past life together while in the primary school, David could see himself moving into the realms of reality; he could see that his dreams of achieving success and coming to take his family out of poverty, was close to him as his expectations became high. "Having good friends is seeking a good future." He was so happy to be mingling with these boys whom he was referring to be his friends. He saw them just like people who thinks making a rational decision is necessary; he saw how he was beginning to believe in them more than he was believing in himself.

That morning, when he and his friends arrived their newly hope-to-be school, he could see that the school was full of many people moving around—some from one office to another. Students on uniforms, teachers and all the school administrations, parents who came with their kids to help them with their admission procedures—maybe because they were afraid their children would not be able to do it themselves, and then there were also the new students to be admitted.

The bell rang, and all the students hurried down to the assembly. And after awhile, speeches were made by the principal, followed by the Lord's prayer which was said together by all the students, and after that, the country's national anthem was sung, and then, the school anthem. Information of the events of the school were also later discussed, and at the end, bands and other various kinds of musical instruments like the tambourine were played and the students all marched to their various classrooms, singing songs of praises along. At the course of this event, all the new students and some parents who accompanied their children there, watched in amazement and exhilaration, cheerfully hoping and believing to be parts of it soon. This brought pride to the students and the school administrations, as they saw other people praised and admired them. David, on his own, could feel something in his mind already—that it was God who brought him there. He could not wait for himself to be one of them; he wanted the admission procedure to commence immediately, so were the other new students. It was a day in his life that he thought he could not forget as he took a look back at his epic struggle and being able to reach this place. He thought that, there is nothing in his life that he could set his mind to do that he cannot do.

The new students were assembled inside the school lecture hall to receive a lecture about the rules and regulations of the school. They were also lectured on how to achieve their aims and objectives in the future. As first-year students, everything seemed new and complex to them. Everyone of them were later given an admission form to fill—which they were ask to return the next day with the school fees and other fees included to be paid, and lastly, a prospectus so that they can obtain more information about the school—this prospectus which they all paid for.

That evening at home, David brought the prospectus and the admission form out to show to his parents. His mother read every of the forms and prospectus, but at the end of it all, she was took by surprise when she saw how much the expenses was. She knew there was no way they could afford this together with another one which David's elder sister who had just been admitted into another school also as a first-year student. It was a complicated issue for his parents at this time when they were having all their children in school, and they all needed their parents only assistance. It was then, a filthy mood of pessimism started to grow in a man's life, a man who once thought he could fly so high to touch the sky, a man who thought success was his portion in life, a man who believed in what he sees and sees that what he sees is real, but he could see that reality was already turning into a fantasy. It was at this period, he started to believe that, "Money can give a man what he really need in life. Money should not have to be evil, rather it has to be a blessing. It should have to be a friend more than being a foe."

CHAPTER 12

T HE NEXT DAY CAME AFTER David had collected the admission form and filled it, expecting to return it back to the school with the fees included. He was at home doing nothing due to the fact that his parents were unable to afford the money for the fees and other requirements needed for him to be admitted fully into the school. The next day, he decided to go and assist his father with the farm work. It was a good day for him and he was full of joy, even if he was supposed to have been in school with his friends, working on the process of his admission into his new school. Following that day, he was in the farm again and again and again. Finally, the third day came, and his father who was satisfied with the work he has done by assisting him to do the farm work, called him and asked him how much he really need for all the expenses. Immediately he told him, he went inside his house to bring the money out and then called his mother and gave her the money, pleading with her to make sure she assist him to the school the next day to pay all the fees. David, thrilled and released from his suspended doubt, thanked him. The one thing he learnt was that, "Patience is a thing that brings you happiness at the time you might not expect it." He was beginning to regain his lost senses back, thinking of a better life ahead of him again as he will not cease having hope for the future. He could recall in a song by one local musician living in his city, "When there's life, there's hope." As long as a man is alive, he is bound to have hope, because, "when a man die, that is when his hope also die." "Hope here, can be an expectation, a desire without assurance. An unseen thing that keeps us moving but with no certainty of fulfilling what we are dreaming of." But it is a good thing to have hope and David will not quit having it. He had read in the bible long time ago in Romans 8:24-25—which says, "For in hope we have been saved, but hope that is seen is not hope; for why does one also hope for what he sees? But if we hope for what we do not see, with perseverance we wait eagerly for it."

As David and his mother both arrived his new school compound that morning, his mother insisted on going to see one of the teachers—a brother to David's step mother whom she thought might be able to help her in getting the admission procedures worked out easily and fast, because she saw that many people were doing the same with the influence of the people working there. Although David warned her not to fret herself over this, but she declined to listen to him, thinking herself to be wiser than her son, and moreover, she thought it was a an opportunity for her to place David in this teacher's control. David has to obey, so they went searching for the man even when it appeared they do not know where to find him. But she kept asking some of the teachers she met by using the man's surname. She did so for almost one hour until she finally met someone who told them where to find him. They went, still looking for the man, and the moment she saw him from a distance, she started running towards where he was, and all David could do was to run after her, shouting and calling her to wait for him which she had refused to do until she finally reached where the man was. From a distance he could see how cheerfully his mother was and how she and the man had both greeted each other. He could not actually fathom the reason why his mother would be so excited about this, only to watch them in wonderment. But it was later when he grew up, he came to comprehend that they were both in a society—one of the most powerful secret society that was running the country.

David greeted the man too, half-kneeling or rather bowing his head in accordance to their tradition which states that you must bow or kneel or prostrate when greeting your elder to show a sign of respect. Later, in his future life, this is a thing that impelled David to be more serious and sensible when he arrived in the western world, seeing a teenage person jocularly insulting an elderly person—and yet, they will both end it up, laughing with each other. For this, he fell in love with the white man's world, as he saw with them a distinctive culture which he believe to be more advanced. Many that practices this, might referred it to be a tradition. But, he also could believe that there is nothing wrong with respecting your elders. Here comes respect which has to be a thing of choice rather than being a thing of obligation. Not to mention, as in the place where he was born, this is somehow referred to as (disrespect) and it is unlawful—and there is a punishment for this. He came to learn that, in this place where he was born, in reference to tradition, people are respected, obeyed, and admired in regards to how old or wealthy they are. But he thought this idea to be wrong not just for these people, but also for everybody living on the planet, Earth. He thought it will be more idealistic to see that respects and admiration should be given to the people with a thinking power to move the world forward, people that are inventive, innovative, creative, and then to the generous and philanthropists. He affirmed that respect must be given to elderly people, but not to all, since some really does not deserve it. How could a man be so greedy to marry seven wives and then having thirty to forty children, sitting in front of his house everyday, gossiping without a job, and leaving these kids to their mothers to care for them and yet will still want people to respect him? That man does not deserve respect, instead he should be ashamed of being a man; he is a disgrace to humanity because he has failed to comprehend the atrocities he has brought to the life of these kids.

After David had greeted the man, he waited for his mother to bring to closure the discussion he was having with the man. He waited and waited and was tired of waiting, at a time he was about to open his mouth to say something—something he knew that if said, will upset his mother; he wanted to tell her that they should leave and go do what they had actually come to do, but he knew what the consequence might be if he make the mistake to disrespect his mother in the presence of a stranger, so he shut up his mouth and waited patiently to see what was going to happen next. As he waited, staying a little distance of ten meters away from them so as not to cause them any considerable inconvenience, he saw from the distance where he was standing to wait, when the man wrote something in a piece of paper and handed it over to his mother—and he saw that she was smiling. He was dumb-struck, but still not knowing what exactly it was that was written in the piece of paper that was given to his mother. But, when the man was about to leave, he called him to advise him. David ran to meet him. 'My son, you are new here I know, but one thing is that you have to know the reason why your parents has sent you here to study. You have to be very serious about your education. Your parents love you, so that is the reasons they managed to raise this money to pay the fees. You know it is not easy to get this money, and it is not every parents whom their children found their names on the list here are able to sponsor them. I am going to be honest with you. This school is meant for the rich kids as you can see, it is very expensive, so you cannot expect your father to be spending all his time, doing that laborious job in the farm and coming to spend it on you here without you knowing the reason you are sent here.' 'Thank you so much,' replied David. Then, he continued, 'you do not have to thank me. All I want from you is for you to show to me how serious you are, not to put your father to shame, because I have heard of you several times. I have been told you were very intelligent while you were in the primary school, but now that you are here, you have to prove it, because this is the best place for you to prove how high your intelligence is.' David was about to blurted out something when his mother interrupted him. 'Did you hear what he had just said?' she asked, with her voice somehow threatening. 'I heard him,' said David, lowering his voice. 'O.k. You know we are poor, but we will do the best we can to make sure you succeed but you have to prove yourself.'

When they were about to leave, they bade the man good-bye and he did the same, but he later called David back and said to him again, 'all my four children are studying here in this school. One of them graduated already and had traveled abroad. One of them just gained an admission just like you. You can always look for me so I might be able to introduce you to my children.' Bringing out a piece of paper, he wrote in it, his name and surname, the class where he teaches and the office where he usually stay when he is not teaching. He handed it to David and bade him good-bye again.

David whose brain was already full of all the advises he was given, walked hurriedly to go meet his mother who was seeking information from one of the teacher she came across on her way to the office, showing her the written piece of paper the man had given her, but when David walked closer to meet with her, he saw that his mother and the woman were embracing each other just as if they knew each other for long. He was astounded, not knowing how to intrude, but the first thing he did was to greet the lady half-kneeling. 'This is my son I was telling you about,' said his mother, pointing directly to him. 'Oh! I hope you are here to study and make your parents be proud of you,' she asked, facing him. 'Yes,' replied David. 'This is my sister, 'said his mother. David who knew his mother's sisters and brothers, knew this woman was not a member of his mother's family that he knew, so after they left her, he asked his mother again, 'how is she your sister?' 'Shut up your mouth, "A little child has nothing to say where elders are in conversation." He did obeyed and shut his mouth up.

Before he could know what was happening, his mother was already in front of th bursar, the man in charge of the management of the school financial affair. They greeted each other while his mother presented the piece of paper which she was given before by the other man to him. He read it and said a word to her—this word which David could not understand, but he could see his mother replied him. Standing on his feet to greet her very well, he had asked her not to bother herself to wait there, that she should go and wait outside, but to drop the money and the forms which she did exactly the way she was told—and then called David to follow her outside.

In not up to twenty minutes, the man came out, leaving his job and the people who were waiting in a queue for him. He handed the forms and the receipts back to David's mother, greeting her and bidding them good-bye. David who was supposed to have been so excited that he was now a student of this school, became concerned with how his mother had become so famous that people should be respecting her that much. He was overpowered by dismay as he could see a long deep hole dug into his heart by some unknown demons. He could not help explain to himself what he was seeing, but he kept his mouth shut until they arrived home, and immediately they arrived, he swiftly jumped into the bed and slept off.

Finally, as David gained the admission and was able to complete all the normal procedure and paid all the fees required to be paid which was admissible by his new school—where he was already a student. Although, it had been a very difficult task for his father, but in conclusion, the old man was able to raise the money necessary to meet with the requirements. It is a thing he had always promised to do for David—to ensure him with a better future with education, but in return, logically and basically, David was to always assist him with the farm work since that was his only means of getting the money.

The school had just commenced and David was already in a new class, a new school, and with new classmates. His other friends who also gained admission there in that school, were all in another class.

It was his first day in that new school as a student with a new school uniform in a classroom of about thirty students. All he could do was to be staring around the class, trying to observe the buildings, the furniture, the blackboards, and the behavior of his new classmates. He could see that there was a dissimilarity between this school where he was and his former school. All the students, the way he could see them, were all neat on their uniforms and were speaking better English grammar, probably because most of them were from better primary schools and came out with distinctions just like him. He watched as various teachers entered the classroom to teach. He could see how his new classmates respond quickly to the questions they were asked, then he new how competitive everybody in the class were. He fathomed how hard he need to study to be able to compete with them. He tried to affix himself and to communicate with some of them, who just shoved him away because he was not from the same school with them. That actually was beginning to make him loathe himself, knowing that he was the only student in that class that was from another school not actually recognized by the other students. He was beginning to have this inferiority complex on himself. Something extraneous about these new classmates that he was having was that almost all of them were book-worms. At first, when David tried to observe them, he thought they were only trying to impress the teachers by being competitive most especially when answering questions, but he later got at the fact that they were exaggerating not just because of the teachers but also to improve their skills in book learning. He saw that whenever the teachers were not around, that is when these boys would even want to prove themselves better by engaging and devoting themselves to set-up debates on different topics, arguing, and challenging each other. It was a thing he always dreamed of, but it was now becoming a curse to him as he was sitting alone, holding a book but not concentrating on what he was reading. He looked so forlorn, thinking he wish life can be revised back. He was beginning to put into considerations his father's financial and health conditions, knowing there were less possibilities of him able to move forward like these other boys whom he did believed their parents would always be there for them financially when in need. He knew how hard he would have to assist his father in the farm work. He also understood that his father responsibilities for every of his children most particularly the ones in school will probably impoverish him even further. He comprehend that for him to be able to compete with these other boys, he would have to study harder, and to study harder, he need to have the key—the key which are the textbooks. But how could he get this books when his father could not afford them? His father thought that the text books used by his elder brother will still be of use at that time, forgetting things change and new teaching syllabus were issued out by the country's ministry of education. During this time, as he was still sitting alone, thinking about his life and what he should better do with it, one of the teachers entered the classroom, introducing himself to be the students new mathematics teacher and at the same time, their form teacher. The teacher was indeed a very friendly man. He told all of them to start introducing themselves by mentioning their names and surnames. As they do, he would make fun with the names and everyone would laugh, but when it was David's turn to introduce himself, he could not do so since he had already started laughing. He tried to stop laughing and just say something, but he still could not, and when he finally did, he mentioned his first name and then his surname. His surname was very interesting to the man when he heard it. He repeated it for almost five times, and at the end, he changed it from (Idahosa) to (Idaho). Idaho—which everyone of them except David, understood to be a state in the United States. In conclusion, he informed them of the exam that will be taking place in not less than one week; this exam which was intended for only the students who had graduated with distinctions from their previous schools. He then asked anybody that came there with distinction to raise his hand up—which David and five other students in the class did.

David raising his hand up, made him looked to himself to be eccentric, seeing all eyes in the classroom turned to stare at him—showing their disbelief. He could not help resist this discreditable situation. All he could see was his demons coming around him, stripping out from him his happiness and then installing fear. Although, he was so unhappy about this and he did not show it, instead he pretended not to have felt anything by joining everybody to laugh it up and forget about it.

That day was his first day with his new classmates, and it was also his first time to receive lessons from secondary school teachers, but it was also a horrible day for him. Immediately he arrived home, he went straight to his father to ask him for some money to buy some of the textbooks listed for them, but when he saw his father, pity would not be a word to describe how he felt about him. He paused and changed his mind and greeted him and left to go read his book. Anyone who takes time to look at his father very well that day, could see that he had endured his long life of poverty with stoicism. He actually would have like to study so to become a doctor or a lawyer or an engineer, but how could he do this when his father—the only person that he thought will be responsible for his financial assistance, was having too many children with no good source of income and at the same time, was in a bad health condition? Every a time he take a look back at his past life when he grew older, he would put blames away and confront what is ahead of him. He sees that he could find no fault in his father or his mother or himself. He believe that is how life was meant to be for him. The universe had also later made him to understand that, "Every man has to structure his own life to his own taste." For this reason he wrote a poem while he was in jail.

FORCE OF NATURE

Take a look at me and see,
If God would have to blame me.
This wildest dreams I'm having, I care to protect,
While in every reasons, I cursed and live to regret
Every of the evil deeds I did.
But, I did so as to out-last and out-live.
Please, judge me not, I was a victim,
Seeing my destiny, leading me to my will and pleasure.
It's a force of nature.

David who was already pessimistic again about his future, could see that he needed something to revive him back to life, so he picked up a novel to read—this novel which he had read several times before, and never got tired to read. This novel entitled, OLIVER TWIST written by the great Charles Dickens. He said he found pleasure in reading this book—as it is a story of a boy, a miserable and a sad story, but very interesting as it was with a happy-ending. It is about survival, and it is the life being experienced by most kids born into a vicious cycle of poverty. After he read this novel, which he did in six days, he thought his strength was back and that he could do what is necessary for him to do; he thought he could see a brighter future again and will be able to achieve the success he would not stop dreaming to have. He said to himself, "I am born into this world not only to see people, but also to be seen by others. I will keep my dream up and I know I will achieve that success." How he was going to achieve that success, that was the question he was asking himself everyday while he was sleeping, while he was eating or even while he was in the toilet—and he kept asking himself this same question.

Reading OLIVER TWIST novel was not just a thing he did to amused himself, but he read it and also took the oath to act upon it. He knew it was the time for him to start to believe and be doing something different from the way his parents would have want him to be raised up. He thought it was the time for him to drive himself along the fearsome and perilous route in life—this idea had then became an illusion to him as he kept thinking about his future, and how he was going to succeed.

That day, as he was still alone by himself, thinking of what to do, he thought he could hear someone saying something to him, "Dream a dream, do not walk away from it. Let it be what you think everyday, but deviate from evil." And immediately he heard this voice, he felt a wave of relief came running through his body. But how could he deviate from evil when he could see the evil doers getting richer, living extravagantly, while the righteous are becoming more poorer? This was another question he could not get to the bottom of. Anyway, when he thought deep about this theme, he also came to ascertain that "Evil cannot yield good and lasting life." Then he said to himself. "I will do the right thing and avoid evil, if only it will lead me to my goal."

When he arrived school the next day which was his second day as a new student, he knew the right thing for him to do was not to be a dormant and stick in the mud, instead to get himself involve in some activities with some of his new classmates maybe by peace if they choose to or by force. Not quite long, he saw that the boy whom they were both sitting together, left to meet some other group of boys since they were all from the same primary school, and then, they started debating on a very interesting topic in literature which had a very magnetizing effect on him, besotting him to intrude, but as he did, one of the boys yelled at him, insulting him and repulsively asking him to leave. The boy then asked his friends not to interact with him and he then started calling him names—making him a figure of fun, mocking and scoffing him. Since David could not resist this longer, he bounced on the boy and started hitting him and they both started fighting as the rest of the boys watched and applauded. But, when the rattling noise became louder, it soon reached the office of the administration where an order was issued for a summon to be served, bringing the both of them together to be punished.

Kneeling down with the boy who was fighting with him and waiting for judgement to be passed before the administration finally will know what to do with them, David was already judging himself, regretting why he did what he just did. This was making him skeptical about his chances of achieving his goal in that school. Inside him he started praying for God to deliver him out of this trouble, vowing never to repeat it again. But at the end, the administration finally ordered them to be flogged in public by one of the school teacher who was known for his no-tolerance-actions. He flogged the both of them until they were almost bleeding. That, to him was to give a fair warning to all the new students who actually think they were being admitted into the school to come to stage themselves in fighting each others. He tried to inform all of them of the consequences they would have to face if ever caught fighting. At the end of it all, he suspended the both of them from receiving lectures for three days.

Later, that evening when David arrived home, he was ashamed to reveal to anybody the story of how he was flogged. What he did was to boil some water and used it to shower and went to sleep. But after three days when he returned back to school, all the boys were staring at him as he entered into the classroom. He automatically became a hero; he started to associate himself with the other boys without approval. There inside him, he still could feel something like happiness mingled with regrets, but his sense of his own importance and value—mostly known as dignity, augmented. He could feel it right into his bone, and from that day onward he was then recognized and had beginning to grow new friendship with his new classmates.

A day before the day he was to sit for the exam graded for all the new students who graduated from their primary schools with distinction, he arrived home from their village where he and his bothers had went to spend two days in assisting their parents in doing their farm work. He came home to see that the electricity in their house has been disconnected since his father had failed to pay the bills, leaving them to be in total darkness. He could not help describe this situation, knowing how it had made him feel separated from the world that was surrounding him. He knew he was about to lose the strength he needed to fight the evil that was beginning to grow inside of him. He knew the battle was about to be lost. That night before he went to bed, he prayed to God to intervene in this crisis that he was facing personally. "There is sometimes in life when you are enclosed in an adverse circumstance, with no one for you to call on, but your God Whom you cannot even see or do not even know if actually He's existing." "But the fact is that we all have to believe in something, and continuously believing, hoping it to be our guardian, and by believing and hoping, it will always be there for us."

David went to school the next day without preparing for the exam, knowing already there was no way he could pass it. He was in the classroom with the other boys who were fully prepared for the exam. And as he sat there writing, his mind was at home, thinking if only he could get home to see that there was light in their house, and he was also thinking if maybe he could get home to see that his elder half-brother in Germany arrived home with cars and money and other luxurious things; he was thinking what if he get home to see that a letter was dropped inside their post box, informing him to get prepared to go and live in the United States, as he has written more than a thousand letters to some of the churches there, narrating to them the situation he was, pleading to them to send him a visa to go over there and live. Although, he received several letters from some of them who did sent him some cassettes, bibles, and tracks to read, but none of them had actually written to tell him of the good news he had always hoped for. He was also thinking if he could get home to see a parcel sent to him by his the same elder half-brother in Germany—a parcel that might be consisting of sport wears made in Germany or West Germany as it was called at that time. He was still thinking, when the exam bell rang for them to summit their answer sheets. He hurriedly finished it and when to summit and left, not waiting to discuss it with the other boys.

He went home that day unhappy, but still living in hope to meet one of his expectations. Getting home, he was met with another tragic situation. From a distance, he could see people gathered together in their house. He first sensed that a supreme good had visited his home. He was almost at the point to start to rejoice when he asked a boy he knew live in their house what was happening. He was told that one of his nephew had just be killed in a car accident. Immediately he heard this, terror struck him as he could feel his heart pounding in his chest. He did not know what else to do, only to keep walking till he get to where his mother was who then disclosed to him everything that has happened, and how his nephew whom they were both born on the same day, was traveling with his mother and two other sisters to their family house in another village to settle a dispute they were having between themselves, and how the driver had mistakenly passed the wrong side of the road to hit another car. But the only person that was killed was his nephew and he was the youngest among every other people that was in the car. David suddenly burst into tears. He could see the end of the world come right in front of him. He opened his eyes to see if he could wake up from this tremendous nightmare, but he only realized he was in a real world, a world that he thought is real but not real, a world that favor evil more than good, a world that the wicked had gained the power to suppress the innocents, a world where people you love and cherish could disappear without you ever seeing them again, a world he chooses not to live because of the too much of tragedies. He was still crying when he recalled how he and the boy used to play together round their house anytime the mother bring him for visit. He cried, but he knew no matter how he was going to keep crying, his nephew was never going to come back to live again. So he walked away from all the people there who were also crying, and went to his favorite secluded reading spot. When he arrived there, the first thing he did was to look around if there was anybody that might be there close to where he was. He could not find anybody, so he came back to the spot, open his hands, uplifting them high to the sky, then he called, 'O God, why would you allow this to happen to me, why, why, O God, why, O God? I believed in you, I trusted you, but see what has happened now. Why me?.' The truth is that one week before that day, he dreamed that someone had died and everybody was crying, but in that dream he could not recognize the face of the decease since he was not allowed to see it being that he was still too young. He told his mother about this dream, but his mother has referred it to be a dream. So when he received this news of the death of his nephew, it came to his mind that he would have been able to save him if he had known he was to be the one. He knew most things he had dreamed about many times has come to happen, but he was always afraid to say it out so as for people not to call him a witch. He felt a deep sadness about this and with the too much uneasiness and discomfort that he had throughout that week, he thought it will be best for him to commit suicide. But how is he going to do this was the question. As he kept propounding on which way will be easier and faster for him to go take his life, he cried out again, calling God. Suddenly, there arose a violent storm with thunder and lightning, and he ran swiftly, climbing down through the step leading to the uncompleted story building toward where everybody were hiding in their house. Because it was raining and the electricity had been disconnected, leaving them in total darkness, so it was difficult for him to even find a way to enter his room, meanwhile he was still wearing his school uniform.

Fear had took him to an average height when he first heard the noise of the thunder, he thought he had arouse the wrath of God and he was about to be punished. After then he vow never to question God again no matter what the situation is, but this he did repeat several times again whenever he meet up with difficulties.

As this mood of melancholy descended on him, and he was in the middle of life and death, his belief and trust in God was beginning to fade way. He has always believed God to be the giver and the taker of life, so why would He take the life of an innocent child whom he had loved so much. But when he other met people and discussed this subject matter with them, he came to learn from them that God is not a wicked God to allow someone you love to be taken away from you. He was also given a lesson by one of his friend who dedicated his life to serve God and was a regular church goer. He was taught by the boy that, it is the devil who is actually responsible for all our misfortunes, and God who is responsible for all the good things that come to our ways. David did agree with this theory, but this could not satisfy his curiosity, making him ask the boy why the vicious experiences good life all the time, and the innocents live in pains and sufferings. The boy who definitely was indeed with a shrewd idea and has dedicated his life in studying the bible, quoted some verses from the bible. He quoted from the books of Isaiah 3:10-11, which says, "Tell the righteous it will be well with them, for they will enjoy the fruit of their deeds; Woe unto the wicked! Disaster is upon them! They will be paid back for what their hands have done." and also Jeremiah 31:30, which says, "Instead, everyone will die for his own sin; Whoever eats sour-grapes-his own teeth will be set on edge." and also

Proverbs 22:8, which says, "He who sows wickedness reaps trouble, and the rod of his fury will be destroyed." and lastly Ezekiel 7:11, which says, "Violence has grown into a rod to punish wickedness: none of the people will be left, none of that crowd-no wealth, nothing of value." These quotes perambulated round David's medulla oblongata, making him rethink of how to be converted into a Christian immediately, seeing that to be the only way he could be happy again. He told the boy he wanted to become a Christian and the boy was so pleased with it, encouraging him to come to their place of worship the next day.

David's nephew who was killed, was supposed to be a bond of relationship between his family and the mother of the boy who actually in previous time had been having a long-running feud with David's entire family. The father of the boy who was David's father first son, but died long time ago of kidney failure even before he, David was born. He was survived by two daughters and a son. After his death, David's father was to be in possession of the house property and to be responsible for the kids upbringing while they were to be in their mother's custody. But because the only boy among them was dead, there were beginning to arise a strong doubt of any reconciliation between David's family and the mother of the kids, since the two of the kids left alive were women, because, in Africa, having a male child could create a good means for a woman to get access to his husband's properties, but having female children gives a woman a lesser chance. This was an idea that David later had took a decision to fight against when he grew up and traveled abroad to see how women were considered equal with men in the western world. He also knew that it has long be a very hard struggle for so many women in the western world to have been able to reach to their wants. And he still believe there is much more for the women to do to lift themselves higher than they already are, and also to fight this gender discrimination everywhere in the world. He saw the people in the western world more tolerance and more learned because they were able to tried to make some changes on how women are been disregarded in the society. But he thought he still believe there are lots more to be done that has not be done, because he said he could still see that, even in the western world where he postulate civilization to be pronounced, he could recognize the violation of the so-called fundamental human rights, as women were never given the chances of becoming head of the catholic churches or to become a pope or to earn equal wages with men. He said he believe that women should be treated with polite regard, respected, estimated and honored if not for any reason but for one reason that, "Every man and woman born into this world is been given a life by a woman." He also recognize that very few women actually realize their dreams of becoming what they intend to become in the societies where they live, purposely because most men sees them to be incompetent. This idea which does violate the article No 1 of the Universal Declaration of Human Rights which states: All human beings are born free and equal in dignity and rights. They are endowed with reason and conscience and should act towards one another in a spirit of brotherhood.

After some days of grief, David finally returned back to school, staying more closer to himself because the memory of his nephew's death was still running around inside his brain. He was informed of the results of the distinction exam he took some days ago—the day his nephew died. It was said that he had failed the exam, and that the exam was conducted for the purpose of selecting the best out of the bests. The boy that had scored the highest mark won a scholarship to study in the school for three years without paying for the school fees. David knew how brilliant that boy was and he knew he did deserved it. As for him, he thought this was a precise moment for him to give his life to God just when he just became a member of his school C.U (Christian Union), an organisation in the school set to learn about the word of God, to study and to teach other people to be near to God. At first when he became a member of this organisation, he found it very interesting because, it gave him an opportunity to be able to study the bible and quote verses without looking at it. He found it interesting, because he felt he was being strengthened by the word of God to fight against the evil that was almost overcoming his thoughts. He was glad he became a member and tried to be able to share this experience with other people, preaching to them the good news of Jesus Christ. But, along the way, he saw that he was left in an agony of suspense as he could see his fellow members preach by warning people about the proximity to doomsday. He tried not to get involved in confronting these fellows, but when he could not resist it, he thought it was the time for him to start to reject this idea since he could see it not just as a warning but as a threat—the way people were putting it. He called his friend whom he think was more learned and was interested in learning about the different ways of life of other people. 'Hey brother, what do you think about the doomsday that we have been warning people of?' David asked. 'I think it is near and we all have to get ourselves prepared for it,' said the boy. This affirmation did startled David who expected something different to be said. So he decided not to prolong this discussion, instead he turned to leave, but remained dumb, not uttering any other word. As he was leaving, the boy called him back and asked him, 'brother, what is the matter?' 'Nothing,' replied David. 'Well I think it is good you say what is in your mind so that we can discuss it and learn from each other.' Immediately David heard that, he waited. 'Yes, there is something I would like to say to you.' 'You are very free brother,' said the boy, coming closer to him and offering him a seat to sit and sitting close to him. When the both of them were seated, he said to him, 'please do not be annoyed at the question I am about to ask you.' 'No, I would not.' 'O.k. Can I ask you the reason why you are studying very hard to pass your exams and further your education by going to the university?' 'Yes,' said the boy, 'it is because I want to be successful. I have told you before that I want to become a doctor.' 'You want to become a doctor?' asked David again, standing up. 'Why should you be studying to become a doctor when you know the world is going to end soon?' asked David, showing his disappointments in the boy. 'This is what is written in the bible,' replied the boy. 'This is just how it is. Preaching the word of God does not stop us from making plans for our own future.' And when David heard this, he walked away, without waiting for the boy to give a further explanation about this; he knew already this way of life that he was about to follow on was wrong as he was beginning to see how people mock their fellow human beings with the help of religious beliefs; he said he could see how people preach one thing and do a different thing far from what they preach. He said he could see that, "People who thinks themselves to be sinners might even be more righteous than those who claimed to be saints because of their strong religious beliefs—that is leading them to fanaticism" This questions about religion later became a very controversial and crucial issue he intends to deal with privately and secretly. Religion which is said to be the belief in the existence of a supernatural being, now, he said he had come to understand it to be a propaganda. Yes it is to those who thinks they are smart enough to fool people around, using religions campaign deliberately for their own benefits. Religion is the same as politics if actually we take a good look at it. It is a way for people to proclaim themselves better than others. It is an exhibition of pride. David said, with much applications of different types of religion, he had come to see that everyone of them is saying something about God, the creator—which means God is one. And if God is one, why is it that people are now killing themselves to prove that their religions are better? Does the same God not said something about being righteous? And do we have to prove how righteous we are by killing, taking souls that does belong to God, The Most High? This experience he had, later affected his thinking on the matters of religion throughout his life. He said he always feel ashamed that he was born in a place where people believe more in religion than in philosophy and science. He said, "He is proud and will always be proud of who he is and where he come from, but he regret to have witnessed that the people whom he loved so much are still very blind to see, even when the light keep shining." He said, the funniest thing is that, in the place where he come from, he could see how the Muslims and Christians are fighting and killing themselves, because, each one is trying to prove the superiority of his religion; a religion that was brought to them by people from other continents to exploit and even enslaved them and took them to another parts of the world where they never wished to be—to go and work and die in plantations." The Arabs were the first people to have come to Africa for slavery with the Islamic religion, followed by the Europeans with the Christian Catholic religion. But yet, these Africans has to make that same religion become a complex and a contradictory problem they are unable to get a solution to. They are unable to solve this problem because they declined to acknowledge what their real problem is. David said he wish to see another beautiful days in Africa. These beautiful days can only be seen if these Africans could put the problems of religion behind them and focus on fighting corruption and investing on education. They need education instead of religion. They need inspiration to be inventive, creative, and innovative as to be able to move their world forward. David also recognize the facts that, believing in religion helps us get closer to God, but we do not need to be too fanatic. "Anything we do too much has its consequence." The westerners who actually had extended the Christian religion to every parts of the world, had also come to believe more in science and technology, and are living a better and more peaceful life with it, while those who were taught to believe, still remain being fanatics, living in poverty, fighting and killing themselves. It could be better if everyone can have the right to practice any type of religion he or she wish to. Worship what you like. Before the coming of the Arabs and the White people into Africa, the people there had their own religions, but they have chosen to adopt other people's religions, because they saw that it was more advanced mostly because it is documented and they also see a better future in it, but now that science has become a new religion, they seemed not to want to believe. Believing in science does not stop anyone from believing in the existence of a Supernatural Being, but it makes us not to be religious fanatics. And religious fanaticism, they say, comes not from deep faith, but lack of it. How could people be so fanatic about a thing they really do not know the course of its existence? David said he believe it is a right thing to do to believe in a Supernatural Being, because he had seen that even all the great scientist that had lived and died and most who are still living, know God exist. "A little bit of everything can lead us to wherever we wish to be." Popularly known as the father of modern physics, a German-born Albert Einstein stated "I do not believe in personal God and I have never denied this but have expressed it clearly. If something is in me which can be called religious then it is the unbounded admiration for the structure of the world so far as our science reveal it." Then again, he stated, "A knowledge of the existence of something we cannot penetrate, of the manifestations of the profoundest reason and the most radiant beauty—It is the knowledge and this emotion that constitute the truly religious attitude; in this sense and in this alone, I am a deeply religious man." Or, why should we not follow the route to the great and wonderful Sir Isaac Newton, an English physicist, mathematician, astronomer, natural philosopher, alchemist, and theologian who stated, "The supreme God is a Being eternal, infinite, absolutely perfect, but a being, however perfect, without dominion, cannot be said to be Lord God—and from his true dominion it follows that the true God is a living, intelligent, and powerful Being; and, from his other perfection, that he is supreme, or most perfect. He is eternal and infinite, omnipotent and omniscient; that is, his duration reaches from eternity to eternity, his presence from infinity to infinity; he governs all things, and knows all things that are or can be done—we know him only by his most wise and excellent contrivances of things, and final causes; we admire him for his perfections; but we reverence and adore him on account of his domination; for we adore him as his servants; and a god without dominion, providence, and final causes, is nothing else but faith and Nature—and thus much concerning God; to discourse of whom from the appearance of things does certainly belong to Natural philosophy."

David was becoming well thought of, illustrious, having many friends, and always absent from the classroom. He was becoming more vehement—developing new ideas—which were transforming him gradually into something different from what he used to be. The demon inside him was developing and reaching maturity and was ready to be active. He started by disobeying his parents, then, lying to extract money from them. He could have been able to fight this demon and won if only he was obedient to his parents and listen to their advises. He could have been able to win that battle if he had not come to that school and meet those new friends that he was mingling with. He sat for the first term exam, when the result was out, he saw that he scored a very low mark and came out 13th in his class, and he was very happy, but when his old friends whom they had come together from the same primary school saw this, they were startled and knew something was going wrong. When they tried to ask him about this, he despised them, comparing them to lunatics, because of how he was always seeing them studying, spending money in purchasing many expensive text-books. He saw himself far better than others who were not prepared to live that hyperbolic and rhetorical life he was living. Although he was not so delight with this new life that he was almost about to commence, but the evil inside him was coming and he was unable to rebuke it. He tried so much to get along with his parents, but it was not an easy task because he had already thought of how to modify his father's ingenious contrivance of how he should assist him with the farm work to get his school financial support. He said he deeply and bitterly resented the way he was being treated by his own father, making of him and his other brothers held responsible for the mistakes he had made long time ago by going to borrow some money for his nephew. David knew it had come to the precise time for him to choose whether to elongate this responsibility the way his father was making it to be or to build a new and more prosperous way of life. Even when he kept assisting him in doing the farm work, he still was not able to meet up in providing him with the text-books he wanted. He was concerned about his health and how he could pay all his debts, but how in the height of absurdity to see that his father was still investing the little money he managed to get in building other houses? David saw that his own career was already in jeopardy as he would have to have much time to work in the farm than to study and not being able to afford most of his needs at school.

"Having one problem is easy for you to get a solution for, but having more will make you lose hope." This was how things were with David. He came back home one day to see that his mother was having a conflict or rather a fight with one of his elder half-sister who was married twice before and had later come and be staying in their father's house since she could not fix herself with one of her husbands; but at the same time will be inviting men to come visit her in this same house where she was living with four children. She never at once paid any bill in that house and yet she was wreaking havoc on everybody living in the house and near-by and sending everybody into the depths of despair. She was rather to be compared to a demon that even hell will reject her. She was happy in causing people pains and was always proud—proud of the things that belongs to her father or her brothers and sisters. She hated David's mother even right from the day she stepped her feet into that house, for coming to marry her father the way she had hated every woman that had tried to. David said it was not his position to blame her for any thing she did, but to blame his father, for marrying his mother in addition to the woman he married before. This same problem happens to many Africans who are born into polygamous family, and with this, most of them who fortunately happen to see themselves abroad and see how the white people are enjoying monogamy way of life, will learn a lesson never to continue with that same life they were living while in Africa

As David came home to meet this conflict, he left immediately, not wanting to interfere. His heart was boiling, forming bubbles and turning into steam; he wished there were any means for him to slay his father for having caused him, his brothers and sisters, and his mother so much pains in life. He knew his half-sisters and brothers had always hated them for some reasons that seemed uncomprehending. But his father had cautioned them not to say a word and if anyone does, the word will be used against him or her. Many days and months went-by, arriving home to meet people trying to resolve the quarrel between his mother and his elder half-sister—which was then becoming an addiction to him. There was nothing he could do about it as he was still very young, but this situation continued the way it was at a time it became worse, that his mother had cautioned all of them to be cautious not to be poisoned. His mother who was so horrified with the situation, had decided to leave the house with her children to go and live in the village, meanwhile their father who has been so quiet, came to apprehend that something has to be done for peace to reign. David's mother who was not a Christian, thought there was a need for her to protect her children, then she chose to consult some soothsayers to ask them what she can do to protect her children. She was given some soaps to bath and lots of concoction to drink, and the same with David and the rest of his brothers and sisters. At nights, she will take them to some herbalist house to bath them with the smelling soaps and some smelling leaves, soaked in the water some days before that day. While bathing them, she will be reciting incantations, calling some strange names of the gods and goddesses, and praying to them. She kept doing this every time, spending the little money she earn from the tedious laborious farm work she was doing. She was doing this, because those witch doctors as they call themselves, had told her that David's elder half-sister was a witch, and that she seek to kill all of them. At that time, David believed just the way he was told that witches possesses some demonic powers given to them by the devil, and with these powers, they are capable of changing anybody into an animal at night while the person is still asleep and later killing this animal, roasting it to become a good meat and bringing it from their coven down to the real world to eat it. They were also said to fly at nights with wings on their backs and has the power to place a curse on people as well. Even when he tried not to believe it, but he saw so many of them confessed of having been responsible for the killing of their children and some others more. It was also said that these witches finds it easier to kill their children or people relating to them. This dreadful situation had hampered David's ability to concentrate on his studies in school, and because he could see that nobody was in the position to do something about it, the rage inside of him as he could not control it, exploded into a thing like a bomb, that one day when his elder half-sister was insulting his mother, he pounced on her and beat her up, running away from the house, knowing his father was going to be very upset. From that day on, he had become a monster. He was no longer afraid of anybody in their house anymore.

The second term exam came and was gone, he scored very low marks and never bothered himself with it. The third and promotion exam came, he did it by cheating, sneaking with him a text-book into the exam hall and when the result came, he passed very well and was promoted to the next grade—the second grade. He told his father there was no way he could sit at the back of his bicycle anymore, so he preferred to walk to the farm so as not to be seen by his friends whenever he was with his father who was always dressed in filthy clothes. He started chasing girls around, attending extra evening lesson—not to go to study but to look for girls, putting on good attires he bought with the money his father had given him for his school fees, and also spending little in going to the cinemas to watch some Chinese and porn movies. He was becoming the real man he thought he was about to be. Most time his father would have to negotiate with him on whether to give him some certain amount of money before he would agree to assist him in doing the farm work. He was moving too fast than the world around him, looking for a way to break free from the demons he thought hold him tight to his father and to poverty, since he has always believed himself to be a go-getter, he thought he could still be, even without education. During this time, he was beginning to associate himself with some group of criminals inside his former primary school building during weekends when there will be nobody. These group of criminals who were usually coming there to smoke marijuana, but at that time he was just a cigarette smoker and was afraid to smoke marijuana with them, thinking it will make him become mad. These criminals were constantly sending them to go and buy them cigarettes and writing pads for wrapping the marijuana, and later giving them some sticks out of it. The more he was getting closer to these people, the more he could hear them discuss how they had robbed some banks and praised their mentor, Lawrence Nomayangbon—alias Anini, a one time Nigerian bandit that did terrorized the city and the entire nation, and was later captured and killed some years before then. Anini who migrated to the city from a near-by village to work as a driver, later became a professional driver for criminal gangs and thieves. He then extended this act to other cities and became famous across the country, and they were robbing banks. His success was based on most police supports because of the bribes they were being offered, but he later became a hater of anyone that has a thing to do with the police force, because they killed some of his gangs that were arrested despite his warnings. In revenge, he killed nine police men in return. He was said to have been the Robin Hood in Africa by stealing money from the banks and splitting them into the air for the poor people. When he was later arrested with his right-hand man, Monday Osunbor, they both confessed of how they were aided by some superintendent of police, who were later tried along with them, prosecuted and executed.

Just as David was still sitting, listening to these criminals discussed about Anini, it was then he knew he was sitting close to some habitual criminals, meanwhile he had first thought they were just gamblers due to how they were usually coming there to gamble and smoke. Fear seized him, and he immediately lied to them he was going home to see his sick mother. He left them running to his house and when he reached, he swiftly went to shower and fell inside his bed and slept off. The next day, he heard that the four criminals were shot dead by the police inside the school compound where he had left them some hours before the incident. It was a heinous news, but he rejoiced that he was so lucky to have left the very time he did, if not he will probably be among the dead criminals, because in his country, any body seen with a criminal is equally a criminal, and the police there actually do not know how to arrest a thief, all they do is to shoot because the criminals might shoot first if the police failed to.

Time was moving very fast and David was growing older and wiser and wayward. He became a terror to his entire family, not afraid of anybody, and not listening to anyone's advice, not even his mother who used to beat him up and rubbing her fingers with ground hot chili peppers and putting it in his eyes when he does something wrong at the time he was still a little boy. His father was afraid to tell him to assist him in doing the farm work. He became the boss of his own, and was also responsible for most of his needs. With the training he had from his father on how to work in the farm, he and his elder brother, Ken, were able to go work for another farmers and get paid, and some of this money were spent in purchasing new out-fits since they both love to dress in the latest fashion and be in that world. They would save money together to purchase clothes and be using them together. They were two brothers who loved themselves, but they were different. It is when it come to fashion and lying to their father to extract money from him that you will see them sharing ideas together. Ken, who was able to convince David to continue to assist their father in doing the farm work so as for them to always have an entrance to their father's pocket where they believe there is always money and always will be. But their father who was smart as well, was smarter than how they thought and even more than them, knew what their intentions were, so he sought a way to despise them. They kept living like this, on and on and on with less trust and confident for each other, but they were still happy in their distress and poverty. Ken, rationally, would have wanted David to be getting closer to him so that they could be working on the same crucial issue of their life which is, having a better future, because he knew David was a man with vision and was prepared to do anything to reach the mountain peak, but David, on his own has already seen the light coming from a different angle the moment he started mingling with his classmates who were from rich families.

That year was an unfortunate, tough, and rough year but was also a wonderful and unforgettable year for David and his family. Not up to a year that he had just lost his nephew who died on a car accident. It was 05:00 a.m that day when he was woken up by the distinctive noise of his elderly half-sister, whom he had constantly referred to as a witch. He could hear her cursing two of her grown up sons, asking them to leave the house to go and live with their father. Not only that she had cursed them, but she was also chasing them around the house that morning, just to make sure She was not seeing them, and that they leave. These kids whom the eldest was two years older than David and the other one was born the same year with David, had both been living with their mother and their two younger brothers of which the youngest of them was born to another man. Their father who also had married another woman and was having other kids with her, was an irresponsible man who could not cater for his children, then leaving them for this woman, who because of the hardship and her another unsuccessful marriage, had come to hate these kids, cursing them every time and driving them out of the house. These kids who were left with no choice and not knowing which way to go and what to do in life as victims of child abuse, could see themselves like kids living in the street rather than kids with a house. This situation had lead them to be vulnerable to crime, stealing money and food from anybody and from anywhere, not even afraid to be poisoned. They became more radical and lack of brains, causing a public nuisance. David who knew something about these kids and what they were encountering in life, could best describe them as the dead among the living as well as the living among the dead. He said he could have been able to save a life close to him if he had not declined to lend a hand to a drowning man whom he had seen in his dream. So, that morning when he woke up, seeing these kids being chased around the house by their mother, he tried to stop them not to go to anywhere, that he was planning of how to go kill a rabbit inside the moat at the back of their house, which they agreed to help him do later in the day, but when their mother kept pressurizing them, they decided to leave. In not more than one hour, a strange danger-like florid loud noise boom like an explosion came through the air, and everybody were frightened with that noise, and there was a stampede broke-out of people wanting to go see what exactly was happening. When David arrived at the scene, he saw that it was one of his nephew that the mother drove away from the house who was gravely trampled by a lorry against a house. It was a dreadful accident as David watched it in awed silence. In his mind, he could ask himself whether there is anything in the world worth living for if he could be standing and seeing two of his nephew born the same year with him die in just one year. He saw death knocking at his own door, asking him to follow them since he was the next person. What enraged him and made him soak himself into a deep sea of hatred for his family, was that immediately after the boy's death, people were gathered in their house to mourn and to console the mother who was now weeping uncontrollably, rolling herself on the floor to show how painful it was for her to have just lost a son whom she has just driven to be killed in less than one hour ago. As David watched this scene, he thought it will be better for him to get a grenade and throw it in the scene so that everybody there to die. He could listen to their different comments about these kids on how they had been suffering. 'But why these comments?' murmured David to himself. Because he knew everybody there had seen these kids suffering and dying without lending them a helpful hand. The only person he could not blame was his father, because he knew the old man had did the best he could to help those kids by providing the little he has for them and by allowing them stay in his house with their mother, which is not actually allowed by many men. The person that became David worst enemy that day was his most eldest half-sister who was born of the same mother with the mother of the kids. Seeing her weep made David detest her, knowing she was capable of providing every of their needs because she was married to a very wealthy man and was living extravagantly with her husband and children, and yet sometimes, she will want to take away the little that belongs to their father. This situation made David think the world to be so wicked as he keep asking himself, "How could people be rich and be happy when the people around them are starving to death?" It is a thing he could not comprehend even when he grew up to see the world better than he used to sees it and see that greed and selfishness is what we are all living for. This sometimes make him think of not blaming the world richest countries for not giving aids to the world poorest countries when he could see this happening even in his own family and nothing he was able to do about it.

He was still mourning his dead nephew after eight months when he arrived home one day to see people gathering in their house again. With fear that something awful and terrific had betide a member of his family once again since anytime he sees a scene like this, it has always been in a misery. But when he drew closer to ask people around what was happening, he was told that his elderly half-brother, Sunny, who had traveled to the then West-Germany two years ago, had just arrived. He could not believe what he was hearing that his elder half-brother had returned from Europe. He asked the lad standing near him, 'are you saying Sunny is back from Europe?' 'yes,' replied the lad. 'He is there, are you not seeing him?' 'Where is he?' asked David, gesturing at the direction where there were many people. 'That is him over there' said the lad, pointing to a huge shining black skin man wearing a white designed singlet and a blue designed short and white American made converse sneakers. Definitely, when you see him, you will know he is not living in Africa because of how his skin shines. He was well to be compared to the black Americans; his black skin was different from that of any other person close to him and he had become so immense and weighty. Although, he has been very tall before he left to Europe, but he was very slim. David heart was full to the brim with excitement. It was the best moment he has experienced in life since it was the only time he knew he was having a family and that things might change to be better for him and his family. As he looked at his brother, his hope returned back to him and he became proud of the family he was born into for the first time in his life. He was proud not because of what he thought his brother had brought from abroad, but because of the prestigious life he will be placed in as a brother to a man that has just returned from Europe.

Already in school, David was very proud of himself and was able to associate himself with the people he thinks matters. He started registering his name in some of the school voluntary organizations like the music clubs and the press clubs, just to get more chances and opportunity to be able to participate in music conferences held by all the schools in the city—where girls and boys usually get together to discuss issues relating to music. He became interested in visiting his friends with rich family background at home so as to join them in watching music videos and movies. They will visit the zoo and the amusement parks and the stadium together, looking for girls around. These new friends that he was having, were all spending their parents money, but since he could not get that opportunity, he deliberately chose to work harder, doing daily jobs and getting paid for it. He and his elder brother, Ken were getting close to their father again, believing it to be the only way their father could help them, by sponsoring them to go live abroad. His elderly half-brother, Sunny, who returned from abroad was emboldened by their most eldest sister, as David was told, not to come and live with their father, instead to live with them. But to David, he understood that was a lie, he knew Sunny was lured by the luxurious house and the good things around it, so he had preferred to live there than come to live in a filthy, crowded, and noisy house. Sunny called for Ken and gave him some American made sneakers and some other clothes he brought along with him, but Ken had expected more than he was given. David never went to see him, because he was never called for. He did not even see him face to face since he was always concealing himself from him. He thought there were no reasons for him to go see him, since their eldest sister was the one to be telling him what to be doing and what not to be doing. Sunny shared everything he brought from abroad within their eldest sister children, including electronics. David said, it seemed unimaginable and unfair to see, "Why some greedy rich people would want to have what they see going to a poor man's hand, even when they already have more than enough in their hands." This attitude conducted by Sunny and their eldest sister had angered David's father to an extent, he called David and Ken together to expose the secret of how he had contributed a large sum of money in sponsoring Sunny to travel abroad. This secret was concealed for them not to know he was having such money with him, but it took David by surprise when he heard this. His father then promised to sponsor Ken to also travel abroad, maybe to fulfill the promises he made with their mother long time ago since he loved her so much and was always found of her, because they were both members of one of the highest and most powerful secret society in the country. Although, these promises made by their father to sponsor Ken to travel abroad, was what later brought them hopes and unity again.

With the clothes and sneakers Ken was given, David became renowned for his good dressing when he will put them on and walk along the street and inside the school compound with a warm feeling of pride inside his heart. He was becoming the talk of the town among young girls and boys. His classmates were beginning to envy him, and wanting to be like him. Most of them were showing him regards, knowing that he was related to Sunny and his most eldest sister's husband, who was a very famous man in the street where he was living mostly for his house and the big satellite dish he installed in his compound.

Everything were moving on well with him, he came back to his senses once more, getting serious to study—and to pass his exams, reuniting with his family, and the dead of his two nephews fading away from his memory; he was becoming a man again, he was becoming Joseph the dreamer again. Frankly speaking, he thought of asking for his father's forgiveness before he called them to break the news of his new promises to them. That they were reunited, he was curious to know much about the secret society his father belonged to, because he read little about them in a book—that it was formed by men of intellectual and was meant to help unite people and to improve the life of the believers and worshipers of the creator of Heaven and Earth—the only true and living God. But many people outside this secret society had said many horrible things about them. Some claimed they perform rituals with human beings, while some even claimed they had seen them cutting some parts of the bodies of some of their dead members. Most people then referred to them as evil. David, who had seen his father to be a righteous person, could not believe what he was hearing about them, but when he tried to learn things about them from his father, he refused to disclosed it to him, instead he encouraged him to start to have the interest of being a member when he grow up. David actually became very afraid of his both parents because of this, and relinquished the idea of seeking more information, but he knew they cannot be evil, and after much observation and studying the reasons why they made that choice to become members, he came to fathom that they had done so—so as for them to know eminent people, and to become predominant features in the society or community where they were living. He came to understand it to be a thing to do with power and influence. He knew they did so—also to protect their children; he also knew it would have be more better and easier for them if they had chosen the Christian way of life, and think of bequeathing their problems to God. But, whom among us actually know the right thing to be doing?

At about 11:00 p.m on Sunday, the day was dark and the moon and stars were the only source of light as there was an electric light failure which every Nigerian is accustomed to. David and the other people in their house, including his both parents, were outside the front of their house, discussing and chanting happily, hoping to see the light come back. Suddenly, someone drove a black Mercedes Benz car into the spaced compound in a very speedy manner, and coming out of it, was David's nephew, the fourth born of his eldest half-sister. He came to deliver a very sad news to David's father, of how their house was mistakenly set ablaze with a gas-lamp. When the news reached their father, he screamed to break the news to everybody, even to the people living in the near-by house. The lad did actually came to beg them to follow him to their house to help them take care of their properties, so as for other people not to steal them. In less than one hour, David and his other two brothers and his nephew, the elder brother of the one who died some months ago, were already in their eldest half-sister's house. His father and some other people who were living close to their house, were all presented to assist in helping them bring out the little remaining things inside the house, and to help them watch-over the properties. They were all very busy throughout that night, working with no rest. It was David's first time of seeing that house, and it was his first time of coming across his elder half-brother, Sunny, since he returned from abroad. When he first saw David, he was shocked, knowing already he had offended him. David who wrote a letter and sent it to him at the time he was still in Germany and he never replied him, but, as he was seeing him for the first time after so many years that he left him, he was left with no word. All he could do was to thank him for coming to assist them in their bad time.

The next day, after much hard-work and no sleep, David and his other nephew, Uyi, manged to go to one of the nearest house to go and shower and returned back. The house was fenced round with the gate locked, making unknown people outside the family not able to get into the compound to help or to steal. People who were watching from outside the compound were wondering how this had happened—some of them amid who tried to even jump through the fence into the compound, possibly to steal. But David and his nephew were always vigilant not to allow them to. They worked and worked and later went back home to sleep, leaving the rest things for them to take care of as they were having to take care of their own problems as well. Meanwhile, David's nephew, Uyi, decided to stay because he was customary to going there to live and to spend some days with them, and also to be able to steal some of what he had hidden somewhere already.

Getting back to school the next day, some of David's classmates who saw him at the compound where the house was burning, came to meet him to ask him if he was relating to that family. When he told them he was, they all started respecting him, looking at him to be a man who was from a wealthy family, not knowing his most eldest half-sister does not even recognize him not to say the husband. Meanwhile, at that point, he could see what it means, "When you are related to rich people, even when you do not benefit any material things from them, but you still can benefit how people regard you, seeing you with these rich people." For this reason, he came to understand that, "A wealthy man does not help you to become rich like himself, instead he entices you with that—which is mutilated or characterized by superfluity, showing you pride and vain-glory, with a gross exaggeration, and at the end, demanding from you, flattering attentions and praises." But he also came to understand that, "We have to always pray for a wealthy man, as everybody who are fortunate to have their house close to his, can also relish the splendor illumination that come from his house." This same issue, he thought he could see in realness with the countries that are very near to some wealthy countries around the world—like Jamaica, Bahamas and Mexico are—to the United States or Solomon Island and New Guinea Papua are—to Australia.

David who just finished his third and last term exam, and was waiting for his result so as to be promoted to the next grade; he was beginning to spoil his relationship with his parents after two months that he reunited with them, because they asked him to go and spend the holidays with them in the village. It was still his second year in the secondary school. His bitter and sweet year—the year he lost his nephew whom they were both born the same year, the year, his elder half-brother returned from Europe, and the same year, his most eldest half-sister's house was mistakenly set ablaze and they had lost very many expensive properties, including the ones his elder half-brother, Sunny had brought from abroad. He had made a mistake to have seek a fame that does not correspond to his family's standard, by lying to some of his classmates about his family background, telling them they were rich and he was living in a better and more decent house than the one he was living. Anytime they tried to visit him at home, he was always trying to avoid it and was giving them different excuses. At the time that his parents had set-out to the village with their two youngest kids and leaving behind David, his elder brother, Ken, and his elder sister who was already so confident in herself and financially independent as she was into small scale businesses of buying fruits and selling them in front of their house. David and Ken were then obliged to cater for themselves—which they did by going to do some daily jobs and getting paid. Sometimes, they would travel to their village to assist their parents for one or two days and return back to the city with lots of food and little money given to them by their parents. This way, they both decided to live their lives, and were very much happy with it. David, whom the evil inside him was developing rapidly, was secretly in quest of pleasure, tempting this evil to grow more faster. He was paying frequent visits to some of his classmates who were already in the world of black Americans rap music, which were so interesting to him anytime he acquire an access to listen to them. He came to fall in love with this rap music being that he never had the access to do so before, but it was also resulting into what was leading him to a self-destruction, generating his moral philosophical interest of life into new ideas. During his primary school life, he had loved literature and was always interested in poetry; he saw that rap music was full to the brim with it, and it was a meticulous fairway, and brilliant scenery, for people to tell stories about their attitudes and way of life. To satisfy his curiosity, he continued to associate himself with so many rich men children who were bestowed upon with the means of getting magazines and video-cassettes of most American music. He would read these magazines and watched the videos, seeing the fabulous life these musicians were living, and how women were always around the men, crying to hold them. He knew this was what he wanted in life, but how was he going to get to America—the place at that time, they all believed to be the heaven on Earth. Trying to imitate what he was seeing in the video and magazines, he thought of drawing his own plan of a journey, getting himself close to some arrogant that were living in his street who had taught him how to live a new way of life to become a nuisance. The more closer he gets to these lads, the more he was interested in their ways of life mostly in the music aspect, even when his gods tried to control him, he still could not live the life that first came inside of him while he was still very young and was learning to become a good child and having much interest in literature. This time, he became a man struggling to survive, and thought of meeting the people of his choice—who actually were the wrong people that later promised to help him destroy his own life. The first time he was given a wrapped marijuana to smoke, refused, but they mocked him, calling him names, letting him know how weak he was. When he took the marijuana from one of the lads and smoked it, he was seeing something different from what he was seeing; he could see the world turning upside-down, the whole structure of his brain and how it works was changed automatically, and he was so hungry and wanted to cry out for help. But he knew his friends were going to mock him more and later narrate it to other people who were not there, so he tried to resist it. Resisting it was causing him distortion and he could not move from where he was sitting and was not hearing anything that his friends were saying about him; all he could do was to be staring at a particular distance from where he was. As he kept staring, his instinct was interpreting to him the reason he was born and he thought he could see the world clearly as he look deep into it. You see "Sometimes you see the world so clearly as you look deep into it, knowing that what you are doing is wrong, and it is not the right thing that you should have been doing. But you just cannot help yourself in finding an answer to it as you keep asking yourself, why you are doing what you are doing." At this very time, it was still impossible for him to predict what the eventual outcome and consequences will be. After he got home and had eaten and slept and woken up, he looked at himself with pride. He saw that he was able to smoke the so-called marijuana he had heard people criticized—saying it makes anybody who smoke it null and void. some even said the first day you smoke it, that is when your madness begins. He was looking at himself to be a hero who had just returned back from a deadly war; he tried to recall everything that happened while smoking it; he thought it was all fun and there was a great pleasure in it. What he enjoyed most while smoking it, was how the music he was listening to had pierced through his ear and moving up to his brain and later down to his heart, helping him to receive the message and interpreting it clearly. He thought it will be better if he choose to smoke it once more to see if he could feel the same way, but he barely recognized the gravity of the situation which he was about to place himself.

As time, days, and months went-by, he was already getting himself accustomed to this life-style of marijuana—smoking and listening to music so as to derive meanings from the lyrics. A time came when the country where he was born and where he was still living, was beginning to feel deeply the effects of stress and tension of another civil war. He then voluntarily joined some radical groups in his school, who with the help and supports of the university students and some pro-democracy and human right groups all over the country, have said it was time for them to fight for their rights as citizens of the country, first, by embarking on a peaceful protest, and when they could not find an answer to their questions, they decided to turn it into a riot, setting fires on most of the government premises and fighting with the police. It was really a hard time political and economic crisis for everybody in the country since there were no hopes for a better future most especially for the youths. It was during a military regime of one General Ibrahim Badamasi Babangida, popularly referred to as (I.B.B), who was a Nigerian Army Officer that later became the country's military ruler after he had plot a bloodless coup to overthrow General Mohammadu Buahari, the then president in the year 1985. Although, Babangida had been a coup plotter some years before this second time which finally, he had come to succeed. He studied at the India military school, the Royal Armored center. He also took the the Advance Armored Officers course at Armored School, the Senior Officers course, Armed Forces Command and Staff College, and the Senior International Defense Management course, Naval Post-graduate School, U.s. in 1980. As a man who had achieved education and had traveled abroad, he should have fathom the needs for people to have some basic human rights and live a better life in their country just as he had seen it abroad, which was what he proclaimed, led him to overthrow the former president since he could not show restraint to see him abusing human rights, but immediately, after he gained power, he started, by embezzling the country's oil wealth, setting people on a trail of precedent corrupt life. He launched a Structural Adjustment Program (S.A.P), to build-up supports for austerity measures enhanced by the IMF and the World Bank. He was said to have conducted a lot of unresolved political assassinations by sending them letter bombs, which to anyone who could see well, is the worst human rights abuse, and there was no conviction, not for him or for his ministers who were involved in these acts. To show how strong he really was, to an extent, some years later after he left power, he decided to come back to rule the country, this time under a democratic political party, and was still winning supports from his many fans who thought they benefited from his corrupt and bribery way of life in aiding frauds being done outside the country. This same president had set-up an election for the country, after his eight years of rule to return back to democracy, what come after it was annulment with no vindication or whatsoever. During this riot, David and his friends also took the advantage of destroying and robbing most private and government business premises, but they had fought hard to make sure their voices were heard. In one of the contest between the police and the youths, one of the lads walking beside him was shot twice and died at the spot, and when he saw this, he went straight to his house and never make the attempt to participate again till the end of the riot—which encompassed a wide range of police brutality, chaos everywhere in the streets of the cities all over the country. People were crying as police were shooting and innocent youths were dying. Long before the commencement of this riot that was about to break into a civil war, there has been a long time dejected, dreary and cheerless starvation, every nights what they get accustomed to, was nothing than hearing gun shots—gun shots of armed robbers, leaving everybody in fear and despair. David said the only thing that came to his mind was that, he has to run away from the country as he could see his heart was on fire, but there was no way he could do it since he was still very young and penniless. He saw that no one was trying to stop the crimes, since the people governing them were saying, there is no solution. All the cities were full of corruption and with much population, inflation, bribery, nepotism, ethnicity and religious conflicts. Everyday was a day starts and end with misery as everyone's life was at stake, no jobs, and people could not afford to study as long as they were not having the finance to do so. As the situation continued, and was cast in this same mold, offering no space for a change, many of the youths lost their integrity as human being, driving them to start to make a choice of whether to proceed with this hazardous life or to travel to another part of the world to have a life. At this period of time when the nation was about to start learning of how to be self-reliant, which would have draw the youths nearer to civilization and the invention of different forms of technologies since there were much wealth being fetched from the country's oil exports, but with this horrible and frustrating situation, most of them were impulse in sending themselves into self-imposed exile.

David was for another time, hopeless once again, but still full of energy to fight his demons and send them back to where they came from, but how could he do this? How could he afford to when he had become very headstrong, proud, and lazy, and not assisting his father in doing his farm-works so that he can in return assist him financially in paying his school fees and also providing for him, his school materials. He was beginning to encounter formidable life, getting himself involved with some desperado friends in conducting wrong doings and partying, which mostly leads to fighting other group over girls with knives ax, hatchet and sometimes, guns. Although, he had never in life hold a gun or assault a woman, neither has he be a member of any secret cult, but he was a friend to so many cult members, criminals and arm robbers who were capable of committing any kind of crime. He learnt how to go into a plantain plantation to steal plantains. He also became perfect on how to steal live chickens and hens, strangled them, and used them to cook yam or plantain porridge which he sometimes serve to his elder brother, Ken, who was always afraid to support the killings but always happy to show his supports when ever the meal is served. He became a good liar, even better than Ken, who taught him of how he could extract money from their father. He became very perfect in lying till he could even lie to himself and God, the Supernatural Being he believed created him. This manner and attitudes adopted by David was then leading him to meet with different rogues who were planning to travel out of the country in search for a better future. He made lots of efforts, trying to convince Ken about his new conception on how they could both pressurize their father to sponsor one of them to travel abroad, since they already lost hopes of their half-brother, Sunny coming to help them. But Ken, who has always inclined to the conception—that life should be taken easily, refused to join effort with him, leaving him to be standing alone in the middle of irremediable despondency. He knew it was the precise time for him not to follow his brother's footsteps by being pampered and told what to do and what not to do, so he came to conclude it will be better for him to to despise him and walk farther away from him than he has always thought of.

As a day that has passed can never wait for us, time was moving very fast, and time became his only enemy and only friend. He thought he was getting too old to still be living in poverty and waiting for his father or his elder half-brother to decide his destiny for him. He thought he would have to make himself a man and move himself forward, but he understood he was still very young and penniless.

Sunny, his elderly half-brother left back to Europe, this time to the U.k. after many of his properties that he brought from Germany and his elder sister's house where he was living were all burnt, and after he suffered to raise money and waited for almost two years to finally get a visa. David and his father were more separated more than they had ever been, because of his radical and too desperate to make it life. He was in his fifth grade in the secondary school, (S.S.S II) Senior Secondary School, second grade as it was in the nation's newly adopted educational system known as the 6-3-3-4 system that stands for—6 years in the primary school, 3 years in the junior secondary school, 3 years in the senior secondary school, and then, 4 years in the university level to become a graduate, but anyone who intend to, might further advance h/his educational career if they want to. David, who was already getting addicted to smoking marijuana and drinking and partying every time, could not concentrate on his studies anymore. He barely had time to pick up any of his text-book or a novel and read. He was having more friends and friends and friends, visiting them, but never allowed any of them to visit him, because he was ashamed of his home and his family poor background. He lied to some of his friends that his father was his grandfather and that his father was dead and that he was the first male born of his father, even telling them that his elder sister was in Europe. Music then became the only way he could console his soul as he was enjoying spending more time with his friends, smoking marijuana and listening to some reggae music than reading or spending time with his families. His family became his worst enemies, most especially his father whom he always referred to as old man. He once asked his father where he was when some of the richest men in his country were getting rich. He was always blaming his parents for his misfortunes and was rude to them, showing how much he did loathe them. When it came to the time for him to sit for the promotion exam to the sixth grade (S.S.S III), his last exam before the General Certificate Examination (G.C.E) or the West African Examination Council (W.A.E.C)—the two exams for all the final year students to pass before being allowed to sit for the Joint Admission and Matriculation Board (J.A.M.B), and after this, before they will finally be admitted into the university. He knew what he was about to get himself into. He knew it was not going to be a plain sailing procedure to get to the university, and even if he manged to get there, will he be able to afford it? Who was going to fund the school bills for him? He quickly gave up the prospect of ever stepping his feet there and embraced the prospect of transforming his destiny to what he thought will be best for him—which he himself could not describe what it is or what it might look like, but with faith, he knew his gods will be there always to watch over him and lead him to the right direction to reach his destiny that he has always preached about to his father whenever he asked him to leave his house to go find life for himself. This exam to him had made him propound failure for himself as he was not prepared for it, even when some of his friends cautioned him about how his life was going to be affected if he fail the exam. Yet he made no attempt to study, believing he could still have a way to cheat on the exam day. When the day came, he tried to do the best he could to cheat, but the security there in the exam hall was too tight, so he gave up the idea, and when the result finally came out, he saw that he has failed. He did not make any mistake to show it to his friends; he left and walked home to think about what he should be doing next, without showing it to his parents as well, since he believed nobody was prepared to show a sign of concerns to his problems.

With so many thoughts in his mind of what he was going to do with his life since he already failed his exam, he decided to come closer to his family by asking his father to forgive him and promising to assist him in doing his farm-work, but this time, voluntarily. He became very frequent at home and used to relax inside the room of one of his elder half-brothers—the last born of his step-mother, just to listen music. His elder half-brother was old enough to look for life for himself, but refused to because he was not smart enough to do a thing like that. He was nicknamed Tolongo, a name even David never knew what it meant, but did understood it was a name to describe a person with a low I.Q. Tolongo was quiet, vigorous and industrious, and because of this, many people took the advantage in cheating him. He had spent much effort in helping David's father in cultivating a large scale of farm land, but when he made the decision to quit and wanted to live on his own, his father was upset and wanted to disown him. He was upset not just because Tolongo had decided to quit helping him, but also because Tolongo had decided to quit learning to be a mechanic—a profession he had chosen to learn many years ago by making his father paid a large sum of money for it to his master and owner of the workshop where he was learning this work. David father was also paying him for assisting him in doing the farm-work. He wanted him to have a future, since he was a dullard and could not write or read his name, and moreover, he was disregarded by all his age-mates whom they both grew up together. Although the whole world were looking at him to be a no-genius, feeble-minded person, but David saw in him, a great sense of humor, as he was friendly and was a person who tolerate; he was a man with a strong passion for listening to music, but not to become a musician. David who also was having that same passion, would sneak into his room on his absence to listen to some of the cassettes he had bought. Tolongo was a good collector of music cassettes and was a good singer and was having good taste in music. He was always singing along with the music anytime he hears it playing. He usually purchased different kind of music, some, David never think exist at that time since he was still very young. He was very familiar most especially with country musi—which was his favorite, followed by reggae music, then jazz, rhythm and blues, and little pop, from 70s to 80s, but he was not familiar with African traditional or local music. With him, David had first realized the existence of musicians like America, Bruce Springsteen, Phil Collins, Michael Button, Skeeter Davis, Bobby Bare, Peter Tosh, Bob Marley and the Wailers, and so on. Among all these music that David was already having the opportunity to listen to, he found Bob Marley's music very unique, because of the lyrics which were about a need for a revolution among the poor countries in the world, most particularly, in Africa.

There was this other fellow, who was living in a house right after or before the house of David's father, depending on which side of the street you are coming from. His name is Daniel, and his father died some years ago, maybe six years before then. And before he died, he has chased this fellow and his mother out of his house with a gun, cursing them and vowing to get them killed anytime he sees them around his house. Since then Daniel did not return back to that house until his father was dead and buried. He was the last child of his mother who was already having two other children with another man before coming to marry this man who was already having five children with another two women who left him because of his arrogance and selfish life. Daniel was of the same age with David's elder half-brother, Sunny, who had just left back to Europe. He was very friendly, gracious, and non-hostile to David, not mindful of the age differences between the two of them. David, on his own had respected this privilege by not being impolite to him whenever he was with him. He was a very intelligent fellow just like his father and the rest of his five half brothers. He was too intelligent that most time he found it impracticable to cope with the society which he was living in. Although he had never been to the university, but he was more intelligent than any graduate that David had met. He was to David, a man of considerable intellect but still remain poor and was unable to further his educational career because he could not raise the fund to finance himself. Most time, when David looked at him, he felt pity for him, knowing him to be somebody who wants to study but nobody was there to assist him financially. With this, he grasped that, "Only a congenital cretin never make plans. We all make plans, but earning supports to execute our plans is what is most essential in life." But when David came to understand that his half brothers were rich—one of them who was a lawyer, a journalist, and an actor, and was capable of sponsoring him to study in the university. Another one, the first born among them who was living in the country's capital city with his wife and kids, would have also been able to assist him. Then, there was another one who was living abroad but with his wife and kids still living in that same house where Daniel was. He was beginning to be curious to know the reasons why they were not willing to help their youngest brother to study since they all love education in that family.

Since David already failed his exam, he was calm and decided to change his life to become a better person his family will be proud of, not that wayward and devilish child he was almost turning into. He was then visiting Daniel frequently in his house as he was always having the opportunities to read some of the books, magazines and newspapers that Daniel was purchasing for himself. Daniel was at that same time, doing a part time job and studying more in one private school, and also at home. It was then David initially came to understand something about self-education. He was then happy again with this new life he was having. He was enjoying the good music he usually go to listen to inside Tolongo's room and the knowledge he was receiving from Daniel. He saw that, as he continuously draw himself closer to this new life, his lost memories were also coming back to him—his memories of how he dreamed of how he was going to become a prominent figure in the society where he was born, and also how he was going to succeed in achieving a good educational and career goals, and having a dexterous profession in the future.

"In everything that we are doing in life, we have to look at our mentor, and see what they have achieved, to see that we are not doing the wrong thing." David looked at these two people and saw that they were both living a miserable and unfortunate life, then he tried to speculate about this and provide an answer to it alone on his own. He saw that Tolongo was just a man with a strong passion for music but was not having any ambition to become a musician and was a very hard-working man that people are taking an advantage of. Daniel, on the other side was a shrewd and intelligent man who declined the assistance of his other brothers to study and to become a greater person in life. So many a time when David had brought this topic to discuss it with him, he would pretend to be doing a different thing. The problem with Daniel was that he was proud to his brothers; he thought he could make life all by himself; he was ashamed to cry even when he was been beaten. This actually made David to come to comprehend that "What we really want could be here close to us, but we just cannot realize it, and even when we do, we just would not admit it because of pride. And this pride that they say it comes before a fall."

Just when David was on the verge of commencing a different and more suitable life, something terrible and heinous happened again. After the then military president of his country—the so-called (I.B.B) annulment of the election, causing a massive uproar and a life of poverty and hardship among the millions of citizens in the country and outside, and left without handling power to the winner of the election, then arrived an interim government before they could know what to do next, as the country was already on a brink of civil war. A one time chief of army staff and later minister of defense, General Sani Abacha, with a military coup, deposed the then president under the interim government from power, making the country return back to live under a military dictatorship. He silenced the citizens uproar by ordering soldiers around every cities to beat the hell out of anyone who is heard say something about the president. People who were blaming the former dictator (I.B.B) for his misconducts and corrupt life came to believe he was a good man as they all saw Abacha come into power with a zero tolerance for citizens right. During this period of time, life became more complex for everybody, more poverty and starvation with more crimes and any criminal caught was killed instantly without any trial even if it were to be a mistake. Soldiers were then in the position of the police for security purposes; they were everything in the country. Anybody could be arrested for wearing boots since nobody has the right to do so apart from the soldiers. They were at then having power more than they usually were.

With this melange of several different enigma moving around the upper storey of his head, and was creating a mood of melancholy—which descended on him. He was forced to cease thinking about having a future, instead he was thinking about survival. How was he going to survive all these tragedies that he already seen laid await for him and the millions of youths that were living in the country. Some years back, their father would gather them and start to tell them stories about the last civil war that engulfed the country many years ago. Having heard this, he was already been able to picture what exactly war might be looking like. He knew he was not going to experience it and for him not to, he knew he would have to do anything to leave the country to anywhere, even if it happened to be the near-by country, no matter how poor or rich the country might be. He knew something should have to be done since he already seen youths like him traveling out of the country—some with their parents supports, while some were without the consent of their parents. His bitter-feelings towards Ken, his elder brother rose again, because he was seeing him as a man who was weak and not prepared to lead even when he was having the opportunity to. Ken was unable to meet his father to persuade him to sponsor him to travel abroad by land even when he was hearing news of how many youths were doing so, instead he was waiting for his father to call him to tell him his visa was prepared to come and travel abroad. Many times he object the prospect when David tried to talk to him about it. And at this very time, David's immediate elder sister had left to an unknown country with an unknown person handled over to by his most elder sister, Julie, the second child of his mother, who got pregnant while she was still in the secondary school. David said he was rather sad, one day, as he watched his brother, Ken, dancing and rejoicing because his own younger sister was leaving home to travel abroad to go work as a prostitute to pay the sponsor the sum of 40,000.00 dollars before she could think of coming to help her family. David said how he wish he could see his brother die, seeing how he care much about himself and not caring for others.

On a very warm evening when David returned back from outside where he had just finished smoking marijuana with some of his arrogant friends, he was looking for something to eat since he was very hungry and needed to eat something. He checked the cooking pots their mother used to leave in the cupboard and saw that there was food in one of them. But when he brought it out to serve it on the plate so that he could start eating it, Ken came hurriedly, snatching the food from him and started fighting and insulting him. They say, "A hungry man is an angry man." David, knowing he could not withstand the fight anymore as he was still very hungry and needed to regain his strength back only by eating that food, he picked up an empty bottle of beer and burst it, using the left-over piece still in his hand in stabbing him twice at the back of his shoulder. He said he wanted to keep stabbing him until he could see him fall down as he listened to the demons inside him praised him, saying, kill him, kill him, he is of no value to you or to anybody.

The next two days after he stabbed his brother, he came out from where he was hiding meanwhile he was told that Ken was discharged already from the hospital and that he had had many stitches and was so lucky he was rushed there, if not he would have died. David was so happy that he did not committed murder and also to hear he was still alive and talking and able to raise his hand up, because if he died, there was no assurance that he was not going to be killed also according to the law of the country. But after the incident, he became a hero as people were afraid to intimidate him. They were praising and calling him names like Gaddhafi, killer, bad boy, mudiaga, Castro, e.t.c. He became very pompous and proud of his misdeed. You see, "People will praise you when they see you doing evil, because they know you will die soon for it." He was then having more friends more than he was having before, attending different parties and fighting and bursting more bottles. He left home to go and be staying with some new friends he just met with. Anytime his mother would see him, she would shed tears and begged him to return back home.

For another time, he merged with another group of friends—which he was fond of doing every time, by moving from one group of friends to another, because he said he believe, "Friends are meant to come and go, and more over, you have friends so that you can learn something from them that might help you in the future, but not to be kept, since they can never help you define your fate." He said he really do not believe in keeping friends or embarking his trust on them, because he might not have them when he is in need of their help. So there is really no reason for keeping them. "Meeting a new friend is like meeting a new life." That he has just met this new group of friends, he discovered something new once again—this time about how to convince a woman to come to your house—a thing which he has never done before, even when he spent his last money in purchasing some of the best attires a boy of his standard could afford. This group were specialize in partying, spending the little money with them in purchasing some attires and getting themselves involved with different kind of women. So, this had led him several times to encounter troubles that he was never prepared for. There had also been fight break-out and contentions between them and some other groups over the issues of women. There was always a competition among this groups on who gets the most beautiful girl. They were all like a family, although they were living in the same street. David who was good in lying, never told them the truth about himself, even when he was living with them as part of the family. Amid this group, he chose one of them called Billy, to be his best friend, yet he never told him so many things that he should have told him.

When the time for him to enroll for his Senior Secondary School Certificate Examination came, he went home to his father to plead for money for the exam. His father, who has constantly wanted him to study to achieve that education that he himself never had a chance to have, forgave him and gave him the money, without demanding for his last school result—this money which he later spent in buying some clothes since it was already near Christmas period. The rest, he spent in going to eat in a restaurant everyday throughout a week with his new best friend, Billy. When it came to the day of the exam, he went to a village where he told his parents he had enrolled for the exams, to spend two weeks and returned back home, telling everybody, including his so-called best friend, Billy, that he has participated in writing the exams.

After when he tricked his father and collected money from him to enroll in an exam and later spent the money for himself, he returned back home to meet with a very good and hopeful news that his elder half-brother, Sunny, was back from the U.k. Despite how delighted he was, but he knew it was of no benefit to him, since he fathomed there was no way he could rely on any of them, as he was on his own, ready to confront any obstacle that might be on his way to success. He immediately decided to modify his attitudes. He started first and foremost, by eliminating pride and deciding to choose for himself the kind of friends that will be of good advantage to him. He chose some new friends, one of them whose father had a delivery van and was dealing on plywood in a sawmill close to his house. Although his new friends were not sociable but were more hard-working and were earning little money for themselves. These new group of friends were all happy to see him in their midst probably because they were all aware of who he was—from his past innocent life to his present monster-like life. Starting a new life with these new friends he just met and earning little money to feed himself, was beginning to make him have a thought of regret of some of his past attitudes towards other people by disregarding and threatening them. But he knew there was no need for him to regret it, because he has learn so many things from his past and from his former arrogant friends—things like music and dancing and how to approach women and convince them and bring them home to have sex with them.

Not quite long, as life was about to be a little bit sweet and smooth for him, his other nephew, the elder brother to the one that was killed in an accident some years ago, died during a surgical operation. This was the saddest day of his life, the day that no matter what he become in future and how he survived all the tragedies in life, this memory will remain occlude inside his brain. He loved this boy so much that many years after his death, he was still appearing to him in dreams, warning him of the danger in struggling to achieve success. They were both friends and enemies, but understood each other more than twins do; they were more than just brothers or friends—they were like lovers.

With a new uprising against the government of the dictator of his country once again, the cities were overwhelmed by chaos, activists brutally beaten and sent to prisons, and the country was with a high level of inflation and the continuous lack of employment, making many youths homeless and to become ensnared in a life of crime. Abacha, the military dictator who was the most corrupt president in the country's history, was also a wager of war. He was not ready to step down as a president even with much international pressure from mostly Great Britain and the United States and later the United Nations. Abacha remained where he was and continued to siphoned billions of dollars out of the country's coffers to other parts of the world mostly Switzerland, and he was aiding his families and ministers in looting several public funds. During his regime, a lot of political activists were killed by hanging. The former democratic political aspirant was imprisoned, but he later died of a heart attack a month after Abacha's death. Some other political activist and aspirants were charged with treason and sent directly to prison to be executed; some died while waiting for trial and execution. The whole country was in an absolute state of mayhem.

David, who never knew anything about politics, was beginning to put his ears down so that he could hear what people were predicting about the future of the country. All he could hear, was war! war! war! war!. And all these voices he was hearing were voices of well educated old men and women living in agony and frustration. David knew war was not going to lead the country to peace except division, but division would have been better since the Northerners decided to take power on their hands to punish the Southerners, forgetting how much joy and happiness that has been and were to be taken from the youths who were already left with little faiths to survive. This division that he believed could be better, how could it be achieved? Do we have to use violence in achieving everything we really want in life? It is not that he is not a person who believe co-operation is the key to success, but he saw how the northerners were striving for power, that he came to believe something else must be done for both (northerners and southerners) to achieve their goals of living peacefully.

As he proceeded with his investigation, he could hear people talk about unity, but he disagreed with this idea, because he said he believe, "People cannot be united and be living in pains and agony, so it will be better if divided and live in peace and harmony." "Tolerance is vital when living with people that are not of the same ethnic or religion or race or gender or class with you, but there are things sometimes we cannot tolerate which is not our fault but because it is of nature, so for there not to be a dispute, we can move a little bit away so that these people too can live a convenient life as we too also live our own convenient life." From a sight he said he could see the world sinking as he could explain it better, "It is simple to say that man's attitude towards one another has brought man to a high level of fear, that man could no longer trust his wife or his brother or even his son or daughter."

CHAPTER 13

F OR THE SECOND TIME, HE was falling in love with a girl after he had once loved his class teacher whom he could not even touch or think of making love to, because he was just an innocent little boy carried away with the love to achieve knowledge from a decent woman that was as beautiful as gold—a woman he was never going to see again in his life. This time it was real love that he felt for this girl, love with a deep affection and emotion. Although he has made love to other girls before, but he had never truly understand what it means to be in love. Being in love is like being possessed by a very strong spiritual power. It can take you to anywhere. It can take you to the land that you never wished to be. It drives you crazy like hell. Everything happened when he started visiting his new friends at home. She had long heard things about him, but she had never really seen him. Then she was surprised to meet him face to face. Although she was dating someone else who was spending his father's money on her just to win her heart. Seeing him for the first time, she fell in love with him. She was very smart not to had allowed him to make love to her at the time he had wanted to, knowing he was going to run away after that. She did so, because she wanted him to stay—to stay and live with her till death do them both.

Initially, David's intention was not to love her, but to have fun with her and dump her just like he had done to some other girls he had met before he met her. But everything changed one day after the girl's mother died and they were preparing for the funeral. Actually, some days before that day, they both quarreled. He was sad and penniless and could not do anything than smoke marijuana, and when intoxicated, he fell down to sleep on the floor in front of a pit toilet roofed and built of zinc, inhaling the smells of the excrement coming from the pit without knowing it, since he was unconscious and not knowing what exactly he was doing. Meanwhile, the other boy, who was spending money on this girl, buying her watches, jewelries, and other exorbitant material things, also spent a lot of money to assist this girl in organizing the funeral to a good taste. He invited a lot of people and hired a video camera and a music band to play throughout the night of the funeral. But at night, the girl thanked him and left him to go look for David, and when she found him, she woke him up, took him to a dark hidden place and started kissing him, knowing the hardship he was passing through. The next two days after the funeral, she came to David's house to visit him, to surrender her body to him and let him do anything he wish with it, to let him know how much she want him in her life. As there was a lack of communication at that time and the people were still not exposed to the use of mobile phones and telephones at home, she came without calling him to know if he was at home, and getting there, she met his absence and waited and waited till at the time she was tired and left to go back home. When David was later told the time he arrived home of how the girl came and waited and waited, he was almost at the point of shedding tears, knowing that was his opportunity to make love to her. But he felt something in his heart, something he had never felt before for a woman of his age except for his primary school form teacher who was old enough to be his eldest sister, he felt love.

Some days after the day she came to visit David and not meeting him at home, she was astonished when she saw him in front of her house, meanwhile, she had sent a message to him through some of his friends who were living close to her house, asking him to come and see her. Immediately she saw him, she felt a shiver of excitement and was so happy, and this was noticed by some of David's friend who helped her delivered the message to him. That day, he was able to convinced her to follow him to the house of one of his friend where he was partly living. When they finally arrived there, he wanted to make love to her but only to realize that she was on her menstrual period. He was riled and unhappy about this, but she begged him to be patient and that there was still more time ahead for the both of them. David who believed the girl was already in love with him, was becoming more conceited, and after two days, he went having a date with another girl who was a friend to this same girl that was in love with him. He actually never intended to, but he did so because he did not know they were friends, and it was the other girl that seduced him, and since he already knew her to be a spoiled and loose woman, he wanted to have sex with her once and dump her. But, it was impossible for him to predict what the eventual outcome and consequences will be. In spite that he did not make love to her, but the news soon get to the girl and she felt hurt, disrespected, humiliated, and unloved. She could not bear it as she found it intriguing, so she started looking for a way to pay him back of this disgracing moment of her life. As time went on, David tried to meet her so as to apologize to her, but she refused to listen to him. With the help and supports of David's friends who were aware of everything, she was able to meet another boy, who was living close to his house, and at that same time, the boy's elder brother in Europe just returned and was staying in one of the most expensive hotel in the city. The boy who was able to enticed her with money by taking her to the hotel where his elder brother was lodging, then finally succeeded in making love to her. The girl's elder sister who has always hated David and opposed her sister's notion of falling in love with him, was so delighted when she saw the both of them split. David, who already had an intuition that something awful was going to happen, persisted, not blaming himself, instead he knew he was to get himself out of this infinity pool where he had sunk himself. He knew that was not what he should be striving for; he knew there was much more for him to accomplish, and this was the appropriate time for him to get started. He said the memory of what he read in a book came running around his head and he heard a voice speaking to him, "A man's greatest pleasure comes when he is able to achieve his dreams." As the voice spoke to him, he swiftly realized there was a need for him to turn his grief into ambition. He would have to live if he can, if he cannot, he would have to welcome what life brings. He knew somehow, some days, someone will have to love him again.

CHAPTER 14

AFTER SOME DAYS THAT HE lost the girl, he was beginning to think she could be the woman of his life. He was still striving to have no recollection of it, but the memory of the many times they had met and kissed and hold each other, promising to love and cherish one another till death do them, kept running back to him. But, he also understood that life is too short and there is no need for him to wait too long. Although, he had heard people say, "Patience dog eats the fattest bone," and also, "Too much hard work does not bring riches." He said, he agreed, and at the same time, he also disagreed, as he read in the bible, that, "All hard work brings a profit, but mere talks leads only to poverty." And moreover, he also read that, 'It is wise men who knows the value of hard work," not to mention when he was told that, riches are the rewards to a hard work wisely done. He said he knew he will achieve his dreams if he start working towards it. The only question he was asking himself was if then was the right time as he was penniless and lack some financial supports. He said, he had once read in a book that, "The right thing to do is also the most obvious thing to do." He knew he could either succeed or lose his life, knowing already, the most important mainstays in life are patience, supports, and encouragements—which he was lacking. But this voice kept speaking to him, "If you cannot stand the damage, do not try to mange. Move along or stay behind." The whole incident was then to him like a life of fairy tales.

One bright sunny afternoon, as he was heading home from one of his friend's house where he had been for two days, he walked passed an art school and gallery—which was situated at the road where he usually take to his school, and was with a name carefully and neatly written on a board in front and also designed on top of the roof, (CREATIVE ART GALLERY AND SCHOOL). Apparently lost in thought, something made him to stop and take a good look at the art work done and placed outside the gallery for exhibition. Although, he was not having much interest in fine art and he had never ever thought of becoming a fine art artist in his life, but when he stopped to look at this beautiful art works displayed there, something came to his mind, "You are an artist in every form. You can be artist and a designer, if you wish to." He could not help get this voice out of his head and mind as it was beginning to accumulate there. The next question he was already asking himself was, 'how do I get this done?' He walked directly into the gallery, and when he reached inside, he met the secretary and asked her what it takes to become a student of the school. But when he was told the amount for the registration fees, he knew he was never going to be able to afford it.

Getting home sad because he knew this time nobody was ever going to financially support him in any plan that he would have to lay his hand, he went into his room to meditate on what to do next then that he was planning for his future. An idea walked straight to his mind, ringing and uttering a word, "'STEALING." Where was he going to steal the money from? He could not wait to get the answer from anybody since he knew it was only his father that could be having that amount of money but be pretending to be penniless.

At that very time, he was living in a room close to his father's room where Ken, his elder brother was living before he left to go and be living with their grandmother in her beautiful, inestimable, and high worth apartment furnished and payed for by their aunt who was prostituting in Italy. He knew that his father was not at home and it will take him maybe another three hours before returning back home. So he removed one of the ceiling inside his room and climbed the top of the roof and crawled to the side of his father's room, then removed the ceiling from inside and jumped down, landing inside his father's room. He walked straight to where the bed was and raised the pillow, and when he did, he saw some money. Without waiting to count them, he put everything in his pocket of his trouser and left, taking the same way back to his room and placing the ceilings back in order the way he had met them before.

Already in his room, he counted the money which was exactly the same amount of what he required for paying the registration fees. The next day, he was already at the front of the door of the gallery and waiting for them to open it. When the secretary came to meet him, she laughed and opened the door, then asked him to sit down and wait for her boss. As he waited, he could watch in amazement how the students were tripping in—all of them, properly dressed and neat with files on their hands. Deep down inside of him, he knew this was the right place for him to be and it was God, Who sent him to be there. When the secretary finally told him that most of the students there were from universities and polytechnic colleges who had come to do their industrial training, he was so delighted to hear this as he waited for the proprietor and boss to arrive. But when the man arrived, he was too busy to attend to him, so he asked him to return back the next day. The next day, same time, he was there again, sitting and waiting at the secretary's office. When the man came to meet him again, though was still busy but has to attend to him. He called him into his office and gave him the information of the school and and the materials and tools that he was to provide, which to David, were things he knew he could not afford. He left and went back home sobering. He knew he was not going to spend that money he stole from his father unnecessarily, which already was causing an havoc in his house. Apparently, he was not the prime suspect since his younger brother had become very stubborn and was stealing from all sources to lavish on young pretty girls.

After another two days, he met with his neighbor and friend, Daniel—the smart, quick thinking genius. He asked him to assist him to another art gallery, pretending to be his elder brother who came to help him pay the registration fees. This time, it was not a school but a workshop or rather to be referred to as a studio. When they arrived there, everything went as planned. He paid the fees and was accepted as one of the apprentices that he came to meet there. Since the studio was near his former secondary school were he just left—where he failed the last exam he did, walking to get there everyday was not a thing he was not accustomed to.

The first day he started, he thought it was going to be like the other art school where you would have to go with all the required art materials for drawing, painting, and sculpting, but this place was quite different. He was first asked to sweep and tidy the workshop continuously for one week without learning anything he had come for. The boss, who was not concerned about what was happening in the workshop, had left the place for his younger brother and his senior apprentice to take care of. David, who was already in a deep sense of unease because he was not being taught what he had come to learn, instead being converted to a person for cleaning and tidying the workshop everyday. Although, he managed to buy some art materials and clay to practice at home on how to sculpt. He fell in love with sculpting, because of the creative idea that it was making him develop. After some weeks, he commenced with the real lessons by following them to the building sites to sculpt some various designs of wall reliefs. He was happy with this, since he had always love things relating to creativity. He was devoting his time to learn this work and spurning his friends. The more he was continuously having interest in this work, the more he was meeting new artists and making friends with them, knowing what exactly was appropriate for him to be doing. He ignored what his old friends were saying about him. He said he could use this opportunity to advise any body who is making a decision to live a new and better life from the one he had been living, that, "We do not need to wait for tomorrow to start making our plans when we can make it now, as we might not know what is ahead of the next hour," and that, "We should forget about what people think about us and what we are doing. We should keep doing what we are doing, knowing it to be the appropriate thing to do. People will see what we are doing, only if we do it well and enough."

As he successively devote his interest and passion to art, his boss discerned this and decided to help him build that creative power that he saw inside of him, by sending him to his other workshop were he could learn metal sculpting which was more important and was in vogue and was more demanding by the wealthy people in the society. The very moment he saw this work, he lost his passion for other form of art and embraced this. It was involved with welding and structuring of metal to become designed Queen Elizabethan's-like gate. The location where the workshop was built was very far from his house that he had to walk five miles everyday before getting there. He saw that it was far, and when he discovered a new place where the work was been done better and seeing that it was nearer to his house, he decided to register himself there.

One of his elder sister who has been his enemy for long was then getting close to him since her husband has advised her to do so, letting her know that, David was a smart and intelligent boy who need an assistance to do some greater things in life. He believed in him as he learn more about his childhood life and compared it with his recent life. He saw the fire in his eyes and he comprehend his passion for this work and he knew he had to lend him a hand.

One day, he called David to discuss issues relating to his work with him and to ask him what he actually needed. David who had already saved some money from his very small landscape farm harvest and had went to steal from his father again, begged the man to assist him in going to register in a new place so that he could learn that work very well. After said and done, he was assisted and then started working as a new apprentice in this new place where the owner just died some months ago and the person in charge was his bereaved wife, who was a family friend to David and was in love and had been having a relationship with one of his sister's husband. After six months that he was registered as one of the apprentice here in this workshop or rather referred to as an art gallery which was five times bigger than the one he left before coming over to this place, and with more staffs and apprentice artists five times the number of the other workshop. He was enjoying this place and was learning the work better than some of the lads that he came to meet there. Some of them were very serious and some were not. Those that were serious were the ones with poor family backgrounds and were there to learn the work to build a future for themselves, while the ones that were not serious were the ones that were having supports from their families and were there to have fun and to pass away their time, by making this work an ingenious contrivance to get their parents to trust them and plan to sponsor them to travel abroad. He was beginning to meet with some great and famous artist who were well known for their painting and sculpting skills, and with them, he was beginning to obtain more knowledge about art and designs since almost all of them were graduated students from the universities and polytechnic colleges. From them, he received some historical art books which he read to know many past events in the history of art of his country and the rest part of the world. He also used this opportunity to read some books about some of the world most famous artist that has lived and died like Leornado Da Vinci, Boticelli, Michelangelo, Galileo Galilei, Vincent Van Gogh and many more. The most fascinating history of art that he read was the (FESTAC), a festival that was hosted by oil rich Nigeria when oil was newly discovered in the country and money was flowing everywhere. It was the second Africa festival for art and culture held to solemnize individuality, antiquity and the power of the black and African world. It was meant to display different art works from the different countries around the continent. It was also meant to learn on how to cope with the new era of modern technology and industrialism among the African countries. The logo of this festival was an ivory mask of Queen Idia, (Iyoba ne Esigie), which means, the Queen mother of one King Esigie who lived a legendary life and was a heroine who helped protected and ruled the Benin Kingdom, one of the greatest kingdom that were in Africa—the same city where he was born and bred. He also read that the original work of this ivory mask was stolen by the British during the time of their colony. For this reason, he said, "How sad it was for him to see how the British has exploited them." But when he became older and was already living in the western world, traveling from one country to another, and with the help of the English language, he was being able to communicate with different people around the world, then he said. "How glad he is to see that his country was colonized by the British." He said he came to realize one thing that, "Even if the British had exploited them—which is true, but they have also given to them wisdom and exposed them to the real world—also known as civilization. He said, sometimes he believe if the British were still in Nigeria at the time oil was discovered, they would have refused their independence, and it would have been better if they have done so. They would have exploited them, and at the same time, spend some part of the money in developing the country, which would have been more better than the way the country was. Because these Nigerians eyes were full of greediness and could not see the futility of this greed and self-indulgence, as they discovered oil, they decided to make all the British still dwelling there to leave. But, now that it is an independent country and is oil rich, for more than five decades, they are still depending on technologies and other manufactured goods from around the world, there has been more starvation, ethnic, religion, political, and economic crisis. There is also an essential need for infrastructural developments and none of the leaders has ever thought about it. For decades, they are still struggling on how to restore democracy by fighting and killing each others. The worst of it all, corruption. The leaders are wise enough to see that with no fear, they can embezzle the nation's money and lavish it for themselves and their family, while the normal citizens are starving to death. Greed and Self-indulgence, see how it works and how much damages it had caused. The attested truth is that, they lack the the inborn aptitude to govern and treat themselves in the right and proper manners, and they need people to modify them. You see, "Fretting about your arduous and complicated situation won't help, except you get up and stand on your feet and call on someone to lend you a hand. But, who are you to call on, when everybody is entangled in a series of Herculean task." No one actually was going to respond to the call and listen to them. "They have also forgotten that, helping others solve their problems make us forget about our own problem for awhile and rejoice and applaud our good deeds."

David, who felt cosy doing the work of art that he was doing, was already developing more skills in art generally, by traveling with the company where he was working to different states in the country to work with them. With this, he was beginning to know other places and was beginning to meet some very rich and famous people face to face as they were working for them. He became happy that his life had changed due to the fact he was no longer smoking marijuana or hanging around with friends. He became very close to his grandmother by following her to the church to worship and praise God. Sometimes he could then fast and pray to God to empower and give him the confidence to quit having relationships with friends who will ruin his life. His grandmother who was formerly a member of a strong secret society, was already converted into a born-again christian despite the warnings she received from David's parents who were also members and some other people who knew what the consequences might be for doing what she just did. David, who was also enjoying some financial supports from her, was becoming interested in attending the church all too often. The man, who assisted him in going to register for the second time in the place where he was working—the man who married one of his elder sisters, was also giving him some little financial supports.

They say, "Good luck come to those who does not include it in their plans," this is how it was to David. He met a boy who had invited him to another state to work for them, meanwhile it was rumored that that state was the center were people were using human beings for rituals in making money, which was popularly known to be blood-money in Nigeria. David's mother and his sister warned him not to travel to that state, but because he was money-conscious and thought of not losing the opportunity to become rich, he left for the job. Getting there with one of his co-worker and friend, they were able to meet the man who was an architect, a building engineer, and a landscape planner. The man's heart was replenished with joy immediately he saw them. He has seen the job done before by the company where they work, and there was no way he could hire that company to work for him because he will never be able to afford to pay them, knowing them to be the best in all over the country in designing and structuring the Queen Elizabethan's-like gate. Because this company had earned a high level of reputation, they had come to make it clear that they could only work for the rich and classy people.

David and his friend were still afraid that one day, they were going to be killed for rituals in making money even as the man tend to be nice to them—to convince them of thinking positively about him, knowing already what was in their mind. Despite all these, David and his friend were still able to do some of the work and brought out the good qualities of their work to the man and the entire city, exhibiting a different design and form of gate to attract their attentions. As the man saw this, he refused to pay them their money, because, he was afraid they were going to run away, and if they do, it will definitely cause him a big loss as he was still having so many other sites where he needed to build houses and install these new design and form of gates. David, so money-conscious, was not prepared to go back home. He was ready to stay and commence a new life over there as he was thrilled with joy and exaltation with is new life, seeing himself being useful to the society. Every time, they were given money to feed and and to take good proper care of themselves, with beautiful accommodation they were not paying for. He was prepared to live his life there, knowing one day he would be elevated and dazzled. He was able to dine in one of the university students canteen everyday which he find delights in doing since he could have the chance to get close to the university students. He knew he has wronged so many people and that they want him dead, that this opportunity had arrived, he did not want to take it on granted. But, the problem was his friend whom they were both working together—who started that work two years before David, but he was later learning some new skills from him, whom with his shrewd idea and the little education he had acquired, believed he could be able to change water into wine and was proving it by being able to do whatever he laid his hands upon to do. His friend who was a Muslim and had grew up, living with the owner and proprietor of their company who later died some months before David's arrival, was always satisfied with the little things he was having and was not money-conscious, but the problem about him was that he was poor and always needed help from other people even when he was praised by everybody for his sincerity and horse-power life style. Having calculated the total money they had worked and were supposed to be paid, he begged David to let them go back home, lying to him that he was sick and needed to go get some treatments before finally returning back to stay. The man who came to like David and trust him, maybe because of his talent and creative skills in bringing out new designs to beautify the jobs and make it different from what has been done before or for his rationalism, at a time, he wanted him to befriend his only sister who was a student in the university and was living in the campus and had come to visit him during her holiday period. Because of this, he gave them all the money they had worked for, and in addition, he gave them some extra money for transportation for going and coming back, pleading to them and expecting them to return back soon, so that they could finish the projects in time. Immediately they received the money, they went straight to the city's bus station or rather referred to as a park to get a bus to go back home.

Reaching home, David and his friend left each other and scheduled to meet again the next three days. David reached his house and presented to his mother some of the bread and a roasted meat he bought for her. She was so contented, not because of what he bought for her, but because of how she was seeing him transformed his life back to the innocent little boy she gave birth to; she was so happy for him.

He was becoming a talk of the town as many mothers were then pointing to him as an object lesson for their children to emulate. Everything he was doing, he was doing with self-admiration. He was becoming a man he always dreamed to be as he could spend his own money without fear or favor. Some days after he enjoyed himself and has met with his friend again to inquire of how and when they will be returning back to go and finish the projects they already laid down. The boy entreated him to give him more time and promised not to disappoint him. But the more he meet him to inquire, the more he kept promising and promising, and the more he was spending the little money that was left with him.

One day, on a cool evening with the stars and moon shining from the sky. He went to visit one of his old friend who believed he was concealing himself from them because he was making money from his work. He tried to soothe him by accepting to follow him to go and smoke marijuana in one of their favorite smoking spot, where he vowed never to step his feet again. Reaching there, he met some of his other friends. He greeted them and ordered and paid for more marijuana to be served for all of them which he was praised for. As he sat in one of the chair, smoking and listening to Fela Anikulapo's music with them, seeing more people coming in and some going out, he tried to listen carefully to see if he could grasp what exactly the message was. He came to comprehend that Fela was trying to tell the youths of the country most especially, that there was a need for a revolution even if the government intend to stop it by dispatching soldiers all over the cities in the country. The more he was listening, he came to hear him sing about democracy and describing it as a demonstration of craze—crazy demonstration. He was also been able to delineate how the rich are using the poor just like their tools. David said, he knew he was saying the truth about the problem in the country and he was the only one who was not afraid to speak out on behalf of the people even when the government kept arresting and jailing him, but he kept singing, because music was his weapon, the only way he could reach out to everybody in the country to fathom what was going on, and how the government were violating their rights as citizens and as human beings.

When he heard him sing about democracy and describe it to be a demonstration of craze, what came to his head was how could democracy be a demonstration of craze when he had heard and read in some books and newspapers that, democracy is the best form of government, and moreover since he understood that the U.s and Great Britain and other countries in the west were practising this democracy, so he believed it could only be a demonstration of craze in Africa but not in these countries mentioned above. He has not actually experienced what democracy was at that time since he was just a little kid who could neither speak or hear what was happening around him when his country once experienced it. But, he was told that the so-called democratic government was a government that was terminated with the devastation of the country's economy, with corruption and mismanagement, and then leading them to both political and economic crisis just like the military regime did. It was in his later life in the future when he was living in the western world where he had once believed democracy can be best explained as, government of the people, by the people, and for the people. In other words, it can be explained as, the treatments of every citizens in a country fairly and equally, and their rights and willingness to participate in deciding their choice in leadership. But, he came to observe that, even in the western world including the U.s. that this democracy that has been preached was never ever been practiced.

Long time ago in the U.s. where people pretend to acknowledge the existence of this democracy, black people were not allowed to vote. Just because of their color of race, they were being denied their rights as citizens of the country where they were born and live. David said, he was asking himself if that was what democracy was truly about. He said as he continued to scan through this word DEMOCRACY and what it truly stands for, he came to agree with this musician, Fela Anikulapo's Kuti's formulated theory, as he sees the living burying the living with different foul political strategies, calling it democracy, which actually is a demonstration of crazibility, as he may refer it to be in his advance English grammar. David said, he keep asking himself when will people ever think of changing this democracy of how the rich get richer and the poor die of starvation? But David also said,"It is more better to have an unfair democracy than to have a good dictator, because, if that dictator is good, he would not want that power for himself alone, knowing it to be a life of greed and insane ideology."

Because of his friend's delay, they finally gave up the conception of going back to finish the projects they left behind, and the landscape planner who was sponsoring it was infuriated and decided to look for another set of workers to get it finished, making David to lose the big opportunity he thought was going to lead him to his dream. They say, "Friends can assist you to the place where you can achieve your dream, but they can also make you lose everything you have worked for all of your life and lead you to your grave," this was how it was to David.

He was beginning to be close to his old friends again, spending the money he was been paid for his art work lavishly for himself and for his friends who became very close to him. He was been able to encouraged some of them to get themselves useful by learning a professional job like his own. Some of them who were tickled by the money he was making and how he was spending it, quickly made a decision to follow his foot step to learn the same work with him or learn a different one. He said, as he saw this, his heart was ease and brimmed with felicity as he could see that he was able to make an impact on other people's life to become useful to their families and the society just as he did to his own life. As he continued to strive to become useful to his family and to the society where he was living, he also thought it was a good thing if he does not abstain himself from his vicious friends, instead try to help them build their lives by preaching to them the benefits to be achieved for many hard-work and good plans for the future. One day, as he continued by visiting one of their favorite smoking spot to smoke marijuana, he met with one of his old friend who use to demand from him, money for buying marijuana. He thought at the beginning when he first saw him, that he was going to ask him for money, but he was astounded to see the lad ordered for marijuana for everybody and paid for it. David, who understood this to be very strange, immediately decided to leave the spot, lying to them he was going to meet someone for a new job. The next day, he was informed of how the police had come to that spot to arrest some of the lads and shot the very lad that paid for his marijuana because he was trying to escape. From that day onward, he finally decided to quit going to that spot to smoke, instead he will buy it and take it home to hide in a covered place at night where no one could see him and smoke. His parents knew he was smoking marijuana, but had never seen him doing it even when people repeatedly inform them about it.

Traveling from one state to another, doing his work and making more money that he has never seen before in his life, he was then been able to afford good and expensive attires, having relationships with different girls and also saving some money with his father who became very proud of what he had become and forgiving him and helping him plan on how to establish his own company. Even as his life was becoming better with more money and good friends and different lovers, he was still unable to flush from his heart, the memory of how he loved the girl he once loved—that later disappointed him.

It was getting to three years that his immediate elder sister has arrived Spain and was married to one Spaniard because she needed a document to live there. With the prostitution work she was doing over there, she was able to affix almost the whole of her family with some of their vital needs. David and his family were starting to live happily better than they usually were. It was then David called his elder brother, ken, for the last time to inform him again of his plan for him.

He told him there was a means for him to leave the country to Europe by passing through land. Ken, who was so lured with the money his sister was sending to them and was always afraid to risk his life, refused to listen to him, thinking him to be insane for saying he could travel by land to Europe.

David who was a great thinker, called some of his friends several times to smoke marijuana, and at the spot, he will inform and desired their opinions upon the prospect of success for them in the future. He also explained to them what his future plan was and how rich he was going to become with the art work he was doing, not knowing his plans were making them unhappy as they could see him to be too ambitious in life. His friends were already hating him more and more, but still pretending to be his friends by not showing him the face of hate. The boy, who befriend the only girl he had loved and was unable to make love to, was able to get a visa to travel to Holland with the help of his elder brother who returned from Europe and was financially loaded. He was calling the girl, beseeching of her to wait for him to return back, and was also warning her not to ever think of starting a relationship with another man. But, the girl was still in love with David and she could not help herself to forget about him, so she tried to plead for forgiveness more and more by coming to his house to see him, even when he kept rejecting her and disapproving of renewing the relationship.

From the money he saved with his father, in addition to the money his elder sister in Spain, Tina sent to him to buy some of his working tools; he was also able to design and structure a very expensive gate and placed it for sale, with the price five times the money he spent. He was so pleased with himself that he did this, and so was his family and his friends who admired his brilliant work and lauded him for it. As he was waiting for the gate to be sold and for him to invest the money on another gate and have his own workshop and purchase some of the tools he might needed for his work, he met one of his former schoolmate Harrison, whom they had both be friends right from his childhood in the primary school and in the secondary school. The both of them were so delighted when they met each other for the first time after more than two years. They were two people whose their souls merged, but because of his arrogant life in the secondary school, the relationship was impaired and he never saw him again since he failed his exam and left the school. But, instantly when he saw him, he said he wish he did not.

His friend Harrison was already in his second year at the university, and was just returning back from school when they both met. He was so ashamed that his friend was telling him about his school life which he had always wanted to have and was unable to. Harrison was also able to mention the list of the names of all their former schoolmates who were also studying at the university, not knowing how much pains he was about to bring to his friend's life. After he met and discussed about school with him, his life never became the same again. He could no longer travel to work, but he was able to spend the little money with him with his friends to smoke marijuana, drink beer, and meditate and preach to his arrogant friends about his visions for the future—which was becoming too obvious, making them hate him more and more, thinking he was just bragging and wanting to fool them.

One day, he came back home to meet Ken, his elder brother complaining to his father about his grandmother, saying, he was tired of living with her and that it will be better if he can go rent another house and be living alone. But, when David asked him who was going to be responsible for the funds, he was told his elder sister, Tina had already promised to do it. He was deeply hurt inside and was ashamed of Ken for doing what he was doing, always wanting to be a receiver and not a giver, He could not help explain how his brother would ever think of waiting for his younger sister to travel to Europe to be using her body to be working as a prostitute and later sending them the money to live an extravagant life there in Africa. He knew this was just a way many families around the country, mostly in the city were he was born and was living, were exploiting their children, particularly the girls.

It was at the middle of the year when the news broke out about the sudden death of the military dictator, General Sani Abacha. It was rumored that he was poisoned by some of the India prostitutes imported to him by his close chum and then minister of defense and later minister of the Federal capital territory (F.C.T), Lt-General J.T Useni. But after some days of investigation, it was later discovered that he did not die of poison, instead of Viagra which he took to have sex with the prostitutes. Indeed, no one actually believed that, but the mystery of his death remained unsolved till this day and no one cares because his death brought joy and merry making to the entire nation.

It was almost at the same period of time that the country were participating for the first time in the World Cup football competition which was hosted by the French. Everybody were celebrating as the national team won their match with Spain, because Spain was leading by 2-1, and later lost the match to Nigerians by 2-3. The last goal which was a notable and unforgettable goal to all Nigerians drove them mad to celebration and jubilation, and for awhile made them to be oblivious of their adversity. Every time he said he recollects this memory, he could reckon the existence of gods that guides and trail along with the game, particularly at the time of victory. He said, he could see football (soccer) to be the most interesting sport in the world and how the competitions are encompassed with a high spirit. It is the most populous and enjoyable sport in the world as it could bring people together even in their time of conflicts, but can also split people depends on how fanatic they are. But, when everybody were celebrating the victory over Spain, David was alone at the back of their house, smoking marijuana and meditating. He said the demons that he thought he had once defeated and cast into the lake of fire and watched them burning, came back flying directly, piercing through his heart down to his soul, and he was unable to be in control of himself. Every problems that he was undergoing, were making him detest his life and think of resolving the problem, only by traveling out of the country. He said he could see his heart burning at the time he saw people celebrating when there was an herculean task awaits for them to tackle as a new transition government was already in power and the entire nation was waiting for an election to be conducted, so that power can be restored back to a democratic government, which he himself was skeptical about because there was never he could take his leaders at their words. All these subjects of thoughts accumulated and turned into a maelstrom, quickly made him to take the decision of running away to a land he had no idea where.

First, in the context of his brother Ken, lavishing his sister's money and continuously to hope and depend on her, and was blissfully unaware what the future outcome will be. Secondly, the inferiority complex he felt about himself because it was rumored that the boy who befriend the girl he had loved and later traveled to Holland, was about to return back to marry her and take her away. Thirdly, he saw that majority of his Secondary Schoolmates were about to become graduates from the various universities around the nation, and no matter how much he make there, he will never be able to fit into their midst. The last and the worst agenda that unease him more than any other person living in the country—which he prayed not to experience, was the political crisis that he thought was probably going to or less extend to an outbreak of war. But, during this period, most of the citizens were showing more optimism about the future of the country, believing in democracy, and believing it was at the right time, and with faith, believing it was surely coming to them. David said, with this situation, he came to believe that Fela Anikulapo was right when he said the people were living in a life of suffering and smiling. But, he also believe that people should not cease to have faith, particularly when it come to a political and economic crisis of any country if only they are able to achieve democracy first, because democracy as they say, is a state of mind and idea, and it does takes time to mature and be prosperous, and when it does, good things will always come out of it.

With his mind already preoccupied, he knew he had to leave the country; he knew it was the right time and the right thing for him to do, even if he understood that, "No one know the right thing to do, as the right thing to do can be the wrong thing, and the wrong thing can also be the right thing to do."

He said, with good observation, he could visualize how the the country was going to look like in the next years, since the leaders will not acknowledge the rights of the common citizens. He saw that there was nothing these median citizens could actually do about the corrupt and mismanagement of their leaders, except for them to be advert and be attentive as these leaders progressively and uninterruptedly with their unkind hearts of stone, commits these atrocious and mischievous deeds.

How could he get the money to travel out of the country to anywhere became the questions he was asking himself every time, dumping his job, selling his electronics sets and clothes to his friends and later spending the money in purchasing marijuana for himself and for his friends. When he tried to sell the gate he invested his money and could not, because the materials he used in structuring the gate was too expensive and he did not intend to sell it cheap so as to make some profits out of it. The energy, time, and the money he spent should not have to be a waste, so he thought—as he went to see his former schoolmate Harrison, whom he trusted, cherish, and loved not just as friend but also as a brother all his life, from his primary school years till his secondary school. His reason to meet with him was to disclose to him, his problems and see how he could help him think of what to do about it. He also discern that Harrison's eldest sister in Italy was building a house, so, he thought they might need the gate. But when he met him and explained his problems to him, what he expected of him was for him to say his sister will be very much interested in buying it or the people that his father was working for that were said to be wealthy people and might be interested as well, instead he took him to meet his father who was an herbalist and a soothsayer that predicts to people what their problems are and how to puzzle them out. Getting to Harrison's father, what he was seeing was the man doing some incantations, spitting out words he had never in his whole life heard before, and later telling him he has seen his future shuttered by fame and fortune. He later asked him to take a bath with the soap he said he specially prepared for him, knowing he was going to come to meet him, and at the end, demanding money from him.

As he arrived home that night unable to sleep, he sat down and started thinking. He said he could recollect how he loathe his mother long time ago for doing this, now it was his turn. Then, he immediately recalled a quote from the great Shakespeare's play MACBETH, which says, "The forces of evil often tell us the truth in order to destroy us." Although, he never believed in these people or has he ever had the faith, maybe that was the reason it was not working for him, even when he has heard many people laud and worship them for their works.

Five days later after he had waited hopelessly to dispose off his gate and still could not, he quit using the soap to bath the way he was instructed by the witch doctor, and decided to go and confess his sins to God, doing so by going to meet a Reverend father in the catholic church which he was invited by a friend to attend and he later fell in love with the way and method that they worship. He said, attending the catholic church had really made him to beginning to have more interest in worshiping God as a christian as he could see them pray silently and preach the gospel with a very calm and mature manner and with audible voices, unlike when he was attending the pentecostal church with his grandmother, hearing them preach and pray with their voices so high that he barely hear what they say; he said sometimes it could drive him crazy. What impresses him most about the catholic church was how they sing their hymns. He was not a religious person, neither was he a pagan. He believed in everything, probably to benefit from it or to generate pleasure. That was the truth, the substantial truth, he was money-conscious and was willing to do anything to succeed.

Getting to the church and having an appointment with one Reverend Father Francis, whom he confessed all his sins to and asking him to pray for him. But after Father Francis finished praying for him, he beseeched him to help him to look for someone to purchase his gate. Father Francis, who knew his intentions already of how much he needed that money to travel out of the country, berated him, but later called him back to advise him to be patience, so as for God to manifest to him the right direction to take.

So many days went by and David still was unable to sell the gate. Pessimism and frustration overtook him, and he thought of choosing a different direction. "It is probable to see you come across formidable obstacles when you are on the verge of achieving your goal, because of the impatience and anxiety that might be involved in it." It was not that he could not have sold the gate very easily, but because he was in a hurry to do so, so it was delayed.

One morning immediately he woke up, he went to meet his elder sister, whom her husband was very supportive in raising funds for him to purchase one fellow-used welding machine, which he later sold and spent the money in buying marijuana and smoking it with his friends. He thought it will be better if he uncover his heart and make her know his plans to travel abroad. But, before he could open his mouth to say something, she was already telling him not to bother himself to, that she planned to take him to their so-called spiritual leader of the Cherubim and Seraphim church she was attending. David did agreed to follow her there the next day, but when he returned home, he quickly went to stand in front of a mirror and watched himself very well and shed tears. He cried because, he was becoming a foe to almost all of his friends again at the time that he was penniless and hopeless. His family were also suspecting him of the different crimes that was being postured in his house. He became a nuisance and a laughing stock once again.

As he followed his sister to meet the spiritual man the next day, what he experienced there was a thing he knew was happening to many young young boys and girls around the world who feels it is a wise decision to take—to seek their fortune from a fortune-tellers or psychics and assign their lives to them after being extracted of their little money, providing them with rules that could possibly drive them to their graves. When he met with the man, he was told, next time he was coming to meet him to provide for him some seven white pieces of clothes, candles, feathers of chickens and so many other things David knew he could not afford as he was totally, financially broke. The truth was that, he actually did not come there to think of spending more money, but to seek for help of how he could sell his gate to raise funds for himself to prepare his documents to leave the country. At first, he thought it was a conspiracy between the so-called spiritual leader and his sister, but after he thought it all over again and again, he came to conclude that his sister will not be able to do a thing like that. He left, promising to return back within some few days, but deep inside his heart, he knew nothing was bringing him back there. He knew these people were just impostors and that they can only fool some people sometimes, but they cannot fool all the people all the time, according to the great Bob Marley.

Meanwhile, a month before then, he wrote a letter to his elder sister, Tina, the one living in Spain, whom he had a quarrel with, dropping the phone on her and telling her never to ever call him again, as he had unveiled to her his plans of traveling abroad and she had not approved of it. Getting home that night, his father came to meet him inside his room and calm him down, giving him her address in Spain and asking him to write a letter and send it to her. His father knew he could write to convince his sister of his plan, and he also knew it was a good and profitable plan not for him alone but for the whole of the family. His father knew his elder brother, Ken was not prepared to lead, and that David was, and that was what he wanted. David who took the address from him, sat down and wrote the letter, explaining to her the situation she was to face in the future if she continue to believe in using her body to make money. He also wrote to let her know that a man was supposed to be the one to be responsible to stand for the family not a woman. Furthermore what he said in the letter that touched her, was that she cannot continue to use her body, so she needed his assistance to eject out the whole family from their adversity. He made her also to think of being truthful to the man she had married and think of having a baby for him and not to lay her life to rescue her family by inflicting on herself the exertion of force, which might later cause her a cry of despair. He made her understand that she was not Jesus Christ who had come to die for the sins of the world.

That evening when he returned back home from the so-called spiritual leader or prophet the way his sister used to call him, the weather was a bit hot and he could not sleep, so he went to shower with the cold water he fetched from the tap. And, as he was about to lie down to sleep, someone knocked on his door, and when he opened to see who the person was, he found out it was his father, who sneaked into his room to whisper to him, not wanting to let anyone hear him break the news to him. He told him of how his sister sent a message to him to wait for her phone call. Immediately he heard this, he conceived the reason why she wanted to speak to him, and he knew it was all about how she was going to sponsor his trip to Europe.

Two days later, the money his sister sent to him through Ken, who did not fathom what was happening between the two of them, because he scandalized him in the letter he wrote to her and she knew already he was a parasite. In not up to one week, he was already having his passport in his hand, preparing to go and meet the man who was to prepare his traveling documents from Mali to Europe the way he was told. Since he had never left his country to another country before, he did not know what to do, but he knew he needed someone to give him some information on which route to take to Mali. There was nobody he could meet except his friend, Billy, who had stolen some money from his father and had tried to use it in sponsoring himself to Europe through land, but could not succeed because he became ill along the way and decided to return back home to wait for his mother who was living in the U.k. to come and take him there. Billy who has been one of the best friend he he was having, was the only person he thought he could trust to break the news to, and moreover, because he was having an experience of the trip and he understood the route better than any other person who has travel out of the country before.

It was 05:00 a.m, a very cool weather at the middle of February, the very time the country usually experience the best weather when it is not too hot. He picked up his hand luggage which was containing some of his few clothes—the hand luggage he bought a day before that day. Passing through the backyard of their house, he went to the place where he took a bus to the bus station, where he later stayed and waited for a luxury bus to take him to Lagos, the capital city and also the border town between Nigeria and the Republic of Benin. Before he left his state, at the bus station, he raised his head up and looked up to the sky and prayed silently inside his heart, saying, O' lord, it is your will that I have to leave to the land where I can go to achieve my dreams to return back here successfully to invest in my art work and become one of the most recognized and richest artist here in this country. Let Thy will be done O' lord. He finished praying and immediately get into the bus and they left.

When they arrived at Lagos, he took a taxi that was going to the capital city of Benin, known as Cotonou. Inside the taxi, there were another three girls and one boy. When they reached the border between the two countries, the immigration officers there, demanded for their passports which they all brought out and presented to them, but they were later asked to come down from the taxi so that they could be searched, and when they did, the immigration officers kept asking them questions of where they were going to and the reasons they were going there. Not to waste too much time, the driver of the taxi asked them to bring out some money so that they could present it along with the passport for the second time when they demanded for it, because that was exactly what they wanted. But when they gave them the money, they kept asking for more and more until they were satisfied and allowed them to pass with the taxi to the other side. When they arrived at the other side of the border, which was another country, the same incident occurred and the same bribery procedure were repeated. This was how it was repeated over and over until he was able to pass through four country's border and finally getting to Bamako, the capital city of Mali, where he was told by his sister to meet someone who was going to prepare his documents to leave to Europe.

As he arrived at the dusty, filthy, and crowded bus station, he stayed and waited for the boy to pick him up for more than two hours. Since it was his first time to be in that country, and was informed that the police there were not to be compared with the ones in his country who never care to show a sign of concerns on the issues of immigrants—legal or illegal. He could not wait more than he had already waited, since the people whom they had come together with the same bus, were advising him to follow them to the place where they were going to stay so that they can help him the next day to contact and locate the boy that he had come to meet. He knew that was the appropriate thing he would have to do, so he followed them. But, when they arrived there, he saw that it was a woman who owns the house and she was using it as a business place for prostitution. After he took his bath and was given a bed to sleep, he refused to eat anything, because it was too late for him to do so as the time was about 02.00 a.m, so, he fell asleep immediately.

The next morning when he woke up from sleep, he was astounded by the different girls he was seeing, dressing on panties and bras, with noises of the gist of arguments inside the room. He was given some food to eat and water to shower again, as the weather was too hot for him to resist, twice hotter than the one in his country. When the woman who owns the house finally succeeded in helping him contact the boy he came to meet, she called him to advise him of the many awful things that were happening there, telling him to be smart and wise. The boy, who later came with some of his other three friends, did not care to ask how the journey was, instead, he thanked the woman and came to meet him, asking him to enter the car, and when he did, the car drove off.

He was alone in a room which was given to him to be staying with another boy who was always absent in the house, leaving him behind and threatening him not to go out so as not to be arrested by the Malian policemen, who were always hunting for illegal immigrants, mostly Nigerians, to be deported back to their country of origin, due to how the European Union, the Moroccans, the Algerians, and the Libyans were said to be sponsoring and mounting pressure on them to prevent more Immigrants from coming to Europe—from what he was told, but the facts remain concealed since he never care to to know much about who were responsible. Although, he was very unhappy about this situation, how these people were hunting for them, whereas they were very many in his country and nobody cares what they were doing there or why they have come there. He came to understand that his country, Nigeria was a very free country where nobody show concerns on the issues of immigrants unlike these countries where he had passed to come to Mali, including Mali itself. He could see how their citizens were all having their identity cards to show they live there, and how the police were always controlling people, asking them to present their I.D cards. He saw that these countries were twice or thrice poorer than his country and yet they were still concerned about immigration control. It was not like he was not in support of the issuing of the I.D cards, but he was strictly against the control of immigrants who actually were of the same color of race and was in a country who with the same agreement signed by all the West African Countries, have the right to travel to any of these countries to live. He thought these countries should see it to be a good fortune as they see other people come into their country, because they will never come there to get any benefit except to spend more, maybe for tourism or for business. He knew the control was not just for security reasons, instead, for humiliating other Africans like them, because the police there, were never in the position to cause an impediment to people from other continents like the Asians or Europeans or Australians or Americans. They were not at all concerned about immigrants who were rich, but just immigrants who were on their own, passing by to another country. He said, he was so worried about this situation, because if Africans can degrade and humiliate other Africans like them, then what do they expect from the westerners who are rich and would want to protect their wealth. The country that he said astonished him most, was Burkina Faso, as he could see the people and the country enveloped in a huge and true life of poverty. In his future life, he said when he recalled back this memory and asked himself, "If the world will be free one day, to see that people will now have the right to move from one country to another without a legal document." He said, "How glad and satisfied he will be, to see that every citizens of every country is also a citizen of the world with no legal document to prove it."

Three days later, with the help of the boy he came to meet, the middleman and also the planning the trip with the traffickers, he was able to talk to his sister on phone. His sister had then promised him not to fret himself about the situation, encouraging and promising him of a new advancement of the processing of the documents which he needed to board a plane to Morocco. She also told him she was going to pay the boy 3,000.00 dollars to get him there, and another 1,000.00 dollars to another person who will be responsible for getting him to refugee camp located in Ceuta, Spain. Hearing the amount of money mentioned by his sister, he was shocked, because he was afraid these boys were impostors and could trick her to collect this money from her, and at the end, dumping him there in an unknown country to find life for himself. It was not just what he thought about them, but it was what exactly was happening there. He knew something has to be done to prevent her sister from losing that money all for his sake.

More weeks came and passed while he was still staying at home without going out, because he was afraid not to be arrested by the police. He woke up one morning and could not find the boy they were both staying together in the same room. He decided to leave the house to go to the city center to take a view at the city and see what it looks like. When he arrived there, he saw that it was a busy place and there were not much police control just the way he was threatened. So luckily for him, he met some other people who were from the same country with him. Immediately they saw him, they knew he was a Nigerian like them, so they called him to introduce themselves to him and let him do the same. They later told him to be heedful not to be arrested by the police there or he will be sent back to his country. They also told him to always bring himself closer to them so as to get the day to day information on how to travel through land to Morocco. One last advise he was given was that, he should not allow his sister to be duped by the boy he referred to as the middleman.

When he reached home that day, his heart became troubled as he started thinking about his life again and what made him develop that thought of leaving his country and coming to end up there and getting his sister to be duped by an impostor. Even when he kept trying to erase this thoughts of trouble of dismay that was already stock-piled in his heart, he saw himself to be an innocent fool, who was weakened and deflated, and could not stand up like a man to defend himself or rather his sister from the impostor. From that moment, he thought of traveling through land with the other boys who had promised to take him along. He knew the trip was not going to be easy as he was well-informed by his new friends—the danger in traveling through the desert. But how could he trust them, knowing that they were all still there because they were not having the money to leave where they were. He knew he would have to leave, but not with them.

The next morning, he went out for the the second time and returned back home more hopefully of getting his plan executed—his plan of leaving and moving forth to where he actually left home to go, putting fear aside of him. He was continuously going out and coming back home with more hopes and more hopes, even when his friend whom they were both living together became aware of it and kept warning him to be careful of the police. One day, as he went out to meet his new friends whom then they were planning to leave together, he met another boy with three girls who were just coming from Nigeria and had just arrived the city, but were looking for a very cheap hotel to lodge. He actually volunteered to help them by showing them around the city and getting them to a very cheap hotel. At the beginning what he was told was that, they had first thought he was among those boys who were usually going to make deals with the police to arrest Nigerians who were just arriving the country newly, so that they can extort money from them and shared it with them. After they had introduced themselves and understood the reasons why they were both there and saw that they could render each other a help, they finally decided to take the trip together with another boy who was younger than the rest of them and was having lots of money sent to him by his two sisters in Italy. David knew inside him, he was never going to trust any of them, but he did not show it to them. After they had concluded to meet the next day to set on the trip, he went home to prepare himself, lying to the boy whom they were both living together, that he was returning back to his country and was no longer interested in traveling abroad. The boy felt sorry for him and even begged him to help him to deliver a message to his family in Nigeria. Before, he made this decisions to plan this trip, he had initially called his sister to inform her of his plans and warned her not to send any of them the money they all demanded for. That night, a night before the day he was to leave that place, his last night in that city tormented with the fear of police every time, he knelt down in the middle of the night and said a prayer secretly and quietly to God, Whom he always believe will send his guardian angel to guide him and not lead him astray. For that reason, he later wrote a poem at the time he was held behind bars in Italy.

SETTING ON THIS STRENUOUS JOURNEY OF MINE.

Rough and tough and narrow road
Full of thorns—this choice was mine.
My guardian angels protecting and guiding me to my dream,
To a time, my life I drove into a misery,
Seeking the beautiful things in it.
The horrible boring land where I depart,
To sail through the world of my imagination.
Heading to the place my soul belong,
Where everything could seem wonderful.
But the eyes of the people near me, I see
Piercing into my very soul.
My destiny to structure, one step to lose my life.
In my heart, I still can follow where it leads.
With my true faith, this I preach,
To outlast, not only with a horse-power,
But also, with sensibility and tenderness.

CHAPTER 15

I T WAS AT ABOUT 10:00 p.m, after a hot windy day, David and his friends were already prepared to leave the city to Gao, the border town of Mali with Algeria. With them, they were having five Malian passports they bought from some Malian policemen, which were hidden inside the underwear of one of the girls. The journey was scheduled to be at night as they could not do it at daytime for a simple reason not to be seen by people who will inform the police of it. Locked up in the back of a truck with some other people, say, twenty to twenty-five, with everyone head and face tied with a robe so as to prevent them from the dust and from being recognized by the police along the road-side as Nigerians. But, one thing they could not prevent was the susceptible, high sun heat, which was about forty-eight degrees centigrade. As they were all inside the truck, they were cautioned never to utter a word so as not to draw anyone's attention to themselves. Following the rules and conditions given to them, they were all able to reach to the end of the road, and were waiting for the truck to enter in a ferry, and to be taken to the other side of the road—the actual place they were going to. But, immediately they arrived, they were all stunned with a ray of hopelessness as the police there arrived to arrest everyone of them and took them to the police station and locked them up in a cell until the man that they were supposed to go meet finally came to settle the policemen with some money to free them. But after some days passed, it was finally revealed that the same man had set them up with the police so as to use this to install a little fear in their hearts, and to extract more money from them for the trip as he was to be their trafficker.

After staying for twenty days in this town called Gao, with a very hot weather of about forty-eight to fifty degrees centigrade, David could no longer resist the heat and was confused of what to do next, thinking if there was any way he could return back home. And, also there was still no way he could move further since he had already given some part of his money to the trafficker, and was only left with the little money that he had wrapped with a cellophane and was hiding it inside his anus, which might not take him to Morocco, his first destination before finally looking for a way to enter Spain. Meanwhile, he was smart enough to be able to seek and received the best information of how to travel through the Sahara desert to Algeria and later to Morocco. He wanted to leave on his own, knowing he was wasting his time there, and every person he encounter there seemed to rile him. He could no longer feed himself, and he could no longer think of asking his sister to send him more money, knowing the means of receiving money there was unreliable, as the person to receive the money was to be a person who is holding the country's national identity card—so he was informed.

He wanted to take a decision that he knew was appropriate for him at that very time, but he also knew if he did, there will be a consequence and he would have to pay a very big price maybe with his own life. So he decided to be patient and wait till the man said to be the trafficker was ready to leave. With a calm and confident manner—he was able to convince the trafficker that he will be paying him more money that he asked for, since he already knew he was having somebody abroad to send him the money.

It was twenty-nine days since they arrived in the town and he was almost bored to death. He woke up that morning, packed his few belongings together and was tensed in a great state of agitation and poised to return back to his country when the trafficker called him to relax and informed him that they will be leaving the next day to Algeria. He was electrified when he heard this. At first, he thought it to be a joke because he has heard it several times and demanded for his money to be refunded—an idea which the trafficker always responded to with a sharp rebuff. He asked him again and again so as to be very sure of what he was told, but all he could hear from him was, 'relax, we are moving tomorrow. But make sure you call your sister to get the money ready, o.k?'

The next day, he saw everybody in the house where he was living, busy getting themselves prepared to embark on a cohesive and grisly journey that they all set for themselves. He knew it was true that they were finally leaving that town brimmed with adversity, chaos and fear. But another thing came straight to his mind—something he was told that he tried not to recall—the desert.

He was informed many times by some other boys and girls who have tried to pass through the desert and were unable to succeed, that many people had lost their lives in the desert due to the too much heat and lack of water to drink and food to eat. He could not allow this to change is mind from sticking firmly to his dream of traveling to Europe. He was not in the position to give up this dream; he was prepared to make that sacrifice, pushing fear to rest there in Gao, with faith that the Lord God, Whom he believed in his name and trusted to always be at his back, guarding and protecting him.

The trafficker, who was having about thirty-six passengers including him, ordered for two old and one new range-rover jeeps to take them through the desert. He knew it was the right time for them to leave that town, as he too was tired of bribing the police there everyday. He has delayed them because he was waiting for his passengers to call their families and pimps who were living abroad to send him some part of the money before he could set up for the journey. He was a very smart man who has been in that business for more than six years with his wife and daughter they both had in that route. He was smart enough to an extent that the police in every border in the cities and towns came to recognize and respect him for his unlawful and bribery ways of life, as they were all constantly happy to see him come to give them money. David said, it was just all about demanding for money everywhere they arrived and everybody they were encountered with, without an excuse and much to argue about—just money, money, money, money, money and money everywhere they were and it was everything they were always demanding for.

Before he left his country to come to these places, he has always believed Muslims to be the most righteous people on Earth and will be unwilling to take bribes. He witnessed this at the time he traveled to some parts of the Northern states in his country, but as he now found this, he was beginning to come to understand the reason why people always say,"Traveling is a part of education." "Yes, it is true that we do not have to judge people when we do not go close to them to really know more about them."

Midnight at about 11:00 p.m, as the three range rover jeeps, loaded with the thirty-six passengers, each carrying twelve passengers, set-off for the journey which began with dust and mud as the jeeps drove along the dirt road. David with his face covered with robe, was beginning to think death was near him, as he experienced a wide range of suffocation which was unbearable to him. He wanted to give up and cry for help but he could not, believing if he did, he will be punished by being thrown out. He saw the girls inside and asked himself, how they could possibly resist this hazardous situation when he a man could not. He became very afraid of everybody there, knowing they were all desperate to get to Europe—but too desperate.

In this vast hot desert, where they might be seeking for help from some other people who were traveling too or the police who were close to the borders, here, they were still running from everybody so as not to be seen and be deported back—making the drivers plunge into the most extraneous and dangerous road, with rueful smiles, warned everybody not to utter a word. Speeding without rest, these drivers commonly referred to as Buzu, were kind of displaying their skills in driving, competing with themselves and doing it with joy and excitement, while the passengers inside the jeeps laments as they could all see themselves dig their own graves.

The journey continued till at a time the drivers decided to stop for awhile and take a rest and pray. And, as they finished praying, start up again with a dispute between themselves and were about to fight for something irrelevant as David was told by the trafficker. It all continued this same way with the same attitude until they were able to reach the place they were to sleep that night which was just for two hours. It was said that, in that desert, there were so many different kind of dangerous snakes, which drove more fears into David's mind, making him unable to close his eyes and sleep; he was vigilant and was very careful not to utter any word of offence to anybody, most particularly the drivers who he could always see as men with their hands stained with blood, seeing them bringing out their long sharp knives out every time and threatening to kill themselves; he was very afraid of them, knowing them to be barbarians and were capable of committing a felony and getting free since nobody was there to defend him or anybody who might fall a victim. He had long heard of these barbarians as murderers from so many people who have traveled passed that desert before. Inside him, he kept praying secretly to his God, still believing and trusting Him and laying all his faith in Him—and this was making him to be confident of reaching for victory.

As they finally arrived in Tamanrasett, Algeria's border town with Mali, a city with a population of about 150,000 people with a majority of them being the Tuareg people.

Long ago when he was a kid and was studying in the primary school, he has heard about these people and has seen their pictures in some books of how they look like, but he never really believed they exist until when he finally saw himself standing with them face to face and talking to them even if they could not understand what he was saying. He was very happy he was having this experience and felt a shiver of excitement, seeing what he thought many of his friends whom he left back in his home town would only be told as a tale.

In Tamanrasett, all the thirty-six passengers including David were all locked-up in a house fenced round by the trafficker who brought them there and also threatened them of the danger in that city. It was said that, in that city were police was always patrolling day and night, searching for the African immigrants to be deported back to the desert where they could either find their way back home or return sneaking back to the city.

The wall of the fence which was about thirteen feet high, was so high that no one could be able to see what was happening outside the compound of the house. It was to many of the people inside that compound, a dream turned into a nightmare as days went by and they continue to live in a lack of confidence in the man trafficking them and were all overwhelmed by a deep sense of despair.

Three weeks after they arrived Tamanrasett and were still complaining and disputing with the trafficker who already knew there was no way they could leave the city without him approving of it. He was smart enough to have used this opportunity once again to demand for more money from their families and pimps.

It was a cold, windy morning, at about 3:00 am when the whole world might have been asleep. A group of armed police men in their dark khaki uniforms with all their faces masked and unable to be recognized, dismantled the small iron gate and broke into the house were David and the other thirty-six passengers and the trafficker were living. With guns pointed to their faces, they were all woken up, bruised and beaten and were forced to stand, facing the wall and with their hands raised above their heads. But, immediately these policemen were aware that there was a little girl of six-year old among them, they felt pity for her and called the father who was the trafficker and demanded for some money which they were given and left them. Although, they were all supposed to be deported back to the desert, but because of the little girl, they were left and warned of the next tragedy that will shutter them.

That the man trafficking them has seen the handwriting on the wall, he took a swift decision to leave that town and to move forward, knowing if anyone there is deported back to the desert, his own money will be lost.

Just some few days after the raid, the trafficker gathered twenty of them, leaving behind sixteen and with the help of some of the policemen in that town, he was able to smuggle them out with three cars used as the city's taxi and headed to the next town, placing in their hands different country's passports. As they move forth to pass the tollgate between Tamanrasett, which was the border town with Mali and still was not considered as one of the states in Algeria, everything became very complex and complicated as they reached the tollgate of Regan, and were being controlled and examined one after the other by the policemen in the border, who could not actually confirm if the passports were truly for them—maybe because they were illiterates or because they preferred to obtain bribe and let them pass to where they were going to. From the many stories David was told about that border and how difficult it was, he was astonished as they all succeeded in passing through the tollgate easily without any obstruction.

Still moving ahead, succeeding in passing through many other difficult tollgates like Adras and Gadaya, and finally arriving in the country's capital city known as Algiers. There in Algiers, David said, he thought he was already in Europe and thought of not leaving there until when he later returned back to his senses to know that he was illegal there and, if caught by the police, he will definitely be deported back to the desert which he sworn never to return back to, and if unfortunately he did, he would take a new decision to give up the journey and return back to his country of origin.

That night was a night he knew he was close to his dream of seeing Europe and stepping his feet in it, as he climbed the luxury bus and sat in it and wait for the driver to start the bus and get them going. He saw that the bus was clean and was fully air conditioned, unlike when they were all bundled together like crayfish inside a small old range-rover jeep and driven through the dusty and sunny desert which he referred to as the hell on Earth.

As the bus drove from Algiers passed some smaller cities and later to Oran—one of the largest and most beautiful city in Algeria, if not in Africa, David said he saw that "The world is a beautiful place, and that we can only explore this beauty if only we leave where we are and go to see other places." He sat inside the luxury bus like a tourist: he came to see that, as he watched and enjoy the cities side attractions, he was reaping the rewards of the adverse circumstances and the weary way he just succeeded to pave a way through. He watched in wonderment and recall how he was in the desert, and as he did, he fell asleep till he finally arrived in Magnaya—the border town of Algeria with Morocco.

In Magnaya, there was no need for them to be in a hotel as long as there was a very wide and long valley where they could all build a hut and sleep inside—which already, more than three hundred people were living, most especially, Africans from Nigeria, Mali, Senegal, Ghana, Cameron and some few Algerians who were junkies and some others who already made it a tradition in coming there to sell hashish for some of the boys who were already getting addicted to it.

In that place, there were boys—some—who were deported from trying to find a way to enter Ceuta, where the refugee camp was—and some—who were living in Morocco before, but were penniless and have decided to come there to take some passengers to Morocco so that they could be able to raise some money to pay the middlemen there who will hand-over them to the Moroccan guides to take them to Ceuta.

As David and the other passengers arrived the valley, they were hailed by the people there, as the trafficker who brought them, popularly known as Papa Sabrina was recognized by very many of them. They were all given an already-built tent to stay, knowing business had come for them. For more than a week, they were still there, as the trafficker drew plans on how to leave there to beat the border of Morocco and go to Rabat, the second largest and populous city in Morocco. The trafficker who became a professional in this business, knew what was best for him to do, as he was having many passengers and wanted all of them to succeed in reaching where he promised them, so that he could be paid for his services rendered. He waited in that valley, trying to get more information on how the route was like and whether there were more police raids near the border between Algeria and Morocco. He knew he needed some professional guides with much experience to lead him and his passengers to pass that border to Rabat, so he ordered and begged them to come from different places they were in Morocco, using telephones to call them.

As the guides arrived to help him, they demanded for money first, knowing him to be a man of deception. He begged and begged until they finally agreed to help him after being paid some parts of the money he promised. All these stimulated his anger to make him demand for more money from his passengers before they could leave for the trip. Some of them were able to call their families and pimps abroad and ask them for money, but some were unable to—and among them was David, who already knew, no matter what, he will be able to reach his destination without the help of the man trafficking them, but he only promised to pay him when they arrive in Rabat, meanwhile, he had hidden some money inside his anus.

Two days after the guides the trafficker called arrived, they all set-off for the trip to go to Rabat, taking with them some bottles filled with water and milk and some loaves of bread. As they went on along the road, trekking twelve to sixteen hours a day without resting. It was the worst of all the journey David has made in his life, as they would have to hide from the policemen patrolling the bush and the borders. The very first night as they left, trekking thirteen hours, he was about to give up, but he could not, because there was nobody to care for him if he did. He saw death calling him and as he went close to meet him, he saw a very bright light shine from the darkness where death was hiding, and a voice called his name to return back. It was then he knew it was not going to be as easy as he thought before he started it. At night, as they all find a place to rest and to relax themselves before setting-off again, he left everybody, walking far from them and in the dusty bush, he knelt down and started praying. As they relentlessly trekked through this bush, beating one border to enter another, dogs barking at them and chasing them, hiding from the police and the citizens who were accustomed to this and were fond of screaming to draw the police attentions, some of the girls were raped first by some of the Algerian policemen and later by some of the Moroccan policemen, just to allow them pass without being deported back to Magnaya, they finally arrived at one of the train station, completely exhausted and rendered insensible. There at the train station, as they waited to enter one of the train scheduled to get them to Rabat, the police arrived with their cars chasing them and making them run in a helter-skelter dash, in a form of a random, zigzag motion, scattered all over the bush. David, who was now left with no food and no water, fainted, not knowing the time some passers-by Moroccan men and women in that village called Oujda, who saw him and took him to their house to feed and give him water until he regained back his lost strength and became fully conscious again and was able to go back to the train station where he met the rest of them again and finally took the train with them to go to Rabat. But, unexpectedly for him, another problem occurred while they were inside the train. About six to ten policemen walked, pumped themselves into the train, searching for them. He ran to the toilet to quickly conceal himself there, but unfortunately for him, someone was already there running from the the same policemen he was running from. He lost his faith in his God, thinking he was being abandoned until he could hear the whistle inside the train blow, showing a sign that the train was about to stop for people to come down. He prayed in his heart not to be caught as he was a Christian and could not utter it out in the midst of all the Moroccans there, who were ninety-six percents Muslim. But when the train stopped, he saw in surprise, as the policemen all came down, waving their hands to them and bidding them safe journey to their destinations.

It was 11:00 am, early in the morning as they arrived in Rabat, everyone of them rejoiced as their hearts were all full of joy and happiness, knowing they were near to their dreams and were in the pathway to a better future. Seeing Europe and stepping their feet there were their real goal, but that they had succeeded in reaching Morocco, there was a need for a good celebration first before thinking of any other thing in their present life and in the future. The man trafficking, who was still having some money with him, did not waste a single minute to send some of the boys who owned the house they were to stay, in going to the market to purchase some food stuffs for them to make a meal for themselves. Immediately they arrived from the market, in less than thirty minutes the food was already on fire, boiling and was ready to be served. They did not wait for the food to get cool-off before starting to eat it, as they were all at the point of starving to death. To the whole of them, they were already in Europe, as they could see themselves eat the legs and hands of the chickens they have begged from the Moroccan butchers who for long usually throw them away, but, as they see these

Sub-Saharan or the black skin African immigrants rush to have them, some of them decided to be making money with it by selling them. But the black skin Africans who, in their country could not afford to have legs of chickens for meat in their food, as it was very expensive over there, used this opportunity in getting them in a large quantity to cook and eat. David confessed the first time he started eating fifteen legs of chicken in a day—that was when he knew his dream of reaching Europe was not going to be a dream in a short period of time, but a reality. He also said, he knew he will be able to afford better meal and meat when he gets there—and that was what invigorated him to keep scuffling and struggling to get there in Europe, the wonderland he had dreamed of.

Sitting down together and eating mashed potato turned into what they refer to as fufu and tomatoes stew cooked with many legs of chicken, they were all enjoying the nice, tasty, savory, flavored, palatable and worth eating food, and at the same time, discussing about the tremendous and dangerous lives they had all lived in the desert. To David, it was sad and funny though, but it was very interesting, making him to believe,"In this world that we live, we all have to make a sacrifice in striving to have a better life for ourselves."

After two days that they arrived, the trafficker was prepared to return back to Tamanrasett, so as to go and bring some of the passengers he left there including his wife and daughter. Getting all of the passengers he brought to Rabat to pay all the money they agreed on became a very serious problem he could not address, as so many of them were not willing to pay but had agreed to the terms that were being given while in the desert just to make sure they arrive at their destinations. Among them was David, who was still having with him 300.00 dollars he was hiding in his anus. He had also borrowed to one of his friends another 200.00 dollars, but by the time he demanded for that money, his friend was upset and threatened to unveil this secret to everybody. David, knowing what the repercussion will be if the boy mistakenly tell the trafficker about this, quickly begged his friend to forget about the money, but the boy later paid him back the money and went straight to the trafficker to reveal everything to him. Reporting him to the trafficker was not enough for the boy David had lend money to, but fighting him was the best option to prove how much he did hated him and how he had vowed to take his revenge on him for having secretly had sex with one of the girls that was with them whom he was in love with and has spent so much for her. When David recollect what he did and how he made a promise to pay the trafficker the money he asked for, he knew he was about to be beaten by some gang of thugs hired by the man to beat up and stab anybody who refused to pay him his money. Although, he was told before how these people were stabbing and killing boys and girls that have offended them, so he knew it was time for him to get away from that city, since he was not ready to comply with anyone's rules. He paid the money he thought was necessary for him to pay, not what the trafficker demanded for, and he paid it with the little money he was hiding inside his anus—and promised to pay the rest immediately he was sent some money by his elder sister in Europe just to let peace reign and to have enough time for himself to think of what actually will be best for him to do next.

A week after they arrived in Ṭakadum which was a small city, outskirts of Rabat and was not very far from it. Takadum, being the cheapest area where they could live, seemed to be purposely designed to harbor the unemployed people, gangs of robbers, hashish dealers, smokers and illegal immigrants. It was a place where living was mispronounced for violence. Everyday was the same without news not being told of how a Moroccan boy stabbed his fellow Moroccan over an argument, or a Moroccan bandit tried to extort money from one African, stabbing him with a knife, or a Moroccan bandit threatening to kill his fellow Moroccan friend or an African boy or girl, first by stabbing himself. It was all violence everywhere in Takadum, that David said sometimes he wished he has not left his home to come over there to be slain by those Moroccan bandits who were not even afraid of the police, as they were been abandoned and were prepared to do whatever comes their way just to subsist. David saw that it was a problem the government of Morocco ignored, but needed an attention and a solution; he saw that the country was beautiful many times than the country he came from, but there were much hunger and starvation which was leading to different types of crimes. Every citizen's dream was to flee the country to another country, and the vast numbers of the people working and could offer themselves a meal were three times less than the unemployed who could neither feed themselves or plan for a future; he saw crime in that place like a thing which is appropriate for everyone to do and to survive, and it was done with pride. He knew there was no way he could withstand this threat of been beaten and robbed, so he collected the money which his sister had sent to him without bothering to pay the balance money he owed his the man who trafficked them to that place; he left after settling some of the boys he was living with and arrived in Tanger, where he started looking for how to get a connection to meet a middleman or a negogiator who will handle him to a guide to take him to Ceuta.

The longer he was living in Tanger, the faster is money was reducing to nothing—as he would have to pay more bills and hotel rents. He was afraid to pay the connections he met and was waiting to meet with the right connection so as not to be duped. He knew he should have to be very mindful and heedful to avoid being duped, because, if he mistakenly fall a victim, that will send him directly to meet his doom. Then he continued watching and warding, trying to get the best and to make the best out of his plans not to fall in the hands of impostors, thinking he was smart enough to have been able to reach where he was and moving foward would not be any cause for an alarm. Although he was advised by some of his friends who knew he was a generous person and might succeed and later be the one to send them money to pay for the same connection. He waited and came to realize that his money was almost finished, then he made up a choice not to wait too long for a trustworthy, commendable and honest man his friends were advising him to wait for, so he paid to another man.

.

CHAPTER 16

D AVID THEN ARRIVED IN SPAIN to deliver the wrapped hashish he swallowed in Ceuta to the house where he was told to go. He and his friends whom they both boarded the ship together were all inside a bus going to Malaga, one of the most populous drug city as he was told while he was still in the camp. The hashish he swallowed was beginning to show a sign of effect even when he tried not to complain by pretending everything was fine with him. He then entered into the toilet which was inside the bus just to try and see if he could poop out some of them as he could feel everything he swallowed pushing down to his anus and was ready to come out. He was deranged and could not sit in his seat and could not been able to poop it out when he visited the toilet, so he tried to be calm for a while and not to think about it so as for the situation to get better for him, but the more he intend to do so, the worse the situation became. So he thought it was best for him to call on the driver and report himself, because he was afraid that it might explode inside his stomach and if it does as he was told, that will be the end of him as a human being.

As he was about to go and meet the driver to inform him of his problem, one of the lads saw him and quickly ran to him, pleading to him not to do it, knowing they will all be implicated and that might outflow them from the bus and tie them up in jail. The boy started begging him for more than thirty minutes and he was still begging till at a time David could realize the problem was getting over and he was becoming himself again, free from the discomfort he was having. He then went back to his seat, relaxed himself and prayed for God to be with him, but vowed never to repeat this again in his life.

As he regained his strength back and could see and observe what was happening around him, he watched surprisingly from the bus when a teenage boy was kissing his girlfriend—a thing he was not accustomed to—that almost made him scream. He also could see how beautiful the roads and the cities were all like, and deep inside his mind, he was beginning to fall in love with what his eyes were seeing. He saw that civilization was to be referred to as a blessing rather than seeing it as a curse and condemning it. He immediately came to a conclusion to praise himself for all the sacrifices he has made to be where he was; he knew his dream was already been twisted out of poverty to a better future. In his heart, he rejoiced and felt a sign of hope come into his life for once again.

With the too much joy and happiness that was ready to stimulate inside his body, he was able to resist the pains and sufferings he was encountering till the bus then reached the bus station—their destination.

As they reached the bus station, they were all divided in groups, walking from one end of the bus station to the other end, patiently waiting for someone to call them and to pick them up from there to a house where they could discharge the wrapped hashish inside their stomach. In about thirty minutes a girl called one of them and asked him if he has arrived at the bus station and as the boy answered the phone and told her they were there, so she came out of the coffee bar near them and called a taxi to take her and the boy and two others to the house where people were already on await for the hashish to be delivered. In not more than thirty minutes since the first girl came, another two girls came, one of them walked straight to David and two of his friends whom they were standing together and asked them to follow her, and as they did, he saw that a car was already parked a hundred meters from the bus station to take them to a house.

Arriving the house which the girl showed to them by entering first—the first thing that occurred to David, was—what if the police now traced them to this place and see all the different and many drugs that was in that house? What will he say to his elder sister who has financially made this possible for him or his parents who were already waiting for him to come back home with abundant wealth?

Inside the house—were two girls and two other boys, David and his two other friends that they both came to deliver the hashish. Immediately they entered the house, they were given chilled milk to drink and mashed potato turned into what they usually refer to as fufu with soup and meat. In not more than ten minutes, as they finished eating the food, David said, he felt all the food he had eaten pushed down to his anus, that he thought something was added to it to purge everything in their stomach out. He ran straight to the toilet and started pooping the hashish out. He pooped out sixteen out of the fifty he had swallowed and went to relax in one of the couch in the parlor, and as he was sitting down and relaxing, one of the girls called him to come over to the toilet again and as he reached, she, with a quiet voice told him to wash the wrapped hashish with his hand, showing him some hand-gloves hung on the wall. David, who never knew this is how it was, was beginning to lament and regret the reason he had brought himself into this dangerous course which was very tempting and susceptible. With his hand, he washed the feces from all the wrapped hashish he pooped out and saw that it was clean and kept them in a bowl placed there for each and every one of them that had come for discharging. As he finished, he went to the parlor to relaxed and was watching he television as another boy went into the toilet to carry on with the same task he had set for himself, meanwhile, as David was sitting down watching the television, then appeared 2nd David. 'Wake up,' he shouted loudly at him. David who had forgotten he was the only person who could hear him, woke up from the trauma he was starting to practiced and getting used to. 'What is your problem?'asked 1st David oblivious he was with other people. Immediately he said this, one of the boys who was with him thought he was talking to him, so he quickly answered in a very low and calm voice. 'I did not say anything,' said the boy. 'O.k, I thought you were talking to me,' replied David, pretending he was not talking to a ghost which no other person could see except him alone. He quickly took an excuse to go down-stairs to buy something, and as he reached, he went straight to a park not far from where he had come down from and started his conversation with 2nd David, first, asking him to please live him alone so he could live his life. 'You are not going to live your life the way you want it,' replied 2nd David, moving closer to him as he was now alone by himself. 'I have come to remind you of the deal you signed with me.' 'The deal I signed with you, did I signed any deal with you?' he asked, riled and poised to pounce on him. Moving an inch backward and standing himself properly, 2nd David uttered his last word,'Was this your dream?'—and he vanished into the air. As David saw this, he could not help himself to resist what he had just experienced; he quickly ran away from the park and went straight to where he was to discharged the hashish he brought that was still remaining in his stomach. He opened the fridge and took out some milk and started drinking it so it could help him poop everything out easily and fast.

At about 3:00 a.m the next day, David woke up from where he was sleeping, ran swiftly to where the toilet was, opened the door and went in and started pooping. He pooped and pooped and pooped till he was weak and weary and was almost about to pass out. But when he finally stood up to wash and count how many he had pooped out, he saw that it was thirty-four and adding them to the sixteen that he kept in the bowl before, it became the total sum of fifty which he swallowed. He was elated with the thrill of his success and could not in any way help explain this—how he felt as he went to the parlor to break this news to everybody that he was prepared to leave that house the next morning after he might have been paid for the job well done.

Waking up in the morning at about 9:00 a.m, he accelerated passed the other boys to the bathroom to shower and got dressed and was waiting for the boss to come and pay him off. The other boys looked at him without uttering out a word, even as he greeted them and wanted to wish them good luck on their self-assured errand. One of the boys who swallowed a hundred pieces and was just a half-way of the process of discharging, called him and went close to him and hugged him and went back to the room he was sleeping. Then arrived the boss who complimented him on his job well done and paid him a hundred thousand pesetas which is equivalent to about 600.00 euros. With that money, he knew he could start his life, so he left the house without wasting more time to discuss anything with anybody and went straight to the bus station where he bought a ticket of the bus going to Vitoria, northern part of Spain where his sister was married and living with one Spaniard called Joaquin.

Leaving Malaga, a city in the south Spain to Vitoria, a city in the north was to him, like you are leaving Europe to Australia, as he was told the journey was going to take him eleven hours and that he would have to change his bus in Madrid. He quickly called sister on phone to inform her that he was already on his way to her house. Instantly, as she received that call, she said, as she later told David, all her heart was brimmed with joy and happiness and her eyes too were brimmed with tears, joyful tears, a thing we normally experience when we are able to achieve a goal after much sufferings and despairs. She said she thought it was a joke that her younger brother was coming to see her after many years that they had not seen each other.

David was so wearisome that he could not leave the seat he was sitting, even at the time the bus stopped for everybody to come down so as for them drink and eat for twenty minutes before getting back on the high-way leading to Madrid. He was inside the bus, thinking about everything—everything that he had experienced and the last word uttered by 2nd David. Although he knew exactly what 2nd David was trying to say to him, he knew he had come to warn him of this dangerous life he was about preparing for emplacement. He knew it was dangerous and that he tasted from it because he was desperate and most probably, he was a man who love adventure and always want to try everything—good and awful. But, he also knew pursuing his dream and knowing the reason he came to Europe was supposed to be his prior consent.

Reaching Madrid, he started asking questions on how to change a bus to Vitoria, even when he could not say a word in the spanish language and nobody around there was prepared to speak with him since almost all of them were stark illiterate when it comes to speaking and understanding English. He managed to talk to the taxi drivers about what exactly he was looking for, even if one of them could not utter a word in English, but he knew David was new in Spain and could not speak their language and he needed to go to the bus station where he could get a bus to Vitoria, so he called him to get into the taxi and drove him there. Reaching there after David had paid him, he parked his car somewhere near the bus station and followed him to where the bus to Vitoria was and helped him book a ticket and even assisted and followed him to the bus and begged the driver to put his eyes on him and he left. David, who was so excited to see his sister but was a little bit confused, as he could see himself tread warily into a world where English is not understood, a world where he thought people know it all but was seeing for himself that very many of them were less concerned about life and what it matters in reality. This actually prompted an increase of despairs in his heart, regarding these people to be ignorant.

Inside the bus, his sister had called him on phone for more than eight times and was asking him when the bus was going to reach Vitoria's bus station. Instantly, as the bus reached the bus station, David took his bag, hanging it on his arm and walked round the bust station. As he continued his strolling and sight-seeing, he saw his phone ringing and picked it up, and as he did, it was his sister who was already at the station waiting for him to come down. He then quickly walked to where she was, and as they saw each other, they embraced and hold themselves with tears of joy and happiness running down to their both cheeks.

His first night in Vitoria, he said he could recall, was a day he saw light defeat darkness as he could see himself in his sister's house with her husband, Joaquin. He saw Joaquin as a good man, a perfect gentleman and a salt of the Earth. Instantly, he liked him. He liked him, first, because he saw him as a kind person for marrying his sister so as for her to be legal and be able to stay in Spain. Secondly, because he was industrious. And thirdly, because he saw the way he was respecting his sister as a woman. He was convinced with this man's attitudes that the white people were very far from Africans. He saw that their ways of reasoning was quite different from that of the Africans, most especially when Joaquin asked him to come to the balcony to smoke with him and they laughed and talked even if they could both not understand each other's language. But, as time went on, with the help of his sister who was always at the middle between the two of them to be doing the interpretation, David was beginning to comprehend him more and know what he was capable of doing. He said he was astounded when he first learnt that his sister's husband was not too good at doing with books and he saw in his parlor, a shelf loaded with books. He also learnt that he was a workaholic which made him liked him, knowing he will be able to provide his sister's needs. But he as a smoker could see how Joaquin smoke and drink coffee and disliked him for that. The more he became closer to him, he felt pity for him, as he recalled how his family have structured a plan and have asked his sister for his pictures so they could take it to a juju priest so he can give them something to send to her to put in his food, and anytime she demand for anything from him, he will do it.

After David had spent three days with his sister and her husband, he knew it was time for him to decide for himself what to do, so he was worried and wanted to start working so he could earn money, because that was the reason he risked his life to come to Europe. He was tired of waking up every morning and not seeing Joaquin around because he went to work. He was also tired of waking up to be served tea and milk and butter and bread by his sister. He was beginning to see himself as a weak person who could not fight for himself. What if he was not having anybody in Spain like some other boys he knew while in camp, but were all working in the farm in Valencia and Murcia? He wanted to leave his sister and move ahead and go search for life for himself, and as he could not bear this state of feeling bored any longer, he wanted to leave, leave to a very far place where he was not having anybody, where he could find his future for himself, where no one he knew will be advising him of what is right and what is wrong, he wanted to see the world for himself, he wanted to be free as a bird and fly to everywhere around the four corners of the earth, he wanted to explore the beauty of the world.

He called his sister to tell him of his plan of traveling to Switzerland or England or if possible, to the United States. He needed help from his sister and her husband, Joaquin to move ahead. But his sister, who thought he was too much in a hurry, begged him to be patient so she could find a way for him to get a job there in Vitoria. In spite they knew, getting a job in Vitoria was as difficult as traveling to the moon basically because he could not speak the spanish language and most especially, there were very few black people there at that time and the people there were unfamiliar to other people's ways of life. There were few Moroccans and and south Americans who were not even friendly to black people. David said, he had beginning to hate this city, because he sees the way people stared at him while walking on the street, and immediately, he knew it was not a place he could stay as every moment he looked around him, everybody he sees were whites. He tried hiding this feelings inside him anytime he was with Joaquin and see people stare at them, but he could not, so he voiced out to his sister how humiliating it was for him. His sister who already had the same experience, knew what he was passing through and asked him to be patient for her husband to help him get a job so he can start working.

It seemed his sister told Joaquin all about David and how he was willing to leave to go find life for himself, so he called him to a coffee bar to have a conversation with him even if they both could not speak each other's language but with they were both demonstrating everything they meant to say with their hands—and at the end, they both understood what the other was trying to say. At the bar, David disclosed everything to him, opening his mind to him to see what he was about to say, but Joaquin only advised him to be patient and promised to take him to some places where he could lengthen his welding work which he thought he was perfect in doing. After they left there, they went to pick his sister with the delivery van joaquin was working with and then they all went to the biggest and largest supermarket in that city to shop. Getting to the supermarket and after they finished shopping, Joaquin asked David to choose anything he might like best. He walked around and could not see anything that he liked there, because he was already in a mood of melancholy. He tried to be make himself feel happy by going too close to where the music was coming from, in amazement he gazed at some of the cd's placed in a shelf for a moment, not knowing whether to pick some up or move away from there till joaquin saw him and walked closer to him and asked him to pick any one among them that he would want to listen to. He immediately picked up one of Bob Marley's cd's from the album of (uprising). He knew he needed a disc-man to play it, so he picked up one made by Sony and slotted in the cd and started playing it. As the sound of the music went to his brain, he felt a sense of relief and all his heart was brimmed with felicity. He was revived back to life by this music—and, as he was listening, he was singing along with it loudly but unaware that the people there were hearing him. joaquin who was completely astounded by this attitude, quickly asked his wife, Tina to call his brother to inform him that they were in a public place. Tina did what was right by calling him to a corner to edify him of how to live in Europe, letting him know that Europe was a different place unlike in Africa where everybody were habituated to noises and whispers.

To David, it was an embarrassment, as he was not allowed to do what he thinks pleases him most—which is listening to music and singing along with it. He wanted to go home, so he told his sister who too understood how he felt and asked Joaquin to pay for the things they bought and drive them home. Getting home, he went straight into one of the room in the apartment that his sister gave him, placing the earphone in his ear, he lied himself in the bed and started listening to Bob Marley's music. He was really enjoying this music because it was long he wanted to since he left his country and have not been able to get this very album and to listen to it. He said he believed too much on Bob's songs that a time it was almost driving him to a realm of becoming a fanatic. He said he loved Bob's music because what he expressed was wide spread and was not just songs but messages to most especially to Africans and to their once colonies. He said he fell in love with his beautiful and evocative music because he saw the truth in it, and being that he was already living with the whites, he was becoming to realize how discriminating many were when back at the time he was in Africa, he had believed every white people to be saints. He was beginning to regret why he was there and saw that life was more valuable than just playing with it; he was beginning to feel inferior and think of how to prove his color of race to be a superior one. But how could he ever think of this and how could he ever commence with this idea of looking to white people as a racist, when Joaquin, his sister's husband was always nice and kind to him and had loved his sister and cherished her not minding her color of race. As these thoughts came stumbling in his mind, he came to learn that, not every White person is bad just as not every Black or Indian or Chinese is. He said he knew it will be a very inappropriate thing for him to do by letting that idea of race be his problem, so he instantly took the decision to let it go out of his brain so he could focus on the real problems that brought him to Europe, which is money.

The next morning, his sister asked him to come with her to Bilbao, a city one hundred and fifty kilometers from Vitoria, so that they can go and purchase some ingredients to cook. David was astounded when he heard this, knowing they could get anything they want there in the supermarkets in Vitoria; he hesitated and wanted to stay at home, but his sister begged him to follow her.

At 9:00 a.m they were already in Bilbao. He saw that his sister was recognized by so many Africans there in calle San Francisco—the street mostly dominated by black Africans from Nigeria and Senegal and then Moroccans and Spaniards who were junkies. David who was so curious to know what was happening around there, watched and observed that drug dealing was the reason why too many Moroccans and these black Africans were perambulating. Along the street were different African shops were African foods and ingredients were sold. Moroccans meat shops and restaurants were in everywhere. And, as David continuously to watch with outstanding powers of observation, he saw how the business was going, how drug were purchased and paid for and how police on mufti were also observing from distance and how some of the drug dealers were arrested and taken away. The whole thing, though was unfamiliar to him but was also abnormal and extraneous to him, making him feel bewildered, dubious and uncertain about his future. It was weird to him as he recalled how he and his friends back at the time he was in the refugee camp in Ceuta, have discussed the issue of being a drug dealer. He saw the risks in it and how difficult it was to get things done without being caught by the police. He saw that the money was not worth it no matter how much you might be making from it, so he walked quickly to the shop where his sister was buying some African foods and told her he wanted to return back home immediately. His sister, who already knew what was happening, quickly finished with her shopping and took him back to Vitoria. From that day on, David searched his heart and come to find peace in it even when he was still very poor without a job and no means of getting money to start a life he had long wished for. He knew from the little experience he had had in that street—calle San Francisco that he was not fit to do a job like that and that he had not dreamed of being imprisoned for having sold drugs. He knew he could get a job if actually he will go finding in the place where there are very many Africans working in the farm in the southern part of Spain, so he was worried and wanted to leave to another place, anywhere but not in Vitoria where he was left with no hope of finding a job or Bilbao where he might be tempted to join the business of drug dealing.

So, he called his sister that night to let her know of his plan of traveling to Murcia, the southern part of Spain to find a job in the farm. Although he knew his sister wanted him to stay near her there in Vitoria or in Bilbao, but he also grasp what his future was going to become in jail if he decide to stay in Bilbao. He begged her to lend him some money and as she did, the next morning he took a bus and traveled to Murcia. In Murcia, he met some of his friends he knew back at the time they were in camp. Since they were all new in Europe and were all struggling to achieve the same life just like him, so he joined them and they went straight to a village where there was a possibility for them to work in the farm. As they reached, it was not as they were told. Things became more complex to an extent he was unable to handle it.

The first night he spent in that village called Torre Pacheco, it was like he has visited hell as he was unable to get a place to sleep and he and his friends had slept outside in the cold weather of winter during November period. He regretted it and had asked his God the reason He had made him to come to Europe. That same night he regretted why he was born black as he could see how his fellow Nigerians had drove them out of the house built inside a farm with no light which nobody was even paying for, allowing them to go and sleep in the cold winter. He hated them for that and swore never in his life to marry a black woman, because he said he thought at that time that a white person would not do that to his fellow white person, but later when he stayed longer in Europe, he came to see that a white person could do worse than that to his fellow white person. He saw the absurdity of the situation he was and thought that, to be black was to be evil as black people could not even help him when he was already beginning to view the racial injustice in the new world where he just placed himself. The next morning, since he and his friends were able to survive the strong winter cold, the next thing they could do was to leave that village seeing there was no hope living there to be blessed and cursed by God with cold driven into their bloods and veins. They left back to the city of Murcia, searching for the red cross for food and shelter. Meanwhile, as they were still searching, one of them became weak and was tired of having walked so many miles and still unable to locate where the red cross was. He called David and his other friends telling them he was buying a ticket and was traveling to Holland where his family were living. Just like a joke they entered one of the ticket office nearby and ask for the price of the ticket for the same day. He saw that his money was completed and he bought it and left to the airport immediately.

After David and his other friends spent two days with the red cross and were still unable to find a job for themselves, they were recommended to *albergue*, meaning shelter. There, they were able to shower and eat and sleep for another four days until most of them gave up the hope of getting a job there and left to other places. David continued to stay and search for a job everywhere in Murcia in no avail and later decided to return back to Vitoria as he ran out of cash to be living with is sister again.

He was so unhappy as he arrived Vitoria and was now living with his sister again. He tried to be patience due to how Joaquin was constantly encouraging him to be and was always providing for him everything he wanted like cigarettes and coffee which he was now getting accustomed to. He loved Joaquin for everything he was doing for him, but he disliked his sister because of her attitudes towards her husband and how she was cheating on him. He came to fathom that his own sister was not actually in love with Joaquin her husband, instead she was in love with another Spaniard called Alberto whom David liked but hated for knowing that his sister was married and was still trying to do everything he could to get her away from her husband. David was not pleased with this and was prepared to leave so as not to be seeing what his sister was doing. He wanted to leave to anywhere where he would be free and will not be seen by his sister. With this attitudes of his sister and what he has heard about women who were prostitutes, he came to a conclusion that "Marrying a whore was just like digging a grave to lie inside to be buried." He saw that there was no way anyone can please them than reap-out his soul and handle it to them. Although, Alberto did helped him in so many ways, trying to please him, knowing he was not co-operating, seeing him with his sister because she was married. He also understood that David liked him and would have been so glad to see him and his sister together if maybe she was not married.

David, who became so fretful since he could not get a job or get himself hook-up with something doing to raise money, was starting to dislike everybody living around him. He thought he could do better if he was not living with his sister, but where is he going to when he was not having anybody somewhere? He knew something had to be done, but what? He saw his life turned into a well of sorrows and hopelessness as he tried to search for a job and was still unable to come out a with a good result. He tried to plead with his sister once again for an assistance to leave to Switzerland or to the U.k. or even to the United States, but there was no way she could render that help as she had not even traveled out of Spain before and was not familiar with issues like this or how to handle it. Joaquin, who also was not having a good educational background could not provide any means of help for him, and moreover he was not happy at all that his brother in-law was not happy with the life he had met with in Spain. He thought it necessary for David to be thankful and grateful to his God that he was in Spain, but he was astonished as the little boy aim was not actually to live in Spain and was too ambitious to leave to anywhere not minding what he will encounter there. He was so concerned about this issue and tried to oppose this idea and make him believe Spain, for long was not good at harboring immigrants, but also promised him, with time everything will be different and Africans and other immigrants will be seen everywhere just as it was in France, Holland and other countries David was willing to go and live.

After much dissension between him and his sister for some days, she finally decided to inform Alberto to assist them to the police station to get an information of what type of document his brother might need to travel to the places he wished to go to. Alberto, whom to David, would have been far better to be pronounced his sister's husband not Joaquin because he was more social and the family have wanted him to marry his sister, unlike Joaquin whom his family had opposed the relationship and did not appear at his wedding day with David's sister. He said he saw in the both of them good humor and caring for his sister and they were both having a job, but Alberto was an addicted marijuana and hashish smoker—making him not to think of him, a man who can make a good father. Joaquin, on the other side was closed to his family more than he was closed to his wife.

At the police station, he was asked to provide some requirements to enable him to be able to apply for a refugee travel document (*titulo de viaje*) which he needed in addition to the registration certificate, residence, and working permit he was issued when he was in the refugee camp. But he was told to wait until a letter will be sent to them for him to come over to station to get it.

David, who waited for one week, could not wait any longer, as he was then thinking this was a way for them to hold him down not to travel to where he wished to go. He begged his sister for another money and left to Valencia, where he went sleeping in *albergue*, (shelter)—a place owned by some catholic for the homeless who were mostly junkies. After spending one week there with some other immigrants from all over the world, mostly Africans, Moroccans, Europeans from East Europe and Asians, and were still without jobs, they were all driven out to go get life on their own. Then he went sleeping under the bridge in the artificial made valley not far from the bus station. Inside the valley at night, many things were happening, things he was scared of—drug dealings and prostitution. He said he never thought he would succeed in getting out of that valley when he was sleeping there in a strong December winter cold, days after days and weeks after weeks, eating garbage from the dust-bins.

After he searched for a job with no avail, he decided to come back to his sister again to celebrate the Christmas and New year which he enjoyed as never before, because it was his first time of experiencing it in a western world. It was splendid, he said. He, his sister and Joaquin went to shop in different shopping centers and supermarkets and at night they gathered together, opened a bottle of champagne, served themselves, drank and celebrated. He was happy even with no money in his pocket, as Joaquin and his sister were always responsible for buying him packets of Marlborough cigarette and the next day, Joaquin cooked a good, palatable Spanish food which he was almost getting to love and preferred more than African foods. But after his sister and her husband went inside their room to sleep and he was then all alone by himself, he looked from the window to the street very far as to the Mercedes Benz manufacturing company not too far from their house, he saw that the street was gleaming with lights of different color. As he continued to take this view and saw flash of lights and colors shining from bright surfaces all around the roads and cities, he became happy again and hope crawled back into is heart, knowing the lights glorifies hope. Instantly he recollect the details of how he spent his last Christmas and New year back in his country when there was a total blackout and he could not find the candle he has since hidden inside his room to see what was happening around him. As his memory came back to him, he left where he was standing and watching from the window, then reclining on a sofa and started doing a hard thinking of his past and present life and which is better. The lights which he could see showed there was still a possibility for him to achieve his dream, and as he continued this thought, joy and exaltation filled his heart and he was happy once again.

Two days after Christmas, David left his sister's house to return back to Valencia to continue with the job searching. Luckily for him he was offered a job in a village two hundred kilometers from Valencia by a group of social assistance. He was given a contract to sign to work for three months in an onion farm. He was so excited as he signed the contract and waited to commence with his new job the next morning. He quickly called his sister to break the news to her. His sister was so happy for him that he had found a job, but she also advised him to be careful and to be tolerant as she knew he might go there to face some racists who might insult him.

The next morning, he bought a ticket and was already inside the train going to his new place of work. Inside the train, he had met with some other people who were going towards the same direction. He went closer to them, showing to them the address he was given and asking them how he could locate the farm, fortunately for him, he saw that he was talking to some of the people who were already working there. He was happy that things were moving smoothly for him and he was beginning to realize the essence of being patient and keep moving in search of what you want in life. He could not wait to start working like a jackass, even when he was not ordered to. The first day was a very long day for him, but he worked more than any other person there even since he was a new person and was having a little or no experience on how the job was done. He was working too hard more than the rest of the workers only because he was trying to convince his boss of how capable and hardworking he really was, so he could be given an opportunity to stay and work there forever. He was so contented most especially as he received his first weekly salary.

With money already in his hand, he first bought a jacket, as the weather was still very cold and he was still sleeping in an open space under the bridge in the valley. He was sleeping one night, covered with a blanket when a very pretty white girl walked closer to him and wake him up, asking if he was with cocaine to sell for her. He shouted on her as he was very upset being disturbed from his sleep. But, he was very surprised, as the girl spoke fluently in English, telling him she was sorry, and that she thought he was one of the Africans who usually come over to the valley to sell drugs for them. He saw that she was beautiful, but he was sad to hear that she was into drugs. He brought out a cigarette and lit it with fire, and as he did, the girl asked him for one. He gave her a cigarette and she collected and lit it and sat down with him and continued to smoke her cigarette and interact with him in English language. After she finished smoking, she asked him if he was having some money with him, so that he could offer it and make love to her. He swiftly and carefully brought out 2,000.00 pesetas out, claiming that to be the only money he was having with him. She took it from him and stripped herself naked, inviting him to have sex with her. It was his first time to see a white girl naked and he was too excited to have sex with her, starting first by licking all her body and later fixed his penis inside her already wet cunt and ride on her crazily as she scream and scream and scream and hold him tight and closed to her body till she cum first and he later cum and the both of them fell from each others body and relaxed on top of his own-made bed inside the winter cold under the bridge. After she left, he was happy that she had come to revive him after many months that he had not had sex. He was the most happiest human being, because he had had sex and most especially, he had had it with a white woman. The next day, he thought it will be appropriate for him to get a place to live that he was working and was getting paid. The thing he did was to look for some of his fellow country people who already knew he was working, and for that reason had given him a chance to be sleeping in the sitting room and be paying 20,000 pesetas, the then Spanish currency which if converted to euro, will be approximately 120.00 euros. He was happy with his new life and was beginning to call his families and some of his friends in Africa, letting them know he was already in Europe and in few time will be coming back home with money in his pockets. As he continued to call them, one of his friends demanded for his phone number and gave it to one of their friends living in Holland.

One evening, immediately he closed from work, he washed his body and was in a hurry to go home to purchase some food stuffs before the supermarket will be closed. His phone ringed and he picked it up to see who was calling, but, as he raised the phone very well to see the number, he saw that it was a call coming from another country in Europe. He picked it up ans asked,'who is this?' Then he heard a voice called his name, 'it's me Chelsea.' He was shocked and stood for some seconds motionless and dumb. 'Hello, are you hearing me?' cried the voice. 'Yes, I am hearing you replied David, and then they started talking—talking about their past lives and friends. David would have been the most happiest person to have heard someone tell him to come to Holland to be staying with him so he could get a job and live there, but this phone call set him in another life to make him see himself unfortunate and unhappy—unfortunate and unhappy, because Chelsea was one of his greatest enemy in life. He disliked him, because he was able to enticed his girlfriend with money and had sex with her when they were still in Africa. David, who decided to travel abroad because of the political situation of his country, has also wanted to prove to the woman he has loved and never been able to have sex with, that he was born to make it. And then, he was seeing himself having a conversation on phone with the man who has been behind the whole problems. He could remember how he shed tears for so many days because this boy enticed his girlfriend, won her heart, and had sex with her, left to abroad and was still communicating and making promises on how to return back home to marry her. He was in a state of confusion when he dropped the phone and sat in a chair along one of the streets in Valencia, thinking of how to overcome this temptation that was just beginning to become a way for him to change his plans. Holland, France, Switzerland, Germany, the U.k. and the U.s—were the countries he had chosen to go to live right before he arrived in Spain. He wanted to reject this offer and change his phone number so that there will be no means Chelsea could communicate with him, but he thought it over and over again and came to conclude that for Chelsea to offer him this opportunity when he knew how he disliked him since he took his girlfriend away from him, maybe it was a way for reconciliation, as Chelsea might have felt guilty. He has heard things about one of the smallest and mightiest country in Europe, called Holland, and this was an opportunity for him to be there, so why should he lose it because of a woman whom he once loved and later hated—a woman who caused him pains and adversity which he overcame. He searched his heart very well to know that he was moving towards the right direction if he decide to go to Holland, since he heard there were more job opportunities there and life will be more simple for him because Chelsea has told him everybody there speaks English. That same evening, he broke the news to his friends that they both living in the same apartment, telling them he was living, and the next morning he left Valencia and returned back to Vitoria where his sister was, to get himself prepared to go to Holland. Although, he was beginning to like his work, as the Spaniards there were good to him and were always trying to render him help in anyway he had wanted it. One of the girls had fell in love with him and had tried to communicate with him by demonstrating it with her hands since the both of them could not speak each others language.

To his sister's surprise, David called her to inform her that he was already in Vitoria and was waiting at the door. It was absolutely frightful, as she first heard this, thinking he was being arrested and brought there by the police, but when she opened the door and saw him alone with his bag on his hand, she was calm and called him inside. David, who knew how awkward it will be for him to inform his sister and her husband, Joaquin, of his decision to leave Spain to Holland, also knew what he would have to say to convince them that what he was doing, was the appropriate thing for him to be doing. He went straight to shower and after then he sat down quietly to tell his sister everything. She could not believe what she was hearing, but insisted he should have to wait to explain it better to Joaquin when he returns back from work. But when Joaquin arrived home and had taken his bath and had finished eating the food he was served, he called David and they both went to a coffee bar to discuss this issue. Joaquin who was a very hardworking truck driver, thought bringing him there to talk to him might facilitate everything. He thought he will be able to preach to him the good attitudes possessed by the Spaniards if that was the problem he was encountering, or he thought he will be able to analyse more on the hope of job and economic growth within some days and months in Spain. He tried in every way he could to convince him to stay, prophesying to him the prosperity that is installed for him if he agree to live in Spain. But his heart was already made up and he knew no-one was going to try to stop him. So, with the little money he had saved from the farm work he had just quit, without his sister's approval, he went to a ticket office to purchase a ticket of a flight scheduled for the next day. His sister, who could see how determined to leave he was, knew there was nothing she could do to stop him, she then took to a decision to support this plan and advised him to be careful.

It was the same day that he purchased a flight ticket to Amsterdam, the same day at about 09:00 p.m he left to Madrid, the capital city of Spain where he will be boarding his flight. Before 02:00 to 03:00 a.m, he was already at the bus station in Madrid. Since there was no transport means at that hour and he was not having anybody to call on or that he could go to his or her house, he slept there in the bus station and wake up early as 07:00 a.m to leave to the airport. At the airport, he waited till 05:00 p.m when his flight was to leave Madrid. Before he was given a boarding pass to board the flight, he was almost exhausted because it was the first time in his life that he was traveling by air and there was nobody there to assist him, making everything more complex, since he could not communicate with the people in their language. He ravel out the complicated moment and finally succeeded in getting himself into the flight and left to Holland. He said he had never seen a thing like that before, how the flight took-off and ascended into the sky and later descended and landed at the ground. It was funny-peculiar and was fascinating and was also enjoyable, because it was his first time to experience it.

When he arrived at Schiphol airport, he saw that everything were automatically changed and he was already in a different world—a world different from where he was coming from—a world where he could see everybody to be one. He was so delighted as he watched and observed the situations of how people were communicating with each others not regarding the color of race. He said, he saw Chinese, Blacks, Whites, Indians and Hispanics chat and giggled at jokes together. He also said he saw different people of different race work in the airport; and he quickly step into a strong conviction that all will be well in this new country that he has come to live. He was alleviated as he walked round the airport and did not come across anyone who asked him to present his documents. He then tried to walk out of the airport, since he was afraid not to meet with any of the immigration, but he was totally mystified by the signs directing him to exit. As he uninterruptedly walked round and could not find a way out, he went straight to the two black and one white policemen patrolling there and asked them boldly in English of how to exit the airport. Immediately they heard him speak, they knew already, he was new in Holland, so one of them asked him to come with him then, leading him out of the airport's exit gate. He asked him which city exactly he was going to. He also asked him to present out his documents and as he took a careful look at them and handled them back to him, he advised him not to ever come to Holland again without having his passport attached to the documents he was having. It was at then, David realized that his documents were still not complete even when he thought he was having everything already and could travel to anywhere without getting to encounter in an argument with the immigration.

As he walked out of the airport's gate, what he saw first was the big, large television screen outside Schiphol airport. He watched in wonderment as people of different ethnics walked, cycled, entered into the public transports, cars passed, tram passed, train moved passed, and many stood to watch the big, large television screen just like him. He stood agape, not knowing what to do then, but he fell in love with the country and the kind of people he believed all of them to be. 'Heaven is here on Earth,' he murmured to himself, still unable to move an inch.

After spending much time and yet still was unable to decide on what else needed to be done, he left were he was standing and walked hurriedly to one of the phone booth and slot some coins inside to call his friend, Chelsea, whom he came to meet. He dialed the numbers several times and could not reach him, not knowing he was supposed to add zero to the nine digit numbers he was dialing. He repeatedly dialed the numbers and was upset that it was not going, thinking his friend has wanted him to take the consequences of what happened between the two of them some years ago back in Africa. He was unhappy and lamented why he has not been heedful even to comprehend that his friend hated him because of the girl they have both loved. He regretted why he inflicted on himself these heavy casualties of complications and aggravations. In his own perspective, it was a humiliating defeat by his friend, and there was no way he could return back to Spain immediately, and there was no other person he knew as a friend or a member of his family that was living in Holland. He did not know what else to do, so he went to buy a ticket of the train going to Amsterdam. Getting there, he came down from the train and walked out of the train station, going to a place still unknown, but with faith, he continuously to walk along the road just like any other person living there before. As he walked some meters away from the station, he turned back to take a good look at it and saw Amsterdam Centraal Station, boldly written. It was later, when David was staying longer in Europe and was traveling to other places, that he came to learn that this Centraal Station was one of the most largest and busiest train station in Europe. He loved it, as he stood and watched it in awed silence. Standing was never going to do him any good than harm, he knew, so he continued to walk and watch the different lives people were living and how he could learn from them on how to live in one of the smallest but mightiest country in Europe called Holland. He said the thing that brought him joy, to make him be oblivious of the adversity he was, was that everywhere he set his eyes or stepped his feet, were black people, not just black people as they were in Spain, but distinguished black people. He saw himself to be a happy and a complete man, as he was ecstatic about what he was seeing. He said, with that, he came to believe that, "Everyone feels more comfortable when they are surrounded by people that looks like them."

In his later life in Europe, when he was in prison in Italy, as he recalled this day and how he felt about Amsterdam the first day he arrived there, he wrote a poem with a title Amsterdam.

AMSTERDAM.

Lowland surrounded by water.
The water overflow into a chamber
With beam bridges built across the flowing water,
And the boats sails passed the canals and under the bridges,
As the rain drops, sun shines on the surface and water's edge.
The lights everywhere gleam in colors
Of blue, red, green, yellow, grey,
Violet and pink, and all with a ray,
A ray of hope to revive the city's splendors,
As faces of people of different race:
Europeans, Arabs, Asians, Africans, and Hispanics all embrace
An attitude to tolerate, love, and cherish one another.
Even, as many from far have come for shelter.
Christians, Muslims, Atheists, Jews, and Buddhists
Conducts and participates in a like-wise feast.
Colors of flags, blue, white, and orange;
Orange, a symbol of the Dutch.
One and all seem perfect in cycling like it commence from the stone age.
From the different museums, walking along with faith to the church,
To the mosque, and then to the synagogues, and temples
While I quake and shiver, as my eyes set on nipples
Of half-naked whores, beautiful, and tempting
Inside a decorated, clean covered-glass house surrounded by red lights.
From the coffee shops, music blasts, smoke of weeds perceived as I come in a sight
To illustrate and create views of my innocent life still sleeping.
The heart of the Dutch,
A place to be, the land to touch.
To know it and explore it, come then to see
Where evil and good is mixed, so please take a heed.
This is where everyone meets,
A city with something for everyone.
This is Amsterdam.

He has never actually experienced cold the way he was experiencing it, as he walked along from one street of Amsterdam to another, not knowing exactly where to go to, as the day was getting darker and it was coming to night. Although, he fortified himself against the cold as he repeatedly buy and drink hot coffee *(koffie met melk)* along, still putting his bag passed his right arm. He knew there was no-way he was going to survive the cold, so he went into one of the coffee shop to smoke marijuana, because he was told before it was legal for anyone to step in to buy and to smoke. He did not actually know how to spend the Netherlands currency, so he asked one of the black Suriname boy he met there whom he also told his problems, and he was advised to go to Rotterdam or Den Haag where he could find many sympathetic Nigerians like him to help him to stay and get a job. It was the same boy who had let him know that in Holland, it is mandatory to dial any phone numbers starting with zero, making him come to believe he was wrong for accusing his friend for having let him come to Holland to be stranded and frustrated. But at the time he wanted to bring his phone out of his bag to dial the numbers again, that his when he found that he had lost it and that was where he had stored all his friends and families phone numbers. "So many people are ashamed to cry out when they are in problems thinking others might mock them, but there are still very many people who would want to help, if not financially, might be with words of advice."

He bought another train ticket and was already inside a train going to Rotterdam. After some minutes that the train left and stopped in several train stations and very many people were coming down, he stood up from where he was sitting to meet a very young lad, standing and was waiting for the train to halt so he could come down. He asked him in English, which stop was Rotterdam, but he was told it was the next stop. So, as the train reached, he hurriedly stepped down from the train not even raising his head up to look at the signboard to read the signs and to know where he was. But it was after he came out of the station that he came to read what was written on the top of the stations building and found he was in Den Haag. He was so disappointed, as he was so exhausted and it was almost night and all the money he was having with him were almost finished. He cried in silence and said a prayer to his God, believing, He will send His angels to lead him out of the bondage he was seeing himself. As he prayed silently, sitting on one of the chair outside the train station alone on his own, there arrived 2nd David once again—saying to him, "You can never see the light if you do not see darkness first." He was shocked and wanted to warned him never to come near him again, when he heard him saying again, 'It will be well with you, you are blessed.' As he finished saying this, he disappeared into the air and David, relieved from his fear, stood up and walked towards where there were many people, and, as he progressively walk and stare at the street, he saw a cafe bar and went inside to order for another cup of *koffie met melk*. Inside the bar, he saw a fat advance black woman of say forty-year old, sitting in a chair, drinking coffee, and at the same time was talking on her cell phone. He walked closer to where she was sitting and sat closer to her, letting her finished her talking on phone and then approached her, first by greeting her 'good morning.' 'Good morning,' she responded. 'What do you want?' she demanded. 'I am sorry if I am inconveniencing you. The truth is that your face looks very familiar and I thought I might have seen you before somewhere else.' I do not think so,' she replied, annoyingly, wanting to get up from where she was sitting to leave. 'Please, I am really sorry to have come to inconvenience you.' He too stood up, carrying his bag and was about to leave. She called him back and ordered for another coffee for him. He then sat down, as they both started a conversation in their native language, first, by introducing himself and how and where he recognized her to be his neighbor some years ago in his home town. He told her of his problems and how he had lost her phone and was in a very critical situation and not knowing where to put his head that night, as he was not having anybody there. Despite all he said, she was in doubts that he was not telling the truth. She was afraid of him, as he was a stranger and a black man and moreover, a Nigerian, whom she later said she found very hard to trust, because she has been dealt with several times by most of them she has tried to help. When they finished drinking their coffee, she asked him to follow her to the red light where she was working as a prostitute in the place popularly known as Holland Spoor—which actually was the second name for the train station. He was appalled at this when he first saw that she was still prostituting after she was in Holland for almost twelve years and had come to Africa several times and helped all of her family, some to come to Europe and setting a business for others. She was thought to be a very rich woman, since David has seen her to be and from the way she was respected back in their country. He could not in anyway believe what he was seeing, as she apparently removed her dress, then putting on her working attires which made her very attractive to David, even if he knew she might be too old for him, as she was in her forties and he was still twenty-two-year-old. She knew he liked what he was seeing and was purposely posing herself in the right manner to seduce him more and more. The way she was dressed was completely indecent, as he watched her in surprise as she rubbed her body against his, pretending it to be a mistake—making him miscalculate his steps, when he walked to the toilet to urinate. He was beginning to spew out some sperms when he entered into the toilet. He knew this was going to be tough for him, knowing he was with a prostitute who is capable of doing anything, maybe kicking him out into the cold weather if he refused to follow instructions. He paused and waited inside the toilet until the time she called him out. She was not prepared to work, and he knew this due to how he saw her closed her window to show she was unavailable at that moment. She spent time with him, asking him about the people they both knew back at their home, and later picked up a phone that night, calling some other people she knew, who could help her locate Chelsea, the boy David had come to meet there in Holland. When she finally succeeded in reaching Chelsea, who admitted it was true David has come to see him, she was convinced he was telling the truth, and then moved him to another of his friend's room who at that very time had left to her house, due to some problems she was having with her boyfriend who was five years younger than she was, and she has given him money to go and buy some African foodstuffs and creams and cosmetic goods for her in the U.k, but the lad has decided to run away to Canada with the money, since he was already having a citizenship there in Holland and could travel to anywhere in the western world without a visa. In that room, he was given soaps and creams to rub his body after he might have taken is bath and showed a bathroom to wash his body with warm water. After showing him this, she went back to her place of work to look for money. Immediately he finished cleaning up and using the cream, he fell asleep in the bed with his trouser and shirt still on.

The next morning at about 05:00 a.m, she came to wake him up to come to her room, and when they reached, she ordered him to pull off his trousers and shirts before he could be able to get into her bed—which he did with no exemption, and later she slept beside him, the both of their bodies touching each other. He did not want to start it, because he still was not convinced of what he was thinking of her and what might happen if she was not thinking what he was thinking. He was afraid not to do anything stupid so as not to be kicked out, so he waited for her to start, and, as he waited, he fell asleep and slept off, snoring very hard that he could be heard at the other side of the building.

It was almost noon, when she woke up and also woke him up, then made a lemon tea for the both of them to drink, and, as they did, she brought out her phone to call one of his friend who owned a very large African food shop and was also rich and has stayed long there in Holland and was married to a Dutch and was also a citizen there. She called her and pleaded with her to accept him as an assistant in her shop. First, she refused to, but when she continued to plead and plead, telling her he was from Spain and was with a document, she agreed and asked her to send him to wait for her. David was very happy that he was about to get a job, even when he has not spent more than a day there in Holland. He saw his dream about to come true. He thanked her, showing how much he appreciated her efforts to make sure he gets a job; he was about to lie himself down for her to walk on top. He knew it was the right decision he made to have left Spain to come to Holland, and he was glad he did.

The next day, he was already made an assistant in the large Afro-shop, being showed how everything was done; he learnt quickly and was beginning to enjoy the environment and the new people he was now associating his life with. He saw that most of his fellow Nigerians and other Africans there were dedicated to working and working, while some were still into business of different kinds, legal and illegal—as to drug dealings and merchandising, but, very few of them were studying to have a degree. They say, "Tell me your friends and let me tell you who you are." David said, in his later life, he had come to fathom the reasons why most kids born into a home where their families are all educated, are always motivated to do the same. He said, it made him believe, "In the beginning of any child's life, the society where he finds himself/herself can also be of a profound impact."

As time went-by, he still was happy and had refused to go and meet Chelsea and some of his other friends who were calling him on phone, saying he was being very lazy and was afraid to face a challenge in dealing with the matters of life. At first, he did not listen to them and he did not want to leave where he was to go meet these people, knowing already they were just being envious as he was living a good life where he was. He was given a free room arrayed with electronic equipment, and at the front of the house he was staying, was the shop were he was working as a salesman. He saw his dreams not far from where he was standing, and he wanted to grab it and hold it very tight. But, human are never to be trusted, most especially when they are blacks. His plan actually as he got that job, was to be able to change his way of life around to be truthful, strive to possess some fine qualities in life that other people will admire and be doing what he believe is appropriate—seeing it to be the precise time for him to build his own future. He proposed doing this, but was that what others wanted? He thought life was going to be sweet as a candy as he was promised by his boss—regarding to the wages and benefits he will be receiving at the end of every months ahead to come.

His life was about to go astray, as he continued to wake up every morning to go to the shop to tidy it up and sell the foodstuffs and other things inside, keeping the money for his boss and at the end of the month not getting paid. Confusion mixed with frustration once again in his life and he knew "Humans could never be trusted, so we all have to keep struggling on our own to achieve everything we dreamed of, and quit the ideas to wait for others to do it for us." He did not know what to do when at the end of the first month his boss had refused to pay him, promising and promising, days after days. He called the woman who had introduced him to her to report the matter, thinking, she was the only person that could help him beg her friend to pay him his salary. Although, he was anxious to get that money not because he needed it to feed as there were always food and drinks for him every time, but he needed the money so he could send them to his parents in Africa. After much arguments between the two women, his boss finally agreed to pay him his first month salary, which she did not pay to him directly, but was sent to his parents the way he instructed her to, despite the warnings she gave him. He thought there was a need for his parents to start to receive money from him because of how he promised to change their poverty lives to a better one.

Months after months, things became more complex for him as formidable obstacles was now tearing him apart from his boss due to a financial crisis. She was not prepared to keep to her many promises and he was still receiving phone calls from his friends to leave the job and come to meet them so they could fix him up with a job that he will be paid better even if he has to go there to work with another person's document. He tried to overcome this temptation, knowing "Patience, supports and encouragements to be the most important mainstays in life." But the problem was that he lacked these three qualities in life and could not deal with the problem. He wanted to start working or doing anything else just like his other friends so he could raise money to send to his family; he wanted to make it within a twinkle of an eye and go back to Africa to invest on the work which he was already having a vacation for. His joy of having come to Holland and in a short time found a job, was already turning into sadnesses as his boss continuously refuses to pay him his salaries. At that time, he vowed not to smoke marijuana or hashish again, but when life continue to bring him misfortune, he thought it was not yet time for him to quit smoking, so, one night, he strolled down to one of the coffee shop just five minutes walk from his house, purchased two joints and went back home to smoke one out of it. But, when he finished smoking, he was intoxicated and could not move his body out of the bed, so he relaxed while Tupac's music was blasting. It was a wonderful night as he listened to the lyrics and come to think that he was been fooled by his boss, and that something should have to be done for him to quit this life of working and not being paid. Tupac was never a coward, so why would he? That night, he wanted to take all the money he had sold and run away to go and meet his friends who were already proffering to him the better and more progressive life he could have if he quits the job he was doing and come to meet them. He wanted to be able to stand on his own as a man by working to raise money for himself; he was tired of being instructed by a whore who was only good at lying and cheating. He wanted to be free from a woman, who he had first saw as his savior but was later becoming his only and one enemy he thought of strangling with his bare hands. As he woke up the next morning, Tupac's music still playing repeatedly the way he programmed it to be, he was strengthless and invalid, but managed to stand on his feet and open the door to go to the washroom; he met with his boss when he opened the door of his room. 'Good morning,' she greeted him, 'good morning' replied David, trying to hide his face from her. For more than a minute, they were both standing, discussing about the sales of the previous day. Her eyes gleamed with happiness, like she has won a lottery and was about to be paid. She passed him and went straight into his room which, apparently she was the one paying for it. She then sat down, telling him to go to the washroom to go do whatever it is he was going to do there and return back, because there were things they needed to talk about. He hurried to clean his face with water and returned back to hear what she was about to say. Getting there, she ordered him to sit in the same bed where she was also sitting, and as he sat down and they were close, he raised his face up to listen to what she was going to say, only to see that she was looking straight into his eyes. After awhile she commenced with her story of life on how her husband, an old Dutch man had given her enormous amount of money and the money was later duped by her Nigerian boyfriend. She was at the point of shedding tears, as she continued to narrate her sad story of life. What came first to David's mind was sympathy. Sympathy came first, as he listened to her, not knowing what else to do. He wanted to hold her close to his body to console and comfort her, but he knew from the way she was looking at him and the way they had both talked and laughed and even smoke cigarettes together—that she was feeling something for him—something strong—maybe love or just she wanted to have sex. But what if he make up his mind to give it to her the way she will want it, rough and smooth, slow and steady and hot? Another thing was, what will be the effect since he comprehend how the other woman who introduced him to her was also in love with him even when he refused to make love to her several times they have met and have slept in the same bed? That morning, he wanted to hold her, squeeze her, and drive her like a car since it was long time he never had sex and was sex starved. But one thing he came to understand was that, "Whores are women who have chosen prostitution to be their profession rightfully because of the money and most especially because they seem to like it for fun." He could not help comprehend the reason they both wanted him, even when there were so many other grown up boys like him that were running after them simply because of their money. He was so perplexed, when he sat down and think of how he could be loved by a woman of his mother's age. He apparently came to believe in what people always said about whores that,"Once a whore, is always going to be a whore." Yes, it is true that, "No matter what you do to cherish and love a whore, she is never going to be honest and be sincere with you, or else you are able to satisfy her financial and sexual needs which to her, are the most essential things in life."

David was happy again, since he was being able to feed himself with the money he was ordered to spend by his boss, but what made him happy most, was the pleasure he relished from music, since he was having an access to smoke weed and listen to every kind of music, most especially Tupac's music which was beginning to send a message of hope and inspiration to him. He was happy and quit the idea of running away, as he has once wanted to. He was happy because he was able to watch good programs in the television; he was happy because he could watch CNN, BBC, Discovery channel and more than three music channels and other good channels he constantly love to watch, since the government of the country already made it very easy for them to be receiving these channels without having to fix a satellite. It was just as easy as buying a television, plugging it, and the next thing you see is everything is already be done for you. He was happy he was in Holland, because he could see himself getting closer again in life to education and civilization unlike when he was in Spain and was unable to watch CNN throughout the time he stayed there.

When he reported the the issue of how his boss refused to be paying him to her friend who introduced him to her, but she was not in a situation of helping him as long as he was not ready to comply with her request, so he thought of waiting there till when God will intervene. But, it was when he reported this matter to one of the girls that was prostituting to pay his boss the sum of 50,000.00 dollars for bringing her to Europe just only with 6,000.00 dollars. David, who thought himself to be the only person with problems, when he was told by the girl how she was arrested by the police and kept in a deportation camp to be deported back to Africa, he shed tears as he was listening, but advised her to travel to Spain so as to be able to get a document. He also told her to make sure she was sending her boss the money she was owing her because, if she refused to do so, something terrible and awful might happen to her family back in Africa. But trying to help another person while you yourself—your problems are just more than you that you cannot even think of how to solve it. It was ridiculous how he could do that when actually he was financially zero. He almost quit trying to help and advise her, knowing it was going to be impossible, but she was already in love with him and wanted to have him since they were living in the same apartment and were always alone together at home in the morning when everyone might have gone to work and him too is getting himself ready to go to the shop to continue with his daily routine and they were always together every time he was back from the shop. She was the one cooking for him; she was the one he will call when there is a need to call anyone; he was beginning to develop a thing referred to as love for her, when it happened the day he wanted to tell it to her face that he was in love with her just as she was already in love with him and was always in the mood of making love to him, something obnoxious and nasty happened. She was arrested and taken away while she was walking along the roadside by the police who were following her for long without she knowing it. For long both of them have wanted to have sex, but there was another boy living with them and he was trying to get the girl's attention even when his wife was in Dublin, Ireland, and has given birth to a baby and the Irish government had issued a document for the kid and the mother. The boy left Holland the previous day to Dublin to reunite with his family there, but David's boss came to meet him that same day, warning him not to let her see him get closer to the girl anymore, since she was already suspecting the both of them. Although, David and the girl were both living in the same apartment rented and paid for by their boss and mistress whom at that time was still living with her Dutch husband and was still prostituting despite she was having up to six to seven girls still paying and were to pay 50,000.00 dollars each. From what David was told, the both women—his boss and the woman who introduced him to her, were very rich people and were professionals in the pimp business, yet, were not prepared to give it up. David was so perplexed, the way he saw "Africans enslaving themselves all for the sake of money even when the whole world decries it, knowing it was the worst atrocity that men have imposed on their fellow men." "Everyone who knew something about slavery, knew it was evil and was inhuman." Now that the people of world have come to see it so, and have abolished it, people have decided to re-introduce it through a different way, calling it business, punishing themselves while the whole world watch and laugh at them because they think them insane and greedy.

After much thoughts and thoughts and weed smoking and Tupac's music which was really giving him inspiration and stating explicitly that the system and the society we live are to be blamed for our own problems. Although, in his later future life, he found this theory to be true and also to be false. The message he was receiving from the music was that he was in Europe and could survive with or without any aid from his boss. The more he was listening to Tupac's lyrics, the more the inspiration was coming to him. He swiftly took a decision to leave to go and meet his friends so he could get a job and raise money to send to his family in Africa.

One night, it was on Sunday, a day after the girl he was advising to travel to Spain was arrested, he was alone in the apartment and was fretful. That night after smoking weed and listening to Tupac's song titled LIFE GOES ON, he knew he had to leave if not to be compared to a coward, so he packed all his belongings and some of the things that he knew was high worth bought by his boss former Nigerian boyfriend who duped her and ran away but later returned back to Holland and was pleading for her to accept him back with all the money already lavished. He took three of the VERSACE jackets and some other ritzy clothes and JEAN PAUL GUALTIER'S perfumes and loaded everything in his big bag and kept it for the next morning trip. In the morning, he left some of the money he sold for almost a week in his room, locked it and left the key under the foot-match and went hurriedly, straight to the train station. There he bought a ticket to Madrid, Spain and left.

He arrived in Madrid very late but was still very lucky to had met with the last bus going to Vitoria—which was scheduled to be at 01:00 a.m. Meanwhile, he has called his sister to inform her he was on his way to Spain for the refugee travel document he applied for some months ago before he left to Holland. The document has arrived some days ago and his sister has called him on phone to tell him. He arrived Vitoria that morning and that same morning, he was at the police station without anybody assisting him, since he was already smart enough to do it on his own, even when he knew he could not speak fluent Spanish language which was a vital thing for an immigrant living in Spain to be good at. After he was given the document, he went home to meet his sister who squealed with delights, as she saw him come back to Spain. That he came to Spain, apparently was not to stay and live but purposely for him to get the refugee travel document which he needed to add to his other documents so he could return back to live in Holland legally. But, his sister wanted him to stay; she wanted him to get life for himself and be happy in Spain. How could this be when he was so money-conscious and wanted to make it and return back home to his family? He knew he was deeply indebted to his parents and the rest members of his families, and he thought there were no means for him to think of bringing that dream to become a reality as long as he was in Spain. He wanted to return to where his heart was, where he thought life will be more convenience; he wanted to go on the highway; he wanted to see life for himself in a country he already fell in love with the culture and the people. He thought living there was like living in a free world which he always dreamed of—he wanted to live in Holland. At home, with his sister and her husband, there was always a dispute, since he could not quit smoking cigarette which his sister was always against, and the worst of it when he was watching the television and could only listen to everything in the Spanish language. He was furious with himself and he was upset for having come back to Spain for the document instead of him going to meet his friends who has proffered to him a better life by helping him to get a job there. He tried to call his boss to tell her he was sorry for his misdeed, but she shunned him, calling him a thief and telling him to send her the money he stole. He was enraged and could not keep with his rage, so he called his friends who wanted him to come over there to inform them of the day he will be returning back.

It was the third day since he returned back to Spain and was still very unhappy, blaming himself for having made that mistake of coming back. He knew he needed something to wake him up from his sleep, because he was seeing himself as a weak and indecisive man, so he embarked on what he thought was right for him which was to follow a dream, a dream that he saw was given to him by Tupac. As he listened to the first track of the cd he brought with him from Holland, he could hear the voice of his mentor preach to him . . . . 'Makevali in this—Killuminati, all through your body. The blow's like a twelve gauge shotty uhh, feel me! And God said he should send his only begotten son to lead the wild into the ways of the man. Follow me; eat my flesh and my flesh' . . . Following these, he heard the chorus . . . 'Come with me, Hail Mary Run quick see, what do we have here Now, do you wanna ride or die, La dadadada, lalala' . . . . David, whose Tupac's music was already having a profound impact on his life, could not help resist this song HAIL MARY. He did not wait to listen to the music farther, as he stood up, took his bath, with his bag already around his arm, and was poised to leave. His sister was appalled when she saw him holding his bag, saying he was prepared to leave back to Holland. She did not know what to say—only to tell him to be careful.

Within some few hours, David was already in Madrid train station where he bought a ticket of the train going to Eindhoven, the fifth largest city in Holland and was one of the recognized industrial town in the country. When he reached Holland, his friend, Chelsea whom he went to meet at the first time but was unable to see him due to some circumstances that he misplaced his phone and was unable to call him, came to pick him up at the train station to his house. When he first saw him, he could not recognize him, since it was more than three years he last saw him and he was now bigger and mature than he used to be, but still with no sensible attitude. They embraced each other with excitements and left to one of the Mcdonalds near the train station to eat. After they finished eating, Chelsea paid for everything and called a taxi to take them to his house, and getting home, he took him to one of the coffee shop near his house to smoke weed. David, who hated him for having taken his girlfriend away from him some years ago back at the time they were in Africa, knew it was time for him to forgive his friend, as he did not want that to be an obstruction to his progress in life. For so many times, he could people say, "We cannot bite the fingers that fed us,"—which he then think it was time for him to put it to practice. He was glad he was in Holland again, and was with a childhood friend who could assist him in getting a job since he too was working. He tried, calling the woman who introduced him to his boss to plead with her to forgive him because he knew she will not be happy that he has taken a decision to leave without informing her of it. She was glad he called, and she then begged him to return back that she was prepared to help him to get another job. He wanted to return back so he could have sex with her, because he already see that she was deeply in love with him and was ready to do anything for him to survive and live there in Holland. He did appreciated it, but what will be the end if he return back to her? Was it all about sex? What about his dream of living a life his mentor Tupac lived, a life of do or die? He knew his interest in her was only for mercenary reasons, which to him was a foolish and nonsensical thing to do when he knew he could make life by working or if it come to the worst, he will sell drugs in the street the way he saw some boys do it while he was in his boss shop in Dorsaalaan, one of the worst street for selling drugs in Mashaven, Rotterdam. Although, she called him several times to let him know of how rich she was which was a financial inducement for him to fall in love with her, but he declined her invitation because he detested the prostitution work she was doing. He stopped calling her on phone and even changed the SIM card in his phone so that he could see himself do without her. But he was so astonished when Chelsea and one other of his friend called R. Kelly, who was also a close relation of Chelsea and was from the same street with David—searched his phone, took the woman's number and started calling her, telling her he was interested in having a relationship with her. She was so smart to have noticed that David changed the SIM card in his phone, so when the boy called her, she begged him to passed the phone to David, but he refused, letting her know David was not having anything to do with her and also letting her know how much he decries prostitution and has vowed never to have sex with any of them.

After some weeks passed and these boys were still unable to help him find a job, he then knew they were not his friends, instead they were his ill-wishers. He saw that they were only proffering to him a better life just to keep him hold down while they were working, making money and bragging about the many things they have achieved. It was almost becoming a competition between them of who will make it first to return back to Africa. He was surprised, since he could not help grasp what was wrong with him getting close to people he thought were his friends. As things got worse and he was still unable to get a job, he called the woman—the whore he thought was already becoming a pest to his life. He called to tell her of the formidable life he was living since he could not find a job. It was then she revealed to him how one of them had called her, telling her how he, David had denounced and decried her because she was a whore, and how he also wanted her. He was ashamed when he heard this, but what will he do to outlast this situation? She told him she forgave him and still wanted him to come back to her, so that she could help him get a job. David, who was regretful, was also confused as his life was conquered by misfortune and the only person to set him free from this misery was a whore, a whore who loved him and wanted to assist him to achieve his goal in life, a whore he condemned, calling her different sorts of names, thinking she needed a cure for her sickness of sex. You see, "We the people of the world are accustomed to passing verdicts on our fellow human beings from what we see them doing, and because of what other people say about them. We will not even think of getting to know them before arriving at a conclusion." David, who after he came to learn the truth that his friends were upset with him because he was new in Europe and was having a document while they who were already there some many years before him, were still afraid anytime they sees a policeman and were unable to travel to anywhere because they were illegal. He came to believed in everything the woman told him about friends in Europe and how envious they are to see that you are about to be better than them. He was already learning a lesson of life, as he sat down to think of the next step to take in life—to return back to the woman who was there to help him or to keep staying with foes he first thought to be his friends. As the days passed and he was still jobless, several times, he was told when he would ask the reason things were not working the way he was promised, the answers he gets, was that there was nobody to give him a document to work. He could only watch his friends bring women home to have sex with them, leave to work, go to parties, return back home, only to preach to him the same old quotes from the bible that said, "Thy shalt love thy neighbors as thyself." As this proceed without a solution emitted to put an end to it, he picked up a pen and commenced with writing his autobiography which also added a fuel to the whole issue, making it worse. He wanted to go back to the whore, knowing he will be welcomed with sex as he was already sex-starved and needed it badly and wanted to have it. He wanted to go back to her so as to be able to run away from the enemies he called his friends that he was living with. He said he came to also had a different view of life, as he continuously, increasingly think about the whore, that "Whores are full of lies and are decisive and are thieves, but they can also help save a life of a miserable lonely man whom death has built his house near him." He came to fathom something in life that he once thought was not worth thinking. The truth. "Yes, we the people of the world are afraid to utter the truth because we are afraid of what the consequences might be, mostly when it become a thing we cannot prove, and also for us to hide the horrible side of our lives that is not worth seeing." "The truth is bitter and you have to know the truth before you judge, but knowing the truth, you have to dig deeper." "The substantial truth is that, whores are evil, but some are also angels that have saved the lives of so many men in the world where we live."

Still living with his friends and still jobless, one day when he came home to meet his friend discussing an issue with another of his friend on how he was going to start a business where he will be making more than five thousand dollars in a week, first, David thought the boy was joking, but, as the boy continued to say it and was making plans on how to get it started the next day, he knew he was serious and was up to something different from what he was thinking of him. David became curious and wanted to know what the business was and where and how and when it was going to get started.

The next day, he was already in the boy's house, watching him called one of Holland's telephone company to come to his house to install six eight house-phones, giving them the name of a person with a residence permit holder and his bank account, meanwhile it was all forged. In not less than three hours some people knocked on the door and the door was opened for them to come in and they were showed where to install the telephones, and in not more than thirty minutes, the phones were already installed. One hour after the phones were installed, the boy who ordered it called David to come closer and to watch the way he was communicating with the phones. David was surprised when he saw the boy calling people in Kuwait, Saudi Arabia, Iran, Yemen, United Arab Emirates, and even Iraq, connecting them to be using the lines in communicating with anybody anywhere around the world. At the end of the day, these people in these countries mentioned above gave him account of the calls and the next morning, money was sent to him through Western Union. At the beginning, it was funny to him, since it was his first time of coming around with intelligent criminals like this boy, but since he was not working and needed to be doing something—anything to raise money for himself, he joined in doing the business. He did not only learn how to get in contact with these people in the middle east that were in need of people to connect them with phone lines to be doing their business and paying less fees, he also became perfect and was lauded by his friends. They continued with the business for one week, when they woke up one day to commence with their evil work, and as they dialed the first phone number to see if it was still working, they found it was with no line. It was blocked by the telephone company and a letter was sent to them to come pay the bills before they could continue using it. It was at that time David knew his life was endangered, as his friend quickly pack his little belongings, telling him to be quick and that they were to leave that house immediately to another place so that they will not to get caught by the police. At that very moment, he was confused, as fear drove quietly into his mind. He could not move his leg, neither could he move his body, and he saw himself fall into a trance and his friend knew what was happening to him, so he quickly hit him, begging him to follow him. After they left the house, packing everything inside out to another place which the boy rented and paid for, knowing already what was going to happen, David sat down and was thinking of how he was going to continue with this and if ever he was going to survive it. He came to understand crime to be a very easy way to make an enormous amount of money, but he also came to understand how perilous it is to be living a life with crime, running every time from the police. He knew this was not what he came to Holland to do, and he knew he was being mislead and the only way he could get out of it was to get himself a job.

The next day, he left early in the morning with the fake document of another person he was given by his friends to go and look for a job, as he had accused them of forcing him to be doing what he never intended to do. He went looking for a job all day, going to different offices of temporary employment agents, presenting the fake document he was given. But, he was told to wait for them to call him, even when he begged them, almost kneeling down for them to call him. There was a little chance for him, although, since he could not speak the Dutch language which was a good advantage for people who are looking for jobs. But with faith and the way some of them had promised to help him, he went home to meet his friends to tell them of what had happened. As he arrived home, he heard one of his friend has traveled to London illegally to go and stay there since he was having his brothers and sisters there and has been in Holland for more than three years and was still illegal and the police have arrested him several times and tried to deport him back to his country, but he has always been so lucky to escape it. David was touched when he received this news. He loved him no matter what he was encountering and even when he knew he was the one who tried to separate him from the whore by calling her and telling her different things he that he said about her and also telling her he was interested in having a relationship with her. He missed the boy because he saw him to be a serious and shrewd person who was industrious and was always running away from crime. He was nicknamed R. Kelly because he was a great fan of the R 'n' B music artist. But he was happy for him, as he had succeeded to enter the U.k. illegally without being caught by the immigration. He was so happy when they talked on phone. This lad also advised him to be careful and to be patient and try to continue to search for a job, letting him have the belief that he was always going to make it there in Holland, as long as he was having his documents with him. David, who was worried about his situation, but was also glad to see that he was legal in Europe and for that reason, he knew he was also indebted to the Spanish government for them being sympathetic and issuing out documents for many immigrants to live and work in Spain and also to be able to travel with it. How could he pay them back for what they did for him? How could he loathe the people that have given him the opportunity to travel to other European countries to see life for himself? Although, he was always complaining about the situation why the Spanish government were in no way assisting their own immigrants both financially and morally unlike in Holland where even refugees were provided with shelter and some other life's basic amenities. But, as time went on when he came to meet with many Spaniards in Holland and had a discussion with them, he came to get to the bottom of the matter that many Spaniards have decided to travel out of their country to other places in Europe so to seek a better future. He was so perplexed when he was beginning to learn that the Spanish economy was not as good as he thought even before coming to Europe. He was afraid of the future, as he saw many Spaniards in Holland looking for a better future just as he came to look for his own future there. Instantly, he was able to predict how the future outcome was going to look like in Spain. He became afraid of going back to Spain to live, since he could see the light of the future look dim from a very far distance where he was standing.

For four days he went looking for a job and there was still no hope for him due to the fact that he could not speak the language—that was said to be a barrier; he finally gave up the idea of waiting to starve himself to death, knowing that his money was about to get finished—the little money he was paid for the dubious work of crime he associated himself in doing with his friends. He knew he would have to run away to meet one of his friends who was living in Amsterdam and was into drug business and was already promising him of a marvelous life he will be living if he made up his mind to come and be staying with him there. But, when he was about to take a new step to leave to Amsterdam, his friend who introduced him to Bruce—the same boy who was installing phones and using them to connect to other people around the world, calling it business, also called him to inform him of the latest business the boy was planing to carry out. When he heard this, he knew he was not going to miss it even if he was still unsatisfied with the payment. 'Half bread is better than none,' he said to himself. He agreed to wait for the boy to come around that evening he was told. He waited alone at home at the place he was sharing with his friend till 08:00 p.m that day. He waited and was tired and was about to leave with his bag already around his arm, when his friend called him from his place of work to inform of where to go and wait for the boy. As he reached the place, he saw the boy and one other boy sitting and discussing something he did not care to know about, as it was not his concerns to know. He greeted them by shaking them and excused the boy he came to meet to tell him of the reason he was there, but the boy asked him to sit with them and then introduced him to the other boy who actually was legal there in Holland and was there for more than six years and was also in Germany for three years before coming to Holland. After they talked about what they were planning to do, that was when David came to comprehend how they were running it and also came to understand that the new boy he was seeing, Lekbahibi, from what people were calling him, was the boss and was the person financing the projects and was also the person with the biggest share. He was asked to follow them to the coffee shop were they went to smoke weed and drink and later went to a restaurant to eat before he was taken with a car to his house to sleep and wait for the business to get started the next day.

The next day, they were already in their telephone business, connecting people. Days after days went by and money were being sent to them through Western Union. Things were getting better for everyone and life was as sweet as candy. After two weeks that they operated the business, the telephone company known as KPN, sent them the bills, asking them to pay it before they could get them connected again, but the boy David was working with, was very smart and witty and was not the type who gets frightened when he is into a deal. He picked up the phone and called the company, telling them to get the phone connected, and that he was ready to pay all the bills in less than three days. He called them several times, and as they refused to do what he demanded for, he bounced the phone on them and told David, 'man, is over'. That night, when the boy who was sponsoring the business returned to join them, they went to their favorite coffee shop to smoke, and as they were smoking, they were discussing about life and their plans for the future. It was then David knew Bruce, the boy whom he thought to be a criminal for life, was a person with a plan to go to Dublin, Ireland to go and study to become a doctor.

The phone business was over and David was left alone at home doing nothing once again, but was still staying with his friend, Chelsea who was still working with his elder brother's document and was receiving an enormous amount of money, yet the Dutch government was responsible for his rent and feeding because he was a refugee and was granted a residence permit to live but not allowed to work since he was still seventeen and underage. Bruce, their criminal friend finally succeeded in getting himself to Dublin with his Dutch girlfriend who was still seventeen years old and could not marry him, as the law stated. But, when they arrived Dublin and seek asylum, they were allowed to marry and the both of them later decided to study there. David was later told Bruce studied and became a doctor and his girlfriend who was once a drug addict when they knew each other, later studied and became a nurse. Lekbahibi left to be living with his wife, leaving David and Chelsea to their fates. Chelsea's girlfriend who has lived in Italy before and has come to visit his brother in Holland and decided not to return back, was always coming to Chelsea's house and leaving, but one day she decided to stay because she was ready to get married to him, and before she could do so, she must be able to study him very well to know if actually he was the man of his life. Meanwhile David was still without a job and was almost becoming a man with no place to put his head, since anytime Chelsea's girlfriend was around he would have to sleep in the bathroom.

One day, he was called for a job by one of the temporary employment agents. When he reached there, he was offered a job in a place which was four miles from his house. He started working the next day, going there with the bus prepared for workers by the agent to assist all of them who could not make it to their place of work. Meanwhile, he was still writing his autobiography every time he will return back from work in a cool, locked room. He will open the door since it was formerly the room they had rented for their phone business, but because the police had called the owner and told him of the bills that someone who rented it was to pay and there was no-way he could locate that someone who actually was Lekbahibi, he decided to lock it, but was unaware that David was still holding some of the keys. So he will enter the room when everybody might be asleep and will be writing. He proceeded like this to live in that room for more than a month untill one day when he woke up and went to work, forgetting he did not put the light off, and when the owner passed by and saw it, he came to change the locks—making him homeless again and to be sleeping in the bathroom every night. With the little money he made from the work he was doing after paying for the document even as it was fake, he decided to go and rent a room, but who told him to start having that idea of renting a house? His friend called him to tell him the document was to be given to another person who was to be paying better for it. Then he knew there was no way he could raise money for his rent if he dares think of going to live on his own, and he was asking himself when this unpleasant situation was going to change for him. He started accusing himself for not being able to change this situation for good, thinking it was his bad habits or behavior that led him into these many tragedies. He was beginning to loathe himself for every of his misfortunes. He also knew that men were unreliable, as he could see that people who were his friends, were also the people that were causing him mischief just because they knew he was going to be better than them. How was he going to escape this? How was he going to break that yoke that was hanged around his neck to become free once again and be living with joy and happiness? Something has to be done he said to himself, when he woke up one morning and went straight to meet the agent who was calling him on phone to know what his problems was and why he has not be coming to work. He went there, and when he met the Dutch man who was so sympathetic and was always in the position of rendering people helping hands even if he was doing it to get his money, because the more workers he was having, the more money he was making as well. When he reached the office and was questioned why he has quit the job he was offered, he told him everything from A-Z, how he was sleeping inside a bathroom and how his friends has taken away the fake document he was given before away from him. When the Dutch man listened, he was almost shedding tears, seeing how black people were treating themselves. Later, after David revealed everything to him and letting him know he was having a Spanish document with him, the man demanded for it to see if it was true, and, when he saw it and knew he was not lying, he promised him not to fret himself much and that he was going to help him get a working and a residence permit to live and work in Holland. He also cautioned him to be mindful and heedful of what he says and do with his friends, as he could see that they were covetous because he was talented and was going to have a better future than them. He has seen him singing many times and even advised him, jocularly to go and register in one of the music school there in Eindhoven. He took the documents from him, photocopied them and immediately told him to start working with him the next day in a slaughter house—a company that was not far from his house and he could ride a bicycle to reach everyday. He was the most happiest person, as he was told to start working the next day in that company where he knew the payment was almost two times better than where he was working before. He went home happily with the proposal he was given and was so excited, as he knew he was going to start working with his own documents, meaning the man was going to help him change his Spanish residence to become Holland residence and working permits. How could this be? He thought it to be a dream or rather a joke not until the next morning when he woke up to meet the man who took him with his private car to his new place of work, showing him to the foreman who was in charge. What he did was wrong, despite the warnings he was given by his friends, but he could not help resist the excitement inside of him when he went home that day to deliver the good news to his friends about his new job and how he was going to be working with his documents. Hearing this was so strange, as he watched them gazed at him in amazement, repeating the phrase one after the other again and again, 'You are going to be working with your documents now.'

Some days after he was employed in his new place of work and was paid for the first week a reasonable amount of money, he looked at himself and saw what his forthcoming life will be. He was oblivious of the warnings he was given before by his then boss and angel who had come to rescue him out of the the mouth of a dragon. He forgot his friends were not very happy of how he was progressing with life. "Money can make people regard you and respect you for whom you really are." Immediately he received his salary and started living like a real and noble man, his friend, Chelsea's girlfriend was beginning to fall in love with him and after she had tempted him several times and was unable to get his attentions, she called him gay and that made him thought of proving it to her he was not. As he was sleeping one day in Chelsea's bed, she came from outside and opened the door and sneaked into the room, got herself naked and slept with him and was using her legs to scratch his legs. When he woke up to see that she was lying with him in the bed, pretending to be far asleep, he started touching her from her breast down to where her cunt was, putting his fingers inside, as he heard her let out a sigh. He removed his finger and immediately her phone started ringing, she picked it up and was talking to her friend. He swiftly stood up from the bed and left the room to urinate and never return back until Chelsea was back from work and the three of them were together again laughing and cheering. With this attitude, as he, the girl, and Chelsea were laughing together, he said he came to understand women to be very deceitful and evil, since they can separate two friends and cause them to kill themselves even if they still are referred to as the mother of creation. He watched her laugh with her boyfriend yet her mind was far from there.

As time went on, he was taken to the foreign office by his boss to apply for a residence and a working permit in Holland after the man had provided all of the requirements he needed to apply for it. They were told to come back in another two weeks for an interview before he will be issued everything he had demanded for, meanwhile he was still working and earning his salaries every week.

Four days before he was to go for the interview, he was preparing himself to leave his friend to rent a house for himself. But he was begging him to still stay for awhile with him even when he was beginning to suspect his girlfriend of having an affair with him; he thought he was done with the life they were living as he needed more space and time for himself to proceed with his autobiography and also to be able to watch MTV and other good programs in the television that he loved. His passion for music was becoming stronger as he continued to watch MTV and play Tupac's music which was inspiring him and driving him to think of imitating him in everything he did in his life time. The girl saw that he was industrious, smart, and was also creative but was less concerned with the issues of women, so she thought it was best for her to seduce him and win his heart and then dump his boyfriend who also it was rumored he was still in love with the girl he left in their country, the same girl David loved and has never been able to make love to—the same girl that drove him to get life for himself because he came to never think of trusting a woman since he could see them to be wicked and heartless. David was prepared to do it, have sex with her as a payback for what his friend did to him some years ago back at home in Africa. But how could someone think of paying evil with evil? Why not leave everything for God to judge? Has he come to Europe to pay his friend back what he did sometimes ago or was he here to find a future for himself? "We all know that right is right and wrong is wrong, if we really think we know, why not leave vengeance for God?"

It all happened when Chelsea became sick and asked him to go to Burger King to help him purchase two big Macs and a strawberry milkshake. As he went with his bicycle, thinking his wallet was still in his back jeans pocket, he was later surprised at the time he wanted to take from the money inside his wallet to pay for what he ordered for, that was when he knew he has lost his wallet. He did not wait, but rode fast back home to search for hit. Getting home, he searched everywhere and could not find his wallet. He knew the devil was at work again. His documents were there, meaning there was no way he could be given a residence in Holland since he will not be able to provide them. Did he lost it or someone saw it fall from his back pocket there in their house and kept it? He was beginning to ask himself these strange questions, as he had never trusted them and he was also very careless because of the too much masturbation he was doing that was causing him a self-destruction. How could this be when it was the very time he had got a job and was very happy with his life and was already on the trail to a beautiful life that he dreamed to live in one of the freest country in the world, Holland—a country he was already in love with and was ready to live all the rest of his life there. Was it Tupac's music that was bringing him misfortune or the movies he was watching that was inspiring and bringing him misfortune? Was it inspiration or was it madness that he was achieving with this dream he was beginning to dream? Why always him? Why not another person this time? He did not know how to conquer this insanity that was driving him to the road built with devastation.

When it came to the day he was to have the interview, he took his bath, get dressed and set for it with the photocopies of his documents in his hands, and at this time he was left alone since his boss could not assist him any longer because he said he was having a problem dealing with David's problems. When he met the man who was to interview him, he was asked to present his documents, but he could only present the photocopies and the worst of it all when he was asked the residence number—which he did not know because he never thought it to be an important thing to know. Since he could not provide his documents, there was no way they could interview him and there was no way he will be issued a residence and a working permit in Holland. It was over for him. When the interviewer asked him to leave to go and get his documents before he could return back for the interview, he asked the man boldly, 'Is there God?' The man was so astounded at this question and could not provide an answer to it, instead he responded by telling him to ask himself. Since he was in DenHaag for the interview, he did not want to return back to Eindhoven until he finds a solution on how to get the documents back. When he called his boss to tell him how everything were going, he was advised to go the Spanish consulate with the photocopies of his documents and a copy of the complaints to see what they could do for him to get his documents back. But when he reached there to give an explanation before the consul on how his documents got lost, he was told there was nothing they could do to help him as long as he was not a Spanish citizen. The worst of all, he could not even do the explanation in Spanish, instead he was doing it in English, forgetting he was going to get someone crossed for not coming to plead for help with a language that could be understood. He thought he was smart, not knowing he was fooling himself by showing to the consul some of the papers he was given by the Dutch authority for applying for a residence and a working permit there in Holland. Since he was told there was nothing they could do to help him get his document back, he decided to return back to Eindhoven, and when he reached, he packed his clothes, telling his friends he was returning back to Spain to go see if he could get his documents back. Some of them did advised him to stay and go seek asylum there so that he could be entitled to some of the Dutch government social-welfare. Some others advised him to get a connection and travel to the U.k. or Ireland, since there were very many opportunities for him to get there, and at that time, many immigrants were pumping there because of the plenty of job opportunities and better salaries were earned. Some even advised him to buy a passport from some Nigerians there who were already citizens and were holding the Dutch passport and could travel to the U.s. and Canada without having to apply for a visa. At that time, many immigrants in Europe were leaving to Canada and the U.s. with other people's documents, and it was easy because of the less security in the airports. He was in a poignant moment and was profoundly confused about everything, not knowing which of the advice will be best for him to follow. He knew he had to take a decision, but he also understood that he was to be very cautious of any decision he was to take—which means he would have to need some days to think it over before jumping to a conclusion. He called the Dutch man, his new boss—the man who was helping him. The man knew there were always going to be a solution to that problem as long as he was having the photocopies of the documents with him, so he advised him to stay and proceed with his work, and save some money for himself, since in the foreign office, they had asked him to come back by giving him another appointment date.

So, David continued to work there in the slaughter-house with all his strength and might, knowing that was the only way he could convince the company he was good at the job he was doing, which actually was the most dubious work there that others were afraid to do. But he was getting to enjoy it, because of the salary and most especially when he knew he was working with his own documents and was on the pathway to get the Netherlands residence, which only can be issued if you get married to one of the citizens or you are being granted asylum—which was always impossible because the country has long did so and has welcomed a very large numbers of immigrants and was almost getting tired. He wanted to live there in Holland because he said he was experiencing a very profound and opened life of freedom. Freedom and equality among every of the citizens, that is what he thought was the reason why he fell in love with the country, and moreover, the financial assistance that the citizens and immigrants were receiving from their governments. He wanted to become a part of it all in every aspect. Though, he was afraid to return back to Spain, because he understood what it meant to be living in a place where you are being disregarded simply because of your color of race. He was happy, seeing different people of different race in Holland as it was not seen in Spain. He saw civilization in Holland than it was in Spain. He saw a life with a future there the way he has not sensed it when he was in Spain, sleeping outside in the cold weather inside a valley and eating from the dust-bins. Nothing he could do about it, so, one day, when he was with a friend who was telling him of our many years he had been in Europe with no document, he quickly grasped he was having something special in his hand that he was about to lose—a document. It was then he knew the good life the Spaniards had prepared for him by giving him a document to be living and traveling around Europe.

One morning, at about 08:00 a.m, as he woke up from sleep when he was supposed to wake up by 05:00 a.m and go to work, but because he had thought of going back to Spain to get his documents back, he packed his clothes in his bag, called Chelsea and told him he was leaving and was returning back to Spain. So he took his bath, dressed-up and left. At 01:00 p.m, he purchased a ticket and was already inside the train going to Madrid, Spain. The train which passed through Belgium and had stopped at different cities and had later entered France, stopped at different cities before getting to Paris where they were told to come down to change a train to the one going to Madrid. As he came down from the train in Paris, everywhere he set his eyes were very many black people working, traveling, walking and sitting. He thought he was already in Africa when he looked around him and saw a group of black people chanting in french language. He was so happy at the things he was seeing, and how people were living together with peace, love and harmony. From where he was standing, when he moved an inch, he saw another group mixed with Chinese, Arabs, Blacks and Whites, all chanting and singing songs of praise in french which he did not understand, but could read their leaps and with the way he was seeing them, he knew they were all in a happy mood. As he watched unceasingly, tears began to fall down from his eyes. He cleaned his eyes with an hand-kerchief, and went asking people on how to get an underground train to the train station where he was said to await the train he was to take to Madrid. Asking people questions in Paris in English language was causing him to begin to like Holland better as the french were very bad in English and were very proud of it, since most of them thought the french language was supposed to be the most important language if not in the world but at least in Europe. He could not understand what people were saying and could not communicate with anyone when he came across some policemen who were already watching him since he stepped down from the train. They stopped him and commenced with questioning on where he was coming from and where he was going to. He showed them his ticket, and the black one among them demanded for his documents and he gave them the photocopies of his documents, then trying to explain to them in English how he lost his documents and was on his way back to Spain to see if he will be able to retain it. The policemen were very sympathetic and asked him to leave, but also warned him never to pass through France again without his original documents. One of them whom his English was fluent, called him and gave him a map of the underground train and explained it very well to him how he could get to the train station. He also cautioned him to be cautious and bade him goodbye.

David who was getting sick of the French due to the fact that he could not interact with anyone who speaks English, decided not to ask anybody any question, but to his astonishment, someone tapped him on his back, asking him if he speaks English. When he raised his head up, he saw a white French of about twenty-five to twenty-eight year old, smiling at him and offering his hand out to shake him. He offered his hand too, and as they shook each other, what he heard first was 'hello,' 'hello,' David said back to him. 'Nice meeting you,' 'I am David, nice meeting you too,' 'I am Charles,' said the boy, taking his eyes away from David's eyes and facing where he was heading to, inviting him to follow him since he was also going to the same train station where David was to go take the train going to Madrid. 'Are you Charles de Gaulle?' asked David as he walked swiftly, following him and they went conversing and chit-chatting from the underground transport till they finally reached the train station. What baffled David most about Charles was that he volunteered to pay for the transports for the both of them, and when they reached the train station, he saw that David was still having enough time left before his train arrived, he took him to a coffee bar and bought two cups of *cafe avec lait* for him and for himself. David was stunned with silence as he watched him talk about how he had traveled to the U.k. and to the U.s. and was very happy that he is meeting someone who could interact with him in English language. After they both left the coffee bar and the boy shook and hugged him and left, leaving him there to wait for his train to Madrid. David could not believe what he was seeing. He could not help sought an answer to his own question of why white people in Spain hate and disregard black people. Immediately the boy left him, he was beginning to believe that it was not all white people that are wicked; he was beginning to notice how some white people are even more sympathetic and are willing to help him more than his fellow black people who were causing him pains out of grudge and enviousness. He recalled how Joaquin, his sister's husband has tried to assist him. He also recalled how he met one English man who was working in Philip electronic company in Eindhoven, and the man had volunteered to help him get a job there, and had also promised to help him to travel to the U.k. He then recalled how the Dutch man who employed him has tried to help him get a residence and a working permit for him to be able to be living and working in Holland, and later, it was Charles, a young french who volunteered to pay for all his tickets and also invited him to a bar and paid for everything, and most of all, he showed him how to get to his destination. From that very moment, his love for white people was beginning to grow. He was beginning to believe that, "There are always good people as there are bad people as well in every part of the world, not minding the color of race or their gender." He was beginning to believe that, "Hatred are possessed within individuals not regarding to the color of race."

He was inside the train going to Madrid when the ticket agent—a beautiful Spanish girl, walked into the coach where he was sleeping. She woke him up, demanding for his documents so as for her to collect it and present it to the police at the border. He brought out the photocopies which was left with him and gave it to the agent who was so infuriated as she saw him bringing out photocopies and explaining how he lost his documents in Holland and was coming back to Spain. She yelled at him, telling him there was no way he could pass that border without a document. The worst thing was, when she asked him a question in their language and he could not respond, then she knew he could not speak the language of the country where he was issued a document and yet he was claiming to have lived in Spain before and had went to Holland to look for a job and has mistakenly lost his everything and was now coming to get them back. She left him there and went doing her job till when the train arrived at the border town, and it was time for the Spanish immigration to cross-checked the passengers coming into their country. They were not after drugs or any other thing, except for documents reasons. David was astounded when he was called out at the border by the Spanish *guardia civiles*. He went to meet them to give his explanation, but he was ignored and ordered to come down with his bag and wait in a locked room with some other three people—two men that were coming from Greece and were supposed to be Egyptians but were holding with them, Greek's passport, and another Nigerian woman that was coming directly from Africa, but had claimed to be living in Spain before and was speaking fluent Spanish, but she complained she had also lost her documents. As they waited inside the room for more than four hours after the train left, they were all escorted by six Spanish immigration, *guardia civles* and *policia nacional* mixed. David and the other three people were deported back to France and left there in the French custody for them to deal with the problem. He was disheartened, seeing the Spanish police warn the French *gendarmeries*, not to allow people beat their border to enter Spain illegally. In his mind, 'who the hell do they think they are, to be preventing people from entering their country illegally when the Dutch, Belgians and, the French had allowed him to pass their borders without much questionings, then, it was the Spaniards whom he sees to be poor and less civilized, that had decided to deport him back to France, pleading to them to make sure they were deported to their countries of origin.' It was disappointing to see that a country where he was said to be legal, was also the same country that was rejecting him, purposely because he was given a document to work and he left with it to another country, and later, he was returning back to tell them everything got lost and was pleading to come in illegally. David could not help resist this incident and pretended to be who he was not, instead, he proved himself by insulting the Spanish police, calling them sorts of names in English. They dropped them and left, but as they left, the French gendarmeries, left them, but warned them not to go back to that border. Some of the *gendarmeries* even advised him not to go back to Spain, instead, they gave him some addresses to go to Paris to seek asylum there. He was wayward and wanted to return back to Spain, so he called his boss in Holland who advised him to return back to Holland, promising to assist him in anything he would want. He also called his sister and Joaquin who could not help in anyway but told him to look for life for himself. Since there was nothing he could do, he went to meet one of the French *gendarmeries* to beg him to give him a route to get to Spain. Although, the man was startled at this question at first when he first opened his mouth to say it, but later, he saw how desperate he was, so he advised him to purchase a ticket going to Portbou, the border town, and as the train gets there where the police would want to get inside to do their checking, he should come down there and follow an underground to the other side where he could purchase another ticket going to Barcelona. He did exactly as he was told, and within some few hours, he was already in Barcelona. In Barcelona, he was not having anybody there, so he purchased another bus ticket from there and went to Valencia, thinking it will be easy for him to go fight for his documents back there. But, as he arrived there and went to look for his friends whom he left there, he saw that everyone of them had left that house and he was not having anyone he could call for a help, since he was not prepared to repeat what happened before he left Spain to Holland by sleeping outside in the cold weather, so he left to Madrid, and when he arrived in Madrid, he stayed in the train station, thinking he was going to meet someone he might know and asked him to render him a helping hand, since he was still having some money with him. He waited in Madrid for two weeks, sleeping in a very small and cheap hotel, tending to get a lawyer there to see if there was anyway they could help him get his documents back. First, he tried to look for his fellow country people who might help and advise him of what to do about his documents, but he did not find any, since most of them were living in the out-skirts of Madrid, but not in Madrid the capital city. He knew his money was going to get finished and if he was not careful, he will end up without any money in his pocket. But no matter how he tried, the money got finished and there was no alternative for him rather than to be sleeping in the garden, covering himself with cartons and walking around, searching for some left over garbage to eat from the dust-bins. He did so for three days until he finally met someone he knew before in his country who purchased a ticket for him to leave Madrid to Vitoria where his sister was living. The first time he met his fellow Nigerians there in Madrid was the day he walked into one of the most beautiful and largest park in Spain, and was in Madrid—a pleasant garden that is said to have originated between 1630 and 1640. There in the park, were many tourists and citizens among those who usually visit there everyday mostly at summertime. When he first saw his country people, he ran towards where they were all standing, chanting and giggling. But, as he got nearer to them, they were running from him because he was so filthy and they already knew he was stranded and they were not in the position to help him out. He was ashamed of himself when he saw this, so he left them and could not explain his problems to them to see if they will help him. As he saw one white girl sitting and reading a novel, he knew she was a tourist there in Spain, so he went straight to meet her and said to her, 'hi,' sitting close to her and offering his hand to shake her. She immediately held out her hand to shake him too. 'Hi,' she replied as they both shook hands. Within some minutes, they were already deep in conversation, facing each other and laughing and looking at each other's eyes. Inside him, she was an angel sent by God from heaven. Her smiles were twisting his brain and he was already in love with her and was at the point of uttering it to her, when one of his fellow country lad intruded. The boy came, first greeting the girl to know where she was from, and instantly when he discovered she was American, he called David to where he was standing, to ask him of his problem, but when he finished narrating it to him, he gave him 200.00 pesetas which is equivalent to 1.00 euro and 20 cents. He told him to leave the girl for him and to go use the money to call his sister to beg her to send him some money, so he will be able to purchase a ticket for himself to go and meet her in Vitoria. Although, he took the money and left quickly to purchase something to eat, because he was almost starving to death, but in his mind, he knew he was being humiliated by another black man like him with the same nationality. "It is inhuman and also very frustrating, to see yourself being deprived of what you want and need most at a very critical situation of life by a person you referred to as a brother." He did not say a word. He left and was still watching from far, how the lad was still trying to continue with the conversation for him, but unfortunately, the girl left him there in shame in the presents of his other friends who were then mocking him. Not quite long as he was still watching, he saw four policemen came with their bikes, coming down and asking all of the Nigerians standing there to present their documents, and when they did, the police started to radio, and after awhile, they called the police with the car and took two lads away, including the one that was trying to snatch a woman from him. It was at that moment, David came to fathom what was happening there in the garden and why most of his country people were always coming around there. He knew it was drug-dealing.

CHAPTER 17

BEFORE NIGHTFALL, HE WAS ALREADY in Vitoria as he left Madrid at about 02:00 p.m. He called his sister who told him to enter a bus from the train station and come home. When he reached, after greeting his sister and Joaquin, her husband, he went straight into the bathroom, took his bath and opened the fridge and brought out some African food already prepared by his sister and started eating like a hungry dog. He could not wait to wash the plates the way he normally does anytime he finished eating, he instantly fell into the bed that was already prepared for him by his sister and slept off until the next morning when he woke up to find himself inside a very large and neat bed, his body covered with a smooth blanket not a carton.

As the days went by, and he was penniless and was already starting to look for how to get himself a job with the photocopies of his lost documents. His sister's house was not far from where there were many factories and companies, so, early as 07:00 a.m, he would wake up, brush his teeth and went looking for job from the beginning of the city to the end of it. It was hard for him to get a job, because he could not speak the language, and moreover, the people there were not habituated to immigrants, and they were still very afraid of them. He did not know at the beginning that there were very many temporary employment agencies in that city. He wanted to give up looking for a job there in Vitoria, and he was about leave to go to other cities and go try. He was at the point of losing his faith in his God Whom he always believed in—the God he always prayed to whenever he was encountering difficulties—the God Who has always be there for him when he was in need of someone to assist him—the God he ignored and has begged for His mercies several times—the God he disputed with and later reconciled with several times, pleading for forgiveness, knowing he would be forgiven as he also believed Him to be the merciful One, according to what he read in the bible. He was no longer interested in believing in anything, seeing himself drawn into a life he did not wished for himself, and without him being able to find a way-out. Where was his God? Where was this God when all these misfortunes were constricting him. He could not provide an answer to these questions, so he decided to quit praying and believing in the existence of this Supernatural Being, but the more he quit this belief, the more he found himself in a worse situation and was unable to find a solution to all these problems. He swiftly forgot how he used to pray to his God to lead him out of difficulties, and because he believed he had always come out successfully. In his later life in the future he came to understand religion as, "Praying, believing and achieving." He also came to understand that, "We pray to an unknown God, gods and goddesses to assist us in anything that we are doing in life, and because we believe and have faith in these deities, some of the things we ask for is being granted to us." He said he sees it that people of the world had come to use this opportunities to make religion to become politics as everyone and each strive to make his/her own, the more better and trusted religion for others to look on to and become a part of it. He said he also came to understand that religion should have to be voluntarily not an obligation the way most people are trying to make it to be.

Since he could not get a job, he could not also raise money to get himself out of the deep hole he was already in.

One morning when his sister went out of the house to go to the supermarket, he slotted in one of the Tupac's music disc he brought from Holland to listen to the lyrics, and as it played, he was singing along with it, not knowing his sister had jammed door, pretended to have left but was still there listening and was talking alone to himself and singing. She opened the door and went straight in, confronting and insulting him, telling him he was lazy and to go get a job for himself. He was ashamed as she continuously pour insults on him and called him names. At first, he did not say a word, but she did not stop. She took out the the disc he was listening to and struck it at the wall which was resentful to David, because he knew the cds were the only properties he was having in life, and were also the only thing that could give him pleasure. So he pushed her away to prevent her from destroying his cds. But why did he has to push her when he knew already she was upset with him and could throw him out of her matrimonial home at anytime? She instantly demanded he should leave her house or else she was going to call the police. He did not wait for her to call the police, so he packed her little belongings in his bag and left to an unknown destination. Although, before then, he sensed this incident and knew something like this was going to happen, because he understood his sister to be a very harsh person and could do anything stupid at anytime; he left and went walking along the railroad track alone where found a little house built five meters away from the railroad track. That day when he left, he went to the city center, thinking he might find any black person who might volunteer to help him. He walked for more than three hours and was beginning to get tired and weary still unable to meet anyone, so, he finally decided to go to the little house he had seen before close to the railroad track and was almost at the outskirt of the city, and he was to walk almost forty-five minutes to get there. When he reached, he took one of the left-over broken doors and placed it on top of some concrete blocks, taking out the wool jacket, one of the high-priced jackets he left with from his former boss in Rotterdam—where he was working as a sales boy. He laid some clothes on top of the wooden door and placed his bag to be a pillow and laid himself down and slept, covering his body with the wool jacket, with his shoes still on. But, he was unaware that there were dried carcasses and feces in that same room. Factually, he failed to perceive the smells of the dried carcasses and feces, because he was exhausted, freezing to death, and was very hungry, and was not not in the mood to look around where he laid his head to sleep.

The next morning at about 09:00 a.m, he woke up to see that he was sleeping in a very dirty and smelling room, so he quickly rose from his self-made bed and left the room to look for a job. As he walked passed his sister's house to go and look for a job, he looked up at the building and the very apartment where his sister would probably be eating her breakfast since it was always at that very hour she always prefer it. He started to blame himself for everything that had happened and was regretting why he had not been quiet not to have utter the word that had provoked her. He also knew there was no way he could have avoid it rather than trying to go get a job for himself so as to raise money to start his own life.

It was the third factory he visited that morning, and there he was offered a job, but the boss had demanded for a report from the police to prove his documents were valid to work there. He left to the police station presenting the written note to them and he was given a paper stamped by them to prove the documents he was having with him was all valid to work in the whole of Spain. As he returned back to the factory to present the approval, he was asked by the boss to start working immediately. He could not believe what he was hearing as he went straight to where the foreman was, who took him to where he was to start working. He was showed how it goes and how everything functions and he was given some hand-gloves to start working with his clothes still on. The company was a small company for recycling papers and cartons, but because he could not speak or understand the language and none of them could speak English, he was bored because he was being laughed at by all the Spaniards there working with him. He was calm and did not mind what they were saying about him, even when he did not hear them but from their lips and their attitudes, he knew he was being mocked. That evening after a long day arduous work, as he reached the little house—his new house, to rest. He was very weak and at the same time, was very hungry due to how he had worked eight hours and another four hours overtime tirelessly without eating anything, apart from the excessive water he was drinking frequently. Since he could not withstand this hunger any longer, so he rose from his bed and walked slowly and faintly into a site near where his new house was. He walked round the site, picking the left-over bread and other garbage he found on the floor and started eating them intensely to quench the hunger. When he passed by and saw a bottle filled with water, he picked it up and started to drink it. After the meal, he was happy again as he regained his strength back and was beginning to hope for a better life within some few days, since he was already working and knew sooner or later, he will be paid some money. It was true that he was going to be paid some money, but how is he going to continue doing this job without eating or without anybody to give him something to eat or to drink? Yet, he was glad that he was having a job and was putting more efforts in doing this work to convince his boss that he was capable of doing it. He became so happy as he continued to work and get his daily meals from the street dust-bins and the dust-bin that was in his working place—where he was caught one day by his co-worker as he was eating some of the garbage, even when he begged him not to let others hear of this, but the lad declined to conceal what he saw and revealed it to the rest of them who then make it a laughing matter every time he was there to work.

One night as he walked into the site, talking to himself, his ghost, his soul, his second life, and his best friend, 2nd David—to look for some garbage, he came across the night watchman responsible for guarding the site to prevent people from going to steal the tools left there. The man who at first was startled when he listened attentively to him speaking to himself alone, said to him, '*como estas?*' offering his right hand out to shake him. '*Stoy bien,*' he replied as he shook his new neighbor and friend and was glad to see he was able to utter out some easy words he had learned in Spanish language. The man said something to him in Spanish that he did not understand but nodded his head to it. Then, the man immediately knew he could not speak Spanish, and he said to him in English language, 'who were you talking to when you were coming towards this place?' 'I have seen and heard you several times when you are talking to yourself inside that little house.' It was so surprising when he was told this; he did not know how to respond to the questions, so he bent down his head and started to cry, knowing that the man speaks English and then continued to narrate his stories of life in sorrow and grief to him on how he was working with no food in his stomach. The man felt so sorry for him that he invited him to his office and offered him a very hot *cafe con leche*. As they were both drinking and discussing in English language, the man opened up to him about his past life too; he told him of how he traveled to Switzerland at his young age, and had slept in the street there before he could get a job to start his life; he also begged him not to allow this situation drive him to think there is no God. He told him not to let misfortunes rob him of his faith in God; he told him to continue to believe in God as He is the Alpha and Omega, the Beginner and the Finisher of our sins, the Only true God, the creator of Heaven and Earth, the One that had sent his only begotten son to come die for the sins of the world.

Since the day David met with the night watchman and he was advised to keep believing in God, things automatically changed from bad to good, and he was becoming a believer again even when he continued to feed from the dust-bins and was still working. One day when he went to the city center, he saw a young black lad and quickly ran to meet him, since black people were hardly seen there in that city. As he reached where the lad was, he saw that the he was someone he knew before when they were in the refugee camp in Ceuta, and they had both slept outside in the cold weather in Murcia when he first arrived in Spain and traveled to look for a job there. Now, he was standing face to face with his friend whom his sister had saw and interacted with and had motivated her to kick him out of her house, thinking he was not serious in life to get himself a job as the lad had told her there were very many jobs there in Vitoria. After they greeted each other and discussed about their past, he opened up to him that he was homeless and was working, and all he needed was just a place he could be putting his head before he could get his own place. But to his astonishment, this lad refused to help him, telling him he was sharing the apartment with another lad and a lady who rented it. He claimed he will be thrown out of the house if he mistakenly bring another person into the house to live with him. David, who was bitterly disappointed, could not utter another word than to bid him good-bye and left. Inside him, his thoughts was getting dark about his fellow black people. He looked at himself as he sat down in his well designed bed inside his new and lonely stinking house and recall how he was treated by his friends in Holland and how a white man tried to help him out and the discussions he had with the young french lad, the french gendarmeries and this Spaniard who was helping him every night by bringing him hot *cafe con leche*, he was beginning to dislike his race, believing there was no good thing going to come out of being close to them. He was beginning to be afraid of them just like he was afraid of wild beasts. He knew it was time he should run away from friends as it was not doing him good, but trouble. He was told by the night watchman to go to the city town hall to complain his situations to them there. He assured him he was going to be given a place to be living for awhile as long as he was working. So, he went there and he was given a card to go live in *albergue*—meaning shelter, for one month. There, he was entitled to breakfast and supper everyday. This place was then making him get accustomed to so many Spanish food which he was beginning to fall in love with.

One day, he called his sister's husband Joaquin to inform him of his new job and his plan of getting a house. They both met in a coffee bar and he explained his situation to him and told him he needed his assistance on how to rent and share a room with some Spaniards. Joaquin, who was so happy that he was working, volunteered to help him get a place, even when his sister still refused to allow him to. He started buying newspapers and calling many people who were ready to lease a room in their apartments out to somebody, but it was very hard for him to quickly get someone to accept him simply because he was an immigrant and black for that matter. Meanwhile, David had filed a lawsuit against the company where he was working, because he had worked too hard and was paid a very small amount of money by his boss, who thought because he was an immigrant, then tried to cheat him. But, when David went to report this to one organization who was responsible for dealing with this issue, he was given a government lawyer who stood for him and make sure he was paid the right amount of money. He was also paid an out-of-court settlement, making him been able to raise money for more than four months rents before he could get another job for himself. But, luckily for him, he had another job and was working with Michelin, a company known for manufacturing tires and rubbers, but David was under a subcontracted company and was employed for loading and offloading tires into trucks in different warehouses in that city. Life was getting better for him as he was now living with two Spaniards in a shared apartment and was earning good salaries because he was always working overtime.

In spite of the good life he was living, he was still not happy that he was in Spain because he thought it would have been better if he was in Holland and was working there with his documents. He loved Holland that he thought there will never be a place like that where he could stay and live a life to the brim of felicity. He wanted to return back to Holland, meanwhile his documents were expired and he needed to renew them before he could leave to anywhere. During this period, many immigrants were migrating to Vitoria as many immigrants were also migrating to Spain. Moroccans and Nigerians were becoming very many in that city and houses were leased to many of them since construction works were booming the economy and was the most common work you could get in everywhere in Spain. "The more you allow people to get near you, the better you will know what they are capable of doing." As many immigrants arrived in this city and were prepared to work and there were job opportunities for them, with the help of the Basque government giving social assistance to all who were in need, the population was increasing everyday. People from other cities were rushing down as higher salaries were paid to workers and their rights were recognized. Although, David's heart was still not in Spain, but he fell in love with the city as he could quit one job and get another one the next day. Smile returned back to his face once again as he was able to work, more wages were earned and he was able to start sending money to his family at home in Africa. He loved his family too much that he thought he wish he could turn everything around for them. So as he receive, that was how he was giving, still promising them not to fret themselves—that he was prepared to sacrifice his life to make sure he put a halt to their poverty life. While in Jail in Italy, when this memory came back running to his head, he wrote a poem for this.

MOTHER AND FATHER, MY PRECIOUS GOLD.

Mother and Father think I love them not,
Precious gold, to me, always they are.
Deep down in my heart, they make a nest,
While day and night, to my God I request.
When shall He, on me, His blessings shower
So, on my parents, I can also shower?

He said he wrote this poem because he knew how his family really did needed his assistance at that very period and he was unable to provide it. He was unhappy as he could not help assist them, but none of them was able to see how much he cared and loved them. Sending them money to feed was not what he dreamed of, but establishing a small scale business for them to be running and taking care of themselves. He could not do all these things that he promised inside his heart, because he was not having the opportunity to do so.

As things went smoothly well for him: He was having a good job and was earning a reasonable amount of money and was able to assist his family in Africa, even if it was small. The best of all, he was able to reconcile with his sister who kicked him out of the house, and he saw that she was pregnant and was about to give birth. One thing he was worried about was, whether he will be able to reconcile with other black people, since he was beginning to see them to be wicked people who would want to see you in pains, and when you run to them for aid, they will start to mock and call you names. He thought it was better if he desert, despise and abstain from them. Instead, he was spending more time at home, watching the television—which was getting him to start chasing a dream—THE AMERICAN DREAM. The more time he spent watching the television, the more he came to love America and the people there. The Hollywood movies and the documentaries he was watching, became a school for him to study. He was beginning to learn more about the American history of how they saved the world from the hands of the Nazis during the second world war. He also learnt that the U.s. was a place where opportunities were given to everybody not regarding your ethnicity or where you are originally from. From his point of view, he saw the place, America—as the heaven on Earth, and he wanted to step his feet into that land—a land he thought was the right place for him to be—a place where he thought he could have a chance to become something more greater than what he was—the land of hope for all, not regarding of where you come from. He wished he never had this dream, maybe things would have went well for him because, since the beginning he had it, he was beginning to act differently, regarding other people who were not Americans to be inferior even when he has traveled and lived in Holland for awhile to see that the people there were also smart and intelligent just like the Americans might be since he could not guess how they really are, because he had not been there to see for himself. "Seeing is believing," but he already believed even when he has not seen.

Tupac, his mentor's music, became another source of inspiration in addition to the movies and documentaries he was watching. He thought he could make it to the U.s. and start to sing like him and become famous and be recognized world-wide. But how was that ever going to eventuate when he was still in Europe as an immigrant and could not get any means of getting himself there in the U.s. Even if he was able to get there, who will be the one to harbor and take care of him? Who would want to sponsor him to become a musician? It was not a question he was able to get an answer to, but what mattered to him was to get there first, then other problems will be solved. Since he had started dreaming and was willing to do anything, anything to make sure his dream becomes a reality, everybody living in Spain was automatically a nuisance to him as he wanted to be communicating in English and be creative—writing songs like Tupac and singing it and seeing that the world listens to his songs.

As many immigrants pumped into the city and were given an opportunity to be working and be living there, they were informing their friends in other cities about the place, inviting them to come over to live and enjoy the good life there with them. The numbers of immigrants coming there were increasing day after day and there was a need for the indigenous people to start leasing out their houses to them, since they were there to work, but based on a condition that a Spaniard like them would have to guarantee for the immigrants with his/her documents just in case there is a problem of say—they were unable to continuously paying the rent or the house is not properly maintained. They say, "Two heads are better than one," that was how these Africans were grouping themselves together to rent the houses. Three or four people with jobs might team up to rent an apartment with the supports of maybe their boss standing as a guarantor for them. Although the city was very expensive, in fact at that time, it was the second most expensive in the country followed by San Sabestian, another beautiful city also in the Basque country. But the wages were high and people were able to live a comfortable life and still have enough for them to save. Things were getting better and more immigrants were pumping in and the economy of the Basque country and the entire Spain was booming.

David, whom his sister was married to a Spaniard and was working and receiving good salaries as he was doing more overtime, was in a more opportune moment to rent an apartment and give the rooms out to his fellow country people to be living and paying, but he declined to do so simply because he thought it will not be appropriate for him to live with his fellow black people. He was afraid of black people since he has learnt lessons from his past life with his friends in Holland and in many other occasions, other Nigerians like him. He was seen as a racist by many of his fellow Nigerians and was called different names. It was even rumored he was gay and was having sex with his landlord who actually was a policeman and was a good Spaniard who had tried to fix him up with one Spaniard blonde lady—which he firmly rejected, because he thought it was not the right thing for him to do, since his will was to go to the U.s. to go live his life, not in Spain. The only thing that mattered to him and was his only interest and vocation in life which was his dream of getting himself to his promise land, America, and becoming a renowned artist. He was ambitious and believed he was going to succeed since he has always been a man that was born with success. The most distorting thing about him which was also outrageous, was that he believed too much in himself. He said he thought,"Believing in yourself might be the only key to any dreamers success." This belief that he had too much in himself also led him not to always believe in the existence of a Supernatural Being which was a wrong idea he should not have adopted. David, who was so ambitious and believed he could reach where he set his feet to go, also had it wrong since he could not foresee the obstacles that might fall his way or even think if his aim in life was exactly what he thought it was. "To be ambitious is a great thing in life, but to be too ambitious, that is where danger lies."

He was oblivious of the people around him and how they sees and listen whenever he was alone and was in a conversation with 2nd David. Many people were beginning to think it to be madness since he could not change his attitudes and was too desperate to see his promise land, America.

One day, when the other Nigerians assembled themselves to celebrate and invited him to come over to their house, setting him up with one of his friends whom he had known for long while in the camp and they had both met when he newly arrived in Spain and had went searching for a job in Murcia together. When he first met him, the lad told him he was in Austria before, selling drugs and has just returned back to Spain because his documents were about to be expired. David, who was so ashamed to disclose to him how he lost his documents, decided to lie to him, telling him he was caught with drugs in Holland and his documents were impounded by the police there and he was later evicted from the country and was warned never to return back there again. This same lie he continued to stand on and telling every of his friends in his later life in Europe, just only to prove himself to be a tough and smart habitual criminal who is never going to give it up. He lied about this to his friends because he sees that his fellow country people sees a man commits crime and laud him for it. It was all about bragging rights, and he knew it and also knew how to play the game with them. As he arrived at the house, he was surprised to see people dancing as the music play. He wanted to turn back to leave since he was not told when he was invited that he was coming to a party. He was told he was coming to see his friend who returned from Austria and was sick. Getting there, his friends took him to the balcony and wrapped a joint of hashish for him to smoke and as he smoked, another of his friend came in and greeted all of them. As they were smoking, the boy started to narrate how he had swallowed hundred balls of wrapped cocaine and tried to traffic them into Austria to be paid 4,000.00 dollars, but unfortunately for him, he was caught by the immigration and was imprisoned. When David first heard this, he was stunned and dumbfounded for awhile, unaware that he was in the house of the lad who refused to help him when he was still sleeping outside in the cold. He did not know how to react to this, so he quickly dropped the joint of hashish and wanted to leave. But his friends would not allow him to, instead they started mocking him, saying he was gay and a racist to black people and that he deserved to be flogged. Although, he was calm as he could not recognize all of them even when he was told they were all living in that city. There were many girls in that house and the boys were dancing with them, playing the music he disliked and would not want to listen to—which were his native music. He was already intoxicated with the hashish and the little beer he drank and was unable to leave there to his house. He was wearisome and could not utter any word as he was listening to their different conversation on how he was being mocked and called a madman. The only time he felt relieved was when one of them said he understand that he was having a dream to leave Spain to the U.s. to become a star. He swiftly stood up and tried to stand on his feet and leave. After some hours had passed and the boy who was imprisoned in Austria decided to slot in one of Tupac's cds, it was like you wake a lion up to eat a meat already slaughtered with blood all around the body. He stood up from the couch where he was lying and started singing and dancing. It was then all of them knew why he was different from the rest of them. They came to understand that it was true the way it was said by some that Tupac was his mentor and his dream was actually to become another Tupac and to be famous just like him. Jealousy was a word too good to describe their reaction when they saw that he was inspired by Tupac whom they all believe to be a legend and were very proud of him because he was a black man who was not afraid to utter the truth about racial discrimination in the western world. But how could a man who does not like his fellow black people be inspired by Tupac who was ready to die for fifty niggers as it was tattooed round his body. It was ludicrous and it was also unusual for them to see that a boy who passed through the desert to come to Europe, a boy who was from a wretched family like them to think of becoming one of the world most famous musician. Not showing concerns on what was happening around him, David, with tendency, tirelessly, increasingly, unremittingly, persistently, continued to sing along with Tupac's music to an extent they could not listen anymore and decided to stop the music and the party. David said he learnt a lesson that day that, "When people envy you and try to bring you down, you do not need to relent, just keep doing what you are doing, knowing it to be the the appropriate thing that you should be doing." After he left there that night when he was going home alone, then came 2nd David, appearing in front of him. 'Good job you did there,' he said to him as he walked side by side with him. 'Really?' asked 1st David, smiling with his face like that of a man who just won a battle and was returning back home with exaltation. "Look! Life is tough, but not too tough," so said the Americans. 'But, have you not told me this before? asked 1st David again. 'Yes of course,' I have said it before and I will keep saying it to you. It is just a way for me to encourage you to keep up with what you are doing because I know you are making the right plan to travel to the U.s. and become a star, because it will be hard for you to live all your life in Europe. The U.s is just the right place for you to be ok? New York, the land to be seen and lived, California, or Washington D.C.' When these states were mentioned, 1st David could not bear to wait to ask how he could get there immediately if not even the next hours. 'Apparently, how can I get there?' asked 1st David. 'It is easy if only you wish to do it. All you need to do is try a green card lottery and see if you will not be there soon.' 'I do not know how to do that, o.k.' 'what about getting someones documents to get there, I mean any black man that looks like you with any European passport, I bet you are going to succeed,' said 2nd David, and vanished into the air. At that very moment, he knew it was time for him to commit himself into this dream he was already dreaming and that was ruining his life. He knew nothing was going to stop him not to become an artist as he could see the universe drawing him closer and closer and his gods calling on him to come with them to the beautiful wonderland he could have a life to fullest.

His sister who was pregnant, finally gave birth to a baby girl, and Joaquin her husband called him to come around to the hospital Txagoritzu where she was put to bed. When he arrived there, he saw that she was still lying on the bed weak. He greeted her and stood there with Joaquin and watched as the nurses and doctors come in and out to attend to her. After awhile, he was given the baby to hold on his arms and when he hold the little creature, he felt a strange power came into his life, and it was the power of love, the love for an interracial relationship. He saw that his own sister's baby was white and he was pleased and was happy. He watched the baby the way she turned her body with the black curly hair in her head just like he was still dreaming and was wanting to wake up from the dream. After he stayed there for some hours, he was told to go home. Joaquin who was rejoicing that his wife has given birth and her brother was there to visit her, decided to go drop him with his *furgoneta* (van). That day was one of his most happiest day just when he has also forgotten how his sister drove him out of her house to go and sleep inside the cold winter. He was glad that she has given birth and was in a good condition of health. When he arrived home, he broke the the news to his landlord, who was also happy for him. That evening, he called his parents in Africa even when his sister has informed him that she already called them before to deliver the good news to them. He was beginning to think how he wish he was having a white woman who will give birth to an half-caste baby for him. From that very moment, the conception of having a white woman so that he could have an half-caste baby his niece came into his mind. It came into his mind that he could not control it any longer—making him dislike having a relationship with any black girl.

Some days passed and later months and he was still there in Vitoria working and was lucky to have renewed his documents and was given a two years residence and working permits to live and work in Spain. He was also in a good relationship with his sister, her husband, and Maite the new born baby girl, and was having a good job, still working in Michelin, but he was still not having a girlfriend since he could not hang around with any of his fellow country girls who mostly were prostitutes and could help him financially if he was with them. He tried all his possibly best, searching for a Spanish girl to love and to marry, but it seemed difficult more than he thought, making him beginning to dislike them because they could not speak English and were too proud to think of going out with a black person, seeing they were all from Africa and have come to Spain through the desert to Morocco and later crossing the Mediterranean sea to Spain the way it was shown everyday in the news in the televisions. It was really degrading to many other black people in Spain at that time when they will be watching the television, seeing their fellow Africans striving to come to Spain by crossing the sea and some getting drowned and died. The more this picture and videos were shown, the more the Spaniards were using it to humiliate the black people there, calling them names, saying they were starving to death—that was the reason they strive to come to Spain for a better life. David was beginning to hate the situation again when he looked into the matter very well, seeing that he was trying to love the people who were mocking him and calling him names. In his place of work, there was a very high level of discrimination and it was bothering him even when he tried and tried to make them love him and never went close to his fellow black women, but the more he tried to go closer to the Spanish girls, the more he was rejected and mocked. But how could he turn back to meet his fellow black girls when actually he could not feel love for them or say he could make love to them. What he did not wish to see was he going out with a black woman whom everybody already sees to be a prostitute the way it was shown everyday in the television. Then another thing was that prostitutes have these attitudes of disrespect for their men all because of money and were also known to be always in a talkative mood and wayward and ill-mannered and uneducated. The situation became very boring and sad for him even when he kept trying and was shoved away by many Spanish girls many times he tried to. He did not know which way to go to since his fellow Nigerians were also laughing at him for being so lonely and not having a girlfriend, not to talk of getting married to start to have kids. In the place where he was working, there was a dispute between him and some Spaniards over a girl that he tried to love because he sees in her a future that he could leap into and be happy even if she was not educated and was an unskilled laborer just like he was. He wanted to love her and treat her right. He also thought by loving her and marrying her so they could both have kids and raise them together there in Spain even when he knew if he do so, that will stop him from realizing his American dream. He thought by doing this—he could be able to help develop love for the country and the people, and could be able to support and nurture the culture that they love so much, and how to help them extend it far to everywhere on Earth. But, he came to understand that the same people were not in supports of having him as a family or a friend. They were not against the idea of seeing him and the rest immigrants go back to their countries. Then, he remember his dream of going to the U.s.—the land of liberty and freedom to live and die. There was a time in his mind, he thought it will be more better for him to be in jail in the U.s. than be in a free world in Spain as he became more preoccupied with the way immigrants were been treated with disrespect everyday and everywhere around the country. This situation was beginning to provoke hatred inside of him and since he could not resist it or pretend to love them when he knew deep down inside his heart how much he loathe them because of the wicked attitudes majority of them possessed. In his place of work, everyday to him was a tragedy since he could not put up with the insults of many of them, telling him to go back to his country if he feels the place was not good enough for him. Why should he return back to his country when he has already tasted from the honey of civilization and was dreaming to make it to the top to become a hero? He fathom by going back to his country was a way for him to give up his American dream, so he called one of his friends in Holland to help him get a Nigerian with a Dutch passport that might have the same face like his own so that he could travel with it to the U.s. He was asked to send them money before they could send him the passport which he did by sending them 170,000 pesetas which is equivalent to approximately 1,060 euros. But the passport was never sent to him and he did not say it out to anyone because he was ashamed to. Since he thought seeing the land America was his dream, he did not want to give it up, so he begged another of his friend who came straight from Holland with a passport and gave it to him to travel to the U.s. but when he arrived in Paris airport with the ticket he bought 128,000 pesetas, about 800.00 euros, he discovered the passport was fake—said to be transplanted one and he was supposed to go to jail there in France, but the immigration left him, knowing he was being duped by his friends just when he explained everything to them of how he was having an American dream and wanted to see the land. They thought he was insane and let him leave without problems. He said at that very moment when he continued to watch many documentaries and movies about some many great Americans and legends, and at the same time was listening to Tupac's music, he saw that he needed to to find an outlet for his many talents and interest, and it was only In the U.s. he believed there was a possibility for him to do so. He wanted to leave Spain to another place in the world so as for him to stop developing hatred for the people who have helped him to see his future. He saw that racism was been pronounced in the country where he live.

One day, his sister called him to inform him of how some Nigerians met her and pleaded with her to help them talk to Joaquin, her husband so as he can assist them by standing as a guarantor for them for an apartment to be lease to them by an estate agent. Meanwhile, the same boys had also pleaded with him to help them talk to Joaquin about this issue.

So when his sister called to inform him, he could only corroborated and offer his full supports for Joaquin to help them, but when Joaquin asked him if he was willing to join his friends in renting the apartment so that he could live with them, he refused. He said living with his country people was like living with demons, as they never liked him because they understood he preferred to live with the white people and moreover he had embraced the white culture and was ready to get married to their women and have kids with them. After the house was given to them and he was exempted from it since he did not want it, one of his friends who they both lived in Holland before and was at that time also living in Vitoria and has heard of him many times and was looking for how to meet him, ceased this opportunity to get his phone numbers from these other boys and called him on phone to beg him to come around to where he was living so they could meet to discuss things about life. He did not refuse the consent to meet with him since he has known him to be a man with foresight and has lived in Holland and was also planning to go and live in Canada. As time went on, this boy, Igie, became his only friend in that city and was also able to bring him closer to other black people and tried to make him understand more about life than he had thought it to be. Igie became the only person that was also able to make him discover many other talents by letting him know that Tupac's music was not the only source he could acquire inspiration from. He also gave him one Tracy Chapman's cd to play and immediately he listened to it, his life was no longer the same again as he had also come to learn that Tupac's music was inspiring him and at the same time, was also misleading him by making him think himself to be prodigious and by being haughty and lofty.

He was beginning to change his life around since he met this boy who was apparently becoming his new adviser. He assimilated learning from this boy and came to see that it was absurd that he was only thinking the U.s. was the only place he could realize his dream. The boy who also came to let him see into life that he could also try other places like Canada and the U.k. The boy who was a good lover and was interested in loving both white and black women. Later, David and Igie became two good friends who were in favor of the idea of interracial relationship and has tried to drawn some other black boys to indulge in their cause, because they thought that was the only way they could mend the gap between the black people in that city with the white indigenous people. But Igie later quit that idea and started inviting some African black women who were prostitutes from Holland, Italy and everywhere to have sex with them and called them his African queens since the Spanish girls were not willing to reciprocate maybe because of ignorance or because they did not meet the right ones who might be interested in having a relationship with black lads or simply because racism was their way of life or they were always listening to the devilish advice of their parents. Another thing that made David always fond of his friend Igie was that they were both lovers of fashion and were always purchasing the good names in the world of fashion and designs.

One Sunday morning as David, Tina, his sister and her husband Joaquin together with the rest members of Joaquin's family from his mother to his in-laws were all gathered in one of the catholic church near their house for the baptism of their daughter Maite whom David came to love so much and thought of having a child like her. David was her godfather, so also was Joaquin's niece her god mother and she was almost nineteen years old. It was David's first time to experience a baptism in a western world. At first, he wanted to exempt himself from this great event because he knew all joaquin's family were going to be present there and he was not in the mood to see them as his sister has told him of how the entire family hated her and were against her marriage with Joaquin. She also told him that Joaquin's mother has insulted her and called her a whore and an African witch. But, it was his sister who also begged him to assist her as she had tried to make the relationship work by forgiving them and reconciling with them just because of her daughter. To David, he could not blame Joaquin's mother for this because he thought she was trying to protect her child from a whore who was also a stranger. But, in accordance with fact, she intentionally hated her because she was black not because of her profession. "In anyway it might be, it is not fair for people to condemn other people purposely because of their color of race or where they come from."

So it happened when they were all in the church for the baptism, David standing beside his sister and Joaquin's niece standing beside her uncle to present the baby to the church Reverend father who poured water on the child and blessed her and prayed for them all. When they finished inside, they all went out, shaking hands, pecking each other cheek, and hugging each other, and snapping pictures happily, and later going to the restaurants for the reception to dine together. And, as they dine, they chant and sing and discuss very important issues about each other culture and traditions since some were curious and were willing to be edified more on what they think of Africa. It was an opportunity for them to introduce themselves and get to know each other better. The better part of it was that the girl who was representing Maite as her god-mother, was willing to converse with David in English language since she was desperate to learn the language and has traveled to the U.k and Holland and was smart and intelligent and was an admirer and supporter of interracial relationship the way David could see when he look into her eyes. He had even wanted to ask her out, but he thought she might be too young for him. Her family saw the chemistry in their conversation and were in supports of anything that it might result into. That day was full of fun and merriment and it was generally reckoned a success as it marked the beginning of unity and understandings between some white Europeans and two black Africans. As David left the scene to go meet his friends when he was called, he felt joy inside of him, seeing that he was with his sisters family and they were all whites and had got long with each other happily. Tears started falling from his eyes as he recalled how he has wanted to experience a life like this and has never been able to. He said he believed it is just so easy to see that people keep outside racial difference and do what is right to each others. "We can all be happy if we do not look back to anger and decide to have a good time with our neighbors."

After that wonderful event, David had seized this opportunity not to give up his pursuit for happiness to get married to a Spanish girl as he also wait in forlorn hope to see his American dream become a reality. Although, he did not know which one to choose. His American dream or getting married to a Spanish girl, but he knew everything depends on where the wind blow him to since he still believe his God will not lead him astray. As he continued to believe in what he already believed in that love can be the only way-out of all these tragedies, he met one

Spanish girl whose name is Klara and was a bar waiter and she gave him her phone numbers and when he called her, she responded and invited him to meet her friends. He fell in love with the girl, thinking he was going to marry her since she was interested in having a relationship with him. But, while he thought he has met the woman of her life even when he knew she was still very young and was at the age of twenty-one, he found out he was in love with a drug addict whose aim in life was to smoke hashish and marijuana. When he first met Klara, he thought she was serious about life because he met her working as a waiter in a bar, but later when he came closer to her and her friends, he saw that she was a little girl without parents and has crippled into the life of drugs with her friends. He did smoke marijuana with her several times and did not tried to make love to her or even say it. He knew he was to take time to study her to really know her. But when he saw that she was an illiterate and was from a different city and has come there alone to look for her future by living with some friends who were also junkies like her, he tried to change her, and by so doing, she stopped picking his phone calls. He continued to call and call and see that she was not ready to talk to him no matter the many text messages he sent to her and how he tend to convince her to win her love so they could be together. He quit calling her and decided to focus on his aims in life. He could not wait to be told what to do when at that same period he lost his job and has started another work in the construction as an unskilled laborer and was working too hard in a company owned by a Portuguese who tried to cheat him by paying him less than the rest workers because he saw him as black and thought there was nothing he could do about it. Stung with wrath, David insulted him and was about to beat him up when his co-workers arrived at the scene to separate the two of them when they were holding each others. David quickly met with an organization for workers commissions there who gave him a lawyer that helped him filed a lawsuit against the construction company who later gave him his severance package and then sett off. Also in the house where he was living with two Spaniards, he was given fifteen days to leave because he confronted the landlord who was also a policeman, for raising the price of his one room rent. He loved that house even when he knew the lad whom he was living with was a policeman. In that house, inside his room he could do whatever he wants with it even to an extent he used to smoke hashish inside. Many times he has hidden some balls of hashish in a container and placed it inside the fridge and every morning he could get them out and take it to work to sell for his co-workers who were his regular and only customers.

After he lost his job and was bored being at home in his sister's house and was looking for another job and a house to rent, he found himself being duped by one of his parents family friend in Nigeria who was living in the U.s. He sent more than 200.00 dollars to the man and called him on phone with more than the money he sent to him because he said he helped his elder brother, Kennedy, to apply for a green card lottery there in the U.s—and that the boy had won the lottery, and he needed that money to process some documents there to get him to go and live in the U.s. David who was also a smart lad, fell a victim because of the trust he was having for the man who was the same age as David's mother and was very related to them. He traveled to the U.s. with one of his daughter who also was David's age mate. He has left five years before David left his country to come to Europe. Although his children were still there in Africa and were almost starving to death since their father could not send them money from the U.s. to feed. Most time, David's mother was always responsible for their feeding due to the fact that they have lost their mother who died after more than five years that the man left to the U.s.

Everything became complicated for David again, since he did not know which way to go to and was about to give up his American dream and was still very lonely and could not find a white woman to love and was not prepared to go out with his fellow black women, living there even when he could see three women fighting for one man. He was beginning to hate himself for who he was and was blaming himself for being born and also blaming his mother for having given birth to him. He did not know actually how and what to do to console himself. He could not comport himself as a man any longer since his dream was fading away and he was about to lose his dignity as a man. He tried to listen to Tupac's music but it would not help. He tried to proceed with his biographical life writing, he could not, because he saw himself incompetent since he was not a graduate and did not even finished his secondary school grades. Life became miserable for him that he thought he could commit suicide so he could not witness his own future which he always predicted to be success and was apparently turning into failure. He called his friend, Igie, to seek advice from him, only to be told that some of their other friends who were there, among the group that invited him to a party to mock him. He was told that four of them had left to Austria to go and sell drugs to make easy and quick money, since they were fed up with the lives they were living there in Vitoria. But, when he asked the reasons they were fed up, he was told it was because they lost their house and were unable to get someone to lease out another apartment for them. Igie was also getting himself preparing to leave to join their friends sincehe too was in need of money to travel to Canada to go and live with his sister over there.

Confusion was about to be born, when he thought it over and over again, not knowing which way to head to. He wanted to return back to Holland since he was already having his documents, but how could he return back when he has lost his documents there and regretted his life for having traveled there? He was still in love with Holland, but he wanted to try something new—something different, as he was an adventurer and was prepared to go to any length to see that his dream become a reality. He went to the U.s. embassy in Madrid to get some information on how to get a tourist visa to travel there, knowing he was not going to return back since he could seek asylum. He was given a phone number to call to get every information he might needed. He called the phone several times and he was told to fill out a form in the internet and at that time he was still an internet illiterate who does not know how to touch a mouse or rather he could brows. He gave up the idea of traveling to the U.s. so he went to the German embassy also in Madrid, and getting there he lied to them that he was having a member of his family there and wanted to go there to work as an artist who was specialized in metal design gates. He told them he was having many years of experience in welding works, showing them some of the pictures he took while he was still in Africa, posing with some of the gates he designed and structured. But, tell him he was talking to the Germans not the Moroccans. The lad he met asked him if he speaks German and he said no, so the lad told him it was no problem, when he gets to Germany that will be an easy thing for him to do, but it was necessary for him to provide some certificates for them to be assure he was having some skills and experience in the profession which he claimed to be an expert. The truth was that they knew he was having a residence and a working permit and was ready to go and work in Germany, not to go there to become a nuisance. They encouraged him and really wanted to help him if only he was able to meet up with the requirements which were too much for him, because they also required his birth certificate and his bachelor's hood certificate. He tried to provide them even when he was not born in an hospital and did not actually know the date he was born not to talk of having a birth certificate. He called one of his sister in Nigeria who tried to forge some of the documents and sent it to him. Still he was unable to meet up with all of them. He saw that it was an herculean task for him, so he relinquished that idea and thought of another thing to do. While still in his sister's house with money in his pocket, he was called for a job not far from where he was living, and he went to do the job which was only for some few days. He saw that there was no need for him to wait to rent an apartment and continue to work. So one day as he was watching a documentary of Norway and how the people there were living, he remembered how one of his friend in Holland had wanted to travel there to seek asylum. The boy also said something about the Norwegian girls to be very intelligent and always in need of men not minding where you come from or your color of race. Immediately, something came to his mind to try Norway. The next day he talked to his sister about it and that same day, he went to meet an agent to purchase a ticket to Oslo and was prepared to leave Spain to Norway. His major aim was actually to go and look for a blonde girl there to marry and live the rest of his life with her. He knew it was not going to be easy and smooth, but he also knew it will be a progress for him to leave to discover new things in his life since he was having the opportunity which was the documents the Spanish government gave him. At the agent's office, the girl who sold the ticket for him looked at him and asked him, '*para que quieres ir al Noruega?para vivir o para hacer una visita?*' '*para vivir,*' he replied courageously as the ticket was handed to him. He shook her hand and left.

He was already in Bilbao's airport waiting for the flight going to Paris, France, since he purchased an Air France ticket and was going to transit there to take another flight to Oslo, Norway. He entered into the washroom and since there were nobody inside, he knelt down and prayed to his God to assist him in his journey to a place where he actually did not know anybody who was to receive him there. Although, he knew he was going to seek asylum. But, how was he going to hide his documents and to whom? Or, what if his asylum is not accepted and he was kicked out into the street to sleep inside the cold, as it was the beginning of September and autumn when he was told Norway was one of the most coldest place to live in Europe as it is a Nordic country? Or, what if the police there find out he was having a document in Spain, what will be the consequence? He did not lose faith in his God, Whom he believed to be his creator because he believed He will always be there for him whenever he was in a complicated situation like that. There was a time he thought to quit this belief when the night guard in Vitoria, Spain, at the place he was sleeping when he was homeless, came to wake him up by preaching to him about the good fortune one can always have if only he could believe in the existence of God. He was having faith that his journey was going to be successful since he has traveled to Holland before and had lost his friends phone numbers and later met a woman who came to his rescue. He believed he was definitely going to meet another woman who will come to his rescue again. After he finished praying and boarded the flight and was inside, he saw himself sitting next to one courteous young German man who was also transiting in Paris and was going to Germany. He was lucky the man was speaking fluent English, as he offered out his hand for a shake. When they finished shaking hands and have introduced themselves, the man asked him where he was going to and he told him he was going to Oslo, Norway. First, the man was startled when he heard the word Norway. He repeated the question and David replied him for the second time, 'I am traveling to Norway.' 'Do you live there?' asked the man, sitting himself well so he could hear clearly. 'Yes of course,' lied David repulsively, thinking in his mind, why is he doubting him or, does black people not live in Norway? 'It is a nice place,' said the man, looking straight into his eyes like he was seeing a black Norwegian. 'Yes it is,' said David, still pretending to be a black Norwegian. 'That country is rich I heard,' said the man. 'Are you working over there?' he asked again. 'Actually, I am a student, but I am also doing a part-time job there,' replied David, feeling very uncomfortable, as the questions were getting too much for him and his lies were about to be unveiled. 'They say is cold over there, how do you like it?' 'Yes of course, it is cold, but I am accustomed to it,' said David, wanting to get himself out of the bondage he already placed himself by pretending he was not hearing the man very well when he was asking his questions. 'Where exactly where you born?' the man asked again. 'Anyway I was born in Nigeria,' replied David. 'Nigeria?' the man asked. 'Is it long you have been living in Norway?' 'Yes, I have been there for more than six years now and I am happy to be living in a country like Norway,' said David, excusing himself, as he stood up to go to the toilet. Inside the toilet, he met 2nd David who also was waiting to edify him of the new steps to take to overcome the burden he was receiving from the young German. 'You do not need to be lying to people because you do not know who is who, and if you are caught lying, it might become a problem to you. So you better say the truth and see if anyone might be willing to help you,' he said. 'Look, I thought you were going to say something more reasonable, but see how you are advising me to be truthful. Do you believe I can get any help for being sincere,' asked 1st David, sitting in the toilet, pretending to be pooping. Then a man knocked at the door—making him quickly take from the roll of the tissue papers to clean his anus, and when he opened the door to come out, the man looked at him in surprise since he did not see any other person with him as he thought he was there talking to another person, not knowing he was talking to his soul, his best friend. When they arrived at Paris airport, he bade his new German friend good-bye and left, running to meet up with the flight going to Oslo. Inside the flight going to Oslo, he was sitting down with one fat pretty blonde lady whom from her look you can see that she was living a good life. 'Good evening,' he greeted her, 'good evening,' 'how are you doing?' asked the fat lady. 'I am doing well.' 'Are you a Norwegian?' asked David, trying to be friendly, and at the same time trying to know if she was interested in talking to a black person. 'My Dad is a Norwegian, but my Mom is an American,' said the woman. From her American English accent, he already knew he was talking to an American lady. 'Wow! You are American, he said. 'That's right,' said the fat, blonde woman. 'Are you going to Norway for vacation?' 'Nope, I'm going to visit my parents, they both live there, but I'm living in the U.s.' Her English seemed to be too fast for David to understand, since this was his first time in his life to be talking to a mature and wealthy American woman face to face and was a little bit confused and was stammering even when this very one was friendly. Inside his heart he has fallen in love with her just because she said she was American. 'How I wish she can tell me she wants to marry me,' he murmured to himself. 'Were you talking to me?' asked the woman. 'Nope,' said David, trying to imitate her American accent of English. 'You are beautiful,' looking into her eyes. 'Thank you,' said the woman, shutting her mouth, immediately she saw the air hostess bring the food to serve them. As the flight landed and all the passengers came down and walked to the baggage reclaim hall, he saw the fat blonde woman also waiting for her luggage as he was also waiting for his one bag which he checked in. Putting the handle of the bag round his arm, he walked to the arrival hall and there, he met the fat blonde woman again. He walked straight to her and greeted her. She greeted him too, asking him where he was going to pass the night. He lied for another time that his friend was coming to pick him up. She stood for some minutes and gazed at him, and then said to him. 'Look, actually I'm not going to my parents house this night. I'll be passing the night in a hotel in Oslo, what about you?' David was stunned with her question and wanted to unveil his situation of life to her, but he thought he was going to let himself down to her, and moreover, he saw that she has taken out the wedding ring she was wearing before. He knew immediately she was married. But was she thinking of having an affair with him and dumping him? He did not know how to tell her he was interested in her, so he bade her good-bye, as she continue to look at him as he walked away. From the airport, he took a bus to Oslo, the capital city. There in the bus station, he met some black people who actually were from Somalia, and immediately he ran to meet them to ask them of how to get a cheap hotel to lodge. One of them told him to follow him and took him to a hotel, which to David, was not cheap, but could be one of the cheapest in Oslo. There inside the room in the hotel where he was, he knelt down and prayed to his God, asking Him to send his angels to guide and protect him, since he was in a new place and was not having anybody there to care for him, and when he finished praying, he slept till the next morning, as he woke up to see that it was almost 08:00 a.m. He quickly brushed his teeth and went to the dining hall just the way he was instructed by one of the workers, to have his breakfast which was made of butter tarts muffins, cinnamon rolls, pan cakes, sandwiches and wraps, breakfast pastries, egg dishes, breakfast biscuits, crispy and creamy doughnuts, fruits, beverages, milk and many more to be mentioned. When he sat down with many other men and women to enjoy this wonderful breakfast of serve yourself, he found himself to be the only black person there, and he was stunned and looked at the people there very well, and saw that they were all distinguished gentle men and ladies of high class. Why did the Somalian boy brought him there to come lavish his money when he knew the place was for rich people? But he also forgot he told the boy he wanted to lodge in a hotel, instead of him to have said he wanted to lodge in a pension. But the boy was supposed to know he could not afford a hotel as expensive as that. How could he ever know that, when he saw him dressed like a wealthy man's son who just arrived from Houston, Texas, and has come to Oslo for tourism? He was wearing a western boots worth a hundred and fifty dollars, a Levi's jeans trouser, a Jean Paul Gaultier's sweatshirt he stole from his boss's boyfriend in Holland, and a golden necklace worth 400.00 dollars. Who will ever think he was coming to Norway to seek asylum? With this experience he had, he came to really understand that, "Many people who are fashion-conscious might not know the implications they are bringing to themselves when they might be thinking they are only drawing attentions of people just to see them as good looking people."

Two days since David arrived in Norway, he still was homeless and not having a place to sleep even when two Nigerian boys helped him for the first day and later told him to go look for a life for himself because he did not tell them the truth that he came to seek asylum, and moreover, he also told them he was good in drug trafficking just to impress them, not knowing these were different Nigerians from the ones he has met in Holland and in Spain. One morning at about 11:00 p.m, he was still roaming about the bus station, not knowing where to go or who to call on. He was wearing his leather jacket since it was getting too cold than he expected even at the beginning of September when it was still very sunny in Spain. A black man walked closer to him to ask him where he was going to, and he was happy that someone finally cared to ask him that. He swiftly turned from what he was doing to respond to him, thinking God has sent his angel to deliver him out of his misery and frustration. When he first asked the man who he was and where he came from in Africa, and he was told he was from Somalia. First thing that came to his mind was, is Norway a home for the Somalians? After awhile, the man took him to a nearby coffee bar and ordered for two cups of coffee and after then, he took him to his house, saying he was rendering him that help because Allah has said so. David was happy apparently, because he thought God has sent His Holy angel to rescue him from the miserable and stranded situation. He was beginning to think Muslims to be the most sympathetic people in the world since nobody was ready to give him a helping hand except the Somalian man whom he thought Allah sent to him. At the man's house, he showed him the bathroom to shower and gave him a new towel to dry his body with it and when he was done with the cleaning, he showed him the bed so he could sleep to regain some of his strength back. While he was asleep, he felt something like he was having sex all alone by himself with nobody. He thought he was dreaming, so he swiftly woke up from the deep sleep he fell into due to the fact that he was very hungry and was both physically and mentally fatigued. As he woke up, he saw the man removing his hand from his penis. First, he thought he could wake up from his dream, but as he wiped his eyes with his hand to see that he was seeing clearly and that what he was seeing was real, he drew the man closer to himself and asked him to turn his back so he could have sex with him since it was more than a year since he last had sex. The man was delighted and swiftly picked up a condom and gave it to him and turned his back for him. He wore the condom and pushes his penis into his anus and pushed it hard as he screamed and screamed, he continuously pushes it harder and harder until he was about to faint and stood up as he released the sperm on top of the mattress because the condom was already broken. After some minutes when the man was able to get himself back, he brought out some money from his pocket and offered it to him, then he opened the door and ordered him out of the house. As David walked out of the apartment with his bag still around his shoulder, he did not know what to do and he did not know how he could get himself back to the bus station where the boy picked him up, then he remembered Spain to be a country where he would have been working, earning some wages and living his peaceful life, instead of him coming to see himself in an unknown land where he was starting to learn a new life that he has never in his life thought he could experience not to say he was already practicing it. He recalled how he was even about to kill his co-worker, a Portuguese by throwing at him a big stone, because he jocularly touched his penis and said he loved him. He saw that he was practicing homosexuality which to many Africans was a taboo. A thing he will regret in his life to see that if any of his friends in Spain was aware of, he would find himself been buried by shame and insults. He was beginning to see his life drawn into a horrible and awkward feeling of maelstrom situation. He saw that life was so deep as his father has once said. "It is not just the way we look at life to be that it truly is."

Back in the bus station, he knew there was no time for him to waste, since his money was finished and he was almost beginning to starve to death as hunger finally found a way into his life and the strong windy Norwegian September cold was beginning to haunt him and finding a way to cripple him to the pathway that will lead to his grave. He quickly decide on what to do, knowing that the Norwegian government were capable of restoring him back to life the way they did for many others who were there, living lives with glamour. He went to hide his documents in a near-by bush not very far from where the police station was without anyone seeing him do so. He went to the police station just the way he was advised, and then seek asylum with a different name and age entirely from the name and age he was bearing in his documents in Spain, which actually was not also the rightful date of birth but was the real name he was christened by his parents. In Norway, immediately he became a refugee and was sent to the refugee camp where he could stay before he could be transferred to any other place later, as he undertook different task to pass through the necessary procedures on whether to be granted asylum or be denied. His new name when he was first asked, was Godffrey, since he has mistakenly wrote it, but two days later, he found it was wrong and decided to change it to be Geoffrey with a middle name of Cass and a surname, Oviawe. He forgot he was making the authority responsible for dealing with every matter relating to refugees starting to suspect him of lying of where exactly he was coming from, and lying about the problems that really drove him to come seek asylum there in Norway, because it was very uncommon for Africans to bear names like that. He chose these names because he read them in a book long time ago when he was still very young and was in the primary school. He read these names in Oliver Twist novel and has first thought of changing his name at that very time, but was unable to. He thought this was a golden opportunity for him to do so. One week after he applied for asylum and was in the camp not too far from Oslo, the capital city. There, he was with some new friends and was quite happy with them and the way they were being treated and cared for by the Norwegian refugee council. He was bored there in the camp, as he found it difficult to meet the woman of his dream—which was his major aim of coming to Norway. He thought it will be better for him if he could go to Oslo to have fun and search for his desired object. He sneaked into a train without paying to Oslo city-center. As he sat down, near the train station and watch a happy spectators or he could rather say a crowd of happy people surrounding some tall beautiful young men playing volleyball in a beach volleyball court in the frontage of the country's largest and most beautiful train station, he fell in love with the country where he was and the people in it. He was brimmed with a sensation of pleasure seeing what he long dreamed of even right from his youth. He saw that life was worth living even when he has regretted why he left Spain when he first arrived there and was frustrated, not knowing what to do and which way to go. He saw young men and women frolicking here and there to their different destinations. From what he was seeing, he could believe there was an obvious contrast between the people in Spain and the people there in Norway—the new place where he was living. He saw that the Norwegians were more open to communication with strangers, and that almost all of them speaks English, unlike the Spaniards who were tight and closed and do not speak English or say—not willing to learn to, because they still believed the Spanish language to be fundamental. He said, he was always unhappy with the Spanish girls to see that they were not always in a good mood to have a conversation with strangers most especially when that stranger appears to be a person from a third world country. He said he could see that, "To be open to communication with strangers can help us create a beautiful atmosphere where the both sides could benefit from it, as it is a way for everyone of us to learn from others, things that we have not seen and places that we have not been." He was glad he was in Norway since almost all the girls he come across with, could have a time to talk to him when he insist. He was glad as he could see them and excuse them so that they could talk. The vital part of it was that many of the girls he met and had conversations with, were all with knowledge and understandings, and have traveled to more than ten countries around the world—which impelled him to have fallen in love with almost all of them. There in the city center near the train station, he sat and watched the crowd of happy people and the volleyball match, and was also seeing around the corners some junkies with dirty clothes on, perambulating. Not far from where he was sitting, he saw two pretty young girls kissing themselves, and he walked closer to where they were and sat close to them, telling them in English. 'Look, if you need a man,

I am very much available.' When they saw that he was very serious with what he was saying, they left him there to be talking to himself. When he looked around, he saw a pretty blonde girl, sitting alone and smoking a cigarette. He waited for more than ten minutes to see if someone was going to meet her, but no one came and she was still there all alone by herself. He left where he was sitting and went to meet her. 'Hello,' he said to the girl. 'Hello, how are you?' replied the girl, offering her hand out for a shake. He raised his hand and shook her and then asked her, 'please can I sit with you?' 'Yes, you are very free,' said the girl, as she smiled at him. He smiled back and sat down near her. From her accent of English, he knew she was not a Norwegian. 'Are you English?' he asked, smilingly. 'Apparently, I am from Australia, I am not English,' said the pretty girl. The moment he heard she was Australian, he quickly change his accent of English, trying to brighten it up so she could hear him clearly. 'Australia? That is so amazing, I heard it is very cold there,' he said, looking into her eyes to see if he could see himself inside. She stood up and walked to go and sit in another position, calling him to come over and sit with her. 'Australia is not that cold anyway, its a bit hot at summer and not too cold at winter,' she said, looking back into his eyes. 'I am waiting for my boyfriend,' she said. 'He is from Kuwait and he is living here in Norway. But we both met in London.' 'You mean your boyfriend that you are waiting for is a Muslim? asked David, like she just committed a crime for saying her boyfriend was from Kuwait. He brought out his necklace out, as it was hidden by is jacket. His 400.00 dollars necklace with a cross locket worth a hundred dollars. 'You see, I am a Christian and I believe Christ has come to die for all of our sins,' he said, raising the cross locket up so she could see it very clearly. 'I am here in Norway for a vacation and I will be going back to Spain soon where I am working.' He brought out his niece picture to show to her that he was a man who already was having a relation with a mixed color race. He wanted her to know that she was not supposed to be with a Muslim man, instead she was supposed to be with a man like him who believe in Christ and would love her till death do them part. He saw that she was not the discriminating type and was very open in communication to strangers like the other Norwegian girls he had met. 'Look, pretty girl! you are sensitive and you are a caring person, and you are so simple yet insightful.' 'Thank you for the compliments, said the girl, bringing out two sticks of cigarettes and offering him one, 'do you smoke?' she asked. 'Yes I do,' taking it from her and bringing out his own lighter to light the cigarette for himself and for her. 'Thank you,' she said, moving her body to face him. 'I like you, but the truth is that I am already in love with someone else and I just cannot do it.' 'But, why do you prefer to be with a Kuwaiti? or don't you know these Muslims are evil doers who are prepared to kill themselves and a million people more? 'You said your name is David, right?' 'yes my name is David.' 'Look, David, "There are things in life that many people in the world with eyes cannot see apart from the few ones who are willing to dig into it so they could see it." 'What do you mean by that?' asked David, sitting himself well, trying to pay more attention to what she was about to say. 'I know you hate Muslims because of the suicide bombers in Palestine and many other Arab countries.' 'Yes,'said David. 'Why should they do that?' 'Why? Or, is that a strategy to create fear in our world so people could be afraid of them?' asked David, his face dark with rage. 'Calm down,' said the girl, sitting more closer to him and looking into his eyes. 'These Palestinians believe that to be the only way they could avenge themselves since there is nobody who is willing to support them in achieving their goal of creating a Palestinian state.' 'Creating a Palestinian state?' 'Yes,' said the girl. 'I can see that you are new to this.' 'I am knew to what?' asked David, opening his hear very well to hear her preach her sermon. 'Do not believe in everything that you read from the newspapers and books or everything that you see in the televisions.' 'I watch CNN and BBC,' said David. 'You just said CNN and BBC?' 'Yes,' replied David boldly. 'I like you because you are curious and want to learn,' said the girl. 'Do you know who owns them? 'No, said David. 'O.k, you don't. Let me tell you. They are owned by the Americans and the British, and who are the Americans and the British? The Jews if you do not know, know it now. The Jews owns the largest wealth in the world and they are mostly based in these countries and with their wealth, these countries have been able to achieve everything they have wished for, which is power.' David who was so astonished with these words, since he has never heard of these stories before, was calm and unable to move like a man in a trance. But the more quiet and calm he was, the more she continued with her sermons. 'Have you read anything about apartheid in South Africa before or the segregation in the U.s. or the slave trade or the Crusade in Ancient Europe? Everything was not just about hatred but a strive for power to rule and govern. Can you tell me the meaning of the word PROFITEERING?' she asked. 'No,' said David, since he has never in life heard of the word and do not know what it meant. She brought out a small Oxford dictionary and showed it to him to read, and he saw that profiteering is the act of making a lot of money in an unfair way, for example by demanding very high prices for things that are hard to get. 'And that is exactly what the Americans and other countries in the western word, mostly Europeans are doing to the third world countries. They make excessive profits from the goods supplied to them from these third world countries, but when they are selling to them, they sell to them in high prices. Is that not exploitation?' she asked. David stunned in silence, tried to grasp what she was trying to preach to him by listening more carefully to her—to the beautiful stranger he was already falling in love with, seeing that she was the perfect woman for him, his desired object, the hidden treasure he has come to search for in Norway. This time, she came sitting closer and closer to him, and stretching her right hand towards his neck, she touched the necklace he was wearing and the cross head locket, and said, 'this is beautiful, and after that, she dropped it and looked into his eyes again and said, "But some days to come I know you will see the truth clearly with your eyes and then be able to judge who is right and who is wrong." As she said this, a car drove in and she stood up and pecked him on the both cheeks and left to meet the Arab man in the car waiting for him and was still waving him goodbye, even when she was already seated. The last words uttered by the girl was so outrageous to David, when he sat down and continued to think about it. How could she be in support of evil doers? he asked himself. I hope she finds a better and well educated man and leave that dumb ass Muslim to go and kill himself with a bomb. But deep down inside his heart, he was trembled as he repeatedly utter the word PROFITEERING and think about what she just said to him about this power that men seek.

CHAPTER 18

I T WAS ON SEPTEMBER 11TH, 2001. David woke up as early as 06:00 a.m to wash and clean the floor, as he was scheduled to do so by the refugee camp authority. When he finished the task he was given to do which took him just one hour, he went back to the small room in the camp which he was sharing with another boy who also was from Ghana, but was claiming to be a Rwandan, because he thought he could be accepted by the Norwegian refugee council since Rwanda was still in a political crisis and Ghana was not—meaning there was less chance for him if he was a Ghanaian. He entered the small room to see that his room mate has left to the construction work he was doing—which also was a black job since he was employed by one Norwegian illegally. He quickly climbed to the top where his bed was and slept off. He slept off for more than seven hours, and when he woke up at about 02:00 p.m, and was very hungry and needed to eat something, he hurried to the toilet first, to urinate and poop before he could think of what else to do. There in the toilet, he heard some Somalians and other Arab speaking people murmuring, muttering and grumbling, and he could understand it was all about something, but what exactly it was, he did not know, but he could see clearly, as they all stare at the cross head locket attached to his necklace—that it was something relating to religion. So he walked out of the toilet before they get him killed. Getting himself out of the big camp toilet, he went closer to the television room, where there were many people watching CNN, and, when he joined them to watch, he saw two skyscrapers(World Trade Center) in New York brought down by planes flown in by some hijackers who were said to be terrorists and were named with a title (Al-Qaeda). He stood for awhile and gazed in awe silence and after that, he saw that another flight was also flown into pentagon, and another to Pennsylvania. He knew it was meant to be a war against the Americans, so he screamed in wonder and, as he did, everybody there including the guards, turned to watch him, knowing he was in a horror of agony. He was devastated as he watched this in the television. He did not know what to do as he watched the many innocent men and women get killed, all because some people have decided to commit suicide and took the pains to kill other innocent people of every religions and tribes around the globe. He thought he could wake up from the dream he was dreaming since he was still not believing what he was seeing, happening to the people he loved so much—the Americans. He immediately understood there was no way he was going to achieve his American dream, since the insane religious fundamentalist have blocked his way of getting into the land he long dreamed of—to travel to and to live the rest of his life. Immediately, he knew many countries were going to pass an anti-terrorism legislation and expand their laws on immigration and provide more security and traffic control inside and outside the airports. How could people be as so wicked in the name of religion to have been able to develop this ideology of hate and think of how to cause a great devastation and also a confusion among the good people of this world like this? he screamed out as everyone there in the room turned to look at him and as tears fell from his eyes to his cheeks and dropped down on the floor. As he wept for the people and the families of those that were dead and the ones that were injured, some Arabs and Somalians there were happy it happened in America, causing him to recollect what he was told by the beautiful stranger he met in the city center the previous day. He knew there was something wrong somewhere and it should be fixed, and if not, something more unpleasant and weird was going to happen sooner or later. In David's later future life when he was in prison in Italy, he came to write a poem about this bizarre incident of the terrorists attacks.

IN THE DARK HEARTS OF EVIL MEN.

In the dark hearts of evil men,
Lies the ideology of hatred.
Leading them to their evil deeds,
Causing a great devastation.
While killing innocents men and women,
And believing it to be the will of their God,
Whom they adore and worship.
Creating fear among everyone who lives in our world,
Bringing to us all, division and confusion,
And impelling others to think of this religion to be radical and aggressive.

There was no way David could erase this incident out of his mind when already some days before he arrived in Norway, it was said that in his country where he was born and brought up, there has always been a religious conflict among the citizens; and it all commenced when some radical Islamic group decided to set the churches ablaze and also killed some of the members in one of the state where the majority were Muslims, thrusting on the Christians to take a retributory action. This issue of religious differences has been a part of the most frequent and recurring issues in his country's body politics since the independence was granted and even before then and yet this issue had yet been able to be resolved. The religious conflict has led to a great jeopardy physically, psychologically, politically, economically, and as well as to the cultural lives of many of the citizens. To an extent at a time, a (sharia law) was about to be imposed nationwide, which also has brought another division among the citizens, provoking some to stand up for their rights of living as citizens of a republic country with freedom and liberty—which actually is deserved by humankind. David, on his own, knew it was time for him to stand up and fight not only for the thousands of innocent people that were killed and maimed in the attacks on the world trade center, but also for the innocent men and women that lost their lives in these violence religious conflicts in his country. But how could he think of fighting these evil doers that he thought every Muslims were, when actually he has come to Europe to work to earn some money and return back home to invest on his creative art work he was doing before he left his country? Or, how could he fight, when his dream was to become a great and renowned artist? He could not help change this idea of hating every Muslim, even as he tried several times and failed and kept trying and trying. When he went for an interview and was inquired by the Norwegian refugee council to write a statement of the reason he left his country to come seek asylum there, he wrote that he was formerly a member of an organised group who believed in freedom and liberty and was with an objective to eliminate every Muslim living in the southern part of the country where he claimed to be the place he came from. This statement which later had an effect on him as some of the workers there in the camp studied and observed him to see that he was truly against the Islamic religion—maybe because of the religious conflicts in his country, not knowing he was lying to be accepted there in Norway as a refugee who actually fled his country to come to Norway for refuge. He was swiftly transferred to another city called Bergen—a city very far from Oslo, since he also told them he was having a girlfriend there when asked by the authority which other place in Norway apart from Oslo that will be suitable for him to live. He was upset with the Norwegians because he saw how they were in favor and supports of the many people who were from the Arab countries and other Muslim countries in Africa and Asia to seek asylum there. The tangible truth was that every refugee there were being accepted, nurtured, and cared for, but asylum were granted to the people from countries with political crisis. The fact was because they were Muslims, he thought it differently from another way round, putting him to be questioning himself, why the Scandinavians preferred and considered Muslims more than the non-Muslims?

It came to the day he was to leave Oslo to Bergen, a new refugee camp he would have to go and live since he has deliberately chosen it for himself when he was asked to do so. He could not imagine how on Earth one of his friends called Njuma, who was a Muslim and was from Burundi, also decided to choose the same Bergen for himself, even when he knew David was not in support of any Islamic doctrine that he has tried to preach to him just to convince him to be a part of them and hate the Americans. From the time David arrived there in that refugee camp, they were both friends because he saw that he too has stayed in Germany before and was having a child with one German woman, but has decided to come to Norway to seek asylum with the prospect he will be given an opportunity to stay there because of the war in Burundi. David came to hate him right from the day the terrorists attacked the world trade center. He actually loathe and detested him more than he has to Osama bin Laden, the master minder who claimed to have been responsible for this mischief. Although to David at that time, Osama bin Laden remains the Satan that was said to be the cause of all evil according to the bible. David said he saw him as a mischievous man with evil conduct, who was trying to draw other souls to it. But, the worst thing about this issue was that many Muslims including his friend Njuma, were so blind to see that Bin Laden was not a messiah as he claimed to be, instead he was a thief who has come to steal and to destroy the human dignity. He came to cause confusion among people of different religion and proclaiming himself the chosen one who actually was to lead every of his believer astray. When the then United

States president George W. Bush declared the war on terror and attacked Afghanistan as the first step to commence since the U.s. secret intelligence believed Bin Laden was living there, David did supported him and thought of going to enlist in the U.s. army so as to make sure these evil doers he supposed were all the Muslims everywhere in the world to be brought to justice. Njuma actually mourned those who died in the attack and condemned it, but he tried to edify David, his friend of the past history on how the Catholic church declared an holy war known as the crusade to eliminate the Muslims and to eradicate the Islamic religion. He also tried to lecture him of how the Muslims came to declare Jihad—their only war to fight to resist the Christians. But David, who apparently has not heard of all these stories before, thought it to be lies and did not want to listen to him—instead he was beginning to shun him. So, it was so surprising when David saw his friend packed his belongings and was getting himself prepared to take the same train with him to his hope-to-be new camp. He thought if he could vanished from the planet Earth to another planet since he was beginning to think it was a conspiracy between the Norwegian Refugee Council and his friend Njuma due to the fact he already knew everyone there in that camp knew he was against every Muslim and was trying to avoid them. Njuma has been his good friend before the world trade center incident. He has been financially supporting him mostly when he was in need of cigarettes. How could this be that they were going to be together again even when he believed he could avoid being his friend if only he leave that camp to the one in Bergen? Inside the train, when he was sitting opposite him and they were both having a discussion of how their new camp might look like, David recalled he has concealed his passport and the Spanish residence and working permit he used in traveling to Norway inside the pocket of one of his trouser before they left the camp. He brought out all his clothes and started searching them one after the other to see if he could find them, but, he did not. He searched again and again to see if he was mistaken, yet he could not. His mind went back to the time he left his room with his friend Njuma, who came to wait for him early that morning and helped him to pack his clothes into his bag. He became suspicious of his friend having stolen his documents just to punish him for having the belief that Islamic religion is haughty and arrogance and simply cannot countenance the idea of keeping to itself—a phrase, they both read in a newspaper together—that made him finally concluded he was against his religion. David could not help control himself as he was chafed—seeing that he had landed himself into frustration once again. What if he was not accepted by the Norwegian Refugee Council so as to be able to stay there in Norway? How was he going to leave there to another country? He uttered out some words that he was being punished for not willing to accept a life that he thought was so miserable for him to live in. It was so absurd, but when Njuma heard this, he went close to him to console him, knowing he had become a prime suspect. As David and Njuma reached Bergen when it was almost dark and waited at the train station for someone to pick them up and the person has refused to come at the right time because it was raining, Njuma brought out his packet of Malboro cigarettes which was David's brand and offered him one. At that very time he was a cigarette addict and could not do without smoking, so it was very easy for anyone to befriend him if that person was a smoker. Later that night as they arrived the camp and were showed to their room and the toilets and bathroom and were left alone to do the rest on their own, they both prepared coffee for themselves and started smoking and chanting just as they were at the very first time they met each other before the world trade center bombing. The next day, early that morning, a woman knocked at the door of their room and she was asked to come in. David who was covering himself with a blanket and was wearing a white singlet and a blue bursar, was so shy to get up in her present, but could only talk to her from where he was lying. She sat down in the chair and first introduced herself to them as Toni, the second in command in that camp. The beautiful blonde Norwegian woman who probably will be more than forty-five-year-old, was still there talking to him like she was interviewing him. But Njuma, his friend was astonished at the way the lady was conversing with David and not turning to face him even when he tried to distract her attention away to his bedside. Instantly, David was beginning to feel something inside his heart that the lady was having some interest in him. He could not concentrate on anything as he wished she could leave so that he could get up from his bed and get himself dressed. But, when she later decided to leave, he thanked his God and quickly get himself up and dressed up and took his tooth brush out, pressed the toothpaste in it and went to the washroom to brush his teeth, meanwhile his friend Njuma was already dressed even at the present of the woman, stripping himself so as for her to see him very well. From the very first time that morning when David saw her and had a conversation with her as he was still lying inside the wooden bed covering his naked body with a blanket and she was sitting down looking into his two eyes; he has seen her to be an angel that has come to deliver him from the hands of the daredevils. He felt something for her and thought of loving her and living the rest of his life with her—which was a thing that he was fond of doing best when he sees any white woman who finds no problem in having a relationship with a dark skin man like him. He thought he was falling in love with her or he thought he thought it was passion not love and that he was mistaken one for the other as he could not even distinguish between the two. He saw that she was so sympathetic and was a God-fearing person because of how she apologized to them for not coming to pick them up at the right time when they arrived at the train station and it was raining heavily. Their new camp was a two storey building house with more than twelve rooms, meaning, it was a building with three floors. Those with families were given a one bedroom apartment to live while a single person was allowed to share a room with one other person—maybe of the same race or nationality but, it has to be of the same sex—all these were to evade frictions and clashes among them. David and his friend Njuma were in the same room and since they were in accord with each other apart from the little difference of misunderstanding each other's religion, but they were moving on well and were at the top of the building. At the second floor, was the office of the workers and directors headed by a woman who also was at her forties and speak fluent English as well. Down at the house were three television rooms and in one of the rooms, was a billiard table and the television there was with a satellite. Another room was meant for watching movies borrowed from the public libraries which was also free as long as they were all entitled to a library card which also was free including their every monthly bus transportation card. Inside that same room, was a piano, a keyboard, a guitar and some other musical instruments, but the television was without a satellite. The other room was only for watching television and was also with a satellite, which was later installed there for English speaking people among them, because of how David has disputed with the Arabs and Muslim Africans there since he was not allowed to watch CNN, BBC, and other American and British movies and documentaries, even with these people's aggressive threats and fights, was unable to be forced to relinquish control of the television. He was so contented with the new life he was living in this new camp in Ytre Arne—which was situated six miles from Bergen—a small settlement with a population of about two thousand people and was surrounded by a fjord and was always raining just the way Bergen was always raining. From the window of the room where David and his friend Njuma was living, they could watch the boats pass the fjord since the camp was on a hill. Two days after their arrival, David and his friend were given a monthly bus card so that they could go to Bergen, as they were also enrolled there by the Refugee Council into a (a school for new comers in Norway for learning the Norwegian language). Ten meters from their camp, there was a library, which was shown to them by Toni, the lady who came to introduce herself to them before and was showing a sign of love to David by always looking into his eyes whenever they were talking to each other. She also drove them to Bergen with her car to enroll them in a school and took them to the big library there, to register them and gave them both, library cards so that they can always go there to borrow books, video-cassettes, and cds. David saw that she was good and kindhearted and was in love with him from the looks in her eyes. But, how could he love her when he knew that she was older than him and there was no way she could have a baby for him again since she was already having two grown up children almost the same age as the age David claimed to be there as an asylum seeker. He wanted to love her for her generosity and her good attitudes towards others, most especially immigrants. He wanted to love her and make her happy all the rest of her life. But he needed a woman who can have an half-caste baby for him. He needed a younger girl, whom he could love and get married to—not for money or for documents reasons. He saw that she was willing to do everything for him to make him happy and to live in Norway and be a part of them as she had seen in him a successful future. Some days later, Njuma, his friend and roommate called him to inform him that another of their friend whom they had left in the camp in Oslo had sent him some of his belonging which he left there, and amid them, there he had found the documents David had lost and was still looking for. It was so surprising as he heard this, but yet, he thanked him and collected the documents from him, knowing he was lying to him. He knew he stole it and had wanted to use them to travel maybe back to Germany as his wife was always calling him on phone to return back to

Germany so she could marry him to get the German stay. When David first arrived there in the camp, he saw that the place was populated with mainly Arab people from Iraq, Iran, Afghanistan, Kurdistan, and other Africans, mostly from Somalia. There were also some few white people from eastern Europe like Macedonia, Georgia and Ukraine. The idea that Norwegians were always in favor of Muslims, came back to him. But there was nothing he could do about this issue as he continuously take a rightful and stable view at how Muslims were accepted more than other people of different religions even when he purposefully bought some tickets with his monthly feeding allowance, and traveled to Copenhagen, Denmark and Stockholm, Sweden—to see that it was the same in all these Scandinavian countries. He ascertain the fact that there was something he could not fathom how it came to be in existence. He became very upset, this time not with the Muslims, but with the Scandinavians, for allowing them come there and practice their religion, and even supporting them in building mosques everywhere. He was bitterly upset the way they were all accepted into this civilized society which many Muslim fundamentalists were preaching against. *Nygard skole* In another building just about two hundred meters from were David's refugee camp was situated, there were eight other refugees. Four of them were from Albania and were one family, and were living in one apartment, and at the opposite apartment, were some Norwegians, two men and a young beautiful lady. The Norwegians have rented that place and were all working and studying. On top of these two apartments, was a four bedroom duplex, and inside, were three Nigerians and Twaha, a boy from Burundi—the same place with Njuma, and he too was also a Muslim, but was not fanatic and does not pray unlike Njuma, who was always prayerful, and yet was with an immoral lifestyle not minding what the consequence might be. Among the three Nigerians, was a boy called Onyx. Onyx has actually lived in France as a refugee for two years and was not granted asylum there before he decided to come to Norway to try his fortune to see if things will turn to good for him. Onyx, was from the Igbo speaking part of Nigeria, and was desperate in doing anything in order to make money. He was a good lad the way David saw him and came to sense that they were of the the same type and were having so many things in common. He was pleased when he met him there at the he visited them in the building where he was. He saw that Onyx was also very intelligent and was a graduate in one of the universities in his country, and was also possessing some of those great natural qualities just the same as he was. Moreover, he was a smoker and Marlboro cigarettes were his brand just like him and Njuma. He came to like him and prefer him more than any other person there, because they were of the same age and he was also a Christian, and has seek asylum with just the same problem he too has seek his own. They actually became two good friends that he will leave the building he was, because of the too much noise of the different people of different ethnics and race and religions, and visit him in the building where he was with Twaha and the two other Nigerians who were always working and were always absent at home, making the house very quiet and more comfortable. His going to visit him was mostly for him to stay out of trouble as he could not cope with the stresses and strains he was having being unable to tolerate those many fanatic Muslims who were in the same building with him. The more they were getting together, the more they were getting to like each other and narrates each others past and laugh and drink and listen to Tupac's music which also was Onyx most favorite. But the more he was having this new relationship with Onyx and always absent in the camp, going to meet Onyx or going to the city, the more the people in his camp were developing hatred for him because of how he was scorning them. Among these people, was Njuma, his roommate whom David actually was always trying to avoid, knowing he was against the American politics and policies in dealing with the issues of the world. After some days that he arrived at this new camp in Ytre Arna, Bergen, he applied for a school which was located in the city-center, for learning the Norwegian language and he was given a chance to start. Starting the school, he was also given a monthly bus card so he could go to the city anytime he would want to. This actually made him to be more frequent in the city every time and everyday, meanwhile he had also utilized this opportunity in going to the city to look for Norwegian girls, knowing he might luckily meet anyone who would want to marry him since he already knew there was a little or no chance for a Nigerian there to be granted asylum, because the Norwegian refugee council believed there was no political crisis there, even as the country was about to plunge into a civil war because of the every day religious and ethnics conflicts. It was not because he wanted to stay there and be legal that he was actually looking for a girl he could marry; it was also because it was the most vital life he desired to live, by marrying a white woman and living all the rest of his life with her—and that has been his reason of coming to Norway as he said before and will repeatedly say it again and again. In this new school, he came to meet other people who also were foreigners, but were not refugees like him. First, he found it difficult to be able to cope with them because he was beginning to feel inferior in their midst. But later when he came to understand them to be very good and humble people who regard him for what he was, he became very friendly and attached himself to them and made them his pals. In that class, he was the youngest among them, and was the one with the dottiest attitude. Though he was not very interested in learning the Norwegian language as he found it very difficult, but he was always happy whenever he was there in the classroom chanting with the people and making fun of the language and the teacher. In his class, were three women and seven men including him. Among the women, was one from Ghana who was married, another from Yugoslavia and was still very young at her thirties and was having a boyfriend, while the third woman was a bit older than the second woman and from Albania and was still single. Among the men, was one Egyptian man who might be at his thirties and was married to a Norwegian lady who had brought him from Egypt to Norway so they could come and live there. There was another Nigerian man at his forties and was married to a Norwegian woman in Las Palmas, Spain, but they both came to live there in Norway. The third among them, was a Canadian who also married a Norwegian in Canada and came with her to live in Norway. The fourth one was a Spaniard whom too, his wife was a Norwegian and they have both married in Spain and came to live there in Norway. Then, there was this Italian man, who has lived in the U.s. for fifteen years and could speak fluent American English just like the Americans. He was working in a restaurant owned by another Italian and was also living with a Norwegian woman even if they were not married yet. The sixth and the last of them, was one American from Alaska, but has lived in many other cities in the U.s. He was also married to a Norwegian man and was brought there to live with her, even when he was not happy with the cold weather and was unable to learn the language just like David. The American was the only person amid these people together with David whom actually were not happy with the life there because they both found the language to be a poison. In David's later future, the Norwegian language became a language he wanted to learn while he was already living in another country—but it was too late for him then. As David came to see these people who were far better than him come to live in Norway with their wives, he was surprised and began to ask himself questions of the reason why they have chosen to come live there. It was later when he went further to inquire and to know how much social welfare was rendered to everybody living there as long as you are legal, he came to fathom the reason why people were running to come live there. When he learnt that he was the only man there that was still single, he was ashamed and wanted to do everything so as to quickly have someone he could call his own even if they were not married, but at least, he could present her to be his girlfriend. Since these people (his classmates) were all working and were in good financial condition, they were getting accustomed to hosting themselves for dinners in some restaurants not too fancy and McDonald's. David became ashamed since he could not do the same to them, but he was glad he met them and respected them for who they were just the way they also were not the immodest types. Back in the camp, Toni, the lady who was already in love with him and had wanted him so badly, became upset with him since he was no longer frequent and was always spending more time in the city than he was spending time in the camp with the other refugees. She was beginning to disliked him as he was not showing any sign that he wanted her back just the way she had wanted and loved him, even as other men were running after her. Every men there in the camp including Njuma, David's roommate could see that she was in love with him and he was not ready for her. David knew she was dying to have him, but he could not help her to achieve what she wanted in life, because he felt something more stronger than love for her that he thought he could fall for her, and at the end, dump her for another younger girl who could bear him kids. He knew if he did, it could hurt her so much and she might not be able to withstand the situation. One day when he called her to beg her to replace him in a room where another boy had left in the house where Onyx, his friend was also living, she immediately went to meet her boss and convinced her to allow him to go and be living there. She was glad she was helping him and that they were still interacting with each other. She was glad that he came to ask her to help him and she did helped him so he could be happy and be comfortable. She also organized a billiard competition for them there in the camp and set a prize to be awarded to the best players. The award was worth a hundred kroner for the winner, and for the second position, it was fifty kroner. David actually came to win these awards twice as he thought of the money and what good it will be for him even when he came to that camp as a novice and was not really interested in playing billiards. But as he started it and kept practicing and playing every time, he swiftly developed a talent and passion for it and became perfect and was enjoying it. In his later life when he was staying longer in Europe, billiard became his favorite game. David knew she knew what he wanted and wanted to offer them to him ten times more than he has wanted, but he loved her so much that he did not want to hurt her, and for that simple reason, he refused to fall for her even when she kept trying and trying and he kept resisting her and was not having a girlfriend at that time and was getting accustomed to frequent masturbation inside the bathroom with some porn magazines. Meanwhile, David was still calling Klara, the Spanish girl who was a drug addict and has never wanted to change her life around to live a more responsible life. He kept calling her, trying to make her understand how much he cared about her and would want to have her in his life, but yet, she was warning him never to call her again. David, who was a book lover and always loved to read novels, finally had the opportunity to pick up a book to read when he was issued a library card which permits him to borrow any book or music cd there in the library without paying a dime. Since he has been in Europe and even some years before he left Africa to think of traveling abroad, he has ceased to read because he oblivious of the pleasure he always derive from reading and has also let money conquer his mind and brain. He picked up that book to read because he saw that it was written by an American author, but immediately he finished reading it, he could only see himself pants for more books to read. The memory of his childhood came back to him when he recalled how he loved literature and constantly loved to read books. He could recollect the face of the first woman he once loved and never made love to because she was twice his age and he was just a teenager—it was the face of the woman he was never going to see again—the woman who made him love to read—it was his childhood school teacher. He said he saw the book he was reading revived him back to life, and without delay, he saw the secret of life unfolded to him again, giving him a fresh opportunity in life to think of himself the dreamer he once was during his childhood. He saw that this opportunity was also for him to grow and change from his obsessed life with America and to relieve himself of his self-afflicted adversity. He saw that it was never too late for him to reformulate his idea and think of doing what was necessary to be done. He saw that this opportunity could also allow him to visualize his future and refocus on a plan for a better life if only he could clearly define what his aim in life was. And to define his aim, he knew he needed a power to accomplish it, and that power was inspiration, and he could only acquire that inspiration just by reading. As David, with the help of Toni, moved into a new house, the same house Onyx, his friend was living so as to replace another Nigerian who left the country because the Norwegian government asked him to leave or he will be deported back to his country of origin by force. He knew it was time for him to think of something else that is more important than fighting with the Muslim fanatics there in the camp where he used to live. He saw that there was no way he could reward Toni for what she was doing for him except to pray for her and stay far away from her. But, some few days after he left, she was made the boss and was responsible for every activities there in the camp. He wanted to meet her to tell her how he felt about her so she could always help him in dealing with his problems both financially and morally. The more he thought of going to her, the more words of wisdom he found inside the book he was reading at that same period. As he met her for the very first time since she was named the director of administration, he looked into her eyes when he was speaking to her, to see if he could trust her to let go his dream and follow her to anywhere she wished to take him, and when he was doing this thinking, his mind reflected back to his childhood life of how he loved a girl who later broke his heart by going out with his friend—making him thought of women as treacherous, evil, and unreliable people. Although, he wanted to love her since he could see that by loving her and living with her could make him develop an attitude of a grown-up and a responsible adult. But he was still doubting his mind, knowing a woman's heart is always a deep place to reach, and it is mysterious. After he left her and not utter any word relating to what she might expected as they were alone in her office, he went home to start reading his book from where he stopped, thinking the more quotes he come across might inspire him more than a woman who was not his age and was desperate to have him. The more he tried to concentrate on what he was reading, the more he could see her face and recall how she was helping him. He could not help the situation as he thought about her and also was thinking of his future and wanted to be clear about what he really want in life, and how to set a goal and outline some strategies to achieve it.

It was one cold evening, when David was waiting for a bus in the bus station in Bergen to go to Ytre Arna where he was living. A girl walked passed him and he greeted her. Squealed in surprise, she responded and greeted him back, smiling to him. He could not wait to be told what to do next, but followed her and started talking to her as they both walked out of the bus station and went to sit in a chair near the train station which also was near the bus station. As he was talking to her, he came to see that she was young and pretty, very smart and intelligent and was speaking English fluently. When he asked her what was her name and how old she was, she told him her name was Gitzy and she was just twenty-one. The name was a beautiful name when he heard it and asked her to spell it for him and she did, he could not help wait to conceal his feelings for her, instead he knelt down and begged her to love him. Strike in great surprise when she saw him knelt down to beg her to love him, she asked him to get up and gave her a peck on his cheek, but she made it very clear to him that she was going to think about it very well before she could decide on what to do. So she collected his phone number and stored it in her phone, promising to call him soon to tell him when she will be prepared to meet with him for a dinner. When he told her to give him her phone numbers, she refused because she said she already has a boyfriend and would not allow anybody to call her when she is with him. But when he tried to know things about his boyfriend, she told him he was from Kurdistan, and as he heard that her boyfriend was a Kurd, he fell in an appalled silence, thinking how in life could a girl as intelligent and sympathetic as she was be dating a Muslim. He asked her if she knew Muslims were terrorists, but she replied him with a furious voice. 'Who are you to condemn other people's religion? I have been dating him for more than a year and I know he is not the fanatic type and I love him, but the truth is that he does not speak English and I have made him to learn but he has refused to. You do not need to judge people because of their religion.' David watched her speak, and inside him, he thought if there was a way he could make her leave the boy that same moment so he could prove to her what it meant to be who and what she is. After some hours of discussion and she has scolded and lectured him on the issue of religion and also made him know that she has read the Koran and found it not to be evil as proclaimed by many Christians, they finally left each other and she promised to call him on phone. He thanked her and promised to wait for her to come and love him. But, some few days after they met, and was just five days before Christmas, she called him on his phone to tell him she was prepared to meet with him the next day at McDonald's in the city center. He was agitated with delight and instantly, he began to rejoice and celebrate like he has won a lottery. With too much exultant happiness that he could not hide, his friend Njuma noticed that he was undergoing an emotional sensation of pleasure, he called him to ask him what was happening. When he told him he has received a call from the girl he met some previous day and also told him about, he was happy for him and they both started celebrating and he quickly went to buy a packet of Marlboro cigarette, made some tea, and they started drinking it and smoking their cigarettes. David did not actually thought she was going to call him the way she promised to, because he has met some others before who promised and never called. In his heart he believed she was the angel sent to him to come and heal his wounded soul. The next day he broke the news to one of his classmate called Ignatius who was also a Nigerian and was married to a Norwegian woman and was financially supporting him and was always advising him to look for one to get married to so he could have the chance of staying there in Norway. Ignatius, who was so happy when he heard this news, swiftly put his hand in his pocket and brought out some money and gave it to him to hold when he will be going to meet her. He also used that opportunity to invite the rest of his friends including the Egyptian and the Spaniard to go eat there in McDonald's. After they finished eating and were about to leave, David saw Gitzy and hurriedly went to meet her bidding good-bye to them. They all bade him good-bye as well and were all happy for him that he finally found someone. As they both left to a coffee bar inside the biggest and busiest shopping-center located in the heart of the city which actually she has chosen, he felt very comfortable and secured, walking and talking with her and when they sat down to discuss, she ordered for two cups of coffee and paid for it. She started by introducing herself and telling him everything about herself, and when she finished, she asked him to do the same. He wanted to tell her everything about himself—the truth—the whole truth. He wanted her to love him for who he was and not for what he was, but with his heart filled with fear that he might lose her, he told her what he believed will please her, he told her lies, lies, all lies, from his name to his age and to his family background and what he was doing in Norway. Inside him, he knew she knew he was a refugee, but he thought it was not the right time for him to disclosed it to her because it might scare her away, since many women in Europe at that time believed every refugees are out there for women so as to be able to secure a document that will enhance them and allow them to stay in their country. But inside him, it was love first even if he might needed the document which actually is inevitable since he was still a refugee and was illegal and want to live his life there—seeing the country's economy to be one of the best in the world and the citizens and immigrants were all entitled to equal protection and social welfare. That day was the most happiest day of his life, even when she did not agreed to kiss him as they walked together to the bus station and after much hugs, she watched him take the bus and waved him goodnight and blew him a kiss with her hand. He was happy he met her and was beginning to think she was the right woman for him—the woman to be the mother of his unborn kids. At that time he was already twenty-four, and in his Spanish document, he was already twenty-six, but he lied to her he was twenty-one since that was what was in his document there in Norway. He also showed her his student I.D card and she saw that his name, truly was Geoffrey, and this name she came to fall in love with and was always happy when pronouncing it. After that day, they met again, and again, and she promised him to wait that she was going to break up with her boyfriend soon before she could get to spend more time with him. Although, she loved him out of sympathy, knowing he was in love with her too, and also knowing that he was having a strong passion for music and literature as he tried to make her come into his world and profess to her what the future might be when she decide to come with him to his unseen and unknown when-to-be paradise on Earth. Two days before Christmas, he called her more than ten times and she did not pick the phone. At first he thought she was running from his calls maybe because she thought he was moving too fast and needed him to take a break so that they could get to know each other before anything, but when he continuously call her and her boyfriend picked the phone and warned him never to call again, he was hurt so badly that he thought of going to commit suicide. He was hurt and was also humiliated because he knew the Kurdish boy she was with, did not actually loved her from what she told him of him. He knew from the beginning it was going to have a devastating effect on him if he lose her, so he tried to do everything to please her, everything that will make him have her by spending the little money he was saving from his monthly feeding allowance given to him, on recharging his phone to call her every time. It was very painful as he was a vulnerable person and could be hurt easily. Since there was no way he could resist it, he tried reading a novel and it could not help because every nights, he could hear the scream and hush from a Norwegian girl when having sex with another Nigerian refugee living in one of the rooms in the duplex he was living. At that same time, Onyx, his friend left to Trondheim, another city in the north of Norway. He was left alone at home with the Nigerian man who in reality, graduated as a civil engineer in their country but has come to seek asylum in Norway and was already working, earning good salary in a cleaning job and was waiting for the Norwegian refugee council to grant his asylum. The other boy, Twaha from Burundi, also traveled to Stavanger to visit some of his Norwegian friends. That Christmas eve, as David tried to resist the girl's screaming and failed because the weather was very cold and it was snowing, he decided to visit Njuma whom he left in the other camp. Getting there, he saw that his friend was busy talking with his wife in Germany on phone which might take him two hours to do since it was already a thing he was habituated. He sat down in one of the chair in one of the TV room and was watching CNN, but he was hovered between anger and remorse since the place was noisy and little kids were oscillating restlessly here and there. He saw Toni, their new boss—the woman who actually deserve his love, the woman who knew what he wanted in life. They greeted each other and she left him there to attend to the children who needed her care and supports. After awhile, she came back to meet him, asking him to follow her to where she gave him some chocolates and biscuits and showed him how to design a house with them, using candy gums. He wanted to reject it at first, but when he tried doing it, he discovered that it was fun and interesting, so he continued doing it, and when he finished and returned it back to her, she gave it back to him as a Christmas gift. He could not help explain how she was still showing him love after all he did to her by despising her when he knew she needed him. As he walked back home that night, he began to shed tears. He swore never to forgive Gitzy, for how she treated him that day as he arrived home and slot a cd into a compact disc player that was supposed to be in the parlor, but he decided to leave it inside his room so he could always listen to music since that was the only thing that could heal his wounded and worn-out soul. He slotted in Celine Dion cd and started singing it along as the music was playing. That night which was Christmas eve, he wanted to draw her close to himself and feel the warmth of her body. He needed her and wanted to love and caress her; he needed sex to quench the fire that was burning down inside his heart; he wanted her to come near him and never leave. Since she was not there, and he was repeatedly listening to Celine Dion, he brought out his porn magazine once again and masturbated. He was cold and sad even when the electric heater in his room was on. Later in his later life in prison in Italy, he came to write a poem on how she did hurt him that night.

HOW MUCH YOU'VE HURT ME.

See how you've caused me to go at a trot,
When you fathom, with your love I'm lost.
I sleep my sleep to wake up by the morning light
With my face unable to smile in two directions.
Like a bird whose wing's hurt,
From the sky my heart fell down to be burnt.
How much you've hurt me,
To the world, I just can't explain.
To you, my heart I've rendered
And my heart, you've squeezed.
The fate you've made me lost
Is now becoming their dreams.
My professional philosophy as an expert lover,
When you cry, I cry more.
And yet, you turned my heart into a steam,
A steam of water that boils without ceasing.

Just a day after Christmas, without delay, David decided to visit the library to return some of the books he borrowed and also to borrow some more. That morning, he arrived very early at the library and went straight to the section where he first saw and read little articles about a book of the essence of ancient Egypt culture and reinterpretation of its relation with outsiders throughout its history. The book was also about the culture, monuments, and language of the ancient Egypt. But when he tried searching for the book and could not find it where he met it some few days before, he was disappointed, and a deep feelings of sadness went down on him as he has watched a documentary of an ancient Egypt in the television the previous day and was beginning to develop interest in the study of hieroglyphics, thinking he could be able to read and interprets the Egyptian symbols and pictures of objects. He thought it will be appropriate for him to dig into history so he could know where exactly he came from. His heart filled with disappointments, he returned the borrowed books he was having inside his bag. He wanted to leave to go home, but going to stay at home lonely and reading all those books was already driving him insane. He was bored, really bored, and he needed a company—someone he could talk to. Since he could not go home, and then he decided to spend some time with the computer and browse, and after that he went upstairs of the library to see if maybe he could still find the book. Suddenly he saw a beautiful, tall, slim, blonde girl, and she looked like the girl he met before near where he was living in Ytre Arna. He walked swiftly to meet her and saw that it was the same girl but only that she ha changed because she also changed her attires and her make-ups and was apparently looking more beautiful. He greeted her, and as she turned her back to see him, she was glad and greeted him back, and they started conversing. He has actually met her before and told her she was beautiful and that she was meant to be a queen. He also told her he was interested in being her friend and she did agreed, but when she told him she was still seventeen, he instantly gave up the idea of thinking of having a relationship with her, but he insisted they become friends. She told him she was studying fashion and design and was having a dream of becoming a model, and when he took a close look at her very well, he knew she was fit to be one since she was possessing every quality of a model and a designer from her looks to the way she was dressed. As they were engaged in conversation, he asked her why she was in the library. Then she brought out some of the fashion magazines and books out from her bag and showed it to him, and from that very time on, he knew she was desperate to achieve her dream. After much conversation, they both left to take the bus to return back home since they were living in the same street. Inside the bus, they sat near each other and he was always looking into her eyes, thinking if God would make her think about him the same way he was thinking about her. He opened his heart to her and confessed every of his past life and what his dream was. She later left him to come down and gave him a peck on the both cheeks—making him think heaven was here on Earth. From that day on, he knew it was time for him to be really serious in what exactly he was doing, and as he continuously visit that public library without cease, and came to discover the use of internet and became addicted to it, and with this addiction and the much interest he was having in reading those great books, he was becoming to understand that his dream was to become what he always thought he was, a writer. But he was becoming exasperated with himself, knowing he could never become a writer since he was a mere secondary school drop-out with no school leaving certificate. How could he be dreaming of a thing he knew he was never going to achieve or else he was going to end up being a failure. The more this thoughts were running all over his head, the more books he was reading, and the more he was losing faith in himself and blaming himself for having started reading and getting addicted to it. One day when he was alone, doing his thinking of what he should be doing, then appeared 2nd David, walking close to him and putting his hand around his neck. 'Why are you regretting of being who you are?' he asked. 'Whom am I? asked 1st David, sitting himself well to hear what he was going to say. "You are what you are, you are what you think you are," Have you not heard this saying in the bible that, "As a man thinketh in his heart, so is he?" 1st David being a person who love quotes, quickly rose up from where he was sitting and shouted out, "I know what I am and I know I am a man born to make changes." 'Aha ha aha aha ha ha, make changes?' asked 2nd David, mockingly. Anyway, "If you believe, then you can." But, as becoming a writer, you need to study very hard to achieve it since you are not a graduate and can neither spell every English word correctly not to talk of those grammars and vocabularies you come across when reading books.' 'Then how do I do this?' asked 1st David. 2nd David who was prepared to assist his second life, his soul, on how to become a writer, picked up a pen from the table and sat him down on the chair and started lecturing him. First he advised him to always write down every quotes he come across when reading a book, and later he advised him to write down every words he come across that he does not know the meaning and later check it in a dictionary, and after he did that, he bade him good-bye and disappeared. Since the day he was disappointed by Gitzy, the girl, he loved and sworn never to hurt, he sworn again never to love a woman since he came to believe none of them really deserve his love. He started attending night discos with one of his classmate, Ignatius, a Nigerian who also was married to a Norwegian woman but was a good womanizer and was also dealing on drugs. With this opportunity, David came to see that the Norwegian girls were very easy to get. After he saw that Ignatius was always busy, he decided to be going alone, and since he was a music lover and a good dancer, many girls were throwing themselves at him, asking him to do with them whatever he wished. Many times when he would start to dance with them without asking him questions, they will start to kiss him, and some will take him into the washroom and with a condom, have sex with him. He was starting to enjoy the country as they continued to come, days after days, anytime whenever he was present there in the disco. This was also bringing an attention of many Norwegian young boys to him since he would not stop dancing and the girls will not stop following him. Many people were getting to recognize him there, and for that reason, the owners decided to change the rules by implying new ones and asking people to be paying before entering. He did not quit going even when he would have to spend his feeding allowance for entrance into the disco to dance with the girls and have sex with them anywhere they prefer. When Onyx, his roommate returned back from Trondheim, and was also interested in this new life-style of partying to look for women, they became very frequent in all the disco houses in Bergen. One day, when they were both inside one of the disco, he saw Gitzy, the girl who broke his heart on Christmas-eve, and she was with her friend. He quickly went to meet them to say hello. She was so happy to see him and quickly introduced him to her friend who was a little bit fatter than she was. Although he met her once after the Christmas-eve incident, and she took him to a disco house and they both danced and danced and danced and she tried to apologize for what she did that night and he did forgave her, and later, she threw herself to him, opening her two big nipples for him to caress and fondle with their both lips sucking each other's. But when she proposed to follow him to his house, her boyfriend with some of his other friends came and dragged her away.

So that night when he met her and her friends, after the introduction, she ordered for a drink for him the way she has always been doing it right from the very first time both of them started goingsout together. Inside him, he still was in love with her, but he was tired of waiting for her love. He called Onyx, his friend and also introduced him to them, telling him to pick the other girl out for a dance so he could have a chance to be with her, but the two girls refused to dance with them. He knew it was time for him to display to her his true color and what he was capable of, so he picked up another girl and started dancing with her, and all of a sudden, they started kissing, and as Gitzy saw this, she went closer to him, thinking she knew him very well that when he look to her, he will leave the other girl to come meet her. But he cling to the girl very tight and never loosen his hands from her waist as he fondle her and kissed her smoothly. She was infuriated and called her friend and they both left. That same night, four girls gave him their phone numbers, one of them, he had kissed very well and she also taught him how to kiss better and later followed him to the place he took his bus to go home. She was a university student whom her father was very rich and was just twenty-two, young and pretty and was like an angel with a name more English than Norwegian, Toni-Lil. But, after then, they never met again because he was very busy consuming every of his time, taking a self-education-course. He would have called maybe one of them, but he carelessly lost his phone where he stored the numbers of the other many girls he met in the disco. He was more concerned about his future, knowing there was always time for him to meet his future bride. After then, he was beginning to doubt if really he was not gay since he could see himself enjoy being always alone and living a solitary life and was hating the idea of associating himself with women more than men. One night, when he was walking alone along the street and after leaving the disco where he danced and danced and was almost exhausted, he saw a Norwegian lad sitting, smoking and waiting for a bus; he swiftly went straight to him and asked him for a cigarette. As the lad offered him one, they started discussing about life and music. When the lad saw that he was having a strong passion for music, he advised him to keep to it and never let his talent be squandered. He also told him, music is a money making machine, and it is the easiest way to achieve a dream of a successful life with wealth. David, at that moment recollect how he always dreamed of becoming a musician like

Tupac, and how he also dreamed of going to the U.s. paticularly because of his passion for music, because he could see Los Angeles and New York the right place for him to excel. As he looked into the lad's eyes, and saw how beautiful he was, he wanted to kiss him to show how much he appreciated his encouragement for him to do something good with his talent. He fell in love with the lad, and he knew he did, but he was ashamed to reveal what he truly was to the public. Another time he came to also realize the fact that he was gay, was when he met one Norwegian grown-up man whom they both had a conversation, and he came to see that they were two people of the same philosophy of how life should be. The man who actually has traveled to Athens, Greece and Barcelona, Spain and so many other cities around the world, was kind to him, and had had an amicable relationship with him the day they met each other. The man also took him to his house that night and politely asked him to come take a shower with him inside the bathroom which he refused to do, pretending he was not gay. Over and over, he met so many lads there in Bergen, whom he came to like more than the girls he also met with, because of their moral and ethical behavior. He said it startled him when he could see himself more open and truthful to these men more than he was to the many women he discussed with. But, all and all, he was also hating the idea of him turning himself to become gay as he could look at women and see what beauty means to life, and see that they were more attractive to him. After six months that he was in Norway, and was already in love with the country and with the people and was trying to contrive a plan for his future there. He woke up one morning and was delivered a news that he was having a letter by his Burundi roommate, Twaha, who was already working there in the camp after two years that he had stayed in Norway and was never granted asylum, instead he was asked to leave the country by the Norwegian Refugee Council. But when Toni—the lady who was in love with David was made the head of the camp, she called him to start working even as his chance for staying in the country was just too lean. From the very first time David and Onyx saw him working there, it was strange and they both immediately started to suspect him of working with the Refugee Council as an informant. David and Onyx were very concerned about this issue, making them not discuss anything relating to their asylum case with him, but it was too late for them to do so since he already knew everything about them. Njuma, the other Burundi man decided to come and be leaving with Twaha in the same room, because he said he was finding the situation of coping with the noise and disturbances of the little kids and Arab people there in the other camp unmanageable. David knew he did not come because of that but, because he was missing him and how they always smoke and drink tea together and moreover, the good conversation they used to have. David who thought himself to be very smart by giving Twaha one gram of heroine to sell for him not knowing he was about to get himself nailed to a wood. That one gram of heroine was also given to him by his Nigerian friend, Ignatius, and because he could not sell it and was not interested in looking for how to sell it, but could not return it back to him so that he could not be seen as a coward, instead, he gave it to Twaha to help him sell it since he was claiming to be a drug dealer and was boasting with it. Ignatius, on the other hand was starting to make David his sincere, wise, and trustworthy friend, and for that reason, he was coming to visit him every time in the camp even when David tried to make him to stop coming, but he kept coming. He was beginning to be frequent and was not coming to visit him in the house where he was staying, but always in the bigger camp where Toni was working so he could have an opportunity to get closer to her since David told him how she was dying to have him. David who thought he was smart, was also the dottiest person on Earth to have allowed his friends know about he and Toni and what was going on between the two of them. All of them who heard she was loving him, also utilized that opportunity in trying to get closer to her and to win her love, but she refused to fall for any of them, still waiting for him to come have her. When David arrived at the the office to collect his letter, he saw how everybody there were staring at him—making him instantly knew it was over for him, and when he opened the letter and saw that his asylum was rejected and he was given thirteen days to file an appeal or leave the country or else he would be deported back to his country. He was unable to think with clarity what else he should do to get this issue resolved. He immediately took a bus and went to meet his lawyer to help him do something about it, but as he got there, his lawyer automatically was acting strangely, pretending he was not hearing English—forcing him to make plain what he wanted him to do for him in Norwegian language. Everything was happening very fast and very strange, and he could not believe it was happening to him, thinking he was in a dream. When he finally sat down to puzzle over the whole matter, he came to see why it was happening to him this way. With a deep understanding, he came to see that everybody were watching him in everything that he was doing. He saw that the Norwegians liked him because he was smart and was curious, but they also hated him, because they felt he did not value the life he was living there since he could not quit preaching of the American vision to them. He knew he was to be blamed for everything because he could see them offering him every opportunity that he want in life so he could be happy, and yet he was being ungrateful. What baffled them most about him was that he was not interested in speaking the Norwegian language which he was taking a class for every thrice in a week which he later reduced to twice in a week. Instead, he was beginning to improve his English more and more, spending more time in the library and was always with a dictionary and jolting down quotes on pieces of papers everywhere. Even his school teacher was a young and pretty girl who did the best she could to encourage him to learn the language, and yet he refused. One day when he returned home, he found that they had scattered his room and leaving the many pieces of papers he wrote the many quotes he had read from the books. When he asked his roommates, it was Twaha who told him some of the Refugee Council workers have arrived to search every rooms in the house which was strange because he has never experienced it before—and it was one week after then that the letter came that he should file an appeal or leave the country. As he sat down alone, thinking about everything, trying to comprehend and apprehend how this came to happen, he was shedding tears, knowing this was the end of his stay in a country that had transformed him or he transformed himself or they have helped him transformed himself into something different. He knew they have done enough for him and there was no-way he could thank them for it, only to say, some of the few words he could utter in Norwegian language. He actually loved Norway and was having the intention of achieving his goal there, but his mind still was not prepared to accept him into the society as part of the people living there as he could not learn to speak the language which affix a clue that he was not ready. Even when he was called for an interview, it was different from how his friends were interviewed. He was interviewed in a very quiet room in a very big and expensive hotel by two beautiful blonde girls, one of them who actually tried to help him by coming to him after the interview to talk to him face to face things about life, thinking he will be interested in telling her something sweet, but at that time he was not much interested in women since he was more interested in his dream. After the interview he was denied a working permit by the refugee Council. At that time, every refugee was entitled to a working permit after four months of staying there and immediately after his/her second interview, but he waited and waited and waited, and when he was denied of it, he went looking for a job everyday and everywhere without a working permit and was not offered any, because some who would have want to help him, were afraid they might be penalized for it. As he sat down thinking of what next step to take in his journey of life, he saw that there was still hope for him to stay in Norway—and the only hope was for him to meet and talked to Toni, his boss, who actually was expecting him to come tell him about his problem. He could not do it because his conscience was already judging him of how he would continuously use her to get what he want and never do the right thing that he knew he should have to do, but he also knew he could not persist with this awful situation. He knew it was time for him to leave to go back to Spain since at that very time, his sister was also worried about his Spanish documents getting expired since he was still having some few weeks left to submit them for renewal. His psyche was beginning to speak to him to leave as it was the right time for him to do so—and since the universe wanted it so. He could not wait for thirteen days before he could be deported back to his country, and going to meet Toni was a thing he swore not to do, so he went to her and lied that he needed an advance of his feeding allowance to resolve some problems and she quickly gave it to him, only to ask him to sign. He also called his sister in Spain who sent him some money as well, and after that he tricked Onyx to borrow some money from him, giving him his debit card to collect his feeding allowance which he was already having with him. Before he could leave to Spain, he sent a text message to Toni on her phone—thanking her for all the good things she had done for him, and later he bought a flight ticket and after a week, he flew back to Spain with the many books he borrowed from the library without returning them back. *Jeg elsker Norge—*

CHAPTER 19

D AVID ARRIVED IN SPAIN WITH a flight that transited in Amsterdam, making the Spanish police suspicious he was probably a drug trafficker since Holland was the center for drug traffickers in Europe. With the attires he was putting on, it was very easy and clear that he was a drug dealer as he was dressing on a very expensive leather jacket and a jeans and a Stetson tweed cap to match—all stolen and sold to him by some of the Arab boys living in the same camp with them, except for the black suede boots worth a hundred dollars which in Norway was cheap and was bought only for 200.00 kroners. After the policemen thoroughly checked and ransacked his bag and everything about him and found that he was coming from Norway, they immediately left him to go, and even showed him where to change the Norwegian currency to Euro, as at that time, Europeans were just starting to use the Euro as their currency. He was happy he was back to Spain safely, but at the same time, he was also regretting why he was back, knowing he will fall short of the opportunities of the good life he already started living in Norway. That same night, he took a bus from Madrid and left to Vitoria to meet his sister once again to live with her. In Vitoria, once again, he was faced with judgement from his fellow Nigerians, that he has chosen to travel to Norway so as to look for a white woman to marry—and it was true. When he was asked if he was having a girlfriend in Norway, he lied to them he was living with one who promised to marry him so he could be legal there. He was also asked if he was having the intention of returning back after he might have renewed his documents, and he said yes. At that time, his sister was already having an African shop where cosmetics and African food were sold. He saw that she was always busy, and decided to be giving her a helping hand by waking up every morning to go stay in the shop as a sales boy for her. He was enjoying life again due to how he could call his families in Africa and send them some little money which for long since he left to Norway, was not ideal. He saw that the people he left there in Spain were living more progressively more than he was. They were all having a permanent jobs, earning good salaries as the Spanish economy was becoming very buoyant and were amid the most dynamic economies in the Euro-zone. He was starting to see himself to be a failure, thinking his dream was not doing him any good except to drive him into disarray. He was upset with himself for having chosen to live a life of high adventure. But, when he was sad and upset and picked up one of the books he brought along and started reading it, hope came back to him, and he knew he did the most appropriate thing by leaving to seek for knowledge and wisdom where they were concealed. He was beginning to see his fellow Nigerians who believed and considered themselves to be living life to fullest just because they were having the opportunities of being in Europe and working as unskilled laborers day-in day-out, doing more over-time, only to be sending the money to their families in Africa, a thing, even he himself was fond of doing. He came to ask himself, how long was it going to take for all of them to be struggling and scuffling only to send money to their families whom they do not know what they might be doing with all the money? The more money they were sending home, the more their families were demanding from them without asking them what they were doing to get the money. When he came to sit down and think of it, he came to comprehend that they were all enslaved by their own families. In the real sense, they were doing it to assist them, but these people in Africa took that advantage in dealing mercilessly with their children and families abroad. David said he came to ask himself why every families in the place where he was born had decided to send their children, most particularly girls to abroad, even when they knew they were coming to prostitute. From the many stories he was told of how many families had killed their children when they see them return back home, just because they had lied to them of what they were doing with their money in Africa, and as they arrived there and demanded for those things to be showed to them. David said he felt so unhappy as he returned back to Spain to see that the lives the immigrants were living, were quite incompatible with the lives the immigrants in Norway were living as he met many of his fellow Nigerians there who were doctors and others with professional jobs, but in Spain, everybody he met was either working with a construction company or working in a factory or a warehouse as an unskilled laborer. He also saw how desperate his fellow Nigerians were, as the men became more involved in ridiculous criminal acts and the women continued with prostitution, and all the money they were making were been sent home to their families who were living there and obliging them to get more and more to send to them. He came to fathom that it was not their families who were enslaving them; it was they who were enslaving themselves as he could see them as buffoons who were being deprived of their rights to choose for themselves what is best for them, which he could describe as "free will." Most of the women among them saw prostitution to be the only way-out for them as they were all illiterates and were never in favor of the idea of seeking knowledge. The attested truth was that prostitution has brought them fortune, just as it has brought them disaster, but it has done them more damages than good which they failed to acknowledge. David said he felt pity for himself and these other African immigrants as they became stuck-up, living in the middle of hell and heaven, being unable to go back to their masters and unable to move further into a better future. He said to himself, 'How could it be that many years after slavery was abolished, many Africans are still being manipulated and enslaved by their own families?'

It was just few days before his documents get expired and he still was not able to get a job so he could have a working contract to renew them since it was the law imposed on every immigrant with a residence permit, which says—no working contract, no renewal of residence. The only immigrants who could renew their documents without a working contract, were immigrants with a permanent stay in the country. David was not much preoccupied about it, knowing his sister was going to do that for him. About three days before it expired, his sister called him to accompany her to the office of her legal adviser so she could write a contract for him. As they reached the office, he saw a young, pretty, brunette girl asked her sister to sit down, and as they discussed on how many months the contract was to be and when it was to get started, he watched in amazement since he thought her to be the receptionist while the lady sitting at the other side of the office to be the lawyer. When they were done, they left and went home, and at the time they were going home, he asked his sister if the girl was the lawyer or the lady who was busy playing with his niece, Maite. She told him it was the girl. She also let him know she was not a girl the way he was seeing her, and that she was older than he thought. The next day, since his sister was too busy to accompany him to the office, she told him to go alone, and he went. Reaching there, immediately he opened the door and went inside and as the girl saw him come in, she stood up and came standing near him and looking into his eyes as he speak to her. She pretended she was not understanding his Spanish as he spoke to her, but he kept explaining and demonstrating what he intended to say very well with his hands. David was startled at her behavior and thought she was bluffing. He did not fret himself about what she might want from him or what she was up to, he dismissed her advances. He knew it was not time for him to play games with any Spanish girl since he already knew they were not the type that will want to have a black man as their lovers, most especially, when he saw that she was a lawyer. What will a young Spanish girl who is a lawyer have to do with a black African immigrant who managed to come to Europe by passing through the desert or by crossing the Mediterranean sea? Some few days after he submitted the working contract along with his documents for renewal, he was to wait for another three months to be issued another residence and a working permits. He was bored and thought he could not wait till his document were renewed because he was feeling uncomfortable with the life he was living and was displeased with the attitudes of his fellow Africans towards him, as they all were comparing him to a clown and a threat rather than a person to lead them to a change. But, while waiting for his document and was assisting his sister operate her business, he continued to read all the good books he brought from Norway without ceasing, even when he was doing it secretly so as for his friends not to see him, because if they do, that will be a general topics and will be spread to every corners of the city. No matter how he tried, he was seen by many of them, and immediately they ascertain the facts that he was always reading novels, rumors went so fast and everyone of them began to complain of the new and distinctive mode he had brought to Spain from Norway. Within a short period, everyone in Vitoria were looking for him to see him and know him as the news went round, and after a while, girls (blacks and whites), were tripping into his sister's shop, looking for a way to penetrate into him. The men became jealous and hatred and anger were aroused, but money were coming into his sister's account because of the many customers that were floating in—so were more money and profits they were making. He, his sister and his sister's husband were all happy about the situation, and his sister was thinking of making him her manager and leaving everything in his care. He came to see himself develop another talent in merchandising, as he could lure their customers and entertain them with good music and television programs which he himself had come to install there. As many that were coming in there (black and white), he was beginning to preach to them the need for a life with education since he believed it to be the only key to everyone's success. He was also beginning to preach about the reason why they all need love to survive as he believe, "Love is the basic sacrifice in life to triumph." The more he was doing this, the more he was beginning to experience a strange power being built inside of him and he was beginning to believe he could change people's life the way he once did back at the time he was in Africa. But he was already in Europe, not in Africa. At this very time, he came to also think there was something wrong with his brain as many had said since he could think of changing the world when he could see himself abstain from what he has pledged to do for his family—by getting them out of poverty. How could he change the world when he could not even change the lives of his family by improving it from a bad state to a better one? As these thoughts rings in his brain, and his friends were also coming to brag and lie to him of how much money they were having and what they had achieved in Africa, he came to see that there was no reason he should equate his life with that of his friends when he could see them taking one path to their future, and him, taking another. Since he was becoming too famous in this city and many people were talking about him everywhere, both the black people and the white people, and yet he was still all alone by himself without a girlfriend, some were starting to believe he was emotionally disturbed. Many women were getting close to him and he was pushing them away, lying that he was engaged to one Norwegian girl in Norway, and was waiting to get his document so he could return back to her there. It was this same time, Klara, the Spanish girl he once loved, but had never had sex with her, came to see him. He was astonished the very first time he saw her passed by their shop, and when he saw her, he swiftly stood from where he was sitting and ran to meet her and her friend and they both came into their shop to greet his niece and his sister, and after they left, his sister instantly belittled her, letting him know she was not worth being his girlfriend because she has seen many more beautiful and well to do women coming over there to seduce him to draw his attention to themselves. David said he knew it, but was only trying to play to the rules of love which he believed in that was also making him to hurt himself and making him vulnerable. One afternoon, he and one of his friend decided to pay a visit to a bar owned by one Spanish lady who was already at her thirties and was still single—and was also a friend to David's sister, Tina. She came to their shop twice and always wanted to see him so that they could both talk. His sister also told him of how the lady has long wanted to see him because she was interested in having a relationship with him. That day when he and his friend arrived at the bar owned by this lady, she was absent and had left the bar for her salesgirl, who also with the company of one of her younger sister, came to buy a bottle of Heineken beer and drank it there while having a good chat with him. At the bar, was also David's sister former boyfriend, Alberto, who was also a good friend to David and had helped him so many times, even at the time he newly arrived in Europe and went to apply for his refugee passport. David went to meet Alberto to greet him, he was asked to sit with him and his friends and a bottle of beer was ordered and paid for for him, but he could not abandon his friend whom they both came there together, so he thanked him and left them and went to meet his friend who was too stunned to speak because of what he was seeing because of how he was told before David was more friendly with the white people more than he was to the blacks. He looked at him and said to him " David laughed and gave him a bottle of beer that was paid for by Alberto. As they sat down drinking their beer, Klara and two of her friends walked in. This same girl David has wanted to love and marry even before he left to Norway, and when he was there, he kept calling her on phone, pleading for her to love him, but she refused to. Although they have met once since he returned back. When he first saw her, he thought he was dreaming until she and her friends came to sit near him and his friend, and after greeting them and had ordered for their coffee and milk and began to smoke their hashish and offering him a wrapped joint to smoke, he took it from him and smoked it and quickly returned it back to her since his friend also rejected it. He was intoxicated and wanted to go home to rest, because for long since he left Spain, he had only smoked it once in Norway with some girls, but after then he had decided to quit. Klara would not let him leave until she and her friends snapped some pictures with him. But the salesgirl became very worried and was upset, seeing him sit and discuss with these girls. She thought it was a good opportunity for her to have him since her boss was absent, but her sister had went to inform Klara about David's presence in the bar as she too was interested and was betrayed by her own elder sister.

That same evening, Marijo, the owner of the bar whom David actually went to see, called his sister to report the issue to her. She also begged her for an assistance on how to get him. The next day at the shop where David was helping her sister, she came again to meet him to demonstrate to him what she was capable of doing financially. This time she came with her big beautiful white companion dog which David loved and started playing with, but when she was about to leave as many people were there, she winked at him, giving him a sign and left. Meanwhile, David's friend who followed him to that bar was beginning to get worried and started coming close to David, pleading for his assistance so he could have a chance to get a contact with one Spanish girl since he was illegal and the only way he could be able to have a document was to marry a Spanish woman. David saw that he was desperate and was happy for him for having that thought in mind of getting married to a white woman which also his dream even if he was unable to to achieve it. He supported this idea and persuaded him to learn and accept this conception of interracial marriage since he saw how being tortured, controlled, and humiliated by one Nigerian girl who was a prostitute, all for the sake of love. He started taking him to different places to look for a white woman, and in the later time to come when he stayed longer in Europe, he came to see that with the too much ambition this boy had, he was able succeed in marrying a white woman even after he had had several relationships with many of them and things did not work out. At this very time, Idahosa as he was called by the white people, and Osas by the blacks, became notable and esteemed because of how many women—sisters, friends, employees and employers, blacks and whites were disputing among themselves on who was to have him, and the men, blacks and whites, quests for his friendship. Although at this same time, secretly—he was depressed and his loneliness was killing him, but he was turning his pains into joy all alone on his own. When he came to think how people were getting closer to him all over again and again, he came to grasp the honor that is being achieved when one is trying to make a change for the world to be a better place to live. Then, he knew there was no turning back except for him to achieve his goal of preaching love to the world which he had always asked his God whenever he was praying to Him. He came to think that he can understand the true nature of heroism, and with that belief, he was seeing himself as a hero. But, how could he be a hero when he was penniless and was also jobless?

He took a decision to help himself by having a professional job, so he went to apply for a course which was free in the office of the (National Institute of Statistics), which in Spanish is known as () . After a week he was called for a welding course, which he himself chose because he thought he was having some experience before in this particularly field. He was having a pleasant time at the very first and second day the course started because it was theory, but the next day which was the third day and was for practicals—when they were to try using the welding-machines and electrodes to weld. He forgot how painful it was when you stare at the lights and at night he could not sleep. The next day he saw that he was about to get his eyes blinded, he quickly gave up the idea of becoming a welder and told his sister's husband, Joaquin that he was going to quit the course not knowing he was about to arouse his sister's anger. Although it caused him pains as he took the decision to quit the course, but he was glad he did because he said, "It will be far better for him to starve to death than to see that he was blind and could not afford to read all the great books he intended to read that he could not read." Immediately he quit that course, he was beginning to have some difficulties because his sister and her husband saw him to be a person who was not prepared to be a man and confront his problems all alone on his own. She began to complain of how much profits she was not getting from her shop—that was to say, David was hindering her progress in life and it was time for him to go get life for himself. David knew all what she complained about was false. He knew the only reason why she was upset with him was because of the strange life-style he has adopted in Norway, by dedicating his life to reading and reading and studying and studying. She and her husband were becoming fed up of the whole issue since they were becoming bored mostly of how David was watching television every nights without sleeping. What baffled them most, was how many women were throwing themselves at him, and how he resents them, thinking they were not sensitive enough to be with him. They too were beginning to ask themselves, who he think he was. As David could not withstand the shame of how his sister was reacting to his conducts since they were seeing him as a failure, he knew it was time for him to leave Spain to anywhere in the world to search for something different, something above him as he thought he already saw all the women there not sensitive enough to be loved, and he also looked at himself and saw himself as a person of great insight and with an intense desire for wisdom and knowledge. He knew he was having more to offer to the world than just clinging to a woman who might at the end of everything throw the love away and hurt his feelings. Although, he believed, "Change takes courage, and it is said to be a natural phenomena to be progressive." And that was what he thought his fellow Africans needed at that moment, forgotten he could not change any of them or else he first change himself by getting a profession for himself. But he was not prepared to strain and stress his mind and body for another profession since he already has one and could not listen to his friends even when they tried to edify him of their projects and how he could be a part of it, because he thought they were morons who actually were lost and needed someone to lead them out of darkness to the visible world where the light shines. He continued to read the books he brought from Norway, and as he did, the books were inspiring him and also making him capable of thinking in abstract terms. He was beginning to hear voices from the universe speak to him, and as he listened, he came to see the absurdity of the situations which everyone of them as immigrants were living without bothering to see it clearly from the angle which he was seeing it. He knew it was not his destiny to stay, but to proceed further with his relentless journey to achieve his goal in life. Even at a time when he thought of getting himself a job so he could live and party like his other friends, but he came to see how it will be impossible for him to confront the jealousy and hatred that were emerging from his friends because of his own talent that he has worked so hard to possess—that was also making him become a vagabond. He swiftly made up his mind to leave to anywhere that was not too far from where he was so that he could breathe in a new fresh air once again. He bought a Euro-line bus ticket and left to Paris, France, a place he passed and has never lived before and was not having anybody he could call for a rescue. He was beginning to think, with the experiences he had before by being adventurous and setting on journeys to places he does not know anybody and was able to attain knowledge, he came to believe, with this knowledge he could survive every situation no matter how hard it comes. Undisputedly, he chose France this time because he knew France to be a country that harbors immigrants, and there was no way he was going to starve to death there since he could simply go to seek asylum when the situation get worst. Immediately he arrived France, he fell in love with the city, seeing people of different faces and religions.

He was pleased with what he was seeing, but he was unhappy he found it difficult to communicate with the people there since majority of them were not speaking English. He loved Paris as he took his bag and carried it to walk around the city from the very time he entered the city which was 01:00 p.m till the time when he became hungry and wanted to eat which was already at about 07:00 p.m. He loved the city as well as the beautiful people he was seeing. Later on, when he was in jail in Italy, he came to write a poem with a title, Paris, you're in my heart. *o boy, you like white people?Instituto Nacional de EstadisticasINE*

PARIS, YOU'RE IN MY HEART.

This beautiful city so exquisite.
In the middle of summer, so warm and bright.
Every ethnicity is what you find.
United color of all races and religions.
No matter all the places I've been
And all the things that I've seen.
One place that makes me feel alive,
One place I love to live my life.
Paris, Paris, you're in my heart.

You love to snuff-out the fire in your heart,
You've got to come here to start.
Me as a child of fortune,
I love to live my life in the sunshine.
Paris, Paris, you're in my heart.

Some call it the old and new world in one city.
Some call it the beginning of civilization,
While others claim it to be the real world.
But, all and all, one can see
It's a single city with a thousand names.
Please, come see Paris before you die.

With the little money left in David's hand, he entered a restaurant so he could order for a menu, but when he saw the prize, he stood up from where he was sitting and picked up his bag and left. He never knew Paris to be a very expensive city as it was. He thought it was going to be a little different from Spain; he came to see that the cost of living was very high almost twice as that of Spain. He decided to enter a coffee bar and ordered for a cup of . As he was drinking it and smoking his cigarette, he caught a glimpse of a pretty blonde lady watching him from a distance. He was afraid to meet her since he thought she might be waiting for somebody. But, after almost one hour that he arrived there, she was still there all alone by herself and was lonely just the same way he too was lonely. He then quicklyordered for another, this time with a sandwich, and when he was served and had paid the waitress, he took everything to where the lady was sitting down and said to her " '," she answered. David who does not understand French not to talk of speaking it with a French person, quickly relinquished the idea of pretending to be what he was not and greeted her well in English, with faith, believing she was going to respond, and with a great surprise, she responded. 'How are you doing?' she asked him. 'I am doing good.' 'May I sit down here with you?' he asked, already putting his sandwich and coffee on her table where she was sitting. 'Yes, you can sit here.' After sitting down, he said to her, 'from your accent of English, I guess you are not French.' 'Of course I am,' replied the young pretty young lady, 'but actually I am living in the U.k.' 'You look pretty,' said David, offering her is hand for a shake, and as she brought out her hand to shake him, he grabbed it and kissed the fingers. He was eating and talking at the same time, and after he finished eating his sandwich and drinking his coffee and saw that it was getting too dark, he picked up his bag and wanted to leave. 'Where are you going to?' asked the pretty lady. 'It is dark, and I think I have to go and look for a cheap pension where I am going to sleep tonight,' replied David, reluctantly. 'Sit down, I will help you,' said the pretty lady, drawing the chair she was sitting closer to him as they both gaze into each other's eyes. David quickly looked at her left hand to see if she was wearing a wedding ring in one of the fingers, but she was not. 'Are you married?' asked David. 'Yes I am, but I am separated from him now because he said he is tired of waiting while I am away from home.' 'You mean when you are going to work?' asked David, expecting her to say something he would like. 'No,' said the pretty lady. 'He is tired of waiting while I am traveling around the world.' 'You mean you travel a lot?' 'Yes, I do. I travel a lot,' said the pretty lady. 'By the way, where in Africa are you from?' she asked, still gazing into his eyes.

'I am Nigerian,' said David. 'But, how come you live here in France and don't speak French?' asked the lady. 'I am not living here, I live in Spain for almost three years now, and I just think I am tired of the life I was living and I have decided to come to France to live.' 'Where you legal there in Spain?' 'Yes, I was,' replied David. 'And you have decided to come to France, why not go to England as long as you speak English?' asked the lady, standing from her chair and walking to the washroom. 'I will be back soon, wait me there, o.k.' As she went into the washroom, David was starting to feel some chemistry between the two of them or it was lust. After about three minutes, she returned back, and when she did, she called the waitress and ordered to be served a red wine, and turned to David and asked him, 'what would you like?' 'oh, you mean me?' asked David, not very sure of what was happening and how it was happening so fast. 'Would you like some wine as well?' asked the pretty lady. 'Yes I would, I want wine,' said David happily. 'Tell me something,' requested the lady. 'Why do you like to travel?' 'How do you know I love to travel?' asked David, glaringly. 'I can see it inside your eyes,' said the lady. 'Look, I am a psychic, and I know everything about you.' David was astonished as he heard that she already knew he was coming and that they were going to meet as she claimed that was what the universe wanted. 'Why do you hate the Muslims?' she asked. Because I have seen them and lived with them and I have come to see that they are against western civilization, said David, still not knowing what to do next—whether to leave her there and run away or listen to what she was going to tell him. 'Look, it is the universe that is bringing us together so I can enlighten you about life.' Sitting speechless, David could only look at her in awe as he was already thinking, it was a set-up, and that he was been followed from Spain to where he was. He was beginning to think everybody were out there to come and get him. As she speak, he could not listen very well because he was lost in thought, thinking that it was a conspiracy, and that Europeans were after him because of his obsession with American way of life and visions. He wanted to leave her, but she has already ordered for two menus for the both of them and he was hungry and wanted to eat. But, he was still wondering how his fellow Africans sees him to be a threat and how the Europeans were also coming to see him to be the same threat to them. He was starting to loathe himself for not having lived in Spain and get himself a job, instead of coming to France to see a woman who already knew everything about him and was telling it to his face. He saw how he was severely punishing himself for being stupid and not thinking of working to earn little salaries, instead of him dreaming to be on top of his fellow Africans they both came to Europe together. He was beginning to see it as vanity. *cafe avec laitcafe avec laitbonsoir, comment allez-vous?Je suis bien* As the food were served and they were already eating, he asked her, with decency. 'Do you like Muslims?' 'I love and respect everybody without regard to their religion, race, color, religion, sex, or national origin. And that is how life is supposed to be, son.' When he heard her called him son, he knew she was right as he could see from her face that she might be more than forty-five. 'But, Muslims are violent people and they commits suicide and kill others every time and tried to pose a threat to our everyday society.' 'Yes they do. But do you know the world we live is full of injustice?' asked the woman, leaving the food she was eating and coming closer to him and resting her hand on his lap. 'Look, David, "An innocent man does not have anything to be afraid of." I know who you are and how your destiny is going to be, but never be afraid to utter the truth and keep with you what you already have inside of you.' 'What is it that you think I have,' asked David, curiously. "Love, faith and ambition are the three driving forces of human life," and I know you possessed all of them. Do you have any clue of what led to the world trade center bombing?' asked the lady as she stood up to bring out her Gucci purse out to pay for the food and asked him, 'are you coming?' He dropped the glass full of wine that he was drinking and left with her to a hotel where she was lodging, and when they entered into the room, he dropped her bag and hold her and they started kissing and romancing till they fell on the bed and he made love to her like he has never done to any woman before. He wanted to enter inside her body since she was pretty and her body was scent of mint. That night he made love to her thrice and was never tired and wanted more. After the third time, he asked her if she could divorce her husband so they could get married, but she responded by telling him to go out there to get a woman of his age because she was too old for him and can never bear him a child. He loved her and wanted to love her forever, for whom she was and for coming to teach him things about life. Her name, Monique was like a beautiful diamond to him and he thought he could hold it tight not to lose it. In his later life in the future in prison in Italy, he came to write a poem or rather a song regarding to what happened, and to show how he felt about her that night.

LOVE'S AS SWEET AS HONEY.

O' darling baby, you make my heart delight.
O' lovely darling, you're the apple of my sight.
You with your nipples soft and tight.
O' lovely darling, you with your beautiful face,
Love the way you cover me leaving no space.
O' darling baby, you I've always wanted.
Might not know, for you I was created.
There ain't no other baby in the world
Like my lovely darling baby.
O' Lord, make us together now we fly
And in rejoicing together we die.

To you, this song I'm singing,
Love me honey, and let me drown in honey
Cos, love's as sweet as honey.

To you, this song I'm singing,
Love me honey, and let me drown in honey
Cos, love's as sweet as honey.

The next morning when he woke up from bed and watched her still sleeping, he brought out his tooth-paste and brush and walked into the bathroom to brush his teeth, and when he finished, he quickly showered and dried himself up, rubbed some cream and came back to meet her in the bed. 'Good morning,' he greeted her. 'Good morning,' she replied. 'You were about to destroy my womb last night.' 'I am sorry if I did so.' 'No, you do not need to be sorry, I enjoyed it. You are a superman.' 'Really?' asked David, smiling. 'You are,' replied the lady as she got closer to him and kissed him on his mouth. She walked into the bathroom, brushed her teeth, showered and dried herself up and came back to him inside the bed, naked—and when he saw her, he saw that she was beautiful just like an angel. He grabbed her and started kissing her, licking all her body from head to toe, till he finally put his mouth in her cunt and wanted to eat everything inside till she cum. He drew her close to himself and asked her to suck him and as she did, he hold her well dressed hair and was screaming, seeing himself already living in heaven and angels hovering around him. He made love to her again for the fourth time, and after they were done, they both went into the bathroom to wash their body, and when they were there, he made love to her again and was weak, about to faint. She looked at him and laughed and stood him up and kissed him, dried him up and brought him to the room and placed him in the bed. After a while, he was able to regain his strength; he thanked her and got himself dressed, and when she was already dressed, they both left the hotel and went to a restaurant to eat salad, spaghetti, ribs and a luscious strawberry desserts, and after that, they both drank coffee and she offered him a stick of Marlboro-light cigarette and they began to smoke. As they were smoking, she asked him again, 'do you know why the World Trade Center was bombed?' 'Yes, because Bin Laden, the Al-Qaeda network leader ordered his fellow Muslims to do it,' said David, sitting himself well, paying attention to her. 'Do not use that word Muslims, because it describes every Muslims as terrorists.' 'Yes all of them are terrorists.' Have you ever heard people of other religions commit suicide attacks once?' 'Let me tell you things that you do not know,' said the lady. 'These terrorists are just extremists who misunderstood the Koran and come to think the only way they could fight for justice for their people and religion is by terrorizing the world to create fear, and they are wrong because they are being mislead by their leaders. But the factual truth is that the world is full of injustice. Do you know the Americans supported this so-called Bin Laden and the Taliban some years ago to fight against the Russians?' 'No, I have never heard of that before,' said David. 'I know you have not,' replied the lady. 'Tell me why the Jews had refused to let a Palestinians have their own state?' I do not know, said David. 'That is the reason why you have to stop judging people because you do not know anything about them.' Immediately David heard this, he recalled what he was told by the beautiful stranger he met in Oslo, Norway. David speechless, was beginning to think he was being fooled for having thought he knew too much, whereas he knew nothing. She proceeded with the same subject matter, saying, Bin Laden was fighting stupidly like a coward for the entire Palestinians against the Jews who were being aided by the U.s. government. After the lady finished smoking her cigarette and saw that David too was no longer smoking, she said to him with a polite voice, 'honey are you with me?' 'Yes, I am, just a little bit stunned with what I am hearing now from you.' 'Yeah, I know,' responded the lady. 'Would you like to take a walk?' she demanded, already getting up from where she was sitting. 'Yes, I would love to.' He stood up and followed her, and when they walking, he said to her, 'I need you in my life.' 'I am not going to allow you waste your time because you are still very young and I know you are ambitious to make it in life, but all you need to do is choose a career for yourself.' 'What kind of a career do you think will be appropriate for me to choose in life because I am very confused of what to do with my many talents?' 'You can be a musician, a film actor and you can also be a writer. But I prefer you do the one that is more easier and more prosperous. I mean to say you can go look for a producer to help you produce your music or try look for a film director and try to convince him that you are a screen-writer and an actor.' 'But, how do I get in contact with a music producer or a film director?' asked David. 'I can help you with that,' said the lady, asking him to come with her as they both walked to a park in the center of Paris, where there were many other people—kids, young and old, playing and chanting. They both sat down as she brought out her laptop, opened it, put a phone near it so as for the computer to receive network. It was strange to David since he had never in life used a laptop before and did not know how it functioned. She opened to yahoo, and with a search-machine, she brought list of some famous music producers and film directors in Europe and wrote them down in a piece of paper and gave it to him, but when he read it, he saw that most of them were in Holland, Germany and Belgium. 'What about France,' he demanded since it was not included. 'Because, in France, you cannot do anything or else you speak French fluently, and you cannot travel to the U.k. or else someone invites you there or you get a tourist visa—which you might need to process if only you are working. But this normally happens to immigrants in Spain and Portugal and Greece because these countries are not much regarded in Europe.' David kept the the piece of paper, not knowing what to do with it since he was left with just some little money. How he was going to get the money to travel to Holland or Belgium, was becoming another problem. After they left the park and were walking back to the hotel where she lodged, she asked him, 'David, are you religious?' 'No, I am not,' replied

David. 'I know you are not, you really do not have to be, because it will only make you shrink in poverty.' 'Thank you for the advice,' said David, staring at her like he was looking at the mother he never had. 'You are welcome,' replied the lady. 'But one other thing I love to ask you is,' 'go ahead,' said David, with interruption. 'You see, do you not think it is unfair for the Americans, to be doing whatever they want to other poorer and less developed countries just because they believe they have the power to do so?' 'I do not understand what you are saying,' said David, thinking if she could just not talk about politics and let him go his way.' 'I am not much concerned about politics,' said David, trying to change the content. 'I know you watch CNN and other American news and you are very much in support of the American politics. You do not have to hide it from me, I already know everything about you as I have told you before,' said the lady. 'The Bush administration is planning on how to invade Iraq, because they think Saddam Hussein is allegedly supporting the terrorists in Afghanistan and other places in the Arab world, and he is a dictator and a tyrant and there is no way the citizens will be free from bondage or else they step in. They also think he is possessing weapons of mass destruction which actually is false. As for you, what do you think about this?' asked the lady and opened the door of the hotel and greeted the receptionist and brought out her Gucci purse, to get the keys out, and when they climbed the steps upward to the luxurious hotel suite where she lodged, he followed her in, and when they entered, he saw her threw away her clothes and fell inside the bed. He went to meet her and hold her, saying to her, 'I love you and I want you to marry me.' 'Lets get back to business,' she said. 'You see there is no justice in our world. Do you think there is not enough food to feed everybody in this wide-world?' she asked. 'Yes there is,' responded David. 'If there is, why is it that many children in Africa and other poor countries in Asia and South America are starving to death, and the people in the western world are having enough left for dogs and cats and much more to be dumped in the dust-bins?' David, astounded, did not know what to say. She stood up from the bed, and when she did, he could view her nakedness very well. She was the first pretty, mature lady he has seen completely nude. He stood up and went closer to her and hold her close to himself, I love you, and I want to live all my life with you,' he murmured into her ear. 'Stop it, she screamed, I do not want to be loved, I want to be fucked.' He picked her up and dumped her in the bed and started kissing her, sucking her breasts, and later her cunt, and when she was about to cum, she screamed, and he threw-off his underwear and stuck his penis into her cunt and started riding on her. He did not know the time he slept-off. It was fun, all fun, as he has never experienced life like this before. When he finally woke up, he saw that she was not there, but when he got up from the bed to look for her inside the bathroom, thinking she might be there, he saw some pieces of papers on the floor and he picked them up and started reading. The first one, she wrote—I am very sorry to have done this, I never liked to, but I have to. You are still very young and energetic, and you deserve something better, so please go into the world and excel. The second later, she wrote—Do not let them fool you, do not believe in their twisted lies, and always remember you are an African, the most poorest continent on earth. Stand up and fight for your right not against the righteous, but against those who believe and practices injustice, and also let love be what you worship. When he opened the third piece of paper, he found three hundred Euro notes of fifty each, and in that same piece of paper, he found a note written boldly—SEVEN DAYS THEORY, and at the bottom, she wrote—See you at twilight. The fourth paper which was different from the others because it was plain, she wrote boldly in it—"Let there be light, and there was light. Let them seek wisdom and transform it into whatever they wish it to be that can ensure and improve moral values and wriggled out of inglorious life. And with this wisdom, they will rule the world. Let the wisdom be the light, because where there is light, darkness disappears. This light that we see, will be our pioneer to the real world where we all dreamed to live." After he finished reading, he was calm and did not know what else to do because he actually did not know what exactly she was trying to tell him by that. He swiftly showered and got himself dressed and left the room and went straight to the Euro-line bus station, bought a bus ticket and took a bus and left France to Amsterdam, Holland. Although, he felt it right inside his heart that he has finally lost a woman as special as she was, just within a twinkle of an eye. Once again, David was in Amsterdam, sitting inside a coffee bar, thinking of every thing he was told by the beautiful stranger he met some time ago in Oslo, Norway and what he was told by Monique, the psychic, the woman he believed to be a spy, and has come to lecture him things about life, making him see clearly what was going on in the world of politics. He did not know what to do next. Although he acknowledged the truth about what she said on the issue of the Bush administration planning to invade Iraq and Bin Laden fighting for the rights of the Palestinian people because he saw them helpless and hopeless. He also thought of how many people in the world could be suffering and dying of starvation, while others were living extravagantly and excessively. He was becoming to see the differences between rich and poor people everywhere around the globe, and he asked himself, why? But, he came to believe more in himself as a man with a great power since he was being recognized by an unknown psychic whom he also saw to be a lunatic, because she has said many things that terrified him. Things about metaphysics and mysticism, and has also lectured him about the ILLUMINATI and later about a society she called, a Rosicrucian Order, AMORC, which he has long heard of at the time he was in Africa, and also acknowledge one of his sister's husband to be a member. As he sat down thinking about the whole thing, he came to quickly realized he was having families in Africa that he would like to help, and that was his reason of coming to Europe, not to come change what has been made to be. But he was beginning to think of erasing the idea of every Muslim is a terrorist from his head since he came to get the true picture of how the Palestinians were been oppressed and seeing that by terrorizing the Jews will be the only way they could fight for themselves as nobody was there for them. Leaving the coffee bar, he went to buy a calling card and started calling all the numbers of the music producers and film directors Monique gave him to call in Holland. He continuously to call and none of them picked the phone, making him pissed-off and was about to desist from the idea of pursuing any of the career she has expected of him. When he called one German number, the girl who received the call, told him to send his work to their studio so that they can get to see if they like it, but he was not having anything with him. He tried to explain to the girl that he is a screen-writer, and would have like to meet the boss face to face before he could do anything with them, but she refused, and only demanded he send his work to them whenever he was prepared. He tried calling the music producers who also told him to send some demo of his work to them so they could see if they like it. He was perplexed and thought of returning back to Spain immediately to come get himself a job, but it was already too late for that since he was no longer having any money with him apart from the 20.00 euro left with him—which he was going to spend in purchasing his train ticket to Den Haag, a place he believed he could meet people who might help him to get a place to stay for awhile before he could put himself together. He tried calling the numbers in Holland again, and one of them picked the phone and also told him to send a copy of his work to them or else no deal. Unimpressed with what he was told, he came to comprehend what it means to start a life of fame, as it is never a bread and butter thing. He was beginning to think his passion for music was a misfortune for him. Without hope, he left where he was and started roaming aimlessly about in Amsterdam, but when he saw that he could not resist the cold anymore, he went to the police station to make a report that he was traveling to Africa, and was supposed to transit in Holland for four hours, and as he came out of the airport to see how the city look like, he mistakenly lost his documents and ticket, and for that reason, he needed to wait till his sister in Spain could send him some money for another ticket so he could return back to Spain. When they first heard this, they doubted him, telling him this was not the first time a Nigerian has come there to give the same report, instead of him to just say he had come to Holland to live. David knew it was true as he was told to do so by some Nigerians he met in the bus station when he arrived in Amsterdam and asked them if they could help him. Although, the police later offered him a place to stay and eat for one night as he awaits his sister to send him money. But when he called his sister, she told him to go get life for himself and dropped the phone on him. The next day, he saw that there was no hope for him then, he quickly went to meet the man who was in-charge of the activities in the house meant to serve the homeless Dutch adolescents who might be having a dispute with their family and had decided to stay away from them for awhile. But as he met the man to explain to him, he sent him to another lady at her thirties who actually was the head. When she first saw him, she took him to her office which was quiet and there were no other person there except for the both of them. First, when he saw that there was no other person there, he wanted to use that opportunity to tell her she was beautiful and deserve the man to love and treat her right. He thought it was wrong for him to do that, instead he decided to get back to business—his reason of coming to Holland. He said to her, 'please can you help me to contact a music producer here in Amsterdam? because that is my motive of coming here.' 'Really?' she asked. 'Yes,' said David. 'I cannot help you, o.k?' 'O.k,' said David, leaving the office, and as he left, he turned back to look how she might be feeling and he saw that she was disappointed with what he had come to tell her. He left the house, still leaving his bag there, knowing he was not going to be aloud to sleep there that night, so he thought it will be nice for him to go outside to see if anyone will be able to rescue him out of the miserable life that he was about to face. As he walked along the streets in Amsterdam hopelessly, thinking of where he was going to sleep that night, but with the mix of many talents he thought he possessed, and with experience of living a hard life and with much determination, assurance and confidence, he knew something good was going to come up. As he walked and proceeded with his hard thinking, a blonde, slim girl greeted him, 'hi, how are you?' He ignored her, thinking she was insane, but when she passed him, he recollected a woman had just greeted him, so he ran back to meet her, telling her he was sorry for not responding to her greetings. After introducing themselves, they both started discussing, and she told him she was from Austria, and was in Amsterdam for tourism. He knew immediately she was one of these girls who might be interested in using and dumping men. Even when she insisted he should accompany him to her hotel, he refused, but it was after she left that he came to realize he was being stupid and came to regret the reason for him being judgemental. When he later returned back to the house that evening, he was told to leave, so he waited until the time for supper and joined them to eat, and after supper, he left, carrying his bag and went to the train station and get on the train without purchasing a ticket that night and went to Den Haag. In Den Haag, he decided to take a stroll along the street of red lights, popularly known as Holland Spoor. As he strolled, he saw a black, beautiful, gorgeous girl standing in one of the window, and he immediately knew she was a Nigerian, and he went straight to meet her, but she saw him, and rebuffed him instantly. He did not leave until she was ready to listen to what he was going to tell her, and when she saw how eager he was to talk to her, she opened the door for him to enter. He greeted her and introduced himself to her, and later he did gave her his documents for her to hold so he could go and seek asylum as he was advised by some boys to do so—so as for him to be able to live there in Holland—and so as to be entitled to social welfare—which is basic for every refugees there in Holland, but if you are rejected, that will be a problem, and there was no possibility of him going to be accepted by the Dutch Refugee Council as long as he was from Nigeria, because the Dutch people believe Nigeria to be a wealthy country as it is an oil-rich, with no political conflict—a wrong idea which many other countries believed too. Moreover, many countries in the western world were also becoming tired of Nigerians as they were frightened by their criminal records. Applying for asylum there in Den Haag was going to be a thing he was going to regret, so he was told by some Africans he met. He decided to go to Rotterdam, thinking he could still meet some of his old friends he left there some years ago, but reaching there, he saw that everything became different from the way he left them. The shop where he used to work as a sales boy was later turned into a very large and beautiful barbing and hair-dressing saloon, but still owned by some Africans. Doorsalaan, the street remained the way it was with junkies and drug dealings everywhere just the way he left it. He did not know what else to do, so he returned back to the the railway station and standing in front, watching people coming and going out of the station. He was there, trying to see if he could distinguish between other white people and the Dutch people, and as he tried, he came to see that there were also a difference between the Nordic race and the other Europeans. Immediately, he saw a group of young people coming out of the station, he figured out they were from either Norway or Denmark or Sweden, so he said to them in Norwegian, One of them overheard him and replied, When he heard that, he ran to meet her to converse with her, but she told him they were in a hurry and were in group and she could not leave her friends to stand and continue the discussion. He bade her good-bye as he watched her leave to meet her friends. After staying for more than an hour in the train station, and when he was about to leave, he saw one American dressing on bluish black suit with tie, he instantly knew he was a member of the Mormon church since he has invited many of them to his house before and had had discussions with them and even went to their place of worship several times, so he ran to meet him and stopped him. He told the young missionary he was being loathed and punished for having to love and care for a particular group of people whom he believed has come to show the world the pathway to heaven. He also told the lad that he was not prepared to relinquish and that he was still going to move on to preach to the world the reason he fell in love and was obsessed with this great nation. In return, the lad asked him where in the U.s. was he from? But when he told him he was not an American, he looked at him in astonishment and asked him, 'how come you speak like you were born in the U.s?' He later said to him, "Follow your heart where it's taking you to."*jeg elsker a bo i Norge. var so gut.* With the last five euro that was left with him, he returned back to Doorsalaan, the streeet where he used to live in Marshaaven there in Rotterdam. He decided to go and buy marijuana to smoke—thinking maybe that will energize him to be able to confront the terrible and awful situation he had placed himself. When he reached the coffee shop where he normally go to smoke hashish, he saw that the five euro in his pocket was no longer there, so he unloosed his golden neck-lace and was asking the boys there to buy it for just 30.00 euros, and when he finally found someone who gave him 20.00 euros for it, he sold it to him and spent the money in buying a joint of marijuana and a bottle of orange juice. Immediately he finished smoking the marijuana, he was beginning to see the world more clearly and was thinking the Europeans were after him for taking a trip round Europe and preaching the American dreams to everybody. Meanwhile, it was now his sixth day in Holland since he left France, and a night before that day, he had conversation with one beautiful black Dutch woman with an American English accent, whom actually would have rendered him a help, but he refused to let her know he was suffering and was homeless. He and the lady both debated on the issue of racism in Europe and she was the type who was married to a white Dutch man and was prepared to fight for black people to have their rights everywhere around the world. She also complained about African leaders, blaming them and saying they are the cause of the poverty in Africa. She was the first black woman he has seen to be pretty, smart, and intelligent since he arrived in Europe, for that reason—he wanted to tell her he love her, but he saw that she was married and that will be embarrassing to say she already told him she was married and he was still asking her out. After smoking the marijuana, and was already intoxicated with it, he took a tram not knowing where exactly he was going to, but as he sat inside, watching from one of the windows, he saw some area full of Arab people with their families. He also saw mosques well built and designed; he swiftly came to a conclusion that the Europeans were in favor of the Arab people and were supporting them to be terrorizing the Americans, since that will be the only way they could cause confusion to them and make their economy shrink. He was beginning to ask himself, how could westerners allow Muslims to bring their culture to these civilized society and even build mosques here, whereas, in the Muslim countries, Christians are killed everyday. He was thinking, if would it not be better if the westerners had agreed to apply the same standards to Muslims as it is applied to them when they travel to live in these Muslim countries. He did not know how to eradicate these thoughts from his mind until the tram finally reached the city center of Rotterdam, and he saw the flag of his country, green, white and green, next, was the American flag, and later it was a European union flag and finally the flags of many other different nations. Was this a reality or was it just his imagination? once again, he could not distinguish between the two. He could not understand what was happening, since he came to believe the terrorists attack on the World Trade Center was nothing than a conspiracy. Inside him, when he tried to figure out who and who was involved, a question came straight to his mind. Why are the Europeans so intense to unite and be using the same currency? He saw himself answering the same question, oh, it is true, they are uniting for a purpose—to be the world super power, and since they understand, with a good economy they could be whatever they wish to be, that is why they want the euro currency to be more valuable than the dollar, so it could become powerful and influential world-wide. At this same time, there was also a disagreement between many of the European Union countries including Germany and France on the issue of the Bush administration planning to invade Iraq, even without a resolution being passed by the United Nations Security Council. Although, the United Nations had called for a U.N weapon inspectors, to verify if Saddam Hussein was in possession of weapons of mass destruction and it was clear he was not. David, who was so obsessed with the American way of life, and was with an intense desire to go and live there; he was upset with many European leaders mostly, French, Jacque Chirac and German, Gerhard Schroder, for not being in support of the Bush-supposed American vision to bring every Muslim radicals and extremists said-to-be-terrorists to justice. As David came down from the tram and was walking and talking alone all by himself along the street of some shops brimmed with costly and valuable clothes and jewelries, he thought it was time for him to choose a profession—to work with the American Intelligence group in Europe. From his point of view, Europeans were ungrateful for having forgotten what America did for them during the second world war—for putting an end to the Nazis reign and for rebuilding Europe and their economy after the war. As he was still thinking about all these, suddenly, towards him in a whirl-wind, rolled inexorably bruise-colored storm and he was almost frozen with cold hopelessly, even when it was at the middle of summer. Immediately, he heard a voice from heaven say to him, "Why do you have to bite the fingers that fed you?" It was a strange voice, very strange that fear gripped him, and when he could not resist it, he screamed out loudly, calling for someone to help him. He jumped up to hit the show-glass were there were very expensive jewelries so as to raise awareness of the people around and to bring their attentions to himself, but the glass remained the way it was. So he screamed out louder, and a blonde Dutch lady at her thirties came running towards to help him, and when she held him close to her body, asking him what was his problem, he cried out loud to her, asking, 'please, can you ever forgive me?' 'Forgive you for what?' asked, the pretty lady. 'I mean forgive me for betraying you. Please, forgive me, for having betrayed you, I promised I am going to confess all what I have done if only I can get a church priest here now. I want to confess everything to him, I want to confess, I want to confess, I want to confess.' 'Confess what?' asked the lady again. 'How I have betrayed Europe and the people.' But when the lady tried to grasp what he was talking about, three Moroccans came running towards him and asking him what he really wanted. With fear, he wanted to commence with the confession, but when he saw that the lady was leaving him for these Moroccans, he ran away, thinking they were going to kill him if ever he open his mouth and tell them how he has hated Muslims and their religion. After awhile, as he increasingly scream and everybody there were staring at him in awe, he saw a church priest on a black cassock robe and pectoral cross, came close to him. So he swiftly ran to him, holding him tight and pleading for forgiveness. The priest laid his right-hand on him and said some words which he himself did not know the meaning. In not more than two minutes, he fell asleep—as he could not see very clearly or hear clearly what was said about him by the myriads of people watching him, he thought he was never going to survive the misery. The next morning, when he woke up, he saw that he was in a very big hall where there were many other refugees whose asylums were rejected and were already looking for a way to leave the country or someone to harbor them. When he went to meet the man who was attending to everyone of them one-by-one, he saw that he was being given 300.00 euros, and he was told to use it in purchasing his ticket to return back to Spain. He was glad he was given that money, and immediately he left there, he went straight to the bus station there in Rotterdam and purchased a ticket to Spain. Meanwhile, when he was inside the bus, relaxing and trying to recall what happened to him and how it happened, he came to see that it was just seven days that he spent in Holland; he remembered what he was told by Monique, the French lady he loved and had sex with. He remembered the SEVEN DAYS THEORY.

CHAPTER 20

BACK TO SPAIN, DAVID HAS to start life all over again. He was tensed, poised to face whatever life bring across his way, since he was no longer afraid to leap even without watching whether there is a hole near him. First, he went straight to the town hall, asking for a social assistance, but he was given a card to go to for shelter for one week. And when he was given a chance to stay there, he became very rude and was not prepared to follow instructions and he was later driven out. He met one of his old friend, who volunteered to help him by allowing him come and live with him in an apartment he stopped paying for some months before David's arrival. He knew as a man, he would have to face many challenges and be able to overcome the tragedies awaiting him. His friend, Patrick, whose soul seemed lost and was found in crime, was the most happiest living human-being, because of how he was making money from his drug dealing and his girlfriend, who was a prostitute, was also pumping-in money every morning whenever she return back from work. The sky was his limit, and he was seeing himself as the most smartest man. He saw that David was not having anything he could rely on to make money to sustain a living for himself, so he tried to initiate him into his world. Bu when he refused to join him in this crime-way-of-life, he gave him a job by going to get the job and asking him to go do it and at the end of every months, he could be paying him ten percents of the salary. "Take whatever come to your way that you know could aid you and will not cause you any harm to move your life ahead of where you are to a higher place you wish to be." David, calm, but with much potential energy to work, took the job and started working. Although, he was fed and was living freely in his friends apartment and was not paying, even when he too was not paying to the owner. Day-in, day-out, music was blasting as they smoke hashish and bring-in clients to come buy cocaine. He wanted to run away, due to how pressure was mounted on him by his friends to join their team of drug dealings, but he could not, because if he does, where will he sleep and who will feed him? Although he could see this hashish and other drugs they were smoking to be a thing that could undermine his moral defenses, but he could not abstain from it because he thought or believed he was deriving pleasure from it—which was also destroying him, and he knew it. *albergue* One morning, when David woke up from sleep to go to work, Patrick, his friend came to inform him that he will be packing his belongings to leave the house they were staying since the owner of the house has asked him to do so, rejecting the money he had offered to pay, because he came to believe he rented his house to a rogue, after much complaints were laid against him by his neighbors. David, dumb-founded and unable to think with clarity, knew he was to start sleeping in the street again with nobody to cater for him until he will be paid for the work he was doing with Patrick's document. That day, he was unable to go to work, instead, he decided help his friend sort out this problem. It was at this time, he remembered his sister's legal adviser, Alicia, whom he had once related some issues to and she told him to call on her anytime he needed to consult a lawyer. Without waiting, he informed his friend about her, and as he did, they both went to see her in her office. Reaching there, after Patrick had told her what he was encountering, she told him there was nothing she could do about it except to advise him to leave the house for the owner to do with it whatever he wished. David, who even before then knew what his friend was capable of, did not move any step from him, so as for him not to say anything to her. But, to his inexpectation, he saw him looking into her eyes and asking her if she speaks English, and she replied him,' yes.' Luckily for David, Patrick's phone rang, and he picked it up, excusing himself so as to talk with the person. At that moment, Alicia asked David if he speaks English. David recalled how she had tried to communicate with him in English language before by simply pretending she was not understanding the Spanish he was speaking, and immediately, he looked into her eyes, he saw that she was that woman who needed a man who speaks English, but was not prepared to voice it out to him by asking. He saw that she was hiding under a false appearance, and that she was far different from her look, and was dangerous, but, she was pretty and young and was intelligent and was with a good profession. After some weeks, while David was living with another friend in one room and Patrick and his girlfriend have went to rent a one bedroom in an apartment that they were sharing with one other boy who also was married to a Spanish lady, he was paid the first salary which he spent in purchasing some food-stuffs and paying his bills and the house rent together with his new friend, and the rest, he spent in buying some new clothes as he was not having any, apart from the one he was wearing to work and at the same time, wearing them at home. He lost all his clothes while in Holland at the time of his SEVEN DAY'S THEORY, which he will never forget. When David went to see her in her office, he saw that she was as beautiful as an angel, and there was no-way he could be able to tear his eyes away from her, so he decided to ask her out for a coffee which she agreed to. He came to love her as he had seen that she was pretty and was a lawyer and was prepared to assist him in achieving a better life in the future. He wanted to love her mostly, because he felt sorry for her and did not want her to fall a victim of loving the wrong person, Patrick, his friend, whom he believed to be too smart when it comes to seducing women to fall in love with him. In his heart, he wanted to save her, he wanted to love her and treat her right because he thought she deserved it. When he went to see her in her office, he quickly told her about Patrick and warned her about him. He told her, he was a drug dealer, and was having many girlfriends—many of them whom were Spaniards, and the rest whom were Nigerian prostitutes. But, when she asked him about his sister's relationship with her husband, Joaquin and the reason she wanted to file for a divorce, he opened up and revealed everything to her—letting her know his sister was the type who will do it with other men in her husband's absence, and it was true. His sister was having an affair with another man while her husband was at work. At the same time, he told her she disliked his sister's attitudes and manners on how she was treating her husband, but he made it clear that she was his sister and he still love her. After then, she gave him her phone number and asked him to ring her after ten days so they can go to a coffee bar together, but she also told him she was having a boyfriend. That day, after he went to meet with her and told her everything, when he arrived home, he sent her a text-message, telling her she was as beautiful as an angel, and that she worth more than a sister to him, and also thanked her for giving him the opportunity to be able to see her and talked to her. He never knew it was futile of him to have done so, and it was ludicrous to think he was meeting the love of his life.

It was a day—just after the day she asked him to call her on phone, and he did. She gave him an appointment to meet with her in the city center, and when she finally arrived there and he saw her, he was exultantly proud and joyful as they pecked on both cheeks and he followed her to a coffee bar which she had chosen. When they arrived there, he saw that he was the only black person there and most of the people were old men and women of his parents age, and moreover, the place was clamorous and with a constant noise. Although, he never liked the place, but he could not hesitate and leave or ask her to follow him to a very cool and quiet bar where they could be able to sit down without much noise and talk like mature and responsible people. She ordered for a cup of cider for the both of them, and when he tasted it, he spat it out since it was his first time. He was glad she was there with him and they were speaking English. Deep down inside his heart, his dream of marry a white woman was about to come to a reality. He looked at himself and saw that he was the same lad he was when he was young and was still living in Africa. He saw himself as Joseph the dreamer, whom his dream has always come to be real. He saw his future as bright as the day-light, shining from one angle to the rest. Once again his heart was replenished with joy, seeing the passionate look on her face. At the time, he was about to leave, she promised to lend him a novel to read since he told her he was interested in reading, and did not know how to find a book-shop to buy some novels written in English. She promised to help him look for a job as well—since she was a legal adviser to many entrepreneurs. She also promised to lend him a video-cassette of the movie, TITANIC, because, he told her how much he loved the movie and would want to watch it over and over again. What befuddled David most about this lady, was that they were both of the same age, despite that was not his real age that he had in his documents, and another thing was that they were both having similar taste of music. It was when he told her Oasis, was his favorite band, that she swiftly drew her seat near his, and was staring deep into his two eyes, trying to see if she could see and know everything about him. She saw that he was having strong passion for music and the music he loved most was that of Oasis, so, she asked him his favorite track, and without hiding his feelings for her, he told her it was, STOP CRYING YOUR HEART OUT. But, when she demanded why, he told her it was a song about him, and that he was living a life of the songs and lyrics of the music band, Oasis. Immediately after he left her and told her everything about himself and was waiting for the day to meet her again, as he was alone on his own, he recast his thoughts on the issue they have both discussed and came to see that she knew everything about him even before he could say it to her, but how it happened, he did not know, but, he only thought she might be a psychic, and has seek his fortune, and since it was his will to journey far, she has come to his best influence for him to journey farther even more than he was willing to.

Maybe it was not love that David was having for Alicia, or it was just an illusion that she was in love with him and that they were going to marry each other since they were having so many things in common but, he was completely obsessed with her and wanted to be seeing her every time. He started sending her text-messages, telling her how much he loved her and how he could feel her power over him as the mother of his unborn child. She tried to stop him, but he would not, and when he continued, she grew angry and her anger escalated and turned into a nature of hate that she told him to leave her alone or else she was going to call the police. But David replied her, telling her she could do whatever she think is best for her, and that she was hurting him only because he was loving her. It was true that she was hurting him so badly since she has walked into his life and was not having enough time for him—mostly on weekends when everyone around him was with their partner, he will be watching movies and listening to love music, opening a way for loneliness and it was killing him. The more he was thinking about her, the more he love to listen to love songs and was keeping all his love for her. The worst of it, was that she lent him a book to read, and the book was inspiring him and he was acting upon this inspiration and wanted to write a love-story about the both of them. He wanted to let her taste every drops of his love.

Alicia, the woman David first saw to be the love of his life and the mother of his unborn child became the woman to make him hate his reason of being alive. When David saw that he could not proceed further to read the book she gave him to read, seeing that the book was to inspire him to fight for justice and equality that he always infer to be an agenda that should be dealt with everywhere around the globe, and he has always preached about it, referring to the Americans to be a perfect example to learn from, he returned the book back to her, letting her know he needed something more than that, something to energize him to do anything she wants him to do, something more natural and real to impel him to fulfill his dream of becoming an artist, something he thought he needed at that very instant to quench the fire burning deep down inside his heart which was nothing but the true meaning of love. It was at this moment that she told him his sister was about to divorce her husband, and immediately he heard this, he knew someone was giving her every information about him, and that person was either his sister or his sister's husband, Joaquin. He quickly went to meet his sister where she was in her African cosmetic shops and confronted her, saying, 'Why is it that everything I try to build is what you try to destroy?' She was so perplexed when she heard that, and for that simple reason, they both became enemies and he never went closer to her and she too, never thought of him as a brother, and they became cat and rat once again. Although, she fought hard for him not to get involved in a relationship with any of these African prostitutes, because she knew who and what he was, and has never wanted him to waste his talent and time chasing and living with a whore. Instead she wanted him to practice what he was preaching about interracial relationship, meaning she would have want to see him marry a white woman and have kids with her, knowing that was what he actually wanted in life to be happy.

Time went by, and he was still pleading for Alicia's love and was still prepared to love her till death do him. She knew it, and was prepared to give him that love that he wanted from her, but she wanted to take it slowly, only that he was too obsessed and was afraid he was going to lose her soon. He did not know what was happening to him and what he was doing as he was carried away by her love and was drunk and intoxicated with marijuana he was given by his friends, and started to tell them how she was already in love with him—a thing he does often whenever he smoke marijuana or hashish or when he is drunk, making him sometimes think of himself as a talkative, but, it was just that he was being indiscreet and expansive, and his friends knew it. He thought it was a way to deceive his friends and to impress himself on the issue of how long it was that he had had sex, so he lied to them he was having sex with her only for them to laud him and to mind their business and not being concerned whether he was gay or not, because that was what they all thought of him since they have never heard him say he was having a girlfriend even when he tried to tell them he was.

One evening, at about 05:00 p.m, he was already fifty meters away from her office when he called, telling her he needed to see her to discuss a very crucial issue with her. She permitted him to come around, and when he stepped his feet into her office and saw her sitting, he was immediately released from frustration, and went to meet her, saying nothing. She knew why he wanted to see her, so she brought down the curtains of the window and doors in her office, and went into her toilet, calling him from inside to help her take the dust-bins outside and dump them. He ran as fast as he could, and when he returned back, he saw that she was already closing for the day at about 6.00 p.m which was unusual. He knew what he wanted that day, he knew she wanted him to make love to her there in her office, and he was not prepared to, because he thought it will be be more respectful if she call her on weekend so they could both go out and have a good time, and after then, they can walk to his house or hers and make love. But, she did not see it the way he was seeing it that he respected her too much to make love to her there in her office, she thought he was weak, and was gay, the same thing his friends thought of him.

That evening was good, when she closed from work and strolled with him to the biggest shopping-center in the city at that time. He was the most happiest man on earth, as they both strolled and converse and exchange thoughts on many topics. He saw that she was pretty, smart and intelligent and she deserved to be loved, and so he wanted to give-up his life for her to live, only if she decided to love him the way he loved her. When they finished drinking, he told her he was leaving, since she said her boyfriend will be coming to meet her there—a thing he thought will be so absurd to experience, knowing how men feels when they sees their women with another man. So, he thanked her and left happily as he walked back home alone. Although, she had tried her possibly best to let him know she was in love with him too, but she did it on the wrong form, only by being shy and not wanting to show it to him. He saw that she was in love with him, and immediately he arrived home, he sent her a text-message, telling her he knew she was in love with him, and that she should stop concealing it, and that he loved her more than she thought, not knowing that was a way to drive her crazy, and to provoke her to make her think of quitting the relationship. During this time, David had commenced with his love-story book about the both of them, and she knew what he was doing, because many a time, she had seen him with some pieces of papers that he was using.

At this time, since David was lacking sufficient mental abilities to comprehend the situation he was and how to make the relationship work, he knew it will be better for him to get near his friends and quit living that solitary life he was living so as to stop thinking about her every time and to move on with life and make plans on how to render helps to his families in Africa and also build his own future. The more he gets closer to his friends and tell them his problems, the more pressures they were putting on him to think of the reason why he was in Europe without getting to know that he was writing about the both of them, and he was doing it to have a good love-story book written and to make money. He did not know what to do. Although, he was still passionately and madly in love with her even when his friends were cautioning and alerting him about the consequences he was going to be faced with since everyone of them understood what it meant when an African immigrant living in Spain intend to have a dispute with a Spanish lady who is also a lawyer. Later, while he was in jail in Italy, he came to write a poem for this.

TO THE ONE I LOVE.

Of all the women I have met with,
The most beautiful and wonderful she is.
No words to explain, I wish,
How she makes me really feel.
Everything she wants me do, I'll do
To make her allow me to love her.
To love her, never to hurt her.
In love, I'm fallen for her.
In love, I'm fallen for her.
My eyes on her, accord to rest
From the very first moment.
Like a love potion when I drink,
And, it's running increasingly, uninterruptedly through my veins.
Some say, she's mad and bad,
My ears, full to ear, I say.
In the chaos of grief and remorse, even
That dwell and reside in my mind was
One articulate word, (LOVE).
LOVE, LOVE and LOVE.

David thought he could win Alicia's love only by sending her more text-messages without stop. He sent her a text-message, telling her he was on the run like a fugitive, and that he ain't got no gun—a quote from Bob Marley's song of IRON, LION, ZION. He also sent her another text-message, telling her, he won't let pressure make a panic, and when he get stranded, and things don't go the way he planned it dreaming of riches, in a position to making the difference. He also said, he knew it seem hard sometimes, but he could remember one thing that through every dark nights, there's always a bright day after that, and that, no matter how it get, he was going to stick his chest out, and keep his head up and end it. All these quotes which he listened to in one of Tupac's song, ME AGAINST THE WORLD. He thought he was being smart and creative, not knowing he was only drawing more attentions to himself, and that the possible outcome might be deleterious and disastrous.

One Saturday morning, as he woke up from sleep, he tried to recollect the details of the dream he dreamed that night and came to realized he dreamed that he was being chased by a group of some Spanish men who were his co-workers. 'What have I done that men should have to be chasing me?' he murmured to himself as he tried to get up and get himself prepared for work. But the more he tried, the more he became debilitated and weak and could not raise himself up from bed. Instantly, he knew something was wrong, and that something strange and terrible was going to befall him. He wanted to go back to bed and sleep and not go to work, since he came to grasp why things like that might possible come to happen to him when he took time to meditate and did some hard-thinking and came to realize that he was having a dispute with the woman he loved and thought she loved him too. But, going back to bed was never going to fetch him any money, and moreover, he was new in that work and that was the first time they called him to come to work on Saturday. He also knew it was so absurd for them to have called him to come to work on Saturday, because it was unusual for that company where he was working to give an opportunity like that to a new employee like him. He knew there was no-way he could escape it, and even if he did that day, it might come another time, so he decided to get himself prepared and get ready to welcome anything that come to his way. He dressed-up and left for work. As he was walking along the street that lead to to his place of work, he was beginning to converse with himself, and was talking loudly, forgetting he was talking to himself. Suddenly, a car came to pass near him, about to crush him down. He raised up his head only to see that the man driving the car was as well insulting and cursing him, telling him he was blind and that he should be careful the way he walk and talk alone. David, who knew he was not wrong at all, could not believe what he was hearing the man say and all the accusations that he laid. Although, he used to be very stubborn and way-ward, but this time, he knew his life was short, and death was near him, so he kept quiet and did not utter a word out from his mouth, and left to where he was going to.

Reaching the gate of the Mercedes Benz's company where he was newly employed not more than two weeks by one of the sub-contractors there in Vitoria, many of the Spaniards he came to meet were all staring at him with a wide-eyed gaze as if he was a double-dyed villain. He tried to raise his head up to see what was happening around him, and he saw that they were all still looking directly and fixedly at him. Since he could not resist their wild looks, he swiftly bowed down his head as he presented his identity card to the gate-man and passed through the gate to the company's dressing-room, where he was to be met with more ignorant and judge-mental attitudes of some of the young Spanish lads working there who, immediately as they saw him entered the room, proceeded with their gossips about him. At the time he was changing his clothes to put on his working clothes, he overheard them say something about their politicians, and after that, it was about immigrants most especially Africans. He tried to listen more attentively so he could grasp what the noises were all about, then he heard one of them say, 'if this place is not good for them, why don't they pack their belongings and leave so we could live our lives in peace?' It was at that moment David understood what was happening as he recalled how he had discussed an issue about the Spanish politics with one of his co-workers some days before that day. He recalled how he told the man about what was most important to be done to overcome the most critical and grievous problems that was driving the nation into dismay. He thought himself to be wise as to have went as far as to be interfering into matters that were not his business. He never knew there was going to be a big price-to-paid by an African immigrant like him for having had the audacity to dare interfere into the Spanish political issue. At this same time, there was a very big controversy about whether Spain should be divided because of the too much threat that was coming from the terrorist group in the Basque country, where he himself was living. David, who thought himself to be the good lad to save them from their sins, has once argued with his sister's husband, Joaquin on the same issue, preaching to him the need for unity and peace among the Spaniards. Although, Joaquin, who actually was born in Extremadura but had migrated to the Basque country with his parents, and came to like the place and the people, therefore, has come to believed and support the notion that the country must be divided even more than the people who were born there. It was not just Joaquin alone who thought it was right for them to be separated from Spain, but many others who actually had come from the south and other parts of the country and came to lived there, were also having that same belief that it was time for a separation so as for them to live in peace. Many immigrants amidst whom were also David's friends, believed the same thing should be done because they could see how they were benefiting from the government there. They also believed if the country happened to succeed to have their independence, they will all automatically be granted citizenship—and that will be good.

Fela Anikulapo-Kuti, the Nigerian music artist David loved and respected as not only as a musician, but also as an activist, once said, '*when cat sleep, rat go bite him tail, wetin him dey find? palaver him dey find, palaver him go get him own o, palaver him go get.*' David knew he was already in trouble for having had to interfere in a matter that he was not called for. So that day when it came to the time one of his co-worker tried to discuss the issue of the Spanish politics with him, he declined to respond to it, instead he changed the subject of the conversation. He did so because, he knew his days were numbered as he also believed he was being followed by the police and other secret service men, and that everybody were out there for him. But when his co-worker resumed and was trying with every of his effort to bring up the issue and make him contribute to it, not knowing he was talking to a man who could hear the language of the ants as they converse with each others. David saw how desperate his co-worker was, so he kept quiet and watched and listened to him as he talked alone to himself about the problems that was engulfing the country. Since David did not reply him, he paused and looked deep into his eyes, and when he did, he realized he was betraying him—and he knew what he was doing was wrong.

After he finished working, he went inside the dressing room to change his clothes to leave to his house. But when he entered, he saw that the place was empty and there was nobody. He knew something was wrong since it was the time for all of them to have been supposed to be there to change and leave to their different particular direction. '*que estan pasando con estas maricones que piensa que son mas listos?*' he said loudly, thinking some of them might be hiding themselves around there so they could hear and understand he was not afraid of them anymore. He finished changing his clothes and left the room, walking alone towards the gate, and as he did, a man waited for him near the gate and asked him what direction he could take to go to the city center. The man who was dressing on some filthy outfit and was looking haggard, brought out a cigarette and offered him one and started to utter things about the situation of the country, immigration, and later the problems the world was encountering. This time, he did not hesitate to contribute to the conversation, but he did with a shrewd idea and talked about it with him the way it will suit him, knowing he was talking to a secret serviceman and because he has seen the hand-writing on the wall before then—making him believe his life was in peril. As they both passed the gate and were walking towards the city center, he saw a car passed them and parked by. Seeing that it was his sister's husband, Joaquin's car, he swiftly ran to meet him and when he was offered a lift, he bade the so-thought-to-be secret serviceman good-bye and left with Joaquin.

Inside the car, he was glad he was with him, but in not more than three minutes, he could hear him commenced with the same issue of how the ruling party in Spain was in support of the Bush's campaign on the war on terror. He did not wait to keep himself quiet, pretending he did not know what was happening around him, he intruded and told him that people were accusing him to be the bad lad. When Joaquin heard this, he was astonished and kept his mouth shut, knowing he knew everything already. He wanted to take him home, but at this time, he was having a feud with his sister and could not go to meet her even when he insisted. When Joaquin asked him if he was seeing any woman yet, he said no, but he went on to impart some knowledge of the fact why he was no longer interested in having a relationship with the Spanish women. He also told him Alicia was not the right woman for him since he could see her be a pest to his life. Joaquin disagreed with him on that—telling him it will never be so easy for him to find another woman as educated and pretty and rich as she was. He knew he was right, but he also disagreed with the idea that she was the best he could have when he knew the universe never wanted it so for him, and that his fate was not to be with a woman who will make him stay there in Spain forever. He came down from the car and left, and at the time he was walking to his house, he tried to recollect everything that happened and the reasons why it happened.

That afternoon, when David arrived home and had showered, he quickly fell into his bed unable to close his eyes and sleep as he could not comprehend why he was seen as a bad lad. He knew it was a revolution, and even if he tell the world about it, no one was ever going to believe it, but it was a revolution and it was not televised. When he thought about it, he remembered Gil Scott-Heron's song, THE REVOLUTION WILL NOT BE TELEVISED. To him, because it was not televised, no one would think it happened, but it did happened. He felt certain why it was happening to him, he knew it was because he snubbed Alicia to make her feel she was the one who needed him when he saw her passed-by and they were alone while she was looking at him, thinking he was going to run to meet her to beg her to come back to him. He grasped it was a conspiracy theory, and that the conspirators were his sister, her husband, and Alicia working with the government. He did not know whom he could confide in anymore. He was perplexed and did not know what to do next as the whole theme run around his brain, and was forcibly pressing on him and was urging him to an intensity madness—as said by D. H Lawrence, one of his favorite author.

Lying on his bed alone and going deep into his imaginary mental world created by his thought, he came to realize that there was an investigation going on, and it was all about whether he was a spy working for the Americans as they could see how much hatred he was having for the Muslims—referring them to be terrorists. Although he was concerned about the terrorists imposing fear on everybody, but that was not exactly what he intended to write about, instead he was much more and very concerned about the issue of racism and how the world can put a halt to it. Seeing that people were misjudging him, he was beginning to develop inside of him, the feelings of worthlessness and unwarranted guilt, he was beginning to hate himself for whom he was and why he was living; he did not see any reason why these people could believed him to be a dangerous gad-fly that has come to destroy them; although, he realized he was possessing some great power inside of him, but it was not for him to destroy, instead, to build and repair; it was for him to make an impact on the world as he already was very much concerned on the theme of the problems of the world, and came to think of how we the people of the world can come together to resolve them and make the world a better place to live. Many people around him, who came to later take a good look at him and came to see what he was doing, also came to believe he was a visionary—and that was what he was dreaming to become. With how he was misjudged and being treated, he came to realized a thing he once realized at his early age before he came to Europe and when he was on the trip to Europe and even when he was already in Europe, he came to realize that, "To be ambitious is good, but to be too ambitious, that is where danger lies." He knew he was ambitious, and this ambition was for him to be creative and to make money to help his families. 'Was there any need for all this aggravation?' he asked himself, since he came to see how he was trying to walk himself into the road leading to the world where he could be imaginative and creative—which also was a dangerous one. From memory, he came to recollect the reason he left Spain before to Norway and recast his thoughts on whether it was another chance for him to do so again to relocate himself to another country. But, within his memory, he also came to understand that he has left and returned back, and still has not make a decision to change his way of life that was bringing him all these impediments. Since he already believed that, "Every man is got his own reason for living," and that, "Any man born into this world, is born for a purpose," and he knew his purpose of being born was to be an artist and being able to be creative, so he made a decision to cling to what he has always believed in, and quit the life-of-being-afraid-to-be-killed one day, since he could see himself not as the bad lad, but the one who is striving to find a future for himself even with no one's support. He said he came to realize that, "As the fear starts to grow in you, your dreams starts to run away from you," and that, "Sometimes in life we have to take a tough decision, whether it is right or wrong." He said he came to believe this, because something in him told him that we are all going to die, and when we do, someone would have to ask us what we did with the talent that we possessed that was given to us.

As for Alicia, the girl he loved and thought to be his future wife, but later became the same person to be punishing him for having loved her. She will always be seen to him to be a girl who might as well be a liar, because she never loved really him, but was only pretending to. He said he said so, because with her, he learned something new, and came to understand how people pretend to love you and hurt you, "We cannot love someone and take away their vital needs." His vital need was happiness—which she took away from him.

As David was still inside his bed alone, unable to sleep, and unable to puzzle out what he was supposed to do, fear seized him. He was afraid of the people around him, and was much more afraid of himself because, for so many times he has tried to run away to other places, but he could not run away from his soul which was already in Spain; and when he tried to rejoin this soul with his body, he could not—as living the rest of his life in Spain was something against his will.

Some few days after the incident passed, and David was starting to enjoy life again, since he decided to quit the job he was doing and has reconciled with his sister, and has also found another job where he was earning better wages. He thought it was time for him to walk near his fellow Africans and live the same life with them so he could be happy in life. He met Alicia several times, but declined to talk to her or even looked at her, because most time, she was with a man whom David understood was never her boyfriend. Although, she looked at him most time, but also refused to call him because, as a smart and learned woman with a good profession and money involved, she thought she might be letting herself down to an African immigrant who has come to seek a brighter future in her country. You see, "What we want and need is there waiting for us, but all we need to do is just to stray ourselves into the path that leads to where it is without shame and without pride." And, as for David, he knew he has the opportunity to improve his relationship with her as he could still see it in her eyes that she needed and wanted him more than any other thing or maybe she was pretending to, but he was not willing to, probably because he was afraid of the tragedy the love he was having for her might bring to him in the nearest future.

Despite that he was already working and was enjoying life there, but his plan was still to leave Spain and go to look for a white woman he could marry in another European country. Although, he fathom the fact that Alicia was still in love with him or was pretending, and deep down in his heart he was already indebted to her, and would have want to love her and make her happy. He was asking himself, if he has to walk a thousand miles to get what he want in life when he could see it a hundred meters close to where he was. But what mattered was, if that was what destiny wanted for him. He saw that it was better for him to work and earn a good income and be happy even without a woman by his side. It was making him start to loathe women, and as he did, isolation and loneliness found a way into his life once again, and sadness was holding him in his grip. He saw that the only way he could break away from this punishment that he has inflicted on himself was to stop being awkwardly unsociable and become sociable and having friends and also having fun. So, for that reason, he went closer to his fellow Africans whom he once disliked their ways, and has also complained about their traditions and beliefs; he forgot he once told Alicia, how much he disliked to be with them.

David was welcomed back just when he went closer to his friends; he was received with gratitude, because they were all glad that he made up his mind to return back to them, seeing it to be a battle won. They thought he was taken away from them by the whites since they were all looking upon him to be the hero to lead them and defend them with his voice from some wrong doings by the Spaniards. It was so apparent that he has come to lead them again to fight against oppression and to edify them and define their future for them since he already made himself a preacher, and moreover, he could sing, dance, entertain them and make them happy and also make them sad. They believed in him and thought he could take their distress away even when he could not take his own away first. To him, he was a normal person like them who has seek knowledge and wisdom, and with love, faith, and ambition, came to believe he could fly so high to touch the sky and was making others believe in him and in themselves. He was capable of motivating and engineering people to choose the right path and make a future, when he himself was not capable of eradicating poverty from his family. He became who he was, just by spending more time, seeking information from different sources, and was turning these information into inspiration, then imagination, which was leading him to creativity. He did not stop and he did not not quit no matter the situation due to the fact that he already believed in literary mystery. He has also went on some trips to some strange places many of his friends never thought exist, and that was what made him unique among them that they did not comprehend. Although, he said he was patiently listening to voices, dreaming dreams, and living on fantasies. But, he did not know he was about to sneak into a dark room, and when he did, he switched on the light and saw a bright brown-eye opened, and suddenly, thunder was striking, lightning so brightened, and he heard a strange noise, coming from nowhere.

Not quite long, when David was spotted by the police, mingling with his friends, some whom he once denounced of being criminals and was partying and smoking hashish with them, it became very pronounced he was no longer interested in the relationship with Alicia and was blaming himself for having been too close to the whites than his fellow Africans. When Alicia heard this, she became more annoyed and wanted to make sure he was dealt with or deported back to his country of origin—according to what she told one of David's friend, Patrick whom they have both went to see her for the first time on the issue of how they could file a lawsuit against his landlord. The boy, whom David lied to that he was having an affair with Alicia, met her one day and tried to seduce her again since he thought she already broke up with his friend. Alicia told him she was not having any affair with David, and her aim was to squeeze him and throw him out of Spain so as never to be seen again. When Patrick told David all these, he knew it was true, and he also knew her meeting with his friend was planned by the police, so as for him to be envious. He knew it was true because, he experienced it one day as he was walking home from one of his friend's house to his house, he saw a cash-machine, and decided to withdraw some money, when about five policemen in mufti came rushing him against the wall, 'manos arriba,' they shouted. He was shocked, because it was so appalling, and he was afraid to even turn his face to look at them. He raised his hands up, and when they checked him and could only find a pen-knife with him which he claimed he was using in his place of work when asked what he was doing with it. But, actually he was holding it to defend himself since he was already thinking and believing he was going to be attacked one day by the terrorists there—as many have come to him several times, trying to intimidate him. After the policemen checked him and saw that he was not having any drugs with him, they let him go. He knew it was Alicia doing that to him. He knew she has told the police he was dealing on drugs since he once told her his friends were drug dealers, and later he has decided to return back and reconcile with them. He knew she was looking for a way to pay him back what he did to her by neglecting her when he passed close to her. He knew she was really upset, and was on the verge of doing anything it will take so he could come back and kneel down to beg her for forgiveness. That night when he arrived home, he slotted in his Tracy Chapman's cd and went straight to the track, TALKING ABOUT REVOLUTION and as it was playing, he began to sing along with it.

The next day when he woke up from sleep, he narrated the story to his friends whom they both share the apartment, letting them know he was being followed by the police just because he was having a misunderstanding with a woman. He was never the type who would keep his mouth shut; he was always informing every of his friends and even his families in Africa—that there was a conspiracy to eliminate him—for having loved a woman and later decided to quit the relationship. He knew his sister and her husband were involved, and he was saying it straight to their faces, telling them he knew what was going on around him.

He was beginning to draw more attentions to himself by telling everybody he knew what he was encountering, and the more he was doing this, the more tribulations that was befalling him, and he could see himself yearned for more.

Once again, when he went to the police station to report the lost of his documents, he was arrested and accused of having sold it to another person. He was handcuffed and taken to the cell to be detained with no means for a legal defense. He was later released and driven home by one of the policemen who arrested him. Inside the car, when he was driving, he complained about the illegal immigrants and how they were increasing in numbers everyday. David, who was glad that he was released, supported everything he was saying—only for him to go home and sleep after having had a hard day, and that was his first time for being arrested and hand-cuffed. That was also his first time of being detained, and it was making him experience what it means to be kept in a place where you are being deprived of your freedom—his first experience in a cell since he came to Europe, and it was making him feel he could commit crime and be placed there, and he could survive it since it was not as bad as he once thought it to be—compared with the prison he stayed in Morocco.

When he saw that he was being treated like a felon even when he has not committed any crime and was trying to be the good lad to preach and encourage love and peace among the black and white people living there, since he could see the gap lengthened and he thought it was necessary for him to bring it closer. He saw all these things happening to him, so he decided to choose a different way of life—which was, living the lives his friends were living, believing they were living happily and were committing crimes. And immediately he entered into that life, everything changed and he was no longer seen as the bad lad. He became the good lad and was happy and living life to fullest just like his other fellow Africans. He started purchasing drugs from his friends and selling it to the junkies and was making money from it. He was also working and at the same time, still dealing on cocaine, but with little quantity and was still afraid, despite how he was boasting to his friends of being Al Capone. He was doing more over-time in his place of work and was earning good income and was sending the money to his families at home just like his other friends were doing, and he was glad he was doing so. It was then he knew how to test cocaine with his tongue, to differentiate the good ones from the bad ones. He was getting deep inside, and calling it a game. He thought maybe he could gain some certain notoriety for being a drug dealer. His friends knew he was forcing himself to be doing it, but they were pleased he was doing it, and were encouraging and supporting him more and more.

When the police saw that he was desperate to live like his other friends and was willing to face the consequence of what he was doing, they decided to stop him, knowing that he was gifted with high intuition and sensitivity and was having the capacity to do more greater things in his life. He knew that they were trying to stop him, as he could see some of the policemen he knew before dressed in mufti and walked closer to him almost every time he walked to the area where his friends were selling these drugs. He came to fathom that these people he thought were his enemies and were disturbing him and wanted to destroy him by making him do what he never wanted to do, were not truly his enemies, but were only trying to assist him so he could achieve his dream.

David knew it was time for him to choose a woman for himself, but he was afraid to do so since he already vowed never to befriend another woman there, and was having the intention of going to meet Alicia to beg her to forgive him so that they could be together. He was having this thought because, he saw her as the only intellectually responsible woman and with civility among every other women there, and moreover, her English was good, she was young, she was a lawyer and was also very ambitious and love his kind of music. He thought living with her could make him more happier than living with his fellow African girls who were throwing themselves at him so he could love them. When he made a perfunctory effort to call her on phone to apologize several times, first she received his call and talked to him—making him think she was still interested in the relationship, but after then, she warned him not to call again. He was persistently working and earning good pay, and was sending it to his families while his friends were relishing their lives with their girlfriends and were mocking him, thinking he was impotent or was gay. At that moment, he met a girl called Ayo who came to shop in his sister's Afro-shop and was a Nigerian. She was tall, light-skin, and pretty, and beside that, she was a musician in Nigeria before coming to Europe—so she said. She was also smart and intelligent and could speak fluent English language unlike the other girls who were uneducated. She has refused to prostitute just like the rest because she was not brought to Europe by a pimp to come pay the thousands of euros like them, making David think she was sent to him from above to heal his wounded heart. She was having passion and great love for music, and was a good singer, and was very ambitious to make it with her music career.

At the beginning when David first met Ayo, he never knew she was dating another lad, but as time went on, he came to understand her to be dating more than three men there in the same city, and all were Nigerians. She was so cunning that she almost made David fight with these other lads who were also crazy about her just the way David was, even when they were all spending some parts of their little salary for her. When David saw this, he swiftly relinquished the prospect of having her as a lover. He saw that it will be better for him to think of having a professional qualification so he could get a better job and earn better salaries than to persist-in working like a gofer, and be spending the money on a whore who was an hypocrite, and has come to ruin the lives of his fellow Africans in Europe. She was lazy—never liked to work, but was always spending more than what she could earn, bragging about her previous life in Nigeria. She preferred having a relationship with a man who is married or a man with a girlfriend, so she could ruin the relationship. Although, David did loved her, and tried to have sex with her, but she refused, thinking he was only going to have sex with her and run away. Deep inside his heart, he was in love with her, because she was the only person who tried to make him forget the love he was having for Alicia; she was the one who revived him and made him believe there was still life ahead of him and there were still very many women out there that are intellectually gifted. He wanted to love her so they could both leave where they were to any other place in the world to live their lives.

David, who comprehend the fact that Ayo was smart and educated but was also a girl that was constantly with a lascivious thoughts, knew it will be better for him to run away from her. But the more he was running away from her, the more she was running after him and was extracting money from him even when many other African girls were also running after him and begging him to love them with their hands full of money. He was already seeing himself on the verge of total derangement, as he was accused and mocked by his friends of having loved Ayo, while she was having sex with another Nigerian lad who was married to a Spanish girl. When David confronted her about this issue, she admitted she did it because she thought the lad was making a mistake by thinking of getting married to a white woman. She said they had sex the night before the lad's marriage with the girl, and she did it because she wanted to save a soul. David was sad when he heard this, but that did not stop him from still loving and caring for her even when she followed him into his room and refused to have sex with him twice. He continued to masturbate and was waiting until the day she will be ready for him while news and rumors were spreading he was being used by the girl and was a fool. He was embarrassed and unable to think with clarity what was best for him to be doing.

He walked into a very big shop one day to see if he could find some English books. Immediately he saw them, he quickly search for a good one and came across the LORD OF THE RINGS and picked it up, paid for it and left to his house to start reading it. When he started reading this book, his life became different, and he was no longer interested in any relationship but was more focus on the theme of what he must do in his future time. He became more interested in reading and listening to music inside his room all alone than associating himself with friends or looking for a woman to love. With his dictionary, he was studying and was also writing. He was working, and at the same time, concentrating more on his studies, putting friends and women aside—seeing that he was deriving pleasure from what he was doing. He loved it, and knew his dream of becoming an artist was a thing he should be more interested in doing.

As he continued to stay indoors, and with his self-education tried to improve his English grammars and vocabularies, once again he was seen by his friends as a traitor, and by the Spaniards as a hypocrite. He could see that he was being hated by everybody there, but within him, love was the only thing he could rely on, because he knew it was the key to his happiness. In spite that he was faced with critics from his friends and other people around him, he declined to be told what was best for him to be doing. He tried to enroll himself in a course for playing guitars and singing, but he was told he should have to wait till the next year. He continued with his self-education and was so delighted with it. He saw that the more he was studying, reading books, listening to music, and watching movies, he was beginning to enjoy being lonely, and he felt happy with his life; he was transforming himself, not knowing he was. "The truth is that, no one can transform you, except it is your willingness to let that transformation occur." He out-grown his passion for rap music and other African traditional music, and was becoming more interested in rock 'n' roll music and was getting more inspiration from the music. When his friends saw this, they believed he was being transformed by the white people, and that made them loathe him more than they used to, and as they did, he was more happier because he could see himself climbing and was about to reach while they were still down waiting for him to reach and call them to follow him. And as for the white people, they knew he was good in pretending to be who he was not by always articulating and conjoining himself with his uneducated and benighted friends whereas he could have been more happier, seeing himself with distinguished, educated, and well cultured Englishmen. And it was true that he was a hypocrite, and he knew he was, because most time he was with his friends, he could see that he was unique and should have been with people entirely different. But some of them there that were educated were all married and there was no way he could be closer to them, SINCE he was not having his own love partner, making many other women see him as gay.

One afternoon, when he went to a coffee bar with his friends to drink, and when they were inside the bar drinking and discussing the political problems in their country, a man excused and called him out to a corner and was talking to him. Actually, when he first saw the man, he thought he was a Briton because he was more white and looked more like British than Spanish. Being a person who haS always wanted to listen to everybody, he listened as the man narrated his story of life while he was working in England. The man told him he was being disliked by most Spaniards, because he was associating himself with the English people there. At the end, he advised and shake him, and uttered one last word, 'take life as it comes,'—a word he was told sometime ago by another white person. David listened and went back to where his friends were sitting, letting this advice cling to his brain and mind.

CHAPTER 21

I T WAS AT THE MIDDLE of march 2003, when the U.s.—led coalition troops invaded Iraq. The troops were from the United States, United Kingdom, Australia, Poland and Spain, and they invaded Iraq, and toppled the regime of the dictator and tyrant, Saddam Hussein. Before then, France and Germany had long opposed the war, while Donald Rumsfeld, the then U.s. Defense Secretary, famously distinguished between old Europe and new Europe, a statement which was very provoking to Europe, and was about to split the two continents on the theme of how the both had always worked together in order to achieve a common goal. But at this time it was different, as the United Nations Security Councils did not pass a resolution for Iraq to be invaded. It was said that the war could only occur, if weapons of mass destruction was found in Iraq. The Bush administration did not care, but went further to invade Iraq without the supports of its military allies—which are mostly based in Europe. The administration also forgot that they were about to only force Europe to develop its own foreign policy, and increase its autonomy from the U.s. Although, at later on, the military invasion of Iraq only aggravated the conflict in that country even further.

As the shock-and-awe bombing by the U.s.-led coalition troops began in Iraq, people around the world, including Europe were all angry and then reacted with indignant outrage. The majority of the people in the Basque Country were more outraged, because the ruling party in Spain had also supported the war, claiming it to be a war on terror. From what David himself could understand about this propaganda-on-the-war-on-terror-politics in Spain, was that, the ruling party in Spain had only supported that war because, they thought it was a way to create fear in the minds of the terrorists in Spain, not knowing they were only about to further elevate the conflict and create more fear, misunderstandings and chaos among the innocent citizens and the foreigners living in the country.

At this time when Iraq was invaded, many people in the world were beginning to see the American imperialism to be proving to be an over-riding threat more than to lead the world to achieve peace and a stabilized economic growth. To many Europeans whom David met and had discussions with about this war, it was like the Bush administration was saying, look! It is over the respect the Americans were having for Europe based on their cultural achievements in music, art, literature and other things that dominate, including science and technology. Many also believed they were seen by the Americans as old-cargoes, and it was very disturbing and provoking to them. David who had loved America and believed in everything they do, came to see that he was being mislead by the Bush's campaign war on terror. It was then he knew it was a time for him to rethink on the issue of the three major problems engulfing the world that he was much concerned about—which is war, poverty, and terrorism. He said, when he rethink on this issue, he came to ask himself why is there no solution to these problems when there should be?

Watching the television became a problem to him, because every time he put-on the television to watch the news, what he sees was how many innocent Iraqis and Afghans were killed by bombs, and yet the Americans were still bombing them. He said, as he watched this, he came to recall what he was told by the beautiful Australian stranger he met in Oslo, Norway and also what Monique, the beautiful French woman he has loved and had sex with, and when he recalled these words, and uttered them out repeatedly to himself, he saw darkness crept into his two eyes and a strong clean wind hit him on the face while he was unable to see anything, and the only time he saw something was when the world backed him and walked away. The America he knew and loved, and has long dreamed to go live the rest of his life, was then becoming a wolf he could not run to embrace as he was being chased by his unseen enemies.

David said, from his own perspective on and understanding politics, he saw that George W. Bush, the then president of the United States, did not intended to disregard or neglect Europe. As a politician, he was only trying to prove to the Americans that he was competent enough to lead them through that formidable and tough time when all Americans were stunned and paralyzed with terror. Bush thought it will be best for him to prove himself as a leader of the most powerful country in the world by reacting to the terrorists attack in the World Trade Center. He reacted by invading Afghanistan, and the whole world was in support of the war, knowing that Osama bin Laden, the master-minder of the terrorist group known as Al Qaeda, should be haunted. The whole world believed that those responsible for the attack must be brought to justice. But, Bush over-reacted by thinking it was best for him to fight the war on terror by invading every countries they believed the terrorists were operating. Meanwhile, Bush and his administration were sublimely unaware of the great trouble they were about to cause in the world, and the calamities that they will be bringing to themselves and the entire American citizens there in the States, and also around the world.

As the war in Iraq continued, bombs were falling everywhere in the country, destroying the towns and cities, many of the coalition troops and the Iraqis were killed, and myriads of people around the world were protesting against the war, including vast numbers of Americans who also believed the war to be unjustifiable. David knew it was the right time for him to dig deep to know the hidden truth about some many problems that has enfolded the world. As an adventurer, he thought it will be better for him to start from the place where he was. He sensed that most people were fighting for justice, and they were fighting against oppression.

In an area in the city popularly known as *casco viejo,* (old town), where he used to meet his friends at the time he intended to join them to be dealing on drugs and also to drink and smoke. There, there were also night-clubs and coffee bars, where mostly Spaniards, Moroccans, and few black people were always frequent every weekend and were all permitted to smoke marijuana or hashish. Living in Vitoria, to David, was like living in Holland. Not that smoking of Indian hemp was legalized there, but everybody were free to smoke without any disturbance by the officers of law. It was really strange to David most time he is inside one of these bars, smoking and chanting with his friends. He saw that they were very good and kindhearted people who actually were not the ones to live with a word compared to discrimination. They were very open-minded in terms of living your life in that area the way you like it—be you a Christian or a Muslim, Black or White or Indian or Arab or Chinese, everybody were all welcomed. In this same area, David knew, there were possibilities you can meet very intelligent people there who might be prepared to enlighten outsiders about the reason why they were fighting for their independence. So, he began to visit these bars frequently with his friends more than he used to, and then he began to see things for himself. He saw that these people were promoting devotions to their states, so that nationalism in effect was becoming a religion; they came to believe it was time for them to take it to a higher level, and as they did, the cause was impelling them to fanaticism; and as they became very fanatic to think and believe it was time for them to declare to be free from the Spaniards, they chose to fight by terrorizing the nation since that was the only possibly means they believed they could achieve their independence.

When David came to understand what was happening there as he was also told by some—the stories of how long they have been fighting to have their independence, he remembered the many American movies and documentaries he has watched, and come to see how the black Americans have also fought and struggled to gain their freedom and dignity. He saw that these black Americans who even many years after declaration was made for them to be freed from slavery, they were still victimized by their racist neighbors, the inheritance of the new west but not the native of the land. Although these black people have really fought hard in many ways violently, but never achieved their goal until they came to learn that the only way was to love these neighbors, some of them who were with good hearts supported them, voiced out, and did it peacefully, and as they did, they were able to progress and read a success story. David said he came to understand one thing that, "No matter how these people will keep terrorizing the people around them, they will always be denied what they want, except they choose the right way which is to fight, keeping violence aside." Something David also came to understand from having been too close to these people, was that they were very anxious to gain independence because they could see several other regions in Spain also striving to achieve the same goal. There were people from Catalonia, Galicia, and Canary Island—all with a prospect of having their own country. David said when he came to turn his glance at this, he came to also ask himself, 'if he was a part of Spain, would he not for long have decided to have its own independence, because of how he has never seen himself happy in the country and was always running away?' He said there was no reason they could be blamed, because they believed it to be with good cause.

"To make an impact and influence the people around you with your ideas, there has to be sacrifices we have to make, and these sacrifices can lead you to adverse circumstances and misfortunes." He knew this, but there was no way he could escape it since he already made himself a slave to his dream and could not achieve it and could not in the other hand give it up to live a normal life others were living. He proceeded with his preaching, and the people there who watched him became more upset and displeased, thinking he was provoking them more and there was a need for him to be dealt with. Although he thought what he was doing was the most appropriate thing for him to be doing to think of unifying the people there despite the fact that he knew how the people there—Blacks, Whites, and Arabs loathe him and his ideas, since they could see him as someone who has come to save them when he could not save himself. Music became his weapons, as he preached and sing to them. Every time, when he was walking along the road and will be singing alone. Music became his everything, and when many of them saw this, they felt sorry for him, seeing that he was having a strong passion for it and wanted to render him a helping hand, only if he chooses to do it their ways. But no matter what the circumstances were, he was not prepared to do it in anyone's way. The black people there wanted him to be their new Bob Marley while the whites believed he could be the new Michael Jackson. Everything he was doing became so meaningful to them, as every color of his out-fits also became more meaningful. His passion for black and white color of clothes became a tradition to him as he also became more interested in Michael Jackson songs and pretending to be Michael; he also began to lecture his friends on the issue of racism, cautioning them of the risks and outcomes that could emerge from being a racist; he saw that what he was doing was right, but as time went-by, he came to apprehend that, "Nothing is worse than when you pretend to be what you are not." Many of his friends saw this pretense as a threat to them and tried to lecture him about the past on how black people have suffered much from the hands of the whites. They also laid complaints before him on how they were being ill-treated, but he came to make it clear to them that he was a black person who happened to fall in love with some of the white people's culture not because he was being brainwashed as most of them were thinking. He said intrinsically he has heard enough of how black people were being treated by the whites, and there was no reason for them to look back in anger to what has passed; he said history of slave trade, segregation, and apartheid can never be forgotten, but he was also in supports of most white people who become tired of hearing the word RACISM every day, because he himself could see that any wrong doing by a black person, if complained about might make them look like they are racists in public. "Why is it not so that we can tell the stories as it is." "Anyway, the truth sound insane sometimes."

Not quite long as he proceeded with the life he was living, thinking it was time for him to reconcile with the Arabs and ask them to pardon him for having loathe and condemned majority of Muslims for every wrong deeds. He cling to his music and continued with it without stop, and this was drawing more attentions to him even when he did not want it. Many Spaniards including his sister, her husband, and Alicia, from their points of view, knew he was black but with a white heart. He understood this as many white women came throwing themselves to him, and the men, mostly his co-workers, sharing their secrets with him and requesting his friendship. He saw himself arrived in a state of agitation and despondency, as pressure was being mounted on him to get himself closer to the whites and marry the woman he said he loved and would not desert no matter what she did, the woman he will never stop to love, the same woman he knew was causing him pains, and he was dying of loving her to death, the woman he knew he has to run away from, and she was no other woman than Alicia. The more he tried to forget about her, the more she was appearing to him both physically and when asleep. To him, it was just like they were about to force him to pander to her every whim, and any black person—man and woman who tried to befriend him were bound to encounter problems. With this he was beginning to realize how his own action was now having consequences on other people near him. He knew he was the cause of his own problems, and to turn away from who he already is, was to say he was lying. He knew he could be more comfortable living with Alicia more than living with one Nigerian prostitute whom they might both end up having children without means to cater for them or to send them to the school of his choice. Many a time when he remembered how he first met her, he could feel that deep love he was having for her to be priceless, pure, outstanding, wonderful, and divine. He knew he needed her, and that he was only pretending, and was lying to himself. You see, "We lie too much that we allow ourselves get addicted to it, even to an extent we now lie to ourselves, without knowing we are lying to ourselves."

David who always believed that life should be a thing of adventure, was getting tired of living and working in Spain once again. He knew it was time for him to run the race set before him, and for him to do that, he needed strength, and this strength was wisdom and knowledge. But how was he going to attain this energy to increase this race when he could see that his life was thoroughly miserable, and his own imagination was tormented with misfortune, and as he could also see himself enshrouded in a petrifying darkness. Within him he could see a mix of talent, experience, and determination; he could see how the information he achieved was giving him hope, purpose, and joy—a thing he affirmed and was striving to have so as to live the life he always dreamed to live.

One hot afternoon at the middle of summer, when he returned back home totally exhausted and was experiencing a desire for food, he managed to enter his room and put on his music sets, and wanted to sleep a bit. But he could hear some weird noises coming from the parlor and thought they were arguing over there since that was what his flat-mate was accustomed to, since he was in fact the person who rented the flat. He wanted to go and meet them to tell them to lower their voices when suddenly he met Ayo, sitting with a friend of his flat-mate—another lad who has come there for a visit and has come from another state. He thought it was a dream when he tried to wipe his eyes with his hand to see everything clearly, and when he did, he saw that what he was seeing was real, and it was Ayo, the so-called Nigerian musician, the girl he tried to love, even if he was forcing himself to so as to forget about Alicia, the same girl whom he tried to make love to the previous day but has refused and promised to return back to him another day and also extracted some money from him. From the way he saw them, he knew there was an amazing chemistry between them. He did not know what to say than to return back to his room. When he entered his room again, he tried to resist it and could not, so he went to excused her from the place where she was chanting happily and sleeping on the lad's lap, and when she came to meet him inside his room, he knelt down to beg her to show him some little respect not to do it with the lad there in that house. But she yelled at him and told him he was having no right to tell her what to do, and left to meet his new angel. After about ten minutes he could hear the both of them dragged and shambled themselves into his friend's room, and after some minutes of silence, he heard her scream and scream continuously. He did not know what to do next, so he shut the door of his room, increased the volume of the music so he could not hear her scream, but the more he was increasing the volume, the more louder she was screaming, and it was driving him crazy. He swiftly dressed up, shut his door, and left the house while his other friends laughed. He went to sit in a coffee bar, ordered for a cup of coffee and smoke his Marlboro-light cigarette and was thinking about it. He felt sorry for himself for having wasted his time, energy, and money for her even if he was doing so as to stop thinking about the woman he loved, Alicia, and also to prove to his friends he was not gay. He was hurt once again by a woman—and this time by a black woman. It was a pleasant day for him, and he was so delighted because experienced it, knowing the time for him to leave Spain has finally come.

After some days that Ayo had sex with another lad in the same apartment with him, he returned back home from work and was starving. But when he entered the kitchen to cook some food, he saw that Ayo also came in and was about to start cooking. He quickly left the kitchen for her, but as he did, she started to complain of how she could see it so apparent the way David was avoiding her even when she greeted him several times and he never responded. David who was the most happiest man, seeing that everything was happening for a reason, ignored her and her friend who was also befriending his flat-mate and was the same person harboring Ayo in the house where she was staying with her Spanish husband.

As time went on, David became more happier than he usually was, seeing that it was time for him to move forth to explore the world and find his own destiny—that seemed dim to him there in Spain. He wanted to see how shrewd he was to be able to distinguish between good and bad, and to know who is right and who is wrong—and to do this, he knew he has to study and focus more on how human beings behave, how they think, and how they feel emotionally to the things around their environment and the society where they live. Most of all, he wanted to proceed with his American dream and also to edify people around Europe about what the future holds if there could be a co-operation of every human beings living in the planet, Earth; he wanted to proceed with his message of love and peace.

As time went-by, as he continuously spurned Ayo many times she tried to come near him to apologize, he decided to leave the apartment, packed his belongings and went to be staying with another of his friend who was living in a four bedroom apartment and was using one room of it with the parlor. He kept his electronic-sets there, telling him he was going to travel out of Spain soon. Ayo was still in love with him even when he was having a relationship with another lad or she was pretending. He knew it, and everybody including the lad knew it. David said he grasped why she did what she did, and it was the same reason why Alicia, his sister and her husband, his friends, in fact everybody disliked and hated him. He knew it was because they all with a suspension of disbelief based on ignorance and prejudice, came to a conclusion that he was a self-centered person, because many of them has tried to win his heart and to lure him to unveiled what his dream was to them, but they all failed. Some of his friends did made him intoxicated with marijuana and alcohol, thinking it will work, while some many white people also tried by taking him to visit many different places with their newly-bought cars, playing music inside but at the end of it all, they failed. Some others who believed his dream was to become a musician has also showed him to some musical bands, and yet he declined to be a part of these bands even when some of the musicians brought themselves closer to him. It was at this point the secret-servicemen and the entire people there became very much suspicious and scared of who he was since they thought his dream was to become a musician, and wanted to help him to achieve the dream. People became very much afraid that he was a spy since he was not prepared to help himself to become what he longed to become. His sister was even frightened by his attitude, seeing him not to be the brother he knew; he was a different person far from his own brother. The government there became very afraid, regarding him to be a very dangerous man in that society. Although he was also seen by many as a reluctant hero, but others could not consider him to be, since he was always seen mingling with the vicious, having feasts with the saints. He said he could understand how these people felt about him and were willing to render him a help. But how could he help destroy what has been built that was meant to be? He could not help control his own destiny—that was not willing to accept what was offered to him as he has said several times that, living the rest of his life in Spain was against his will. He would have tried to join some of those musical bands, but he saw that they were not English speaking people, and at that time, he could not be able to write songs alone—which is to say, if they speak English he would have find it easy to communicate and work with them. And another reason was that he saw Spaniards as egoists, and a wide-range of racial discrimination was still existing there, making him think there was never a time they could see you as a black African and believe in anything that you do. He wanted to be respected and honored somewhere else but not in Spain where he could still see people respect other people regarding to their wealth or their countries of origin. And moreover, from his own perspective, he could see the Spaniards to be people who like to exaggerate, and are passionate, and fanatically devoted to their country. Best of all, many of them seemed to believe in chauvinism. It always startled him most time when some of his co-workers relates matters to him of how they have never even left Spain before to another country, even Joaquin, his sister's husband was among them. As for his fellow black people, they were not having anything in similar, because he was already far from them, and there was no way he could return back to force them to learn what they were not willing to learn. He saw that his friends who were meant to be his well-wishers became his ill-wishers, with jealousy and hate written all over their faces. But why all these?—when he was the one creating a world of his own, reading great books to draw inspirations. He was then seeing all the demons envious, tend to murder him, but like a fighting cock, he saw himself fought and won the battle. He said he was waiting for the black hour to cease, and to jump into the kingdom of Earth, keeping his soul up to seek death or wealth. When his dreams could not come to the sky, he has to send his life to live in exile. In the community of all races and religions he got himself fixed, affixed, suffixed, in-fixed, post-fixed. Although he never despised the good things of life—preaching, feasting, masturbating, singing, and praying even if he was not a good believer. In his sufferings and hopelessness he found no-one. So even when they said he was dangerous, he was very much in accord with them.

In his later life in the future while he was in prison in Italy, he came to recall this moment and wrote a poem for this.

WAILING FROM THE WILDERNESS

From my enemies, I'm hiding myself,
Not minding the misery I'm to bring myself.
I'm not the man, but I'm the voice,
Wailing from the wilderness.

Only to commence a fame of being me,
In supreme waters I was purified.
Resting beside the water of comfort.
Humbled, mollified, and sweetened by discomfort.
A situation of horror of agony.
Taking a step to the true history,
To embrace a peculiar and cheerless life.
But still, tribulations unwilling to change my visions.
I'm wailing from the wilderness.

Dreaming to promote the spiritual unity of every souls.
And to possess the connotation of the sermon on the mount.
My Lord the staff which I leaned
And the wings that gave me flight.
With a little secret, smiled to myself.
Climbing a rope cast down to Earth from heaven
To capture the glory that humanity deserves.

Seeing how people were fretting about who he was and how investigations were being carried out to know if he was a spy, he wanted to make them think differently. To do this, he decided to embark on an exciting business of merchandise. He bought a euro-line bus ticket and was traveling to the Naples, Italy to buy some clothes there since he was told it was a place for buying well-designed and cheap clothes made by Italians. Inside the bus, he was traveling with, he met a Canadian girl who actually was born in Quebec city, Quebec. From her look, he thought she was an American when he first saw her, until when he greeted her and chatted with her that she told him she was a Canadian. She introduced herself and narrated the story of her life to him on how she has lived in the U.k. for two years and was already living in Belgium. Her English was fluent, but her French was far better even if he does not speak French and was not hearing everything she said in French, he knew as long as she was from Quebec. She was just twenty-four at that time and was young, beautiful, and was possessing every good qualities of his kind of woman. She was stylish, amiable, affectionate and opened to communication. He liked her and wanted to let her know how he felt having a conversation with her. He also narrated few of his life-story to her, but was very nervous as he looked into her eyes and saw that she was meant to be, and was an angel from heaven to take away his burden. But he was not keen enough to have come down with her when she was dropped from the bus in Rome. He only wrote her email address on a piece of paper which he later misplaced. He promised to email her and also to visit her soon in Brussels. She tried to convince him to think of Brussels as the best place to live in Europe. When he tried to stay to collect her phone numbers, the driver of the bus who was envying him as he saw how he started with her and was ending it well, called him in a hurry to enter the bus or else he was going to leave him there. At later end, he came to regret why he did not collect his bag and let the bus leave. Although he missed that opportunity, because he was in a hurry to go buy the clothes and take them to Amsterdam to sell and to quickly return back to Spain to start working again. Moreover, his main basis for not making that sacrifice that he was supposed to make at that moment, was that he was being pressurized by one Nigerian prostitute living in Amsterdam whom he met before while he was looking for someone to help him hold his documents before he could go to seek asylum at the time he experienced the SEVEN DAYS THEORY. They had both been communicating on phone and she had advised him to start this new business of merchandising, promising to assist him by selling them to her prostitute friends. He thought it was all going to be easy, though he knew what she actually wanted from him and he was ready to give it to her so as to set up a way for himself to be able to go and live in Amsterdam and carry-out his plans.

When he arrived in the Naples, he met his long-time friend who helped him to buy the clothes and even took him to his house to sleep, and the next day, he took a train and left to Amsterdam, not listening to the boy who tried to fixed him up with another rich Nigerian prostitute who could have bought him with thousands of euros. Inside the train, he was reading a novel and playing Oasis cd with a disc-man. It was a nice and wonderful trip and he was enjoying it as he was with a camera, snapping pictures of mountains and fields and houses like a tourist, as the train passed through different towns and villages in Italy to France, Swiss, Luxembourg, Belgium, and finally arriving at Amsterdam Central Station, Holland. Although in Luxembourg, as the train stopped, he saw some men entered and walked straight to where he was, demanded for his documents, and when he presented it to them, they checked them and gave it back to him, but they later took those bags from him and ransacked them to see if he was hiding some drugs inside. He accused them of being racists—and they did not care but proceeded with what they say was their job. They even tore some of the shoes and threw them all out from the bags.

In Amsterdam, he took another train to Holland spoor, Den-Haag—the same place he met the girl prostituting before inside a plain-covered glass with red-lights, but in a different street. When she finished with her work she took him to her Rover 75 1.8 automatic car, and inside, she was jamming new r 'n' b music. David said he saw life to be very splendid and candy. Although after staying with the girl for three days and was unable to make love to her simply because he was afraid he was going to contract a venereal disease from her, and also because he did not know how to tell her—I love you and I want you to be the mother of my unborn child. He said it once to her, but she pretended she was not hearing him and wanted him to repeat it, but he paused and never went further to utter it. She tried to seduced him, but failed. She failed because he was truly afraid, and when he left to return back to Spain, he was full of remorse that he did not do it. Her love for him became hatred, because she had wanted him to love her and have rough sex with her, and he refused to.

Immediately he returned back to Spain, many of his friends saw that the clothes were good and were also extremely inexpensive, so they all came rushing to buy them. The girls had the opportunity to come closer and to offer their body to him for the clothes, but he rebuked and rejected them. He was filled with delights as he counted his money and the profits he made from the business. He was also having enough left for his own use since he was the trendy type. He gave out some freely to some of the girls—one of them who had really helped him at his time of distress.

David who saw that his dream could be real when his mind was ready to accept it, was beginning to act differently in his place of work, requesting to be sacked by his boss who refused to do so. He was asking himself why he was doing a job as tedious as loading cars and lorry tires in trailers and containers when he knew he was having the talent to sing. Some other people were thinking the same thing about him, as they witnessed him sing and dance while working. Others were not seeing him that way, instead they thought he was suffering from a mental and neurological illness that he never realized, and that he needed to be cured by a psychiatrist. For this reason when he visited the hospital and reported the job he was doing to his doctor, hoping he will be entitled to a sick leave for some days, instead of that, another doctor was sent to him for a mental health test. He could see that what he had come for was not what he was doing as he could see the doctor ask him several questions more about depression, and later he saw that the test was more of that of obsessive compulsive disorder, anxiety, and personality. Though, it was funny to him as he also saw three policeman there in the same room where he was, and he was asked to pull-off his clothes and everything he was wearing. He knew they were after him again, and for him to overcome all these problems, he would have to avoid it, and the only way he knew he could avoid it, was to leave that city to another place. Frankly speaking, he realized many people who knew him and were aware of how he was living, believed he was insane. He also believed himself to be insane, and even many of his mentors were, and these are things most people outside the field could not comprehend. "The factual fact is that many writers are insane, but this insanity is based on creativity. Like-wise most scientists are also insane, and this insanity is based on invention."

David said he so much believe, life-span can be lengthened by good surrounding, good medical care, education, and moreover, good spirit and love from your neighbors. But what he was experiencing there in that city made him come to a conclusion that there was no way he was going to reach his thirties. He perceived danger, and beyond doubt he fathomed it was time to move on.

He quit his job, not waiting to be sacked and given a severance package or a termination paycheck. He left Vitoria to Madrid without informing anybody including his sister except his friend, Francis, whom he left some of his clothes and his electronic-sets and cds in his house.

Getting to Madrid, he saw the way some of his friends whom they had both come to Europe at the same time were having much relish and were living lives to the fullest. Some were working and some were not. He wanted to stay in Madrid, seeing that it was a big city, and there were very many black Africans, and they were living happily, partying, and celebrating every weekends. He saw that crime was a profession to some who were never ready to step their feet into a factory and work, while others—some who were working and some who were not—were extracting money from most of the girls who were prostituting. Majority of the lads he met and has known for long were all driving fellow-used flashy cars bought with the money given to them by these prostitutes. He could not help imagine how a girl could be suffering to cater for a lad who wakes up and sleep only to have sex with the girl and be paid for it. It was a good life to live as he saw them enjoy it. He was about to start regretting why he was born into this world to suffer, but when he entered one of the coffee bar to relax himself and drink a cup of coffee, he heard the music of Oasis playing, BORN ON A DIFFERENT CLOUD, and when he heard it, hope came back to him. He knew there was much more to be enjoyed in the future than relying on a whore to feed and cater for him.

After spending three days in Madrid with his friends, he bought a euro-line bus ticket and left to Switzerland. Inside the bus when he was seated, he tried to bring back to memory the life he has lived in Vitoria, and thought it to be a beautiful one since he was able to make an impact on the world by changing the lives of some of the people there. He saw that he had assisted most people to find peace in their hearts, because of how many white people were really worried about what will be the end-results for allowing too many immigrants come to live with them. He said he portrayed a picture of what life they will live in the nearest future if they open their hearts to receive these strangers who were ready to love and assist them to build a world with no violence, but with prosperity. He was also able to lure and convince some of his fellow Africans to think of continuously loving their white neighbors not regarding on how they are ill-treated. He saw that some of what he did was appropriate while some were also weird as many people also could disapproved of it and compared him to be Lucifer.

The bus he took was in actual fact, not going to Swiss. It was to stop in another bus station in France where they would have to change to another one. Inside the bus, where two girls, sitting with their mother and another girl, sitting not far from his seat. The girl sitting near him, conforming to her body type, she was a rather plain-color girl—and was almost like an albino, but was not. She was slim and pretty like a model and was having some tiny black dots all over her face. Initially, she occurred to be a German, but at the time when they all came down to change their buses, he was astounded when she entered the same bus that was going to Swiss with him. He admired her, and tried to look for a way to speak to her. He allowed her to go in first, and when she was seated, he went to sit at her back. At the other side of the seats, was another Nigerian man probably at his forties. David, who was not happy to see the man near him shunned him even when he tried to greet him. He wanted to have the girl's attention and that was what was bothering him. At first, he was afraid to talk to her, knowing he was not his type, and besides that he was a black African. Although he was well dressed and was cute. He was wearing a white linen short-sleeve, a black suede-jeans and a white Reebok with black line canvas. To match, he wore a black leather puma wrist-watch. He was cute, and he knew he was. Everything he was wearing was about a thousand euro including the Jean Paul Gaultier perfume he sprayed in his body every three three hours."Looking cute can give you the courage to meet a woman and ask her out for a date," this has been his policy for chasing a woman even if he chases them for no reason and at the end still unable to catch them. Maybe to him, it s always fun or the universe never wanted him to have them.

The more David tried to talk to the girl, the more she shunned him, pretending she was listening to music. At a time when he finally had her attention and told her he liked the music she was playing. She was stunned to open her mouth, thinking how could a black African love Red Hot Chili Peppers? She thought he was bluffing and was only trying to have her attention, so she wanted to test him by asking him where the band live. He told her they are from California, and proceeded further to analyze on their music and describe them to her. Instantly, she fell for him and commenced with her life-story. She told him his father was a very rich man and was working in one of the Rolex companies. In point of fact, he was not counting on his father's wealth, he was very much concerned about whom she was and her passion for music and books and her ambition to become a musician like him. She knew they were from the same world, and might probably end up together, realizing their dreams of becoming music stars. She told him she was a ballet dancer and was more interested in trance, techno, house and dance music, and at that time he was not very much interested in these kind of music even if he was very good in dancing it the way he learned to in Norway—and when he was dancing in Spain, many Spaniards knew he was not living there, because it is uncommon seeing a black African dance well to these kind of music there.

When they arrived at the bother between France and Swiss, the bus stopped, and David, the other Nigerian man and one other Algerian were all given an order to step down for control by two Swiss immigration officers. It was so plain and clear how the three of them were distinguished from the rest people there. It was a discrimination of race, and it was illegal and unfair. But what can they do? Nothing, just nothing except to take life as it comes so he was told. David's heart was beginning to sink into a deep sea of rage, seeing what it means to be different in a white man's country. He was saddened and was down in the dumps. He saw himself and the two others being humiliated. If he was having a gun, he would have fired at them. After much checking of documents and control, they were asked to go into the toilet so they could check them if they were hiding some drugs in their anus. When he heard that, he could not bear the grudge anymore, so he voiced out and accused them of being racists. He told them it was all because of his color of race that he was being suspected of being a criminal. But when they finished checking him and found nothing with them, they asked them to rearrange their clothes in their bags. The girl who was checking his bag that he had accused of being a racist and was almost about to insult, saw that he was not the type they were looking for—as she saw many books and music cds and a dictionary and some of what he was writing that were all properly concealed. She apologized to him and swiftly dressed her hair properly and was looking deep into his eyes if he could look back at her. Instantly, he knew she was not a racist, and that she was doing her job. When he later returned back to the bus, the beautiful rich man's daughter he was having a conversation with, felt very sorry for him and apologized to him for the misdeeds. But he was already at rage and could not control it, only to go to the back of the seats of the bus to cry and ask God when will people be judged not according to their color of race or their faith? Later when the other

Nigerian friend came to meet him to narrate how he was caught before inside Swiss with 8,000 euro and all the money were confiscated, it was then David knew he was hanging with a dangerous drug peddler already with a criminal reputation. So why was he blaming those police? He realized he was misjudging others as well as many others were also misjudging him. Then, who was he to blame when his fellow black man was almost about to land him into jail? Or what if he was still trafficking more drugs and he was caught? Being that they were from the same country and were sitting close, that might be very implicating. Then he started to query his God about why he was born black. He quickly left the man and went back to his seat, only to see that the girl had went to clean herself up in the washroom and was now looking different with a look of elegance, and was as beautiful as the princess of Wales. He tried to talk to her, but she refused to listen to him, and when the bus stopped in Lausanne, he could only watch in compunction as she came down to meet her young, attractive and handsome boyfriend. From his eyes, tears ran down to his cheek, seeing the both of them embrace, smooch and kiss each other with the boy's car packed near them. He blamed himself for having been a moron to have lost what he was already having in his hand. It was painful, really it was.

CHAPTER 22

IT WAS ALMOST DAWN WHEN he reached Basel and was picked up by a friend he knew long time ago in his native-city. He did not recognize him, but when he mentioned his name, he knew he was the one. He told him he was sent by some girls to pick him up since they were afraid to come over as they were illegal in Swiss. He followed his friend to the house where these girls were living. One of the girls who was his family friend back in Africa, actually was the person who invited him to Swiss. She told him many lads there were making hell of money by selling drugs—and that he could join them too.

In the house where the girl was living, he saw that it was not conducive to a man's habituation, since three other girls were also living there with her in a one bedroom with a kitchen and a toilet. Although, the room was big and could contain all of them, but it was horrifying, seeing these girls were all prostituting, and before they could leave the house to their place of work, they would have to spend time to shower and make up, and every time he watch them do all these, he gets irritated and blamed himself for coming.

After some days, he was shown the refugee camp to go and seek asylum. He thought it was going to be the same as the one in Norway, but reaching there he noticed that the Norwegians were caring for refugees as they were caring for their children and pets. He lingered on for some days before he could regain his lost memories of how he was treated as a refugee in Norway. It was also in this place that he fell in love with the name David—and decided to choose it for himself. In this place, he also changed his surname to a very funny-peculiar and a comical one—which was unusual and unreasonable for a black man to bear. He claimed his surname was Bodeger, and he was from Liberia, Africa. He said he comprehend the name was German, and thought it might enable him conquer these people's heart and find a way for himself there in Switzerland. He forgot he was dealing with people who are twenty times more shrewd and cunning than he was. In his first interview, when he was questioned on the reasons he left his country and to give details of how the people there reacted to the the civil war, he was confused, even when he has read about it in the internet and thought he could pass the interview easily. When he was also asked of the different languages spoken there, he gave them two languages, not knowing there was a Liberian man there who speaks those languages. He ascertained that they already knew he was a Nigerian, so he changed his story—telling them he was born in Liberia, but was brought up in Nigeria. But it was too late for him to do that, as they were very strict and decided to subject him to a penalty for having lied to live there. Although, many Refugee Councils around the world fathom most stories told by many refugees are lies, but it is based on humanitarian reasons that most of the asylums are granted, which many refugees do acknowledge. In the sense that we can only escape wars and seek asylum in a near-by country; not to escape wars to find yourself in a country five thousand miles away from your own country. The whole world knows it, the refugees knows it. "The important honest fact about the reality, is that many people wants to leave and go to places where they are to go live their lives in a different society where they could enjoy some basic amenities and freedom—which they have been deprived of."

David said, every time, when he trekked to the city center of Basel and watched the Swiss people and how they live, he could see that the city was the most beautiful place upon all the places he had visited and had lived. The beauty was at its best probably because it was at the middle of summer. He could see people swim in the clean canals with swimming trunks and bikinis. He saw that these people were living good lives, and it was a life he had always dreamed of.

In the middle of the canal, was a concert stage built for music in an open-air, and from far he could hear the drums and guitars of dazzling sounds; by the sides of the canals were men, women, boys and girls—Blacks, Whites, Asians, Hispanics, Arabs—blondes, brunettes; across the canals, sailing ships and boats passed, and blowing horns echoed and filled the air. David said he could not help resist how tempting it was as he visualized how he will be living there legally with the happy people he was seeing. He decided to take more walk to explore the city, so he crossed the beam bridge to the other side of the canal, and there he saw some black Africans—most of who were with dread-locks like that of Bob Marley, and they were all smoking weeds together with some Swiss white boys and girls. He immediately ran swiftly pass them as he could see he was in the heart of darkness and walked towards the other side where he met one beautiful blonde, holding a pen and a notebook and was writing. It was his first time in life to see a young European girl writing in a public place: he had only watched it in movies. He went closer to sit near her. As she saw him, she stood up and left him there. He saw her walked away and followed her to the other side where she went to sit. He said to her, 'I know you are writing an autobiography, that is a good thing to do.' 'My English is not good,' she replied. 'Do not say that,' instructed David, getting up and sitting more closer to her and peeping at what she was writing, only to discover that she was writing in German. She stood up and bade him good-bye and left. He sat there all alone by himself, watching the canals and the people and the ships that were sailing passed. From a little distance he sighted a Swiss lad probably at his twenties, and he was there alone playing his guitar. He went to meet him and sat with him after having greeted him. The lad stopped playing his guitar and returned the greeting to him. 'I like how you play,' said David to the lad, staring strangely into his eyes like he was a girl and he has never met anyone like her before. 'Thank you,' replied the lad. 'I love Oasis, they are my favorite.' 'Yeah, that is Oasis music I was just playing,' said the lad, about to stand up from where he was sitting. 'Please can you play another one from Oasis for me?' paused, and proceeded, 'because I would love to hear it,' said David, holding his two hands together, pleading like it was ice-cream he was begging for. 'O.k,' said the lad. He started to play his guitar, and was singing WONDER WALL, and as he was singing, he stared deeper into his beautiful eyes, and it was a sign that he was falling in love with him. After singing three songs from Oasis, the lad unexpectedly switched to Bob Marley's I WANNA LOVE YOU. He was barely uninformed of the dubious and uncertain enigma he was about to bring upon himself by playing the type of music he would love to hear. There was no way he could control the feelings he was having inside for him, so he went to sit closer to him and was about to kiss him when two Swiss blondes and another lad appeared from nowhere to meet the lad he was having a conversation with, and one of the girls quickly kissed him on the mouth—a sign that he was her boyfriend. David said, it was like he fell in love with him and so confident they were going to be together forever as he could also see in him passion for music like he was, and in addition to that, he could see that they were both from the same world with the message of love and peace. He wanted to love him the way he never loved a woman before in his life since he could no longer confide more in women: His instincts was letting him know he was born to bring him back to life to come live again as a person who could still find love. He wanted to give him the key of his heart to hold for him, because he could see that he will always be careful with it.

Inside the camp, he was beginning to develop new friends— Whites, Blacks, Gypsies, Arabs and Indians. His best friend was one boy from Sierra-Leone, who also was a Rastafarian with dread-locks. The boy who apparently was upset with the Swiss Refugee Council, for having been informed there was no chance his asylum was going to be granted. He was in Holland, and there his asylum was also rejected and was asked to leave the country or else he was going to be forced to. He became very confused and was unhappy, believing every white people to be wicked. He thought—as long as Sierra-Leon was seen by everybody around the world as a country dangerously afflicted by war—there was no reason his asylum should be denied. He was having a grudge against Europeans for not standing by the laws based on the principles of justice. He was smart and was a person with a high standard of education. When David met him, sympathy came first as they both introduced themselves and narrated their stories to each other. David knew his asylum there was a total failure, but he also knew if he try he could succeed, and the only way he believed he could be able to live there in Switzerland, was to look for a woman to marry so that he could be legal in the country. This same issue he related to his new Sierra-Leonean friend who thought he was a wangler, a swindler and a betrayer like the other Nigerians he has met with before; although he was, but not at that very time. He felt sorry for him and thought the only way he could help him was to help him change what he think about other people and make him choose love instead of hate so as for him to be successful in life. Inside the camp, he also met another friend from Chechnya who was wearing a t-shirt designed all round with an America flag and a golden eagle. It was showing how patriotic he was when actually he was not an American. He was very much concerned with the way refugees were being denied their rights as citizens of the world, and was with a message to the Europeans, CHANGE YOUR WAYS, LOOK TO HOW AMERICA IS A COUNTRY KNOWN

FOR FREEDOM AND LIBERTY. He was about six feet tall and was just twenty-five year old and hated the Russians. His accent of English made him seem like an American, but he was not very cautious when it come to telling stories of how many countries he had actually visited. He and David became two good friends because he found out David could speak little Norwegian since he too was always interested in speaking it even when he knew it was going to cause him some big problems. When David first saw him, he thought he was like the communists, but at the time they both discussed about their pasts, he came to understand him better and liked him—making him his new best friend, and when the Sierra-Leonean saw this, he became envious and was referring him to be as a moron who love white people despite being treated like a vagabond by them. It was from the same Chechen, David learnt that Chechnya was trying to separate from Russia, and for that reason there has been a war between the two.

David knew he was to be expelled soon from Switzerland within some days, and the only way he could guarantee himself to live there was to find a Swiss woman. He decided to take a decision to look for one in the city every time they were on break and he walked out of the camp. He met many young girls whom he tried to interact with, but most of them were not like the Norwegians whom you could meet in the street and convince easily to have a date with them. In Switzerland, everything seem extremely expensive for him, and with the little money he was having, he could not go to a night-club, since the girl who invited him took the money from him, saying he was going to help him save them, and he too had decided to let her save it since he was the thrifty type—who believe in savings, and not wasting unnecessarily because he might need it soon. He tried the best he could and found that it was going to be very tough for him due to the fact that he was having very few days left to be expelled; and the more pressure he was mounting on himself to find a woman, the more women he met with and collect their phone numbers to call them, and as he called, their boyfriends would pick it up and warned him never to call again. The situation became very complicated and problematic for him. He became very doubtful, and thought it will be better if he stay calm and wait for the universe to decide for him what is best and where his destiny should be even if he once believed himself to be the master of his own destiny, but there are things he believed we cannot force to be when the universe does not want it to be.

As he was no longer interested in going out of the camp to search for women, he saw his Sierra-Leonean friend reading a novel and asked him who gave it to him, and he was taken to the offices of some Humanitarian Organisations responsible for aiding and assisting refugees, and providing them with legal advisers who provides them with confidential and independent legal services. When David first arrived there, he saw that they were always very busy and were having many people to attend to. Notwithstanding the immense and massive amount of people coming there for aids, he still wanted to be recognized. He met with a woman called Maria, whom he thought to be the head, because she was very much concerned about the welfare of the refugees, and was doing everything she could to assist them in every ways she could. She was very calming, respectful, and was a compassionate woman. David said she was the type to be describe as a beautiful woman denied of sex appeal. He tried to look into her eyes to see if she will respond, but she never did. He took a book from her to read, and left back to the camp and started to read. It was a bestselling fiction book, and was very interesting. It was a outrageously funny book with desperate couples risking their lives to achieve their dreams, and it was full of romance. As he started to read the book, he derived pleasure from reading it and was no longer bothering himself about what the future holds for him there in Swiss. Many of the workers inside the camp including the security men who saw him to be a very cheerful and contented man when even they could see that he was to face distress in not less than twenty days, were all very astonished and tried to comprehend the reason why. As they all focus their attentions on him, they saw that it was the book he was reading and the music videos he was watching on television. It was strange and bizarre to many as it was also humorous, waggish and silly to others. He became the gossip of the camp, and he was beginning to build a new fame because of how he was fond of singing along with the music coming from the television. He was also very friendly with everybody regardless of their race, and most of all he was chumming and friendly with the little children there to an extent everyone of them were calling him by his name and always want to play with him. He said at that same time, he could judge Michael

Jackson from the life he was experiencing with these little kids. "Getting too close to little kids who actually are not yours is a dangerous thing to do, because your affection might turn into a different thing. But who are we to judge another person?"

The more he was reading his book and barely had time to associate himself with his fellow Nigerians, some of them were beginning to see him as a impostor who was lying to himself and lying to every other people there.

A time came when some white arrogant boys from eastern Europe were having a clash with one Nigerian boy and it turned into a big fight between the Nigerians and these arrogant boys from Macedonia, he did not intrude because he was afraid to fight and get himself injured over matters of a woman who left his Macedonian boyfriend for the Nigerian. He was thinking, what if someone died and later the girl later dump the boy? To him it was stupid, but to the boy, he was fighting for a cause; he was fighting for love. Although David had admired and eyed the girl several times, and he knew she was not in love with the Macedonian, because, he could see it from her eyes. The security there and the Swiss Refugee Council were in support of the Nigerians, and decided to expel some of the Macedonians who were involved in the fight.

Because he did not intrude in the fight, he was later seen by his fellow countrymen as a coward and a traitor. He continued to read his book and sing, and his life was filled of joy. He only earned himself enmity for not having intruded and joined the fight, and he knew this. But he was not ready to apologize to anyone even when he knew he was wrong. He became more happier, seeing his fellow Nigerians despise him. The only person who tried to come closer to him was one Nigerian girl called Becky, who has worked as a clerical accountant before in one popular bank in Nigeria. She was married and was actually traveling to London to meet her husband when she transited in Zurich and missed her flight. But when she tried again, she was detained by the Swiss authority without an unreasonable excuse, and was asked to go seek asylum which she refused to do—so she told David. He neglected her when he first arrived there, because he believed there was no way she could help him, and furthermore, there was no way he believed he could have a relationship with any Nigerian again due to what Ayo did to him before he left Spain. But he was later told Ayo decided to return back to Nigeria when she found out he already left Spain. They said she was regretting for having hurt him, and that she confessed she did it because she loved him too much and wanted to make him jealous. To David, that was not a good excuse—the deed has been done.

When David met this other Nigerian and only girl among them in that camp, he tried not to get close to her. He looked at her like a friend and made her understand he was after a white woman not blacks. Immediately after the fight when others were blaming him for refusing to prop and support them, she came closer to him, and when she did, he embraced her with his heart and made her his friend. As time went-by, and as they were both getting to know each other, they became just more than friends. He saw that she was the educated type not like the prostitutes who would accept many gifts she was being offered for sex by many Swiss men including the security guards in their camp; he tried to control himself, but the more he was trying, the more she was pushing hard to have him by tempting and attracting him and going with him everywhere he went, even when she knew he was more interested in dating a white woman. He knew she has come to ruin everything he planned and has come to cause him a mischief. He detested her for having come into his life at that particular time when he needed help and he was been offered everything—only for him to choose which way will be best for him to hunt his meat.

Before they became friends, he has seduced and flirted with one of the Swiss-German woman working there, but when she began to see him with the black woman, she became very upset with him and instantly, she disliked him, and would have poisoned him if she was given the chance to. One day, she presented her husband, making him grasp what was happening as he too was startled how she changed her attitude towards him and became unfriendly. He let it go, and thought of another woman who was also working there. He saw that she was still young and was pretty and educated. He flirted with her until at a time she invited him to assist him to bring the food from the restaurant where it is being cooked. While they were inside the truck as she was driving, she tried to question him about his past life and whether he was a Nigerian or a Liberian. He refused to tell her the truth, but did made the efforts to make her understand how he felt about her. When they finally arrived at the camp, she bade him good-bye without promising to meet him the next day, making him very pessimistic about whether she was interested or not.

It was just one day before his final interview, the girl who interviewed him for the first time, walked passed where he was playing with two little kids, and when he saw her, he swiftly greeted her, and when he did, she waited for him to come to meet her to say anything he wish to him because she saw him look into her eyes for the first time they met and has scratched her hand when he shook her. He rushed to where she was, but getting there, the little kids he was playing with would not allow him to, as they were disturbing. She told him she was in a hurry and that they will be meeting next time, and left. He really thought she was going to be the one to interview him again, so he kept his words for the next day to come when he will meet her. Although they have both quarreled before because she said there was no proof he was a Liberian since he was not having anything to identify himself as one. And besides that he could not speak any of the languages spoken by Liberians. But he argued and even accused her of being cruel.

'Is it what we wish for in life that we really get?' murmured David to himself since he was in the toilet all alone. He said he could see many possibilities opened for him to achieve his dream of marrying a Swiss woman and living the rest of his life there. But he was afraid if ever it was going to happen that way or as proposed by the universe. Could he be able to ignore that universe and make himself the controller and master of his fate? This became a question he was never able to find a good answer to through-out his whole life as he suffer and wander around Europe unable to find s destination where he could live a happy and humorous life with a woman he love and have kids and see them grow.

The night before his interview, he disputed with the Nigerian girl, because she was not prepared to let him go or else he was going to love him. He tried to apologized for having played with her heart, and he also tried to impart knowledge of some facts to her that they have both come to Europe to seek a better future. He advised her to accept the gifts sent to her by many rich Swiss men who were prepared to marry her and make her legal there in Switzerland, but she was enraged and did not listen, instead she was threatening him of the consequence he was to face with if he ever think of abandoning her. To him, it was strange since he has never seen a thing like it before. He looked at her and saw that she was extremely dangerous. The worst thing was that she was not willing to listen even when he tried to make her understand that the Refugee Council was still investigating her case since she also told them she was going to meet her husband in London. From what David could see, she was not the type to see Europe and be excited, she was from a very rich family and does not care what people in Europe believe. Among the men who were asking her out, was one of the security there who was nicknamed Mobuto after the one-time president and dictator of the Democratic Republic of Congo, who siphoned the country's money and banked it in Switzerland, and after his death, the whole money was confiscated by the Swiss government.

The Swiss man, who was familiar with Africans and was also a good man, wanted to help the Nigerian girl so she could be legal in Swiss. But Becky rejected all his offers, and was insanely in love with David—a boy who could have sex with her just once and dump her.

The day came when he showered and get himself prepared for his interview. Along the line as he was going to the office, he met Maria, the compassionate woman who was voluntarily working for the Humanitarian Organisation. He was full of delights when he saw her. Although, some days before then he told her he will be going for his last interview. He also told her the time, not knowing she will be coming purposely because of him. He saw that she was waiting for him, and as they both shook hands, he scratched her hand and looked into her eyes and blinked his eyes. She saw it and turned her eyes from him. She asked him to sit—and when they were both seated, she began to lecture him of how he could pass the interview. After lecturing him, they shook each other again and he scratched her hand once more. As he left to the interview, she wished him good-luck and told him she will be around to attend to other people, meanwhile Becky was watching them and was very jealous as she was afraid some white women were about to take him away from her.

The interview was short since he decided not to alter the statements he gave before, most particularly on the ground that he said he was from Liberia. They wanted him to tell the truth so as to allow him to stay there in Switzerland for awhile as they could see in him mixed of talents to move the world forward. They loved him and were readily consented despite that he had not told them, but they already knew who he was.

When he came out of the interview hall, the first person he met with to welcomed him back was Becky, but he did not mind her that much. He told her he was going to meet Maria—and when he walked towards where she was and greeted her, she appeased him and consoled him with a blissful smile—to give him hope. He was pleased and was exultantly proud seeing himself to be a man of fortune for having met her. He looked into her eyes, and when he did, he saw that she was the one he has been waiting for all these years. But, all of a sudden, when Becky saw him smiling and flirting with the lady, she stalked and threw in an intrusive question on her. It was beyond control, and she could not wait to be told what to do. David was upset with her, and with a peremptory order, he sent her away and tried to apologized to the lady for having been insulted by a refugee for his sake. Maria, being a calm and a not easily upset person, did not respond to the girl's wrongful conduct. She persisted and was still conversing with him. He looked at her again, and asked her to marry him. She was startled as she heard this. Then she told him she was a nun which made him felt real sorry for her, but he knew she was already in love with him and was prepared to do it just to make him stay in Swiss. After much conversation, she assured him of a better future in the country and encouraged him to stay even if he was asked by the Swiss authority to leave. She gave him her phone number and told him to meet her in her office the day she will be leaving. But as they were still sitting and conversing, Becky became more upset and left them. Another woman came to meet them sitting opposite to each other discussing like they were already couples—and it was the same woman whom he had assisted to the restaurants before. He was perplexed when he saw her and could not stand up from where he was sitting to go meet her, instead he greeted her from there. She only looked at him and ignored the both of them, even Maria. He knew she was hurt and was unhappy, and she could hit him if he walk closer to her, so he sat where he was, and was sad and quiet unable to respond to some of the questions Maria was asking him because, deep in his heart, he could feel a terrible sense of guilt. Maria noticed this and swiftly informed him that the young lady had decided to quit her job. When he heard this, he knew she has done so because of him. He was told before this people working there were not allowed to have a relationship with any refugee or else they would have to quit their job. She told him before of her different plan to quit the job to get another one, but he never believed it will be so quick as it was. He was sad and did not know how to apologize for all his misdeeds if any of them will ever forgive him. He knew he was hurting people, instead of him to be healing them. Maria knew what he was experiencing at that moment, so she decided to leave, but still leaving him with a promise of meeting with him the final day he will be leaving the camp. But before she left she advised him to be very careful not to be influenced and mislead by anybody. She advised him to keep believing in what he believed in. She said that, because at the time they were both discussing, the Chechen lad walked to them and intruded and condemned the Swiss people of being too self-centered, self-indulgent, mercenary, and not acting according to the Human Rights laws. Although he knew he was right about this, but he understood this was happening everywhere around the world not only in Swiss. But the problem was that he was more unease about his welfare, and was finding a way to sort it out. The same lad also advised him some few days before to follow him to Dusseldorf, Germany to seek asylum there, assuring him of a better life and jobs; he lauded the people there and claimed they were having less strict immigration policies. David wanted to go with him to Germany since he has long yearned for a visit to the country. But, he was told by some Nigerians living there of how strict the Germans were when it comes to immigration.

The day David went for his interview, the same day Becky told him she had injured her hand some days ago, and it was swollen and very painful. That same night she left the women's session, crying to come meet him in the men's session. He saw that she was in pain and quickly ran to call one of the security who took her away to a dispensary near the camp for treatment. From that very time, they never met again since she was later transferred from there to another state far from Basel where he was. He became very free from her disturbances and was glad she left. Later when he became very lonely and was bored, he felt it and came to realized how much he was missing her and how she usually run to meet him—calling him by his fake surname, Bodeger! Bodeger! He missed her disturbances, he missed her, and it was like a part of him just left.

A day before he was to leave the camp, he visited the girl who invited him to Swiss at her house. She begged him to stay with her that night so she could not be too lonely as she will not be going to work with her friends. He stayed, not knowing what her aim was. At night when all the other girls were gone, she tried to seduced him so he could make love to her, but he did not respond, and she became very upset thinking he was gay despite they grew up together in Africa. David knew she has long wanted that from him, and that was the reason she invited him. He would have dance to her tune of music if not that she became very fat and was an essex girl.

It was David's last day in the camp, as he was returning back from the house of the girl who invited him to Switzerland. He was walking along the side of the canal, speculating on what might happen next if he was finally asked to leave the country. From a distance he could see some group of people assembled themselves and were chanting and singing along Michael Jackson's song, BLACK AND WHITE, and from the other end of the canal, he could hear the music of Anastacia, SICK AND TIRED. The more he was hearing this music, the more frustrated he was. He fell in love with the country and wanted to live his life there, but how could he do that when in not less than three hours he will be asked by the Swiss Authority to leave? He continued to walk his way to the camp until he finally reached the camp. As he went in to meet with his letter of rejection, he could not help think of any other thing to do except to go to the office of the Humanitarian Organization and wait at the front door. As he was waiting with some other lads who also were expelled from the country within 24 hours, he sat in a chair and watched some young Swiss boys and girls driving their cars to cross the border to Germany, and some young German boys and girls also driving to cross the border to Swiss. He wondered why the policemen were not asking them for documents or search them. He immediately came to fathom what it means for people to be in their country and be free without anyone to harass and molest them for not having a document. He saw that the lives these gang of youths were living was also a life he had expected to live when he arrived in Europe, but it was never as he had planned it. He knew if he was being patient and has been a diligent and an indefatigable worker, maybe he would have been able to achieve that life. Or what if he has linked himself with some criminal friends who might have convey to him several ways to money-making secretly. He was beginning to see himself to be a wimp who was afraid to make easy money and return back home to lavish excessively on flashy cars and pricey clothes and jewelries just the way many of his friends they both came to Europe were doing. He went into the washroom, and when he looked at the mirror and saw himself, he saw that he could see himself to be a clown, a buffoon, a nit-wit. He immediately wanted to leave where he was so as to go meet some of his Nigerian friends who promised to help him get a place to be staying and dealing on cocaine; he wanted to leave to go start a life he did not wished for himself only to see that he was not the mug or the abject coward he could see himself to be. But as he was speculating on which path he might take to achieve success, one of the voluntary workers named David, approached him—asking him what he was still doing there waiting when already he was told to leave the country. He told him he was waiting for Maria, the woman who promised to be around when he will be expelled so she could help him get a place to stay there in Switzerland without any cause for alarm. He waited and waited for Maria to arrive and was fagged and almost sleepy. Then appeared another woman who was also working there, and was at her forties; she was married to one Cuban before and was divorced with two children. David quickly looked into her eyes as he tried to express his feelings to her, but at first she did not respond, knowing he was looking for some means to stay in Switzerland. David, who was so desperate did not want to relinquish his hope of meeting a woman to help him even when he could see his faith about to wear away. He went to meet the other David, the Swiss man who was working there—and was not in favor of Nigerians because he believed everyone of them who had come to Swiss—had come purposely because he wants to deal on drugs. 'You are my name-sake,' said David to his name-sake, David. 'O.k your name is also David,' said the man, putting his face away, trying to ignore him. 'Yes, I am David, and I love and cherish this name because it is named after kings, and moreover, it's a Jewish name,' replied David, walking closer to his name-sake. 'Yeah, I know it is named after kings, and I love the name too, but I detest the Jewish,' said the man, sitting himself well to hear what his name-sake was having to offer about the Jewish people. 'Why do you have to detest these Jewish people?' asked David, poised for debate. 'Because they are the cause of the world's problem. Look at how they are killing these innocent Palestine everyday since they know the Americans will always be at their back.' David did not actually know how to to reply him, because he knew what he just said was logical.

From the way the man was speaking, David said he conceived how he truly detest the Americans and the Jewish, and was not in a condition to hide what he thought and believed about them. David said he could see how so many Europeans he was having conversations relating to the war in Iraq with, felt about the Americans using their veto power to bomb these poor countries with nobody to intervene.

David said, many times as he himself watched this tragic episode in the news, he found it unbelievable to comprehend how America, the country he loved so much could violate human rights and be killing innocent Iraqi citizens—claiming they have come to save them from Saddam Hussein, and later promising to rebuild the country and show them the way to civilization. "But, in everything that we do, we should look to the motive, and find a way not to conclude our judgement only by seeing one side of it." The Bush administration did took an incorrect and regretful decision by invading Iraq, seeing Saddam to be a threat to the United States, which was wrong. After the invasion, George W. Bush, the president did realized he was making a mistake, but he would not admit his error, simply for him to gain his political stand while many U.s. and the coalition soldiers and innocent Iraqi's were killed and buried everyday. Bush, who would have want to withdraw from the war, has decided not to because he was in the furtherance of his three backbones and assistants—the same people who propped and lured him into this war with the prospect that they were going to win the war and exploit the oil there—the then Secretary of Defense, Donald Rumsfeld, then Vice President, Dick Cheney, and the then Senior Security Advisor who later became the Secretary of States, Condoleezza Rice. The only man that was not in support of the war was Collin Powell, the former Secretary of States, who came to acknowledge that the war was unjustifiable and was cruel.

David said he could not help comprehend how he was coming to loathe Americans for having let George W. Bush become the president of the United States, because of how he could see him not qualified to be. He was not qualified because he did not take that awful decision on his own as a president and Commander in Chief, instead he let his ear down to be told what to do, and he was mislead. He said he could see Bush as a very easy-going person who actually was not prepared to make war his objective in life, but he would not refrain from it because it will ruin his future in politics, and he was having no illusion about the difficulties that was to face the country's economy.

David, who believed and will not cease to believe the Americans to be the most wisest people on Earth, thought it will be better if he could inculcate others with a sense of responsibility. He tried to install confidence in them, preaching on how the Americans have saved the world, and how they are perfect in entertaining the world with movies, music, and many other forms of entertainment. He was trying to edify these people about America as a country not to be blamed for the war since many people there in the U.s. were also in contrary to the Bush's doctrine of kill them first before they come to kill you.

Since he could not make the Swiss man understand the validity of this subject matter, he decided to quit and went to meet the woman he was trying to stare at before. But the man came to like him because he came to also understand that he was different from the rest of them.

When he met with the lady again, he was staring deep into her eyes that she could not resist it, and swiftly asked him what exactly that he wanted. He told her he wanted some food and coffee for a girl who had come to beg for it. She was astounded when she saw him with one pretty young Swiss girl at her twenties. She warned him to leave her to go because, she already grasped she was looking for someone to sell some drugs for her. After the girl had eaten the bread and drank her coffee, she left, and David went to meet the lady once again and make an impassioned plea for him to be given her phone number. She gave it to him—asking him to call her the next day.

As David was about to leave the office, he saw his Sierra Leonean friend, and he was no longer carrying the dread-locks in his head but was looking better than he was before. When David saw this, his heart was full to the brim with joy, and he saw that his teachings had made a profound impact on him. He has tried to tell him to get rid of that dread-locks out of his head so he could look neat and charming to women, and also to be bold to talk and flirt with them since the only way was the high-way, and it could definitely be everyone's way.

The day was almost over, and night was near. David was about to leave when Maria arrived. Immediately he saw her, his heart leaped and once again, his life was characterized by good luck.

Maria, in her haste to meet up with time as she has scheduled herself, called David, and told him to get himself prepared so they could both take the bus to the city center. She also spent some few minutes with the Sierra-leonean, and when she saw that he was no longer carrying the dirty dread-locks in his head, she admired his new crew cut out-look and complimented him for having done so. She saw that he was calm and looking more charming than he was before. She liked him, because she could see in him a wonderful future behead. She looked at him, and later turned to look at David, and smiled. She felt like she was satisfied with what she was about to own. From the way David could view everything, he knew the Sierra Leonean was not smart enough, if not he would have been the one to have asked her out for a date. He was very much engaged with the issue of how justice should be served, knowing that he was entitled to be treated and accepted as a refugee by the Swiss Refugee Council, instead of him to think of how to find a woman who could love and assist him to stay there in Switzerland. It was when he saw how David was seducing these women and they were falling for him, that he came to realized that, "There are much more to learn about life than always fighting for our rights to be treated as citizens of the world, when the truth of the matter is that we are being manipulated and mistreated by our own leaders who because of greed make us run away from our homes to be enslaved by outsiders."

After David was given a ticket to travel to anywhere in Switzerland for one day by the same Humanitarian Organisation before he could leave to any other country of his choice, he and Maria took a bus to the city-center. Inside the bus, they were sitting near each other, and as her body touches his body, life became meaningful, despite the fact that he was asked to leave the country which might have taunted him. He saw that an angel was by his side—as his demons that he long time desisted from, came haunting him again. He knew she was already in love with him as he kept asking her to marry him repeatedly, and she was smiling and telling him to call her when he gets to where he was to go and stay that she prepared for him. It was when they were discussing that she gave him a phone number of a church priest to call so he could go and be staying there before things will get better. She made it plain to him to call her every time; she also promised to assist him in every way to make sure he was legal in Swiss, and he understood what she was implying. He stared at her, and would not stop, and was about to kiss her for having been there for him at that very critical situation when he was left in despair. He was both pretty startled and speechless when he heard she was having plans and provisions for him to live in Switzerland. When she was about to leave him, he kissed her on both cheeks, and bade her goodbye while she stood waving her hands to him, still pleading for his phone call.

Inside the train, when David was going to meet the priest whom she had directed him to, he came to think of the need to evaluate how he could possibly be able to stay with a church priest and still achieve his dream of becoming an artist, because he conceived it will be wrong intersecting religion with his pursuit of wealth; he tried to evade the problems encountering wealth when he is able to achieve it, and religion to him could distract anyone from achieving that wealth that he wanted so much in life—and was poised to go to any length.

When he arrived at the railway station in Aarau—which was not far from Basel; he waited for some hours to meet the church priest after having called him on phone. He knew what was best for him to tell him so that the priest could not look at him and think he was insane for letting an opportunity like that pass him by. When the priest finally arrived, he apologized to him for having come late. He told him not to worry that much that he was not prepared to live in Switzerland, and that he was leaving to another country that same night. The church priest, who was also very kind and generous, gave him some more money and wished him the very best of his future life, and they both departed, as he went to take the train back to Basel where the girl who invited him to Switzerland was still living. But when he called the girl, she told him she was out, and that he should wait for her until she will return. He waited for more than three hours, regretting and blaming himself for having being too determined to have taken such an evasive decision to return back to his demons dispersed around him by these little dare-devils he was about to go live with.

That night, when the girl finally arrived to meet him at the threshold of the house, waiting, she opened the door in silence without uttering a word to him as he greeted her. He sensed that something was wrong somewhere, but what exactly it was, was unknown. As they both entered the house, she quickly passed her phone to him, and when he picked the phone to answer the call, he ascertained that he was talking to Becky, the Nigerian girl he met in the refugee camp—that was insanely in love with him. Meanwhile, he forgot how he manged to gave her that phone number, asking her to call him, and promising to always get in contact with her. After he finished talking to her, he returned the phone back to the girl, as he tend to clarify the issue. She did not wait to be told that he was having an affair with another woman when she was there waiting and longing for him to utter a word of love to her. He knew it was over for him there in Switzerland. He asked her if she could still accommodate him for some days before he could get a place for himself, but she refused. She advised him not to fret himself over the issue of how he was going to live in Swiss, as long as there was no one to harbor any illegal immigrant. He knew she was furious for having been deceived, pretending to be gay; he sensed that there was no way he could convince her again for him to stay in that house for two more days, so he came up with an idea that he will be living to Austria in three days time. At first, she gave an ambiguous answer to what he said, but after some hours passed, and he still remained unwilling to alter his decisions about her, she called him by his name, and when he answered, she told him to get some of his belongings prepared to leave to Austria the next morning.

That morning, when he was already prepared to leave, she brought out some of the money he gave her to save for him. He wanted the whole money, but she insisted he take little of it so as not to spend lavishly. He bought a train ticket and left to Austria that same morning expecting to reach before dawn.

CHAPTER 23

I NSIDE TRAIN, WHEN HE WAS going to Vienna, he tried to recollect everything that happened in Swiss, if actually he made any impact on anyone's life there in this formidable journey of life he was setting for himself. He ascertained that he was a clown who was only fooling himself. He tried to get this thought out of his head when he saw some Austrian youths—two girls and a boy, drinking Ottakringer beer. He had long heard about the Austrians and the Germans to be too addictive to beer-drinking, and he has always wanted to have a taste of their best beer, to see if theirs are quite different from the rest he has tasted in Holland, France, and even Spain.

He arrived in Vienna later that evening exhausted and starving. He did not know who to meet and where to go. He wanted to check into a a very cheap and affordable pension, but he was left with just 50.00 euros, and that will not be enough for him to eat and the same time pay for the pension. He came out of Westbahnhof—a major Austrian railway station in the heart of Vienna, the capital city. He knew there was a need for him to locate the refugee camp where he could go and seek asylum that night. Since he did not call anybody before coming or he was not having anyone to call, he decided to wander around the city before he could find any African immigrant that he surmised might take him to where the camp was located. Seeing himself on the brink of misfortune once again, he thought it will be better for him if he could take the risk to sneak into another train going to Germany, but he was fearful of changing his mind and going to the wrong direction. He came back to sit and wait for some hours and left wandering again with his bag around his shoulder and returned back to the exact spot where he was before there in the railway station.

Before he came to Austria, he has long heard about them from his friends. He was told almost everyone there speaks English just like it was in Holland, and the women there were open to conversation with foreigners regardless of race. As a poor African immigrant seeking his future, but with an intellectual curiosity on fire, he has read and studied the history of the country and the people living in it. He has read that the first world war started because of the assassination of the heir to the then Austria-Hungarian throne—an Austrian Archduke, Franz Ferdinand and his wife by one Gavrilo Princip, a patriotic Serb. Although, it was said to be a classic case of ONE THING LED TO ANOTHER, the Treaty Alliance System. David also read about Adolf Hitler, the evil influenced man who lived all his entire life with evil deeds and purposes and was said to be the most wicked, vicious, facinorous, flagitious, scelestious, nefarious, atrocious, shameful, devilish, and good-for-nothing person that has ever lived on Earth. When David entered the country, one thing that came to his mind was that there were going to be a million Hitlers in the streets of Vienna where he was about to go live. But when he arrived the place, he saw that there was a melange of people of different race and religion fluttering and oscillating from one direction to the other. He could not believe what he was seeing when he saw a black man drive a taxi and parked it closer to the other taxis parked there by some other white Austrians and was having a conversation with them. It was a thing very uncommon in Spain. He was astonished and swiftly ran to meet him, and as he went closer, he fathomed the black man was a Nigerian. He greeted him in their pidgin English, and as he responded, he asked him if there was anyway he could help him get to the refugee camp so that he could go seek asylum there. The man told him to go and wait for him thirty meters away from where the taxis were parked. In not less than five minutes, the man came with his taxi where he was waiting, and urged him to enter inside and drove off to the camp.

From just about two hundred meters away from the camp where he was dropped by the black taxi-driver who collected his last 50.00 euros from him, pointed to where the camp was, and left. He stood there watching if there was anyone coming so that he could ask where exactly the camp was. He was glad that the driver had agreed to collect that 50.00 euros from him instead of the 70.00 euro he charged him before for having taking the risk to bring an illegal immigrant close to a refugee camp—which if caught might land him in jail for having violated the country's law. He said he will definitely be charged for human trafficking, and even David himself knew this.

David knew first thing for him to do was to get someone to help him hide his Spanish documents and his Nigerian passport. Since there was nobody he could trust even when he saw many black people roam around that area, he decided to walk closer to the train track, dug a hole in the sand and hid everything there.

After hiding his documents, he walked closer to some other Africans he saw and asked them where the camp was. They told him they were going towards the same direction and ordered him to follow them cautiously to the back of the camp where they lifted him up and let him jump the fence to the other side, while they jumped along with him. They threatened he will be deported if he fail to take the rightful procedure which they were helpful in providing for him. When he was about to leave them to go meet the police, they demanded for some money from him. He begged them to allow him go, promising to pay them more than they have demanded when he return back. They insisted he should pay them first before he could meet the police or do anything there, but as a controversy arose between him and the three lads, and the noise was increasing, drawing other people's attentions, they quickly let him leave.

In the office, were two policemen who took his fingerprints with the help of a computerized scan-machine which he was unfamiliar with. He was later questioned and given blankets and pillows to sleep in one of the rooms with three other Africans and one Georgian since it was almost midnight, and he was drowsy and torpid, and needed to sleep though with an empty stomach.

After spending a week in the refugee camp in Traiskirchen—a town in the district of Baden in lower Austria, and it is located in-between Wienersdorf and Mollersdorf when using a train. It is just about twenty kilometers south of Vienna, and was a place where crime was rampant under the influence of drugs. David said the more he tried to expose himself to this very area mostly the train station, the clearer he was seeing it that addiction to crime already stole the lives of his fellow Nigerians. He was beginning to think if ever there will be a way for him to change this. But as he tried to do so, his newly adopted friends were referring him to be a sleepy dog who needed to wake up, stop chewing a bone and join the moving train heading to a house full chocolates.

Many days passed and David was already issued a refugee identity card—meaning he was already legal and could stay everywhere in Austria temporary without any police disturbance as long as he did not commit a crime. He thought of leaving Vienna to another city where many doors of finding a job might be opened to him since the city was densely populated, and there was a slide possibility or no probability of finding one there. He wanted to run away from what he was seeing there in the city, knowing there was no way he will not be lured into crime; he wanted to keep his soul alive as he could see many souls already taken away and sunk into the blood of crime. Despite the fact that he was anxious to start working and making money, but he was also fortunate enough to have met with some group of Nigerians who shared his interests, and were all men of considerable intellects. He knew he needed them more than they needed him, and for the first time in his life he was proud of being a Nigerian seeing all these people around him full of talents. He went closer to them to find out they were all graduates and were regretful for having left Nigeria to come waste their talents in a refugee camp in Austria. When he tried to know why they all took that decision to come to abroad, he learned that they were being mislead, deceived, and distorted by some of their friends who left the country to abroad, and in a few time returned back home to them with flashy and expensive cars, erecting new buildings and financing new and different projects. To David, he said he could see these people and many others as nincompoops, morons, and buffoons who actually gave up their soul so as to achieve abundance of valuable material resources, which they could never in life have. At later end, after much scuffling and struggling and still unable to find a job, some of them took to the will of joining the moving train and started to deal on drugs—which was the easiest and common job that they were creating for themselves there in Vienna. To them it was a easy thing to do as the jail term was very low—say one month to three months if caught with cocaine. They were all doing the business and were making real good money from it—and were calling their friends living in other countries to come join the game of making quick and easy money, ignoring the facts that they were destroying the youths of that country that volunteered to harbor them.

One morning, one of his friends took him away to the place where he was buying and shipping fellow-used cars to his country, trying to impress himself, and to lure him into his improper conducts. But David, who already knew what he was up to—was looking for a way to leave them to proceed with their business and money making so he could travel to where he could find a job and a woman to love. He managed to evade them, but as he did, he saw himself faced with many criticisms. Although he could see himself to be a brave and strong person who could do anything his friends were doing that they thought was the ultimate in life, but there were much more for him in life he infer he could achieve which might be worth more than selling drugs in the street. His dream was not to build a future just for himself, but also to build a future for his unborn children so as for them to be able to escape that poverty life he also has experienced. Relentlessly, he proceeded with the help of some of his educated friends to try to change their thoughts and to implant a different vision into their subconscious minds. In return, these people were mocking them, calling them cowards, and warning him especially about the dangerous steps he was about to take to lift himself up in the land. He could perceived danger, but he never knew where it was coming from since he assumed he was not a criminal, and there was no need for him to be afraid despite the voices he was hearing, calling him to quit the formidable and complicated life he was setting for himself to come join them to live a beautiful life. Later in his future life in the penitentiary in Italy, he came to write a poem describing how his friends wanted him to come join them live a happier life better than the one he was living.

COME SMILE WITH US.

We're still waiting for you
To come smile with us,
Knowing that you know that
Life's as sweet as candy.
Come right now, come before nightfall.
Come right now and smile with us,
And let your sorrows fly away.

A darkness into which no one ought to peer,
There he's been living his life with no fear.
He said his life like fire was dragon-mouth,
Formidable, you can't snuff-out.
His nights shapeless and filled with chaos,
With no compassion experiencing the cloud-burst.

Someone's there to see into the bottom of his grief,
Knowing to be loved's as good as life itself.
One thing only, is to listen when the songbird cry,
And follow the path that leads to paradise.
Sooner or later, out we're gonna fly.
So you can clean your heart with a smile
And come smile with us.

It was true that he knew some of his friends were desperate to make money, while some others were possessing distinctive characters, disguising the modesty of their achievements. Some of them were also very sensible and at the same time persistent, and would not sell their soul for money or refrain from their dreams of traveling to Canada and England to study, despite they were encountering some major financial problems and were being disregarded by everybody including the Austrian Refugee Council.

As David stayed longer there in the refugee camp, witnessing a substantial number of African immigrants held in jail for drug-trafficking and robbery. He thought he just made the greatest mistake of his life by coming to Austria to seek asylum. Seeing that there were no chances for jobs to be offered to refugees there in Vienna, many of them were demanding to be transferred to other states where they were having their families and friends who could harbor them and even help them find a job. There was also an American non-governmental Humanitarian Organisation set-up and controlled by one American Pentecostal church—and it was dedicated to empowering the less privileged in the society; they were also providing these refugees with legal advisers, lending them bibles and other christian books to read, teaching them the word of God, severely censuring and reprimanding their friends for their criminal acts, and pleading to them to quit. Every Mondays to Fridays, coffee, tea, breads, and biscuits were served in their offices. New and used clothes were also shared among them, and to round it up, they were allowed free access to internet, making many of them able to communicate with their families in other countries, and also to meet single women online for dating. Although, most of them who were attending the meetings were also the ones leading a double-life.

To live in Vienna, two options were opened to almost all of them. It was either you find an Austrian woman to marry and be legal, or sell cocaine in the street and make hell of money if not caught by the police. David could not wait to be told which way will be best for him to walk. Thinking himself to be very romantic and passionate, he was anxious for the company of a love partner, and he was seeing all the women there to be wise and intelligent probably because they all speak fluent English and loved to travel around the world. There was no need for him to compare the Austrians with the Spaniards, because of how he could study their behaviors, since he once read in a book that, "Human Behavior is directly a product of the environment." He apprehend that these people were more skilled and well-informed, and he also saw that they understood better, the distinctions between tradition and modern societies. It was here in Austria he first met teenage white boys and girls say WHAT'S UP to black African immigrants, and it was a very common thing that you see everyday. Even if he could not find a job, and rejected many offers from his friends to be given drugs on credit so he could start to sell and make money, he was still feeling a very powerful and tremendous love for everyone around him.

One afternoon, as he wandered aimlessly around the train station, since it was becoming the only thing he and some other refugees there could wake up to do, and they were getting accustomed to it, from far, he caught sight of a very estimable young lady, and went to meet her where she was sitting. He greeted her in English, and to his astonishment she responded in English. He sat near her and started interacting with her, looking deep into her eyes—a method he was accustomed to when flirting with women. She was beautiful and was a sociable person who like talking to strangers, and was young, almost getting to thirty. When he asked her if she was living near the train station, she told him she was a legal adviser to many refugees there. He was astounded when he heard that she was a legal adviser, remembering how he was being treated by Alicia, another legal adviser in Spain that he tried to love by almost losing his life. He would have thought of it as a favorable moment for him to meet an Austrian woman, but he was beginning to doubt if he was at the right track, by thinking of dating a woman with a legal profession. She did not give him her number, and he was not anxious to have it since he was already fearful not to meet with the life he lived sometime ago in Spain which was horrifying. When he recalled that very incident of how he had trusted and loved her, and at the end of it all he was betrayed and hurt by the same woman who pretended to have loved him but was only doing it so as to extract some information about his private life from him and present it to the police, he regretted having known her, and then came to write a poem for this while he was in prison in Italy. He said he became very much fearful of every European female who are into legal professions, because he was regarding them to be police informants.

HOW SHE MADE ME TURN AWAY.

For so many years she made me turn away.
For so many years, I grasp not what to say.
The life inside of me, I could live not,
Because, to me, my ghost failed to return.
Bottom of her eyes, I cast my experiment,
And with her lies, then I lament.

One morning when he went to check the notice board, he saw that his name was among the refugees to be transferred to other smaller camps far from the city. Demoralized by this, he thought it will be better for him to join some of his friends who were already living there in Vienna than to be transferred to a village where he could no longer gain access to the internet or go to the disco to look for women. Although it was also said that, Austrian responsible women could be found in the village not in the big cities, as most of them in the big cities were already afraid of Nigerians and their attitudes towards life mostly when it come to achieving wealth. At that time he could draw a conclusion of how all of them were being portrayed as drug dealers, and it was true, since almost seventy percents of them were involved.

Joining his friends to live in the city will be extremely good, and it could also alter his life and make him do what he intended not to do. He deliberately refused to participate in the drug business not that he was scared to be imprisoned, but because he once read some books while he was in Norway. He had read these books to draw inspiration to be creative and to strive to be living with decency. David said he saw these books to be useful guidelines to achieving success in life. He thought, selling drugs to these Austrian youths in the street could only make him a destroyer not the builder he always wanted to be—just as he read in ALVIN THE MAKER by Orson Scott Card. For this reason, he decided to let himself be transferred to a far village called Aspang, more than seventy kilometers far from Vienna.

CHAPTER 24

ONE WEEK AFTER HE WAS transferred to Aspang, he ascertained the fact that his life was going to be miserable there, although it was difficult for him to get to this. He disliked the new camp in the small village, seeing how the other refugees there were living. Every morning, they would wake up to meet with breakfasts already prepared for them. At dawn, all of them will also gather themselves in the same dining hall to eat supper. He came to realized that majority of them would go to the city in the morning to return back at night, but where they usually go to and their motive for going out was unknown to him. There were very many people of different race and religion there in the camp. There were mostly white people from eastern Europe—Russians, Moldovan, Romanians, Ukrainians, and many others while there were also few Turkish, Iranians, Iraqis, Kurdish, and Afghans. From Africa, were few people from other countries, but the majority of them were Nigerians, and almost of them were ex-convicts tha came to rest and relax their minds to think of what else will be appropriate to do to out-last. David, who thought he was wiser than them, instead of him to ask the people he came to meet there what they were doing to earn their living, he neglected them, thinking all of them to be desperate fools whose lives already had been affiliated with crimes.

From the refugee camp which was located inside a forest, and was the only house around there, he would have to walk more than two thousand meters to the train station following the sloping tiled roads meant for vehicles. Sometimes, he would have to take the bus if he was having the money to do so. Although, they barely use the transport as they all found it very expensive and meaningless. All and all, it was more easier for them to walk along the train track to another train station which was nearer to their camp, but was very risky, because of how the trains were always very fast, and might crush them if they were not attentive to the noise when coming. The train track which was also very dangerous because of the thick forest they would have to walk passed, hearing noises and cries of unknown animals—and most time at nights. Several times, they were also controlled inside the train—and fined for not purchasing the train tickets. From Aspang train station, he would have to dodge the ticket controllers, dodge and dodge till sometimes being chased by some wicked ones across the train track, while some good ones will simply urged them to come down at the next station, and when they do—it might take them another forty minutes or more to wait for the next train heading towards that same direction.

Reaching Vienna, he would ramble and prowl, searching for Austrian women, and at nights, he would go to Traiskirchen, jumped the fence and entered the camp to sleep with the aid of his friends still living there. But sometimes it became complicated when the guards arrived to check to know who should and who should not be there. Every on Sunday, oblivious of the fact that he will not be having a place to sleep that night and with no excuse, he would attend a church in the center of Vienna—a Pentecostal church owned and controlled by an Austrian, but the majority of the church-goers said to be Nigerians. English and German were spoken and interpreted there and many who were attending this church were doing so to seek assistance and also to look for Austrian women while some drug dealers were using this opportunity in transacting their deals. It was always fun going to that church, since they could sing and dance to praise God and still make money by killing others with cocaine.

One morning inside the church, when David was sitting with some other lads, a slim Austrian girl improperly dressed and was very much pronounced to be a narcotic addict, walked into the church to sit in-between David and his friend. When David first saw her, he was frightened, thinking she was among the many Austrian young men and women who rove around, looking for someone to sell cocaine for them—a thing that was really motivating most Nigerians to get involved in the business—seeing people begging them for it when they were not having it. Sometimes David said he could lay the blame on the Austrian citizens for what led to the whole mess, for luring many of these innocent Africans into drug business. It was obvious the way they were begging them for it—that sometimes those who never intended to do it might find it awkward to see he could make easy money and be living a whole happy life, instead of living in one refugee camp inside a forest and be fed day and night sometimes with their favorite food and sometimes with food they never liked.

After the church service, he ran after the girl waving to her from far to wait for him. When she finally waited, he greeted her and asked if she was in a hurry to go home, but she responded by telling him not to bother about that. After a long time conversation, they were both tired and sat down on the floor facing each others. He narrated the story of his life to her, telling her he was destined to preach love to the world even when he was touching and caressing her body, and she was enjoying it, not uttering a word to make him stop. She also told him about how she had traveled around the world, and has loved India most. She told him she was addicted to drug and was undergoing a therapy to quit. He felt sorry for her and was glad she had taken a firm and strenuous decision to quit the misery she was inflicting on herself. He loved her instantly, and wanted to live all his life with her despite he knew it will be a ridiculous thing for any young man to do—living his life with a drug addict. She was smart, intelligent, and was pretty, although with her face a bit rough still showing signs that she was once an addict to the two most dangerous drugs in the world—cocaine and heroin. He begged her to quit, lauding her willingness to do so, and he promised to meet her the next Sunday there at the church.

The next Sunday he met her again, and after their conversation he tried to make her stay longer with him, not knowing she was not in the mood to to be flirted with and be left alone. He sensed that she wanted him to follow her home the first day they met, but he pretended and rejected the offer, thinking he would want to know her better before going into a deep relationship with her. As he continued to walk along with her, trying to make her understand how he felt about her, not minding the fact that she was an addict, all of a sudden she hollered at him, and then moved on, running and crossing the road to the other side, still roaring while everybody around watched the both of them in awe. With a look of surprise and incredulity, he watched her too as she ran and talked alone to herself. He wanted to leave immediately so as to return back to the camp in Aspang, but he was not having any money with him and was not in the mood to enter any train without a ticket. So he decided to hang around in the city, and later that night he went to jump the fence and slept in Transkirchen.

Early as 07:00 a.m, he was awake, thinking the guards will be around soon to do their checking. He realized that he could not see well with one of his eyes—which was his left eye. He first ran to the washroom, took some water to watch his face very well. When he finished doing so, he saw that everything remained the same, and he could only see half of everything. Suddenly, the blurred vision then starts to widen until he could only see tunnel which was translucent. He thought he was still asleep as he repeatedly robbed his left eye with the back of his hand thinking he might wake up soon from the horrible and revolting nightmare he was having. He swiftly informed his friends about it, but none of them believed he was serious. They all thought he was saying it just to evoke laughter or amusement, so they all laughed and cheered until at a moment he went out of the room. He later returned back to the room to pack some of his books and clothes. They all stood in stunned silence for a moment, knowing it was a serious matter and he was not joking. They felt sorry for him as he packed his books and clothes and left. He still could not believe what was happening to him, when he walked passed the guards standing at the gate unafraid. The guards also watched him passed without showing his identity, and none of them even bothered to call him back, seeing that he was already unhappy and there was no other reason to arouse his anger furthermore.

While he was inside the train alone, going back to the small village his camp was, he was beginning to think about his past life and how the future was going to be with him having one eye. He was also thinking what if the other eye happen to develop the same problem—meaning he could become blind. He did not know who he must call on phone to inform, when he tried all alone by himself to get the drift of how it happened that he could only see with just one eye; he tried to understand the cause of this problem and whe he tried, tears rolled down like rain from his eyes; he was beginning to think how it could be possible for him to succeed in life without his eyes; he immediately lost hope in everything—from becoming a musician to becoming a film actor or becoming a renowned writer and able to speak to the world about love and peace.

Inside the train coach alone, he was still asking himself questions and laying blames on many people he knew and has and seen in life when 2nd David, his soul and only true friend arrived to sit close to him, touching him. 'Hey 1st David, how are you doing?' 'I am doing just fine,' replied 1st David, bitterly. 'I know what you are experiencing now, and I guess this is not the right time for anyone to inconvenient you,' said 2nd David, lifting himself up from where he was sitting with him, jumping up and suspending himself in the air. 'How did you do that?' asked 1st David, also jumping up to try to suspend himself just like he could see his only true friend do, but unfortunately, he fell down, laughing. 'You cannot be like me 1st David, because I am a ghost and you are the only person that can see me. You see, I am seeing how you are suffering, and I have come to let you know that you need to trust and believe in God, and by so doing, you will regain your original eyesight, and it will be as perfect as it was when you were first born into this world, and in everything that you wish to do in life, you will succeed.' 'Thank you for your courage,' responded 1st David. 'But one thing I will warn you about, is that you try to abstain from that girl you met in the church,' said 2nd David, bringing himself down from suspension. 'Why?' asked 1st David. 'Because she is deeply in love with you and she is possessing a kind of evil power,' said 2nd David, and immediately he said that, he disappeared into the air just as usual. When David looked back, he saw that a young Austrian girl just entered the train and was coming to sit in the same coach with him. Then he knew why 2nd David disappeared. He later tried to figure-out what he was just told and came to believe he might be right, because he recalled what the girl told him the first day they met that she has traveled a lot, and at the end she has traveled to India where she was possessed by witchcraft. Immediately he remembered all the conversation he had with her and what she said about herself and India, he realized he has landed himself into a deep hole where he might not be able to come out, and at that very moment, a great fear seized him.

Getting back to the camp, he entered the room which he was sharing with another boy who left to the city to spend some days with his family there. He was alone and was very comfortable, but that day became the saddest day of his life, seeing that there was no-one to talk to at that condition he was.

The next morning he related his problem to their boss, an Austrian, popularly called chief by the refugees—the man who was in charge of the camp and all the activities. The man who was living in another city, and was always absent from the camp, really never had time to deal with crucial issues like this before. But when he was told, he quickly urged him to get ready and took him to the local hospital there in the village. He was later referred to another bigger hospital located in Monikirchen, a bigger and more developed city with more population.

Staying inside the camp in Aspang village, waiting for the appointment date for him to visit the hospital in Monikirchen, he was hopelessly bored and did not know what to do next, seeing himself going blind. He saw himself ravaged by a tremendous depression and anxiety and could not get himself out of it. Masturbation was adding more pains to his sore and he could not put a halt to it, since he thought he was enjoying it, not knowing he was destroying himself.

One day he had a dispute with one of the refugee who was from Afghanistan, not knowing he was about to start a war he could not fight. After about five minutes that he had the dispute with him, the boy climbed up to his room and returned back with a very sharp, long knife like a sword and started chasing him around the camp till at a time he was tired and waited to defend himself, and he was stabbed in the leg. He quickly ran again into one of the rooms, closed the door while the boy jumped and banged on the door, shouting and threatening to kill him. David saw that he was bleeding but he was more concerned about how he was going to be rescued. He waited inside the room until the other Nigerians came rushing over to confront this barbarian that was about to terminate his life. They also called the police, but when the police arrived they took David away to the hospital without making an arrest—a thing that later prompted an angry spasm, making him accused the police and the entire Austrians of being bias and racists. Although after being treated, one of the police sent for her daughter to interpret English for them—the girl who then came to advised him to be calm and file a lawsuit against the hit-man which he refused to do, but was lured to do it for himself and for the Austrian government since the same boy was being reported several times for having fought and stabbed other refugees and other people outside the camp, and the police were looking for evidence to nail him. He then filed the lawsuit and left.

Some days after he was stabbed, he met a girl inside the train near Transkirchen, his former camp, and she was going to Baden. He greeted her and went to sit near her and was discussing with her. She told him her name was Birgit and she has just returned back from Africa. When he asked her if she was single, she said yes, as she raised her hand and pointed to a baby stroller, saying it was her baby boy that was inside. There was no need for him to come down from the train when it stopped at the station where the camp was, so he followed her to Baden. She was glad he did, and he saw her happy mood because she could not conceal it. She disclosed to him how she has traveled to South Africa, Tanzania, and Kenya, and in Kenya, she met a boy there whom she fell in love with and bore the baby. He loved her immediately the moment she told him the baby was an half-caste. He thought he has met the woman of her life, and that the baby was sent to him by God since it was his dream to have an half-caste baby. When they came down from the train, he begged her for her phone number and promised to call her, but when he finally called her the next day, she did not pick the phone. He then continued to call her until she picked—and when she finally picked his call, she apologized for having not done so before.

When the appointed time he was given to meet with the doctors in Monikirchen reached, and he was taken there accompanied by Chief, the man controlling the camp, with his car. There in Monikirchen, he was also referred to another hospital—this time to Vienna, the heart of Austria. The hospital which he was referred to, was Vienna General Hospital and could also be the best and largest hospital in Austria. It was at this point he reckoned his future life a success with no skepticism since his eye was going to be operated there. His belief in God became stronger as he would have to pray every day and night. Although he has long time forgotten God was in existence, but whenever he finds himself in a grave situation like this, that is when he always seek the presence of God—and that is when he believe in Him.

He arrived home that day with Chief, his boss to meet with a new roommate called Kelvin who also happened to be someone he knew long time ago back at the time he was attending a secondary school. They were not good friends then, but they have both met before in Vienna and found out they were both from the same school. He was glad to be seeing him, knowing they both share the same ideas of how to achieve success. He was willing to teach him and also to learn from him because of how he has long waited for this opportunity to share good practice, interchange ideas and experience. He saw himself to be a person who was not stingy with his knowledge. His objective was to give moral guidelines, improve and support civility and also to preserve and enhance civilization. He believed he was going to benefit from what he was doing as he deemed it a success, and also wanted others to do the same.

One day, when he visited Vienna largest public library which was also equipped with the latest electronic resources, he met with many of his camp mates who also came to spend time there. Majority of them were there to use the internet while others were there to borrow musiccds and movies and even listen to the music there, but very few of them were there to borrow books to read. When David first arrived at this library and saw the many English written books there, he began to feel bad about his eyes, thinking he was going to be blind and would not be able to read all the great novels and poetry books he was seeing there. He wanted to ask them to borrow him all the books so he could stay inside the room and read them all; he was hungry for knowledge and the hunger was so very overwhelming; he became frequent there in the library, coming from the village where he was, every three to four days just to come and listen to some of his favorite music cds and borrow books and also return some. It was good for him due to the fact that he was also seizing this opportunity to run away from the camp to experience the cold outside and to also see other people rather than living in fear with the monster from Afghanistan that tried to butcher him, and was still by intimidation, imposing threats on him and some others who were also living there every time with broken bottles and knives. He was also able to avoid the life he was to commence to live, the life of waking up from sleep being bored to drink a can of beer and smoke a cigarette bought based on I-owe-you-madam from one lady who was from east Europe and was in a relationship with another man from Iran—the same woman who later fell in love with David and also did everything she could to make him ask her out, which he refused to do possibly because he was afraid to be butchered by the Iranian. Moreover she was old and could not have a baby for him. He was deriving pleasure from his newly adopted life of taking trains to Vienna from the small village he was living which was very far; he was enjoying life to the fullest as he will sit inside the train and read some good books and draw inspirations from words of wisdom and was delight that he was living for the future. The more he was visiting this library, the more he was building his brain and was expanding his mind; he realized that he was possessing the ability to research, develop, and initiate creative alternative, and it was then he discovered the ideas that he could implement to ensure his success; it was also then he knew he was born to become an artist.

When he called Birgit, the girl with the half-caste baby one day to greet her, she agreed to meet with him in a bar near her house the next day. He arrived near the train station since she promised to be there, waiting for him. When they finally met and went to a coffee bar, he tried to make her understand no one will equal his love for her. He was able to look into her eyes and tell her how much she was in love with her for having had the desire to travel to Africa and even had a baby there with the son of that soil.

The camp where he was, was becoming frightening and potentially dangerous due to how the police became very frequent to arrest some of the refugees for having robbed in the supermarkets or for having got drunk and commence with fights and disturbances. Three young Russian-speaking Moldovans and one Georgian popularly called Big Joe, who were all specialized in burglaries and robbing of cars, became very tough until they were arrested. Many other Nigerians who were freed from prison for having participated in drug related crimes became very many there, since they would have to relax to think of which next country was best for them to go to. Other refugees who were also deported back to Austria from Norway, Finland, Sweden, and other European countries, were increasing in numbers. Most of them left because they could see no future there since it was just staying in the house inside a forest to be fed and watched the television and later go back to bed. The worst thing was that Austria was accepting these refugees back, but they were not in the position to help them plan their lives which to David, it was meaningless, their reasons for accepting them back. He saw that things were being twisted to be the way it was not supposed to be, and he was displeased and riled with this situation as he was seeing most of them forced to do things they never intended to do if maybe they were catered and planned for. Once again everyone could see that, crime can be a product of the law and the lack of social benefit, misbehavior as a side-effect of social repression. He said he was seeing the blotting-out as everything were getting worn-out and many were trying matches to get-out of their misery and were being knocked-out, making them stay where they were, unable to cry-out since they were all scared to be blown-out. David said he was really not in accord with this situation, and since he could not hide his sentiment which was against the law, he was quickly recognized by the people there in the village and also in the hospital in Vienna where he usually go for treatment. He would not give up his dream and was not afraid to preach to them to dump those rules that will not avail, and to think of better rules to prevail. The problem with him was that he was not getting enough no matter how these people were trying, because his aim was to make them do better.

The first book he borrowed from the library that he was reading, was essays written by Ralph Waldo Emerson, the essayist, poet, and lecturer who led the Transcendentalist movement of the mid-19thcentury. He was glad he picked this book and was reading it, making himself believe more in what he was doing than before. With this book, he was able to penetrate more deeply into the American History, and came to realized that his American dream was not a mistake even if George W. Bush and his administration were about to make him think so.

After some weeks that he was stabbed by the boy from Afghanistan, he received a court summon ordering him to appear in court on a given date. Before they left from the camp, the woman who was to testify as a witness, called him to beg him to terminate the case. He did agreed to do so even when the woman turned against him by collaborating with the boy. The woman also begged Chief to beg him, and he agreed to their terms, seeing that he was not going to gain anything for sending the boy to prison. Although, he was informed by the police if he happen to win the case, he will be compensated with money by the Austrian government for being a victim. He would have loved to get that money since money was always his problem, and if he get it, he could leave Austria and return back to Spain where he was legal to invest the money. But he thought he was selling his soul to the devil as he could see himself as a worthless evil-doer who take advantage of everything he come across just for the sake of money. He felt God will not forgive him if he could send that boy to prison, but at the same time he thought he might be disappointed by the Austrian justice at the end of everything without a compensation. He accepted the sincere apology he was offered by all of them even when his friends were disliking him for having done so. When the day came, he was surprised the way the whole of them including the boy turned against him in the court of law, claiming he acted in self-defense. David said he was startled, seeing all of them including the public prosecutor turned against him—claiming he was after the money to be paid to him. He was not even having his own lawyer to see if there was anyone to defend him. He saw himself in an impending danger and thought there was a need for him to save himself from it by talking. When he was finally given a chance to talk, he went straight to his point with no delay, saying in English to the judge and everybody there in the court: 'I would have to forgive him for having apologized to me for his wrong deed; I am not after the money. But one thing that should be taught here today is that, "A place where there is no justice, there can never be love, and where there is no love, there can never be peace." After he finished making that comment, he was asked to leave and as he left, he could see all of them staring at him. That same day, he was later driven home by the same woman who continued to beg him along the way as they were coming home. When he finally met with Chief, he was advised to make peace and let everything go.

His roommate, Kelvin who arrived the camp and after three days met with one Austrian woman who fell in love with him and promised to marry him. The lad left the camp and was staying with the lady, and after some months, they were married and the lad became legal in Austria. It was easy the way everything happened, but when David took time to looked at it, he asked himself why his own life was always marked by misfortune, sorrow, and tragedies, while others were always having what they wish for in life. He has done everything he could to love these women, but he has never been able to make them love him and be with him, or it was the universe that was responsible for this. He wanted to give up the idea of looking for a woman, instead to see to how he will get quick money and return back to his country and live, since he was seeing himself not sent for by the Europeans. He wanted to return back to Africa to start life all again and be happy. But he was afraid if he leave, he will be blind forever since there will be no means of him able to afford to pay for it in Africa, and moreover, he understood there are more better medical experts and equipment in Europe than in Africa—and this was a great opportunity for him to regain his lost sight.

After many calls, he was invited one day by Birgit, the girl with the half-caste baby for a dinner in her house with her mother. When he arrived at the house, what appeared to be his reason for going was to see and carry the baby in his arm. He loved the baby and thought of being the father even when he sensed that the girl's mother was never going to let that happen, seeing that he was not obsessed with her daughter instead with the baby. The girls' mother was beginning to disliked his attitudes not that he was not well-behaved, but because he was too obsessed with carrying the baby. Maybe she thought he was sent to come take the baby back to Africa since the girl experienced a great deal of difficulty while trying to bring the baby to Europe without the father's consent—so said the girl.

Autumn was slowly fading away and winter was approaching at the time he was admitted to AKH (Allgemeines Krankenhaus), a teaching hospital of the university of Vienna, and was said to also be one of the best hospital in Europe. After many days of visiting the hospital for different diagnostic tests, and also for him to present some documents to ensure the Austrian Refugee Council was responsible for his welfare.

His first day there in the hospital was hell due to the fact that he could not speak German and was surrounded by many sick old men and women who could only speak German. He brought with him a bible that he was reading, and every time he could drop it at his bed-side table. It was among the only time he fasted and prayed to God to deliver him out of this unending misery that was forcefully walking into his life. There was no one he could call on phone to tell he was to be taken into the operating theater. There was no one he knew that was aware he was about to undergo eye surgery, no one, no one except his God—who was always with him right there inside his heart and was sometimes confused with his soul, 2nd David.

In this hospital, he knew it was a wonderful opportunity for him to meet the woman of his life. First he was after one of the student doctors who attended to him for the first time. He knew she was a student there and was practicing with his eye, so he took advantage of the opportunity he was having to be seducing her, rubbing his body with her body and staring deep into her eyes. She knew this but was calm and did not utter a word. She was pretty and young and could have been a model if only she did not decide to study and became a doctor. When she finished with him and they both left each other, there was no way he could communicate with her since he was unable to ask her for her phone. He did not ask her because her professor was there and would not turn his eye away for some minutes before he left the both of them to attend to another student who also needed his attention, and when they were alone, fear and lack of confidence descended on him. Although he believed he was always going to meet her again there in the hospital.

After spending two days there in the hospital, he was later discharged because they said they could not operate him yet, and as he arrived back at the refugee camp to meet with commotions and outcries, he wanted to return back to the hospital to live as he was relishing life in the city. With this, once again he was able to apprehend the similarities and dissimilarities between village life and city life.

After some few days, he returned back to the hospital and was glad he did, as he was welcomed with the hospital food which he was starting to like. When he arrived there, he met with one Dr. Maar who was short and was not as beautiful as the student doctor he met with before. She came to sit in his bed to ask him some questions since he could not get up from the bed after having received some injections by different doctors. They say, "The beauty that matter most is not the beauty of the face but of the heart." He would have not even make that attempt to think of falling in love with her, but she made him to. She made him loved her that she came to make him loathe her and also loathe himself for having loved her so much.

The night before his operation, he met another girl there who was a nurse and was an immigrant and has come from the eastern part of Europe and was naturalized in Austria. She also seduced him, making him think she was in love with him and later wrote a letter to tell her he was born to love her. Although she did not reply him and he never saw her again for the many days he was there.

It was the first time in his life to be admitted to a hospital and it was also the first time he was to experience surgery. Although he was more afraid because he was not having anybody there to console him. He asked himself what if he die during the operation, will there be anyone to call his family to inform them? He was questioned by different doctors about whether any of his family was suffering from a diabetic disease, and he answered no, since he has never witnessed or hear of any member of his family suffering from this kind of dangerous disease. Most of the doctors were also believing it to be cataracts, but he denied having a family who has suffered from this either. He was later given general anesthesia by an anesthetist, and the only time he could see anything was when he was taken away from the surgical ward, and lying in a stretcher, he was rolled into the theater to be operated. He saw about six to seven surgeons dressed in their green gowns with masks and hand-gloves, staring at him and were about to start with their experiments. Before then, he was asked several times to touch the eye that was to be operated—so as for them not to mistake his blind eye with the other one. This later became a threat to him because he was scared of losing the both eyes.

He did not know when his eye was operated till at the time he woke up from the anesthesia after more than seven hours. He was told the operation was going to last just two hours, but he was surprised to see that it was more, and there was nobody to tell him what happened during the operation. When he woke up, the first thing he did was to thank and praise God for having sent His angels to guard and protect him. He usually was a man who was afraid of needles and injections and this was noticed there in the hospital because of how he was always crying like a baby whenever he was to be injected or called for blood test. He woke up, thanking God and also thanking and praising the surgeons—saying it loudly for everyone around there to hear that they were next to God.

After some days in the hospital, he decided to call his sister in Spain only to be notified that his beloved grand-mother has passed away. Tears rained down from his eyes as he mourned the death of his grand-mother whom he loved so much and was planning to shower her with money any time he arrive back home. He planned to return back home even before this incident, but his dream of becoming an artist did made him not think much about it. It was painful, seeing that he was never going to see her again, and he was thinking if life could be rewind so as he could see her and hug her. Although the cause of her death was unknown to him until after many years passed when later it was revealed that she died of undiagnosed diabetes-related complications.

He was also told later that his own mother and one of his eldest sister was suffering from the same sickness—which means it was running in their family just as he was told before in that hospital in Vienna.

There in the hospital, there was another doctor who was more educated and was more specialized in this field of diabetic eye problems and ocular diseases. Her English was like that of an American as she could speak it better than him—whom his country was colonized by the British. She wanted to help him, seeing that he was alone with nobody coming to visit him there in the hospital. One morning after much medical experiments and examinations and procedures performed by many doctors around him, she took him away to another room where she used a laser for him—a thing she told him was very expensive, and was not supposed to be done for him, but she was doing it because she felt pity for him and wanted him to regain his eyesight. It was truly gratifying for him to meet her, because she was humane and well-mannered. He asked her if she was a professor, and she said she was studying to be soon. When he heard that, he knew he would have to go after her no matter what. She was still young and was at her thirties and would have make a good wife for him, but there was one problem making everything complicated for him—there was Dr. Maar, a friend to this other doctor who was also doing everything she could to make him happy and was throwing herself to him. He was beginning to see love and romance to be most certainty in his favor there in the hospital. When he looked into her eyes, he saw that she was willing to save a space for him in her heart at that very point that he needed a lot of tender loving care. He immediately fell in love with her, believing he had her already and she was going to be his wife. When he could not respond to the other doctor the way he should have done, tension escalated between the two women, and he was later seen as the bad lad who has come to cause confusion.

He has seen spirits and has met with angels, so what more for him to be afraid of when he knew his vision was already there in await to make him excel. Death—it was death that scared him, seeing how he lost his grand-mother so easily. He was scared of death because he knew if he die, his vision will die with him. But if he live, his vision will also live. He was afraid he could not complete his mission to preach to the world the need for reconciliation between human beings.

After the operation, he could see clearly with his eye and was glad they made him regain his sight. He believed in them and everything worked out just fine just the way he expected it. But before he left the hospital, he was informed that he was going to get blind or else he would have to undergo another operation so as for a silicon oil to be fixed in his eye to heal the wound inside. David who never had any idea what they were talking about, knew it was time for him to do a research on eye diseases and surgeries. From his research, he came to understand that the silicon oil is meant to fix retinal detachment, and this process is called Vitrectomy—a surgical procedures that removes vitreous humor and replace it with saline solution. He also read that this can be done when the eye is infected or it is bleeding or there is a cataract in the eye or glaucoma. When he started to learn all these while going to the library to do his research after he was discharged from the hospital, he swiftly came up with an idea to make sure he was able to have one of these ophthalmologists as a wife so she can always be there for him. He was afraid of getting blind. He knew it was DrMaar, and nobody else. Seeing that all of them there (men and women) received his witticism by showing how much they loved and cared about him and would want him to be a part of that society, he fell in love with Austria and thought of living his life there most especially because of his eye. He loved the hospital and how he was treated by the nurses and doctors. He loved the other patients who were also suffering from the same eyes problems. He loved the way they all meet every time to smoke cigarettes and discus about their problems. He loved it because he was also learning from them more about the causes of eye diseases. The hospital which was well equipped even with music connected to the bed—was a hospital that heal not because the doctors are perfect but because of what you see around you. He hardly regretted why he was there. Sleeping in his bed, he could listen to music and sing along with it when ever he was alone. He loved the place and preferred it better than living in the camp in the village, since he could meet educated and well-behaved medical students, doctors, and nurses everywhere around the building. They also saw in him the quest for knowledge and his attitudes towards other people was acceptable. He was seen mingling with everybody regardless of their race or religion, and for this, he was honored and he knew he was.

It was almost Christmas, and he was lonely and bored and needed someone to share his love with and could not find any. He tried calling Birgit, the girl with the half-caste baby, but she did not pick instead she changed her SIM card, making him think maybe she was cautioned by her mother to be very careful. He saw how Dr. Maar was always looking at him and was poised to render him any kind of help so as for him to succeed in life, so he wrote a letter and bought some Christmas cards with love quotes and poetry written in German by different great writers and sent them to her, using the hospital's address with her name boldly written on the parcel. At his later life in the future while he was in prison in Italy, he came to write a poem to show how much he loved her.

YOUR LOVE'S MY STRENGTH.

Ever I dream of climbing to the top,
Your love I need to get me there.
Even when my mind's filled with horror and dismay,
With your love I shall survive.
Everything then I lay my hands,
With your love I'm competent though.
So please, don't let me alone.
Cos your love's my strength.

We are the images of God,
God's love is your love
And your love I seek.
I'm afraid of nothing, even my enemies
Since your love covereth me.
When I can't stop the train,
I shouldn't have to try.
But with your love I'll prevail.

During Christmas, many people were leaving the camp to meet their families outside to celebrate with them. Some Nigerians and other Africans who were also fortunate to have met some Austrians who helped them rent a house so as for the government to be paying for it—because it was a law passed in their parliament to assist refugees, but only when they are able to rent a house and paid the bond themselves. With the contract that they signed with the landlord, they could meet the Refugee Council who will then be responsible for the rent. This was good for many refugees as they were enjoying it and were able to live their lives in the city without having to deal on drugs to out-last.

Meeting someone to help you rent a house was like waiting to meet the president of Austria since many Austrians would not lease their houses to refugees, probably because they were afraid they could not afford to be paying for it. Some Jehovah witnesses who were always frequent in their camp, were able to help some of these Africans who were ex-convicts and have decided to repent of their sins to serve God and become useful people to the society where they live. Although these boys were all working—working without having to be paid by anybody. They were selling newspapers as vendors in the streets. These newspapers popularly known as*AUGUSTINE* in Austria, were meant only for refugees and for poor people without jobs to sell so as to earn their living. These boys were making money from their work and David never believed them when they were telling him to join them so that he too could be making money on his own and be able to afford anything he needed. He thought they were bluffing when they told him how they were purchasing used cars and buses and were sending them to Africa with the money they were making. He first thought they were all deliberately obtuse and were lacking perception for choosing to become beggars in Europe—a thing he believed they will not do even if they were forced to in their country. He continued to look for jobs everywhere in the village where he was and many cities near it without any hope of anyone ready to employ illegal immigrants. The worst part of it was that he could not speak the language whenever he meet with some of them who pretended they were not speaking English. The more he was looking for jobs around the village, the more he was getting to know the kind of people he was living with, since he was always studying them to know if they like them or not. He saw that some of them were happy to be seeing them, while some were not, and those whose hearts were filled with hate, were not afraid to utter it out to them to leave by simply adhering posters of hate to the walls—and these were found mostly near many railway stations.

In Aspang, there was a public library that was also serving for many other purposes. In this library, there was a lady called Ursula, and she was very caring, supportive and was showing sympathy. She was prepared to assist him to make sure he could secure a job for himself in that village and be living there. She tried helping him in every way so he could learn some of the very important phrases in German to get a job. But while she was doing this, he thought it will be better if she love him and marry him so that he could live the rest of his life with her since that was what he needed to do. He loved her, because she was slim and was like a model and was smart, but he loved her most because she was sensitive, compassionate, calm, respectful, and was perceptive, showing insight and understanding metaphorically and literally, and also believed in the mystical things. Seeing her, he believed she could be the right woman they could both compact life together and raise very smart and responsible children to become very important people to the society. He loved her and would have done anything, anything to win her and make her become his wife if she did not tell him she was married. He continued to bug her until at a time he gave up on the hope of having her love. He later bought a story book with a title DAVID AND URSULA, and gave it to her as a present to read. Although, after several months, after she waited to meet with him again and never set her eyes on him, she wanted to start kissing and hugging him when she saw him. But at that time, he already made up his mind to leave Austria to another place where he could find the love of his life. He was unable to make love to her, but he did many times with imagination and in his dream and loved how they both did it. He later wrote a poem to describe how much he appreciate the way she loved him.

THANK YOU FOR LOVING ME.

I've found you
So I can live my life for you.
For long these words just sticks in my mind,
When you're the only one I find
Creating a world for me
To live and never wonder why
I'm dreaming to reach the sky.

All I really want to say is
Thank you for loving me.

My heart is coming back from Japan
Even at the time I never had a plan.
I'm so proud that you're a work of art.
Whenever I see you, I think in my heart
Your beauty too rich for me to leave undone.
Your nature as a woman grew in sweetness and strength
Till at least, you set yourself to me
To make me see the beauty of the visible world.

Immediately after Christmas and New year, he decided to join his friends in going to sell the newspapers. He saw that they were too many there in Wiener Neustadt bahnhof, so he decided to go to Baden bahnhof. His first day there was a sad day because of how he felt humiliated, standing at the door of the train station, greeting people who were passing-by *Guten morgen, AUGUSTIN*, showing them the newspapers. But when he arrived back at the camp that evening, he was able to buy a can beer for himself and for his friends, and then smoke from the packet of cigarette, yet he was still having 30.00 euros left with him. The next day as early as 006:00 a.m, he woke up and followed his friends as they all walked to the other train station near their camp, passing through the train tack. It was fun as they walked and chant until they reached, and when they were all inside, he left them and went to sit in another coach and started reading his novel—a thing he always find pleasure in doing. He made another 50.00 euros that day, and the next day more and more and more. He was beginning to like the job since he was making money from it, but he was also very ashamed that he was doing it. He thought at that time he could be able to raise money to assist his family for his grand-mother's burial because of how his mother was being pressured by her maternal relatives to take the necessary steps in burying her mother. Although David's mother and others did opposed these steps which was having enough to do with celebration by lavishing money in hiring local musicians, providing enough food and drinks for the local community where they live just to impress them. And because the relatives knew she was having children living abroad, they wanted her to spend more, referring to this as a tradition that cannot be eradicated. They were less concerned about how these people living abroad were making the money—a thing David took a principled stand against and will in time if still alive, fight to eradicate it, because he could see it to be a tradition leading them to more poverty in Africa. This always was to be listened to in one of Fela Anikulapo-Kuti's song when he said *double wahala for deadbody and the owner of deadbody*. It simply means, there is a big problem for the decease and the people who owns it. David said he could not imagine how these Africans inflict on themselves setbacks, adversity, and failure just because they see it to be a tradition. People are being forced to provide the money they do not have to bury their deceased relatives because tradition want it so. But why is that tradition cannot force these relatives to sponsor the bereaved to any kind of school they wish to attend. The truth is really bitter to say that Africans still have a long way to go if they could not sit and think to know what their real problems are.

After all and all, without David's assistance, his grand-mother was finally buried in the Christian way, thanks to his sister in Spain and his aunt in Italy. It was said to have been witnessed as controversial scene between his grand-mother relatives and the church where is she was a deaconess before she died.

Back to the hospital again after Christmas and New year came and gone. He was faced with another question to answer as the letter he sent to Dr. Maar sparked outrage, and everybody were staring at him immediately he stepped into the big hospital. He thought he could hear almost everyone saying something about him, and it was making him feel uncomfortable and scared. He wanted to run away, but he thought about his eye and decided to stay to witness what was going to happen next.

Before Christmas, a letter was already sent to him at the camp in Aspang, informing him of the next appointment with one of the ophthalmologists who happened to be the other doctor that used a laser for him even when she was not supposed to. He was so excited to see her again, but that day he missed the appointment because he could not meet with time and was not having enough money with him to pay for the train ticket and was asked to come down from the train. He could see that she was more pretty and speak better English more than

Dr. Maar could, and from the way he was seeing her when he looked at her fingers, she was single. He did everything he could that day so as to meet with her again, but he failed. When he later went there another time, to his surprise he met Dr. Maar, and that was the reason he wrote that letter and sent it to her.

In this letter, he wrote that he was an asylum seeker and that he needed someone like her to make him stay in Austria, and that she was pretty and deserve a man like him to love and treat her right—a phrase he constantly use to convince women to understand how much he love and want them. In this same letter, he emphasized the need to love regardless of age, race, and religion, and then the importance of everybody living together without fear. He wrote a quote which he read in a book long time ago that, "Love is always open arms. If you close your arms about love, you will find that you are left holding only yourself." He actually did not know he was about to start pulling his legs out to be recognized this time not in Spain or in Holland or in Norway or in France, but in Austria.

He was later discharged without any operation and was told to come another time. He was also given some medicines to ease the pains and eye drops to use which were all free. After then, he continued his self-employed work of selling newspapers or simply begging if he will be sincere. He was enjoying the way he was taking the train every morning to go there as he could purchase a ticket with his money and without fear, sit and cross his legs and read good books which was the only other way he could derive pleasure apart from listening to music and singing along with it.

He saw that he was not making enough money where he was standing at the train station, so he decided to look for another place. Then he found a big super market not far from Wierner Neustadt. The first day he went there, he was able to return home with 70.00 euros which was just almost twice the money he was making at the train station. He could not believe how this was happening, seeing money pouring to him. It was at this time he came to believe what his friends were telling him before of how they were buying used cars and buses and sending them home. He was glad he was doing this job and was making good money, but he was looking to how he was going to end up doing this to get married and have kids and then explain to them how he has lived his life as a beggar. Although many Austrian citizens were also doing this in addition to the social benefits and allowances which was entitled to them. As he continued to stand at this supermarket and was making hell of money and was starting to encounter and enjoy the company of new friends—among them was a young Austrian lad at his twenties, and was the finance secretary of the supermarket—according to what he was told by one of the workers. From the way David was seeing this lad, with no doubt he believed his father might be the owner of the big supermarket. He was a good lad and was so friendly, but he was having a problem of not able to communicate with him in English. The lad could see that he was having a strong passion for music because of how he was dancing and singing along the music coming from the supermarket. Everybody who were coming there to buy something, saw that he was always happy even when it was snowing on him and he was still inside freezing to death. David knew he was having a problem with himself which could not be easily solved as he was stricken by guilt of the ruination he was causing to himself. He believed music was inspiring him, but it was causing him more pains since he could not live without it and was already possessed by it. For long, music has become his life and the only way he could see himself as human, apart from when he is reading a good book. We can have pleasure when having sex, when we are using drugs, or when we are very hungry and eat or even when we are thirsty and drink water, but to him, music was a better way his brain could experience that same pleasure. Music is so emotional to him that sometimes he cannot control it because of the active force behind it. He said he came to understand music to be a great source of inspiration to many people for doing good and also for doing bad depending on the lyrics. The more it gets into the brain, the more he start to believe in the reality of the message of the music. He also said from what he has experienced in life, he came to believe that we can heal our world and make it a better place with this same music. Many people will disagree with him when he said he took a step back to explore history and came to understand that with music, sports and other forms of entertainment, the black Americans were able to reveal to the world the true beauty of the black race and also to able to conquer the hearts of the white and native Americans so as to be accepted into today's American society. How could he live without music when he has seen the natural virtue that can be acquired from it which tend to the good of mankind?

Frankly speaking, he was making a mistake for having let himself possessed by music which later create an enmity between him and this Austrian lad who was once his friend and later became his worst enemy, simply because he saw him flirting with many girls while he needed him for his elder sister who also visited the supermarket several times and did came straight to greet him where he was selling his newspapers. After then, life became miserable for him again when he took a decision to leave that supermarket to another place.

He thought he was done with singing along every music and dancing whenever the music is playing, so he decided to look for some music producers in Vienna, thinking he was going to seize any opportunity that come across his way. He tried calling some of the phone numbers of the different music recording and producing studios he found in the internet, using a search machine, but none of them were prepared to help him. Some of them even asked him to send them some of his song demos which he could not afford to record since there was no one to finance the project for him. He also met some different group of Austrian musicians and related this issue to them and begged to be a part of their music bands, but none of them were interested in working with him, probably because they were afraid he was among the other drug dealers roaming the streets of Vienna. Notwithstanding how difficult things were getting for him, he was still hoping for the opportunity to live the authentic life which he long dream of, since he came to believe, with patience and clarity of words, he could straighten things and walk closer to his goals in life. He believed he could manifest his agony and adversity in his songs. He was ambitious and wanted to excel there in Austria until the day he met another Nigerian who discouraged him, telling him that was never going to happen there in Austria as long as he was a black man. He did not believe him at first when the boy told him this. He wanted to walk away from him, thinking he was a drug dealer and was only trying to lure him to become one of them. When the boy started to narrate a story of how many Nigerians were jailed for two years and more for having protested the death of another Nigerian who was killed inside a flight for having refused to be deported back to his country, he could not believe what he was hearing, seeing that he was living in a land where one could be jailed for having voiced-out matters concerning racism. David said from that hour, he knew that was not the country he dreamed to live, since he could see there is no freedom of speech there. Although it was difficult for him to see the whole picture to know who was wrong or who was right, but he has always believed in freedom of speech, and thought it to be in existence in Europe. In his later future life, he came to understand this issue of illegal immigrants brutally beaten and killed was happening everywhere in Europe and maybe also in the U.s. It was a question he was asking himself, when will there be an end to this? Why is that people still pretend to be saints whereas they remain who they are without any change, only to dress in white attires and have dark hearts? He said he got reports of this same issue in almost everywhere in the western world, and yet no one is actually debating about it, because we all sees it to be completely irrelevant.

After many weeks, since he was still unable to find a place to be selling his newspapers, he gave up and was staying in the camp only to wake up, eat, watch the television, and read the many books he went to borrow from the library. He was warned by Chief, the man who was controlling the camp to stop these activities as they can cause eye strain. He knew he was damaging his eye, but what can he do without television-watching or book-reading? Nothing, definitely nothing. It appeared to him at first that he was having this eye problem due to the too much of television he was watching, but it was later in his future life when he came to find out it was diabetes that killed his grand-mother and that his own mother and elder sister were also suffering from the same disease, that was when he came to believe he was having the same problem.

It came to the time when he has to return back to the hospital for another operation, and when he arrived there, he was stunned by surprise when he saw Dr. Maar dressed distinctively from the way she used to. He knew he could never ever forget what she wore that day. She wore a white mini-skirt, a white doctors overall, and then a pair of high-heeled black shoes—making her look more like a film actress rather than a doctor. It was the first time he was seeing her dressed this way, and she was looking attractive and was pretty and younger than she was when he first knew her. He greeted her and tried to talk to her about the letter he wrote to her, but she was busy and could not stand to talk to him. When he later met her again, he did not know how to explain his feelings to her since there were other people around. He wanted to meet her and talk to her privately, but he never had the chance to do so.

He was operated again, this time, the silicon oil was placed in his eye. He was told it was used in stitching to close the wound in his eye. He was also told it could not be removed until a decision was made to remove it by another operation. They called it a retinal detachment, but they tried to explain it to him in German, making him confused and not able to know the cause of his eye problem and how it was to be treated. When he finally left the hospital and went to do a research, he came to understand that a retinal detachment can be simply described as a wall-paper peeling off the wall. It means the retina was separated from the underlying, inner wall of his eye. When he read this, he knew the darkest part of the story of his life was about to be unfold, and that he was going to get blind. He was afraid of another operation and was beginning to have the sensation that he was the person controlling his own life not the doctors. He was starting to believe a delay there in Austria would be fatal.

Every of the medical treatment and attention were free he knew, but he was depressed and was so lonely and needed to be doing something to raise money for himself instead of sitting at home doing nothing and waiting to be operated different times at the hospital. He was getting tired of everything and was starting to make a decision to leave the country.

Another time came when he went for the third operation. This time he was taken there by Chief with his car, and that was the first time he was accompanied by someone to the hospital and it was a day he said he was never going to forget in his life. Chief became his good friend after he narrated everything to him on how he was in love with Dr. Maar. Although he asked him if he was sure and he said he was. When he returned home, he was shocked and confused as Chief became too friendly with him. He knew the man was being told to do so. While at the hospital, he was questioned by a man who pretended to be a doctor but was not. He knew what was happening around him. He noticed he was being followed as everyone around him became afraid he was a spy to the Americans, because he was preaching to them the need for black people to be accepted into the society just like the Americans did. He knew it was happening, because they all saw him to be different from the many refugees there due to the fact that he would not stop reading and reading and watching the television and playing music. He has once believed the Austrian government abandoned all of them (the refugees) to their fate, but all of a sudden he was seeing how they were caring for him and were trying to do everything they could to help him and to make him stay there. When he saw all these things happening, then he respected America for having inspired him and make him have a dream. At that very time, he was also afraid he will be stalked and killed if he was not careful since he has offended many women and also made them change their love for him to hate.

There were one young girl at her twenties and a lady at her thirties that David knew they hated him more than they could hate Lucifer. He knew this, because he flirted with the both of them and asked them out for a date. The lady was the driver who was supplying them with food in the camp, while the young girl was a drug addict and they were both undergoing therapy in one drug rehabilitation center also owned and controlled by Chief, the same man who was controlling their camp. The two of them disputed and became enemies because of him, and when they later joined together to become friends—they never wanted to see him again.

David was hating himself as every women he met with was turning against him and were ready to eliminate him. He knew he was to be blamed for everything. He was beginning to ask himself if truly he loved all these women he thought he loved and had wanted to live his life with or it was just a mere obsession or it was just his imagination that he thought they all wanted him. After having applied his mind to study this issue and understood it, he came to believe it to be an imagination, and this imagination was ruining his life without him able to find a way to stop it.

After the silicon oil was removed from his eye, he was given an appointment again for another operation, making it the fourth time he will be operated, and when he arrived that day to meet with another Nigerian man who was at his fifties and was also complaining about how his eyes were being used as an experiment for young student doctors there in the teaching hospital. The man who was suffering from cataracts, has purposely left Nigeria to come to Austria, believing he could be treated. But after he undergone many operations and everything remained the way it was, he was starting to hate the people who were doing him good because he said they were doing him harm not good. David who also had discussions with other different patients who were Austrians on this same issue, came to believe what the Nigerian man has said. He knew immediately he was going to leave Austria after the fourth operation, but where he was going to was what he did not know. Under this extremely critical condition—which was about his life and how he was going to survive, he saw that his friends were still envying him for not coming to them to disclose to them what his vision was, forgetting every knowledge he has, acquired had been a result of many years of intensive studies. The Austrians on their own seemed unprepared and flustered, seeing a black African born in Africa coming to lecture them on how they should be living their lives. It was annoying and confusing most especially when he was seen preaching the message of love, and doing it, using the American methods, and the worst of it all, he was taking his personal opinions to be fact and was getting so carried away with his self-assurance—two things he disliked doing, but never quit doing them. He became more afraid of getting killed by his unknown foes every time as he walked through the forest to the camp where he was living. He said he would have wanted to have patience if actually he was living in Vienna with an educated Austrian woman so that he could have time to read all those great books in the library and study more. He foreseen a beautiful and wonderful future await him if only he could break-through and exhibit his talents, but he also knew his life was at stake in the struggle to defend the human race. Seeing himself trapped in a life that was causing him pains, he thought it will be better if he relocate himself or go back to Africa to live peacefully with his family. He later came to write a poem while he was in prison in Italy to describe how he felt about this situation when he was first admitted into that hospital and at the time when he decided to leave the country.

IN THE STRANGE-LAND.

The sage was grey and
Silver and was at the time of autumn.
The late afternoon laced it
With slanting shadows.
And everywhere there,
Was the white of blowing roses

And the purple of asters.
Before me, lay the beauty all around,
Beauty of life I'd never dreamed exist.
Suddenly came a dark cloud,
With the misty rain,
And voices behind me whispering rhythmic tones,
Singing songs no human could understand.

In this strange-land
Where no one is your friend
Neither anyone is a foe.
In this strange-land,
You wish to live, you live.
Take the same way back home
When you're tired of it all.
In this strange-land,
Death's knocking on my door.
I either choose to live or let the door open.
Let the door open if you can't come with me.

After having done a lot of thinking and came to look back into the mythical time of the tale of his miserable life as a good brave man who had a compact with his gods and made his decision to keep his pride by always running away, running away from the ghosts of the many women he has loved, running away from his loneliness and from craziness. He knew he was to run away to the land where he could find his soul, but he was not prepared to go back to Spain since he was never happy living there. He then chose to travel to Finland, a place he believed he could live no matter the cold.

Two weeks before he was to leave Austria, every day he would wear a short-sleeve shirt designed all-round with American flag. He was actually wearing this shirt to convince the Austrians his dream was to go and live in the United States since no one was doing anything to make him live there with them. He was wearing it to make them believe he was a part of the American vision of freedom and world-transformation. He also knew what he was doing was infuriating and could make the people see him as a thankless-wretch, yet he continued to wear the shirt while looking for how to leave to Finland. He wanted to purchase a flight ticket to go there, but his money was not enough, so he decided to go to the bus station to get some information on how to travel there by bus, and when he arrived there, he was told he needed to have a Czech visa in his passport before he could be allowed to use the bus since they would have to pass through there to Finland, and the country was not yet among the Schengen countries. He tried putting all his efforts into applying to one of the London school of art and designs just for him to be able to go there and live and fulfill his dream, but he could not meet up with the requirements, and moreover, he was not having enough money to finance it. He gave up the prospect of going to live in Finland or in the U.k.—and wanted to go and live in Belgium. But he was later advised by his former camp mate and friend, Kelvin—the lad who got married to an Austrian woman and was finding it difficult to quit the marriage because he was already indebted to her for having made him to be legal there. The lad advised him to return back to Spain where he was legally documented to look for a job so he could save some money to travel to Canada and live there. He knew his friend was right since he could work and save money in Spain to try Canada once again. He swiftly went to purchase a bus ticket to return back to Spain and waited for that day to come so that he could leave Austria, a country he once loved and had wanted to live. During this period, he said he found the British detestable for imposing strict visa issuance to them even when they were colonized by them and his country was still a member of the Common Wealth Nations.

It was on Sunday, when he woke up early that morning to get himself prepared for the journey without telling any of his friends there in the camp apart from Kelvin, the same person who advised him to leave. He took the few clothes he was having with him inside a bag and dumped the refugee documents he was having with him inside a dust-bin and left to Vienna. First he went to the church, hoping he could meet the Austrian girl he thought has cast an evil spell on him to make him blind. After the church service, he was surprised to see her there. He quickly ran to meet her to tell her what he was experiencing. Although she felt sorry for him, but not the way he expected. He thought she was going to be shocked by the news, but she was not. She did consoled and encouraged him to be strong and that he will prevail in anything that he was doing. Seeing her, he recalled what he was told by 2nd David, if it will be possible she could be the cause of the eye disease he was suffering from. He refused to believed what was happening around him when he tried further to ask her more questions on how she said she possessed some witchcraft while in India, but she felt unconcerned and was not prepared to enlighten him on that issue. He was still standing and looking into her eyes and loving her for whom she was, when one Nigerian boy he knew before in Switzerland came to meet him. He was glad he was seeing him, but he was not prepared to let the girl go even when the boy advised him to, calling the girl different types of names, referring her to be a drug addict whose life is already a waste and could not get it back to become important to the society. He told her she was leaving Austria and that she was never going to be seeing him again, but she thought he was faking and lying to win her love since she already understood he was passionately in love with her. He kissed her on the both cheeks and let her go as he went to meet his old-time friend whom he has been looking for since he entered Austria. He knew if he had seen him, for long he would have been living in Vienna and would probably be involved in drug business. He has saved this boy's life in Switzerland while they were inside the refugee camp there. The boy—said to be convicted for the possession of two kilograms of cocaine, ran away from Austria to seek asylum in Swiss, not knowing with his finger-prints they might jail him there. The boy later discovered he was to be extradited back to Austria to serve the jail terms waiting for him when he was about to come out of the camp and the security there declined to let him out. He quickly went to meet David who later gave him his documents to leave the camp.

Seeing the boy in Austria again gave him hope, but his mind was made up and he was not prepared to listen to anybody. The boy took him to his new apartment in Vienna, promising to help him so he could make some real good money that he thought he came to look for in Austria, not knowing he was not actually there to deal on drugs to make his fortune. When he arrived at the boy's apartment, he met another of his friend whom they had both lived in the same street back at the time he was in Africa. He embraced the boy and they chatted and started to drink beer and smoke marijuana—a thing he already decide to quit simply because he was not having the money to purchase. They tried to make him feel at home with extravagant promises, but he explained to them the situation he was by lying to them he was traveling to Spain because of his documents. He then left them to carry his bag where he left it in the left luggage office in Westbahnhof and left to take the bus heading to Madrid, Spain. Meanwhile as the bus moved from Vienna, he was afraid they were going to be stopped and controlled because of him, and truly when the bus left Austria not quite long, some policemen ran after the bus with their car and stopped them to check if everyone inside were having the necessary document to travel with it. He saw how the police were looking at him when he presented his documents out and gave it to them. After controlling the documents he gave them and after they called the Spanish to inquire if the documents were real or fake, they later let them go, and he could see that they were disappointed as they all looked at him in surprise.

Inside the bus, he was sitting near one Chinese girl who was also going to Barcelona, Spain, and was speaking fluent English. She told him she was from Shanghai and has come to Europe as a tourist. They had a discussion for more than four hours that he came to like her. He lied to her he was living in Austria but was coming to Spain to visit his sister. He also told her he would want to visit Shanghai some days to come. They became good friends till they reached Barcelona where she dropped from the bus and bade him good-bye. It was his first time to have had a discussion with a Chinese girl, and he was glad he did. He has met a Japanese and a Korean before and interacted with them, but not a Chinese. He wanted to stop there in Barcelona so he could help her locate a cheap hotel and use that privilege in achieving his goal of having sex with an Asian girl, since he has never done it before and has been told they were quite different. But he was left with just some little amount of money that will not get him to Madrid if he decided to stop because of a woman.

CHAPTER 25

D AVID WAS STILL INSIDE THE bus going to Madrid when he called one of his friend who was living in Zaragoza with his phone just to inform him he was in Spain. The boy pleaded with him to come down at the train station in Zaragoza so that they could meet and discuss something very important. He then obeyed and waited for the boy who later came to pick him up with his car and drove him to his house. He thought David was loaded with money as long as he was coming from Austria, not knowing he did not go there to sell drugs, instead he was there for the quest for knowledge.

Back in Spain, David saw that many of his friends were living more better lives than he was, and were able to assist their families in Africa, while he was still struggling to have a place to hide his head. He saw that many of them were married and were with kids and were also having good jobs and apartments of their own which they took a mortgage loan to purchase. He was starting to regret why he left Spain to Austria to waste his time there without any achievement. He was blaming himself for being too much in a hurry to achieve success and finally losing everything. He knew the first thing for him to do was to get a job. He begged his friend to take him to a place where he could get a job and he was driven to an office offering farm works for immigrants—with majority of them illegal in Spain. He started working there in the farm and was also sleeping there until his two months contract was expired and he was able to return back to live in his friend's house with money in his hands. Reaching his friend's house and living with him happily, he was imagining the magic that just brought him back to life after he left Austria to come back to Spain, but he could still foresee his future in Spain filled with sorrows and tragedies.

It was his first time for more than six years to see his niece, Joy who was invited by his sister to Spain to come assist her to take care of her shop. He was exultantly proud and joyful seeing this girl with them in Europe. She did came with a visa letter of invitation from his elder sister, Tina who was also helping him take good care of his mother in Africa by always sending her money. Although Joy came to Spain, bearing the same surname just like David and his sister, but she was their niece and was still very young and was supposed to still be in school. But because there was not enough money for her to study and mostly because that was what her mother wished for, the little girl was brought to Europe. David lauded his sister for having been able to spend time and money to bring her from Africa to Spain. He understood his sister has always been reckless with money, but she has also helped him bear the burden of his families who were always waiting for them to come save them from their sins by sending them money every time.

When David saw her, she was already grown-up and was as big as his elder sister. He shed tears, knowing he was lost and needed to return back to the place he left for some years ago: He needed to see his mother and father. It was at this time he realized his passion for art was leading him to failure; the path of life that he has chosen to live was a life not easy to attain, but it is also a good life to live.

As he left his sister's house that day to visit one of his friend whom he left his electronic sets in his house there in Vitoria before leaving to Switzerland and later to Austria, he saw that the boy was married and was with a kid and was working while his wife was controlling a big Afro-shop. He was glad seeing what he was seeing, and instead of him to be regretting and lamenting for having left the country to waste his time, traveling from one country to another, suddenly something touched him deep down in his soul and he became very contented ecstatic for one reason—that living his life in Spain was against his will. Before he left Vitoria to return back to Zaragoza, he went to meet Alicia in her office to apologize to her, but she rebuffed and sent him out, making him think it was necessary for him to leave Spain to Finland so he could go look for the love of his life. He said he got astonished many times, seeing that his other friends who were in Spain were doing far better than him as they could afford to purchase flight tickets and travel back to their countries to visit their families there and also invest some of their money on different projects, while he was still thinking of how to explore the world, not minding if others were seeing him as a loser. With the little money remaining with him, he tried to purchase a flight ticket to Finland, but it was not enough because of how the price was rising every day. He was confused, seeing himself trapped again in Spain and could not be in the place he wished to be. He tried with every efforts to leave out that spirit of pride, the will to change the world around him so that he could live peacefully just like his friends were doing, but the more he was trying, the more he got tensed up and his conscience was judging him, reproving him from his thoughts and letting him know there was a need for him to move forward with his strength and courage to fulfill his mission in life.

He saw that many of his friends were selling the houses they purchased three years ago and were making profits of 20,000.00 to 30,000.00 euros and were investing the money in other different businesses, while others were involving themselves in taking new mortgage loans to purchase better houses and apartments. He saw all these and came to think himself a lazy fool since he was unable to do what his friends were doing to raise money to start a good business to his country. It came to a time when he came to really sat himself down to view the surrounding where he was living and study the people and how they were living. He saw that there was a buoyant demands for houses and real estate agents were selling, banks were giving out loans and mortgages to people, and interest rates were raised for them, and since there were enough jobs and wages were well paid, people were able to meet up even as they would have to work a bit harder to survive it. The economy was booming and laws were passed in congress to improve the country's social-welfare for the citizens and immigrants, and everybody were enjoying it. Yeah! it was good. Life was good, good for the Spaniards and also for the immigrants living in the country.

While he was still staying with his friend, he was spending more money than he was supposed to, since he became responsible for everything—from feeding to paying of bills. His friend who was not working but was having a car which he was driving everyday. He knew if he he was to live in Spain, he would have to leave his friend to go live with other people, if not, he will be lazy just the way the boy was. Before he left, he had a dispute with the boy because his girlfriend told him that David seduced her to make love to her and she refused. David could not deny the allegation, but he knew in his heart she had lied to the boy because he knew she never loved him but was only pretending to. It was the girl who seduced him but because he did not respond, she disliked him and then thought it will be better if she lied to her boyfriend so that he could tell him to leave his house. David was happy he left them because he had thought of doing the same thing before he was asked to. Although he was also accused of molestation in Austria before by one old lady who was older than his mother and was at her sixties. The old woman who was coming to assist them in the camp and also to spend time with is boyfriend who was a refugee there. She was there several times and did not meet his boyfriend who found another younger girl and decided to dump the old woman. David who thought he was smart and could seduce her and have sex with her and dump her, did not know she was looking for someone to love her at her old age. When he saw that she was taking it to a higher level, he thought it will be better if he despise her and by so doing, she claimed he tried to molest her. He knew they would have send him to jail if not that Chief, the man controlling the camp has decided to quench the matter. When later he saw the old lady, she tried to call him to apologize and also to seduce him again so they could start from where they ended before, but he was already wise enough to know that he will not be jailed because of an old woman who believed in taking advantage of young and healthy refugees to satisfy her sexual desire.

After he left his friend's house, he got a job and his life changed for awhile, as he was beginning to make plans on what next will be appropriate for him to do. He tried to have an apartment so he could live more comfortable, but he found out it was more easier for him to take a mortgage loan to purchase his own apartment than to rent. With just 1,000.00 euros he deposited in his account and gave the real estate agent his account credentials and his three months working contract and also with the help of two of his friends who were working and have come to stand as his guarantors. After some weeks, he was surprised when they called him on phone to ask him to come the next day to sign for the mortgage. When he later went there to sign for the house, he was given a key, and that was how he owned a house in Zaragoza, not knowing he just dug his own grave by his own hands.

He was happy, living in a two bedroom apartment on the fourth floor of a building with no elevator. He was glad he was having his own peace in his own house. He was also given 2,000.00 euro for the appraisal which he spent in purchasing a satellite dish, receiver, a television, and a desktop computer, believing he was going to start writing songs and try to get in contact with some music producing and recording companies. When he lost his job, he applied and was being paid unemployment benefits by the Spanish National Employment Institute. He then decided to take a plumbing course for just three months, but he later quit and then went for another bricklayer course which he also quit after just two weeks. He became so bored and was not happy there since the only friend he was having there, Wellington, has decided to pack his belongings and left to Madrid, cursing all the people in Zaragoza and saying it was not a place for people like him. David knew the boy hated that city because everybody there were serious about their every day jobs and he was always at home not having people to accompany him in smoking hashish and drinking Whiskey. When the boy left, David was beginning to think of renting his house out to another person so that he could go find a job in Madrid and live there, oblivious of the debts he was getting himself involved in. He was proud, seeing himself to be an investor, and as he has always believed it takes money to make money, he thought he was seeing the light shining from the right direction and only if he could be able to work and pay for the house just for two or three years so that he could sell it and make a huge profit. Paying the mortgage was just like eating candy, so he thought when he signed the deeds and mortgage documents he was given to sign without having to read them and understand what was written in them since everything were in Spanish—a language he could barely read and understand everything they mean. The bank manager, the real estate agent, and the notary were all there, but none of them took time to explain that he was about to sign his death warrant, because they were all after the money.

Before he purchased the house, he has worked in more than six different companies and none of them had wanted to keep him and let him stay long because of the way he will be working and be singing and dancing like he was in a party. Although he was a very strong and industrious person, and was poised to work like a gofer, but they all believed he was not devoting too much of his attention to the work even if he was energetic. In spite of the fact that he was being sacked from the different companies where he was employed, he remained unwillingly to change his life-style habit, which he considered to be his strength in doing these hazardous unskilled jobs. Upon all the whining, howling and growling from the foreman of the last company where he worked, he persisted and tried to do everything he could to make them allow him to stay and work so that he could be able to cater for himself and also to be able to pay off his mortgage faster, but at the end of it all, he was sacked—which made him applied for unemployment benefit.

After he purchased the house and was staying at home without doing anything and was earning unemployment benefits and was living a good life without having to go to work, he became bored every time, trying to write songs and could not since he lacks the skills to do so. He wanted to travel to his country to visit his mother since it was almost six years he last saw and met with her, but he thought he could be a jerk for not having fulfilled his promises of erecting a building of his own for her to be the caretaker and be spending the rent for herself. His parents, mostly his mother who was also very worried and tensed to be the caretaker of their son's not-yet-built-house was also implying he send money home for them to erect a building in a land they have long purchased for him which they did without his consent, but only called him to inform him how some of the money he was sending to them to feed was being spent. Although it was one of his sister's husband who brought that idea, but he was said to have also duped him and had purchased that land for him which made David stopped sending him money even if he never believed.

It became a task for him by his parents to do what he was not prepared to do just because many people who traveled to abroad were fond of doing it. He said he came to comprehend how many young Africans who traveled to abroad were being exploited by their families without them knowing it. Despite it was a way they thought it could be appropriate for them to assist their families, but to David, it was totally insane, futile, witless, and dozy because of how he could see these youngsters and adults living in advanced countries being controlled and manipulated by their families who are already old and still living in villages and towns in Africa (a developing continent). David said he could look at it from his point of view to be "Monkey see, monkey do," as he could see almost all of them striving to achieve something so as to invest in housing. He said he understood it to also be a good idea, but he has declined to follow every other people's footsteps, instead to do it his way, to create for himself his own future. And because of the pressure that was being mounted on him to come build his own house when he knew his father was having four houses and his mother was living with him, he decided to avoid them to move on with his dream of becoming an artist, forgetting he could lose them one day and will never find them again. Despite the faults he observed in the relationship he was having with them, but he still loved them.

He said when he looked deep into this issue of exploitation, he came to understand it to be a thing that exist among very many people living on the planet, Earth. He said he could see it everywhere even in both poor and civilized countries, and it could be best described as modern form of slavery. It is in the commercial sex trade, on farms, in factories, in many homes, in every entertainment industry, even in many offices. He said from his point of view, he could see the workers who undertake harder jobs for unreasonable amount of money to be referred to as the slaves, and those who forces their workers into slave labor just because they fathom they need it to outlive and outlast are to be referred to as the slavers. Although many people sees them to be tyrants. David said, "There has never been a time that man has really given a fair treatment to his fellow human being, just because he has always needed more than he really wanted." And this, he said he could understand to be greed. He said he also laud these many immigrants who decided to take the risks of leaving their homes to other places only to be able to struggle to seek their own future and also assist their parents back at home.

As for self-exploitation, it is a thing that is happening to everyone of us. It is happening to the doctors, lawyers, writers, scientists, farmers, bricklayers, and every other human being born into this world. The president of the United States, during his campaign, he has to do whatever it takes by traveling from one state to the others just to get himself to be in the seat. Writers do the same, so are the scientists and other professional workers in our every day society. We all exploit ourselves for a reason to achieve a better life. But one problem with these African prostitutes that have left their countries to abroad to exploit themselves, the way David could understand, was that they were exploiting themselves for no reason rather than to feed themselves, send money to their families in Africa, and wear expensive outfits to attract their fellow African men who actually their aims were always to have sex with them and extract money from them and later dump them. He said he could also see that many immigrants actually left their countries because of the unjust distribution of their country's wealth to be faced with humiliation and degradation by the citizens of the land where they happen to find themselves.

David at this time, knew he was having enough to do to return back to his hometown to meet with his families he left for long ago. When he was later told he had lost one of his older half-sister and another of his older half-brother, that was when he realized he has walked too far away from his families since he did not know for many years what was happening within his families back in his home in Africa. He shed tears mostly because of his older half-brother, Tolongo who was said to have died of HIV/AIDS. He cried because he loved him so much and understood he was never going to see him again in life.

One day he called his friend in Vitoria who later gave him the phone number of one of his sisters who was living in Madrid, advising him to get a woman for himself and settle down to live like a responsible man. And when he called this girl to tell her he was interested in dating her, without questioning why, she agreed and pleaded with him to pay her a visit. When he arrived in Madrid to see her and also to celebrate Christmas and New Year with his friends there, he fell in love with the city once again, seeing that his friends whom he had slept in their house, were living happily while he was battling boredom in Zaragoza. He came to understand that life was too short to miss out as he was seeing his friends drinking together and smoking hashish and marijuana with women around them while he was getting too addicted to masturbation where he came from. He wanted to stay with them and never return back to Zaragoza, but he was having all his belongings there and could not start life without them. When he visited the girl in the house where she was living, he tried to have sex with her there, but she refused and promised to give it to him the way he would want and prefer it and how many times he would want it only if he come to meet her in Miranda, a small village near Vitoria where she said she rented a three bedroom apartment being paid for by one old Spaniard who was almost seventy-year-old and could not make love to her the way she will always prefer it. When he later returned back to Zaragoza, he got himself prepared and went to meet her again in the small village where he stayed for five days, having rough and tough sex with her. He enjoyed it as it was long he never met a woman and had come to meet a prostitute who was ready to settle down with a man so she could start having kids. It was also his second time to be having an affair with a black woman since he left his country. Although she had wanted him to leave his house to come stay with her there, promising to render to him everything he wished for, but he refused and never went back there again because he thought she could kill him with sex.

Back to Zaragoza, he sold everything he was having inside his house except the desktop computer and the satellite dish and receiver which he gave to one of his friends there to keep for him. After that, he met with his lawyer whom he paid for drafting a lease which he signed and his tenant also signed. His lawyer who already knew or thought she knew what was going to come up in time to come, warned him to let it be for six months, but David never listen, instead he made it two years. He said he decided to leave not just because he was bored but also because he was afraid to love another lawyer again as he loved one before and regretted why he did. He also visited the largest and best equipped government hospital there in Zaragoza and became afraid he was never going to be treated with the way he was treated in Austria, so he thought it will be better for him to leave to get a better treatment in the hospital in Madrid since it was the capital of Spain. When he finished the eye drops he took away from Austria and could not find exactly the same written in German to buy there in Zaragoza, he thought he might probably get them in Madrid. He was afraid he was going to get blind soon, and thought there was a need for him to be cautious and be serious with the problem that he was so much preoccupied about and solving it—which was his eye problem.

He knew his lawyer, Manuela was deeply in love with him and he had seduced her several times to make her to. He did asked her out for a date and she agreed but never had time—a thing that led him to also ask another of her friend out just to substantiate his secretly held view that she was or was not in love with him. The both women started a feud later, and the more prettier and younger one of them left the office to go and establish her own legal practice, while the older one remained in her office and never allowed David to come near her. But after many attempts again, she received him back—and she did because she loved him and thought he has come to save her. Frankly speaking, he loved her, but he could not love her to live with her because she was married and that also made the other younger lawyer tried to snatch him away from her.

CHAPTER 26

A S DAVID ARRIVED IN MADRID and was living with his friend, Wellington—the same lad he has lived with in Zaragoza when he first returned back from Austria to Spain. The lad who said to have left Zaragoza to come reside in Madrid capital because he said he found Zaragoza boring and Madrid lively. He rented a very expensive and big apartment with three bedrooms and two toilets and a parlor where David, after leasing his house to one Congolese family in Zaragoza, had come to live, sleeping in the parlor at nights and was paying him a hundred euros monthly. David was having a pleasurable time with the new company of friends he ran into. Life became very meaningful to him as they will all assemble themselves every evening mostly on weekends, to smoke hashish and take their bath in an ocean of beer, whiskey and gin with pretty African women who were mostly prostitutes and were always with money in their hands coming and going out of the house, flopping around like fishes in the water. He loved the life and thought it was best for him to embrace it. Some of the people he came to meet there were working while others were participating in distinctive form of criminal activities and were all living good lives. Food were cooked every day by different women, and parties were being held with music very loud in the house without the commotions from their neighbors who might be seen as racists if any complaint was made. It was all good for everybody as the Spanish economy was growing every day due to the new infrastructure investments proposed by the new Spanish administration under Zapatero, the ruling socialist party leader who happened to succeed in becoming the prime-minister because of the terrorist bombings that rocked Madrid on march 11th 2004 and killed one hundred and ninety people and approximately one thousand five hundred others were seriously wounded, forcing voters to turn to this socialist party as a way out to conquer the fear that was laid on them by the people's party who before the attack, were in power and had joined the U.s.-led coalition, an operation to get Saddam out of Iraq, claiming it to be a war on terror. Zapatero who vowed to pull the country's troop out of Iraq was then preferred the presidential aspirant to win the election, and he won and pulled the troops out.

After David had stayed with his friends for two months and was unable to get the medical treatment he hoped for in Madrid, because he failed to provide some of the documents he was given before and after the operation since he claimed the eye was operated in his country, making the ophthalmologists demands for it. He wanted to admit the whole truth of how he was treated in Austria, but he was also very afraid of what the repercussion might be for him, for having traveled to Austria to seek asylum while he was a resident in Spain. He decided to give up that idea, thinking he might be able to go for an operation in a private hospital whenever he was having the money to do so. He stopped using the eye drops since he was unable to get them there. When he visited a private hospital to get some information on how much he might spend for the operation, he was told maybe he would have to pay 4,000.00 euros, and he knew there was no-way he could get that money at that particular time, so he gave up even when the eye problem became worse and he could not see with it and he saw himself left with one eye while the other was blind. Although, he was later told by a private doctor there was a possibility for them to proceed with the operation without him having to present those documents, but it was true that his social security did not cover an operation as expensive as that, unlike in Austria where he never worked to pay any social security and yet he was operated four times and they were even pleading for him to have more so as to make sure he regain his sight. Anyway he understood Austria was not to be compared to Spain when it come to providing good standard of living for the citizens, as it was a country with social democracy in power with a higher tax and their resources were mostly spent on social welfare like education, medical care, infrastructure maintenance and modernization.

One day, when he sat down to think and was listening to Oasis and also Tracy Chapman's music—the two musical bands that had really inspired him to know that he was having a mission in life to fulfill, he swiftly picked up his phone and called another of his friend so that he could go and rent a room in his apartment and left where he was living before as he was seeing himself living with uneducated morons who thought they were smarter than every other people, not knowing they were digging their own graves. He saw himself as a navigator finding a way across featureless oceans, and that made him think he was different from them—meaning, he could plot his course on Earth. He saw that the whole of them lacked knowledge and were not prepared to search for it where it is, instead they were giving their souls out to the devil in return for wealth and treasure. He said, "If mankind could choose knowledge first before treasures of material things, life will be more easier—and happiness will fill this world, because knowledge is treasure." He said he also understand that, "Knowledge, that is where civilization begins, and he who is without this knowledge, is dead already—his spirits is long time gone from him while his body await to decay."

Three days after he left his friend and moved to another place, he found a job and started working and proceeded with his life. He was able to work and earn better salary to be paying his mortgage and also sending some money home to his mother in Africa. He was also able to find good books to buy and read them to draw more inspiration and await to reap what he was sowing.

As the U.s.-led coalition troops intensified their attacks on the so-called terrorists and violence spilled across Iraq—almost driving the country to the brink of a civil war, people around the world were beginning to loathe the Americans more and increase their criticism for their arrogant and violence characters for having re-elected George Bush for a second term. More threats were coming from the terrorist group, Al Qaeda after having bombed Madrid and London and were still very much prepared to bomb other cities in the countries around the world people considered western. Securities around the world became worthless since these terrorists were in every corners of the Earth, living with their enemies like friends and were operating from underground without signs they were the perpetrators. At this point, many people thought it incomprehensible the reasons why these Islamic extremists were causing confusions among the countries around the world. With observation and inference in terms of human behavior, David came to apply his own understanding and get to the facts that justice was what they believed they were fighting for. But in his later life while he was in prison in Italy and came to read the holy Koran, he came to see these extremists to hypocrites since they were not acting according to what was also written in the book which says, "Beware of extremism, for verily, the nations before you were destroyed because of it." or where it was also written, "God will not be merciful to those who are not merciful to mankind." or where it says, "To overcome evil with good is good, to resist evil by evil is evil." or another verse which says, "Do you love your creator, love your fellow-beings first." or another verse which says, "The strongman is not the good wrestler, the strongman is only the one who controls himself when he is angry." or another verse which says, "But indeed, if anyone shows patience and forgive, that would truly be an affair of great resolution." Of all the quotes David said he read in the holy Koran book, he came to love two most, which says, "Shall I not inform you of a better act than fasting, alms and prayers? Making peace between one another: enmity and malice tear up heavenly rewards by the roots." and another one which says, "Do not say, that if people do good to us, we will do good to them; and if the people oppress us, we will oppress them; but determine that if the people do you good, you will do good to them; and if they oppress you, you will not oppress them."

David said he also get baffled to see most of these said-to-be Islamic fundamentalists persecute many Muslims who intend to live their lives the way they love to, by embracing the western civilization—which also is a way of life to pursue knowledge, when it is also written in the holy Koran, "The search of knowledge is an obligation laid on every Muslims." or "He who leaves home in search of knowledge, walk in the path of God."

Many Muslims who came to believe they were being hated by their neighbors had failed to acknowledge they were being punished by these hypocrites—claiming to be saints. This is to interpret what is also written in the Koran which says, "He is a bad person in the sight of God who does not behave courteously and people shun his company because of bad manners."

David said he also came to fathom many reasons why these fundamentalists have allowed themselves to be indulged in this act of terrorizing our world, and the reason is just simply because they look back to history of the Crusade, a vigorous concerted movement known as the holy war by European Christians that was blessed by the Pope in the 11th, 12th and 13th centuries to recover the said-to-be Holy Land from the Muslims. Although the Jihad, the sacred imperative which to many Muslims were motivated by self-defense was also meant to spread

Islam and to extend Muslim rule by force to different nations around the world.

These fundamentalists have come to see terrorism as a matter of survival resistance, the willingness to defend and protect their religion from those who tried to render it useless, not knowing that the Catholics, their major rival have gone far from being fanatics and have decided to embrace civilization to the extent they even come to believe in technology more than they believe in the bible.

David said, after many research and studies, he came to ask himself why religion which was supposed to be a guideline to people in achieving peace, has come to be an inspiration for fighting and killing each others. He said, from his childhood, he always believed the westerners to be too intelligent and learned, but when he saw how religion has made many of them became insane to think of killing their own neighbors and inflicting on them punishments, he understood that there is no one who is intelligent among us, and that we are only striving to be. He said he love the westerners ideas and visions but he has seen it—to be—and has always been mobilized by greed, power, and lust—which can also be found in politics right from the beginning of time. In matter of fact, religion and politics can be classified as one, since they are both to achieve the same goal. And because of this, where justice was to prevail, injustice has become the answer. Since a lot of people has come to see that there is too much injustice in our world, so they have decided to take vengeance on their hands by flying planes into skyscrapers, killing thousands of innocent souls, believing it to be the only way people can learn from their wicked ways and do justice. But they have forgotten to grasp with certainty that, "An eye for an eye only ends up making the whole world blind," a quote by Mahatma Gandhi.

"An eye for an eye only ends up making the whole world blind," is a philosophy Gandhi has come to preach to everyone of us, which most people still ignore till this time. Gandhi has said this, not because he was afraid to fight, but because he foreseen tragedy as its outcome, as he also foreseen victory by protesting peacefully without violence or bloodshed.

At the time when the World Trade Center was bombed, David had first thought it to be a conspiracy between the Europeans and these terrorists, for a reason he thought was for the European economy to overtake that of the U.s. and to become more powerful, but when he continued to go on his self-determination to investigate this matter by engaging in conversations interchange with many advanced and learned Europeans, he came to understand that Europeans and the Americans are one, and nothing was ever going to disunite them. He saw how the Europeans love and respect the Americans, making him to formulate in his mind how beautiful and gracious it would be if the Americans do the same to them. From history, Europeans are Americans and America is a continuation of Europeans. He then thought of accusing the Russians and the Chinese to be involved in the conspiracy, but when he sat down to meditate, he recalled the many conversations he had had with many people who practice Islam, he swiftly grasp that majority of them hate Americans, and could destroy America if they have the opportunity to do so. It was all passion, jealousy, and rage, and he could see it in their eyes. Although the Chinese were the most happiest people to have been witnessing this, as they seized this opportunity to be building their economy and were mocking the Americans the way they were busy wasting their money in fighting two wars. The intrinsic truth was that many Americans will never admit that the Bush administration has brought more damage to the American image abroad than any other president ever did. Partnership needs trust to survive and last long, and that is what the U.s. and Europeans has that the Bush administration was about to destroy as he was not taking into account the opinions of American allies.

David with a keen desire to know why the Americans were more hated than the Europeans by many Muslims, has went far to engage in conversations with some of them who actually came to unveil the truth to him, that many of them believe humanity could be better off without Israel being in the midst of Arab countries. And seeing how the Americans have been so biased, by upholding the Jews refusal for an independent Palestinian state to be created, they all came to a conclusion to help their fellow Arab country in achieving their goal only by terrorizing and imposing threats.

Looking at everything—and since he could not think of how it could be solved or who is to solve it, David said he wish these Jews and Arabs could keep their conflicts in the desert or in the red sea so as for other people who practices other religions and some without religions might not get hit in the crossfire. He said he is too preoccupied the way Muslim fundamentalism is fast becoming the main threat to global peace and stability, so also is the Israeli's refusal to render to the Palestinians what they deserve, and as the world continue to ignore this conflicts, the world will never experience peace. He said he really cannot comprehend what it means to live in that land that no one is refusing to give up for the other if not for their both beliefs—a thing most scholars regard as a mix of fact, faith, and hope. They call it a Holy Land, but to David, he said he cannot see anything holy in it if they will not prove it to the world that their both religions stand for peace. He said he wish to see a time in his life when he could see a co-operation from all humans to make love be the religion we worship, to save what is about to perish, to enlist in our hearts hopes for a better world that is suitable for us all and for the generation to come. He said he understand that, "If we love, we cannot hate, and if we hate, we cannot love, so it will be better if we teach ourselves to love, because love is always accompanied by peace and harmony."

For more than a year since David took a mortgage loan from the bank to purchase his house, he was still unable to find a constant job. He became accustomed to doing every kind of job and working everywhere as long as he get paid for it. He became "Jack of all trades, master of none," and considering his monthly salary, he knew he could not proceed further to work to earn almost exactly his monthly mortgage payment; he saw himself engaged in a life and death struggle to meet up as the bank was raising interest rates and the tenant living in his house was not working and could not afford to pay his rent. Life became very tough for him because of how he would have to pay his rent in Madrid and also pay the monthly mortgage of his house in Zaragoza all alone without anybody's assistance. It was at this period of time he knew having a mortgage and not having a source of income is a curse to anyone who have decided to walk this path of life. And at that same time, many Spanish banks were loaning out money to their clients like they were giving them water to drink from a well meant never to dry. He took that chance in taking another 3,000.00 euros loan so that he could always add a little of it to pay his mortgage every month. Back at home in Africa, his father who was having stomach ulcer even before he, David was born, became severely ill and was almost at the point of death. The sickness of his mother, who was also having a high blood pressure (hypertension) became worse since she was always having stroke and was always placed in a coma due to the fact that she was already a diabetic patient. Life became very miserable for David as he tried to do everything he could to raise money for himself to visit them and could not. Although, he was able to send the little he was having to them, but his elder sister in Spain became his savior being that she was responsible for every of their hospital bills. His elder sisters and brothers at home were lazy and could not afford to cater for themselves not to think of their parents. Some of them who could have help them, were having children of their own to cater for.

Luckily for David, he found a job where he thought he believed he was going to work for a very long period of time, because he saw many girls and boys from his country working there and were earning double of what he was earning in the last company where he was working before. Many of the girls who were working as prostitutes before and had decided to quit prostitution to come over there to work, were earning good salaries because of the overtime they were doing. Some of the boys who were formerly criminals also decided to turn their lives around to become law abiding citizens, were also very many there, working and getting paid more money than they could be making in crimes. Although there were few Spaniards working there, and they were either meant to be boss or foreman. Seeing how these black Africans were working and how their boss were treating them with extreme disdain, which to David was wrong and unfair. He knew he came there to work to earn money to solve his problems, but he also fathom there was a need for him to bring a change to the lives of these people and make them think of treating their fellow human beings with regards. He saw how a lot of casual racist comments were used every time without dignity, and thought he has to put an end to it, oblivious of his personal problems. First when he tried to caution the foreman on how he should be be using his words, he was told, *vente en tu pais*—a phrase mostly used by many Spaniards to tell them to go back to their country. He could not withstand the insult, so he confronted him, telling him there were many Spaniards living in Holland and Switzerland and other countries around the world. When they saw that he was rude, they decided to keep an eye on him, and as they did, they saw that he was different from the rest of them being that he was always seen looked so forlorn and was not working overtime and was always reading his books at break time. So they all started to respect him. One of the girls who was working in the office that he tried to seduce the very first day he arrived there, knew he was smart and outspoken and there were things about him so spiritual that was making him unique—that she did not know the time she fell in love with him. He also wanted her and tried everything to have her but could not, because the Spaniards there would not relinquish their so-called-rights to conduct themselves properly and maturely and David would not submit to their demands, thinking it will undermine his credibility. He also looked into his heart to see if truly he love her just the way he think he do to many other women he has met before. He came to realize maybe it was not love he was having for them or simply it was obsession or it was a passing infatuation. But he still doubt if it was true that he was imagining it or it was true that they too really wanted him and he could not have them. But, was it that the universe never wanted it?

Behaving ethically is what he has yearned for in life, but he also comprehend there was a need for him to fight for his right by plunging into conflicts if not violently, at least verbally. He said there was no reason for him to keep his mouth shut, as every day, everywhere he go to in Europe, and mostly in Spain, he could see how immigrants were insulted, threatened, and harassed in public by many chauvinist because of their ethnicity or race or creed. The black Africans were suffering it most, followed by the Arabs whom most are afraid to confront directly because they are afraid of what it might result to. He said he will never shut his mouth because, when the Europeans first came to invade and colonized these poorer countries so as to exploit them, nobody ever demanded for it.

The more he tried to preach to the both side of how black and white people could learn to live with each others imperfections in his place of work, the more the black people there were hating him, calling him names since they were always seeing him mingling and interacting with the whites, while the white people were mocking him, saying he has come to play the role of Jesus. But as for him, many a time he bring back to memory the life he has lived in Spain when he first arrived the country and how he has eaten from the dust-bins and slept in the street, it seemed to him he disliked the Spaniards and was pretending he liked them or he liked them and was pretending he disliked them.

Still working and been hated and mocked by the blacks and also by the whites, he saw at no expense was his personal safety determined there. He knew the black people were hating him because they thought he had come to cause confusion and to make them lose their jobs by thinking he was there to fight for them to have their rights when they never asked him to do so as they were all very contented and satisfied with their jobs and the money they were making there. He was afraid of what was going to happen next as his books were stolen twice where they were hidden. In spite of all these, he was glad he was doing what he was doing, because he believed it to be his mission in life, and there was always a way for him to benefit from it, if not then but in the nearest future. He came to write a poem for this while he was in prison in Italy and titled it, Living For Tomorrow.

LIVING FOR TOMORROW

It's better to give than to receive.
The more I'm giving,
Just the more I'm receiving.
I'm harmless but I'm been hunt somewhere.
Now I can be found everywhere but nowhere.
My ghost I know is innocent,
Guiding my movements to a fulfillment.
Together, we raced from the start,
Till we reached the dark part
That lead into the illuminated world.

See now that I'm in a great affliction,
Seeking a devastation
For racial and sexual discrimination.
And with love, I'm seeking my heart desire
To be able to create for myself
A beautiful world.

David later decided to quit that job when he found another one that was more easier and closer to his house where he could go, using a public transport and could have enough time to read his books inside the bus, instead of him to be waiting for people to take him to work with their cars even if he was paying them for it. He said he was so delighted when he left that work since he was seeing himself like a man listening to sounds inside his head, and he thought he could hear people calling for him to save them, but when he tried lending his hand to help, he heard them saying, 'we do not belong to each other'—a phrase he said he would have preferred if said to the devil. He was scared and decided to leave them to their cause since they said they had sold their souls to the devil long time ago.

As time went-by, and David was still struggling to meet up with his monthly mortgage payments even when he was working more overtime and was earning higher wages in a new baking company owned by one American. He loved the job as he was treated with respect even when he was the only immigrant working there. He was able to work there for six months which was the longest time he has worked in any company since he arrived in Madrid; he decided to quit the job, because while working there, he was able to get a licence for driving forklift, and then moved on to be working in one Fiat Company, first as a cleaner, and later he was employed to be driving a forklift since he was having the licence, and it was at this very time he came across a girl who was injured while coming down from the train. When he saw her shedding tears, he went to meet her to try to console her. He thought she was British from her accent, but she later told him she was American, and had come to study in one of the university in Alcala del Henares. Although he has met many American girls in that same city where he was living, many who also have come to study in that same university and he had had conversations with them before, but none of them has actually made him become interested in them. He has met one who followed him for more than thirty minutes and they both went to drink coffee together, but he never asked her out for a date.

A day before he met this fat blonde girl called Heather, he met a black American girl in a bookshop, and when he overheard her speak English, he swiftly went closer to where she was to talk to her. But to his astonishment, she shunned him and walked away making him feel degraded. It was painful not because she was American, but because she was black like him and was also discriminating. This actually was not the first time he was shunned by black Americans, and it made him come to think how the blacks in America could be complaining of racism and will also be discriminating their fellow black people just because they are from different continents.

When he met Heather, it was like he has met an angel who was to make him realize his dream of seeing the land called America. They had a discussion there in the train station as he helped her call a taxi to take her to the hospital. She told him she was leaving to Paris the next day, and after that she will be returning back to her country; she also gave him her phone number, asking him to call her in three days time. He later called her after one week, thinking she was not going to pick his call. When she did, he could not hide it from her how he felt, hearing her voice again. Initially, he did not plan to convince her to love him, but when he saw how she was advising him to visit America, and by so-doing, he might have the opportunity to get married to an American girl and be issued a citizenship, then he knew she wanted him and was prepared to assist him in anyway to achieve his dream. They became lovers even when she was saying she was having a boyfriend and he kept calling her every time at nights and they were both sending emails to each others, and later she promised she was coming back to visit Madrid during Christmas period. When he heard she was coming, he knew she was meant to be the woman to let him see the statue of Liberty and Manhattan.

Time went so fast as he managed to pay for his house for almost two years and decided to sell it, since he was told by the real estate agent he was going to make a profit of more than 19,000.00 euros. A deep feeling of unease spread over him when he thought of the profit he was going to make if he sell the the apartment that he purchased by taking a mortgage and was paying it with tears of misery. He wanted to have that money so he could start doing legitimate small scale business by buying used cars from Europe and taking it to his country for sale since it was more expensive there, and many of his friends who were doing it, were becoming very rich and were living a more happier life. But how could he sell his own house when the Congolese living in it has refused to allow many clients his real estate agent took there to enter the house to see it. The real estate agent also tried to help him with another remortgage deal so that he could sell the house and purchase a small one bedroom with a parlor loft in Madrid where he was living, and will still be able to make a profit of 5,000.00 euros. But the Congolese who was as wicked as the devil, refused to give him this opportunity even when he has to travel to Zaragoza from Madrid every weekend with a bus for one month, to beg him to leave his house for him. When he saw that he could not continue to beg this African man for his own property which he was also paying for, he decided to use violence by fighting him. The man later called the police for him—making him file a lawsuit against him, using the same lawyer who also helped him to write the contract for him and had warned him for the first time of what he was doing. As time went-by, since it took the court time to pass its verdict and decide when the man must leave the house for him and the man continued to live freely inside the house or sometimes pay some amount to his account, he was unable to figure out what his future could hold for him there.

He waited for the chance to meet Heather, the American girl, but when she finally arrived in Spain and they both went for a dinner, he saw how she was unable to control herself while eating, even when she was fat and big. He was afraid he was never going to take that burden upon himself, trying to control any woman on the issue of how she might be feeding herself, so he declined to take her to his house only by pretending his house was very far from the train station when she asked him how far it was. The love he had for her was gone when he came to find out she was the proud type, believing she had everything in life already and as an American, she must be considered the world's first citizen. He loved her and would have done everything to have her if not that he overheard her mother on phone one day, telling her to be careful and that he was one of the illegal African immigrants that has crossed the Mediterranean sea to enter into Spain—and that was how he came to Europe, but he felt humiliated to be told by the mother of a woman he was in love with. He imagined how the future was going to look like when he will be in the U.s. with her, hearing her mother pour words of insults on him everyday, claiming they have come to save him from drowning. Although he knew he will be the most happiest person to have that opportunity to achieve his long-time dream to step his feet into the land called America, but he also wanted to be respected and regarded by his might-be-mother-in-law. He said he loved her with his whole heart and thought of loving her to death, because he also believed she loved him even more than he loved her. With her love, he said he was able to redefine love as the distance and time measured by the hearts. For long, he has always seen himself to be a person who was afraid of being vulnerable, but he also wanted to feel love and be nurtured and nourished by a woman—and seeing her, he thought she was the one to make him live and be happy, but he later came to doubt this because of what he believed the mother was thinking about him, making him come to understand she was not the one he dreamed of, despite he would not stop calling her on phone, telling her he want her when he fathomed there was no way they could ever meet or be together again. He would have try harder, but he knew the mother believed he was a gold digger and most especially, she believed he was after her so that he could be issued a U.s. citizenship. He wrote a poem which he emailed to her just to explain to her what actually he was thinking about the two of them.

NO MATTER THE DISTANCE.

Your wish, I'll always respect.
I've got a wish too, you can't reject:
Shine on me, let me reflect.
I believe we need not to neglect
What we possesses together, instead let's protect.
My love for you is with no effect.
No matter what, we need no retrospect.
Every man needs you, let me be the one you're to select.
You're the one I want to live my life for
If only you can see into my heart.
I'm just like a man in a trance.
If you can recall how we longed to dance
You can just spare me and give me a chance.
You're in my heart, no matter the distance.

After Heather left back to the U.s. and he did not make love to her and never thought it was right to do so as long as the love he once had for her had faded away, he knew what will be right for him to do was to return back to his home in Africa where he was born, so that he could go and see his sick mother and father. And to do so, he needed money. To get the money, he knew he needed to get closer to his friends who might show him the way leading to committing crimes to make real good money since he was already in debts and could not sell his house to get the profit he wanted. He became very sad since he was unable to visit his parents in his country and also to see what is best for him to be doing there as he could not achieve his dream in Europe. He understood his country to be one of the highest oil-producing countries in the world—which means there will be something for him to be doing there only if he try. Many of his friends he left there were said to have graduated from school and were doing quite better than the ones abroad whom most of them could not return back home because they were ashamed to. Before he left, he saw how many of the youths had set-up some innovative projects, but the lack of government financial assistance has always had an adverse effects on these projects, leading them to failure. He wanted to go there to join himself with politics so as to be able to speak for them and also to be recognized in his home, and to do so, money was needed.

One morning when he woke up in the middle of the night to go to the toilet to poop, he saw 2nd David standing and folding his arms, and was staring at him. 'What do you want,' he asked him. 'I have come to say hello to you,' he replied, leaving where he was standing to come sit near him. 'By the way,' he proceeded, touching him on his lap with his left hand. 'I am here to ask you what you really want in life.' 'What I want in life?' asked 1st David, confused about the question he was being asked by his soul and best friend. 'I am saying if you want to live a happy and glorious life or you want to see justice and equal rights for all mankind.' said 2nd David, looking into his two eyes. 'I want all,' replied 1st David. 'Look! you cannot have everything at the same time. You should have to sacrifice one for the other. The only way you can attain that happy and glorious life, is to banish from your thoughts the need for justice and equal rights for all mankind. And to proceed further with your thoughts that one day you could move around the world to spread your message of justice and equal rights to achieve love and peace, know it that it will be hard to accomplish, and moreover you will never have peace within you or think of living a happy and glorious life that you want.' 1st David stunned with what he was hearing, could not utter a word as he sat there trying to figure out what was best for him to be doing and how to reply his soul. 'Do you want that happy and glorious life for yourself and your father and mother?' demanded 2nd David. Immediately 1st David heard him mention his mother and father, he quickly answered, 'yes.' 'O.k,' said 2nd David. 'I will tell you something. You really do not have to add further complication to your journey in life because of mankind's injustice and greed. All you should do is to accept life as it comes, be on the trail and follow the chase to achieve that glorious life full of joy and happiness.' Instantly when he finished saying that, he disappeared.

After 2nd David left, he still could not move an inch from where he was sitting to go poop, so he laid down back to bed and slept until the next morning when he woke up to find his pants very wet of urine. He tried to recall what happened that night if truly it was real or it was his imagination.

It was at the beginning of summer, at the time many staff workers in FIAT company were off to vacation, and the subcontractors were recruiting more workers to replace them. David was newly employed first as a cleaner, and later as a forklift driver and operator because the boss was so kind, and had wanted to help him, moreover he was having a licence which permits him to operate the forklifts; although he was retrained by the workers there since he was not having a long time experience on how to operate them. There were few jobs left in the company—which was for the people cleaning the company. But because his boss liked him due to how he was taking his work seriously, he told him to keep coming to work to assist the other cleaners until the time other workers will resume. David was glad, seeing that the man was prepared to help him so that he could be able to work every time there. The man who was also having many other black Africans as his workers, promised to retain him there only if he continue to work the way he saw him working.

That day was the last day David and his other three black African co-workers were to finish doing the cleaning which they all considered tedious and filthy since they had to go deep underground to remove all the murky water. It was a job that lasted for two weeks. Initially, David had wanted to quit, but he knew he was about to lose a good opportunity to secure a permanent job with better wages, so he persisted, oblivious of the great suffering and distress the cleaning work had caused them. He believed one day, he could transform his suffering into art. But when he arrived his place of work with his co-workers and they were excited being in the last stage of the cleaning, he received a call from his friend. It was a call that he was never supposed to have received, and it was also a call that changed his life forever to make him see the differences between evil and good. He was told by his friend there was a better opportunity for him to earn better salary than the one he was receiving in his place of work, only if he could be able to traffic one kilogram of cocaine from Spain to Italy and be paid 3,500.00 euros a trip. He once trafficked hashish before from the refugee camp he was in Ceuta to the Peninsular—that was when he first arrived in Europe. At first, he was afraid and thought he was sending himself to prison if ever he try to be careless and make a foolish decision and think of going to swallow one kilogram of cocaine to travel to Italy. He thought it was a joke, so he told his friend not to worry—and that he was set for the journey, assuring him to count on him whenever, wherever. But later when he left work to meet his friend, that was when he saw how serious he was as he met another lad there who was the owner of the drugs. That same evening, they st-up on their journey to Zaragoza where he was presented with the already-wrapped cocaine, twelve grams per each, just the same way the hashish he brought to Spain from Ceuta was wrapped and with the same cellophane. The only difference was that the hashish were wrapped a hundred per each while these ones were with twenty grams more per each. Since their flight was leaving by 06:00 p.m the next day, he was to commence with the swallowing of the wrapped balls by 09.00 am. When he first started it, he saw that the odor was quite different, and the odor was bad and was making him vomit when he was swallowing them, and moreover they were bigger than the hashish he swallowed before eight years ago when he first arrived in Europe. He then ordered for a bottle of yogurt, and when they gave it to him, he forced himself to drink it, using it to swallow the wrapped cocaine. As he forcefully swallow the balls, about to rip his esophagus out his throat, he saw death calling for him to pay a visit. He saw that he was unintentionally imposing punishment on himself, and it was suicidal.

For more than three hours, he was still unable to swallow eighty-three balls, instead he swallowed fifty, leaving twenty-three, complaining they were too big for him. But the lad who owned the cocaine knew it was his first time even when he claimed he was an expert in the job.

At 05:00 p.m, they were already at the airport to check-in their luggage and get a boarding-pass so that they could fly together since the lad was accompanying, because he was afraid he was going to run away with the cocaine. Unfortunately, the airline refused to let them board, because they believed the flight ticket was fraudulently purchased by another person's credit card—which actually was true. David became afraid, believing the cocaine was going to explode inside his stomach. Reaching home, after a big controversy between them and a conflict escalated, they both later agreed to purchase another flight ticket-this time, with their money. But at night, David could not sleep as his stomach aches and the cocaine inside his stomach was digesting and was going down to his anus. He was beginning to regret why he had decided to quit his job to walk into the life of crime which actually was not meant to guarantee him safety. That night he thought he was going to die and nothing was going to save him. When he tried to vomit what he has forcefully swallowed, he could not. He thought of getting himself to the hospital, but he knew there was a reasonable prospect he was going to leave the hospital to go live in jail for eight years since it was in Spain. And while he was suffering, the lad who owned the cocaine was busy talking, bragging of the extravagant life he had lived and the properties he was having in Africa and how much money he has spent in rendering help to his friends and well-wishers. It was then David realized he was a clown being used as a tool by another moron who could not even spell his name.

Looking at himself, he saw his pride bringing him down and he was dying slowly. He asked himself if the money really worth it.

The next day came, and to his astonishment, he was still alive and physically powerful. He saw himself as a tenacious man since he could resist all those pains and sufferings. Later that day, they later went to the airport that same time, took a boarding pass and flew to Milan successfully without being caught by the airport policemen.

When they finally reached the house in Genova, and he was able to discharged all the fifty balls he swallowed after three days, and has also washed them with his own hands, he was paid 2.500.00 euros because he could not swallow all of them. That night he went with the lad, who apparently was becoming his new best friend to a brothel where he had sex with a prostitute and was paid for by his new friend and boss. When he finally arrived home that night, after sending 1.000.00 euros out of the money to his family in Africa, and at the time he decided to lie down and sleep, that was when he asked himself why he did what he did. He realized that what he did was out of greed, and he did it, believing he could make easy money and be free from working for his boss in Spain for little money. He came to realized that it was a life of want-it-all that he has always wished to live that impelled him to do it—to have freedom and never to be controlled by any so-called boss in Spain. He later came to see in his later future, the obvious contrast between this very situation of how he wanted too much freedom with the way people around the world also strive for this same freedom and to have and cherishes it to its fullest. He said he could see that people of the world seem not to be aware of the risks of the too much of freedom, as the society where we live is now where we are afraid to be killed by our unknown foes, because we are not denied of the freedom and rights to keep and bear arms, saying we need them for self-defense. Or how do we further elaborate on the issue of teenage boys and girls being featured on sex, drug, and theft related films. Or when we watch many porn stars having sex with dogs and horses. He said, "If men could continue to believe they could have everything they wished for in life, it is not good. This is greed—a thing that can destroy us all." He said, from the beginning of life, man has believed too much in this freedom and thinking he could do anything on his own. Even when God trusted Adam and Eve and entrusted them with the garden of Eden, but because they believed too much in this so-called freedom which is truly out of greed, disdain, and insolence, they lost it all. He said what he meant to say is that freedom as many understand it to be, is an essential characteristic of ethics—meaning it is good for every individual to have freedom. But to him, having it too much can also lead us to a ruination. A libertarian that he is, he has always believed people should have the freedom to act and think as they like, but he also came to understand that, "Too much of everything is bad."

As David returned from his first trip with money in his hand, he was able to pay his monthly mortgage and spend some part of the rest money for himself in going to the brothel to have sex with some beautiful prostitutes. He later went to the house were he left the twenty-three balls he was unable to swallow the other day and swallowed them in less than one hour. He went straight to the airport to board a flight to Italy with the cocaine inside his stomach. When he arrived at the airport in Italy, he was controlled by some policemen who took him into a room to check his luggage. After they searched it and could not find anything inside, they also searched him and could not find anything with him.

He was then interrogated on various issues, from where he was going to and where he was going to sleep and when he be will be returning back to Spain. With calmness and tranquility, he was able to beat the immigration and the policemen and left their office. Although he was so fortunate to have met the good type who saw with him some novels and thought he was a student.

He thought it will be better if he run away with the cocaine so as to go and sell it to another person at a cheaper rate, but when he tried to call some of his friends there in Italy to help him look for someone to purchase them, he could not find anyone he trusted among them, and he was afraid of not to be duped by another person. So he delivered them to the rightful owner who paid him just 1,000.00 euros and also bought him some jeans and shirt worth 300.00 euros. He was still not satisfied since he was supposed to have sold them for almost 9,000.00 euros. But he took the money and was glad he succeeded. The lad also introduced him to a Nigerian girl whom he gave 200.00 euros just for her to stay with him for the night. David showed him some gratitude for everything by promising to continue working for him. He also told him to confide in him, and after some days, he returned back to Spain also with money in his hand. He knew at this point, life was about to start for him. He was enjoying life as he was traveling every time, reading his books inside the flights and visiting different places in Europe with his hand full of money every trip he make to deliver cocaine, and at this time, he could see something about himself, he could see that he was getting trapped in the life of crime. He thought it was better for him to listen to his voice as he recalled the discussion he had with 2nd David when he was told to think of living a happy and glorious life. He came to believe he was living that happy and glorious life, and he was happy he was living it because of the money involved and the different women he was having sex with who were mostly prostitutes. It was then he also came to realize that the lives drug traffickers are living are just lives involving traveling, money, women, and nothing that much. Even when he was getting addicted to crime, he was still dedicating much time for reading since it was the only thing he could not change about himself, believing he was going to make more money and return back to his country soon to join politics, and will be making more money over there. It was then he knew he needed to erect a building for himself there, so he started sending his parents money for a start.

While he was struggling to make a reasonable amount of money so that he could return back to his country to invest or plunge into politics, he saw that the Spaniards were also busy enjoying their lives to the fullest. As he watched the people, he thought there was a need for a change in their lives. But whom will he explain this to when everyone of them were seeing them (black Africans) to be ignorant; how could he explain this to them when he himself could not even change his own life to become a renowned person and be useful to the society. Still watching them, he thought it would have been much more appropriate for them to have been reasoning forth on how the government could improve their standard of living to compete with the ones in other rich and civilized Europeans countries, and also to develop new technologies that can be sold to the world and help grow the economy, instead, they appeared to diverge and were going in different directions—like hating themselves and looking forth to separation. He saw that there were too much corruption in the country as many politicians were engaging in different criminal activities—funneling money from the country's treasury to their own companies, and they were not being queried—which was motivating more politicians to proceed with the acts. Many were also getting involved in money laundering. Some who were being indicted and queried, were later arrested, interrogated, and prosecuted, but later, as they were convicted, they paid enormous amount of money which they were fined and were set free—and this was making the numbers of corrupt politicians in the country increase. David said, to him, it was so illogical and insensible to be seeing a country said to be in a western world, still encountering a problem of corruption like it was in Spain. From that time on, he visualized the country to be faced with a problem of economic crisis if not then but time to come, since he has seen already, the repercussion suffered in his own country where corruption is said to be a way of life. Another thing that he was so much preoccupied about in Spain was, how the government were far less concerned about the subject matter of how to support and invest on innovations and inventions, and how to also set-up community programs to encourage and promote the youths to work harder on more different scientific and technological projects. But it was so plain and fanciful how they were working less hours and spending more time and wasting money in celebrating different feasts relating to their tradition and cultural heritage, and also spending money in erecting more buildings and believing housing investments to be their only source of income. They were also spending more time, beautifying the country, building different parks everywhere, forgetting life should be grabbed by the horn. David said he saw the Spaniards as people who still care about religion and tradition more than they care about the future of the youths in the country due to how he always see them celebrate and participate in different feasts, killing bulls—a thing he is strictly against as he could understand it like many other learned and distinguish men and women to be animal cruelty. Although, many people from South America and some parts of North America has still not been able to put a halt to this—which is uncivilized.

CHAPTER 27

ONE MONDAY MORNING, DAVID RECEIVED a phone call from his friend, Kelvin who was living in Austria and just returned back from Nigeria. He was told there was a business set for him already in Holland to go and traffic one kilogram of cocaine to Italy. The boy who knew him to be a person with a vision to change the world, thought he was bragging when he was first told he has become a drug trafficker. He wanted to see if it was true, so he gave him the phone number of a lad he was to call. When David called the lad, they talked on phone, and after that he was sent 200.00 dollars to purchase a ticket to Amsterdam. And at this very time, he was looking for a job after having stayed at home for a month, doing nothing. One of the girl who was working in one temporary employment agency called him to offer him a job, and when he arrived in the office, he was given a three-months contract to start working the next three days due to the fact that it was on Friday. He saw that the salary was splendid (8.00 euros per-hour) while most companies were paying 6.00 euros per-hour for unskilled labor jobs. He wanted to do that job not because of the money, but because he was in love with the girl who has long been offering him jobs. He has asked her out for a date, but she had wanted him to take it slowly so she could have enough time to watch him if really he was the serious type—a thing most girls in Europe wants to see if the man is a hard-working person. At this same time, he has also met with one Nigerian girl who also was into the business of buying used cars in Spain and sending them to Africa for sales. She also wanted him so they could both be transacting the business. There was another Spanish girl who was working as a real estate agent, and was very much interested in having a relationship with him. He also asked him out for a date, and she had agreed to meet with him the next two days.

David saw himself becoming a man who was leading an immoral life and was always interested in sexual pleasure, instead of the life he has dreamed to live by loving a woman and treating her right. He said he could not blame himself for doing this, because he was done with being hurt by women, and came to see that life is too short, so it is not a bad thing to see himself enjoy it. He said he also came to believe that is what many women deserve since they will not love you except when you lie and deceive them only to have sex with them and dump them.

When he met these two Spanish girls and the Nigerian girl, he wanted to love a woman again, he wanted to love anyone of them that was willing to give him that chance first. But money was still on his mind when he received the 200.00 euros he was sent from Holland. He called his friend whom he was living with to inform him of the new drug deal he was having to transact in Holland, and when the boy heard this, he begged him not to let this opportunity go-by, because it was a way for the both of them to make some real good money, if only he could go there to swallow the one kilogram of cocaine and divert it to sell it to another person who was prepared to pay 25,000.00 dollars for everything. David saw that it was a good idea, since he could start doing business to Africa and also return back home with the money to invest and get involved into politics there; so he bought a ticket and left to Amsterdam, forgetting one of these women that were in love with him was supposed to be the angel to save him from not falling into a pit.

In Amsterdam, he was gratified by his new business friends. They took him to visit different places there in Amsterdam to eat, dine and have sex with prostitutes. He was glad he was living this good life, meanwhile he was still planning to dupe them. He told them to purchase a ticket that will be leaving from Brussels in Belgium so that he could go and meet one of his friend there to sell the drugs. When they went to purchase the ticket of the train that he was to take to Brussels from Amsterdam, he met some young American girls who were tourists and have also come to purchase their tickets to Brussels and were all coming from Germany. One of them liked him as they engaged in a conversation. He wanted to change the departure time of his ticket so that he could have the same time with the girl, because he saw that she was also in love with him and was prepared to do anything with him that night. When he insisted more on changing the time of his tickets, his friends began to caution him of the risks involved when anybody with a mission is also getting himself involved with a woman. He then left sadly, knowing he was never going to see the girl again.

At midnight, he forced himself to swallow the balls of wrapped cocaine and could not, he then put everything inside his luggage, and in the morning, when he was about to set up for the journey, they asked him if he swallowed everything and he told them it did not take him thirty minutes to do that. They believed him and let him leave and even ordered a taxi to take him to Amsterdam Central Station, where he took a train and left to Brussels.

While he was already inside the train, he brought the luggage out to see if everything were still inside, and immediately he saw the wrapped cocaine, fear gripped him. So he swiftly took the luggage and went to dump it in another seat while he was watching it from far. His heart suddenly started to beat so fast and strongly as he saw one of the ticket controller walked closer to where he was sitting. After the man checked his ticket and left, something came into his mind, and he became very afraid the police was the next to enter into the train to check his luggage. Although, since he was born, he has never been that scared as he was that day. He said he thought he saw trouble walking closer to his way, but keeping out of the way not to witness the effects was a thing he could not do or he could do it but declined to, because money was already on his mind.

Instantly, when the train arrived in Antwerp, Belgium, he took his luggage and entered into the washroom and brought out the wrapped cocaine and dumped eighty out of the one hundred balls into the waste-bin and forced the remaining twenty balls deep inside his anus and left back to sit in the same seat where he left before. He became calm and a bit peaceful as he sat down waiting for the train to get to Brussels where he could call his friend to ask him where he was living there so that he could go and meet him and discharged the wrapped cocaine and sell them. But first, he decided to call his friend in Italy who offered him a better price, making him regret why he has thrown the rest away. He fathomed it was going to take him more time to get a buyer in Brussels, so he decided to move on to the airport, but when he looked at the departure time in his ticket, he saw that he was already late. He wanted to go to the airport to call his friend to come pick him up there so as for the lad to think he was just arriving from Spain since he was going to throw the ticket away. When he arrived at the airport, he saw that his flight was delayed. It was so astonishing the way everything were happening that he thought it was meant to be for him to take that trip since he believed it to be the last. He thought he could sell the twenty balls for 6,000.00 euros as he was promised so that he could add the money to the 5,000.00 euros he was already having that he left inside one of his trouser in Spain, and with 11,000.00 euros, he knew he could start a good business to Africa and even stay there to see to the political problems in his country and be a part of the people to voice out the problems engulfing his country to the world. He was desperate to be a politician, believing he could make more money there.

When he called his friend who was living in Brussels, he was told to wait so that he could come pick him up with his car. It was at this very time, his soul also known as 2nd David showed an extreme tendency to spontaneously offer his advice but based on two distinctive views. His soul became two; one pleading with him with a calm and gentle voice not to make that trip, and if he does, he will be seeing himself in a prison in Italy, while the other was also pleading with him with an abrupt voice, prompting him to proceed further since this was his last trip, and if ever he succeeded, he could become very rich in the twinkling of an eye. He said he did not know which path to take as he saw the path leading to success but shrouded in darkness and fear, and the other path leading to failure but shrouded in victory and mystery. He knew he has to keep his pride and do what he needed to do to fulfill his promises to his family back at home, and to do so, there are some sacrifices that he needed to make, things that needed to be done so as to achieve success; and success, he understood does not come very easily, it has to be with exertion, and that was how he intended to live his life—to scuffle and struggle until he was breathless. So he took the dark part by taking the flight to Milan, Italy. Inside the flight, when he was murmuring prayers to his God who was also informing him there was no way he could escape the trouble he has caused for himself, he knew he was already in prison. He brought out the book inside his luggage to read but could not find anything good and interesting about it, so he kept it back. When he was offered food and wine by one of the flight attendants, he refused the wine and ordered for an orange juice, not knowing there was somebody there watching his every footsteps.

As the flight arrived at Malpensa airport, Milan, he went straight to the baggage claim area to collect his luggage, and when he left there and was walking to the airport exit gate, a policeman in mufti stopped him, and with an air of confidence, he stopped and demanded for a reason. The man showed him his police I D. badge, and immediately he saw it, he knew he was already in prison. But how long was he going to be there became a question he was asking himself as the man followed him and showed him into a room where his luggage was ransacked. He was later instructed to undress and every part of his body were searched, and when they could not find anything, they asked him if he was having some cocaine he swallowed inside his stomach. He denied it and accused them of being racists, but they kept insisting and later asked him to sign a document which was written in Italian, informing him they were about to take him to the hospital for x-ray. Some of the policemen who saw the many books and music cds he was having inside his luggage and how he speak fluent English, thought he was innocent, and had wanted him to leave. But one of them believed he was a criminal and decided to take him to the hospital unless he confessed so that he could be sent directly to the prison. He followed them there and everything were done, and yet he was still denying he was not having anything inside his stomach. But because they were all hidden in his anus, they could not find it easily and they were still doubting if actually he was having them. They were also afraid because they could see him as a lawyer who could go further to sue the Italian government.

Inside a room in the hospital, he was showed a bed where he could sleep until the day he will finish discharging all the cocaine they thought was inside his stomach, not knowing they were in his anus. Three policemen were ordered to be guarding him from escaping from the room with a window already enclosed with barbed wires. At about 08:00 p.m after he was given food to eat and he saw the first set of policemen left to be replaced by another set, he understood there was no way he could run away from the room, and he was also afraid it might explode inside his anus, so he called one of the policemen and told him he was having the cocaine inside his anus. They were all startled by the news, because of how most of them already thought he was innocent mainly because of the different novels and cds that he was having inside his luggage and how fluent his English was. They all believed he was a student, and because they could not find the cocaine in his stomach even with the x-ray machine, they became very afraid of what was going to happen next. When he was given a chance to poop, he saw that the flush toilet was also covered with barbed wires to protect the excrement from going into the hole. After pooping, he was given some plastic hand-gloves and was told to wash the balls by himself with his hands—a thing he pretended was disgusting just to make them think it was his first time.

He was able to poop out eleven out of the twenty balls. The next day, he pooped out the remaining nine balls and became free. When one of the policemen who arrested him arrived and was told he has pooped out everything, he was so astonished, seeing that a Nigerians can never be trusted because of how he has argued with his friends about the possibility of him being innocent. The man, seeing that he was having passion for music because of what was inside his luggage, went far to be playing Bob Marley music for him with his phone—the same type of phone they found inside his luggage. Although, he was later told when he arrived in the prison that they suspected him because of that phone, because it was a very expensive phone and was new.

Before he left that room, another two Nigerians were also brought there from the same airport, and they were also denying of the charges laid against them. When he asked them in their native language if truly they were having cocaine inside their stomach and they said yes, he swiftly advised them to admit and go poop them out so they could be sent to the prison, as he was supposed to be waiting for them to get things done in time so that they could all be sent to the prison without much delay. One of them was with nine hundred grams and was coming directly from Germany while the other one was having 1.3 kilograms and was coming from Nigeria but was to transit in Italy.

As he watched and wait for the other two to finish discharging what they have swallowed, he continued to read the book he has started reading some days before, and as it was almost at the point of finishing, it became more interesting to him and he could not waste time to discuss with his new friends, instead he focused on reading. As the policemen watched him always calm and still reading, they felt sorry for him, thinking he was a gullible person and was tricked to commit the crime he just committed, while others were seeing him to be a deceitful Nigerian who thinks he could fool everybody around him. Actually he was calm, knowing time could not be rewind, but he knew he was in a terrible predicament, and the only way for him to inspire himself with hope and to reassure himself that he was going to survive, was to keep reading. This same book he was reading was a book he really could not understand the reason he bought it. The title of the book caught his eye, and when he saw that it was written by one of his favorite author, he picked it up. It was a book he believed was going to have an influence on his life, and it was also a book he loved to read to see what influence it was going to have on his life. It was THE GREAT EXPECTATIONS, written by the great Charles Dickens. David said, he loved this book that he thought it will take him to where he wish to go, as he has long expected something peculiar and miserable to change his point of view about many things in life; he loved this book since he knew there was a great expectation for him—and to have what he expected, he needed to go search for it himself.

CHAPTER 28

F ROM THE HOSPITAL, DAVID AND the other two boys were transferred to Busto Arsizio, Varese, the nearest prison to Milan. There, they were given the necessary treatment and examined for whatever disease they were having, and after then, everyone of them were presented with bed sheets, blankets, pillows, spoons, forks, and stainless plates to take to their each cells. Near the dispensary, they stayed for three days before they were finally sorted and dispatched to different sections of the buildings. There in the large room near the dispensary, the three of them were to stay with a Brazilian man who was an HIV/AIDS patient, and hasbeen there for days, pleading with the Italian Justice department for him to be extradited to his country of origin. Although the Italians denied him of his rights as a sick patient because he was arrested while trafficking three kilograms of cocaine to Italy from Brazil, and was to be sentenced to nine years imprisonment. He was a very learned person and was speaking fluent English probably because he has lived in the U.s. for many years before. The man who actually did not give up his hope to be extradited, did wrote complaints and sent them to the Human Rights Commission in France, and was waiting for their response. David's friend who could not bear to see themselves being held in the same cell with a man having HIV/AIDS, were beginning to grumble and lay their own complaints to the prison authority, saying it was wrong and unfair. David who was the only person communicating with him, was also afraid not to be infected with the virus, so he knew he has to uphold the idea to be removed immediately from that cell. "Discrimination is in everyone of us, only if we accept the fact."

When David left that room, he was taken to a new section where he was joined with two white Italians, Enzos (Lorenzo and Vicenzo). They were very nice to him when he first arrived there, because of how they were rendering him every assistance he needed. They were also responsible for his cigarettes and food. He said he liked them and would have keep up with them if not the fact that they were stark illiterates and he was the opposite side of their kind. Although they gave him

everything he needed except happiness and tranquility, which made him left them after having struggled to spend two weeks with them in that cell.

When he first arrived there, he knew he would have to be possessing a coarse manner and be impolite to others just to create fear on the other prisoners the way he thought it was when watching an Hollywood movie. He started by not associating himself with his fellow black people even when they tried coming close to him to enlighten him of the tragedies he was about to set upon himself. He was a good friend of these two Italians who were also proud of him for refusing to get along well with his fellow blacks.

His first two weeks was rather to be called hell not cell, as waiting for one day to pass-by was like waiting for a hundred years. He watched around him, and everything he could see there in prison was hopelessness and fear. The scariest thing about it, was the violence he could witness everywhere—making him believe it to be a world where reality overpowers fiction. To him, at the beginning, it was clear how people could see themselves being held behind bars and still not regretting why they were there. He wanted to go back to the life he was living before; he wanted to go back to his childhood life so that he could remake his life and never end up where he was seeing himself.

The more he was staying indoors and not willing to go out to play with the other people outside, the more other prisoners and the warders were getting to recognize him pertaining to who he was. Not quite long, he was starting to engage in a dispute with his two cellmates because he would not allow them sleep at nights—he would not allow them sleep because of how bad he snores like a foghorn when sleeping. In spite how he tried to control himself while asleep, he could not, since it is a thing of nature. He laid complaints to the doctors in the dispensary and they told him there was nothing they could do about it, except he would have to undergo an operation—and he would have to pay for it if he insist. Although he was given some medicines for sometime until he forgot about his snoring problem and was complaining about his eye. As he became upset about the way one of his cellmate was troubling him at nights and also controlling him at daytime, he confronted him and applied to be transferred to another cell. Before he was transferred, he had a discussion with another Nigerian who borrowed him a novel to read and also told him to always demand for anything he wanted.

To assuage his grief, he knew he needed music. And since he was not allowed to watch MTV in the television inside his cell by his cellmates, he chose another way to do it by bringing his head out of the cell bars, and singing Oasis songs. From what he concluded in his heart, it was of no doubt, listening to Tupac music and acting upon it was bringing him more grief than happiness, which made him automatically turn his love for him to hatred—a great rap artist he once assumed to be his mentor. And since he could not do without music and the inspiration he derives from it, he decided to adhere to Oasis, making this band his new mentor and loving their songs more than any other music artist's song, as it was bringing back to him the hope which he already lost, seeing himself in prison being controlled by everybody. He came to understand what it means for one to be free even when that person is living in poverty, and at the same time, he could comprehend even the air he was breathing inside there was not free. He saw the demons inside him coming out again to mock him, claiming to have won the longtime battle he has engaged in with them. When he came to recall what 2nd David has promised him about living a happy and glorious life and forgetting about justice and equal rights for all mankind, then he asked himself if being held in jail was where he could find that happiness and glory that he was promised. It was then he started to reconsider if actually 2nd David was his soul or it was just his imagination. He said he thought at that very time, he was able to compare 2nd David to be the voice coming from his own God and sometimes from the devil in him. Which one is it, he still could not find an answer to the question even when he tried to.

After some days that he applied to be transferred, he woke up one morning to be told by one of the warder to park his belongings to the cell he has chosen to go. In the new cell, was one Moroccan, a morally upright Muslim who was being arrested for being illegal in Italy and was waiting to be deported back to his country. He was a very friendly person that David came to think if every Muslim were like him, no one in the whole wide world that will revile the Islamic religion. David saw in him the good reason to believe in the existence of a Supernatural Being. He loved and respected him for who he was, until another Moroccan came to join them. And immediately he came, everything changed, and where he was coming from became thrice better than where he found himself. He was beginning to think in his mind the lad was brought to come stay with them by the prison authority so as to make him feel he was in a prison not in a hotel where he could have time to read his books. The new lad was not even as heinous as the wicked prank called Tarik, who was coming to visit them only to intimidate and cause him trouble. Even the many times the wicked prank came upsetting, insulting, and frightening him, he persisted because he understood his dream was more fascinating. Many of them were coming to tell him he was comfort in distress, but he kept telling them he was happy and full of fun. He knew what he needed to do was to be sure of who he was, where he was going, and what his aims were. When he saw that they became more determined and strong to carry on their tasks, he applied to be transferred once again to another cell to be living with another Nigerian who later was set free after five days, and was then replaced by another Bulgarian who was an impostor and was having enough money with him and was ordering for everything he wanted for him. He was able to drink coffee and smoke his favorite Marlboro light cigarette. He was starting to relish the life he was living there in prison, since he was not having to pay any light bills or house rents or water bills and was able to visit the library to get some good books for free to read. He was beginning to spend more time, educating himself and was writing poems. He was also receiving free medical treatments and every evening, pretty nurses were coming to put eye drops in his two eyes while he was promised to be taken to the hospital for an operation one day. He was smart enough to be touching one of the nurse's breast every time she was around to apply the eye drops, the other one, he was also able to seduced and make her love him—love him to even dump her boyfriend who was also a warder there in the prison yard, and when the other warders heard about it, they thought of how to get rid of him. He continued with his self-education as he could see a remarkable progress in his life inside there. He was so delighted, thinking it was a big opportunity for him to read all the great books in the library just when he was coming across the many books written by his favorite authors. He was reading more books and more books and his mind was taking a mystical turn, and he saw himself going into metaphysics studies and was expanding his knowledge. It was all books and lecturing at a time he came to understand after reading these many books that, "What we write and what we are to write has been written before, only that it is being seen from a different view and achieved from a different source."

Just two days that he was alone after the Bulgarian left the prison, because the man was put under house arrest. In Italian prison, it was all about money and justice is yours. Despite that it was always said in Italian, *La legge e uguale per tutti*, but that is not true, just as it is not true in every other part of the world. This is a thing David said he took a stand for, and he will always do so in every aspect to further appeal to the governments around the world who published this law to think of how to stand by it and abide to it. He said he could see a boy steals a sachet of Uncle Ben's rice, and was held behind bars for six months, while politicians steals millions and are still living freely with their wives after having been fined and paid. He said he could see everywhere even in civilized countries, the way people make laws and not act according to it. He said, if law is a body of rules of conduct of binding legal force and effect, prescribed, recognized, and enforced by controlling authority—which means, every human being is subject to the law as long as law is implemented there where he or she lives. But why are some people above this law? Why do we have to implement them and also violate them? David said he could see it happening everywhere and every day, and it is only meant to punish the impoverished peasants.

Since David was not having anybody to visit him or rather someone whom he could receive his letter and was not allowed to call, because it was prohibited as long as there was no one who came to look for him. A prominent legal adviser, Marco Martini who was hired and paid by the Italian government became his only friend he could write to. The man felt so sorry for him, knowing that he was not having anybody who was offering him help; so he decided to do the best he could for him to be given the minimum jail terms for drug trafficking, which was two years and eight months, and with good behavior, he was to serve just two years.

Immediately after the Bulgarian left, another young man from Morocco who was also detained for some days for being illegal in the country and was to be deported back to his country, was brought to join him. The young man said-to-be practicing with an objective in life to become an Imam, was also very fanatic to an extent he was not allowing him watch anything in the television relating to civilization. He was also American number one enemy. David said something he really does not like about him was how he tried to persuade him to accept his own opinion and views on religion matters. This young man who believed himself to be a scholar, declined to acknowledge that religion should have to be a matter of personal choice. As for the young man, he saw himself more perfect while denouncing other people's religion. The young man also went as far to present to him the holy Koran written in English, and that was how he seized the opportunity to read it—a thing he has long wanted to do. From the way this young man criticized the Americans, David was able to evaluate how tough and severe most Muslims loathe the Americans and the reason why. He wrote a poem to describe what he believe this man thought of the westerners, mostly the Americans.

TELL IT TO A FOOL.

Say you wanna take me to heaven,
Now you drive my brain to run out of my head.
Since then, only I fathom that I can't do it even
As you declined my dream to grow instead.
Like a lion, I tend to live wild
To a time the sun starts to go down.
Say your rules I need to abide,
So I thought before I realized we are both clowns.

Tell it to a fool
That you've come to save me from my sins.
When it's your mission
To inflict on me confliction.
Tell it to a fool
That you've come to save me from my sins.
When you've got everything
And, all I've got is nothing.

When I ceased to walk your way,
I gotta go back to where I can stay.
Better if I drink a beer and smoke a cigarette,
Just this way I think with my sins I can commemorate.
Your teachings more than a threat to me,

But, I ain't scared, cos I'm strong as Bruce Lee.
I guess you didn't hear what I just said
About letting me be as free as a bird,
So we can turn these melodies into happiness.

David said he believe everybody does have his or her own perspective, and from his own, he think it will be better to let the lying dogs lie. So, for this reason, he wrote this poem.

PUSHING FEAR ASIDE.

When noone thought not to be hurt,
So we better depart from the power we've sought.
For me, I love to live my life on Earth,
I don't care if you wanna stay with death.
Few people are gonna be on my side,
To live a life, pushing fear aside.

He said he also came to understand that from how this lad hated the westerners, he could give his own advice to many who would want to listen that, "The earlier we quit the notion of how to conquer the world and make everybody live to our choice, the better for us to live peacefully." He said he prefer to be an upholder of civilization than to kick against it, and he also believe in democracy and every other things that make man achieve a more better life. But we should as well respect other peoples opinions and ways of life. This he said because, in his later life when he returned back to Spain after having been deported to his country from Italy, he read a post in Facebook, saying, "To develop a peaceful society, men must be governed." He said because he is so accord with this idea, he wrote, "Men must be governed. But it has to be built on justice and equal rights for all." He further went to elaborate on the reason why he said so. And he wrote, "To love is easy as to hate, but to love is vital, as it can take us all to paradise, which they spoke of that is here on Earth."

While he was still inside the same cell with this young Islamic fundamentalist of Moroccan origin, he began to feel more uncomfortable and unhappy, as the young man's friends were coming over to intimidate and mock him for always being indoor and not going to the open field to join other people. His fellow Africans, though were also saying things about him at his absence, but were always coming to see him to chat with him. Even the two Italians that he has previously stayed with, reconciled with him, and others who were not his friends became very interested in making friend with him. He was also recognized instantly by the director of the prison and all the other people assigned to work there. When he heard how everybody were spreading rumors and gossips about him, he knew it was an advantageous circumstance for him to try to change the lives of these prisoners. He wanted to let them know they could still turn their lives around to become great people in the future only if they choose to. The prison authorities were also using this chance in trying to reach a message to the other prisoners to think of how they could learn from their mistakes and become law abiding citizens, while David was trying to change the minds of the prison authority to stop believing the prison is built only for business and profits, instead to rethink that the prison should be set to rehabilitate people, not to destroy them. After a while, one Briton, Joe McInulty became his best pal and was exchanging books with him. Joe, said-to-be Scottish, has left London where he was living to go and stay in Banjul, Gambia where he was lured into drug trafficking. He was coming to Italy with three kilograms of cocaine and three kilograms of heroin in his luggage when he was arrested at the airport and brought to the prison. He did marked himself with a knife while fighting for the right to be extradited to his country. The British embassy in Italy also appointed a lawyer to assist him, and also to send him books and many other necessities including money. As for David, his embassy would have requested he work inside there so he could save some money to pay their embassy bills. When David gave Joe the two books he brought along with him to the prison—the GREAT EXPECTATIONS, written by Charles Dickens and ANGELS AND DEMONS, written by Dan Brown, he said he read it and swiftly returned it, complaining of how frightening they were. They both became good friends and made the decision to stay in the same cell with one other Bulgarian who was at his twenties and was arrested for trafficking five kilograms of cocaine together with his girlfriend who also was nineteen.

Life became splendid for David since he started staying with Joe and the Bulgarian. They were all getting along well with each other even when he snores, but because they were all co-operating, things were good for all of them. David, at that time tried to write to his sister in Spain, telling her he was sorry for what he did, and admitting he made a mistake which he was never going to repeat again. But she never replied his letter making him complain to the prison authority that his letters were being seized. He also wrote to one of the girl working with the real estate agent that was supposed to help him sell his house, telling her he was sorry and that she should inform his lawyer there in Zaragoza about it. But she never replied him and never informed the lawyer about it because she was upset he has seduced her several times and asked her out for a date and later neglected her, which made her think he has also done the same to the lawyer.

Living in prison and having no one to pay you a visit, or write to you when you are not allowed to make a phone call, was like saying, you were dead already, as everybody who knew you has long forgotten about you. It was tough for him, making him feel sad, empty, and depressed with no hope of survival. He thought it will be better for him to commit suicide, but when he read some of the poems he wrote, hope returned back to him, this time to stay and never to walk away. To overcome sadness and depression, he engaged himself more in reading and was about to read his eyes out. He also engaged himself in different types of activities—like taking an Italian language course, patisserie and confectionery course, and he was also striving to join the music course—although he was repelled several times, even when he kept trying and trying and was never given a chance, probably because they were all seeing him to be too smart to be turning his life of agony and the tidal waves of adversity that befall him into an ocean of joy. The American movies and TV-shows he was watching on television were also contributing to his happiness, making him laugh and smile when he was supposed to be sad, and for this simple reason, he said there is no way anyone could loathe the Americans, seeing that they were born to entertain the world and make the planet, Earth, a happy place to live if not for the politicians there who believe too much in money and power.

In spite that he was being disliked by many of his fellow prisoners—majority who were Muslims and some others who were atheists, deliberately because he would not omit one Sunday without attending the church to worship God, and also being disliked by the church priest and many of the warders, because they all understood how he intensely disliked the Roman catholic for all their past evil deeds and was enlightening other prisoners about it; he kept doing what he was doing and not listening to talks about him, because he believed everyone has the right to participate in activities of their choice, and the course of him always being frequent in the church was not truly to worship, but to sing the Christian hymns and songs of praises along with the other people, because to him, it was a way for him to free himself from the bondage he was held in; it was his only way of life, a thing he derives pleasure from that makes him happy, and that is music. He was also going there because he believed he could converse with others who were not in the same section with him, so as to learn from them. In most time he was always arguing with them, because he said, "Learning from others does not mean you have to agree with them. You argue to come to the fact," and that is what he was doing that was irritating many others. To him, by so-doing, his ability to see other people's point of view became clearer. The more he strive for a cause in this manner to join these prisoners together, the more everybody were coming to admire and cherish him, and there was an active power like a magnet pulling him in and in, deeper and deeper—making him believe if he could change these delinquents, he could also change the world. But who was he to think of changing the world? An impoverished peasant from Africa? Most people were trying to imitate him, and were trying to give up the idea of bragging about more high-level of crimes they were to commit whenever they become free. His fellow Africans became very proud of him because he is black, and was doing some wonderful works. He later wrote a song about how he felt at that time when he think about the problems engulfing the world and come to comprehend the need for us all, the people of the world to come together and be one, so as to be able to track them down. He said he believe we can, if only there could be a unification of the hearts of every man living on Earth, to see to these problems and do a real soul-searching to know that we are responsible for all these problems, and we are also the ones to solve them. Starvation, he said will not be a problem if we find in our hearts how to eradicate it. Since we are having enough to feed the whole wide world, why do we still allow ourselves to watch others starving to death, why, why? Or why do we fight wars when we can squander that money for manufacturing bombs in better projects to engage in combats against strange diseases and natural disasters? Or why is there terrorism when we can love our neighbors and live freely with them regardless of their race, religion, and national origins. David said, he could see to it that, it is a big disgrace to see that human beings are still living like animals by killing and fighting each others even when we claim how civilization is fast approaching a tipping point; he said he could not comprehend how man could utter out the word civilization from his mouth when we can not love and treat our nearest neighbors the way we wish them love and treat us; he said he believe people should look up to that which we all call civilization, which does include equality among every living human beings; he said he also read about how many people describe human dignity to be seen as the images of God, which is true. We are the images of God. Then how could we believe in God and claim we love Him and not love ourselves? Human dignity, otherwise known as human values. He said he was once told by a great scholar that, if we humans could respect this human dignity to see that we no longer harm and kill ourselves for the sake of attaining power, instead, assisting, caring, and supporting one another, we can be able to achieve and maintain a state of well being. David said he could see himself as a thief, a drug dealer, an impostor, a swindler, beguiler, a wrong doer, and many more, but he could also see himself to be a man who believe he has to make some sacrifices to reach a goal of how the world can be united for a change to heal humanity and the planet he lives in, and to do this, he knew he has to throw himself into a monumental task—heart and soul, so as to do the work which he was sent to do. He said many a time in the prison, he tend to isolate himself and prefers to live a life in seclusion, even when many others disliked him for this. He said he love to, because it was a way for him to envision a world where there will be justice and equal rights for every world citizen, a world where hunger and poverty will not be a problem, a world where people will not be terrorized, a world where there will be no wars and people living with fear, and also, a world where Blacks, Whites, Hispanics, Arabs, Indians, Chinese, Aborigines etc, will see each other as one, because we are truly one. For this, he wrote this song.

WE ARE ONE.

We are one of the Father and Creator.
We are family, we are His children.
We are one, we are the Human Race.

No matter the color of race we belong.
No matter the religion we've adopted.
No matter the gender we belong.
No matter our profession.
No matter the language we speak.
No matter our age differences.
No matter our marital status.
No matter our birthplace.
No matter how wealthy we are.
No matter the poverty class we belong.
No matter the stage we are in life.
No matter where we live.
No matter where we come from.
We are one, we are the Human Race.

He said he believe if truly the people of the world would think of how to contribute to the uplifting of humankind in the solidarity of covenantal oneness, then we must return back to the real principle of life which is the basic principle Jesus Christ preached to us in his Sermon On The Mount, LOVE. "Love is a great thing, and it is the only sacrifice, the only sacrifice to triumph," as he has said several times. David said he could not see the need for a man eating and getting fat that he cannot move from where he is sitting when another man gets thin as he starves to death. That want-it-all thing is likely said to be inhuman, and it is greed, and the outcome is always a ruination. The worst about it, is when we tend to take away from those who are having just little to live with. He said as for him, he does believe, "It is usually more profitable to give to the needy than taking from him, so as for him to have something on his own and never return back, demanding and demanding." He said he could also understand that, "A wealthy man is not he, who earns a lot and lavish it on himself alone, living life to the fullest to attain pride. A wealthy man is he, who earns a little, but still volunteer to help assist the penniless who is starving to death." And after that, he said he could fathom how many poor people view wealthy people and envy them, and that made him said, "A poor man does not have to look at other people who are rich and regret why he is alive. He has to look at himself and be proud of who and whom he is."

CHAPTER 29

D AVID WAS LATER OFFERED A cleaning job which was to last for three months, as it was the rules made by the prison authority for every prisoner who applied to work. He was beginning to feel like he was rebuilt, as he was also having enough time to focus on his studies and poem-writing. He was also doing well in the confectionery course and was almost very perfect in speaking the Italian language—a language he said he found more interesting to speak than speaking Spanish. It was so easy for him to learn to speak it, simply because it is so similar to the Spanish language. But he came to like it better because, he said he found it very romantic and poetic. And to convince his form teacher he was having too much interest in learning it, he wrote a poem for him to read.

Piano, piano caminando intorno alla terra.
Ma, piu veloce di una macchina.

Although this poem impelled his form teacher to be seducing him since he was gay and was already falling in love with him. He also experienced being detested by many other prisoners after having tried so for him to have sex with them and he declined. To become gay was easy there in the prison, and he prayed every day he was not lured into it because of money, as almost everyone including the prison director, popularly known there as Brigadier, were having that same perspective of—it is just a normal thing to do here. They all wanted him, they all believed in him, and they all wanted to be included in his life biography.

He felt delighted when he started working and was paid after the first month. He was able to ordered for himself from his account, everything he needed, which were mostly coffee and cigarettes and potatoes. He was glad he was able to help others who were in need, as many others had helped him. He became too generous, offering cheap hand-rolling tobacco to those who were in need. Despite he was not having enough money in his account, he knew he had to do it, because he knew they needed it. He looked back to the time he arrived and was not having anyone to send him money, but he was being rendered help by different people—Italians, Moroccans, Tunisians, South Americans, Africans, and many others. He knew he was indebted to them all even when he knew he was never going to see them again. The money he had in his wallet when he was arrested was never given back to him despite the many times he wrote to the prison authority to explain his financial situations to them. But with the help of the other prisoners, he was able to survive. He said he so appreciated everything that he was offered by his many prison mates. He appreciated how the Briton, Joe McInulty spent the little money he earned for working to assist him; he appreciated how they share ideas and how they both drink coffee with cream and smoke their hand-roll cigarettes and watch MTV, because these were the many things that kept him alive.

After the first month he started working, Joe was sent away to another prison in Sardinia, leaving him and the Bulgarian, and was later replaced by another Nigerian, Sam whom they quarreled every time even till the last day he left, because he never allowed him and the Bulgarian watch MTV and other programs they have always love to watch before his arrival. Joe's absence was like a part of him was gone, because of how he missed his Scottish accent of English and the many ways they discuss about Britain, Italy, and human rights. He missed Joe, just as he also missed some other prisoners who were always there for him and were the families he never had.

One morning, he woke up to meet a letter that he was to get his belongings together to leave that prison that same day to another prison. He was sad and wished they could let him work for more time to save some money. He was sad, because he knew he was to miss some of his good friends and the life he was already getting adapted to; he knew he was to miss the every Sunday worship in the church; he knew he was to miss the faces of the pretty nurses that were coming to put eye drops in his eyes; he knew he was to miss the social workers coming to render them help, voluntarily; he knew he was to miss the confectionery where he used to eat freshly made and hot pastries; he knew he was to miss the library and all the good books that were inside that he yearned for to read; he knew he was to miss everything about that prison that he loved and was about to make him turn the place into a home. He loved the place, because there, he was able to relax his brain, meditate, and be creative. He loved that prison, because he was recognized and was being respected by majority of the warders and the prison director, who also ordered him to be taken to another larger and more equipped hospital to be treated and also for him to see the light outside the prison yards. Although, he knew they did so, just for him not to be oblivious of the more beautiful and better life he could be living outside.

In the new prison of Vercelli, near Turin, he was welcomed with different people just the way he was also welcomed with different rules and regulations. Life became very miserable just like the first day he was arrested. He was under the illusion he will break out of the prison and run away even when he knew that was just a fictional Hollywood movie. For two weeks, he thought of the many plans he could apply to get himself out of the prison and came to see that there was none. He was beginning to think and believe there were no choices available for him to change the situation which he was, rather than to commit suicide—a thought he once had and has forgotten. He could not keep up with the new life he was living, nor could he keep up with the new people he met there, not to talk of the warders who were seeing him and the other new prisoners as some new delinquents that needed to be dealt with. It was at this time he realized he was in a prison, not a hotel that he thought it was at the time before he left Busto Arsizio. At this time, he tried to talk to his God, and he could not hear His voice answer him; he tried to seek his face, and he could not see it. He disliked who he was and the reason he was seeing himself with different sets of culprits and villains who many of them were having little or no formal education. He asked himself how long he was to proceed with the kind of life he was already living. Then he recalled what he did that led him to where he was. And, when he did, he grasped he was a fool to have dedicated his life to committing crime. He came to be able to interpret the meaning of the phrase GUNS AND ROSES. He saw that guns were for the fools while roses were for the wise, and he was the fool. He wrote a poem to edify others who actually cannot figure out which group they belong to.

GUNS AND ROSES.

A fool eat and fall asleep,
A wise man, to him knowledge is his food.
A fool will say, we need no education,
A wise man, education is the key to success.
A fool will say, tomorrow will think for itself,
A wise man plans for his future and the next generation.
A fool talks and never stop talking,
A wise man does a little talking and meditate always.
A fool's got nothing to give to make him a hero,
A wise man's treasure is what we see today.
A fool despise knowledge and end up in vain,
A wise man seek knowledge before money.
A fool, because of money, he commits every crime,
A wise man, to him, crime is a disease.
A fool hear you talk and talk but never listen,
A wise man, a word is enough.
A fool never learn from his mistakes,
A wise man learns from his mistakes and never repeat it.

Guns are for the fools,
Roses for the wise.
Guns and Roses—is what we've got in this world.

He said when he came to correlate this issue with how he looked into the issue of the rich and poor countries, he came to believe most of the problems encountered by these poor countries are caused by many of their leaders, who out of greed, have decided to be embezzling their countries wealth got from the mineral resources. He said he could look at it from his perspective that everyone of us has had a role to play in the three major problems engulfing our world. He said he could see corruption in most of these poor countries as a major problem to their economic advancement and social stability. And for this to be dealt with, it is the citizens that their voices needed to be heard, and to do so, there has to be a strong financial support from the United Nations to sponsor some of the educated men and women of good reputation to become parts of the political community in the country. But fighting wars can only exacerbate the situation and lead these countries into a more impoverished life, and their standard of living will never improve. He said he believe the United Nations has so many roles to play, first by educating the youths, and later, fostering and supporting them to participate in the elections. He said he could also understand that most of these Islamic fundamentalist who intend to cause confusion among the countries around the world, are said to have lived most parts of their lives in poverty, and when they are conditioned and money is offered to them to live and enjoy life, they accept it and carry out the tasks. David said he could also comprehend that there are much more for the rich countries to do to improve relationships between every countries around the world, not to let everything be done for financial benefit, but also to see others as humans and think of how to assist them. He said he could see many humanitarian assistance from the west to these poor countries being televised, but things still remain the way they were from the beginning of time. He said, better things needed to be done and everyone acknowledge this, but we are still not prepared to do it now, because of greed and the strive for power.

Coming to believe that one day he will be leaving the prison, he swiftly relinquished the notion of escaping the prison. With just little time, he was able to gained access to the library, and when he did, he became more confident with himself and was hopeful for some better days ahead. The first day he visited the library was among the happiest time he ever had in his life, as he saw the many books written in English by most of his favorite English, Irish, and American authors. He wanted to read them all. Immediately, he picked up one of them and started to read it. He kept reading and was also doing his poem-writing, and as he did, he was being recognized by all the warders, and things automatically changed for him without him knowing why. From then on, he was able to grasp the proverbial phrase, "Patience is a virtue." He was glad for not having done the dottiest thing to execute his plan of escaping from the prison. He was happy again, since he already found good books to read and write his poems. To complete his happiness, his Oasis music cds were all returned back to him, and when he finally met one Nigerian there who gave him his disc-man to play the cds, life became sweet. Then he was able to sing loud along Oasis songs all alone when others were in the open field. He came to like his new prison better than where he came from, since they were allowed to shower twice a day unlike where he came from where they were only allowed once and sometimes no shower. Every on Sundays, he was also able to attend the Roman catholic church inside there and the Reverend priest was very sympathetic that he has to share two to three cigarettes for everyone who asked for it—and that was motivating many of them, including the Muslims to be attending the church mass. He was also able to work out in the gymnasium where there were better equipment than the other prison where he was before. At that time, the 22nd nation Olympic game was held in China, and he was able to watch every of the sports and games mostly the basketball. He and the other Nigerian lad who was a great basketball fan and also a player, were able to scream as they watched the U.s. Dream Team crowned champions. It was all good, life was good for him, and he was glad he was still alive. Although, he felt much for his mother and wanted to see her alive. He recalled the last time he talked to her on phone, and how he promised to meet her. He knew for long, she has been sick and might even die because of him. Not quite long, he and his other Nigerian friend were transferred to another section where all the doors were opened 08.00 a.m-08.00 p.m every day, and they were allowed to shower any time they wish. He started a new Italian language course which he later found disturbing, because of their form teacher who thought she could fool him just the way she was fooling the other lads. He knew he was supposed to be teaching her not she teaching him, and for this reason, any time he was in the class, both of them were always engaged in arguments since, "Two captains cannot be in a ship." Although he has previously fought with one Algerian who was brought into his cell and could not tolerate how he was snoring. The Algerian woke up one night and pounced on him, and when he could not resist it, he fought back despite that he was seriously injured with a pen. And that was the only time he was seen fighting by the prison authority, and for that reason, he was not to placed in the prison isolation cell. He also confronted one of the warder who called another black African from Gambia, *nero*, and when the lad warned the warder not to utter the word again, he repeated it. When David heard this, he laughed, believing it to be a joke. But when the warder saw the lad reporting this issue to David, he rushed towards them and ordered the cell doors to be shut. David saw that he was hostile, so he tried to plead with him to be calm, but what he heard was different. The warder urged him not to utter any more word from his mouth, and that made him erupted in anger over the issue. For more than three hours, he was bawling and yelling while everybody were pleading with him to be calm. The warder was later transferred from that section to another one—and that is the only time when he knew justice has prevailed, because it was not wrong to call him *nero* but it was wrong when he kept repeating it even when the Gambian warned him not to. It was like he was mocking him with the color of his skin, which is very childish for a man more than twenty-year-old to be doing.

At that same time, the American election was becoming as said by many people outside the U.s. to be simultaneously entertaining and horrifying. To David, it was just more than that, because of how much he has wanted that change to come over to America and to the other parts of the world. Although he has been very current and topical, as he remained enthusiastic about the election and how it was going to end. He knew at that very time, the Americans needed a better person and more competent and brilliant president to lead them. And when he looked into it, to him, Obama was the most capable qualified aspirant to be the president of the most powerful nation in the world. He saw him as a silver-tongued politician. He loved him, first, because he was black and has come to reveal to the world, a different description of black race. He said this, because many people have long seen the black race to be less intelligent as they could see the insanely high violent crime rate among blacks in America, while the blacks in Africa constantly engage themselves in fighting wars. Secondly he knew he was the man many people, including him have long spoke of many years ago. He could see that the world needed a change, and he knew he would have to do something on his own to bring that change, and to do so, he has wanted to have an half-caste child because he believed, a mixed raced baby was to be the Moses to come lead us out of this bondage. He wrote a poem for this, describing himself and many other music artists as the birds who have come to foretell of this.

THE MOSES TO LEAD US OUT OF EGYPT.

The birds came down from the sky to sing songs,
They sing songs while making friends with us.
Of the Nazis and the Communists, after the fall,
To an end all wars have come, I thought.

I'm sick and tired of what I'm seeing
That's tearing my heart into pieces.
I've got no option, but I've got weapons
To chase these dangerous flies
Back to the city of my forefathers.

My inward thoughts to bring back to life
The Moses to lead us out of Egypt.
We all really need to be calm
Cos, there's no cause for alarm.

Mama say I was born with two souls,
Meaning I can redefine life with words.
When my food's been cooked with dreams
And my breads's been buttered with love.
So we're gonna stop eating our silence
Which is setting smiles of fire in our faces.

When Obama first started his campaign, he knew about him and thought of him. He recalled when he read Martin Luther Kings Jr. I HAVE A DREAM speech, he knew there was going to be a time a black man will be the president of the United States. But he also knew he was going to be a white/black man. He love Obama not only for the reason that he is black, but also because of his great speeches. His message was of hope to pass through the dark night to where the sun shine. His "YES WE CAN" speech, was of no doubt, a speech that motivated every good American to think of doing the right thing at the right time, and not to look into his color of race to elect a leader to lead America and also to lead the world.

It was true that David would have preferred Hillary Clinton, if not that Obama was there. He love Hillary, first, because she was the wife to former president Bill Clinton, a man he could see as one of the greatest president that has ever ruled America, but he later became more controversial and confused during Obama re-election campaign, maybe because he would have wanted his wife to be the president so that he could lecture her very well on how to lead a nation. He has ruled America to install peace and economic stability which every Americans enjoyed. A stable source of funding was created and things were good, good for the Americans and the entire world. Unlike Bush who ruled to bestow upon majority of the Americans poverty and frustration while also creating hatred and enmity among every nations—and yet he is still loved by many Americans who are said-to-be neon-conservatives and warmongers. Secondly, David said he love Hillary, because she is among the type of women that are needed in our every day society. You see, "Many women in our every day society believe in succeeding to achieve everything they desire in life no matter what it takes, even if it comes to giving out their body to achieve it. They also have forgotten that, a woman could succeed in life and make it to the top without having to exploit herself sexually or making fool of herself to men." Hillary is among these women who made it to the top without having to fool herself. But Obama became an inspiration to David, as he watched him speak. In accordance with fact, for long he has wanted to be Leonardo Da Vinci, Galileo Galilei, Aristotle, William Shakespeare, Charles Dickens, D.H Lawrence, Edgar Allan Poe, Oscar Wilde, Ralph Waldo Emerson, Oasis, Tracy Chapman, Bob Marley, Martin Luther King Jr, Nelson Mandela, Robert Kennedy, Michael Jackson, and many other great artists and activists. But when he saw Obama, his heart was captured by his message of hope and change. He believed Obama was going to win the election if truly the Americans were prepared to keep race aside and face the fact that they needed a leader to get them out of the mess the Bush administration landed them. To him, he was deeply disturbed by America's declining influence as a world super power and China's rising influence. And this was what the Bush administration failed to acknowledge as they continued to fight wars while the Chinese were concentrating on building their economy. David said he grasped that the Bush administration did not really know who their real enemies were. "A dangerous fighter that I am afraid of, is not the one with a frown face, but the one who fight with a smiling face." Russia was America's number one contender, as supposed by the Bush administration, but it was China. And because they are smart and were very quiet, the world thought they were foolish. "No one is really foolish. Everybody are getting wiser every day." Even as the Chinese economy was growing faster than it was before, the U.s. Secretary of State, Condoleezza Rice and the Secretary of Defense, Donald Rumsfeld were both campaigning they were going to win the wars in Iraq and Afghanistan, when truly a wise and learned man would look at it and see that there was not any winning of these wars, apart from losing, losing of lives of innocent Afghans and Iraqis, and then losing of lives of the U.s. soldiers and also losing of billions and trillions of dollars. David said he felt so sad about how these soldiers were dying and yet many were being sent and what those who survived the wars gets, were honor and medals of commendation for bravery, but what the fallen soldiers get, cannot be explained.

David was worried he was going to lose his house in Spain to foreclosure—the same house that ruined his life and motivated him to start living a life of crime, even if he could see that he was also greedy. He thought he could be able to sell it and still make some profits, not knowing the Spaniards were already in a financial crisis. He continued to write to his lawyer, pleading with him to help him, since he was told before he was going to fight for him to be extradited to his country. In spite that it was also a law passed in the Italian parliament for every illegal immigrants in the country to be deported back to their countries of origin, while those in prison should be extradited. He kept writing to his lawyer who was also doing everything he could to help him. But he was told he was to stay for at least one year in prison since he was supposed to serve two years out of two years and eight months, depending how good his conducts were, before his case will be heard by the public prosecutor who was in charge. He was writing to him to help him apply for all his properties and money seized by the police to be retrieved, while he was also writing to the former prison where he was before so that they could send all the money he was having in his account there to him. He waited and waited and nothing happened. But he kept writing to the director of his former prison, accusing all of them of being the criminals. He wrote that they were worse than the delinquents being held behind bars. But as time went-by the money left in his account there were sent to him, and when he received it, he was glad, due to the fact he could be able to order cigarettes, coffee and other foodstuffs he needed for himself since he has been suffering and was begging people for it. He got relaxed and was waiting for the day he was to be extradited as promised by his lawyer. At this time, he met with one of the social worker who was from Tunisia, but was granted naturalization as an Italian citizen. He explained everything to him, with faith he was going to help him.

As he continued to watch CNN, purposely because of the U.s. presidential election, he saw it to be more horrifying than entertaining. He was also very much afraid Obama was going to be assassinated before the election day, because of how he took a look back to American history and saw how many great American presidents, politicians, and activists were being assassinated—five of them, he said there is a need for all Americans, mostly blacks should always have to commemorate the anniversaries of their deaths: Abraham Lincoln, John F. Kennedy, Robert F. Kennedy, and Martin Luther King Jr. David said he could see these great people to have sacrificed their lives for freedom and human dignity even if they were not all saints. And when he took a look back to history and see how the black race has suffered and persisted, he wrote, "In realness, deep inside the heart of a black man, if he carries in it, the spirit of goodwill that will make the world a better place, no matter the tribulations, the desolation, the humiliation, and the inductions, he will overcome them and score a success." He said he wrote this willfully, because he saw how Obama was suffering to convince the American voters to comprehend that they cannot continue with the many wars they were fighting and at the same time be expecting an economic growth while many were ignoring him, simply because he was said to belong to another race that were never expected to lead a nation like America. He later wrote a poem to describe how he was seeing him.

ABOUT HIM.

About him there was something,
A sad and a pathetic thing.
He said the world need a change,
Now he's got the chance to get within range.

Suddenly, he fell on the wildest dream.
That was beginning to fade,
Was the light of a sunny afternoon,
And the world seemed to sink so soon.
By a feeling of hopelessness, he was overcome.
Sort of dragging down the spirits he fathom.

After a long time of grieving,
Thought he was done with all.
But always there, the first, sharp, and painful misery
Waiting for just such a moment.
As strongly as ever, it then came back
In waves, sweeping over him.

He jumped into the stream,
And coming out, only to see
A ray of summer sun shining again.
Then he realized there's still life ahead.

O' my wicked world,
How long do we have to wait
For us to let them bring the change?
The change is what I've been waiting for.

When David saw how Sarah Palin, the vice president nominated by John Mccain to be his running mate was causing confusions that was leading to the failure of cognitive ability for the Americans to hold on to their promise of making the world a better place, he wrote a poem to describe whom he believed she was.

JEZEBEL'S BACK TO LIFE.

She lives her life in a great city.
There, she's been made a queen and a lover.
An institution built to promote peace and prosperity,
There she's come to be the destroyer.
The devil that rules your world, now she is,

Cos, with her love, you're all lost.
Why about her, do you have to tell a lie
When you know you're to join the cry?

Jezebel's back to life.
For a repentance, she said she's back,
While all she's planning to do
Is nothing, but to lead the people into frustration.

A soldier, I'm not to fight,
But, a soldier I am in my heart.
So help me help the world
So we can capture and cast her into the fiery furnace,
Cos, that's where she belongs.

Out of the window, the world threw her,
And the demons sent her back.
To a boomerang, she's to be compared.
Dangerous is a boomerang.
With a boomerang, when you fool around,
You've got to know what you're doing.
Cast it away and it will comeback
And hit you in the back of your head.

He said he disliked her for the attitudes she possess to lure the Americans to fight more wars to exploit oils from these poor countries along with John Mccain, when actually Americans were saying—Look! we are done with wars and exploiting others, we can fix our economy without other people's wealth.

The more David was watching the election, the more he became interested in watching it, and the more he came to love America again, as he watch the poll rise in favor of Obama.

His interest in the election was making him not able to sleep at nights, since he would have to watch the TV and also read the new book he borrowed from the library, the book he has read several times and would not quit reading it, because of how he found the story interesting and also inspiring. It was OLIVER TWIST, written by the great Charles Dickens. Although he was being seen by all the warders as a bat who never sleeps at nights, but prefer to sleep at daytime. As he continued to watch the election and read, and was almost about to finish the book, one morning, at about 04:00 a.m, one of the warder came to inform him to pack every of his belongings, and that he was to be taken back to his country. He was startled with this news since he has long forgotten about his extradition and has decided to apply for a job inside there so that he could earn money, and moreover, he was coming to like the place and was thinking of writing his biography. He did not know what to do when he was asked to pack his belongings; he woke his cellmate who was still asleep to inform him. When he finished packing, the warder returned back to open the door for him, and that was how he left the prison.

Inside the flight that was taking him to his country, he met some other Nigerians, mostly girls who were arrested for being illegal and were prostituting in Italy. The only man among them was also a drug dealer who was imprisoned for five years and has served the full sentence, but yet he still was deported back to his country of origin, because Italy has already descended into a political and economic crisis. The then prime-minister, Silvio Belusconi then ordered the deportation of every illegal immigrants and ex-convicts, putting the blame on them while he was living a corrupt and extravagant life without anybody being able to voice out so as for the country to bring him to justice. He was rich, super rich, and powerful that everything he was doing was with no questioning. David said he was so dumbfounded when he saw that Italy, a country said to have once ruled the world during the Roman empire, a country were art and designs are said-to-be reinvented, a country where technology were being invented and was still a source of income, the home of the most of the greatest artists that has ever lived on Earth, the home of Leornado Da Vinci, the home of Galieo Galilei, and many others, was fast becoming only a home for the Mafias under a corrupt government, and no one seemed to be doing anything about it or were not concerned.

The police who were inside the flight with David were all possessing good manners since he was was not handcuffed and was free to go to anywhere he wish to go. One of the lady was more of a friend to him due to how they were always looking into each other's eyes and communicating in English. She later wrote her phone number and placed it inside his jeans pocket without him knowing till he arrived home to find out. He knew she did not inform him because of the other policemen who were around.

When they arrived at the airport, they were handed over to the immigration and police in Nigeria, who welcomed them home and also extracted money from them and set them free. Meanwhile, David's residence permit in Spain was handed over to him before he left Italy, and he swiftly hid it under his leg inside the canvas shoe he was wearing that was offered to him by the Reverend priest inside the penitentiary.

In the airport of his country, he was supposed to be arrested and jailed for possessing a proxy passport, but he was set free while the passport was impounded, because the immigration pitied him, seeing that he was already worn-out. He slept in the airport until the next morning when he finally took a bus and left to his city which is about two hundred kilometers from Lagos, the one-time capital of Nigeria where most of the country's commercial and financial business is carried out. When he arrived home, he could not help himself to resist to shed tears, seeing all of his families again, especially his mother who was getting too old because of her illness and she has not set her eyes on him for more than nine years.

Back in his country, he saw that many young men and women he left were doing far better than he expected, while some were still suffering, looking for their daily meals. Those who were still very poor were those who actually were lazy and tied down with self-esteem and could not stand up on their feet to find a solution to their problems. He was beginning to regret the reason he left his country to go and be living in Europe, as he was seeing many of his old friends living a more better life, married with kids, driving pricey and luxury cars while he still was not able to learn how to drive. He saw that many who also have left the country and returned back, were also living their good lives happily, while spending money on themselves. Many of his families who were demanding for his help when he was living abroad, were living even more better than he expected. Seeing what he was seeing, he knew that he was lost for not returning back to his country every year to visit his families and also to know what best he should be investing his money in. Investment in his country was easier than it was in Europe, because of the fact that it is almost a tax-free country. He knew he would have not stayed too long without returning back to his country if not for the American dream that he was having and that was bringing him a devastation. He hated himself for having wasted his time too long, dreaming when nothing has changed. He hated himself for having dreamed to go and live in America, the same America he later came to dislikebecause of how he saw majority, mostly neon-conservatives believed too much in power and money, causing others pains and griefs and having no regret. He wrote a poem to describe how he felt for having loved America and was being disappointed.

BECAUSE OF YOU.

I don't know what you've put inside of me
Not to make me live the life outside of me.
When you've thought me to run and fly,
I still cannot break the force that took me by.
In your joy, your friends my friends.
In your conflicts, your enemies my enemies.
Tell me your visions takes on love and peace
Cos, I'm born with a love of justice.

Because of you,
I cannot go to the land
That I wish to stand.
Because of you,
My life's been held at stake,
To scare me away from you.
Like they've asked me to break
The oath that I took with you.

Now that my memories are back again,
My strength, I'm waiting to regain.
I'm gotta let you know straight away
That I'm weak and weary of the odd ways.
We've gonna practice what we preach
To give the world what it desire,
Which will make us stronger and go higher
And grab the sweetness to rest beside the still waters.

After some days that he arrived and has traveled to two different cities where he believed might be prosperous, safe, and comfortable for him to live, he found that he needed money to do anything that he wish to do. He thought of associating himself with the politicians so that he could become part of them, but he understood that, to gain a political influence, money was a vital approach in communicating with the people. He also saw that guns, knives, cutlasses were most essential to prove your capability of being a leader in one of the most corrupt country in the world. He swiftly quit the idea and started thinking of how to return back to Europe. Europe, where he was previously living and was complaining about the hardship and the too much stress, was then becoming the heaven that was impossible for him to reach again. When he went to meet his friend who was also deported the same day he was deported to his country, he was advised to be patient so that they could get themselves engaged in something more relevant and invest some money. He did not listen to him, since already, his plans were for him to return back to Europe so that he could go and look for the money he has hidden in his trouser inside his bag together with some other clothes. He thought he might also sell his house and make some little profit, looking back to the days when Spain's economy was still flourishing. He tried to call some of his friends to lend him a hand, but he was unable to reach any of them, and the worst of it, none of them even care to look for him since from the time he was held behind bars. He said he felt disappointed in his friends when he came to comprehend how everyone of them believed in, "Everyone for himself."

He continued to travel to Lagos to meet the immigration so as to get his passport back, but he was warned never to come closer to their office again or he will be thrown into prison. The more time he was spending in his country without having a purpose why he was traveling from one place to the other, the more he was getting to understand where he was and how he missed everything about the country. With this, he grasped that, "No matter what we benefit from civilization, we do not have to be oblivious of our old world—which is also our past, because it is our past and present that can define our future." He also realized that corruption and bribery were still very noticeable and were destroying the country's economy. The inadequate electric power and water supply was also forcing every individual to own an electric generator and bore-wells in their houses, and people in power were left unconcerned and were not doing anything about it since they were all benefiting from these problems. When he recalled how the youths in the western world were always participating in different types of sports, he said he became very much concerned about the lack of the excellent facilities for sports in his country, and he was so ashamed and was asking himself, where is all the oil money? In using modern technology, he saw that his country still lagged behind the world. Armed robbers were in everywhere while the police were hanging around the streets and roads, demanding for bribes, calling it, 'a token.' He was also perplexed, seeing that Nigeria was still not able to introduce a national identity card into the country's national system the way it was done in most African countries and in other parts of the world, which is necessary to prevent more crimes. The more he watched the people around him, the more his thoughts of returning back to Europe invoke. Although, he saw the many good things about the country; he saw how the people were fast in developing talents in music and arts. New music and films were coming out everyday, as music and films industries were making profits and many youths were also having the opportunities to secure jobs for themselves, giving rise to an increase in the country's employment rate. But what baffled him most, was how he watched the president and ministers make speeches and earned hands of applause when they were embezzling money and not doing anything to improve the citizens standard of living. He also watched in the television how the government was launching programs on how to invest more in agriculture—aimed at encouraging many of the local farmers to push forth in taking loans to develop their farms, grow crops and also plan their business future. He was glad it was happening, but deep down in his heart, he knew it was just a propaganda for the people in power to embezzle more money. Seeing everything, he wanted to stay in his country, a place he was born and bred; as a Nigerian, he wanted to live there and get something on to be doing—like going into music and be making money and enjoying himself like others, and as well, to enable him to communicate with the people through music. But he knew his dream was more than just enjoying life; he knew there is already a mission for him to accomplish, and to accomplish this mission, he would have to leave his hometown and walk very far to an unknown place. He said, as he was there, seeing how people were still suffering and smiling, he came to love his country more and also love himself being a Nigerian, one of the most corrupt country in the world, because he could see them as people who never give up their hopes for the future; he love Nigerians for being very tough and desperate to make money by engaging in every criminal acts, but he also believe, if they could turn this zeal they have in committing crimes into innovations and inventions, they will be more greater and better financially, socially, and in many other aspects of life and could one day rule and be the giant of the world, not the giant of Africa they claim to be—which they are not.

Seeing Nigerians imitate the west, mostly America in many aspect of life—like music and art, to David, he said he found it fascinating, but when he came to realize how some of the citizens were also striving for same-sex marriage to be legalized, he laughed and thought it to be a joke, but when he came to understand how most people from many countries in the west were in support of this idea, claiming themselves to be human right activists, it was provoking and was so absurd. He said he could see that Nigerians were having more critical issues to be dealt with—like improving the standard of education and fighting against bribery and corruption, and that should be considered as the first three priorities, while he could not see these human right activists travel to the country to finance a movement to peacefully protest for a change in government. It is not that he is against same-sex marriage, but it is better for us to stand by the fact and utter the truth. Everybody understand these people were having more problems to deal with already, then why the infiltration and interference of international bodies into the nation to cause a confusion for irrelevant issues, when the major issue remain unsolved? David said he still could understand that, even in some parts of these civilized countries, most people still believe homosexuality and lesbianism should not be explained, elaborated or justified since they believe it to be immoral and wrong. David said he will always uphold the idea of people choosing for themselves what they want, but not actually at this time, should a country whereby poverty seem to be an intense problem that need more attention, will be replaced by people fighting for same-sex marriage to be legalized. He said he found it insane—and also when he was seeing how most of the banks in Europe were playing some big roles in keeping the money of most of these corrupt politicians in his country and yet no one is saying anything about it or thinking of stopping them, then people were debating on same-sex marriage to be legalized.

Life could have been very easy and simple for him, if not that he thought that there was an obligation for him to fulfill. He believed he was already intimately involved in a project that was set for him by his unseen and unknown gods and goddesses that were living deep inside his heart, which he was sometimes referring to as his guiding angels.

As time went-by, while he was looking for a way to return back to Europe and was demanding a permission from his family to sell his half-built house so that he could raise money to purchase a ticket to fly back to Europe since his Spanish residence permit was still with him and he was already having a new passport. His niece, Joy who had just arrived in Spain and was spending her third year there, and has volunteered to become a prostitute despite his warnings, took a decision to send him the money. It was so astonishing, seeing how the little girl was doing just fine, having a house of her own and was spoiling his families with money, making them respect her more than they were respecting him and his elder sister, Tina who invited her over there. He could not say a word rather than to accept the money and purchase his ticket to return back to Spain.

One morning, when he woke up to get himself prepared to leave his state to the capital city of his country, he saw in the news that Barack Obama has won the U.s. presidential election—and as he watched the television, tears of joy were running down his cheeks, since he did not know whether to be crying or be happy. The door leading to his heart were all clasped and protected with some mighty rocks of joy. He jumped up and down, celebrating just like a man who won a lottery. He could not believe America, where a black man was not allowed to vote, was now a place where a black man has been voted to be the president. He was overwhelmed with happiness.

Even in his country, he could see that a person from his state was never allowed to become a president. He said he love America, because he believe in them and will not stop believing in them even if they are wrong in some aspects, they will always look for a way to do the right thing again. In matter of fact, he knew it was going to happen this way, but it was one of the few times he believed God is really existing, because of how he has prayed and fasted for many days just for him to experience this. When he later arrived at the bus station to take a bus to where he was going to, he saw how many other people were celebrating and rejoicing, and the only time he has seen his country in this same mood, was when they won the Olympic football tournament. Then he saw that Obama's election victory was not just a victory for him and the Americans, it was a victory for the world, it was a victory for all black people, it was a victory for all Africans, as they could see him as their own.

From what he learnt from the discussion he had with many educated, polished, and literary Nigerians, from what he read from the newspapers, and what was said by many of the political analysts, he fathomed that many Africans were starting to believe that the astronomical distance between the continent and the west, was getting more peripheral everyday and the atomic affinity was also being ruined. These were all happening due to the fact that most Africans were fed up of being exploited and lied to. They were also seeing the laws and culture implemented on them to be threats as it were violating their culture, customs, and traditional rights, and also putting them at risk. When these Africans looked back to slavery and colonial time, they find it formidable to ever confide in them. And because of all these, they have decided to find another way which they believe to be the right one to deal with their complex situations by involving in businesses and signing deals with the Chinese who actually were exploiting them more, by giving them what they never demanded for, for everything they possess.

Seeing Obama won the election was bringing them another hope of renegotiating with the Americans, believing he will not come to exploit them, as an American having with him part of an African heritage. David said he saw that these people were also fed up, dealing with the Chinese, because they understood them to be more treacherous than the British.

It is not that most people around the world, including David does not regard and respect the Chinese for who they are and what they have achieved, but they were seeing them as a rising threat to the global economy and they should be stopped. It is really frustrating to see how the Chinese economy was growing thrice faster than any other countries economy, and yet the people in China are still living in bondage. How could people be happy to see that China is fast becoming a country with the largest economy. What good will it be to the world if China becomes the next world superpower? No good at all, no good, since no one would want to be ruled by tyrants and communists. "Better the devil you know than the one you don't." David said he is more afraid of the Chinese than the terrorists, seeing the way they strive for power and are building their military and also developing new defense technologies, and are not working together with other civilized and advance countries to promote world peace. He said he truly love their everyday efforts to build their economy when others were relishing life. And, because he could see the country to be more modernized, and it is already more integrated in the context of economic partnership agreements among other countries. They started investing on restaurants, and later on technologies, and then on oil and every other financial investments with much hard-work and showing great perseverance. The Chinese brand could be seen coming to the front of other brands and even surpassing all expectations and they are selling to themselves, and mostly selling to the world. But something in life that they failed to acknowledge, is that the lack of human rights and legal protection that is a result of a government run by communists, can lead the country to an economic break down, causing a turmoil. It can separate the country and even lead to a civil war. Many Chinese who are traveling out of the country to invest in another countries, mostly in the west, might find it difficult to return back to live and be governed by the same communists. Their children who might have studied abroad and have adopted the western culture and are exposed to democracy—and seeing that it is a thing of freedom, might return back to fight for their land so as for democracy to be installed.

CHAPTER 30

A LREADY INSIDE THE FLIGHT GOING to Amsterdam, David was praying to his God, for the Dutch immigration not to check his documents to call the Spanish police to inquire of anything from them about him. But when they arrived at the airport and were at the transit gate to Madrid, he gave his documents to the immigration who were very much concerned to check if his passport was original rather than check his European residence permit. After awhile, his documents were returned back to him, and as he headed towards the boarding gate, he was beginning to thank his God, believing in Him more than he has ever did. It was so astonishing, seeing that he was not refused entering by these immigration. He thought because an expulsion order had been issued against him in Italy, there was no way he will be allowed to enter into any of the schengen countries. At first he could see how they were all staring at him, but immediately they checked his Nigerian passport and seeing that it was the new digital type, he was allowed to pass through the gate. When he finally arrived at the Madrid airport with no immigration demanding for his documents to be checked, he went straight into the washroom, and pretending to be pooping inside the toilet, he knelt down and prayed and thanked his God, Whom he could see changing things he thought were impossible to become possible. He vowed never to walk close to his fellow Africans who believe crime is a way of life. He vowed to work even if it happened to be the most tedious job on Earth, all he needed to do was to work, work, and work until he will be able to save some money and travel to Canada to go and live the rest of his life, get married, and have kids over there.

Outside the airport, he went to a tobacco kiosk and bought a packet of Marlboro-light, his brand, lit it and started smoking as he watched everybody going in and coming out of the airport. He thought he was still dreaming, seeing that he was in Spain once again after having left for more than a year and a month. He saw that he was in Europe once again, after having relinquished all hope that he was going to be seeing himself where he was.

He arrived at the house where he once lived, where he left to Holland, and rang the doorbell. When his friends saw him, they embraced and welcomed him back to Spain—which automatically was becoming Pain after the S—which was to signify sweet was taken away to be left with "It is not the right time, not even the right place."

The first thing he did that night after he found out everyone were asleep, was to bring his bag out from where it was kept to search for the 5,000.00 euros that was hidden in his trouser. But while searching, he found that the bag has been searched before. He found that some of his expensive jackets were even missing. He wanted to scream to wake everybody up, but he understood he might be sent out of the house to go and sleep inside the cold—making him shut his mouth and was asking himself why he did not leave the money in his account. But the bank would have taken it for his mortgage. Or if he gave it to his sister to hold for him, she might have used it and not been able to give account of it or return it back to him when he might needed it. Immediately, he knew he was to face with a more terrible life even worse than he faced when he first arrived in Spain and was feeding on garbage. He saw that it will not do him any good to tell anybody since there was no way they were going to believe him—and by informing them was never going to bring the money back to him, so, what was the need to do that if not only to tell your friends you were having that amount of money and was still complaining before you went committing more crimes to make more money that led you to jail?

After some days, he was able to call almost all of his family members to inform them of his successful arrival; he also called one of his friend, who was married to a German and has traveled to visit his families back at home and also to sell some of the fellow used cars he took there to make money, the lad whom he stayed in his house there in Lagos till the last day he left.

He thought it will be better for him to travel to Zaragoza to negotiate with the bank who gave him the mortgage, so that they might sell the house and give him his own profits. But getting there, he was informed of how much he was to be owing the bank if luckily for him the house is sold, since there was no one who was interested in purchasing a house because of the collapse of the housing market that occurred due to higher than expected home that were built all around the cities and villages in the whole of Spain. When he finally returned the key of the house to the same bank manager running the branch where he took the mortgage, and as the bank got the house appraised, he was informed he was to pay 16,000.00 euros for having failed to pay for his monthly mortgage for one year—which was included with the high interest rate and has occurred at the very time he was in jail. Hearing this astounding news made him gave up his faith of still living in Spain. He wanted to leave to another country where he could change his identity. He wanted to travel to Finland to seek asylum. But when he heard how the Finnish government were getting too strict with refugees coming there to seek asylum, he paused and waited for his residence permit to be renewed since it was going to be expired within three months time, so that he could travel to another European country to look for a job. While waiting, he saw himself faced with different and more complicated never-will-be-resolved issues in his life. He was controlled by the police and taken to the police station for investigation, because they believed he was already being expelled from every schengen countries since Italy was a member country. But he was later left alone and was warned by the police never to travel to the country again or he will be detained and jailed. Although, they were able to find out what he did in Italy when they called the Italians and were faxed some documents relating to the crimes he committed. He tried looking for a job, he saw that the money he was spending in doing so will even be enough for him to be feeding himself as he was seeing many Spaniards and immigrants losing their jobs and the unemployment rate all over the country was rising everyday. He tried applying for an unemployment benefit, but he was refused, because the law was changed and he needed to work for at least a month before he could apply. He did not know what to do next, seeing himself in the middle of heaven and hell and did not know which way he was to choose. The more he was thinking about his complex situation, the more the bank was calling him on phone, informing him of the debts he was owing them and demanding for how he will be paying. He became more afraid of himself and the society where he was living, as he was also afraid he was going to die soon of hypertension. Despite how he kept cautioning the bank to stop threatening him of the consequences he will be faced with for failing to pay the debts, they kept calling and calling that he could not withstand it and swiftly threw the phone away. At that very time, he vowed to his unseen God never to commit any crime again, but seeing his friends live happy lives with money always in their pockets while most Spaniards who owns the country were starving to death, he knew he has to recast his thought and do whatever they were doing even if he was sent back to jail, since he was no longer afraid to see himself back to jail to write his autobiography. He was more afraid of living in a world-said-to-be-free but actually was becoming a bondage for him, as he was already seeing himself a beggar, sleeping, and eating in different houses owned by different friends who were also pitying him because they understood his situation to be far worse than just a normal one. As going back to prison became his only option so that he could be given an opportunity to write a book without having to think of how he could be paying his rent and bills, he became very close to his friends whose only plan was to commit crimes and keep committing crimes.

One day, one of his friends called him on phone, and when he went to see him and was given another person's passport and a marriage certificate issued by a catholic church—all owned by another person to take to the civil registration office in a city not too far from Madrid. He was told the owner was not having time to come over to do it himself. He was promised to be paid 200.00 euros if he could go there to apply for an official family record book. Since David was new to this, he thought it might be easy for him to do without being recognized by anybody if truly he was the owner of the passport. Getting there, he did what he was asked to do and returned back without any problem and was paid the money he was promised. He saw that it was good and easy, so he told the boy to always call on him whenever he was needed. And the next week, he was called to do the same, and as he did he was also paid another amount of money. He liked it and was doing it continuously until at a time he was told by another person, that he was risking his life for little change. The boy also told him that every documents he was given was fake, but he thought he was lying. He became very popular for the job, and was being called by another boy to do the same for him.

One day when he went to apply for the same family book at the same civil registration office where he has been to before to apply, thinking the lady there was never going to recognize him again. All of a sudden, two policemen on mufti came close to him and took him away to their office to interrogate him and later dumped him in the cell for having committed forgery. And when the police found that he was already in jail before, they felt sorry for him. They saw that he was very smart and intelligent and was being used when he explained the situation he was to them. They wanted to help him, but they inquired he give them the name of the boy who sent him, and he gave them a wrong name. They later took him to the court and freed him after having spent one night in cell. The public prosecutor was also a good man who should have ordered his deportation, but because he was having a permanent residence permit, he planned to send him back to jail since that is where he preferred to be. His lawyer who was paid for by the government, saw him and also felt sorry for him. She was also able to defend him and asked him to plead guilty so that they could put him on probation till the time the case will be finally investigated and verdict will be passed. He was to report himself every twice in a month in every police court around the country. He was glad he was freed not knowing he was to start living a life worse than that of a person in prison. He knew the police did pity him, because of the many papers they saw in his bag—which were papers of the many music recording studios in Holland and Germany. One of them even told him he did not need to travel that far before he could become a musician. He advised him to look for some in Spain since there are very many studios, mostly in Madrid. In a matter of fact, at the initial time he was caught and arrested, he insulted them and the entire Spaniards—blaming them for his problems. But when he later came to see how he was treated more or less like a citizen of the country, he regretted for having said some of what he said. He came to love Spain, and thought he could succeed in making his dream become a reality there. He came to see Spain as his home. He came to fathom the reason why he has ran away several times and returned back only to meet with the same life and people whom he believe to be his worst enemies and also his best friends. He came to understand he is indebted to them. He said he knew no matter where he is and where he will be, he will always keep with him in his heart, the many good life that was bestowed upon him in Spain, and not think much about the adversity he was faced with.

After some weeks that he was detained and was put on probation, he was still living and feeding from one friend's house to another. He saw how they were operating their-so-called business. Some of them were after the prostitutes who were showering them with money, while some were into drugs, and the others were into credit cards—a new crime that was fetching them money more than any other crime. He saw that many hackers in India, China, and other Asia countries were sending personal data and credit card details of many Americans and Europeans to these Nigerians, and they were using them in purchasing goods and mostly flight tickets online. Some were cloning them on their personal debit cards and were taking it to the shops to buy electronics and mostly foodstuffs. David said when he watched this happening, he knew immediately the reasons why the Americans and other Europeans were having a more serious problem of a financial crisis. He knew there was a war worse than the war on terror that most people do not believe to be a threat. He knew there is a cyber war, and if the world cannot fight it, there will be no change in the financial and economic crisis in mostly the U.s. and Europe. He said he knew this, because most of these countries where these hackers were gaining ground, were in Asia, and he believed nobody over there is much concerned on this issue not to think of how to fight against it. He said it will continuously be an impediment to many countries economy or else they quit the use of credit cards.

David found himself still starving and was afraid to involve himself with these sets of friends who were dealing on credit cards and were making enormous amount of money. He was afraid, because he was already on probation and if caught with any crime again, that might send him to many years in prison. So when his friend, the same boy who sent him to the civil registration office called him to inform him of the new deal that was to come, he agreed to the terms and condition, just only for him to have some money to feed himself only by renting his document and passport out for 1,200.00 euros—the money which he spent to rent a room in one of his friends apartment and also to buy foodstuffs. But at the long run, the document was never returned back to him, making him become one of the illegal immigrant in Spain. When he entered one of the police station to report the missing document, he was arrested and was about to be deported back to his country, because they did look into his crime record and instantly believed he sold it. Although they later let him leave, thinking he was insane. And at this time, he was not just only frustrated and confused, he was insane, and the more he tried to observe his friends carefully, he came to see that almost all of them were uneducated, uninformed, ignorant, and uncultured. But he got baffled, seeing that these people were living happily and good, with money in their pockets and women always by their side. He said with this observation, he came to understand that, "We do not need to be too educated or clever to be in a wealthy position in life."

Renewing his document became a weighty problem that he could not solve since his passport was the new digital passport his country introduced and there was no way it could be re-issued to him in his country's embassy, except that he has to return back to his country to get it, and going back to his country, he was supposed to be having a residence permit or else he was thinking of not returning back to Europe—the same residence permit that was already expired and he has rented it out. When he took time to look at the boy who was luring him into these acts that were causing him mental agony only for him to make his own profit, with a suspension of disbelief, he saw himself as a fool, a big fool, but he was calm, waiting for that day to come, that day when he would have to prove to the little mouse, he was far wiser than he thought.

After having tried so hard to convince some of the consular officials in his embassy to help him get a solution to his problem and none of them were willing to, he ordered for another proxy passport from his country, and when he presented it in the same police station where he reported his former passport to be missing, forgetting he already left the photocopies with them before. The lady he met screamed and walked him out, although he was supposed to be arrested and sent to jail for possessing two different passports with almost the same dates. The lady was a good woman he knew, so he went to meet her again to try to explain his problem to her, but she demanded for another passport with a different date. He later ordered for another proxy passport and presented it to her for the third time and everything were done and his document was renewed. He knew she knew what he did, but she has decided to help him, because she could see that he was frustrated and was almost on the verge of committing suicide. When she collected the passport and the photocopies and other documents required to be issued a new residence permit, he fell on his knees in front of her to show his gratitude, because he knew she knew that he knew she knew what was happening. After one month, he went straight to the police station to get his document back, meanwhile he was waiting for his friend who lured him into this, because his machination was to retaliate by knocking him down, but how he was going to do it, was unknown.

During the time he was looking for how to get a new passport to renew his document, he was left without money and has wanted it so bad that he got himself involved in another deal by traveling with one of his friend to a city called Puerto de Santa Maria, near Cadiz. There, they were put into a hotel and were fed like kings, but at night they were asked to go and discharge some bags of hashish that was smuggled into the country from Morocco by some Moroccans, with promises they were going to be paid 4,000.00 per person, which was to be prompt and it will be helpful for him to solve many of his problems. Three of them who were Nigerians were joined with three Moroccans and five other Spaniards in this operation.

At night, he saw himself with these ten other men sneaked into the sea to be discharging sacks of hashish weighed ten kilos each. It was so heavy that he almost fell inside the sea when he picked one of it. The hardest part was when he grabbed hold of it and was carrying it, walking inside the sea to come out to meet with a beach, and later with a mountain where he would have to climb to get the hashish out to another person already waiting for him to take it to the truck packed in-wait to be loaded. Doing this, they were to be be very fast as they could so as to elude the Spanish *guardia civiles*, who were always patrolling that area. Although he was told the deal was being ordered by one of them who has met with some of his colleagues and has bribed them with some money.

All of a sudden, David said he heard someone calling *policia! policia!* and what he saw next, were people dropping the sacks and fleeing for their lives. When he looked back, he saw the *guardia civil* patrol boat coming towards where they were with the shining light pointing towards them. He also heard the spinning of rotor blades of an helicopter—thump-thump-thump-thump-thump, then he knew he would have to run. But when he tried to run, he became more feeble and frail and could not move his both legs from the water, so he fell down, stood up, fell and stood again until he regained his strength and was able to walk out of the water and beach and started climbing the mountain. On top of the mountain, he saw stampeding grown men fell and hit each other as they ran to escape and were all heading towards the same house where they have eaten and drank wine and beer before leaving for the mission by jumping through the fence so as not to be seen by their neighbors. Reaching the house, the gate was closed and there was no way they could get inside, meanwhile some of them were cautioning them not to get closer to the house because of the police. They all ran passed the house, and all of a sudden, he was no longer seeing any of them. He could only see some of them jumped into their already parked cars, leaving him and the two other Nigerians behind to keep wandering on their own, not knowing where to hide or what to do next since it was their first time of entering that area and it was at night. When coming to that area, they were also smuggled-in so as not to draw suspicion from the people around, seeing three black men with other white men—a thing that was very uncommon since black people were hardly seen around there. Before the commencement of this operation, he heard the other Moroccans and the Spaniards bragged about the many times they were getting involved in operations like this, and it was a profession they have all chosen for themselves.

As the three of them were still running and wandering, dogs were barking and most of the neighbors were coming out of their fenced houses to see to what was happening in their street, suddenly, a police car came, racing towards them, and when they saw it, they diverted and ran through the road heading to a farm where they jumped the high barbed wires used in fencing the farm and swiftly went to hide themselves, lying down along the muddy floor of the farm with all their entire body already soaked with water and sweat. The car then stopped and turned to the same direction they took, pointing their front-lights on the farm. They hid there, unable to move their body, but when the police came out and were walking towards the farm, they started to run again with their wet bodies towards the other side of the big farm. But as they continued to run and were exhausted, they waited for awhile, and when they turned to see if the people chasing them were still very far from where they were, they saw that they have turned back and were heading towards their parked car.

After having waited for more than one hour and nobody came for them, they stood up from the muddy floor they were lying, sneaked out of the farm and crept towards the gate of the house where they have first assembled themselves and had dinner. Reaching the gate, they saw some of the other men who have escaped before jumped through the fence to the other side of the compound. So they jumped along with them and entered the house where all of them were assembled again with the boss—whom he never once set his eyes on, seeing him complaining about their failure not to have been able to secure one sack of the ten kilos of hashish for him. The more he watched him complain, the more he loathe himself for having come to participate in an operation like this. But he was also thinking it might be better if he could strangle him to death. After the boss left with his big fat stomach, he saw many of them hurried out of the house to go and search for the sacks of hashish while he sat, trembling with rage, waiting for them to return back. He said he came to see himself being used as a tool again for nothing to be compared to what he was possessing inside of him that he realized and just cannot be able to exhibit to the world—his talent.

The next day when they finally returned back to Madrid with still no money to process his document, he called his niece, who later sent him 500.00 euros.

After much continuous struggle and effort to get a job, he became more hopeless and was helpless. He knew he was to do anything his friends were doing to subsist. He knew he was to let fear not tremble into his life, so he engaged himself more in many criminal activities and was beginning to make money and was able to pay his rent and bills, while he was also planning on how to travel to Canada. He started to hang around with friends who were going to rob their fellow countrymen that were having kilograms of cocaine in their houses. He was able to travel to different states in Spain, lodging in hotels and using cloned credit cards in purchasing clothes and electronics. He was also able to dupe some of his friends, including the boy who made him rent his document out before—just a way to tell him he was the smartest. Although it later backfired on him, as people were ordered to go and threaten and murder his mother and father at his home in Africa. He later saw that it will be unheard of to see that his both parents were killed because of his stupid act, so he decided to change his life around and do a different thing for a living. That was how he met a boy who took him to the place he was helping people show them a parking space to park their cars and wait for them to give him money. As he was doing this and could not afford to pay his rent and bills, he moved to be staying with one of his friends, making the couch in the parlor his sleeping bed. He loved it there and was glad he was still alive.

One day, he was invited to work with one Spaniard called Miguel who owns a bookshop. His friend who was seen by the man, begging and has decided to help him by calling him to come and assist him to work in his bookshop. The lad who was not very interested in doing that job, because he said the money he was earning there was not enough to be compared to the one he was earning while begging. He decided to introduce David to the man and left for his permanent work of begging. David who was the most happiest person to have met this man, became very much serious about the job and was working tirelessly for the man to retain him as a permanent worker. But the man was seizing this opportunity in making him work more than he was supposed to and was paying him 5.00 per hour since it was a black job and no contract was written and signed. David was happy he was doing it not just because of the money, but because it was drawing him closer to his dream of becoming a writer again. He was also happy he met this man, because he could see him to be very liberal with his money and not very modest about his success—a thing he hardly seen in the Spaniards when dealing with their workers, mostly when it come to immigrants. He was seeing him as a friend not as his boss, because of how they were always together with one other Romanian, who happened to be his driver, traveling to purchase used books and along the way, listening to music as he sings along with it and also discuss about world politics and mostly about Spain and the economic crisis. David said he came to admire him too much that he wanted to make him his elder brother. Many times he decided to work for him for free, as many times the man did also took him to the coffee bar to buy him coffee and food for free without him working for him. David was also able to have access to many free books written in English language that he could not purchase with his money or might not know where to get them, and as he started reading these great books again, he was able to see the dreams and hopes that were once his, coming back to him. He said the more time he was spending in that bookshop and with Miguel, the more he was believing in himself and also seeing himself to be a writer.

One night, he had a nightmare or say a dream, seeing himself having a conversation with his dead grand-mother, and after she left him, he saw himself grew white wings and was flying through the sky. He woke up from sleep and was worried. He tried to interpret what it meant to himself, and as he tried, he fell back to sleep and what he was seeing again was, himself turning into a natural force like a wind. And this wind was changing colors with any color of thing that it come across just like chameleons. A man came to obstruct and queried the wind for changing his colors like a chameleon. And as it was unable to move passed the man because of how strong the man has trapped it down, suddenly, heaven opened and thunder was striking, strong wind was blowing and heavy rain began to fall, then a voice came from heaven, saying, 'you cannot stop what has been said to exist.' And immediately the voice said that, he saw the wind mixed with another dirty wind and it became a tornado. But as the tornado was about to stop, he saw the wind again mixed with water and it became a tsunami. As the tsunami was getting finished, he saw again as the same wind mixed—this time with fire and it was running through the Earth, folded with thick-red wind—but like a volcano. He woke up from sleep and found that he was sleeping on the couch in his friend's parlor. He was unable to go back to sleep, as fear descended on him and he was trying to interpret the meaning of this nightmare or a dream. But after much estimation of probability of what he might believed it to be, he came to understand the wind to be a very powerful natural force to be able to change into anything. He came to see it as his own creative power which actually has been hindered by different obstacles and yet it remained indestructible, because it has been said to exist to promote love, peace, and justice among all men born into the world where he lives, and anybody whosoever think of trying to stop him, will suffer the penalty and bear the consequences. As for the white wings he grew, it was for him to fly to wherever he wish to be to triumph.

As the days went-by and David was almost getting fed up with the life of despair that he was living. He knew it will be better if he struggle to save some money to travel to Canada so as to go and live and study there since he said he was done with Europe and the economic crisis which many believed, was caused by faulty mathematical models that did encouraged excessive risk taking by many of the central banks in lending out borrowed money with no effective control and regulations. He said he understood that, "We know what our problems are, we will overcome"—a new philosophy that he believed many Europeans have decided to adopt, which him, David, said he could see as just a way to assuage oneself. The truth was that, this crisis was having a profound effect on every of the Euro-zone members just as it was in every other parts of the world. But when the Americans and many other countries took a step forward to risk more money on many banks and industries bailout and also to stimulate the economy, Spain under the so-called Zapatero administration also took the same step by adding more debts to the country's debts calling it *Plan Espanol para el Estimulo de la Economia y el Empleo (PLAN E)*. He said he saw all these, and because he could not help show his concerns about the political and social situation of the country by mobilizing people to protest against this plans, he laughed—he laughed, because he was seeing the Spaniards as herds of sheep being guided by a blind shepherd. He said he said this because of his own situation and the situation of the poor, hungry, and homeless that happened to be in vast multitudes in Spain who were automatically getting accustomed to begging, while this administration was spending heaps of money on renewing and maintaining roads, saying he was creating jobs while the rate of unemployment kept rising.

At this very time when the crisis was heading to a point when almost everybody were gloomy about prospects for the world economy, many actually have come to believe it was the end of the world. But as for David, pessimism was not to be in his agenda, since he has always believed in America to be able to overcome fear of threat and to be able to fix their economy again and also stretch their hands to Europe and the rest parts of the world. Watching Obama and listening to him, an indelicate question David asked himself was, if Obama will be able to confront an indelicate economy he met with as the present incumbent of the white house. He also wanted to know if he will be acting according to his many speeches, despite he knew he walked into this mess which was caused by the Bush administration, not to mention the two wars they left him to inherit and the bad image they chose to portray America. First thing he saw was Obama, an indefatigable defender of civil rights, signed into law, the Lilly Ledbetter Fair Pay Act and Equal Pay, approving legislation that expands workers rights to sue over pay discrimination—ending it with a great speech saying, "It's about justice. It's about who we are. And on this wonderful day, we are getting a step closer to both of those things." He went on to say, "Ultimately equal pay isn't just an economic issue for millions of Americans and their families, it's a question of who we are—and whether we're truly living up to our fundamental ideas." He also said, "Whether we'll do our part, as generation before us, to ensure those words put on paper two hundred years ago really mean something—to breathe new life into them with a more enlightened understanding that is appropriate for our time." Immediately he finished with the speech, David said, tears ran down his face. Obama also signed order to close Guantanamo Bay facility in Cuba within a year, saying, "The order was issued in order to restore the standards of due process and the core constitutional values that have made America great even in the midst of war, even in dealing with terrorism." Although it became a promise which was later unfulfilled, because of how the republicans who have always be his ferocious opposition stood against it, claiming there was no place in the U.s. where these detainees would be held. Even many democrats, his own party were able to block the money that would have funded the closing of the facility. And later when David intended to write about this, he said he shed more tears, as he recalled how the Bush administration authorized the use of enhanced interrogation techniques and water boarding on terrorist suspect detained in Guantanamo, and yet, he still was lauded for his great work of disrespecting and disregarding humanity. He said he knew that is not who the Americans are—the monsters who intend to always show their disregard for the laws and human rights.

Obama also made lots of efforts to tighten regulations and control of the business in wall street and banks to avoid another global economic turmoil—which to many who believed money should be squandered, were coming to see him as a communist. He later decided not to push too hard and believe in wall street and the banks to be people who will learn from their past mistakes and think of doing the right thing. But as time went on, more bailouts were needed by this same corporations only to drive the Americans into more debts and later leaving these taxpayers to work twice harder, while they reap extravagant, excessive wealth, and induce others to make preparation to prevent hardships and sufferings. David said he looked at this and came to understand how this GREED is not going to lead us to where we intend to be. He said he could see this corporate capitalism as a system that is mainly benefited by very few while the rest of us suffers and suffers and yet, we still cannot afford to pay our rents or feed ourselves. He said he could see that we are being ruined by the same system that we the same people have always uphold to expand—that is said to exploit us and lead us into a deep hole of frustration—and the only way he said we can overcome this, is to fight to replace it with social democracy, which will be beneficial for all not for the few.

Another great accomplishment he saw Obama made was, when with the help of Nancy Pelosi, Harry Reid, Joe Biden, and many other democrats and with fewer supports of independent voters in the U.s. congress, was able to sign the Health Care Reform, a legislation to increase insurance coverage of pre-existing conditions, expands access to insurance to thirty million Americans, and to increase projected national medical spending while lowering projected medicare spending. But while this was a victory to Obama, democrats in congress and other millions of Americans who were to benefit from it, then many others who believed good life should be meant for them alone, mobilized by the so-called tea party, took to the streets to protest against it. David said he knew instantly this was linked with the fact that Obama was black and has come to change America. He said he watched in the televisions how many hate groups and patriot groups were beginning to quickly expand to large numbers, many of them who do not share beliefs and conducts, people who are quite old and cannot keep up with time, people who actually cannot believe the world is changing everyday and we must change with it—as said by Obama, people who are seen confusing patriotism with nationalism—these same people who were aided by neon-conservatives to cause confusion.

And not quite long, a midterm election was held to vote for members of the United States congress, and to David's astonishment, those who won were mostly republicans and the so-called tea party. At this very moment, he said he came to see the Americans as people who are very shrewd when covering their impatience. He said he knew how confusing and frustrating it was for many at this very time, as they decided to castigate Obama, because he was spending more time, trying to get the health care bill passed while many were losing their jobs and were becoming homeless. Although, he said he could see that they were also brainwashed to have not stick to their promises of change by voting these republicans and tea party to gain control of the congress, only to clog the change that was promised, without they knowing it. He said he came to apprehend that, "People are coming to depend on lies rather than the truth in their everyday lives." The economy which was already broken by the former administration needed to be fixed, but it needed time. "You can destroy a house in one day, but you cannot build that same house in one day." Bush who spent more time in fighting to win wars, has allowed the American economy to collapse, leaving Obama to confront it since he said he was capable of fixing it. And this was what many Americans failed to acknowledge, as many of them were thinking everything were going to be automatically turned around as Obama took office. Everyone were all complaining about their different formidable life problems and were blaming the president for everything. He said he listened to Obama inaugural's speech when he said, "Today I say to you that the challenges we face are real. They are serious and they are many. They will not be met easily or in a short span of time. But know this America—they will be met." David said he knew Obama knew all Americans problems and think everyday of how to fix it, but he needed time and co-operation of all Americans including the neon-conservatives. He needed it to rebuild America and the economy and also to portray a better image of America to the rest parts of the world.

Another thing Obama did that made David come to believe he is more capable of being the leader of the most powerful country on Earth, was when he was able to make the U.s. and Russia to sign the Nuclear Arms Treaty, believing a nuclear weapons-free world to be a good try in a long lost cause which was meant for the both countries to further reduce their nuclear weapons and also to discourage other countries nuclear weapons programs said to be major barriers to this treaty. Although this was historic, as no other president has ever been able to do so, but it was later said to be of no importance, since the Americans were unable to foster a friendly co-operative, honest, and trustworthy relationship with the Russians, making these people think of how to increase their military spending and renewing military and economic ties with the Chinese.

CHAPTER 31

A S THE FINANCIAL CRISIS IN Spain proceeded and many more were losing their jobs, many were also unable to thrive in the struggling economy and were complaining. Pressures were mounted on the country's ruling party by the opposition party to step down so as for the country to convene and elect a new leader. Europe and their currency were also in peril, as many of the central banks were trying to find one way or the other out of a debt crisis. David said he was as well seeing his own life in peril, since he could neither proceed to beg to feed or return back to his country to start a new life again. when he could not withstand the situation, he decided to walk closer to his friends once again to seek advice of what criminal activity will be easy for him to participate in. Before going back to them, he took time to listen to Tupac's music once again—the same music he has for long decided to quit listening to, because of how he was always afraid the inspiration he derives from it was going to lead him to his own death. But he could not do without this inspiration, mostly when he saw that Tupac, just like him was a struggler, a fighter, and a soldier. He knew he like him and there was no way he could not, because he comprehend the late rap artist would have been a better man than he was if he has seen people who have decided to financially support him to get a good education during the time his mother was penniless and could not afford to take all of his responsibilities.

When he got near his friends, he saw that many who were formerly making money in their pimps and prostitute business, were packing their belongings and were planning to leave Spain to other European countries and to Canada, while some were returning back to their countries—many who were having enough debts to pay to the many Spanish banks who gave them loans and mortgages, and because everything changed and money were no longer coming in. This same issue, when David took his time to have a good look at it, he came to see that almost all the immigrants were leaving just the way his fellow country people were leaving. He said he could see how many of these immigrants have also contributed to the country's financial and economic crisis, as many have come to work and borrowed money and left without paying. He said he could see immigration problem to be a grievous problem which many cannot find a solution to. He said, with what he experienced, he came to understand that we cannot do without it, but we are to be very careful on this issue and how it affects us. He said he could understand that, it depends on how we want it and how we want them to live with us, as it can improve the country's economic growth and also destroy it. He said he saw the Spaniards to be selfish and self-centered for not fully integrating these immigrants. Because if they did, most of them would have not think of how to add more injuries to their injuries by failing to pay back the debts that they were owing. He said he could see how other countries in Europe, including the country with the largest economy, Germany were integrating immigrants, allowing them to be properly examined so as to get them naturalized. Anyone who is naturalized cannot think of running away with his debt, because they could be seeing themselves as the community and can participate in every of the activities. David said he saw most of these immigrants, mostly Romanians, Africans, South Americans who have deliberately borrowed money from the Spanish banks so as to take to their country to invest with the intention of not returning back to live in Spain. Spaniards who actually were giving themselves a self-congratulatory hand of applause by lending out money to these immigrants and raising interest rates—even when they understood they were not having permanent jobs that might enable them to continue paying. But they forgot these people were also having their own plans.

The more David was getting close to his friends, the more he was coming to see that he was only wasting his time and his talent. He knew what he was supposed to be doing was developing his spirit of creativity, since actually that is the source of his inner bliss and joy. He also knew how difficult it will be for him to succeed if the financial aspect is bad. But he would have to start from somewhere, so he met with Miguel, the owner of the bookshop were he seldom go to work, to ask him for a favor by writing a contract of one month for him so that he could use that opportunity to file for his unemployment benefit which he was being denied because the law permits anyone to be eligible for the benefit before fifteen days from the day the person is being dismissed, depending on the circumstances, probably if the person could provide the last company's certificate. The man agreed to render him that, based on the condition that David was to pay the social security to him before he could allow his legal adviser to process the necessary documents. David agreed, believing he was going to pay the man maybe 200.00 euros, but he was surprised when the man demanded for 350.00 euros and he was asked to pay everything once. Not knowing how to get the money, he gave up, but when he later continued his begging work and was able to get the money, he swiftly went to pay the money and waited for the result.

Later, when David went to apply for the unemployment benefit and he was told he was entitled to just six months instead of the two years he was expecting, he argued with the lady he met there, but he was told it was the new law—and the only way he would be able to get it was to comply. He did what he was told to do and waited till the next month to receive his first payment, and when he did, his heart was full of joy since he came to believe everything he dreamed about was coming to be a reality. He instantly came to believe he was already on the trail of achieving his dream of becoming an artist since he was to be receiving 960.00 euros every month for six months. But while his scheme was to fulfill his heart desire only by seeing himself writing, he saw his friends searching for him everywhere so that they could go partying. He knew it was time for him to choose his own destiny and this was a great opportunity for him to do so. The more he spurn them, the more they were with him to encourage him to think of investing the little money he was being paid into some kind of business that might even send him to jail again. But as for him, he was not prepared to return back to jail since he has come to see it as a place that can devastate anyone's life and make that person lose hope in himself or herself. He knew if he was ever going to succeed, first, he was to abstain from having these insincere and evil-minded friends. He said, "It is a great misfortune in life to see that sometimes, when you intend to turn your life around and become a better person to the society, you find yourself drawn to unlawful desires, with villains proffering to you a tantalizing glimpse of the future." To describe how he felt about himself, his friends, and his passion for art, and how he could start his project of life and seek God's aid, he wrote this poem.

STAND BY ME O' LORD.

I'm gonna bring to life my innovation,
Beyond the idea of my imagination.
Long, I've loved to study the reality
That's been concealed with a firm security.

All that stampede me instead,
Is that sooner the world might end.
And yet, I'm still unable to drive to my will
And do the things I love to do.

I dream to eliminate the situation,
Believing it to be the enemy of my vision.
Right is right and wrong is wrong.
I wish to see that day,
That lovely day with a bright blue sky.

When my body lies,
My spirit rose and starts to sing:
Stand by me, stay with me O' Lord.
Stand by me, stay with me O' Lord.

Seeing himself pick up a pen once again in his life and was about to commence to write, he felt joy inside of him because creativity has always been a dream to him, and to fulfill it, he knew there was a need for him to dedicate his life to it.

He wrote the first page and tore it up, believing it was going to end up the same way it has always ended up several times he intended to write. He continued to write and tore it up, making him loathe himself for who he truly was and what his prime objective in life truly was, if not to speak to others about what he believe in—that is also causing him pains. Within him, he ascertain the fact that it will be better if he re-position himself in the life of crime. So he went closer to his friends once again, leaving his dream behind, as he was seeing himself not competent of being what he intend to be—a writer. He thought the only way he could be like Shakespeare or Dickens or D. H Lawrence, was when he will be establishing himself in literary circles, and the only way that could be, would be the time he will be living in an apartment near Oxford and also studying there amid other pedants and scholars. He wanted to run very far that he will not be seeing his friends or mingling with them, but how could he achieve that goal when they were the only people who were showing him the road leading to a means of survival.

Reaching to his friends for aid and also to learn more, he saw that many were already on their way to hell, since the Europeans were tightening their security and implementing stricter laws to halt the tremendous rise in crime. He saw that the money these villains have previously made were of nowhere to be found just as his was of no where to be seen. He saw that those who succeeded in making thousands of euros were becoming poor, helpless, and miserable wretch. He said he came to ascertain that, "To succeed is one thing, but keeping that success is another." He came to learn a lesson when the economic despair in Spain got worse and the citizens were fleeing for survival to other countries in Europe and outside Europe. Although, tough as it was, many Nigerians were still battling to hold their positions in the ground where they found themselves. Majority of them, including him, became beggars, seeing it to be a new source of income, while the others chose their different ways and logic in finding their future. With this, he said he understood that, "It is not how much money we make. It is how much money we are able to save, and how we utilize it."

Coming back to his life, and thinking of how to move forth on his own to accomplish his mission in life which he barely believe he was ever going to survive, he commenced with online dating sites where he met Donna, a white American girl who was at her thirties, and was living in Virginia. He thought she was going to be the one to make him see his future and realize his dreams in the U.s. He was spending the little unemployment benefit he was receiving in calling her every nights on phone and also having online sex with her. He tried everything he could to make her love him so as for her to pay him a visit in Europe even when she insisted he should come around to come get her in the U.s. and was denying never to have walked into an airplane, not to think of traveling to Europe. He also wrote a poem and sent it to her, with his pictures just as she instructed, although, this same poem he wrote at the time he was in prison in Italy, and has actually wrote it for the woman he loved so much and was unable to make love to—his childhood form teacher.

When he finally received her pictures, he was stunned by awe and aversion, seeing that she was thrice bigger and larger than he was. How could he swallow his words back and say, 'I never loved you,' instead of, 'I love you and I want you to be the mother of my unborn child,'—sweet words women love to hear from the men they are dating, and he was always familiar with it. He wanted to know if she was the type he could sacrifice for by loving her despite she was suffering from obesity and was being admitted in different hospitals for different operations. When he decided to use a different nickname to meet with her in the same site and seduced her, she fell for him, and immediately he saw that, he was upset and also came to believe she was unfaithful and not worthy to be loved. She begged him, shedding crocodile tears, but he said his mind was made up. He was no longer interested in all her promises to help him talk to a music producer in the U.s. He later declined to record a demo and send it to her since that was what she wanted and has demanded for. He said he later came to see her as a gold digger who actually was primed to exploit him.

Just some weeks after he broke up with Donna by changing his phone number, he met with another woman, Maria Goretti, who actually was born and bred in Solomon's Island and was living in New Zealand with her two daughters after having divorced her husband who was a biologist and was working in Australia. She was nice and was the woman that he believed really loved him from the bottom of her heart. He loved her back and wanted to live the rest of his life with her just as he has wanted to live his life with the many other women he has met that he thought loved him or were just making fun of him. But when he saw how earnest she was and was getting too serious about the relationship, he decided to quit by calling her and informing her about his plan to return back to his country. He also wanted the both of them to be friends not lovers; he loved her and also came to detest her for being too selfish for not thinking of how she could send him an invitation so as for him to be able to obtain a visa to travel to New Zealand to go live there without ever dreaming of returning back to Europe or Africa, because of how he has always been so keen to travel to the end of the world. How could he proceed to love her, when he knew there was no way they could be together because of the distance. He loved her for who she was as a woman who was having passion for snapping pictures and studying plants and animals wherever, whenever.

Nickole, a woman at her thirties, living in Philadelphia, was still childless and was abiding to his mother's rules of conduct, and according to her, she was still a virgin. She was the third woman he met online. Although they have met for long and disputed several times and also reconciled—making him feel he was indebted to her. But when he tried to seduce her on phone to make love to her, she spurned him and called him a pervert. Although she loved him, and he knew she did, but he thought she might be the kind of woman with a lower sex drive and may not be able to satisfy his sexual desire in bed. So he called her one day to disclose the news to her about how he believe they could be friends rather than being lovers. And as she could not resist it, she insulted him and called him names while crying. He said, out of all these three women he dated online, he found that they were not meant to be his wife, because if truly they were, nothing would have stopped him from not marrying them. He also understood that he may be able to have physical and emotional sex with them if they ever meet, but deep in his heart, he wanted them to stretch their hands to him to get him to the place he wish to be before he could start to write his book. It was not love. It was just the only means he believed he could use in getting to the position where he ought to be—climbing another person to reach. The fact that he was always with self-esteem and was always ashamed to tell them his problems, instead he was telling them he was a writer, meanwhile he was still unable to write a page in his up-coming-to-be memoir book.

After much sacrifices that he has seen himself made and the price he has paid to think of becoming a writer, he saw that he was about to throw away what he possess inside of him that was worth millions that he himself failed to acknowledge. He understood he underestimated his own capability of becoming a writer, but he knew he would have to choose between his death or his dream, so he quit every online relationship he was having and took a decision to be paying to have sex with prostitutes. The more he was visiting these prostitutes, the more he was interested in them and was getting addicted to the new way of life—that was making him squander his money, unknowingly. He was also seizing this opportunity to travel around Spain, visiting different clubhouses and brothels where he could find beautiful prostitutes that can satisfy his sexual desire. And after six months that he sent almost all the money back to his families in Africa and lavished it on whores, he was informed that his unemployment benefit was over. He started to think of where to run to, and since he could not find a place, he swiftly ran to his friends who gave him some guidelines to follow on how to extend his unemployment benefit or was said to be allowance for job-seekers, which was reduced to 426.00 to be renewed every six months for two years while he was to be paying 230.00 for his rent and bills. It was at this time he decided to quit every other thing he was doing to focus on his dream of becoming a writer and never let his talent be a waste.

CHAPTER 32

AFTER TWO MONTHS THAT DAVID started writing his book, he was also offered a free plumbing course by the Spanish, *Instituto Nacional de Empleo(INEM)*. "It is better for you not to set on a journey that you know you are never going to complete," this was his situation. He thought it was only going to take less than six months before he will get to the end of it. Starting the plumbing course posed no difficulty till at a time when he came to discern the fact that he was not learning as an apprentice in Africa. Although this was his first time of going for a training course and really prepared to finish it and get a certificate to work with it. But it became eminently clear that he was in Europe and the type of profession he has chosen to work with, was not a profession meant for dullards. He saw that it was going to be a formidable tax for him to be able to synthesize complex ideas to achieve two principal aims. Writing is not just a bread and butter thing, especially when you are poor and could hardly feed yourself and your mind is set on everything, everywhere to outlive the situation you found yourself. At the other hand, taking a plumbing course, to him and many others, is complicated because of the too much calculations and equations that needed attentions and concentrations to solve while you are poor. He remembered at the time he was young and was still in the secondary school and has began to accompany himself with some rogues, he came to dislike mathematics because of the too much and distinctive equations he was coming across, and mostly the ones he was being told by his friends who were genius—which he disliked and has made him deviated and take a walk closer to art and come to embrace it. He said he recalled how his classmates were singing with linear equations, quadratic equations, algebraic equations, simultaneous equations, and then Pythagorean theorem. He said every time he heard about these equations, it makes him feel completely insane even more than it does to him when he is meditating and trying to figure out why the planet Earth is filled with evil doers. Although, he love scientists and respect them for their works of invention, but he love art more than science, as it is the field where he developed his talent, and most of all, he has great passion for it.

Linking the book he was writing with the too much simultaneous equations and practical aspect of the plumbing course, he saw himself playing insane asylum games and it was distressful and startling. He found himself in a state of perplexity that required a choice between the plumbing course and the book he already sacrificed his life for. He wanted to quit one so that he could concentrate on the other, but one of his friends, who was keen to finish the course and get his certificate so that he could travel to Germany or other European country to look for a job, was cheering and encouraging him to persevere, thinking it was just the plumbing course that was stressing and hassling him not knowing he was also working on a project to shape his future. He also applied for a graphic design course so that he could use the opportunity to learn more about designs, but he could not finish it, because he was not able to meet up with the other students who started some weeks before him. Before taking these courses, he applied for another six months course which was not free, and it was a course he could learn to design, build, operate, and maintain wind power and solar energy systems. And at this time, Spain was number two in solar energy world-wide and the biggest wind power producer in Europe, ahead of Germany. He knew this course was going to be profitable when he return back to his country, but the problem was he could not afford the enrollment fees which was just 250.00 euros, while he pleaded with the man who visited him at home to accept 200.00 euros, as he could pay the remaining 50.00 euros the next month with the monthly fees which was to be 150.00 euros. But the man refused, because he too was instructed to do so. He wanted to take that risk to be paying his bills, rents, and feeding with that 426.00 euros so that he could swiftly achieve something and step out from the sinking ship which he voluntarily boarded.

If dealing with these many issues was his only problem, it would have not to be seen as a problem, but when it happened that the house he was living before was foreclosed by the bank, and he decided to move to rent another one bedroom in another of his friend's apartment, that is when he actually came to understand the reasons why Africans are said to be cursed. He saw how he could not fit, living with them, as their most priority was to show him a depth of enviousness. He saw how many complaints were made against him of how he was always indoor with his computer and many books and papers and pen. Actually, for him to afford a laptop computer, it was like killing a lion with your bare hands. Since he could not afford the bigger one, he purchased a smaller and cheaper one even when his friends were mocking him. During this time, one Nigerian prostitute who was living in Denmark and has come to Spain to look for a way to apply for a residence permit—since it is more easier in Spain, but more costly, because in Spain, it is said-to-be "have your money, have everything you want." She was introduced to him by her cousin who was also his friend and was a gigolo. The boy became afraid when his sister arrived, because he thought David was also going to play the game he too was playing with other women. So he tried to caution her and keep her away from him. But she was already in love and wanted to have a taste of him. When she came around to visit him in the house where he was living, they had sex for two days and she left back to her brother's house. He knew he has to do anything to subsist just like his other friends by looking for a better city for a prostitute to make money and lavish it on them. He did, and the end result was good, as she became his source of income, prostituting and sending him the money. It was at this time he came to understand them better as fools who are being tricked to do anything they are not willing to do; he came to see them as people who loathe the truth and embrace lies. And lying to them make them love and squander their money on men. It was unfair what he was doing to her, but he needed the little help she was rendering to him. He later went to visit her once in Lanzarote, where he thought he might be able to trick her again to use her and obtain money from her. But she became smart and was not willing to give him a penny, because she knew he was after her money. She would have lavished all her money on him, if not that he was serious in letting her know they were not of the same class. Deep in his heart, he knew he was never going to marry her, but he hoped to help her back if ever he make his dream materialized. And to do this, he needed to put more effort and time in his project. He was also very much afraid he was going to contract a venereal disease, having sex with her without using a condom. And moreover, for long he has vowed never to marry a whore and he was fond of telling all his friends, "You cannot make a whore a housewife."

After he finished the plumbing course and was waiting for his certificate, the only thing that became very important to him was to finish writing his book, since that was the only thing he came to believe he could be known and be recognized for by a vast myriad of people; he also understood this to be the only way he could be able to extricate himself from the life he was already living; he said he saw that it was left up to him to decide which way he should go, and for long he has chosen to go the way that leads to creativity and prosperity. He said he came to really understand that the life of crime that he was living was not foisted on him by his friends, it was foisted on him by himself, and there was a chance for him to quit any time he decide to. But in as much as his family needed his assistance, he was willing to give it to them just like many other poor Africans who were also experiencing the same problems of traveling to Europe only to sacrifice all their time and energy for their families, instead of them to be sacrificing that time and energy in building their own futures. It is a sad thing though, but it is more sadder than the way people are seeing it, when you cannot plan a future on your own except you have to live a life foisted on you by your families. It is not that these people actually love their children to be depending on them in every aspect of financial difficulties, it is just that they are being lazy and cannot plan for themselves the same way they have been unable to plan for their children to give them the proper education they might have needed to become great people in their own countries. David said he could look at it and see the reason why many of these African parents are not seeing it as a shameful thing to be depending on their children for everything. He said he could see that they are willfully and totally ignorant.

Even when David was scuffling with his book-writing and was also very worried about his one eye that was already blind, and yet he was still spending time using the computer—even when it was affecting his eye—making him shed tears every time. He came to ask himself a question, if actually he died along the way some years ago, would not his families in Africa still be living? After he asked himself this question, he also came to respond to it, saying, they will be living, definitely they will; they will mourn him for some weeks, but after then, he will be forgotten and life will keep moving again. "The dead is dead, so the living must live." When he looked deep into this subject matter, he decided to focus more on his project and stop sending money to his families in Africa.

CHAPTER 33

MANY MONTHS AHEAD WERE THOUGHT to be a commencement of the financial growth in Spain, but it became worse than predicted by some economists. What became very prevalent in Spain, was the closure of many Spanish shops and banks, since the people were unable to continue with their businesses, while many Chinese were re-opening the shops and were establishing new businesses everyday, and the outstanding thing about them was that they were working too hard, days and nights, making sacrifices for their future economic growth, while most Spaniards were mocking them—saying, *ahi que trabajar para vivir, no vivir para trabajar*. David said when he saw this, he was beginning to feel the sign of a war threat in the global economy. He was beginning to see that, the increase in demand for the Chinese products, was what was leading to the less demand for the American and European products—which means, the faster the Chinese economy was growing, the easier it was for the Americans and Europeans to experience more financial and economic crisis. But even when this continued without stop, the Americans and Europeans were still more preoccupied about the war in Afghanistan while their citizens were deprived of the rights to live and own a house of their own. Banks were throwing out people into the streets because they could not afford to pay their mortgages.

He came to see that even in the western world, there is still no justice, seeing congress and parliaments in the U.s. and Europe making laws for their own benefits. He asked himself, what if politicians who led their countries into economic and financial crises are being prosecuted, and if convicted, should be sent to jail? People like George Bush, Condoleeza Rice, Donald Rumsfeld and Dick Cheney who were supposed to be serving jail terms in the same Guantanamo they believed was meant for terrorists suspects. David said he wish to see these people sent there to live, because of the fact that they were incompetent of ruling the country with the largest economy in the world. He said he saw the Bush administration making mistakes repeatedly and never admitted it. He said he could see that Bush's mistakes were too austere that he should be prosecuted for it—to show an example to many other world leaders. Yet, the Bush administration are still being left to enjoy impunity.

From his own perspective, he said if we wish to celebrate a new millennium for hope, we have to start laying a foundation to build it. We have to re-establish relationship of equality, pursue peace, seek freedom, and justice for all, and above all, love our neighbors. Because without these, he said he believe hope will be lost—and when there is no hope, bad things happen. He said, when he continued to watch these politicians and how they were deliberately disrespecting and disregarding their fellow human beings to make them feel resentment and indignation, he came to think there is a need to repel them and send them to where they never wished to live. He said he believe there is a need and there is always a need for us to fight for our basic rights as human beings, because that is what democracy stands for—a government of the people, by the people, and for the people. He decided to write this poem to best describe what he intended to speak about. He said he also understand the risk he is taking to utter the truth out to the vast majority who share the same idea just like him and also believe we all can heal humanity. But he said, he is done with all, and he is no longer scared of what might befall him, because the life he is already living is not worth a penny—and it will be better if he waste it, trying to lure people to revolt against the democracy we now have, and change it to a distinctive one that was promised in the name of that same democracy that we all believe in. He said he has seen it long time ago that in a decade to come when there will be a revolution everywhere around the globe. Citizens from every nation will come out to demonstrate they are willing to stand for their rights and voice out. He said he could see that it seem people are beginning to get tired of this capitalist system, that they cannot withstand it any longer and can only stand to change it and make it better than it is. Capitalism is greed, and we should not further argue or elaborate on it. He said the true democracy he believe in, is when capitalism is mixed with socialism, so as for everybody in every nation to relish the good source of the country's income. He said he is fed up with the whole issues of how many wealthy people, mostly right-wing parties in many countries in the west—especially republicans in the U.s. still supports many banks that are repeatedly making decisions that has led them to losses, and after then, asking the governments to bail them out with the taxpayers money.

WE'VE GOT TO STAND FOR OUR RIGHTS.

Have you ever sit down to think
That to their self-interest they click?
When half the world's about to sink.
Everyone's notion is to see to a solution
To the problems leading to a devastation.
To my neighbors, do I have to be a friend
Or, do I continue to be a foe?

When the day is still bright,
We need not the moonlight to fight.
So, we're gotta stand for our rights
To promote a democracy that is right,
Since we still can see the future from a sight.

Tell me where do I put my sorrow now
When the wind is starting to blow?
Why I need not a second revolution,
So, I care won't go for a contradiction.
Please, push me not against the *muro*,
Cos when the trouble comes, it's gonna be double.
About you my thoughts start to get dark,
And my feelings I can't express at nights.

Immediately after he wrote this poem, he saw how many people in the Us. were holding to their own protests to revolt against corporate greed in wall street. They thought it will help them to put an end to the greed and corruption of wealthy people in America—which are mostly neon-conservatives. These people took to the street because they came to believe they were being treated like animals by their fellow country people who believe good life is meant for them alone while they watch the rate of poverty increase in the same country where they live and were born. Although, he witnessed the Spanish uprising(15M) *indignados* and the Arab spring. He saw the Spaniards as weak people who prefer to celebrate their *fiestas* rather than causing havoc that might send them to jail. He also saw most of the Arab nations who were fighting for their rights and freedom to be hypocritical, since majority of them were always going to prefer religious leaders to rule them with Islamic laws under sharia than well educated politicians who have embraced ideas about civilization—which will simply be referred to as theocracy. So why do we have to call it democracy when actually we are in a country where people cannot accept other race and religion into their community? But he also support the perception that the youths revolted against these dictators so as for them to be free. But they have to practice it fully so that they could be able to enjoy the good things about democracy. This is not too bad for a start that will take a bit long to achieve the major purpose. David said he find it absurd, unbelievable, and derisory to see that, America—a wealthy, privileged, industrialized nation is the same place where many people are penniless, jobless, and homeless, while few others are getting richer everyday and would not feel pity for their fellow Americans, just because they are accustomed to living the life of want-it-all. He said it is a big disgrace to a nation like America, to see that the government still cannot tackle the issue of social and economic inequality, corruption, fascism, undue influence of the government and large corporations. He said he is so ashamed to see that America, the founder of the modern day democracy, is now turning itself into a system of plutocracy just like we are having theocracy, monarchy, aristocracy, oligarchy, tyranny e.t.c. He said he sometimes lose hope in humanity when he come to see that if these wealthiest people cannot render to their fellow country people what they deserve, then how could they think of finding a solution to the problems in poorer countries where conflicts and malnutrition is said-to-be a general term?He said what baffles him most was how these same greedy and corrupt people are still the same people who preferred to assist many to fight wars instead of using diplomacy in resolving disputes, simply because of the profits they make for selling arms to these poor countries to be killing themselves. These same people, he believed to be money lovers are the same people selling America for their own profits; they are keen to doing anything to raise more money for themselves and for their next generation, as they are more preoccupied about their own empire and power than they should be giving a helping hand to their fellow country people. He said he get confused with everything in and around the planet Earth where he live—that sometimes, he think of cutting his own heart out and feeding it to the lions. From how people tend to always manipulate their fellow human beings, then, to considering the continuing rapid advancement in science and technology and the negative effects of it; he said when men could travel to other planets and into space—if only we can turn this drive towards exploring our planet, Earth and finding a solution to some of the problems causing natural disasters, that is when we will be praised and honored for our good works; he said he love science and technology and cherish the good things humanity has benefited from it. But one question he keep asking himself is, where exactly is this too much of science and technology leading humanity to?—a better world or a destructive world? He said he could see that almost all of us (human) are indebted to science and technology that we do not even know if it is going to let us down, since it has become our strength and light as well as a new religion that lives in our hearts. As for him, he could see the damages it has done to our planet Earth, and yet he cannot explain it better. He said he will never give up to know if what it preaches to us about the future is true—and he has decided to drive to go meet the pope to ask him if there is still a hope. He said he love this Earth and believe it to be the home of every man, and that he believe we can do a lot to make it be, since we cannot walk away from this situation. He wrote a poem long-time ago about this issue at the time he was still in prison.

WE CAN'T WALK AWAY FROM THIS SITUATION.

The Earth is our planet.
Cover it, we should with safety and protection.
Now, we've possessed every micron of information.
To understand it, we need a co-operation.
My belief in science is strong,
But I'm not putting humanity and God aside.
Pour forth the full explanation,
Only when I'm allowed time and opportunity,
Though, not with the words of mouth.
We spill-out some certain precautions
For you not to give everything for greed,
Since it's leaving us on consternation.

The little they have,
We intend to take away.
Don't ever think us to be cynics
As we only choose and accept from various sources.
We pay billions for space tour,
While they are starving to death.
Do you ever agree with me
That crime can be a product of the law
And as the lack of social benefits?
Misbehavior as side-effects of social repression?
See that the too much technologies we acquire,
Is precociously driving us insane.
As we now make God a predecessor
And religion is fast becoming politics.
Global warming is threatening me
When I've seen so much of natural disasters.
See now that the many technologies we invent,
Some are turning into weapons of mass destruction.

We can't walk away from this situation.
We've got to make a consideration.
I don't know what to do now,
Cos, my mind's just a maelstrom
Of hopelessly and conflicting emotions.

CHAPTER 34

ONE MORNING, WHEN DAVID WOKE up to check his account balance with his debit card, he found that he was not paid the job-seeker allowance he was supposed to be paid that day. Without knowing what to do, he left to the apartment which he was sharing with one of his friends. He could not help figure out the reason why. He later requested an appointment to meet with the *Instituto Nacional de Empleo (INEM)* which was to take him another week before he could be attended to. He was unwilling to wait till the appointment day, so he went straight to the office to get some information on why he was not paid. Reaching there, he was not allowed to meet with anybody in-charge and was asked to come back the day of his appointment. He could not wait, so he insisted he was going to meet with one of them, and as he waited and tried again, he was able to meet with one of the women who told him he was supposed to come with some requirements to submit so that they will be able to extend his job-seeker allowance which was already expired. Actually, he did everything and wanted to submit them when a lady there told him it was of no use, and that he could always wait to be paid. When he was later told the reason he was not paid, he was upset and went straight to the same woman whom he met before and has advised him not to fret himself about providing all the requirements. He wanted to eat her alive until one of the man said-to-be the head came out to apologize for the mistakes. David knew in his heart that it was not a mistake, because many other immigrants have always complained about this same woman who actually was always unhappy, seeing them as immigrants coming to apply for the benefits. He later left the office and went home to wait for the appointment date. When the day finally arrived, he went to the same office where many other papers were also demanded again, and as he ran to get them, he saw that it was impossible for him. He was weak and bored, thinking it was time for him to leave Spain. But when he read some parts of the unfinished book he was writing, he became confused of whether to proceed with the sufferings or leave to Switzerland to join some of his friends whom he called on phone and have promised him a better life there only when he intend to sell drugs in the street. He did not know which way to go, seeing his faith and fear becoming inseparable. He knew he will prevail only if he was able to get some financial assistance so that he could be able to pay his rent, his bills, and also feed himself. He continued to go to all the offices, demanding for different documents to present so as for him to be given what he believed he was entitled to that he also knew he was not entitled to. He began to pray to his God and was a constant in the catholic church near his house, where he started worshiping every on Sundays due to the fact that he was beginning to disbelieve in his God, and his faith in Him became weaker day after day. When he went to get the certificate for personal income tax, he was denied simply because it was said he has not paid his income tax returns some years ago—which was 1,460.00 euros and a surcharge was also being added to it, when actually he could barely feed for a day and nobody cared about his situation. He also later saw that the reason he was to pay this money was because the bank, which gave him the mortgage to purchase his house long time ago, has finally sold the house and was claiming he was given the profit of 8,000.00 euros—which he did not see with his only one eye left. The worst of it all, when he went to the bank to demand for the money, he was told he was still owing them some very large amount of money. Although, he was beginning to think he was suffering the resultant actions of his past misdeeds by going to that same office to declare he was having a wife and a daughter in Africa and also providing forged documents so as to be offered this benefit for two years when it was supposed to be for six months because he is without a wife and a kid. But deep down in his heart, he was glad he did so, because it was what he was supposed to do to survive the crisis and get himself out of it. He said many a time when he looked deep into this subject matter, he came to believe, "One does not really have to be too upright and honest, because it can lead us to an impoverished life we can never be able to escape." He said he believe in the saying, "Man made man to be wicked, man was not made to be wicked." From his own experience in life, he came to believe that the monopoly system is biased and it is driving us all insane. He said when he came to learn how this system was first introduced by the Jews, he disliked them for it. He said he could see this system to be very destructive and dangerous to humans.

After having waited for three months without being paid the allowances, he was no longer having a place to live not to think of how to proceed with the book he was writing. He went back to the place he was always going to beg by helping people park their cars only to be able to earn some money to feed himself and also feed the lad who accepted him into his apartment—a foreclosed home without light or hot water to shower. Despite the fact that he was frustrated, he did what he had to do, traveling from one state to another to provide all the requirements needed to be receiving the benefits; he also postponed the payments of the income tax return and was to be paying 170.00 euros every month out of the 426.00 euros he was to be receiving—which he agreed.

David woke up one morning at about 06:00 a.m just the same time everybody living in Spain were going to their banks to check their accounts to see if their unemployment benefits were paid. As he slotted his debit card into the automated teller machine and waited ten seconds, he heard some noises—tah tah tah tah tah tah tah tah tah—like the sound of a gun fire coming out of the automated teller machine, and after another ten seconds, he saw some euro banknotes like golden leaves came out. He quickly grab hold of the money, and when he counted them, it was one 50.00 euros note, two 20.00 euros notes, and one 10.00 euros note—all together, it was hundred; he withdrew his debit card, and as he turned to leave, he raised his head and looked up into the sky; although it was still very early in the morning. He saw the stars shinning, and he called upon his God Whom he believed to be living there in the sky and said, 'Thank You O' Lord for this money, now I believe that You are real.' At this very moment, he came to believe that money is power, the power to move the world forward.

It was just two hours after David went to check his account to know that he was having some money inside. But when he went back to check the statement of the account and the balance, he found that he was having 1,050.00 euros inside, meaning he was paid some months that has been omitted before. He did not know what else to do with the money, since he has long planned to travel to Switzerland or Belgium during the time he was suffering and was homeless, which was not less than three months. First, he went to buy hashish and smoked it. He recalled how for one year he has decided to start writing his book, and that same year he has quit smoking cigarettes and could only smoke hashish or marijuana maybe once in three months depending on when he meet with his friend who was an addict. Quitting cigarette was a thing that was not easy for him to do, but he did it because of his willingness to. He also recalled how he has suffered to take the plumbing course and at the same time he was also struggling to get his book written. After then, he decided to watch SOCIAL NETWORK, a film based on Mark Zuckerberg when he was struggling with his friends in Harvard, trying to launch what everybody now recognize as Facebook. He saw himself watching this film repeatedly, because he was acquiring inspirations to keep him motivated to proceed with what he was doing and never relinquish no matter the circumstances he was to face. He came to believe more in himself more than ever, as he wake up every day to read some of the pages already written in his book. He knew one day he will be able to finish writing it, and if he does, it will help him design and shape a world that he will live that he has always dreamed to live. So he quickly quit the prospect of going to sell drugs in Switzerland or traveling to Belgium to seek asylum or returning back to his country. He decided to go and rent a room so that he could pay for his computer to be connected to the internet, and then he could proceed further to write his book. But he was beginning to feel guilty to leave his friend to be living alone in the foreclosed house without light or hot water, and moreover the lad was penniless and was not working and has also declined to beg like many others were doing. He called him to ask him how much he needed to pay for the light bill and gave it to him even when he knew he might pay it and never get the light back because of the fact that the lad already lost every of the documents relating to the house and moreover he was trying to renew his residence permit which was already been denied by the Spanish Immigration Ministry, because of the too much debt he was owing to pay for his personal income tax return which was more than 8,000.00 euros. After they paid the bill, and in not more than a week, the light was installed and they were both happy to see that, having light was having life. But, there was also another lad who was living with them before, when he started begging and was earning money, he decided to move away to look for a room to rent, leaving the two of them inside the darkness.

When David saw that he could not get his computer connected to the internet, he decided to continue going to the city's library since there was a free WIFI there and it is being installed by the city council in Torrejon de Ardoz. Even though he started going there when they were not having light in their house, but he never liked it due to how many Spaniards were always staring at him, trying to know what he was doing with the many books and a small laptop being that he is black and moreover, a Nigerian—people who prefer to speak English, probably because they believe the Spanish language is not worth dying to learn, and to many Spaniards, it was annoying. He later started gambling with his money till it was almost finished. And the only thing he said he apprehended from gambling—going from one betting hall to another, was that it was meant for rich people to become wretched and for poor people to become rich or more poorer; he also came to understand that gamblers are liable to die young, because of how they can easily develop hypertension.

As David continued to go to that library, all of a sudden he was told that his mother was seriously ill and was almost at the point of death. He was confused again, thinking there was a need for him to be paying to get his computer connected so as for him to finish writing his book in time and travel to his country to see his mother. He quickly sent her money twice and promised to send her more. But after two months, he was called on phone by his sister in Spain, Tina, to be delivered a message that his mother was dead.

The death of his mother was a thing he could not resist as a man—making him grief-stricken and demoralized. He saw himself shedding tears along the street and was frustrated, not knowing whether to still proceed with his dream of becoming an artist or giving it up to do a different thing. He tried to imagine how it will look like, seeing that one day he will arrive in his home not to see his mother embrace him and saying, you are welcome back home, my son. It was the most painful thing he has experienced in life, even if one of his eyes was blind and he has lost his grandmother and some of his half-brothers and half-sisters. He was sad, knowing she was never coming back to live again. He saw himself scuffling and struggling, but for what reason was he doing all these, if not for the only one person in his heart that he truly love and was never going to meet again; the one person that took his love and hold it close to herself that made him not believe there was ever going to be another woman he could trust and cherish; the one person that he will be glad to see carry his own baby in her hands and say, my son, you are a man; the one person that he believe gave up her life for him to succeed in life and never to be afraid of death, because she already died for him to live. That one person was his mother, his half-soul and body.

When David came to take a good look at himself and to compare and contrast the life he was living with the ones so many other people in Europe and America were living, then he came to comprehend why many were trembling with rage, as they believe Obama broke his many promises. But David said he also disagreed with Obama in many aspects, especially when he saw how he was sending more troops to Afghanistan and also fostering other NATO members to send more. David said he never championed this notion, because he could see it was making America spending more money only to fight wars and go deeper in debts when there was a need for an economic growth and job creation—which he, David believed was to be Obama's top priority when he became the president of the United States. He said he believe if Robert F. Kennedy was alive, he would have think of how to solve the problems that were faced by the jobless and homeless in America, starvation in Africa, and other poor countries, and not spending the money in fighting more wars. But unfortunately, R.F.K was assassinated. You see, "Good people never last." He said how in life would it be that R.F.K has become the president of the United States? The world would have been three hundred times better than it is already. To David, he believe it will be better to practice pacifism and throw away prussianism, and that was what he expected from Obama that he failed to do for him—and that was the reason he was awarded a noble peace prize. It was not that he did not take some precautionary measures to create jobs and provide economic relief which were to get people out from the worse recession, as he was also spending too much and was adding to the country's debt. But he did what he should do for his first term as a president and was waiting to be re-elected to do more better than he already did. His major plan to reduce deficit and pay some of the country's debt and to raise taxes on the wealthiest Americans and giving a chance for an economic growth before cutting taxes to increase revenue. Most people still cannot fathom the effect that can occur when cutting taxes in a recession, and that effect is what the president is trying to avoid that he believe could be done after the recession—at the time the economy will be a bit stable. As for immigration, the president has many good plans, and that is the reason he is having more haters—because these people believe his immigration policies is going to be in favor of these illegal immigrants trying to find their ways into a better world.

Obama aim, is actually to rebuild America, but there are very many people who does not want this change, because they are too greedy to allow their fellow human beings live like them. The time David said he became more afraid to see humans wanting everything they wish for and stopping anyone who intend to step in their ways and doing it without remorse, was when republicans were voted into congress, their speech was plain and simple—their number one goal was to defeat Obama and never give him that chance to be re-elected. To David, he said he could see that the unceasing partisan gridlock in Washington is not doing Americans any good, except to hurt the economic growth in the U.s. And when these politicians are doing it, they are doing it for their own political gain.

As for choosing the commander-in-chief, Obama has done far better than the Bush administration who preferred bombardments than getting better at intelligence gathering and intelligence sharing. For eight years, Bush was the president, but he was unable to order the killing of Osama bin Laden. When Obama became the president, for two years he took a very tough decision and ordered the killing of Osama bin Laden. Although the death of Bin Laden was sensationalized by Obama, but it marked the end of an epoch in the world history. Obama has been called all kind of names: An illegitimate president, Marxist, Socialist, Fascist, Un-American, Anti-religion, Radical, Unconstitutional, Worst president in history, A Muslim, and many more. But Bush who led the world into one of the worst financial crisis was still writing his book and people were going to buy it. He was also invited to make speech to earn thousands of dollars. David said he could see how people always prefer to play fast and loose with the truth by calling Obama names and believing Bush to be a saint.

It is not that Obama is perfect in dealing with all issues, but the fact that he is quite better than all the other candidates in supporting and caring for the middle class citizens and working people. He might not have the best economy policies, but the American economy is doing well, only that many Americans are being tricked by these rich Christian-supposed-be politicians who actually has come to finish the work Bush already started that is going to lead America into more crisis. As a civil right activist, Obama also supported and called for marriage equality, saying—"I want everybody treated fairly." David said the two hings Bush was accused of that he did not uphold, was that he is a racist and that he violated the citizens right by ordering wire tapping. Bush, to David, is not and was never a racist, as he was able to have Collin Powell as his first Secretary of States and later Condoleeza Rice as formerly his National Security Advisor and later his second Secretary of States. Bush also was forced to order wire tapping since it was necessary for the security of the citizens as well as to fight crime and also to fight terrorism. But Obama is more competent, because he believe America should not be using their veto power in dealing with issues, instead they should always comply with the United Nations resolution. War is not a good thing, and Obama understand this—which made him thought it will be better if the American troops are being returned from Afghanistan and Iraq so as for him to focus more on the economy and improve the Americans standard of living—that is said-to-be his top priority. He also believe the money spent on wars should be meant for other purposes. David also said he is afraid after the election Obama might ordered Iran to be bombed, because he could no longer trust any politician, seeing what they have all done in the past. He said if Ron Paul has come out as the GOP presidential candidate, he would have supported him, because of his plans to bring all American troops back home and focus on the countries economy instead of going to waste the tax payers money in fighting wars and policing the world while the economy shrinks. He said he will never support Romney, because he already could see him as a man who can only, with his religious faith, go fight Iran and waste more money there, and instead of him to think of rebuilding America, he will be thinking of rebuilding his businesses. He said he could see that this same Romney does not have the full complement of becoming the president of the United States as of now when the economy is just springing and little jobs are being created. America has come far away to return back to that desert the conservatives wanted it to stay during the Bush regime. America need Obama, and they need him now, because he is the man who will best lead America at the right direction. In dealing with China increasingly posing military threats to its neighbors in Asia and also to others, Obama as the commander-in-chief, with Julia Gillard, the Australian prime-minister, they unveiled plans to deepen the U.s. military presence in the Asia-Pacific—a thing David regard with aversion, seeing that Obama won a noble peace-prize which he believed might restrain him not to follow the steps taken by the neon-conservatives in deploying more American troops around the world. He said he gave up his hope of finding peace in his heart since he could not see the world find peace. But as he tried to find a reason why Obama was doing this, he came to get to the bottom after finding a way back to history and came to ascertain that, if there had been a NATO or American military base in France or Holland or Belgium, it would have been very difficult for Adolf Hitler to have succeeded in invading Europe. He said he believe Obama did the right thing as a commander-in-chief, but he also loathe him for doing it, because he believe we should always think of the positive outcome not the negative outcome, because everything that is said to have its advantage might also be having its disadvantage. He said he said this, because he also came to understand that what led to the first world war was militarism, alliances, imperialism, and nationalism. "So we should be heedful of what we do and not to keep repeating the same thing that caused us adversity and remorse before, because, if we do not learn, we are then to be compared to animals." He said he also understand we should not be too judgemental, seeing our leaders taking tough decisions because of what he once read in a book that, "In every leadership, there is a secret to be kept, and that secret is a dangerous one." David said he has seen it all that war cannot be the answer to every of our problems. He also came to understand that, "If we keep fighting wars and resolving problems with violence and cannot find a good outcome to it, why not turn around, changing our ways to see if we can resolve it, using diplomacy?" Obama has been able to prove this to him when dealing with North Korea and Iran and that is what he dreamed of that could make his heart be at peace. To prove that people should be fairly treated with dignity, Obama administration pledged his support for the establishment of a Palestinian state—an idea supported by almost every other person living in the world except the Jews, that making peace with your neighbor is the only way-out and it is quite better than bombing the innocent children. Although he also restore confidence in the U.s. long-standing supports for Israel, saying, "America's commitment to Israel security to Israel is unshakable, our friendship with Israel is deep and enduring." Despite the fact that

Obama understand what it might cost him to be re-elected by not fully supporting Israelis perception on how to deal with this conflict, he urges Israel to go back to 1967 borders which was to support Palestinian demand for borders of its future state while also encouraging Israel to accept that they can never have a truly peaceful nation based on permanent occupation—an idea denounced by many Jews and their leader, Netanyahu. But Obama, who is seen as a politician and would not want to lose his election, because of this, his administration has decided to take a step to obstruct plans for Palestinians to seek recognition as a state at the United Nations. Although, a proposal has been made for peace talks to be renewed. In this case, will Mahmoud Abbas ever take a step back when all the world is already in support? To David, it is a thing he said he could not comprehend that he keep asking himself, if America is being ruled by Israel since no one could actually step forward to utter the truth and let a Palestinian state be created so as for peace to reign in the Middle East and also in every corners of the Earth. And as for the war-mongering conservatives who are mostly Jews, their aims are to make Israel continuously be hated by many others around the world. These people also make political hay to fight more wars, as they send young American soldiers into war-fronts, while their children attend the best schools and travel around the world. What David said he will do was to make people grasp what he believe about the people who voice their opinions on the conflict in Gaza and west bank, is to further elaborate on this issue that these people should not been seen as anti-Semitics. He said he believe it is the Jews that has to be blame for not asking themselves the reason why they are being hated by many others around the world simply because they are not prepared to allow peace reign by giving what belongs to Caesar to Caesar and giving what belongs to God to God. The occupation and discrimination in the west bank and Gaza is unacceptable, and there is no way they could live freely without being disturbed if they cannot come to their senses to put religion and pride away to restore peace for now and for the next generation. As for Iran, there will be a time when the citizens will be fed up with their insane tyrant and they will stand up to revolt against their government just as it is already in Egypt and Tunisia, but it will be so senseless and moronic to see Israel strike Iran, and it will be destructive for all the Jews not only in Israel but in every countries in the world. David said he understand the intense effect of technology to the human mind is that humans trust technology too much that they fail to acknowledge there are limitations on every technology that we invent. The Jews believe they have too much technology to defeat Iran, but they have forgotten if they are fighting Iran, they are also going to be fighting millions of terrorists in every Jewish community around the world. Striking Iran can cause a great devastation to the entire Jews and also get America back to war and then increase the government financial spending. Sometimes, David said he could see that Israel is about to lure America into another war, and when another economic turmoil emerge, they will be nowhere to be found. So for that reason, America must be very attentive in the way they deal with issues relating to Israel. Israel is America, and America is Israel and will always be at their back. But, making peace can be the comprehensive solution to their problems and they have to let it be so, or else the consequences of being too proud, vulgar, offensive, and aggressive to your neighbors is what no one can predict.

One dark hour in the middle of the night, David woke up from sleep, since he was fretful and did not know what to do. He began to ask himself questions about how the Americans could possibly think of even listening to Mitt Romney, who actually has mixed religious faith with wealth—showing how hypocritical he is. He said it sounded to him the Americans actually does not know what they want at this very time if they cannot ignore Romney to think of having another person as a president. Ron Paul was good and he was never chosen, which means it is not just being a republican that matters, it was making America been disliked by others around the world and more gridlocks and corporate greed in Washington and wall streets. To choose a leader, he said he still do not believe people understand what it means.

A leader is like a guide, he shows and leads the way to the right direction. Then, as for leadership, it is the art of motivating and inspiring some group of people to act towards achieving a desired object or a common goal. But David said, it was one person who described LEADERSHIP as the wise use of POWER. And this person also described POWER as the capacity to translate intentions into reality and sustain it. David who is so accord with this idea, have come to think there is a need and it is good for him to further enlighten people about this POWER. He said he think, "We should be heedful the way we handle this POWER and the way we strive to have it. And that, doing what is right to humanity at the appropriate time with this POWER that we possess, the Lord God who owns it and has allowed us to possess it for awhile, will be pleased with us; but disregarding humanity because of this POWER, God will allow it turn against us, and if it does, it will destroy us."

CHAPTER 35

AVID'S WHO CONTINUED TO MOURN his dead mother, was seeing himself faced with distinctive problems drawn up. First he knew he was never going to meet his mother again. Secondly, he knew he needed money for his mother's burial, being that it was said-to-be a tradition in Africa to lavish money on funerals. He that could hardly feed himself was beginning to think of how to send money home for his mother's funeral. The intrinsic truth was that his families in Africa were aware of the economic hardship in Spain, but they insisted on sending him and his sister bills. When he sat down to think about this whole issue, he saw himself as a fool who will only get himself into prison if he is not careful on how he intended to deal with it. At first he thought of purchasing a ticket to going back home to go and pay his mother her last respect. He love her so much and has only saw her once for more than thirteen years. How could he ever live his life and tell this to his unborn children in the future? He knew it will be the right thing for him to do by going home at that very time, but where was he going to get the money to purchase a ticket worth 800.00 euros not to talk of the money he was going to spend there that will not be less than 4,000.00 euros? To get that money, he knew he has to do anything. So he started calling his friends whom for long he spurned, and was pleading with them to call him for any type of criminal activity so that he could participate and make money. The more he was calling them and they were also calling him and telling him they were sorry his mother was dead without any help on how he could get the money to purchase a ticket or even send them money over there for the funeral, the more he came to detest his fellow Nigerians for their lack of supports and co-operation in dealing with each other when any of them is caught up in a dreary life situation like the one he was. Although, he has also rendered help to many he could when it happened to them, but when it came to his turn, none of them were there for him. Many would have helped him, but due to the fact that he was always lying and bragging about how rich his families were, he saw all of them standing offshore and watching while he was drowning in the sea. He wanted to do anything—anything to raise money to return back to his country to say *adios* to his dead mother, the woman of his heart that he was never going to see again. When he puzzled out the whole thing and came to understand that he could be seeing himself in jail while others will be weeping and burying his mother, so he decided to make an attempt to do a different thing to soothe himself. He tried everything that he thought might help, from smoking marijuana to drinking wine and whiskey and gin, and the end results were all zero, and even worsen his problems. But when he tried to write, he saw that inspiration was pouring in more than it has ever been, and it startled him and was making him feel his mother will be the most happiest person where she already was to see that he was able to accomplish his dream of becoming a writer. He became happier and thrilled as he proceeded with his writing and was deriving pleasure from it more than it has always be. He loved himself for what he was doing, knowing that he was doing it for his mother who was always with him, watching and guiding him. She became his guiding angel and was always in his brain and mind, directing, leading, and fortifying him to go and live in the land he wished to.

At the moment in his life when he became less determined, was also the time he lost his mother and was trying to overcome the despair, and at this same time, he appeared to be in a much more blissful state and was glad he was alive even if his mother was dead. Despite that he was happy and not feeling too bad about his mother's death, but he was much more afraid of what was going to happen next when he stop receiving the benefit he was receiving. He decided to quit watching the news in Spain, because of how it was scaring, hearing tragic news—like a man killed his wife, a man killed his son, or a son killed his father to inherit his wealth, police caught some criminals and took them to jail, prostitutes and pimps were arrested, and then, worst of it all, how the Spanish deficits and debts problems could be solved following the German chancellor's rules and regulations. To David, the more he was hearing how the German chancellor laud the Spanish prime-minister's plan to reduce spending while unemployment rates were rising every day and many Spaniards were left homeless and penniless, the more he came to believe he was still living in a third world country where the government still were ruled by another government said to be in the same continent but not in the same country. It was not that he did not uphold the new prime-minister, Mariano Rajoy's plans to reduce government spending, but it was obvious the way many workers were being sacked and it was meaningless, as job creation should have been first thing before any other thing. He said he said this, because he believe when more people are able to secure jobs, more consumer will definitely have money to spend—and when consumers do not spend, then how can the economy grow? The fact that Europe still cannot believe that the only way to sort-out the problem of the economic crisis, is to give more chances for jobs to be created. A severe austerity is not actually needed in the middle of a recession or rather said to be a depression. They still believe the great recession ended some years ago. To David, he could sense the beginning if they are unable to let jobs be created. Although what the prime-minister was doing was supposed to be done by the last administration, who actually squandered the money without control and regulations. It may seem really biased and slanted if the government was proposing a severe austerity cuts, and could not reduce the politicians salaries by fifty percents, instead they were thinking they could do it in the education sector—which was to be the country's only hope of recovery—that is when they can invest on innovation and invention. David said when he saw this, he came to believe there is nowhere in the world that he could see fairness. He said what he keep seeing, is how people still earn more than what they deserve, while many others continuously earn less than what they deserve. He said he still cannot get to the land where he wish to live to see meritocracy being practiced. Another thing was that the new administration in Spain was said to be a party with the highest rate of corruption in the country and yet no one was doing anything about it, even if they were trying, but were still not doing enough to create fear on these perpetrators. David said he was also beginning to see himself experience a different form of imperialism in Europe, as he was seeing German Angela Merkel taking Euro-zone to an extreme level, to think she can dictate for other countries what to do and what not to do. She forgot that, imposing your own will on others against their own will, is just to say you are enslaving them, and it is unfair. The factual fact was that Europeans have no idea on how to deal with this mess that was caused long time ago due to the fact that they have all spent excessively and lavishly, borrowing and borrowing without strict regulations. But he said he is so concerned about this matter, that he asked himself if Europe was ever going to restore its dignity. He said he believe they should start from somewhere and put shame aside and face the fact that, at this very time, Euro-zone is just a calamity, and the only way European Union can be stronger is when there is no more Euro-zone. Yes, it is. The better the Europeans acknowledge this, the better for the world's economy. Everybody should return back to his own currency and try to get things regulated and come back to form Euro-zone again, and it will have to be for only those who could meet up with the set-up strict measures. But the way it is already, it is always going to be problematic. "It is good to admit defeats, get stronger and fight again." There is no need for anyone to be ashamed to cry out. Why should the German unemployed who might want to be, not because he is unable to find a job still be living life to the fullest because of the social assistance he is receiving from his government, while Greeks and Spaniards who are unemployed and have done everything they could to get a job and could not, will be homeless and starving to death because he is not receiving any social assistance from his government? That is unfair if we take a good look at it. "We should hold hands together while we are walking through the stony dark path that lead to progress." David said he also found it absurd when the Greeks were referring to Angela Merkel as the new Hitler. He said he could understand their frustration, but they have also forgotten how they are to pay a big price for being too lazy and corrupt. The problem in Greece was not caused by the Germans which the whole world can testify to. It was caused by the Greeks themselves. They have decided to live the lives that were not fit for them, and at the end, the outcome became a nightmare. David said he did uphold the fiscal treaty proposed by Merkozy, as it will be the only way to stand the Euro-zone, but one thing is, will every country who signed the treaty be able to do what they promised? Although, as for him, German chancellor is not to be blamed for the problems in Europe, but it will be far better if she take a decision to pay more attention to her country's problem for awhile rather than dictating for other countries and advising them on how they can recover from the economic breakdown. She is to be seen as the most powerful woman leader of our time. She is popular and is well regarded as a leader. She has been able to lead a country with the largest economy in Europe even in the time of an economic crisis. And from what many immigrants in Germany have said about her, she is seen to be the only German leader with the prospect that Germany is ready for a change and she has also been able to prove it—by integrating more immigrants into the new German society. She is doing this because she believes in multiculturalism. David said he could see her as a great woman to set a precedent for many other women, but she must be very careful not to ruin everything she has worked for, only because she is dictating for others on the basis of what might be good for all of them which might also be disastrous. David said he understand that a serious austerity measure has to be taken, but in a staggering economy, it could only weaken and destabilize it. It is not that disintegration is not going to cause the Union a great devastation, but what is needed to be done, needed to be done and quick and effective decisions should be made. Actually, it was said that the Union was formed to prevent wars, bring political unity, and for economic growth among member states, but to David, he said he does believe these goals will never be met, because, looking back to history and seeing how Europeans have fought many wars among themselves, we can see that no one is trusting anyone— which is to say, there is no way for a more political union that is really needed to make Europe to be strongly united, which could have been far better if they could do so. There is still that inequality among member states, not to talk of the extreme cultural and nationalistic differences which is also a great impediment. But for Europe to be together and to be able to overcome this crisis, lots of sacrifices must be made mostly by the core member, Germans, who actually could acknowledge how they needs the Euro-currency more than the currency needs them, because of the fact that the country is export-driven and the economy is growing faster than the rest—and thanks to the euro.

"To overcome adversity, is also to let pride not dwell too much in us." In many years, Europe has been Africa best companions and pals. In spite that they have exploited, enslaved, and colonized them, but they have also taught them how to live and die. It can be noted for some decades how these masters have come to ignore these Africans, because they could see that they are wet behind the ears and untaught. But this is after when they have benefited a lot from them. It is easy if they could go back to Africa to reap what they have sowed, instead of living the Chinese to reap where they did not sow. But this time, it has to be with conditions and generosity of spirit. There is still much more to explore in that continent that cannot be seen in Europe, only if there is an accord with the both, and there should be. The world is changing everyday, and it is better we put aside our little differences and come together as one to solve some of the problems engulfing all of us, render to each other a helping hand when in need and let our souls come together and also implant in our hearts the will to tolerate and respect each other for who we are as human beings—so as to live a more prosperous life, and for peace to reign. We should let rest on the floor that hatred and rivalry and think of how to heal our wounded world. It is not that the invasion and colonization of the British and French in Africa, or the Spanish and Portuguese invasion and colonization in South America, was not said-to-be a curse, it was also said-to-be a blessing and many witty Africans and South Americans comprehend this, as they could also link it with greed. But it will be more easier and friendly if they apologize for their many wrong deeds, and also if these people should be awarded compensations by their colonies—and to do this, they could make trade be fair, and go back to invest, innovate, invent, and help them develop these countries. This could be a step forward in dealing with the issue of how we could make the world a better and peaceful place to live. From what David has experienced and from the discussion he had with many Africans and other immigrants like him, he could still see that grudge, making many feel happy—seeing that their former colonial masters and slavers are undergoing what they believe to be predicaments even when they too were still very far and cannot reach the same position and yet are suffering. Many Europeans who are not born with silver spoons on their mouths are also having this grudge, because they are fed up with the life of poverty they have been living right from their childhood, while they watch others live extravagantly.

One day in Madrid city center, he met an Indian American who disliked almost every rich people around the world, since he too has suffered a lot and has traveled around the world and came to believe Qatar was the only place he could be able to live a peaceful life. When they both went to a coffee bar to drink coffee and also to converse, he saw that the lad was just the same person as he was. He was the brother he never had and would want to live with so that he could be able to learn more from him, being that he was a very educated person. Although he promised to go live with him in Qatar if he ever succeed in achieving what he want in life and think of settling down. The lad wrote a full page to describe the economic crises as a punishment for many things being done by wealthy people in the past and gave it to him to read; he wrote—woe unto these wicked and rich people, as they will weep and wail because of the misery that is coming. I see their wealth as it rot and moth eating their clothes. Their golds and silvers will corrode, and their corrosion will testify against them and eat their flesh like fire. They have hoarded wealth in the last days. Look! The wages they failed to pay the workers who mowed their fields are crying out against them. The cries of the harvesters have reached the ears of the Lord Almighty. They have lived on Earth luxury and self-indulgence. They have fattened themselves in the days of slaughter. They have condemned and murdered the innocent ones who was not opposing them. Only if they repent and ask for forgiveness that they might see the sun-light again.

To David, it was like this man was the same as he was, and they were two different people having the same beliefs, and thinking the world should be healed. He said he love this lad and also wrote his poem and later posted it to the address he was given in Qatar, and he also promised to meet with him and live there some years to come. But he waited for so long and never got a reply from him. He wrote the poem to explain how he felt about him.

I KNOW YOU KNOW.

I know you know.
I know you know that I love you
And care about you, and will always do.
I know you know that we're one,
And we're from the same creator
And we will always be.
I know you know He loves us
And want me to love you
And for you to also love me,
So that we can both fly away
To the land we ought to be,
And live a life full of peace and harmony.
I know you know.

I know you know that love's the only remedy,
A thing to give and to receive.
And it can fortify us to sail
Across the seas and the oceans
Where wild fishes swim and live.
I know you know.
I know you know that some days,
We will suffer and prosper, run and win.
We will be chased by enemies we can't see.
And with love, we will cast them into a furnace of fire,
And keep moving till we reach the end path.
I know you know that we're our own strength and light,
And we're capable of sending the wind of change
To blow away the grim and dreary in our world,
And chase these hearts of stone
Into hell, where they can live their lives alone.
I know you know.
I know you know you and I are to be the one
To heal the world where we live,
Even as we cry and smile,
Die and live,
Weep and rejoice,
And walk like the living ghosts.
I know you know we will overcome,
As we stand in awe in the middle of heaven and hell,
And read the handwriting on the wall.
I know you know.
I know you know, in the darkness, thick and dangerous,
We will walk and tremble.
And then, have a feast
In the season when thunder sleep,
As we see our fame shine, attracting attentions
And our destiny's stead-fast as the steered-by stars.

CHAPTER 36

A S DAVID CONTINUED TO WRITE, he was able to associate himself with his friends to be doing everything he could to save some money to send to his families in Africa for his mother's funeral. Although he could not send them everything they demanded for, but he was able to send them the little he was having with him, since he could not kill himself to become the money to send to them. He stopped paying his personal income tax return which he postponed and was paying monthly, approximately 170.00 euros. Since he was still staying in his friend's foreclosed house and was not paying rent, he was able to seized that opportunity only to starve himself for awhile and became more focused on his book. He decided to quit visiting the social network, Facebook where he was having more than two hundred friends around the world that he cherished, because of how many of them have contributed to the urgency and seriousness for him to proceed writing and get it done. With these people, whom most of them were Americans and Canadians and Indians and some very few Africans, he was able to edify himself more on how to become a good writer. Although he is never a good writer, but his willingness to become one was inevitable by sharing ideas with his dearly beloved friends, and mostly, learning from them, as majority where universities graduates who were mostly writers and poets. He said he will never forget his Facebook friends who helped him turn his creative vision into reality, as he saw many of them published their books and came to believe he could do the same. They are the type of friends that want a better life for their fellow human beings. Although he knew most of them detest him for his bigmouth, but he could see that many were also in support of what he was doing that he believe in and will not stop believing in. As educated people, they believe he was just speaking from his own perspective. The more he was writing, the more he was also learning better grammars and vocabularies, and the more he was relishing what he was doing. He came to understand that, "To become a writer, you must not continue to read to draw inspiration, instead you must write to start learning and to become perfect and also inspire others." He said there is no way he could thank his Facebook friends for everything he learnt from them, but first, he would have to thank Mark Zuckenberg for having founded Facebook, a social network to connect people and make them seek and share ideas, thoughts, and knowledge. He love all his friends, the book people, writers, poets, activists. These people will always be there in his heart. These people were to him, the brothers and sisters he believe he already have, and some of them who are with beautiful names like—Inna de Graaf, Dewey Dirk, Brian Coscione, Robert Gibbons, Philip Harris, Subrata Ray, George Russel, Jullia Stepanchenko, Opoyemi Olanihun, Ujjol Kamal, Timothy Gega, Rob Diggy, Gil Van Wagner, Laila J. Mila, Osaretin Iyen, Jan Mielke Schwartz, and many many more.

As he continued to post and share comments on Facebook, he became very much afraid many people were after him because of the more difficulties that he was encountering. He was thinking many believed he was against civilization, not knowing that he was just driving himself to the land where insanity dwells. This made him lie to many of them he was living in Holland while he was in Spain. And to explain it better how he prefer civilization to primitiveness and would want people to practice what they preach and prove what civilization really is if not love and peace, he wrote this poem.

WE'RE GONNA COME WITH THEM.

They've been digging into us a hole,
When all they profited a tempest of woe.
In the secret valley where we weep,
There, we gotta lay our heads and sleep.
The most potent factor of our visions
To develop our nature with enormous sensation.
Where they roll is heaven or hell,
Need not ask whom I'm to tell.
That they've come to set us free
From the demons that hang us to the tree.
We're gonna come with them.
Wherever they go, we're there with them.
Only if they make a pact
And stand by the fact.
Cos, we're born with the names of justice

And to preach the need for peace.
The devil, we're gonna send to where it dwell,
Since that's where the bad beast belong.
After all the days that has yet to come,
We might see the sun-light without a storm.
When a new hope was born-out,
They still wanna blow our minds-out.
But love we kept alive in our hearts.
Love in our hearts, and love only.

And to indicate in a way that he is among many other wrongdoers who is trying to find his way into the road leading to perfection and also to lure others to walk with him along the same road, he wrote a poem for this.

THE PERFECTION OF MAN.

I'm a saint.
I'm a sinner.
I'm not a saint,
Neither am I a sinner.
None among us that is perfect.
A perfect man lives beneath the Earth.
In this Earth, our hidden will, the first aspect.
The wind and the fire, there was a dearth,
As running water ran from the mountain to treat,
Speak, sit, peep, beat, leach, seize, and teach,
With a formula unknown and was unveiled
To us, as the secret was concealed,
And, as the truth Himself has revealed
To us all, whom with deep and natural affinity,
Possesses the qualities made to heal humanity
Where the souls mingled, faded, dissolved, accelerated,
Incorporated, educated, saluted, painted, planted,
Created, tested, and reacted,
For sure, to structure our future.
Come then the dream
To wake and revive the seed sown some centuries since

That will lure them to strive,
Strive to be,
Strive to become.
Strive to be and to become the converted faiths
To arise the uprising and patronize the perfection of man.

He said he wrote this poem to also be able to distinguish himself from many religious people, mostly Christians who claimed to be perfect and believe in everything they read in the bible. It is not that, it is not a good thing for them to do so, but one thing he would want people to understand is that, "The mystery of the bible can only be solved, if only we prefer to read the new testament more than we intend to centralized on the old testament, because that is where the truth rest." He said he can see the gloomy fate that will befall many Christians who continuously to preach about the second coming of Jesus Christ, and yet their hearts are still filled with rigid ideologies. He said he could recall a baptist church pastor in the U.s. saying, "You've got to kill the terrorists first before the killing stops and I am for the president—chase them all over the world, if it takes ten years, blow them all in the name of the Lord." David said he really cannot understand which Lord this pastor is referring to if not Jesus Christ who gave His life for for everyone to live according to the same bible the pastor said he read and he is preaching his doctrine from.

In Facebook, most people were seeing him as a person who does not welcome the American way of life. But that was not true. He care too much about America that he came to believe Americans can get stronger only if they could see themselves as one. He learnt from what they said, "If a kingdom is divided against itself, that kingdom cannot stand." And from his view, he could see that Americans are getting divided, simply because of Obama, and not that he is not a good president, but for a reason that he is more black than he is white and probably because he believe America must work with others to get peace and economic stability—this is to say, the community must work together or perish. Our world needs unity and understanding to tackle the many problems. He said he could also understand one thing most Americans cannot get to, is that if Obama loses his re-election bid, the world will definitely lose faith in the Americans once again. Obama re-election will be to pay the American debts, but because debt has always been a choice for the Americans, many are afraid he is coming to change it. Americans need to pay their debts to regain the position they stand in the world so as to continue leading. And something many Americans do not understand, is that the Chinese economy is growing too fast everyday while their politicians spend much time in congress, debating on who wins and who loses the next election, and also spending more money having American troops all over the world, instead they should be focusing more on the economy. They seem oblivious that without a good economy, they might lose their complexion in the world—or is it not said that, "Money is power, and power is money?"

David said, not that he hate the Americans. It is that he is so worried—he is so worried about two men grips on power in Moscow, claiming they were democratically elected and are there to unify the people, when actually they are dividing it and causing confusion that will soon lead to a civil war—and they are doing so only to think of a way to invest more on their military defense. He said he is so worried about a communist Chinese practicing capitalism and coming to understand it better than those who started it, and after making too much profits more than its counterparts, has decided to keep grip on power to destroy its neighbors. He is so worried about the Europeans incapable of finding a solution to the economic and financial crisis in Europe that is about to split the Union. David said he is most worried about how many others sees Americans and create for them hatred because of the neon-conservatives conceptions to continuously take what belongs to others. He said he is worried because he love America so much and would not want to see its fall just like it happened to the Romans.

At about 06:00 a.m, David was still writing his book and was about to finish it. Then appeared 2nd David, who for long was not seen. He was lying in David's bed without David knowing because he was with his computer, sitting and writing and was facing the wall. 'Hello 1st David,' he called to him. 1st David was startled, because he thought his mother's ghost has come to haunt him, maybe because he was still writing when he was supposed to be shedding tears as believed by many Africans who think tradition must be kept. 'What are you doing here?' asked 1st David, lowering his voice so as for his other friends in the apartment not to hear him having a conversation with himself. 'I have come to congratulate you for your book,' said 2nd David, rising up from where he was lying and coming to stand near him. 'Thank you,' replied 1st David. 'But I think I am busy now and I would want to finish what I am doing.' 'Please, do not be upset with me because I lured you into committing crimes that led you to jail.' 'Thank you for doing that, you made me suffered,' said 1st David, waiting to hear what his soul and best friend was going to say about what he did that led him to jail. 'Look! that place make people civilized,' said 2nd David, walking around the room. 'Civilized? You mean a prison make people civilized?' asked 1st David, about to scream for people to come. 'Yes, that is what should be called civilization, o.k? Let me tell you something. You think attending Harvard university that will make you civilized? 'Yes,' replied 1st David. 'That will make you civilized I understand, but the prison also gave you something you might have never been able to achieve in the free world that you claim you are, which actually is a wicked world. How could people claim to be civilized when we know what we are supposed to be doing that is appropriate and not doing it? 'What is that? asked 1st David, opening his ears wide to hear what he was to say. 'Everybody believe poverty and wars must be put a halt to, these violent extremists around the world must also be stopped, right?' asked 2nd David. 'Yes, but people should have to help themselves in finding a solution to their own problems,' replied 1st David. 'O.k, let us leave poverty and wars aside, let us talk about these extremist groups,' said 2nd David. 'What about them,' asked 1st David. 2nd David who was very much intense to edify hm, started talking. He said, 'Look! for we to prove that we can put an end to these violent extremist groups, we must start from our homes. Are you not ashamed, seeing the numbers of Neo-Nazis in Europe and in the U.s. increasing everyday? Many Americans believing illegal aliens must be killed so that more will stop coming in. And yet, are you not surprised that no one is considering them to be worse than the terrorists? 'How can they be worse than the terrorists,' asked 1st David, dozing and was almost about to fall asleep. 'They are worse than the terrorists, because they live within our neighborhoods while the terrorists live in the desert and hardly can harm us. To eradicate these extremist groups in the U.s. and Europe—the both continents have to do what it takes to extrude them, and this will make them restore their dignity as people who believe in civilization and practice what they preach. Or, have you forgotten that to love others, that is where civilization started? As 2nd David said that, he disappeared passed the wall and that was his last word. When David thought about what his soul just said, he recalled how seventy-seven people were killed in Norway for embracing multiculturalism and how Gabrielle Giffords, a U.s. democratic representative was shot, simply because she had not backed the immigration law to send all the illegal immigrants back to their countries. He came to believe that what 2nd David was saying was true, since he could see the Earth to be the home of man only if we the people living in it will make it be. And to make it be, everyone little support can be of an effort, as little drops of water can make a mighty ocean. He said he also came to believe that the great God is always in our hearts, when only we allow Him to speak to us. But, as he was almost exhausted and wanted to take a nap, he knew he has to finish the book. When he looked back to his past life to the present time, and how he started and all the formidable problems he has encountered, and yet he was able to endure and fulfill his dream of becoming a writer, then he said to himself, I WAS MY EVERYDAY SUPERMAN, MY SUPERMAN, MY OWN SUPERMAN.